The Fashioning and Functioning of the British Country House

STUDIES IN THE HISTORY OF ART · 25 ·

Center for Advanced Study in the Visual Arts
Symposium Papers X

The Fashioning and Functioning of the British Country House

Edited by Gervase Jackson-Stops
Gordon J. Schochet and Lena Cowen Orlin
Elisabeth Blair MacDougall

National Gallery of Art, Washington

Distributed by the University Press of New England
Hanover and London   1989

This publication was produced by the Editors Office, National Gallery of Art, Washington
Printed by Garamond/Pridemark Press, Inc.
The type is Bembo, set by BG Composition, Baltimore, Maryland
The text paper is LOE Dull, with matching cover

Distributed by the University Press of New England, 17½ Lebanon Street, Hanover, New Hampshire 03755

Abstracted by RILA (International Repertory of the Literature of Art), Williamstown, Massachusetts 01267

ISSN 0091-7338
ISBN 0-89468-128-1

Proceedings of the symposium "The Fashioning and Functioning of the British Country House" jointly sponsored by the Center for Advanced Study in the Visual Arts, National Gallery of Art, Washington, The Folger Institute, The Folger Shakespeare Library, and Program of Studies in Landscape Architecture, Dumbarton Oaks, 5–8 February 1986

Cover: Hardwick Hall, Derbyshire, from the southwest

Frontispiece: The Long Gallery at Chatsworth, Derbyshire

Page 11: Dyrham Park, Gloucestershire

Page 255: The Stone Hall at Houghton, Norfolk

Page 329: The garden at Blenheim Palace, Oxfordshire, with a sphinx modeled on Consuelo Vanderbilt, Duchess of Marlborough. Photographs: James Pipkin

Studies in the History of Art
Published by the National Gallery of Art, Washington

This series includes: Studies in the History of Art, collected papers on objects in the Gallery's collections and other art historical studies (formerly *Report and Studies in the History of Art*); the Monograph Series, a catalogue of stained glass in the United States; and the Symposium Papers, based on symposia sponsored by the Center for Advanced Study in the Visual Arts at the National Gallery of Art.

[1] *Report and Studies in the History of Art*, 1967
[2] *Report and Studies in the History of Art*, 1968
[3] *Report and Studies in the History of Art*, 1969
[In 1970 the National Gallery of Art's annual report became a separate publication.]
[4] *Studies in the History of Art*, 1972
[5] *Studies in the History of Art*, 1973
[The first five volumes are unnumbered.]
6 *Studies in the History of Art*, 1974
7 *Studies in the History of Art*, 1975
8 *Studies in the History of Art*, 1978
9 *Studies in the History of Art*, 1980
10 *Macedonia and Greece in Late Classical and Early Hellenistic Times*, edited by Beryl Barr-Sharrar and Eugene N. Borza. Symposium Series I, 1982
11 *Figures of Thought: El Greco as Interpreter of History, Tradition, and Ideas*, edited by Jonathan Brown, 1982
12 *Studies in the History of Art*, 1982
13 *El Greco: Italy and Spain*, edited by Jonathan Brown and José Manuel Pita Andrade. Symposium Series II, 1984
14 *Claude Lorrain, 1600–1682: A Symposium*, edited by Pamela Askew. Symposium Series III, 1984
15 *Stained Glass before 1700 in American Collections: New England and New York (Corpus Vitrearum Checklist I)*, compiled by Madeline H. Caviness et al. Monograph Series I, 1985
16 *Pictorial Narrative in Antiquity and the Middle Ages*, edited by Herbert L. Kessler and Marianna Shreve Simpson. Symposium Series IV, 1985
17 *Raphael before Rome*, edited by James Beck. Symposium Series V, 1986
18 *Studies in the History of Art*, 1985
19 *James McNeill Whistler: A Reexamination*, edited by Ruth E. Fine. Symposium Papers VI, 1987
[In 1987 Symposium Series became Symposium Papers.]
20 *Retaining the Original: Multiple Originals, Copies, and Reproductions*. Symposium Papers VII, 1989
21 *Italian Medals*, edited by J. Graham Pollard. Symposium Papers VIII, 1987
22 *Italian Plaquettes*, edited by Alison Luchs. Symposium Papers IX, 1989
23 *Stained Glass before 1700 in American Collections: Mid-Atlantic and Southeastern Seaboard States (Corpus Vitrearum Checklist II)*, compiled by Madeline H. Caviness et al. Monograph Series I, 1987
*24 *Studies in the History of Art*
25 *The Fashioning and Functioning of the British Country House*, edited by Gervase Jackson-Stops et al. Symposium Papers X, 1989
*26 *Winslow Homer*, edited by Nicolai Cikovsky, Jr. Symposium Papers XI
*27 *Cultural Differentiation and Cultural Identity in the Visual Arts*, edited by Susan J. Barnes and Walter S. Melion. Symposium Papers XII
28 *Stained Glass before 1700 in American Collections: Midwestern and Western States (Corpus Vitrearum Checklist III)*, compiled by Madeline H. Caviness et al. Monograph Series I, 1989

*Forthcoming

Contents

7   Preface
HENRY A. MILLON

9   Introduction
GERVASE JACKSON-STOPS

13   William Kent and Esher Place
JOHN HARRIS

29   The *Bombé*-Fronted Country House from Talman to Soane
PIERRE DU PREY

51   Pompeian and Etruscan Tastes in the Neo-Classical Country House Interior
JOHN WILTON-ELY

75   The Neo-Classical Transformation of the English Country House
DAMIE STILLMAN

95   Portraits of the English Abroad in Countries Other than Italy
BRINSLEY FORD

121   Old Masters at Petworth
ST. JOHN GORE

133   The Hanging and Display of Pictures, 1700–1850
FRANCIS RUSSELL

155   A Georgian Patchwork
JOHN CORNFORTH

177   Eastern Trade and the Furnishing of the British Country House
OLIVER IMPEY

195   The Nonfunctional Use of Ceramics in the English Country House
During the Eighteenth Century
ANNA SOMERS COCKS

217 A British Parnassus:
Mythology and the Country House
GERVASE JACKSON-STOPS

241 The Eighteenth-Century English Chimneypiece
ALASTAIR LAING

257 Introduction
GORDON J. SCHOCHET and LENA COWEN ORLIN

261 The Lady of the Country-House Poem
BARBARA K. LEWALSKI

277 The Country-House Arcadia
WILLIAM ALEXANDER McCLUNG

289 *The Convivium Philosophicum* and the Civil War:
A Country House and Its Politics
MICHAEL MENDLE

299 Philosophy at the Country House:
The Ideas of the Tew Circle
RICHARD TUCK

305 The Country House and the Country Town
MARK GIROUARD

331 Introduction
ELISABETH BLAIR MacDOUGALL

333 The British Garden and the Grand Tour
JOHN DIXON HUNT

353 The View from the Road:
Joseph Spence's Picturesque Tour
A. A. TAIT

373 History, Myth, and the English Garden
MICHEL BARIDON

395 Gardens, Houses, and the Rhetoric of Description in the English Novel
ALISTAIR M. DUCKWORTH

415 Biographical Sketches

Preface

This volume of *Studies in the History of Art* contains a group of twenty-one papers first presented at a symposium on "The Fashioning and Functioning of the British Country House" in Washington, D.C. on 5–8 February 1986 under auspices of three sister institutions—The Folger Institute at The Folger Shakespeare Library, the Program of Studies in Landscape Architecture at Dumbarton Oaks, and the Center for Advanced Study in the Visual Arts at the National Gallery of Art. This collaborative program took place in conjunction with exhibitions on various aspects of the British country house, including its architecture and landscape, interiors and decoration, libraries and art collections, mounted at The Octagon Museum, The Folger Shakespeare Library, Dumbarton Oaks, and the National Gallery of Art.

The symposium was intended to address two principal issues. The first involved the processes by which the country house came into being and changed over time—its design aspirations, sources, and influences, as well as the standards and sources for its furnishing and the economic base that made it possible. A second, although by no means secondary, concern was the uses of country houses, their furnishings and objects within familial, social, cultural, literary, political, and philosophical contexts. Through a consideration of these issues it was hoped to contribute to increased understanding of the variety of images, associations, and facilities sought by those who built and occupied British country houses in the sixteenth through nineteenth centuries.

The first two days of the symposium, held at the National Gallery on 5–6 February, were devoted to the exterior, interior, and furnishings of the country house, and planned in consultation with John Harris of the Royal Institute of British Architects and Gervase Jackson-Stops of The National Trust. The Trustees of the Gallery ex-

press their appreciation to Joe L. and Barbara B. Allbritton for making these sessions of the symposium possible. The following day's program took place at The Folger Institute and considered the country house with reference to the literature and political thought of the sixteenth to eighteenth centuries. These sessions were constructed by Lena Cowen Orlin of The Folger Institute and Gordon J. Schochet of Rutgers University in collaboration with their colleagues on the steering committee of the Center for the History of British Political Thought, J. G. A. Pocock and Lois G. Schwoerer, and with their fellow members of the central executive committee of The Folger Institute, especially Leeds Barroll and S. K. Heninger. The Folger program was made possible with the generous support of the Honorable and Mrs. Ronald S. Lauder. The final day of the symposium, held at Dumbarton Oaks, was organized by Elisabeth Blair Mac-Dougall, then director of Studies in Landscape Architecture. This session focused on the country house from the multiple perspectives of travel, garden, and park, including the writer's idea of the garden.

The organization of this volume follows the original tripartite scheme of the symposium program. The first set of papers was edited by Gervase Jackson-Stops, the second set by Gordon J. Schochet and Lena Cowen Orlin, and the third by Elisabeth Blair MacDougall. The National Gallery is grateful to these scholars for their willingness to edit the symposium papers and to write the introductions to their respective sections of the volume.

This is the tenth in the symposium series of *Studies in the History of Art,* designed to document gatherings sponsored by the Center for Advanced Study in the Visual Arts and stimulate further research. These collected papers unfortunately do not include those presented by A. A.

Tait at the National Gallery and Robert Williams at Dumbarton Oaks. The Editors Office of the National Gallery produced the volume. Future volumes in the series will chronicle additional symposia, including those held under the joint sponsorship of the Center for Advanced Study in the Visual Arts and sister institutions.

HENRY A. MILLON
Dean, Center for Advanced
Study in the Visual Arts

Introduction

To the Symposium Papers
Presented at the Center for
Advanced Study in the Visual Arts

5–6 February 1986

The aim of the symposium sessions held at the National Gallery of Art in conjunction with the exhibition, "The Treasure Houses of Britain: Five Hundred Years of Private Patronage and Art Collecting," was to examine some of the areas that could not satisfactorily be covered in the show—notably architecture and interior decoration, as well as immovable objects such as chimneypieces and particularly fragile ones such as textiles and lacquer.

Many of the symposium papers suggest new avenues for study in the arrangement and display of such objects, and in the planning and decoration of the country house as a setting specially conceived to contain them—in many ways the ancestor of the modern museum.

The papers are grouped under three main headings: architecture, paintings, and the treatment of interiors. In the first section, Pierre du Prey traces the idea of the bow window as a central elevational feature from baroque architects such as Vanbrugh, Archer, and Talman, through the Palladians (notably William Kent and Sir Robert Taylor), to the neo-classical designs of Adam, Chambers, and Soane. The connection of this idea with the concept of the villa, attempting an integration of the house with its natural setting, was one aspect of the popularity of the bow window, while another was the return to movement in architecture—the quality in Vanbrugh's work that Adam particularly sought to reestablish. The French derivation of the form, implicit in the word *bombé,* remains questionable, however, and it is easier to see Vanbrugh's bows at Blenheim ultimately deriving

from the oriels of Montacute House than from the great domed saloon of Vaux-le-Vicomte.

The rise of the villa is also one of the themes of Damie Stillman's paper, which examines the neo-classical transformation of the English country house in terms of social as well as stylistic change. The increasing importance of the banking, mercantile, and nabob classes may have had something to do with this, but it was more the increasing informality of everyday life that led to wide-scale alterations in existing houses and bolder experiments in the planning of new ones. The Pompeian and Etruscan styles, too often confused in the past, are aspects of this bold experimentation, which John Wilton-Ely discusses in greater depth, relating their development to the continuing archaeological discoveries of the late eighteenth century. Finally in this section, John Harris shows that country house archives can still yield undiscovered treasures: in this case, William Kent's designs for Esher Place, Surrey—not only his largest collection of drawings for any one place, but also of crucial importance in assessing Kent's gothick style and his role as father of the "picturesque."

The second symposium session at the National Gallery, concentrating on pictures, was opened by Sir Brinsley Ford with an investigation into portraits of the English painted abroad—excluding the Grand Tourists in Italy, whose likenesses by Batoni, Mengs, and others have already received much attention. By contrast, the ambassadors and refugees, soldiers and merchants, travelers and explorers, who ventured to other countries in Europe and beyond, have been largely neglected. To have assembled them for the first time, as seen by foreign artists from Dürer and Petrus Christus to Goya and Rodin, is a fascinating exercise, and it is to be hoped that Sir Brinsley's list (with its subsequent appendix) will be regularly updated, as more examples emerge. St. John Gore's case study on the Petworth Collection, based on the inventories of the 10th Earl of Northumberland and the 2nd Earl of Egremont (and the latter's records of his purchases at auction), reveals much about the changing tastes of seventeenth- and eighteenth-century English art collectors, suggesting that connoisseurship had much earlier roots than is often supposed, at least in court circles, and that the London art market was already highly developed long before the age of the museum.

Francis Russell's study of the hanging and display of pictures between 1700 and 1850 points to the immense care with which most country-house owners arranged their acquisitions, again long before the age of the professional museum curator. The suitability of certain pictures for certain rooms, the problems of uniform framing, double hanging, canting, and many other issues, are raised, and will surely stimulate further research into a subject that still has great relevance. The same can be said of John Cornforth's equally important consideration of eighteenth-century furnishing textiles, which opened the third session of the symposium, devoted to interiors. Attitudes to color and pattern (notably a progressive diminution in scale from the saloon to the furthest rooms of the enfilade) and the choice of materials, from rough mohairs and caffoys to the finest silks and cut velvets, all had a complex history of association, quite apart from the laws of supply and demand. In a period when the upholsterer usually had more real power over the country-house interior than the architect, this is indeed a field that would repay further investigation.

The vital part played by the English and Dutch East India Companies in the furnishing of the country house—with carpets, porcelain, lacquer, and wallpapers—is the subject of a paper by Oliver Impey. Using contemporary inventory descriptions, he throws new light on how such objects were kept and used, and how much their form was affected by western demand. The purely ornamental display of ceramics in the eighteenth century, from Oriental pieces to Meissen, Sèvres, and the English manufactories, is discussed by Anna Somers Cocks, with a wealth of illustration from portraits and drawings as well as books and letters of the time. On the whole, porcelain was considered an object of feminine interest (except for some of Wedgwood's chaster neo-classical vases, made for the more masculine libraries and state rooms of the 1770s), and garnitures and figures, jars and pots, were crowded together to continue that sense of the exotic that had first appealed to Queen Mary II and her contemporaries.

The male and female characteristics of the country-house interior are also considered in Alastair Laing's paper on the chimneypiece in the eighteenth century, and in my own paper on the use of mythology as a decorative language. Too often neglected by scholars, perhaps because it falls between the two stools of architecture and sculpture, the chimneypiece represented a major branch of the carver's art in Georgian England, achieving a distinctive form quite at variance with its French counterparts. The terms and caryatids, Persians and atlantes, found in the designs of Kent and Chambers and going back to Inigo Jones, were, for instance, used symbolically—as captives, echoing the triumphs of British overseas expansion—and also archaeologically—as essential members of an order of architecture, following celebrated monuments like the portico of the Erechtheion in Athens. In the same way, the world of classical mythology was plundered by the country house builders for the subjects of decorative paintings, furniture, tapestries, and many other works of art, in an attempt to prove that a new civilization had been constructed from the ruins of the old. A latter-day temple, where taste and standards of behavior were to be taught and appreciated hand in hand, extending the lessons of Plato and Horace, Virgil and Ovid, the British country house once again comes to be seen as the prototype of the modern museum.

I should particularly like to thank Mary Yakush and Ulrike Mills of the National Gallery of Art's editors office, and Barbara Anderman and Maggie Grieve, for their invaluable assistance in preparing the various papers for publication.

GERVASE JACKSON-STOPS

JOHN HARRIS

William Kent and Esher Place

Howard Colvin, author of the *Biographical Dictionary of English Architects,* and I share memories of the company of Rupert Gunnis (1899–1965), the great authority on English sculpture, on our forays to country-house libraries and muniment rooms. What extraordinary treasures were then to be discovered in unopened portfolios! We recollect the 1950s with fond regret, for now, as the years roll by, chance discovery has become a rarity. Therefore, imagine our excitement in the autumn of 1985 when the secretary to Commander Michael Saunders-Watson at Rockingham Castle in Northamptonshire laid before us on a table a portfolio tied with frayed green ribbons. There was that catch of breath as we undid the ties, to discover no less than the largest single collection of architectural and garden designs by William Kent (1685–1748) for any one country house. The plans were for Esher Place, Surrey, built for the Hon. Henry Pelham (1695–1754). Included also were a few designs for Pelham's town house at 22 Arlington Street, London, which was begun by Kent in 1741. But why was all this at such an unlikely place as Rockingham, a great medieval castle with no obvious connections with William Kent? The *Complete Peerage* provides the answer, for in 1752 Grace Pelham, third daughter of Henry Pelham, married Lewis Watson, who became Baron Sondes of Lees Court, Kent, in 1760, having succeeded to the Rockingham estates in 1746. We know nothing of Grace Pelham's personal character, but we may guess that her relationship with the witty and amusing Kent may have been similar to that of Kent and Lady Burlington, who was his constant companion and was taught drawing by him in partial return for her and Lord Burlington's lifelong patronage of this beloved architect. What matters is that had Grace Pelham not taken the drawings away from Esher Place, they might well have passed from Pelham's other two daughters, who were unmar-

ried, to Lewis Thomas Watson, who had become the 2nd Baron Sondes after the death of his father in 1795. The 2nd Baron preferred to live at Lees Court and sold Esher in 1805, bringing many effects to Lees. Had the drawings been among them, they would have been burnt in the terrible fire that gutted the house in 1910 and destroyed all the Esher furnishings.

Esher is not unknown to architectural historians[1] as an example of associational gothick. By *associational* I mean a conscious stylistic addition to an existing gothic building, extending it in a similar style. Upon first scrutiny this style seems to be a manifestation confined to northern Europe. No broad study[2] has been made of the fascinating problem of associational gothick alterations to European cathedrals and greater churches. Such a study, whether its focus were Britain or Europe, would certainly have to consider the matter of survival and revival.[3] The stylistic problem is not confined to northern Europe, as can be seen from the later stages of construction of Milan cathedral, or from the completion of the facade of S. Petronio in Bologna.[4] Baldassarre Peruzzi produced designs for S. Petronio in 1522, Giacomo Barozzi da Vignola did the same in 1545, and Giulio Romano in 1546—all in gothic. Giulio's design, a hybrid of pointed and ogee gothic, is a remarkable forerunner of the style that has come to be known in England as *gothick* with a *k,* conveniently distinguishing real gothic from this form that essentially belongs to the rococo revival.

In England, gothick style can be traced back to a seminal work by Sir Christopher Wren: the completion of the entrance tower (or Tom Tower, as it is called) at Christ Church, Oxford, in 1681, continuing the work begun by Cardinal Wolsey in 1525. Tom Tower stands at the head of a family tree of associational gothick designs, revival rather than survival, including John Talman's unexecuted designs[5] for remodeling the hall and chapel range of All Souls College, Oxford, in 1708, which he described in his own words as "pretty much after ye Italian Gothick."[6] Talman must have known, and may indeed have possessed in his great architectural print collection, Carlo Buzzi's engraved designs for Milan cathedral, dating to about 1654. A great delver into Italian cathedrals, sacristies, and archives, he and Kent roved Italy together from 1709. Not only was Kent a self-confessed admirer of the work of Giulio Romano, but is also known to have respected the "very much Gotic"[7] of St. Marks, Venice.

Eventually All Souls was remodeled by Nicholas Hawksmoor in 1716. Like Giulio Romano, he mixed pointed and ogee forms, but as a baroque master he understood better than Giulio, and certainly better than Kent, the linear energy of medieval gothic. This was equally demonstrated in Hawksmoor's work at Westminster Abbey, not only in the upper parts of the towers of the west front, built in 1734, but also in the lovely drawing[8] Hawksmoor made of the sixteenth-century stalls in Henry VII's Chapel.

Churches and colleges were building types more sympathetic to the associational gothick style, but, to return to country houses, it is worth considering a building comparable in its courtyard plan to Christ Church and again largely rebuilt by Cardinal Wolsey. This is Hampton Court Palace, Middlesex, specifically the east range of the Clock Court.[9] To the untutored eye this might appear to be Wolsey's work of the sixteenth century, but it is not; the range as it appears today is a rebuilding designed by the Master Carpenter of the Works in 1731. The post of master carpenter was titular only, and did not require a practical knowledge of carpentry! The holder of this post in 1731 was none other than William Kent, poised at a crucial moment in his career. Already a painter and decorator, furniture designer and book illustrator, he was now ready to display his prowess as architect and landscape gardener.

Hampton Court was the subject of an interesting comment by Horace Walpole in his *Anecdotes of Painting*.[10] Walpole says that Kent first proposed to rebuild the Clock Court range in a classical style, but was prevailed upon by Sir Robert Walpole to do it in gothick, or rather, in "Tudor" style. Sir Robert was First Lord of the Treasury, ultimately responsible for passing the estimates for the building, and Horace was not only a relative, but knew him intimately; thus

ELEVATION OF TURRETS AT THE EAST SIDE OF THE CLOCK COURT, HAMPTON COURT PALACE.

Fig. 1.
Reconstruction drawing of Kent's gatehouse at Hampton Court before alteration in 1853 (Allan, "Kent at Hampton Court," plate 3; drawing: Daphne Hart)

Fig. 2.
Neo-Palladian villa project for Esher Place by William Kent, c. 1730, pen, ink, and wash (Victoria and Albert Museum)

Fig. 3.
Capriccio of Hampton Court Palace and Esher Place by William Kent, c. 1731, pen, ink, and wash (British Museum)

this tale has the ring of truth. As we shall discover, Kent also at first proposed a classical neo-Palladian villa at Esher Place.

There is an obvious affinity in compositional outline between Tom Tower and Hampton Court, for Kent's task at Hampton Court was to create a gatehouse or through-entry. This affinity is even more strongly established if we compare the Christ Church tower with Kent's gateway before its cupola was removed and windows altered, soon after 1853 (fig. 1). For the details and general character of the fenestration of Kent's work we need look no further than at what Kent could see at Hampton Court itself, with its Henrician cupolas and Tudor mullioned windows. The only alien note was the curious bastard-gothic Venetian window in the second story below the crenellated parapet. It was obviously too whimsical for the Victorian Goths to stomach, so it had to go!

So what of Esher? "Esher I have seen again twice and prefer it to all Villas, even Southcote's, Kent is Kentissime there!" Horace Walpole was to write.[11] Henry Pelham bought the estate from Dennis Bond in 1729, three years after marrying Lady Katherine Manners. His purchase included the gatehouse of the mansion that had been built for Bishop Waynflete in about 1480, of brick, like Hampton Court. It must be assumed that this gatehouse survived from a quadrangular house, in plan a reduced version of Christ Church or Hampton Court. An engraving by Jan Kip, after a drawing by Leonard Knyff,[12]

made about 1700, shows this gatehouse now isolated among simple late seventeenth-century parterres in a formal garden. Kent's first idea for his friend Pelham was to disregard the Waynflete house and to build a classical villa (fig. 2), set not by the river Mole, which flowed near the old gatehouse, but on the nearby hill. Made about 1730, this was, in all probability, Kent's first country-house design. Although it was for a traditional neo-Palladian villa, it already shows Kent's idiosyncratic styling in the flanking pavilions with their cubic form and rusticated entrances. There is a hint, here, of the side elevations of Lord Burlington's villa at Chiswick, where Kent lived, and also of John Webb's Gunnersbury House, 1659, then venerated as a work by Inigo Jones, and not far away from Chiswick.

What can have caused Kent to change his mind so radically about the style of Pelham's new house? Obviously by 1731 the problem of Hampton Court was conflated in his mind with that of Esher, for if in the one he had been creating a gatehouse, in the other he had the possibility of extending a gatehouse. Both were Tudor buildings and both were associated with Wolsey. It would have pleased Kent to have discovered that Esher had been Wolsey's prison in 1529. Sir Robert Walpole's suggestion of a gothick design must also have played a part, for Pelham was "strongly attached" to Walpole and "more personally beloved by him [Walpole] than any man in England," according to Lord Hervey.[13] A capriccio of Hampton Court Palace and Esher Place (fig. 3) aptly links both buildings, for on the left-hand side is Hampton Court, whimsically rebuilt in Kent's gothick style; in the middle background on the hill is a classical rotonda-like temple that may well have been intended for the hill at Esher; and down below on the right by the river Mole is Esher Place with mixed gothick classical wings. Kent's inscriptions are composed from Michael Drayton's *Poly-Olbion* (1612), a famous topographical poem bestowing blessings upon the land of Britain. Clearly this capriccio must have been made soon after Kent offered the classical villa solution to Pelham, because this creation accords perfectly with the architect's first gothick design (fig. 4).

The extraordinary facade in the design deserves a close examination. It can only be described as multifaceted, a succession of square, canted, and octangular bays, only hinting at a classical language in the two triangular pediments. It is a potent example of Kent's obsession

Fig. 4.
Penultimate design for Esher Place by William Kent, c. 1731, pen, ink, and wash   (Victoria and Albert Museum)

Fig. 5.
Design for the courtyard wings at Esher Place in a landscape setting by William Kent, c. 1731, pen, ink, and wash   (Victoria and Albert Museum)

with a staccato or concatenated exterior architecture, achieved through the advance and recession and the breaking-up of the facade into a succession of bays of differing width. Indeed, this is precisely the same theory of facade movement with which Kent was experimenting at the Royal Mews at Charing Cross, designed in 1731.[14] The source of this mannerist affectation must lie in the work of Giulio Romano, in other mannerist works, and perhaps also in the sectional drawings by Andrea Palladio for the reconstruction of the Roman Baths, which Kent had studied first hand in Lord Burlington's collection.[15] One detail needs to be singled out: the

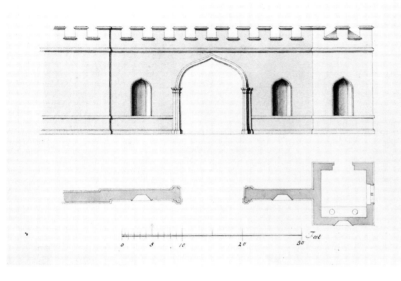

Fig. 6.
Design for the courtyard entrances
at Esher Place by William Kent,
c. 1731, pen, ink, and wash (Victoria
and Albert Museum)

Fig. 7.
Design for gate piers in the park at
Esher Place by William Kent,
c. 1731, pen, ink, and wash
(Wimbledon Public Library)

facade in all its parts is tied together by a sort of
parapet that serves as a string course and is composed of balls set upon concave bases. Kent
picked this up from Palladio, who uses it as a
topping for a screen wall on each side of the west
facade of S. Giorgio Maggiore in Venice, a
church published by Kent in his *The Designs of*

Inigo Jones . . . with Some Additional Designs, 1727.

Another of Kent's sketches dating to this time
(fig. 5) reduces the wings in length and introduces the low, single-story offices that would be
brought forward to flank and screen the entrance. In the Rockingham portfolio there are
several designs (fig. 6) for the court entrances,
and there is a design in Wimbledon Public Library,[16] Surrey, for entrance piers with gothick
niches and octagonal ball finials (fig. 7).

No doubt Kent arrived at an acceptable solution for Esher Place very quickly, once he had
decided upon a gothick style. The penultimate
elevation for the entrance or east front (fig. 8),
also housed at Wimbledon, conforms, except for
minor details, to the front (fig. 9) engraved and
drawn by John Vardy, one of Kent's closest associates in the Office of Works and an admirer of
his style. This engraving and its companion for
the west or garden front (fig. 10) may have been
intended for Vardy's seminal work, *Some Designs
of Mr Inigo Jones & Mr Wm Kent,* 1744, though
for reasons unknown it was never included.

The west front is accompanied by a plan that
requires investigation. Octangular in style, it almost suggests that Kent took the canted bays of
the Tudor gatehouse as a starting point, and developed his own curious plan from it. The
single-story projections on the west, and the
three-story bays on the east, represent rooms
inside the house that are either octagonal or
canted at one end. This is a wondrously felicitous
plan, not a little wild, and freewheeling, and
loose limbed. It would be fascinating to know
how the plan worked above the main floor, for,
with the Tudor gatehouse splitting the house in
two, there must obviously have been some in-
convenience of communication. The planning is
astonishingly prophetic; here, not later than 1732
or 1733, long before Robert Morris gave them an
imprimatur in his *Rural Architecture* of 1750, are
canted bays fronting octagonal rooms. Morris'
textbook is supposed to have given currency to
this type of plan form common to the neo-classic
villa.[17] Because Morris describes himself in his
Essay in Defence of Ancient Architecture (1728) as
"of Twickenham," it is very probable that he
visited the new houses in this part of the Thames
Valley; if so, he could hardly have ignored Esher,
sited on a celebrated tourist circuit of the houses
on the Thames.

As at Hampton Court, the ornamental vocabulary is a simple one—of ogees, drip molds, qua-
trefoils, crenellations, and ogee cupolas. At

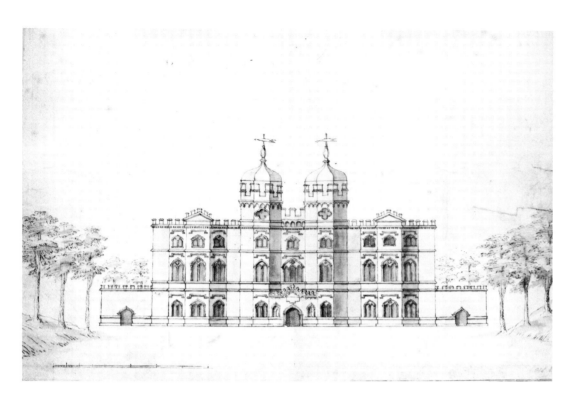

Fig. 8.
Penultimate design for the east front
of Esher Place by William Kent,
c. 1731, pen, ink, and wash
(Wimbledon Public Library)

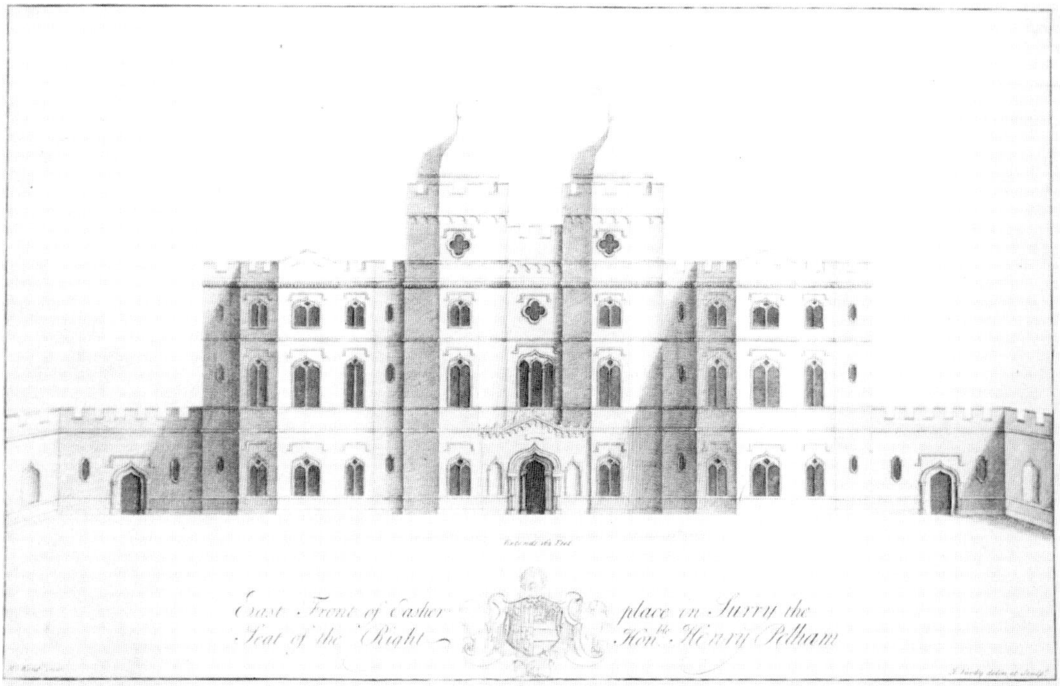

Fig. 9.
Engraved elevation of the east front
of Esher Place by John Vardy
(Photograph: author)

Fig. 10.
Engraved plan of the main floor and elevation of the west front of Esher Place by John Vardy (Photograph: author)

Esher, even more than at Hampton Court, we can observe Kent's delight in the whimsical mixing of classic and gothick ornament, notably in the Greek key friezes that serve as capitals to the gothick orders of the entrance door, whose design (fig. 11), dated to 1733, incorporates a statue of Cardinal Wolsey in one of its niches. Elsewhere this mixture can be seen in the fragmentary remains of interior decoration in the present tower, consisting of fan vaulting and ogee screens, and huge shell motifs set against the staircase; in an engraving by Vardy of a chimneypiece (fig. 12); and in the precious and only surviving design (fig. 13) for one of the interiors, in this case for one of the main-floor octagonal cabinets on the west front. Kent's playful mood is best expressed here, and of note is the extraordinary and willful overmantel to the chimneypiece, where a pediment rests upon the heads of two busts. Kent is playing the mannerist game.

The drawings by Kent in the portfolio are accompanied by a group in a hand that can be identified as that of Stephen Wright. Wright entered Lord Burlington's employ as a draftsman in 1731 and almost certainly drew most of the earl's projects in the early 1730s, including the Chiswick Link Building of 1733 and the wings that were added to Tottenham Park, Wiltshire, in 1737. It is unclear if he was working at Esher during the 1730s or subsequently, for the designs in his hand concern the addition of an office and stable wing that, as far as can be ascertained, were not built in that form. There exists a rather crudely drawn design (fig. 14), either by Kent or Wright, for an enlargement of Esher in an octangular style. The wings that extend forward remind us forcibly of Elizabethan houses of the Cobham Hall, Kent, type. More conservative are Wright's plans for offices and stables (fig. 15), and elevations for both the former in the gothick

Kent Inv.   T. Vardy delin.

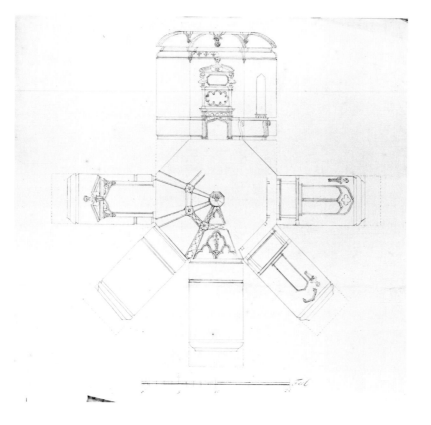

Fig. 11.
Design for the porch entrance on the east front of Esher Place by William Kent, 1733, pen, ink, and wash (Wimbledon Public Library of Merton Library Services)

Fig. 12.
Engraved elevation of a chimney-piece at Esher Place by John Vardy, from *Some Designs of Mr Inigo Jones & Mr Wm Kent*, 1744, plate 36

Fig. 13.
Plan with laid-back walls for an octagonal cabinet at Esher Place by William Kent, c. 1733, pen and ink (Victoria and Albert Museum)

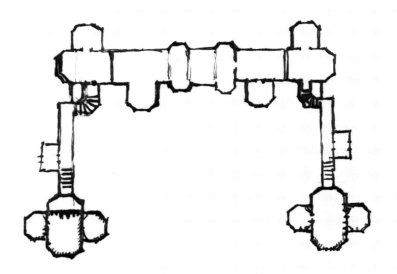

Fig. 14.
Rough plan either for the first house or for later additions at Esher Place by William Kent or Stephen Wright, pen and ink   (Victoria and Albert Museum)

Fig. 15.
Plan for an addition of offices and stables at Esher Place by Stephen Wright   (Victoria and Albert Museum)

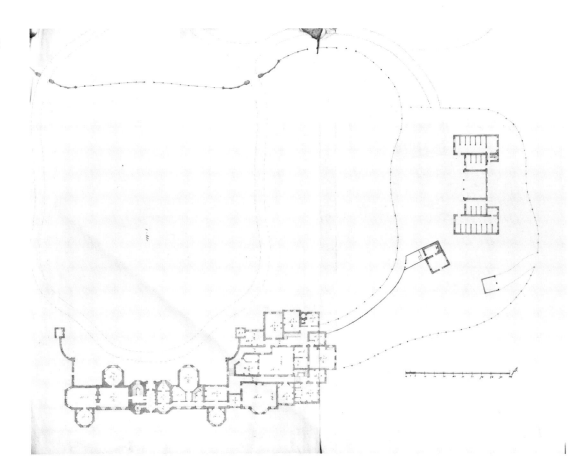

style (fig. 16), and the latter in the classical (fig. 17), although it is difficult to know if these are by Wright for Kent or by Wright alone, even after Kent's death.[18]

This is not the place to discuss in any detail Kent's designs for the garden at Esher. A survey published by the cartographer John Rocque in 1737 shows the house and four of the garden temples set in Rocque's characteristic view boxes (fig. 18). The park studies that survive in the portfolio are among the loveliest and most evocative of all Kent's garden designs. They demonstrate more than any other group just how indebted he was to the art of scenography, and they show how he operated, not with rule or line like other garden designers, but with the eye of the painter. Among these drawings is a remarkable one for a water and flower garden set on an island behind the Fishing Temple, with flowers set in the ground in circular "studs" or boxes (fig. 19), a gothick boathouse, and a temple whose plan seems to match one for a structure that is known to have been built by the lake, shown by Rocque. Other architectural temples or garden ornaments include two de-

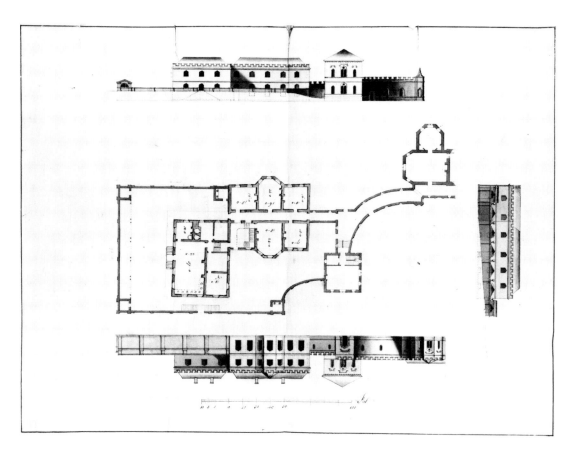

Fig. 16.
Plan and elevations of three facades
for offices at Esher Place by Stephen
Wright, pen, ink, and wash
(Victoria and Albert Museum)

Fig. 17.
Plan and elevation for stables at
Esher Place by Stephen Wright, pen,
ink, and wash   (Victoria and Albert
Museum)

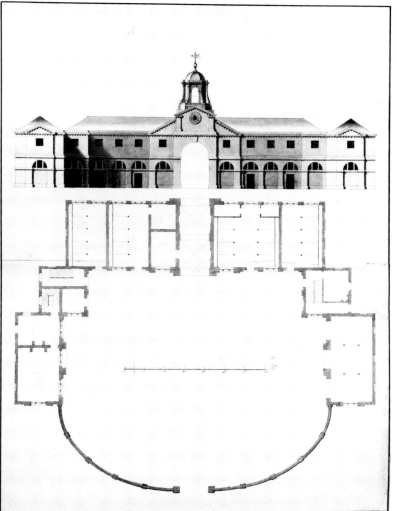

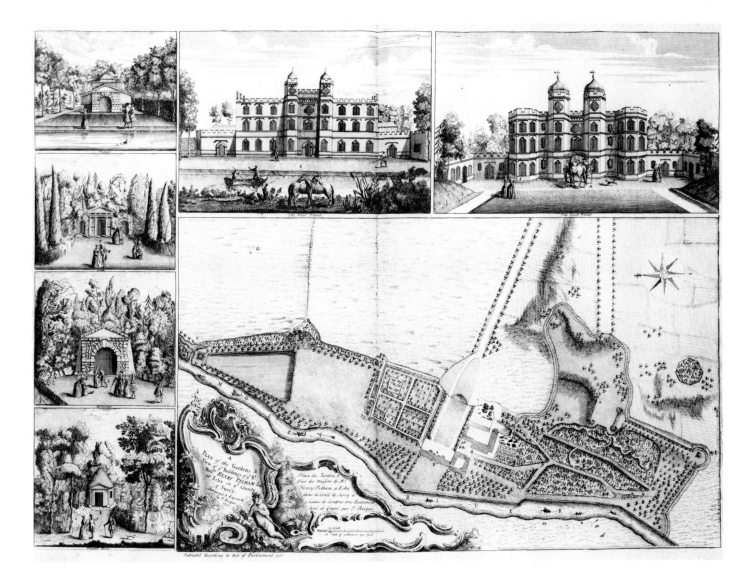

Fig. 18.
Engraved survey of Esher Place by
John Rocque, 1737   (Photograph:
author)

signs for the belvedere on the hill (fig. 20), a
tented pavilion with royal arms (fig. 21), possibly
a festive structure for the reception of George II
and Queen Caroline, and three designs (fig. 22)
for chinoiserie kiosks that must surely be among
the earliest, if not *the* earliest of their kind in
Europe. This is the first evidence we have that
Kent designed in this style, which became popular in the later 1730s.[19] In addition to these Rockingham drawings, mention must be made of another design in Wimbledon Public Library for a
noble temple lit through iron grilles that are set
in the upper part of the rusticated walls (fig. 23).
This may be an abandoned design for the pavilion or fishing temple by the water.[20] Looking at
all these evocative drawings, one is reminded of
Horace Walpole's visit to Esher in 1763 on the
occasion of a party given by Frances Pelham, one
of the two sisters who remained in charge of
Esher. This was a fête champêtre, when "the day
was delightful, the scene transporting, the trees,
lawns, concaves, all in the perfection in which
the ghost of Kent would joy to see them . . . we
walked to the belvedere on the summit of the
hill. . . . From thence we passed into the wood,
and the ladies formed a circle on chairs before the
mouth of the cave which was overhung to a vast
height with woodbines, lilacs and laburnums,
and dignified by those tall shapely cypresses. On
the descent of the hill were placed the French
horns; the abigails, servants and neighbours
wandering below by the river—in short, it was
Parnassus as Watteau would have painted it."[21]

When Lord Sondes sold Esher in 1805, John
Spicer, a London stockbroker, reduced the Kent
house to its original tower and built a new home

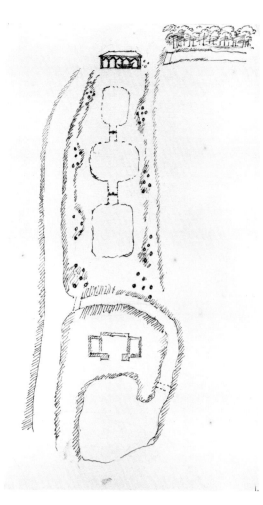

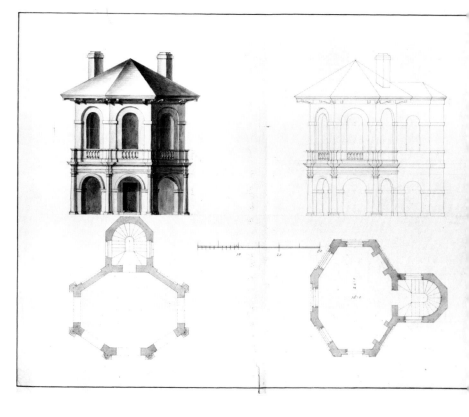

of Grecian severity, designed by Edward Lapidge, on the hill where Kent had first proposed his neo-Palladian villa. This Lapidge house in turn gave way to the present house, built from 1895 for Sir Edgar Vincent. Few estates can have been so split asunder. In the 1920s and 1930s a housing estate divided the Kent tower from the Vincent house, isolated the kitchen garden, and left garden buildings on various parcels of land. In a garden of one house can be found the Grotto; broken stone from the Fishing Temple, a building that survived as late as the 1950s, lies near the triangular basin of water. On Esher Green are handsome brick gate lodges in a Kentian gothick style contemporary with the building of the house, and on the hill is a magnificent pedestal that must have supported a statue of heroic size designed by Kent.

Esher was a triumph. It was for the gothick country house what Holkham Hall in Norfolk

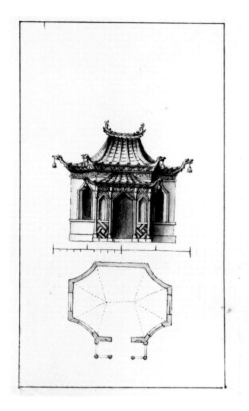
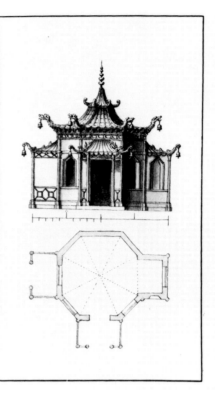
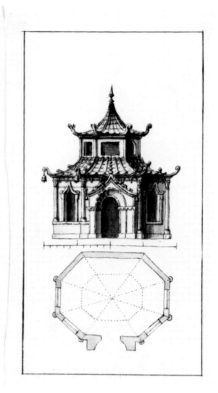

Fig. 22.
Three designs for chinoiserie kiosks by William Kent, pen, ink, and wash   (Victoria and Albert Museum)

Fig. 23.
Design for a temple, possibly the temple by the water at Esher Place, by William Kent, pen, ink, and wash   (Wimbledon Public Library of Merton Library Services)

was for the classical, and we can observe in both, which were built at the same period of time, Kent's attempt to capture movement by the theory of concatenation. Milton Abbey in Dorset of the 1750s, or Tong Castle in Shropshire of 1765, are just two of many gothick country houses that are children of Esher. Today the tower[22] of Esher survives surrounded by small houses in a "stockbroker's Tudor" style. So, if Esher initiated the neo-gothick house in Europe, as it surely did, we can say that on the same estate the circle has now been completed, and the parent is left to brood upon its ugly progeny!

This paper would not have been possible without the companionship of Howard Colvin and the kindness of Commander Michael Saunders-Watson of Rockingham Castle.

1. See John Harris, "A William Kent Discovery," *Country Life* (14 May 1959) 1076–1078; idem, "William Kent's Gothick," in *A Gothick Symposium,* Victoria and Albert Museum (London, 1983); idem, "Esher Place, Surrey," *Country Life* (2 April 1987), 94–97.

2. For a study in a slightly narrower context, see R. Wittkower, *Gothic Versus Classic Architectural Projects in Seventeenth Century Italy* (London, 1974).

3. See Howard Colvin, "Gothic Survival and Gothick Revival," *Architectural Review* 104 (1948), 91–98.

4. For the designs for S. Petronio, see Guido Zucchini, *Disegni antichi e moderni per la facciata di S. Petronio di Bologna* (Bologna, 1933).

5. At Worcester College, Oxford; see Howard Colvin, *Catalogue of Architectural Drawings of the 18th and 19th Centuries in the Library of Worcester College, Oxford* (Oxford, 1964), nos. 40–41, inscribed by Talman.

6. Colvin 1964, no. 42.

7. William Kent, Italian Journal, 1714. Bodleian Library, ms. Rawl. D. 1162.

8. Drawings Collection, Royal Institute of British Architects, London.

9. For a discussion of Hampton Court, I have relied upon Juliet Allan, "New Light on William Kent at Hampton Court Palace," in "Designs and Practice in British Architecture; Studies in Architectural History Presented to Howard Colvin," *Architectural History* 27 (1984), 50–58.

10. Horace Walpole, *Anecdotes of Painting,* 5 vols. (London, 1826), 2:564.

11. Walpole to George Montagu, 11 August 1748, Wilmarth Sheldon Lewis et al., eds., *The Yale Edition of Horace Walpole's Correspondence,* 48 vols. (New Haven, 1937–1983), 9:71.

12. Leonard Knyff, *Britannia Illustrata* (London, 1707), pl. 72.

13. Lord Hervey, *Memoirs,* 3 vols. (London, 1884), 3:358–359.

14. For the Mews, see particularly Kent's designs in Sir John Soane's Museum, London.

15. Now the Burlington-Devonshire Collection, Royal Institute of British Architects, London.

16. See John Dixon Hunt, *William Kent, Landscape Gardener* (London, 1987), no. 112.

17. Sir Robert Taylor was particularly fond of this form. See Marcus Binney, *Sir Robert Taylor: from Rococo to Neoclassicism* (London, 1984).

18. Of course, it is not known if gothic stables had also been proposed. Wright could have made these designs after Pelham died in 1754, for he completed Pelham's house in Arlington Street after 1749, and was working for the 1st Duke of Newcastle, a relation of Pelham's and one of Kent's patrons, at Claremont, Surrey, from 1752.

19. For a recent general account of chinoiserie in Europe, see Patrick Conner, *Oriental Architecture in the West* (London, 1979). Conner cannot locate any chinoiserie garden buildings that can definitely be dated before c. 1740, although there is evidence that in England chinoiserie buildings may have been erected from the mid- to late 1730s. The Kent designs may be for some other garden, but except for one design for a chimneypiece at Holkham Hall all the other designs in the portfolio relate to Pelham either at Esher or at his Arlington Street house.

20. Locating the various buildings at Esher is a problem, because we are reliant upon what Rocque surveyed. Rocque does not show, for example, any of the park south of the temple sited at the apex of the triangular basin of water. This was where an island was formed out of the river Mole, and where Kent laid out (or intended to lay out) the island garden with its studs of flowers. Within the serpentine wilderness to the north of the house one can identify the circular thatched house and possibly the grotto, though this building could equally be the hermitage; the front of it is similar to a rusticated, pedimented entrance in the side of the hill, also with a belvedere (where Kent's classical villa would have been built), in a landscape study by Kent now in the Lambeth Archives Department, Minet Public Library, London (see Hunt 1987, no. 67). Rocque records an oblong building, which he marks E, on one part of this hill.

21. Lewis 1937–1983, 10:72–73.

22. No mention has been made of Pelham's hunting seat at Laughton Lodge, Sussex, likewise a Tudor tower enlarged by Kent in the Esher style; see Roger White, "Saved by the Landmark Trust: Laughton Lodge, East Sussex," *Country Life* (5 May 1983), 1184–1190; correspondence, *Country Life* (9 June 1983), 1561.

The *Bombé*-Fronted Country House from Talman to Soane

Blenheim Palace, Oxfordshire, has been one of the most frequently discussed country houses anywhere in the British Isles, ever since it was begun in 1705 to the designs of John Vanbrugh. The architect, who was also a playwright, a herald, and a soldier who never fired a shot, endowed the building with a special character befitting its owner, Captain General John Churchill, 1st Duke of Marlborough. Previous commentary has evoked Blenheim's theatrical quality, its heraldic symbolism, and its military or castlelike overtones. It is odd, therefore, that such scant attention has been paid to an unusual and prominent feature of the design: the two- or three-story-high bow windows that project from the center of the east and west facades (fig. 1).[1] Their dramatic appearance at Blenheim marks almost their debut in English baroque architecture, although they were not entirely without precedent either at home or abroad.

In 1688 Vanbrugh was traveling in France and was arrested there on charges of spying for the British. In consequence he spent much of the rest of his four years abroad behind the bars of French jails. It could well be that prior to his incarceration he gained some acquaintance with French architecture, particularly with such châteaux as Versailles and Vaux-le-Vicomte, which his fellow architect Christopher Wren had certainly visited as early as 1665.[2] Designed by Louis le Vau, Vaux-le-Vicomte was completed four years before Wren's visit, for the French finance minister, Nicolas Fouquet. One of its most astonishing design innovations was the large oval salon behind the garden facade, breaking forward from the plane of the wall in a semi-elliptical curve. Earlier Italian architecture provides no real antecedent for a feature of this sort and scale. Reverse or re-entrant curves do occur in Italy—the an-

tique Temple of Fortune at Palestrina, Bramante's Renaissance Belvedere Courtyard at the Vatican, and Francesco Maria Ricchino's Milanese Collegio Elvetico of 1627 spring readily to mind. In Italian domestic architecture, however, there is no comparable *convex* facade projection before Guarino Guarini's Palazzo Carignano of 1679, in Turin.[3] The probable French origins of the facade treatment observed at Vaux therefore justifies describing the phenomenon with the French term *bombé,* appropriated from the language of the decorative arts. Louis le Vau, like some skillful *ébéniste,* gracefully warped the stony surfaces of his garden facade as if to form a piece of *bombé* furniture swelling outward in the center. In so doing he achieved several objectives. The *bombé* facade projection displayed an impressive tour de force of masonry; it facilitated curvilinear internal planning; its rounded shape echoed the curving parterres or *rond points* in André le Nôtre's formal gardens (which are similar to the gardens on the east side of Blenheim); and the number of viewpoints over the gardens was increased by the existence of windows set into an arc of nearly 180 degrees.

Whether Vanbrugh was inspired by the *bombé* garden facade of Vaux-le-Vicomte is by no means clear. Equally unclear is whether other influences played a part at the inception of Blenheim in 1705. Slightly earlier, Thomas Archer had begun the *bombé* north facade of Chatsworth in Derbyshire, though it curves more gently forward than Blenheim. Chettle House in Dorset, which was built in the next decade and has been convincingly connected with Archer's name, also uses the *bombé* feature.[4] Archer's travels abroad coincided with those of Vanbrugh but were more extensive, judging from sparse documentary references to his presence in Italy and from the

Fig. 1.
East facade of Blenheim Palace
(Photograph: author)

Italian baroque style of many of his buildings. A link between Chatsworth and Blenheim, the two biggest and most talked-about architectural projects of early eighteenth-century England, cannot be excluded. The existence of the *bombé* facade at Blenheim, however, has yet more ramifications.

In 1699, the untrained Vanbrugh managed to oust the architect William Talman from the most prestigious country-house commission of the day, Lord Carlisle's Castle Howard in Yorkshire. Dean Swift summed up everyone's astonishment in a memorable couplet: "Van's genius, without Thought or Lecture/Is hugely turn'd to architecture."[5] One can well imagine Vanbrugh being a bit panic-stricken, for all his bravado, when faced with the actual design and execution of a complex project like Castle Howard. He probably profited from the previous discussions between Carlisle and Talman, which had ended acrimoniously, a frequent outcome of that architect's high-handed dealings with clients. By great good fortune, some of Talman's preliminary plans survive. One of them features a *bombé,* datable to no later than 1699 (fig. 2). When Vanbrugh arrived on the scene at Castle Howard he could have admired Talman's centralized *bombé* idea, then abandoned it, only to propose doubling the motif by pushing it off to the side facades, as he was later to do at Blenheim Palace. Had the arrangement been preserved,[6] Castle Howard would have remained the earliest emulation in Britain of the French *bombé* fashion.[7]

Talman's unusual Castle Howard plan has been produced as partial evidence for the view that the designer obeyed few norms—in short, that Talman was a rogue or maverick architect in the best baroque tradition of Borromini. The argument concludes that Talman drew upon French published sources, such as the plans of the Château de Turny in the compendium of prints known as the *Grand Marot.*[8] This would not preclude a direct knowledge of Vaux-le-Vicomte on Talman's part, because the degree of his first-hand exposure to continental monuments remains unclear. Be it from Vaux or Turny, from prints or from personal experience, there is an unmistakable baroque Frenchness to his planned *bombé* projection at Castle Howard, reminiscent of a rising soufflé or a bulging *secrétaire.*

Whatever his maverick tendencies, William Talman remained loyal to the *bombé* treatment in his work as the leading country-house architect of the late seventeenth century. In 1699 William III employed Talman in his capacity as Comptroller of the Royal Works to design a regal retreat on the bank of the river Thames opposite Hampton Court Palace. Several schemes by Talman pertaining to this so-called Thames Ditton Trianon have been preserved.[9] One of them has an impressive plan with two *bombé* projections that take the form of a stair hall on the

Fig. 2.
Plan for Castle Howard by William Talman (British Architectural Library, RIBA, Drawings Collection)

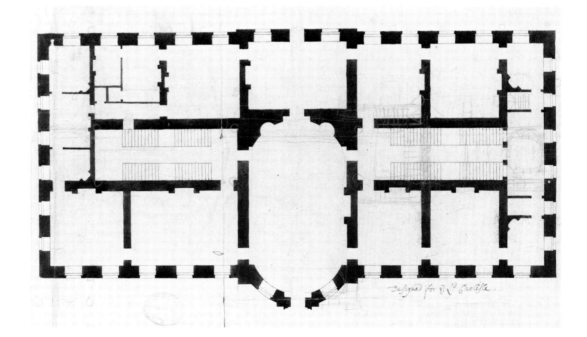

entrance side and an open loggia on the opposite side facing onto the gardens (fig. 3). Another drawing in the same series has an inscription on the frieze which reads in translation: "I avoid the proud thresholds of the state."[10] The words bring to mind the contemporary definition by the amateur architect Roger North: "A villa is quasy a lodge, for the sake of a garden, to retire to, [to] injoy and sleep, without pretence of enterteinement of many persons."[11] The Trianon was obviously intended to be such a lodge, or small retreat for part-time habitation. So, right from the start, the *bombé* treatment was deemed perfectly suitable for those smaller sorts of houses occupied seasonally, which the ancient Romans and their Renaissance Italian successors had called villas. The good sense in this union of style and function was clear. A villa traditionally has an intimate connection with its garden surroundings, which is encouraged by a *bombé* facade.

Although Talman never got the chance to build Castle Howard or the villa at Thames Ditton, toward the very end of his life he had a last opportunity to experiment with the *bombé* facade, at Panton Hall, Lincolnshire, begun in 1719 but sadly demolished in 1960. The central block of the house marked a departure from Talman's work thus far, in that the *bombé* feature was three-sided rather than rounded. Here the canted or faceted variant of the *bombé* takes its first bow.[12] In popularity it equalled or excelled its curved counterpart at Blenheim, and in various buildings associated with the architect Thomas Archer.

Of the three leading turn-of-the-century English country-house architects—Vanbrugh, Archer, and Talman—there can be little doubt that Talman was the earliest and most consistent in the use of the *bombé* feature, even if his designs frequently never left the drawing board. Some of his liking for the motif apparently passed to his son, John, whose extensive studies abroad and collecting forays on the Continent were paid for by his father. John Talman's extraordinarily baroque-looking design of 1708 for the facade of All Souls College, Oxford, derives directly from Guarini's curvaceous Palazzo Carignano.[13] Either young Talman had personally seen it, or he had copied it from prints already available by that time. Whatever its precise sources, the Talmans' exuberant baroque style was founded on a common understanding of the kinetic properties of walls undulating in harmony with changing chiaroscuro effects. Had the elder Talman been

less of a maverick, or his son less of a dilettante, British architecture might have taken a different, more baroque direction. As matters stood, the preference for a *bombé* facade treatment grew sufficiently strong to survive the early demise of the British baroque school of architecture. The reasons become apparent if one considers William Kent's versions of the *bombé* front, which he was able to introduce despite the more rigid, angular geometry of the neo-Palladian movement.

During the heyday of neo-Palladianism in England, the *bombé*-fronted country house was rarely in evidence except in the gothic-revival buildings of William Kent. Besides the newly discovered documentation of the original twist Kent gave the *bombé* feature at Esher Place, Surrey (see Harris, 13), there also exist Kent's neo-Tudor renovations at Hampton Court Palace, and the alterations he carried out at Rousham Park, Oxfordshire, between 1738 and 1741. In all these cases Kent turned for inspiration to polygonal turrets or multi-story bay windows, of which plentiful examples survived from the late-medieval, Elizabethan, and Jacobean periods. Kent must have employed these elements with a view to creating a medieval look in his buildings. Artist that he was, he realized the compositional

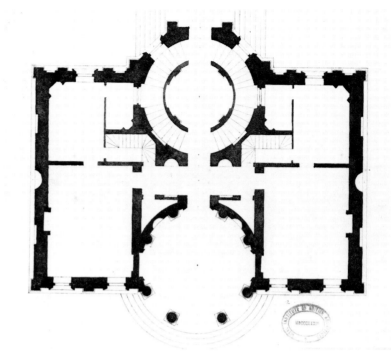

Fig. 3.
Plan for the Thames Ditton Trianon by William Talman (British Architectural Library, RIBA, Drawings Collection)

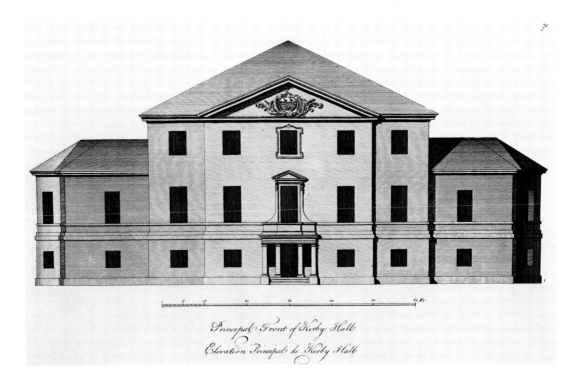

Principal Front of Kirby Hall
Elevation Principale de Kirby Hall

value of a central break or bulge in a facade that might otherwise be flat and dull. In this way—but without resorting to the baroque swagger of his predecessors Talman or Vanbrugh—he kept the *bombé* idea current,[14] simply assigning it a more minor role.

Lord Burlington, leading architect of the neo-Palladian movement and William Kent's patron and friend, was not averse to a subtly modulated but basically flat facade. There appears to be only one documented instance of his use of the *bombé* treatment, at Kirby Hall, Yorkshire, which was begun in about 1750 and subsequently demolished. An engraving of the elevation shows a three-sided *bombé* facade on the extreme right and extreme left ends (fig. 4). The Kirby commission is doubly relevant because the architect Roger Morris carried it out, assisted by a young Yorkshireman named John Carr. Thus, Carr received his baptism in the profession at Kirby.[15] Ever afterward he remained attached to the *bombé* facade, being one of its most frequent exponents. His country houses in this vein, mostly of the 1760s and later, include Tabley House in Cheshire, Constable Burton and Farnley Hall, both in Yorkshire, Basildon Park in Berkshire, and *bombé* extensions to William Talman's own Panton Hall in 1775. At Panton, by a quirk of

fate, Carr literally fused the Talman tradition with the newer style instigated by the Burlington circle.[16]

Another member of the neo-Palladian circle and its chief publicist was Isaac Ware, the translator of Palladio's *I quattro libri dell'architettura.* In his level-headed book of 1756, *A Complete Body of Architecture,* Ware decried the fashion for what he called the "bow window" as an "absurdity that reigns at present."[17] Contrary to what one might surmise from this quotation, Ware favored architectural innovation as long as it obeyed the rules of convenience and common sense. He only opposed bow windows when they were placed in such a way as to command no view, or "prospect" as he put it. And he gave the ridiculous example of two adjacent houses in which the neighbors' *bombé* projections looked straight into each other—eyeball to eyeball, so to speak.

Elsewhere in *A Complete Body of Architecture,* Ware included a country-house design (fig. 5) with a central, three-sided projection crowned with a low dome on a polygonal drum. It is rather as if he were trying his hand at a *bombé* version of his mentor Burlington's famous villa at Chiswick. Whatever Ware's intent, his elevation exemplifies the logical association between a

Fig. 5.
Elevation for a country house by
Isaac Ware, from his *Complete Body
of Architecture,* 1756

dome and a *bombé* facade.[18] This fruitful combination would have ever more frequent repercussions toward the middle of the eighteenth century (figs. 10–12).

The late 1740s and early 1750s saw a resurgence of the *bombé*-fronted country house, largely due to the publication, in 1750, of *Rural Architecture,* a collection of designs by Robert Morris. Morris described himself as an architect of Twickenham and as a kinsman/pupil of Roger Morris, the builder of Kirby Hall. Neither of the Morrises was especially prolific. Robert is primarily remembered as an architectural theorist, lecturer, and poet of doggerel verse. As a designer he had his limitations, but at the same time he proved to be one of the most influential popularizers of the *bombé* facade treatment. The readership of *Rural Architecture,* which was republished five years later as *Select Architecture,* included such leaders in their fields as Thomas Jefferson and John Carr. Carr owned Robert's book of designs by 1758; Jefferson also possessed a copy and acknowledged the debt he owed to it when designing Monticello for his own use.[19] In several respects Monticello can be regarded as a conflation of two plates—numbers 2 and 30—in Morris' *Rural Architecture.* The latter design is described in the text as situated atop a hill, commanding extensive views and with semi-subterranean servants' quarters. The description could be that of Jefferson's home. Plate 2 shows a house plan (fig. 6) prophetically small, compact, and with an intricate sequence of interiors climaxing in a three-sided *bombé* projection, similar to the west facade of Monticello. In his accompanying text, Morris does not attach the name *villa* to either design, although he makes clear that both serve the same seasonal functions as did the villas in antiquity and the Renaissance.[20]

Rural Architecture is one of the most significant publications in the phenomenal first wave of British pattern books that appeared around the middle of the eighteenth century. By 1757 a *bombé* country-house plan by Morris was posthumously contributed to *The Modern Builder's Assistant,* in collaboration with William and John Halfpenny and Timothy Lightoler.[21] These latter three writers figure prominently in the texts printed at this time, which contained a significant number of *bombé* facade projections, usually of the three-sided variety. The 1760s and 1770s saw the greatest outpouring of *bombé* treatments in pattern-book literature.[22] John Crunden's *Convenient and Ornamental Architecture* of 1767, for example, had fifteen such facades; nine can be

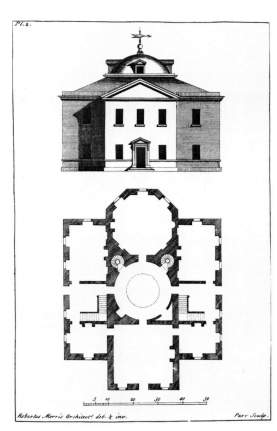

Fig. 6.
Plan and elevation for a country house by Robert Morris, from his *Rural Architecture,* 1750

found in John Carter's *Builders' Magazine* of 1774 to 1778; and ten in John Soane's *Sketches in Architecture* of 1793.

A particularly remarkable efflorescence of the *bombé* facade occurred in the country houses of Robert Taylor. In addition to the knowledge he accrued from his travels abroad, Taylor probably knew the writings of Morris, Ware, the Halfpennys, Lightoler, and others, and was aware of the *bombé* experiments of Lord Burlington at Kirby Park, of Kent at Rousham, and especially of Thomas Wright at Nuthall Temple in 1754.[23] Despite these earlier examples, Taylor's buildings excelled all others in their exploitation of *bombé* facades for multiple purposes. An early Taylor house of 1755, Harleyford Manor on the Thames, is a good example, combining circular and faceted *bombé* facades. Later in date but similarly small in size, Asgill House (1761–1764), downriver at Richmond, has a three-sided *bombé* projection on three of its facades. The jewellike faceted treatment of Asgill's exterior makes up for the building's lack of impressive size. As Crunden remarked in 1767, "a house thus built makes a great figure in the eyes of country peo-

ple."[24] In addition, the windows facing in several directions provided inhabitants with multiple views of the water.

No Taylor house is better planned in relation to its site than Sharpham in Devon. Completed in 1770 if not before,[25] it dominates a curved reach of the river Dart near Totnes (fig. 7). The entire layout of Sharpham is axially related to the *bombé* east front that faces water-borne passersby below. The plan recalls that of Morris' second plate in *Rural Architecture* (fig. 6), except that the cylindrical central space is taken up by a magnificent top-lighted stairhall. The circumstances of the commission are unusual in the annals of the English country house. During the Seven Years War a naval captain, Philemon Pownoll, captured a Spanish treasure-ship laden with gold and silver from Peru. The captain's share of this prize of war was the fabulous sum of £64,000, with which he purchased Sharpham and engaged Taylor to transform the existing house.

The result is a composition that is simple yet stunning from every vantage point, especially from the river. The *bombé* central section of the facade integrates with the landscape, its three faceted sides catching the sun and drawing attention to itself. This is a house from which to view the surroundings; it is also a house that commands respect as a dwelling of substance. Already in the eighteenth century Horace Walpole had articulated this "to see and be seen" aspect,[26] suggesting that it was a novel approach for these smaller yet more aggressively designed houses. In the context of Taylor's lingering Palladianism his *bombé* facade works well, with its rusticated basement, balustraded aedicular windows, crystalline angular geometry, and "staccato rhythms," as Rudolf Wittkower called them.[27] Indeed it fits in so naturally, it is a wonder that Palladio himself never thought of using the motif to enliven his villa designs.

Captain Pownoll's display of new-found wealth was perhaps intensified by the utter restraint of Taylor's art. How different was his approach from the exuberance of Vanbrugh. Compare for a moment Taylor's crisply executed central detail in reddish limestone with the bulging *bombé* at Blenheim (fig. 1). From the window in the middle of Sharpham's facade the land bows to the curve in the river, as if house and surroundings swelled in harmony (fig. 8). This view from the bridge, as it might be described, would have been congenial to Captain Pownoll, even if it never occurred to him that a *bombé*

Fig. 7.
East facade of Sharpham House,
Devon, designed by Robert Taylor,
c. 1770 (Photograph: author)

Fig. 8.
View from the central window of
the east facade of Sharpham
House (Photograph: author)

Fig. 9.
Detail of the east facade of Mersham
le Hatch, Kent, designed by Robert
Adam, c. 1762–1765 (Photograph:
author)

facade projection has a coincidental resemblance
to a ship's prow or poop deck.

When Robert Adam, the architect of
Mersham le Hatch in Kent, returned from Rome
to London in 1758, he found the country-house
trade largely carved up among practitioners like
John Carr and Robert Taylor, who resorted to
smaller houses featuring *bombé* facades. It is not
generally remarked that at an early date, between
1762 and 1765, Adam began his brilliant career
by conforming to the *bombé* fashion.[28] Despite
many differences between Mersham and
Sharpham, particularly the use of a bright red
brick, Adam's design focused on a curving central salon, the windows of which sweep out to a
view of the landscape ending in a distant ridge of
hills beyond a lake (fig. 9).

Originally the effect would have been even
more startling than it is today. Without the
stone portico, which is largely of later date, the
cylinder would have risen up quite sheer and
plain, like a great silo. The pure geometry of the
circular bow is just as much in keeping with
Adam's legato, stripped-down neo-classicism as

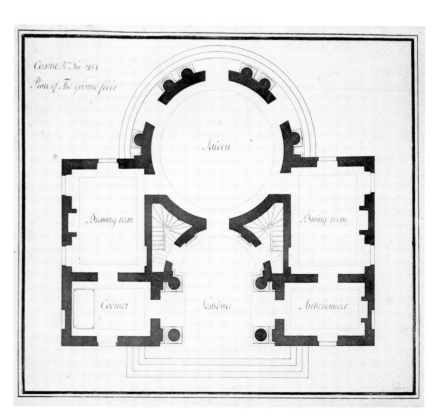

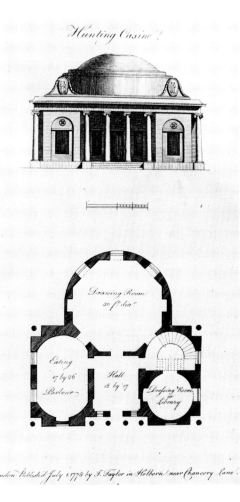

Hunting Casino?

Drawing Room
30 f² dia.

Eating
17 by 26
Parlour

Hall
18 by 17

Dressing Room
or
Library

London Publish'd July 1778 by J. Taylor in Holborn near Chancery Lane.

Fig. 12.
Plan and elevation for a casino by
John Soane, 1778, from his *Designs
in Architecture*

the faceted bow was with Taylor's staccato neo-Palladianism. As Isaac Ware put it, with reference to circular projections, "*there* is composure and beauty, an idea of capacity and an appearance of solidity and strength."[29] He could easily have been describing Mersham.

Elsewhere in his truly astonishing range of works, Adam employed the *bombé* facade treatment on a conspicuously located building in what is now central London: the long-vanished Deputy Ranger's Lodge in Green Park (fig. 10). When Adam constructed it in 1768, it was on the outer fringes of the metropolis and served the park ranger who guarded the land from poachers. It could hardly be described as a country house, considering its suburban location and small size.[30] The best analogy would be a *rendez-vous de chasse* or hunting lodge. A number of elegant ones existed abroad, the closest parallel being Le Butard near Paris, built in 1750 by Ange-Jacques Gabriel for Louis XV. Not unlike

the rangers lodge, it has a *bombé* facade on one side, originally intended to receive a little dome. Despite Adam's admiration for things French, it is unlikely that he knew Le Butard, the design of which was never published.[31]

One individual who could have known the Butard plan—as well as its direct French antecedents like Vaux-le-Vicomte—was William Chambers, who lived and studied in Paris during the year Gabriel completed Le Butard. While subsequently in Rome, where he preceded Robert Adam, Chambers produced a design of his own, dated November 1754, not dissimilar in plan to Le Butard or the Deputy Ranger's Lodge (fig. 11). He called it a "casino," by which Italian word he meant to connote something chic, petite, and perhaps even slightly risqué (in the sense that a casino served for assignations or wild parties). The Italian name is simply a decoy for the ultimate Frenchness of the design, which had been missing from the development of the *bombé* facade in England since the days of Talman.[32] On settling in London to begin his life's work, Chambers took pains to exhibit this and similar casinos. The most notable occasion was at the Royal Academy of Arts in 1773, when he showed his famous casino for Lord Charlemont at Marino near Dublin.

The work of the architect John Soane, a student at the Royal Academy in the 1770s, is of special interest because his career is the best documented of his age, and because his country-house designs revolved around the *bombé* facade concept.[33] In 1772 the Berkshire-born Soane, then in his nineteenth year, entered the employ of the fashionable country-house designer Henry Holland the Younger. In contrast to his architectural brethren, Holland was not at all partial to the *bombé* facade treatment, but his office was located in Half Moon Street, directly across Piccadilly from the Green Park ranger's lodge. Later he moved his operation to nearby Hertford Street, and Soane's first recorded place of lodging was just around the corner on Hamilton Street. Thus, in his daily comings and goings during the period 1772 to 1778, Soane could hardly have escaped noticing Adam's *bombé*-fronted building in the park. Soane came to meet Adam through Henry Holland, and to value the friendship Adam offered younger artists.[34] In emulation of Adam, so it seems, Soane designed what he called a "hunting casino," which he published in London in 1778 (fig. 12). Not only is the function of the building analogous to that of the

Deputy Ranger's Lodge, but the *bombé* shape is seen here for the first time in Soane's work. Soane's use of the name *casino* pays homage to William Chambers, who acted as his unofficial mentor when he was enrolled as a student in the Royal Academy Schools. Chambers and his pupils had a virtual corner on the casino market, having exhibited no less than nine at the Academy shows during the 1770s.[35] A number of these designs no doubt derived from Chambers' prototypical casino plan of French derivation, with *bombé* projection (fig. 11). Soane himself did not exhibit any casino until 1781, but in the meantime he had risen to the position of star pupil at the Academy. In 1778 he received the institution's royal traveling scholarship to Italy, and it was in Rome later that year that he had his momentous encounter with the Earl-Bishop, that most inveterate of English Grand Tourists.

Frederick Hervey, already Bishop of Derry and soon to succeed to the Earldom of Bristol, was a discriminating connoisseur of the arts who liked talent-scouting among the young artists in Rome. He made Soane his protégé, and for him Soane returned to the hunting casino theme in a pair of plans dated 11 November 1779 (fig. 13).[36] The *bombé* facade carries a scalloped-out cornice, which Soane's inscription identifies as inspired by the Temple of the Sun at Baalbec, published by Wood and Dawkins a generation earlier in 1757. It was in displays of this kind of precise archaeological erudition that the Earl-Bishop himself liked to dazzle his listeners, which suggests he might have dabbled with the design. We know he was contemplating the construction of a classical dog kennel at the time, for which Soane supplied some hilarious designs. Soane's hunting casino seems conceived in the same playful spirit—part habitable antique temple, part up-to-date little hunting box. The superrefined elevations can be ascertained from related sketches in Soane's notebook of 1780, which the architect kept when he left Rome to work for the Earl-Bishop in Northern Ireland.[37]

The astonishing thing about the early career of Soane is the speed with which he adopted the Spartan aesthetic we associate with his name, all the while remaining true to the *bombé* facade. His rapid maturation can be judged in his earliest completed country house, the rectory at Saxlingham Nethergate in Norfolk, begun in 1784 (fig. 14). Unlike Soane's student designs, Saxlingham Rectory combines the logical axial planning of Robert Taylor with the simple geometric

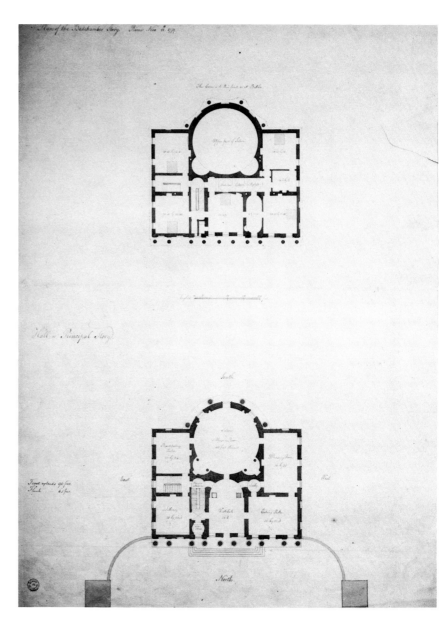

forms of Robert Adam. The *bombé* facade treatment, carried through from front to back, becomes the unifying factor. Externally the smooth *bombé* effect makes an eloquent as well as a sensible statement. Originally the entrance was through the center of the north facade, by what is now a French window. The placement of this window instead of a solid door heightens the original effect by permitting a view straight through the entire house to the echoing southern curve of the drawing room. The simplicity of the axial planning, the smooth lines of the drawing-room cornice moulding, and the austere, geo-

Fig. 13.
Plans for a casino by John Soane, 1779 (Sir John Soane's Museum)

Fig. 14.
South facade of Saxlingham Rectory, Norfolk, designed by John Soane, 1784 (Photograph: author)

Fig. 15.
Interior of the drawing room of
Saxlingham Rectory (Photograph:
Michael Brandon-Jones)

metric chimneypiece (fig. 15) guide the eye in an uninterrupted gliding motion to the lawn, which stretches off to the road just beyond. Ironically, what had begun in 1778 as a youthful design intended for a rich client, ended up being built for the Reverend Mr. John Gooch, who could not pay his bills on time. The whole structure, including materials salvaged from the old rectory and locally baked Suffolk white bricks, cost only £2500. The utter assurance with which this house was conceived, as well as its manageable size in modern terms, has earned the building respect from critics in our own age.[38]

The largest commission undertaken by Soane during his early maturity was Tendring Hall, Suffolk, begun in 1785 at a total cost of £12,000. At Tendring the client was another navy man, Joshua Rowley, Vice Admiral of the Blue and later a baronet. An unpublished preliminary drawing of the ground plan with the two principal facades, complete with a half-height *bombé* projection on the south facade, recalls a Taylor country house (fig. 16).[39] Since the plan is somewhat deeper than that of Saxlingham Rectory, a top-lighted cylindrical stairhall is inserted, as at

Sharpham. Its play of curves forms a fitting prelude to the soft, rounded south facade overlooking a pond in the park fed by the river Stour. In contrast, the shallow projections and recessions of the entrance facade on the north create a more austere appearance.

Echoing the words of Robert Morris of thirty years before, Soane pronounced that the southern *bombé* facade took advantage of the hilltop view "commanding a variety of pleasing objects."[40] The curving center of Tendring housed a drawing room below and Mrs. Rowley's sunny, lemon-yellow dressing room above (fig. 17). If we think back to the Duchess of Marlborough's favorite bow room (fig. 1), it is obvious that a preference for *bombé* facades was by no means restricted to seafaring men, and indeed no precise correlation has emerged between *bombé*-fronted country houses and particular types of clients. As Figure 17 shows, Tendring was a sorry sight in the 1950s after it had been requisitioned by troops during World War II. The lemon-yellow paint had peeled off and dry rot was rampant. Despite the valiant attempts at restoration by the present Sir Joshua Rowley and

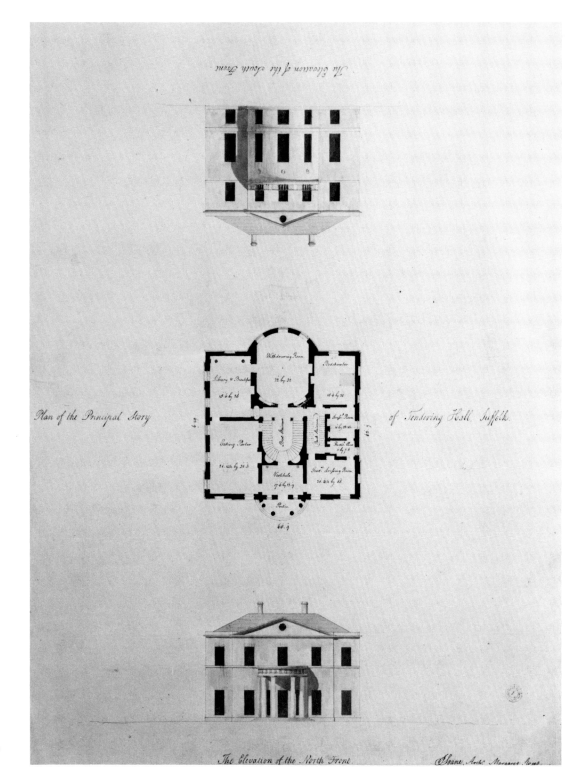

Fig. 16.
Plan and elevations for Tendring
Hall by John Soane, 1785 (Sir John
Soane's Museum)

the late Raymond Erith, a distinguished architect who admired Soane, the house could not be saved.[41] Apart from some haunting photographs, nothing is left of Tendring but the four columns of its entrance porch.

The extent to which Soane's infatuation with the *bombé* theme continued uninterrupted was not recognized until a crucial drawing reemerged recently (fig. 18). Its subject is Soane's next important commission, the rebuilding of Chillington Hall in Staffordshire, from 1786 to 1789. Still the home of the Giffards, a family that goes back to the Norman Conquest, Chillington makes obvious that the *bombé* country house was not restricted to parvenus. The plan and elevation, Soane originals with pentimenti and even a prominent ink spill in the master's own hand, had been in the private collection of the architect Sir Albert Richardson, and had thus escaped attention or publication. Auctioned in 1983, the sheet is now in Montreal at the Canadian Centre for Architecture.[42]

The intrinsic significance of the Chillington drawing in Montreal is far greater than that of the ten other drawings in Sir John Soane's Museum, which are better known.[43] Not only is it in all likelihood the earliest in the sequence, but it is more densely packed with information. In the center of the bottom margin, what at first appears to be a scale bar turns out to be a measured plan of the fenestration pattern of Chillington's existing ten-bay Tudor east facade. The measurements should make it possible to prove or disprove the commonly held belief that Soane

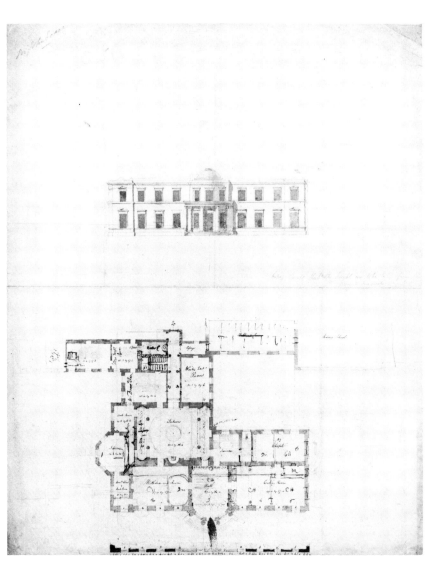

Fig. 17.
Interior of Mrs. Rowley's bedroom,
Tendring Hall   (Photograph: Avery
Colebrook)

Fig. 18.
Plan and elevation for Chillington
Hall by John Soane, c. 1786   (Cana-
dian Centre for Architecture)

Fig. 19.
Perspective view of Tyringham Park
by Joseph Michael Gandy after John
Soane, 1798   (Victoria and Albert
Museum)

extended the east facade,[44] rather than simply reorganizing the number and spacing of the extant windows. The major change would have taken place in the center of the facade, where the Montreal plan calls for two bays to be transformed into a three-bay *bombé* projection leading to the entrance vestibule.

According to the elevation drawing, this central element would have been domed and was probably meant to accommodate a grand master bedroom upstairs. (In fact the Montreal plan of the main floor, as amended by Soane's hasty freehand sketches, has superimposed on it the relative positions of the six principal bedchambers on the story above.) Off to the left of the plan, on the southern facade, already stood a suite of early eighteenth-century rooms, plus a fine staircase. These rooms, attributed to Francis Smith, are still in existence at Chillington, although Soane initially proposed abolishing them in favor of another centrally located *bombé* facade projection, this time of the three-sided variety. Each of the two *bombés* would have led back to a domed and top-lighted salon, larger but more awkwardly arranged than the one Soane eventually built. If the accurate dating of the Montreal sheet is between late 1785 and mid-1786, then this would be the first instance of a monumental top-lighted Soane interior, earlier by five and a half years than his Bank of England interior in London.

Soane received the appointment of surveyor to the Bank of England in 1788, thus inaugurating his career as a designer of public works. His practice as a country-house architect progressively diminished. On occasion, however, he permitted himself a commission on the side, as with Tyringham in Buckinghamshire, perhaps his most famous and best-loved country house. Each time Soane designed such a dwelling he returned to the *bombé* theme, but always with slightly more refined results.[45] The client at Tyringham, William Mackworth Praed, was a banker. No expense was spared. The stone-built house was begun in 1792 and finished five years later. Compared to his earlier brick houses such as Saxlingham, it has a smoother, sleeker, almost French feeling to it, no doubt intensified today by the Edwardian dome of 1909 added by G. F. Rees. The house in its pristine form appears in a visionary watercolor commissioned by Soane from the great architectural draftsman Joseph Michael Gandy (fig. 19).[46] Gandy dramatized the *bombé* bulge by depicting late afternoon sunlight breaking sublimely through the storm clouds, casting shadows and turning the stone to a golden hue. He knew better than anyone how to show off to best advantage the *bombé* aspects of a design, which mattered so much to Soane.

Photographs of Soane's last country house, Pell Wall in Shropshire, in its now-derelict state,

show the building in a way that Soane and Gandy, with their morbid love of ruins, would have admired (fig. 20).[47] Long, slanting rays of sunlight glide across the windows of the northwest-facing facade, dappling the *bombé* front. The tautness of surfaces is intensified by linear grooved pilasters, which give the facade a strangely nervous, almost electric energy. The aged Soane (he was in his early seventies when, in 1822, he designed Pell Wall for a friend) allowed himself a certain eccentricity at the end of his career. He wanted to reinvent the classical language of architecture by replacing the classical orders with his own brand of articulation, sunk below the surface rather than projecting from it. This should not obscure the fact that the central feature at Pell Wall remains that of the *bombé*, inherited by Soane from the previous generation of Chambers, Morris, Taylor, Kent, and Adam. Because of Soane's singleminded pursuit, refinement, and exploitation of the *bombé*-fronted country-house, it is first and foremost with his name that we have come to associate this kind of facade, especially in connection with the North American *bombé* motif.[48]

The *bombé* facade suggested a certain casualness, an integration with nature, and a relaxation of the more straightlaced aspects of the classical tradition. It offered a distinctive, eye-catching profile. Above all, it accomplished these things with verve, and yet was simplicity itself. Perhaps that very simplicity is the reason why the *bombé*-fronted country-house type has not been singled out for the sort of notice it needs or deserves.

Fig. 20.
North facade of Pell Wall, Shropshire, by John Soane, 1822 (Photograph: author)

NOTES

1. The most recent scholarly treatments of Blenheim are Kerry Downes, *Vanbrugh* (London, 1977); idem, *Sir John Vanbrugh: A Biography* (London, 1987).

2. For a detailed discussion of the sights Wren visited abroad, see Margaret Whinney, "Sir Christopher Wren's Visit to Paris," *Gazette des Beaux-Arts* 51 (1958), 229–242. The evolution of the *bombé* facade in France is the subject of a note by Louis Hautecoeur, *Histoire de l'architecture classique en France,* 7 vols. (Paris, 1943–1957), 4:372.

3. In discussion after this paper was delivered, Henry Millon kindly suggested that I might find Italian prototypes for the *bombé* feature among the early proposals of the 1620s and 1630s for the Palazzo Barberini in Rome. Thanks to the generosity of Patricia Waddy I have been able to consult her "Palazzo Barberini: Early Proposals" (Ph.D. diss., New York University, 1973). Although an oval *salone* features prominently in a number of the palazzo schemes discussed and illustrated by Waddy, none of the ovals breaks forward from the wall plane in a *bombé* projection. Professor Thomas Glen of McGill University suggested to me in conversation that evidence exists to link Louis le Vau's château of Vaux with Borromini's partly executed church of S. Agnese in Piazza Navona, Rome, whose curvaceous facade was under construction in 1652. The truly problematic connection is between the *bombé* facade at Vaux and Gian Lorenzo Bernini's first project for the east facade of the Louvre, made in 1664. If Bernini's plan was too late in date for Le Vau to make use of, it was almost certainly seen by Christopher Wren in 1665 and could have reinforced his personal impressions of the *bombé* facade at Vaux-le-Vicomte. See note 2, on Wren.

4. For Archer's career, see Marcus Whiffen, *Thomas Archer: Architect of the English Baroque,* 2d ed. (Los Angeles, 1973). Chettle House and Chatsworth are also described in James Lees-Milne, *English Country Houses: Baroque 1685–1715* (London, 1970).

5. Downes 1977, 14, cites Swift and gives a brief history of the Castle Howard commission. See also, more recently, John Harris, *William Talman, Maverick Architect* (London, 1982); Downes 1987, 530–533.

6. Colen Campbell, *Vitruvius Britannicus,* 3 vols. (London, 1715–1725), 1: pls. 63–64, show only one *bombé* facade variously located at the east or west end, respectively; but 3: pls. 5–6 is an aerial perspective view with a *bombé* projection on *both* end facades. This discrepancy and the engraved plans by Campbell showing single or double *bombé* facades are published in Paul Breman and Denise Addis, *Guide to Vitruvius Britannicus* (New York, 1972), 74.

7. There is a possibility that the Castle Howard plans may have been preceded by the enigmatic ones for Abbotstone House, Hampshire, attributed to Talman. Abbotstone House is an interesting case study of scholarly peregrinations about a monument. Howard Colvin in his *A Biographical Dictionary of English Architects 1660–1840* (London, 1954), 593, pointed out the existence at Oxford of two drawings for Abbotstone, "possibly . . . by [William] Talman." In his expanded *A Biographical Dictionary of British Architects 1600–1840* (London, 1978), 807, Colvin noted that the designs would have to have preceded the death of the Duke of Bolton in 1699. He dated Abbotstone to c. 1685. Meanwhile John Summerson, in "The Classical Country House in Eighteenth-Century England," *Journal of the Royal Society of Arts* 107 (1959), 586, n. 26, acknowledged that the drawings had been brought to his attention by John Harris,

who attributed them to Talman, pre 1726. Summerson focused on the fact that the plan for Abbotstone had four three-sided *bombé* projections, one on each facade; although accepting Harris' attribution and date, he preferred to see the design feature as "Burlingtonian" in origin. Finally, Harris himself in Harris 1982, 22, withdrew his attribution to John Talman and stated that the design might date to as early as 1689. It is to be hoped that one day these drawings, that have given rise to so many interpretations, will be published.

8. Harris 1982, 33, 36–37.

9. These designs in the Drawings Collection, Royal Institute of British Architects, have been dealt with at length in John Harris "The Hampton Court Trianon Designs of William and John Talman," *Journal of the Warburg and Courtauld Institutes* 23 (1960), 139–149; Harris 1982, 36–37. I do not entirely agree with the latter publication's reading of the trianon elevation (fig. 54), only the lower story of which seems to me to be *bombé* faceded.

10. Translation by Howard Colvin, *Royal Buildings* (London, 1968), 26.

11. Howard Colvin and John Newman, eds., *Of Building: Roger North's Writings on Architecture* (Oxford, 1981), 62. I have previously used North's definition to underscore the relation of villa to garden; see Pierre de la Ruffinière du Prey, "Four Cardinal Points of a Villa," *Architecture Québec* 15 (1983), 16–22.

12. Alastair Laing remarked in the question period following this paper that *bombé* as a word was only adequate to cover the rounded not the faceted variety of facade projection. In response to this I would like to stress that no really suitable term in English exists to answer my needs, so I have pressed *bombé* into service. In the seventeenth and eighteenth century and ever since, the words "bay window" and "bow window" have been employed almost interchangeably and with no precision. Laing's complaint equally applies to Isaac Ware's use of "angulated" bow window in *A Complete Body of Architecture* (London, 1756), 423, or to John Crunden's "octangular bow windows" in *Convenient and Ornamental Architecture* (London, 1767), 6. Both these expressions of the period are awkward turns of phrase; I persist in preferring the term *bombé*.

13. Howard Colvin, *Unbuilt Oxford* (New Haven and London, 1983), 37, pl. 1, discusses the Talman drawing in terms of Guarini and illustrates it.

14. Downes 1977, 69, links Blenheim's side facade projections to Vanbrugh's interest in the Elizabethan and Jacobean prodigy house tradition, which also manifests itself in the architect's use of variegated roof lines.

15. Colvin 1978, 189; see p. 131 for the building history of Kirby.

16. Panton Hall was first discussed by John Harris and Nikolaus Pevsner in *The Buildings of England: Lincolnshire* (Harmondsworth, 1964), 335. A plan reconstruction by Jeremy Lever of the Talman part of the house has been published in Harris 1982, fig. 77, but the caption to the Panton plan incorrectly suggests a resemblance to Talman's Castle Howard plan. The facade of the latter is round, whereas that of the former is faceted.

17. Ware 1756, 300. In the text, the words "Venetian window" instead of bow window are used by mistake, as Ware's errata list makes clear.

18. Ware was quite proud of his combination of dome and *bombé* facade. He had Andrea Soldi the artist portray him with the motif—as used at Wrotham Park, Hertfordshire—prominently displayed in the background. Perhaps coincidentally Ware is shown pointing to the same motif on a plan and

elevation of Wrotham spread out on a table before him. The portrait hangs in the Drawings Collection, Royal Institute of British Architects. Ware may have been inspired by the similar end-pavilion treatment intended for Rokeby Park, Yorkshire, according to Michael McCarthy, "Sir Thomas Robinson: an Original English Palladian," *Architectura* 10 (1980), 38–57.

19. Jefferson's use of Morris is well known and has been commented upon by Adolf K. Placzek in his foreword to the reprint edition of *Select Architecture* (New York, 1973); see also William Bainter O'Neal, *Jefferson's Fine Arts Library: His Selections for the University of Virginia Together with His Own Architecture Books* (Charlottesville, 1976), 231–237. Colvin 1978, 189, remarks upon the signed Carr copy of *Select Architecture* in Sir John Soane's Museum, London (Architectural Library, Case 39A). The copy is dated 1758 in Carr's hand.

20. I have investigated the architectural use of the term villa in eighteenth-century Britain in Pierre de la Ruffinière du Prey, *John Soane: The Making of an Architect* (Chicago, 1982), 265–269.

21. Morris supplied pl. 35. The date was misprinted on the original title page, but can be confidently assigned to 1757, according to John Archer, *The Literature of British Domestic Architecture 1715–1842* (Cambridge, Mass., 1985), 404.

22. Using Archer 1985 as a starting point, Jennifer Trant, a graduate student in the History of Art at Queen's University, Kingston, has searched for *bombé* facades in the period 1715–1802. Of the 173 books listed by Archer she has studied some 75 titles and has come up with just over 240 designs with one or more *bombé* facades. A certain proportion of these, however, represent structures other than country houses. Nevertheless, her unpublished survey indicates the prevalence of the *bombé* device at this time. Her conclusions also tend to indicate that William Halfpenny had a more important role to play in the whole development of the *bombé* facade than I have given him credit for here. The topic deserves a full study.

23. In a recent paper, read at the symposium "The Villa: Expanding Definitions and Methodologies" held at Queen's University, Kingston, Michael McCarthy argued for Taylor's reliance on precedent, with special reference to pattern books. The characteristic Taylor motif of a *bombé* projection surmounted by a Serlian window can be traced back to Wright's Nuthall drawings in the Avery Architectural Library, Columbia University, New York; see Eileen Harris' introductory essay to Thomas Wright, *Designs of Arbours; Designs of Grottos* (reprint ed., London, 1979). Some but not all of this borrowing of motifs has been acknowledged by Marcus Binney in *Sir Robert Taylor: From Rococo to Neoclassicism* (London, 1984); see also idem, "The Villas of Sir Robert Taylor," *Country Life* 142 (1967), 17–21, 78–82.

24. Crunden 1767, 6. The passage has previously been cited by Summerson 1959, 586, n. 26. The aspect of cheerfulness within, and the views without, which Crunden makes much of, is also emphasized by Christopher Hussey, *English Country Houses: Early Georgians 1715–1760*, 2d ed. (London, 1963), 27. Hussey considers the *bombé* facade a "rococo characteristic" because of the implied closer link to nature. Hussey's study is the only one previously to have isolated the *bombé* feature for consideration, albeit very cursorily.

25. Binney 1984, 36–37, 53–54, discusses Sharpham. A somewhat fuller account is to be found in Marcus Binney, "Sharpham House, Devon," *Country Life* 145 (1969), 952–954, 1014–1017. During my visit to Sharpham the owners, Mr. Maurice Ash and the late Ruth Ash, showed me photographs of an extraordinary pair of before and after views of Sharpham painted in 1769 by one P. Lewis. The picture showing the Taylor south facade, which is now quite flat, reveals that originally

that front, too, had a characteristic central *bombé* positioned exactly where the former Jacobean multi-story bay window had been! Breaks in the masonry at Sharpham prove that the second *bombé* projection was built. I am most grateful to the Ashes for welcoming me and sharing their knowledge of their beautiful home.

26. Quoted in Binney 1984, 39. Walpole is actually speaking of an older house and one can deduce that a "modern" house according to him would "see and be seen." I adduced this principle of the villa in du Prey 1983, 18–19, without knowing of the Walpole quotation.

27. Rudolf Wittkower, "Lord Burlington and William Kent," *Archaeological Journal* 102 (1945), 151–164.

28. Mersham le Hatch is discussed by Christopher Hussey, *English Country Houses: Mid Georgian, 1760–1800,* 2d ed. (London, 1963), 98–104. Although relatively uncommon in Adam's built oeuvre, the *bombé* facade treatment occurs frequently in his designs, as can be seen from a glance at Alistair Rowan, *Designs for Castles and Country Villas by Robert and James Adam* (London, 1985).

29. Ware 1756, 305. The italics are mine.

30. See Joseph and Anne Rykwert, *Robert and James Adam: The Men and the Style* (New York, 1985), 144–145. The lodge, demolished in 1841, was about 60' long by 30' deep, not including the *bombé* projection. See n. 38 for the dimensions of Soane's Saxlingham Rectory.

31. Christopher Tadgell, *Ange-Jacques Gabriel* (London, 1978), 43, 163, gives the history of the Le Butard commission. Plate 135 shows the low domed penultimate project.

32. John Harris, *Sir William Chambers, Knight of the Polar Star* (London, 1970), 30, 42, 52 fig. 5a, alludes to Chambers' Franco-Italian casino schemes. I have published a redrawn version of one of them in du Prey 1982, 273, fig. 13.4. The Victoria and Albert Museum acquisition number of this drawing is 3359. Related to it are 3416 and 3417 for a "Casino in The Style of Baldasar Peruzzi," done in 1753 in Rome.

33. The literature on individual *bombé*-fronted country houses by Soane's contemporaries is vast and dispersed. The following merely suggests the wealth of material: on James Paine's Stockeld Park, Yorkshire, see Marcus Binney, "The Villas of James Paine," *Country Life* (20 February 1969), 406–410, 466–470; the Robert Mylne drawings for The Wick near Richmond Hill, Surrey, are now in the Canadian Centre for Architecture, Montreal; James Gandon's Carriglas in Ireland has been discussed by Edward McParland, *James Gandon Vitruvius Hibernicus* (London, 1985); Heaton Hall, Lancashire, and Doddington Hall, Cheshire, by the Wyatts figure in Hussey 1963; I have mentioned Sadborrow in Dorset by John Johnson in du Prey 1982, chapter 13.

34. On Soane's various places of work and residence in London and on the topic of his friendship with Robert Adam, see du Prey 1982; Dorothy Stroud, *Henry Holland* (London, 1966).

35. Algernon Graves' published lists of the exhibitors at the Royal Society of Artists and the Royal Academy of Arts tabulate the casino designs exhibited by Chambers and his pupils Thomas Hardwick, Edward Stevens, and John Yenn.

36. These plans are enlarged versions of an engraved scheme of 1778.

37. I have discussed the dog kennel and related casino designs for the Earl-Bishop in Pierre de la Ruffinière du Prey, " 'Je N'Oublieraj Jamais:' John Soane and Downhill," *Bulletin of the Irish Georgian Society* 21 (1978), 17–40.

38. Saxlingham Rectory's dimensions are 57$\frac{1}{2}$' wide by 27$\frac{1}{2}$' deep, not including the *bombé* projections. In the sensitive res-

toration and enlargement of the house, completed in 1971 by the firm of Fielden and Mawson, the square footage on the main floor was almost doubled by the addition of a kitchen and guest wing roughly on the site intended by Soane for a service court. I owe my familiarity with Saxlingham Rectory to the hospitality of its former owner/restorers, Mr. and Mrs. J. H. R. Carver.

39. Tendring is the subject of du Prey 1982, chap. 14. The drawing in fig. 16 is in Sir John Soane's Museum, drawer 28, set 3, item 1.

40. Compare John Soane, *Plans, Elevations and Sections of Buildings* (London, 1788), unpaginated, with Robert Morris, *Rural Architecture* (London, 1750), 5.

41. Lucy Archer, daughter of Raymond Erith, discusses and illustrates her father's scheme of 1953 to save Tendring in *Raymond Erith Architect* (London, 1985), 31, 130, pl. 86.

42. See *Important Architectural Drawings and Watercolors I. Sir Albert Richardson Collection* [sale cat., Christie's] (London, 30 November 1983), lot 74. The CCA accession number is DR1983:853.

43. Sir John Soane's Museum, drawer 29, set 1, items 1–10.

44. Dorothy Stroud, *Sir John Soane Architect* (London, 1984), 130. One of the preliminary ground plans for Chillington is illustrated in Hussey 1963, 224.

45. Apart from the country houses mentioned in this article, the following fourteen can be added to Soane's *bombé* oeuvre: Barons Court, County Tyrone, Ireland; Burn Hall, County Durham; Chilton Lodge, Berkshire; William Colhoun House, Thetford, Norfolk; Combe House, Devonshire; Letton House, Norfolk; villa at Mottram, Cheshire; Spencerwood, Berkshire; Sydney Lodge, Hampshire; a design for Lady Granard in Ireland (John Soane, *Sketches in Architecture* [London, 1793] pl. 22); two designs for houses in County Durham (Soane 1793, pls. 20, 26); an unlocated casino design (Soane 1793, pl. 30); a small villa design (Soane 1793, pls. 34–35).

46. I have discussed this Gandy watercolor in Pierre de la Ruffinière du Prey, *Catalogues of Architectural Drawings in the Victoria and Albert Museum: Sir John Soane* (London, 1985), 59–62.

47. See Giles Worsley, "Pell Wall Hall, Staffordshire," *Country Life* 182 (1988), 134–137.

48. Recent literature in which Soane's name is evoked in connection with North American *bombé*-fronted houses includes: Richard J. Betts, "The Woodlands," *Winterthur Portfolio* 14 (1979), 213–234; Edward F. Zimmer and Pamela Scott, "Alexander Parris, B. Henry Latrobe, and the John Wickham House in Richmond, Virginia," *Journal of the Society of Architectural Historians* 41 (1982), 202–211; Robert H. Hubbard, *Rideau Hall* (Ottawa, 1967); Janet Wright, *Architecture of the Picturesque in Canada* (Ottawa, 1984).

JOHN WILTON-ELY

Pompeian and Etruscan Tastes in the Neo-Classical Country-House Interior

The painted interior, together with its integrated furniture and fittings as an expression of antique taste, is among the most original aspects of neo-classical design. Although Italy was the key source of inspiration, England—followed by France and Germany—was the pioneer of this approach, largely due to the archaeologically based culture that was established early in the eighteenth century by Lord Burlington and William Kent. This taste was developed further in the second half of the century by several country-house owners and designers, some of them closely associated with the Society of Dilettanti and its archaeological activities.[1]

Between 1760 and 1790—the three-decade period covered by this particular study—a remarkable series of imaginative experiments were carried out in country houses or associated town houses in London, in which owners, architects, decorative painters, and a variety of craftsmen played a collaborative role rarely paralleled in interior design. The very fact that several of the painted interiors to be discussed are still designated as Pompeian or Roman or Etruscan by different scholars underlines the fruitful artistic licence involved, as well as the interweaving of various antique sources from the 1760s onward. Even before the new inspiration from southern Italy had begun to take effect, antique painted decoration had entered the repertoire of English designers in the form of the "grotesque" style of Raphael, Giulio Romano, Giovanni da Udine, and their followers. Introduced by William Kent at Kensington Palace between 1722 and 1727 and again by him at Rousham, Oxfordshire, between 1738 and 1741, this highly imaginative transcription of antique forms, sustained by a sense of fantasy shared with the rococo, provided a major decorative language in the early neo-classical schemes I shall consider.[2]

Predictably, the discoveries of Roman domestic taste at Herculaneum and Pompeii, from 1738 and 1748 respectively, awakened a fresh interest in modes of interior design as part of a wider search for a contemporary style of expression.[3] Long familiar accounts of painting in classical antiquity by authors such as Pliny were now to be matched by an increasing quantity of material evidence. The impact of these finds on the visual arts was extremely slow to take effect, because access to the *scavi,* let alone opportunities to record the finds at Herculaneum, were notoriously difficult. While random illustrations appeared in early accounts, the principal paintings brought to light in the 1740s and early 1750s were only intermittently published in the official *Le antichità di Ercolano esposti* from 1757 onward, when the first of four volumes devoted to paintings appeared.[4] Even then, the fragmentary nature of the frescoes depicted was often the result of the physical constraints of the underground site or the crude methods of recovery.[5] While providing little idea of entire room schemes, these reproductions at least allowed considerable scope for creative interpretation.

In 1759 William Chambers, in his *Treatise on Civil Architecture,* asserted that "painted ceilings which constitute one of the greatest embellishments of Italian and French structures . . . are not in use among us," and went on to say that "the prejudices of our connoisseurs hath excluded all modern paintings from our houses."[6] That same year, however, James Stuart was creating a room with an extensive scheme of painted decoration, and was incorporating in it an impressive set of furniture in the antique taste. This room can lay claim to being among the first comprehensive neo-classical interiors in Europe.

Stuart's Painted Room (figs. 1, 2) formed part

Fig. 1.
North and east walls of the Painted Room at Spencer House, London, designed by James Stuart in 1759, before dispersal of the furniture
(Photograph: National Monuments Record)

Fig. 2.
South end of the Painted Room at Spencer House (Photograph: National Monuments Record)

of a suite of lavish state interiors on the upper floor of Spencer House, London, built by Kent's disciple, John Vardy, between 1756 and 1765 for John, Baron Spencer of Althorp, created Viscount in 1761 and Earl Spencer in 1765.[7] In 1765 Spencer became a member of the Society of Dilettanti, and it was the society's secretary, Colonel George Gray, who supervised the design of the house. Gray clearly intended that the Palladian structure should benefit from new approaches to contemporary design inspired by antiquity. These were fostered by the Dilettanti and exemplified by Stuart, who had undertaken his own research in Italy (1742–1751) and, more importantly, in Greece (1751–1755). The Greek expedition of Stuart and his colleague Nicholas Revett was supported financially by the society, which had elected them its first artist members in 1751. Stuart was also to work for other Dilettanti, such as Thomas Anson at Shugborough and at 15 St. James's Square, London, and for the 1st Earl Harcourt at Nuneham Courtenay. Besides Lord Spencer's other house at Wimbledon, Stuart also produced interior designs for the 2nd Marquess of Rockingham at Wentworth Woodhouse, and for Sir Nathaniel Curzon at Kedleston Hall.

The scheme for the Painted Room at Spencer House, as represented by a surviving elevation of the north wall, dated 1759, in the British Museum (fig. 3), shows the grotesque system of ornament firmly controlled within an architectonic framework of pilasters and enriched with painted panels.[8] On the east wall (fig. 1) a series of plaster reliefs are set above a monumental chimneypiece with terminal figures and a small copy of *The Aldobrandini Wedding* fresco on its frieze. The learned display of classical ornament throughout the room is derived from Roman sources—already used by William Kent in Palladian interiors, such as that at Holkham Hall—as much as from Stuart's recent studies in Greece. Indeed, considering the room's total effect, Kent is the prime source of inspiration that comes to mind, particularly his early essay in 1722, to devise an impressive Roman *tablinum* in the Cupola Room at Kensington Palace.[9] While Stuart's handling of classical elements reflects the growing contemporary taste for shallower and more linear forms, his use of a columnar screen closing off the apsidal southern end of the room (fig. 2)—the screen's capitals and soffit taken from the Temple of Antoninus and Faustina in Rome—as well as his amplification of the wall system by pieces of furniture, are equally indebted to Kent.

Stuart's skills as a decorative artist are shown in the fleshly vigor of the painted arabesques on the walls, with fanciful figurative details that are clearly derived from the grotesques of Raphael's murals in the Vatican *loggie.* These are set off by a blue-green ground and picked out with much gilding. Apart from the small landscape panels on the north wall, many of the roundels and lunettes feature compositions derived from *Le antichità di Ercolano esposti,* particularly the centaurs and dancing figures illustrated in the first volume.[10] Other such figures, along with wreaths of flowers and foliage, appear on the ceiling, which is divided into nine compartments. These set off the central motif of zodiac symbols in twelve grisaille roundels forming a circle.

Sadly missing today from this outstanding room is its original suite of furniture, which has been dispersed between Althorp, Kenwood, and the Victoria and Albert Museum.[11] The two *torchères,* which originally stood between the Corinthian columns and the side walls (fig. 2) are among the earliest pieces of neo-classical furniture decorated with painted panels in a mode later adopted by Robert Adam and James Wyatt. These candlestands, which supported exquisite ormolu tripods derived from the "Lanthorn of Demosthenes" in Athens and bore candle sconces and central incense burners, were to prove of seminal importance for the later work of Adam.[12] (According to the British Museum drawing [fig. 3], a similar tripod is shown on the pier table flanking the north door, but there is no evidence to suggest that this and its pendant were actually produced.) The splendor of Stuart's room was further amplified by four mirrors with carved and gilded frames bearing friezes derived from the Colonnade of the Incantada at Salonika. This source is also echoed in the lintels of the door cases on the east wall. Two of the mirrors flanked the west window, facing the chimneypiece, and the others, with curved frames, were set between the bow windows of the apse. In addition to six large gilded armchairs with claw feet, clearly the most remarkable pieces in the ensemble were four opulent sofas with winged-lion ends (fig. 4), two set against the apse walls and the others on either side of the west window beneath the mirrors. These were among the earliest attempts anywhere to revive the monumental forms of classical seat furniture,

Fig. 4.
Detail of one of four gilt sofas originally from the Painted Room at Spencer House, c. 1760 (Victoria and Albert Museum, on loan to the Iveagh Bequest, Kenwood)

which were developed far later by Thomas Hope and Charles Heathcote Tatham in the Regency period and by Charles Percier and Pierre-François Fontaine during the Napoleonic empire.[13]

Striking parallels have rightly been discerned between the Spencer House furniture and monumental pieces in the *goût grec* produced by the painter Louis-Joseph le Lorrain for the Parisian connoisseur Lalive de Jully between about 1756 and 1757.[14] These were subsequently featured in the *Cabinet flamand* of this patron's house on the rue de Menars, which was decorated during the early 1760s in the classical taste. (It has since disappeared.) However, the direct inspiration of antiquity is far more in evidence in Stuart's work than in this commission, and Le Lorrain's designs, for all their learned ornament, show stronger debts to the decorative conventions of the *style Louis XIV.* In strictly archaeological terms the total composition of the Painted Room, like that of its French counterparts, amounts to an unresolved mixture of traditional and novel elements and styles, but the breadth of artistic conception behind Stuart's design reveals him as one of the seminal figures of his generation in Europe.

Robert and James Adam, as close rivals of Stuart, were quick to grasp the potential of the Spencer House interiors. After seeing them in 1758, Robert had dismissed the early stages as

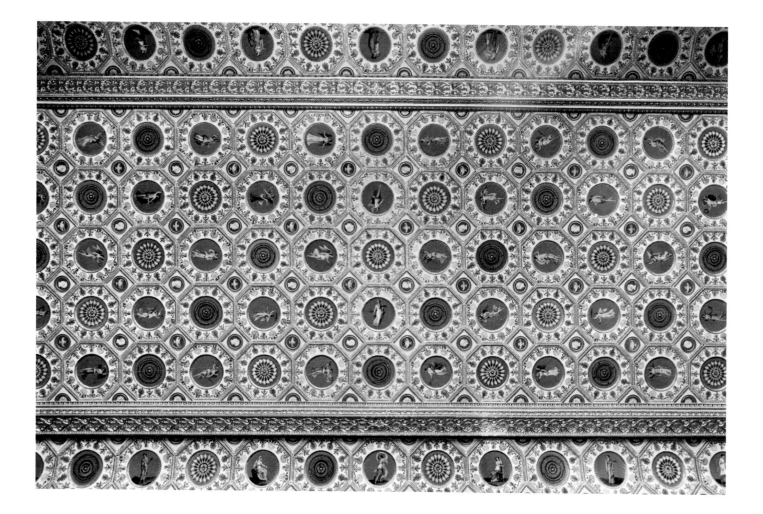

Fig. 5.
Detail of the ceiling of the Red
Drawing Room at Syon House,
Middlesex, with painted decoration
by Giovanni Battista Cipriani, 1764–
1765 (Photograph: National Monuments
Record)

"pityfulissimo" in a letter to James, then in Italy.[15] However, although Robert had been equally unimpressed by the finds at Herculaneum during his own visit there with Charles-Louis Clérisseau in 1755, he was soon anxious to catch up with Stuart and wrote to his brother:

I should be glad to know if you picked up any sketches of any painted ceilings at Herculaneum or had any ancient paintings copied by Zucchi. I should think this as useful work as he could be employed about, as we are much at a loss for their colouring and much we shall want of it about a palace and other places, as I see that taste must come in and will be a good branch for two or three clever hands.[16]

Robert Adam's initial response to this form of decoration is found among the later interiors of Syon House, Middlesex, carried out for the Earl of Northumberland. In addition to a highly complex painted and stucco scheme ingeniously offsetting the tunnellike space of the sixteenth-century Long Gallery, Adam produced an equally elaborate ceiling for the Red Drawing Room (fig. 5).[17] The heavily gilded framework of the coffering derives a certain richness from the vaulting patterns of Raphael's Villa Madama. However, the figured roundels painted on canvas by the Florentine artist Giovanni Battista Cipriani, who completed these in 1764, are directly inspired by the same centaurs and dancers of *Le antichità di Ercolano esposti* used by Stuart. Sir William Chambers referred to these as "skied dinner plates," and inveighed against "the trifling, gaudy, ceilings now in fashion: which, composed as they are of little rounds, squares, octagons, hexagons and ovals; excite no other idea, than that of a desert: upon the plates of which are dished out, bad copies of indifferent antiques."[18]

In the Small Drawing Room at Audley End, Essex (fig. 6), remodeled for Field Marshal Sir John Griffin, Adam avoided the error of placing

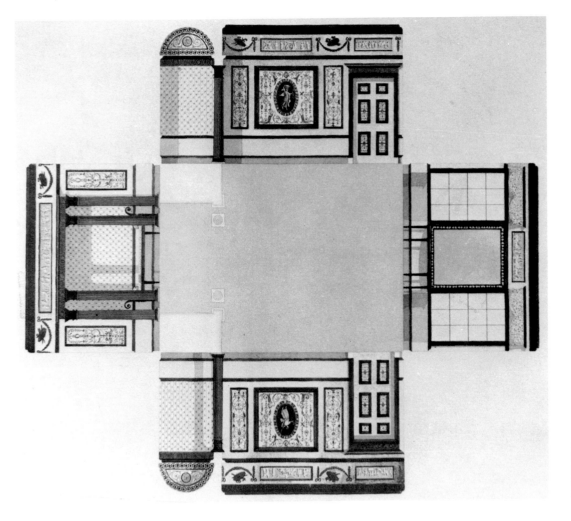

Fig. 6.
Design for the Small Drawing Room at Audley End, Essex, by Placido Columbani after Robert Adam, 1763, watercolor (English Heritage)

such subtle paintings high up within a large space. Instead he applied a delicate system of arabesques to match the room's intimate scale. A drawing for the intricate painted plaster ceiling of this room, dated 1763, is inscribed "Design of a Ceiling in the Style of the Paintings of the Ancients," and closely follows an antique ceiling from the Baths of Augustus in Rome.[19] The panels of grotesques and fictive friezes on the walls, which accompany interlaced medallions on the ceiling and a central tondo depicting Jupiter, Mercury, and Venus, were eventually carried out by Biagio Rebecca.[20] Born near Ancona, this painter had trained at the Accademia di San Luca in Rome before arriving in England in 1761, where he completed his studies at the newly founded Royal Academy in 1769. As one of the leading decorators of the Adam period, Rebecca was to win great acclaim for his command of the grotesque style and feigned bas-reliefs, and was

to play a key role in the evolution of the painted interior.

The swift maturing of Adam's arabesque manner into a versatile system for enhancing relatively intimate rooms is shown in unexecuted designs of 1768 for the two corner pavilions intended to complete the south front of Kedleston Hall, Derbyshire, for the 1st Lord Scarsdale. A Painted Breakfasting Room (fig. 7) was devised to follow the existing State Dressing Room at the west corner of the main block, balanced by a Book Room in the same style adjoining the Library to the east.[21] The Breakfasting Room, reflecting in miniature the nearby Saloon, is circular in form, some twenty-five feet in diameter with four alcove niches. It is articulated by an elegant framework of filigree pilaster strips and lunettes predominantly in gilt and bronze green against a pale gray background. Heralding the controversial Adam style of the 1770s, this

composition shows the potential uses of a select repertoire of decorative motifs—candelabra, bu-crania, paterae, wreaths, husks, palmettes, and anthemia—applied to a variety of painted sur-faces. Only the prominent roundel over the deli-cate mirror frame and sconces above the chim-neypiece, and the pairs of figures flanking candelabra on the ceiling spandrels retain certain affinities with the florid forms of Stuart's decora-tive manner of some ten years earlier.

While no artist's name is recorded for these proposed schemes, it is possible that Rebecca would have been required to execute such highly sophisticated decorations. According to an in-ventory of 1802, Adam's Italian draftsman, Agostino Brunias, carried out "fresco paintings and antique ornaments, after the Baths of Dio-cletian" in an earlier Painted Breakfast Room. This room was situated in the existing northeast wing at Kedleston, but the paintings, to a design by Adam of 1760, do not appear to have been a great success and were subsequently removed.[22]

The relatively sudden emergence of James Wyatt on the architectural scene in the early 1770s was to pose a serious threat to Adam, particularly in the instances when the younger man was able to develop Adam's ideas with a more acceptable restraint, in keeping with con-temporary taste. Wyatt based the magnificent Cupola Room at Heaton Hall, Lancashire (fig. 8), on the circular, domed form of Adam's Breakfasting Room, with its orchestration of grotesque ornament within a system of pilasters and niches. Wyatt's source is easily traced to Kedleston, for not only was his brother Samuel acting as Adam's Clerk of Works there, but the southern facade of Heaton, with its prominent domed bow front (containing the Cupola Room on the upper floor), is clearly derived from James Paine's rejected design for the south front of the Derbyshire house.[23]

The Cupola Room, which was the dressing room of the dowager Lady Egerton, mother of the owner of Heaton, the 1st Earl of Wilton,

Fig. 8.
The Cupola Room at Heaton Hall,
Lancashire, designed by James
Wyatt, with painted decoration by
Biagio Rebecca, c. 1772–1784
(Photograph: A. F. Kersting)

formed the climax to a set of rooms in the house reconstructed by Wyatt from 1772 onward.[24] The strikingly reticent scheme of painted decoration, set off against pale green and buff colored fields, was executed in oil on paper by Rebecca between 1775 and 1784. The repertoire of motifs,

used also at Kedleston and Audley End, reflects some contemporary publications as well as antique sources. Ideas from the Vatican *loggie* were taken from plates in the *Loggie di Rafaele nel Vaticano,* a folio volume of 1776 by Savorelli and Camporesi (fig. 9).[25] Inspiration for Rebecca's

Num II

Fig. 9.
Engraved detail of the Vatican *loggie*
by Raphael, from D. Savorelli and P.
Camporesi, *Loggie di Rafaele nel
Vaticano,* 1776   (Sir John Soane's Museum)

Virtues and Elements, in the ovals and lozenges, respectively, on the dome, were likely to have been derived from the *Antiquities of Herculaneum* by Thomas Martyn and John Lettice, issued in 1773. This translation of the first four volumes of *Le antichità di Ercolano esposti* was more accessible than the Italian original at this time, since the official publication was only available if one had influence at the court of Naples.[26]

Wyatt's decorative treatment of the Cupola

Room challenged Stuart's comprehensiveness at Spencer House. Not only did Rebecca provide painted compositions on the drawn window blinds to match those in the niches flanking the main door opposite, but a circular Axminster carpet to Wyatt's design (since vanished) was manufactured by Thomas Moore of Moorfields in London, who also produced several of Adam's integrated floor coverings, such as that for the Syon House Red Drawing Room of 1769.[27] Like the dispersal of the furniture at Spencer House, the dismantling of Wyatt's carefully coordinated ensemble at Heaton was tragic. A sale in 1902 disposed of fourteen white and gilt chairs, together with sofas and window seats and a set of tripod *torchères* originally placed in front of the mirrors.

A few years prior to the reconstruction at Heaton, Wyatt made a particularly original contribution to the painted interior with a modest scheme for a Thames-side fishing temple at Fawley Court in Buckinghamshire. This interior, carried out according to a drawing with plan and laid-out elevations for all four walls (fig. 10), was executed in October 1771, also probably by Rebecca. With its pale green walls decorated as though hung or inlaid with antique black and terra-cotta figured medallions and plaques, this interior has recently been recognized as the earliest known example of the Etruscan style, subsequently developed with much publicity by the Adam brothers.[28]

While its delicate, linear framework of husks and ribbons derives from earlier schemes, Wyatt's design also reveals fresh sources of inspiration—the hand-colored plates of Sir William Hamilton's *Collection of Etruscan, Greek and Roman Antiquities,* issued in four volumes between 1766 and 1776, as well as the so-called Etruscan ware which Josiah Wedgwood began to manufacture in 1768, prompted by Hamilton's publication.[29] As Eileen Harris and John Martin Robinson have suggested, this adaptation of motifs from Hamilton's collection to decorative schemes owed much to the actual engravings of the vase paintings in their circular, square, or rectangular frames.[30] The Fawley interior (which closely follows the drawing) also imitates the "antique" plaques and large cameos made in "black basaltes with Etruscan red burnt-in grounds, and in polished Biscuits with brown and grey grounds," produced by Wedgwood's new factory at Etruria in Staffordshire from 1769 onward.[31] Harris and Robinson have drawn attention to a reference in the first catalogue of Wedgwood and Boulton in 1773 in which "Etruscan" ornaments were advertised as "fit either for inlaying, as Medallions, in the Pannels of Rooms, as Tablets for Chimney Pieces, or for hanging up as ornaments in libraries . . . or as Pictures for Dressing Rooms."[32]

Use of the term *Etruscan*—as applied by Hamilton to his vases and by his contemporaries to painted schemes after the antique—stemmed from a revival of scholarly interest in Etruscan civilization during the first half of the eighteenth century. Pioneering works by Thomas Dempster, Anton Francesco Gori, Giovanni Battista Passeri, and Mario Guarnacci, among others, were furthered by the publications of the Accademia Etrusca, founded at Cortona in southern Tuscany in 1726.[33] Somewhat later, in 1761, the British dealer Thomas Jenkins began excavating at Corneto (Tarquinia), and after visiting tombs there Giovanni Battista Piranesi published three etchings of wall decorations in 1765.[34] This, in turn, was to inspire the antiquarian James Byres with the idea of publishing a "History of the Etruscans," with plates based on drawings he made at Corneto. According to his correspondence with Hamilton, work on the engravings was already in progress by 1766.[35] Due to financial difficulties, however, the text of Byers' *Hypogaei* was never published, but the plates were certainly familiar to his circle, even if issued posthumously, as late as 1842.[36]

Notwithstanding this evidence, considerable misconceptions were to continue about the definition of "Etruscan." These ranged from popular to scholarly comments on material as diverse as the Raphael grotesques and Greek vase paintings. Two quotations will suffice to underline the persistence of this confusion from the 1770s virtually to the end of the century.

It would appear that the engraved plates of the folio volume on the Vatican *loggie* by Savorelli and Camporesi were already in circulation two years prior to their publication in 1776. According to Father Thorpe, writing from Rome to his patron, the 8th Lord Arundell of Wardour, on 27 August 1774:

Since the Vatican Pilasters have been printed & coloured, their ornaments are now put upon every thing. Coaches, Picture Frames, & all kind of furniture are dressed up with them: I have even seen Priests Vestments & the Antependiums of Altars entirely composed of them. These Ornaments & others in the Etruscan stile [sic] engross all the taste of the Gentry in this country; many of the little orders

for Chimney Pieces intended for England are to be executed after the Etruscan manner in coloured Scagliuola [sic], a platform for a grand Desart [sic] is just finished in the same material & manner.[37]

In 1791 Hamilton published in four volumes his second collection of vases, with line illustrations by Johann Tischbein. By now Hamilton had begun to recognize the Greek origin of the vases and in his first volume set out his arguments justifying his change of mind.[38] However, some five years later, on 4 April 1796, the young designer Charles Heathcote Tatham was to write to his employer, the architect Henry Holland, as follows:

Referring again to internal Decorations, I had almost forgot a modern invention set on foot by a Man at Naples of the name of Tischbein, who has published certain prints, bordures, hangings & such like, in the etruscan style, precisely copied from Sir Willm Hamilton's Vases and adapted to small Rooms and Cabinets. . . . you can scarce imagine how successful and new such ornaments appear."[39]

The election of Hamilton to the Society of Dilettanti in 1777 thus marked another important link in the fruitful connection between archaeological discoveries and the painted interior. A key intention behind his publication of the correct measurements and accurate depictions of the vase paintings in his *Antiquities* (a volume

Fig. 10.
Detail of the wall design for the Fishing Temple at Fawley Court, Buckinghamshire, by James Wyatt, 1771 (Private collection; photograph: Christie's, London)

prominently featured in Sir Joshua Reynolds' group portrait of 1779 commemorating Hamilton's reception by the Dilettanti) was that they should contribute to the improvement of contemporary design in England. In a letter to Wedgwood in 1786, fourteen years after he sold his first vase collection to the nation, Hamilton looked back with considerable enthusiasm to some of the consequences:

It is with infinite satisfaction that I reflect upon having been in some measure instrumental in introducing a purer taste of form and ornaments by having placed my collection of Antiquities in the British Museum, but a Wedgwood and Bentley were necessary to diffuse that taste so universally, and it is to their liberal way of thinking and industry that so good a taste prevails at present in Great Britain, I have always and will always do them that justice.[40]

Given the new evidence concerning Fawley, the Adam brothers' categorical claim in the second volume of their *Works in Architecture*, 1779, to have invented the Etruscan mode of room decoration ("we have not been able to discover, either in our researches into antiquity, or in the works of modern artists, any idea of applying this taste to the decoration of appartments"[41]) is bound to ring hollow. However, in introducing their engraved designs for the ceiling and chimneypiece of the Dressing Room for the Countess of Derby's London house in Grosvenor Square in 1773, they did at least name the style and attempt a definition of its essential characteristics as involving color (i.e., terra-cotta and black) and style of the ornament, "both evidently taken from the vases and urns of the Etruscans."[42] Furthermore, in a sequence of at least eight such interiors, produced between 1773 and 1780, the Adam brothers popularized a coherent mode of expression capable of application to a wide range of decorative features and fittings.[43] This achievement should be appreciated as a conscious response (albeit a somewhat mercenary one) to the call for a modern style of expression made by their friend Piranesi a few years earlier.

Damie Stillman has noted close resemblances between the wall design of the finest surviving Etruscan room, at Osterley Park, Middlesex (fig. 11), and certain of Piranesi's designs in his *Diverse maniere d'adornare i cammini* of 1769 (fig. 12).[44] During the 1760s the Italian designer became deeply embroiled in the opening exchanges of the Graeco-Roman controversy involving Marc-Antoine Laugier, Julien-David Le Roy, and Johann Winckelmann. In his polemical publications, Piranesi gave increasing emphasis to the

fundamental importance of the Etruscans as a source of indigenous artistic inspiration to the Romans.[45] Well before the appearance of the *Diverse maniere,* however, he discarded the antiquarian niceties of debate for a much larger issue and one more suited to his inclinations for complexity and richness of effect. As of 1765, when his dialogue *Parere su l'Architettura* was published, he advocated the necessity of a vital contemporary system of design growing out of a broadly based use of the past.[46] The *Diverse maniere,* while reiterating his central belief in the creative heritage of the Etruscans, provided often extremely eclectic engraved designs for chimneypieces and furniture, combining Greek and Egyptian as well as Etruscan and Roman motifs. As Piranesi's prefatory essay concludes:

an artist, who would do himself honour, and acquire a name, must not content himself with copying faithfully the ancients, but studying their works he ought to shew himself of an inventive, and, I had almost said, of a Creating Genius; and by prudently combining the Grecian, the Tuscan, and the Egyptian together, he ought to open himself a road to the finding out of new ornaments and new manners.[47]

Like Wedgwood, Piranesi also recognized the possibilities of using vase motifs for other decorative purposes ("neither ought I to be reproached for having taken ornaments from urns, bases and other such works, and transferred them to walls"), but those plates in the *Diverse maniere* that appear to have had the greatest impact on the Osterley interior show a considerable debt to the pergola or trellislike themes of second-style Roman wall paintings.[48] Indeed, a visitor to Osterley in 1788 observed that "all the designs were taken from Herculaneum."[49] The distinction between the Roman and so-called Etruscan contributions to the painted interior continued to be as unclear as the sources of Piranesi's own creative eclecticism.

These stylistic considerations apart, Robert Adam's assiduous effort to achieve coherence in the Osterley Etruscan Room is revealed in over thirty-five drawings, most of them dated between 1772 and 1779, now in Sir John Soane's Museum.[50] As a dressing room, the Etruscan Room concluded a sequence of new apartments, which included an antechamber with Gobelin tapestries and a state bedchamber for the banker Robert Child and his wife, the latter of whom took a close interest in the designs. The earliest drawings are for the ceiling in 1772, followed three years later by studies for all four walls as well as for the carpet (no longer extant), and in

Fig. 11.
The Etruscan Room at Osterley
Park, Middlesex, designed by
Robert Adam, with painted decora-
tions attributed to Pietro Maria
Borgnis and Antonio Zucchi,
c. 1775–1776   (Photograph:
A. F. Kersting)

1776 for the "curtain cornices" and the chairs. The sheer thoroughness of control over details is underlined by four alternative designs for the chimneyboard alone (which was used to complete the room's surface appearance during the summer months) between January 1777 and August 1778, and no less than eight drawings connected with the pole firescreen, the setting for a silk panel of Mrs. Child's needlework to Adam's design, made between November 1776 and April 1779.

The room's painted decoration, on sheets of

Fig. 12.
Engraved design for a chimneypiece
and wall decoration from Giovanni
Battista Piranesi, *Diverse maniere,*
1769, plate 2 (Private collection)

paper pasted onto canvas, was carried out mainly
in terra-cotta color and black on a pale blue-gray
ground, incorporating a series of highly colored
medallions of classical subjects. Apart from the
central roundel on the ceiling featuring a Homeric theme by Antonio Zucchi, the main painting, which extended to the furnishing, was
probably undertaken by the artist Pietro Maria
Borgnis.[51] His father, Giuseppe Mattia, had arrived in England from the Domodossola area of

northern Italy in the 1750s to work on interiors
for Sir Francis Dashwood at West Wycombe
Park in Buckinghamshire, thereby founding a
dynasty of decorative painters that lasted well
into the nineteenth century.[52] Unlike similar
commissions undertaken by Rebecca, in which a
degree of initiative was left to the artist, in this
case Adam probably chose a less established
painter because he required a strict observance of
detail in order to coordinate the total effect.

John Hardy has demonstrated that floral ornament is a unifying theme throughout Osterley
Park.[53] As was customary with Adam, the furnishings, which were probably made by the firm
of John Linnell of Berkeley Square, are tied to
the room's surface decoration in a variety of
ways. The eight painted chairs (fig. 13) were
developed from a pattern first produced by Adam
for Lord Stanley at Derby House in 1775.[54] Of
the two surviving chair designs for Osterley, the
earlier one, for a black chair with terra-cotta
details and arms in the form of heraldic birds,
was rejected in favor of a more restrained version, more appropriate to the wall decoration
above.

Adam's adventurous solution at Osterley met
with sharp criticism. The now familiar and
waspish comments of Horace Walpole in a letter
of 1778 to the Reverend William Mason are
worth repeating in full because of the comprehensive nature of his dismissal:

*The last chamber . . . chills you: it is called the Etruscan,
and is painted all over like Wedgwood's ware, with black
and yellow small grotesques. Even the chairs are of painted
wood. It would be a pretty waiting room in a garden. I
never saw such a profound tumble into the Bathos. It is going out of a palace into a potter's field. Tapestry, carpets,
glass, velvet, satin, are all attributes of winter. There could
be no excuse for such a cold termination, but its containing
a cold bath next to the bed-chamber:—and it is called taste
to join these incongruities.[55]*

Another designer's application of the short-
lived Adam version of the Etruscan style can best
be seen at Woodhall Park, Hertfordshire, where
Thomas Leverton provided a former Governor
of Madras, Sir Thomas Rumbold, with a saloon
(fig. 14) during the late 1770s.[56] Here the main
emphasis is on a handsome umbrella dome with
appropriate terra-cotta and black ornaments over
a relatively modest area, twenty-four by twenty-
two feet, paved in black and white marble. The
arrangement of panels and medallions on canvas
attached to the walls, depicting the Cupid and
Psyche story and probably by Pietro Maria

Borgnis, is comparable to the effect of the Print Room of 1782 at Woodhall,[57] where engravings of classical monuments and antiquities are displayed in an illusionistic manner as if suspended by ribbons from nails. The marble chimneypiece in the Saloon at Woodhall has not only painted panels, but scagliola inlay—a technique using colored synthetic marble, often termed Bossi work—found in a number of Adam's Etruscan rooms, such as those at Derby House and at Home House, in London.

By the 1780s, painted interiors in the grotesque mode had been introduced into the Louis XVI style by artists such as Charles-Louis Clérisseau, who himself had played an important part in educating the Adam brothers in the decorative potential of antiquity. While he is recorded in 1764 as having produced an Etruscan room for Cardinal Albani in Rome, nothing resembling this survives. However, the two salon interiors Clérisseau provided for the administrator Grimod de la Reynière in Paris between 1773 and 1774 and between 1779 and 1781 were evidently both in the grotesque style. The latter, as recorded in drawings by the Polish architect Kamsetzer, shows no indication of the ingenuity of Adam or any evidence of fresh inspiration from antiquity.[58]

In England, meanwhile, the Etruscan style received a new and astringent interpretation by James Wyatt in a small ante room at Heveningham Hall, Suffolk (fig. 15), Sir Robert Taylor's building for the merchant banker Sir Gerald Vanneck. The ante room formed part of an extensive decorative scheme for the interior of Heveningham, completed shortly before 1784.[59] In what may be considered the definitive expression of Etruscan taste, Wyatt, probably in collaboration with Rebecca, purged the last traces of illusionistic devices derived from Herculaneum and from Renaissance sources. Pale green walls with white wood or plaster enrichments provide the austere context for a series of terra-cotta-colored figures from vases, matched by an equally reticent ceiling with carefully placed figurative panels. No longer is any attempt made to amplify space by means of fictive plaques or trellis construction. Wyatt's total control of the interior extended to a set of painted furniture en suite—oval-backed chairs, two sofas, and a pair of highly idiosyncratic candelabra set in opposing niches, each candelabrum taking the form of a tapering pedestal surmounted by a vase, with metal candle branches attached to rams' heads at

Fig. 13.
Painted chair from the Etruscan Room at Osterley Park, Middlesex, designed by Robert Adam, 1776
(Victoria and Albert Museum)

the angles of the pedestal. In what was intended as a mere *salle de passage,* Wyatt and Rebecca in concert achieved a balance between ingenuity of detail and overall restraint, which makes the later Etruscan interiors of Adam, such as the Great Dining Room at Cumberland House, London, of 1780, appear effete and overwrought by comparison.[60]

By the later eighteenth century archaeology had begun to open up new perspectives on the decorative achievements of Roman antiquity. As the focus of excavations shifted from Herculaneum to the newly identified Pompeii (hitherto known as Cività) during the early 1760s, the more accessible nature of the latter site enabled considerable portions, if not entire painted interiors, to be examined in situ for the first time.

This, in turn, encouraged a new interest in documenting antique painted interiors elsewhere, as well as a desire to reconstruct total decorative schemes from the available evidence. Characteristic of the new attitude was the folio volume *The Baths of the Romans,* published in 1772 by the Scottish architect Charles Cameron, a follower and admirer of Adam and Clérisseau.[61] The fruits of Cameron's researches in Rome from about 1766 to 1769 were to provide the basis of extremely lavish interiors *al antica* for Catherine the Great in Russia during the 1780s. Cameron's enquiries prompted more detailed investigations, as represented by a series of colored engravings of thermal paintings in the *Vestaglia delle Terme di Tito e loro interne pitture,* published between 1770 and 1776 by Franciszek Smuglewicz and Vicenzo Brenna.[62] Most thorough of all, however, was the study by the French artist M. Ponce in *Description des Bains de Titus ou Collection des Peintures Trouvées dans les Ruines des Thermes de cet Empereur,* published in Paris in 1786.[63] This work not only illustrated painted images and their entire wall context, but also attempted to reconstruct the complex patterns and moldings of the relevant vaulting.

Fig. 14.
The Etruscan Saloon at Woodhall Park, Hertfordshire, designed by Thomas Leverton, with painted decoration attributed to Pietro Maria Borgnis, c. 1778–1782   *(Country Life)*

Fig. 15.
The Etruscan Ante Room at Heveningham Hall, Suffolk, designed by James Wyatt, with painted decoration attributed to Biagio Rebecca, c. 1780–1784
(National Monuments Record)

In 1775 the Society of Antiquaries of London, which in May 1765 had approached the Spanish ambassador at Naples to obtain a "compleat set of the Herculaneum publications," began to receive illustrated accounts of the new discoveries at Pompeii from their Fellow, Sir William Hamilton.[64] Such was the interest this aroused that on 6 April 1775 the president called a special council at short notice to report a letter from Hamilton "wherein he is pleased to grant the permission, so much wished for by the Society, and them, of publishing in the course of their 'Archaeologia' the drawings and Account of the discoveries transmitted by him of the Ruins of Pompeii."[65] This account, first read to the Society at meetings in late January and early February 1775, eventually appeared in the fourth volume of *Archaeologia* in 1786, supported by twelve plates based on the original sketches supplied by Sir William.[66]

While most of these illustrations show external views of domestic or public buildings, including the newly uncovered Temple of Isis, plate 15 (fig. 16) represents the interior of a "Court with several rooms opening to it, one of which is thirty feet long by fifteen, the largest room as yet discovered at Pompeii."[67] The wall decorations consist of a low skirting division surmounted by painted panels defined by decorative borders. The majority of the panels contain small oval medallions, but the caption headed by the letters B.B.B., which refers to the fact that "the paintings of which were very elegant," laments that "the best parts have been cut out and transported to the Museum at Portici."[68] The original watercolor sketch, however, which was passed around at the 1775 meeting, indicates the strong red coloring surviving on certain walls, particularly of the second room to the left, opening off the main space.

Among those listening to Sir William's reports was a fellow member of the Dilettanti, whose artistic as well as scholarly interests inspired him to create a landmark in the history of the neo-classical painted interior. Heneage Finch, 4th Earl of Aylesford, who was elected to the Dilettanti in 1776, had been trained in draftsmanship while up at Christ Church, Oxford. His keen interest in architecture is shown by surviving sketches made in Rome, probably between 1771 and 1773. In addition to Piranesi's compositions, for which Aylesford had great admiration, a strong formative influence on him was provided by the Roman architect Joseph

Bonomi, who became Aylesford's architectural tutor and subsequent collaborator on various projects at Packington Hall, his Warwickshire seat.[69]

Bonomi first arrived in England in 1767 at the invitation of the Adam brothers. He worked for them until the early 1770s, when he transferred to the office of Thomas Leverton.[70] There he helped in the development of Bedford Square, London, and probably also in the interior design of Woodhall Park. Shortly before a brief return to Italy in 1783, possibly in the company of Aylesford himself, Bonomi began work on the redecoration of Packington Hall, originally built for the 3rd Earl by the elder Matthew Brettingham between 1766 and 1772. The initial designs (represented by surviving drawings in the house and in the Pierpont Morgan Library, New York), such as those for the Saloon or Music Room, show debts both to Adam and to Leverton, but the novel treatment of the large room originally intended as a sculpture gallery, which runs the full length of the south wing, was in dramatic contrast to these.[71] This monumental space (fig. 17), divided into three areas by screens of Corinthian columns toward either end, was invested with a remarkably authentic Pompeian character, marking a sharp break with past attempts to recreate the feeling of antiquity.

The full glory of this unique scheme has been

Fig. 16.
Engraved view of an excavated interior at Pompeii, from Sir William Hamilton's report to the Society of Antiquaries, 1774, published in *Archaeologia* 4 (1786) (Society of Antiquaries of London)

Fig. 17.
The Pompeian Gallery at Packington Hall, Warwickshire, designed by Joseph Bonomi and the
4th Earl of Aylesford, decorated by a
team of artists led by John Francis
Rigaud, 1785–1788   (National
Monuments Record)

largely recovered after extensive restoration in
the 1960s, undertaken by the present Earl of
Aylesford with his estate craftsmen, who applied
throughout, to the extent possible, the original
egg tempera formula. The main walls of the
Pompeian Gallery are covered with scagliola in
imitation of *giallo antico* and porphyry, after the
fashion of Pompeian rooms, up to the mantelshelf level of the Piranesian marble chimneypiece,
itself an essay in the adaptation of antique forms.
The upper walls are divided into panels featuring
figure and animal compositions, painted on a

lustrous black ground and bordered with grotesque ornament on a bright red ground in the
manner of third-style Pompeian wall schemes.
The ceiling (fig. 18) is boldly divided into a series
of recessed panels featuring figures on a black
ground similar to those on the upper walls. The
cornice, together with the capitals of the columnar screens, is also painted as if of *giallo antico*,
and picked out in gilt. The main ribs of the
ceiling, meanwhile, are executed in a vivid combination of Wedgwood blue and gray-green,
with ornamental details in white and gold. To

complete the total impression, the windows were originally hung with curtains formed of broad strips of red and black heavy satin, partly reused at a later date to cover chairs in the entrance hall.

Subsequent to the researches of Marcus Binney, Desmond Fitzgerald established the precise source and date of this impressive interior, finding, in his publication of 1972, that Aylesford and Bonomi had plagiarized a wall scheme (fig. 19) as well as figurative compositions from Ponce's publication of 1786 on the Baths of Titus.[72] A surviving account book, moreover, records various payments made between 1785 and 1788 to a group of decorative artists staying at Packington, thus establishing this Pompeian Gallery as the earliest of its kind in Europe, and

anticipating by over half a century similar reconstructions in Germany and France.

Among the artists recorded in the Packington accounts were Dominic Bartoli, manufacturer of scagliola, Joseph Rose, Jr., the Adam brothers' celebrated plaster worker, and the painters Benedetto Pastorini and Giovanni Borgnis, the latter the elder brother of the artist associated with the Osterley Etruscan Room.[73] The dominant figure, however, was the Turinese painter John Francis Rigaud, who had come to England by way of Paris in 1771. A full Royal Academician by 1784, he was to provide decorative schemes for the Council Chamber of the Guildhall and for the main staircase of Trinity House in London between 1795 and 1796. Rigaud was responsible for the richly modeled figures of the Pom-

Fig. 18.
Detail of wall, ceiling, and columnar screen in the Pompeian Gallery at Packington Hall   (National Monuments Record)

Fig. 19.
Engraving of a Roman wall decoration, from M. Ponce, *Description des Bains de Titus*, 1786, plate 2 (Sir John Soane's Museum)

Fig. 20.
One of the set of gilt *klismos* chairs originally in the Pompeian Gallery at Packington Hall, designed by Joseph Bonomi and the 4th Earl of Aylesford, c. 1788 *(Connoisseur)*

peian Gallery's walls and ceiling, reviving a system of encaustic painting from antiquity.[74] He subsequently contributed an altarpiece in fresco for the equally remarkable neo-classical church at Packington with its early use of the Paestum Doric order, built to designs by Aylesford and Bonomi between 1789 and 1792.[75]

Aylesford's choice of a Pompeian theme can largely be attributed to the fact that his gallery was intended to display a considerable collection of Etruscan and Greek vases, which in itself accounts for another striking innovation. Placed along the walls as an integral part of the pictorial scheme were seven (or possibly eight) *klismos* chairs (fig. 20), based on examples in antique vase and wall paintings.[76] Sadly, only one chair survives from a set that marks the earliest revival of this classical furniture type, far simpler than anything illustrated decades later in Thomas Hope's *Household Furniture* (1807).[77] Not only was the form of each gilded pine chair determined by a concern for archaeological accuracy, but the black and red velvet squabs were embroidered (tradition has it by Aylesford's wife, Louisa Thynne, whom he married in 1781) with identical copies of the Roman-style paintings decorating the walls immediately above.

Although aspects of the painted interior after the antique continued to be explored well into the nineteenth century, the gallery at Packington marks the end of an exceptional period of sustained originality, giving weight to the view that the most creative phase of neo-classicism preceded the political revolution of 1789. Thomas Hope, Charles Heathcote Tatham, and John Soane, among Regency designers, were to build on these initiatives, and far later still several attempts were made to reconstruct Pompeian interiors with greater fidelity, such as at Ludwig I's Pompeianum at Aschaffenburg in the 1840s, Prince Jérôme Napoléon's house in Paris in the 1850s, and J. P. Crace's painted interior at Ickworth, Suffolk, as late as 1879.[78]

By the opening of the nineteenth century, however, the delicate balance between patron, designer, specialist painter, and skilled craftsman was to be affected by new factors. Principal among these was the comprehensive control over all aspects of detail by the professional architect, the wider social range of patronage, and, most critical of all, an inhibiting emphasis on greater archaeological accuracy. During the three decades of experiment discussed here, from 1760 to 1790, the sheer imaginative vitality of painted interiors, from Spencer House to Packington Hall, owed much to the eclectic nature of English patronage and design. This eclecticism was largely determined by the highly catholic interests of members of the Society of Dilettanti, their sponsoring of archaeological research, and their active encouragement, thereby, of contemporary design. Such fruitful eclecticism is succinctly summed up by one of the traditional toasts of the Dilettanti: "Grecian Taste and Roman Spirit!"

NOTES

I am greatly indebted to the many publications and researches referred to below. For particular advice and help I should like to thank the Earl of Aylesford, Dr. Geoffrey Beard, Robert Bennett, Marcus Binney, Edith Clay, John Cornforth, Cara D. Denison, Paul Drury, Sir Brinsley Ford, Joe Friedman, Robin Griffith-Jones, John Hardy, Dr. Eileen Harris, John Hopkins, Professor Thomas J. McCormick, Henrietta Manners, Professor Peter Murray, Nicholas Playfair, Margaret Richardson, Christine Scull, Elizabeth Shrigley, Dr. Cinzia Sicca, Felice Stampfle, Valerie M. Thornhill, Peter Thornton, and Dr. David Watkin.

1. Lionel Cust and Sidney Colvin, *History of the Society of Dilettanti* (London, 1914); J. Mordaunt Crook, *The Greek Revival* (London, 1972), 6–62.

2. Cinzia Sicca, "William Kent: Architecture and Landscape," in John Wilton-Ely, ed., *A Tercentenary Tribute to William Kent* [exh. cat., Ferens Art Gallery] (Hull, 1985), 15. John Talman appears to have initiated Kent's interest in this cinquecento mode and urged him to paint a ceiling for his Lincolnshire patron, Burrell Massingberd, "after ye Grotesk manner" in 1717. Sicca also points out that while Kent did not follow this suggestion, three out of ten rooms decorated at Kensington Palace between 1722 and 1727 were in "Grotesque Painting," though only that of the Presence Chamber survives.

3. Robert Rosenblum, *Transformations in Late Eighteenth Century Art* (Princeton, 1967), 3–7, 109–111; Hugh Honour, *Neoclassicism* (Harmondsworth, 1968), 43–50; Mario Praz, *On Neoclassicism* (London, 1969), 70–90; Edward Croft-Murray, *Decorative Painting in England,* 2 vols. (London, 1970), 2: 47–59; Arts Council of Great Britain, *Age of Neoclassicism* [exh. cat., Royal Academy] (London, 1972); Susan Panitz, ed., *Pompeii as Source and Inspiration* [exh. cat., University of Michigan Museum of Art] (Ann Arbor, 1977); see also Francis Haskell and Nicholas Penny, *Taste and the Antique* (London, 1981), 74–78.

4. Accademia Ercolanese di Archeologia, *Le antichità di Ercolano esposti,* 8 vols. (Naples, 1757–1792).

5. See Horace Walpole's graphic account of his visit of 14 June 1740 to the Herculaneum *scavi;* quoted in Panitz 1977, 13–14.

6. William Chambers, *Treatise on Civil Architecture* (London, 1759), 135. The author ignores the painted interiors of an earlier generation in houses like Boughton and Burghley.

7. David Watkin, *Athenian Stuart: Pioneer of the Greek Revival* (London, 1982), 35–41.

8. Edward Croft-Murray, "A Drawing by 'Athenian' Stuart for the Painted Room at Spencer House," *British Museum Quarterly* 21 (1957), 14–15; Croft-Murray 1970, 50, 284.

9. Sicca 1985, 16 ("In this room Kent strove to recreate a vision of an antique *tablinum,* the main room in the Roman house. The result is both unusual and novel: its antique, classical feeling is achieved by the abundant use of architectural elements such as niches and aedicules with busts and full-sized statuary after the antique").

10. Accademia Ercolanese 1757–1792, 1: pls. 17–28.

11. Peter Thornton and John Hardy, "The Spencer Furniture at Althorp," *Apollo* 87 (June 1968), 440–451; Watkin 1982, 37–40.

12. Nicholas Goodison, "Mr. Stuart's Tripod," *Burlington Magazine* 114 (1972), 695–704; Gervase Jackson-Stops, ed., *The Treasure Houses of Britain* [exh. cat., National Gallery of Art] (Washington, 1986), no. 461. The "Lanthorn of Demosthenes," a contemporary name for what is now recognized as the Choragic Monument of Lysicrates, was illustrated in James Stuart and Nicholas Revett, *Antiquities of Athens,* 4 vols. (London, 1762–1816), 1: chap. 4, pls. I–XXVI, together with a reconstruction of its missing tripod (36) which was the direct source for the pieces in question.

13. Jackson-Stops 1986, no. 269.

14. Svend Eriksen, *Early Neoclassicism in France* (London, 1974), 39–40, 49–50, 60–61, 68–74, 311–312, 379; Watkin 1982, 40.

15. John Fleming, *Robert Adam and His Circle in Edinburgh and Rome* (London, 1962), 258. The ceilings might be "Greek to the teeth," wrote Robert Adam, "but by God they are not handsome." By 1773, however, he was prepared to acknowledge publicly in *Works in Architecture,* 3 vols. (1773–1822), 1: preface, that "Mr. Stuart, with his usual elegance and taste, has contributed towards introducing the true style of antique decoration."

16. Fleming 1962, 370–371. In this letter Robert also refers to *The Aldobrandini Wedding,* the small copy of which he could have seen incorporated into the chimneypiece of Stuart's Painted Room. In another letter, written from Rome in October 1762, James tells his brother of "three very fine drawings . . . of antique ceilings in what they call Livia's Baths."

17. Damie Stillman, *The Decorative Work of Robert Adam* (London, 1966), 98; Geoffrey Beard, *Craftsmen and Interior Decoration in England, 1660–1820* (London, 1981), 102.

18. William Chambers, *Treatise on the Decorative Part of Civil Architecture,* (London, 1791), 135. While recognizing that painted interiors had been introduced in England since he wrote his *Treatise on Civil Architecture* in 1759, Chambers felt it necessary in this revised edition, to censure the excesses of novelty. See Eileen Harris, "The Treatise on Civil Architecture," in John Harris, *Sir William Chambers* (London, 1970), 139.

19. Stillman 1966, 98–99. The bill for the ceiling, dated August 1763, described the design as "in the Taste of the Paintings of the Ancients."

20. Croft-Murray 1970, 258–262. Rebecca carried out decorations in several rooms at Audley End, including five chimneyboards (together with some picture restoration) for which he was paid twenty guineas in December 1769, the date when he probably also received £50 for work in the Little Drawing Room. See also Jackson-Stops 1986, no. 290.

21. Stillman 1966, 71; Jackson-Stops 1986, no. 359.

22. Croft-Murray 1970, 260; John Hardy and Helena Hayward, "Kedleston Hall, Derbyshire—1," *Country Life* (26 January 1978), 196, fig. 4, reproduce a surviving drawing by Adam of 1760 for a wall of the Painted Breakfast Room in the northeast wing. Two of five paintings produced in distemper by Adam's draftsman Agostino Brunias in 1761, and now in the Victoria and Albert Museum, are set within a framework of heavy arabesques. The novel decoration of this eighteen-foot-square room did not appeal to the Duchess of Northumberland on a visit in August 1766, who found the painting "after the antique . . . sadly executed."

23. John Martin Robinson, *The Wyatts: An Architectural Dynasty* (Oxford, 1979), 23–25.

24. Timothy Clifford and Ivan Hall, *Heaton Hall, Manchester: Bicentenary Exhibition, 1772–1972* [exh. cat., Heaton Hall] (Manchester, 1972); James Lomax, "The First and Second Earls of Wilton and Heaton House," *Transactions of the Lancashire and Cheshire Antiquarian Society* 82 (1983), 58–81.

25. D. Savorelli and P. Camporesi, *Loggie di Rafaele nel Vaticano* (Rome, 1776); Lomax 1983, 77, suggests that another source of cinquecento decoration for the Cupola Room may have been Giovanni Stern's book of 1784 on the Villa Giulia, Rome,

which Lord Grey de Wilton bought from his friend Charles Townley in 1785.

26. The publication of the first (and, as it transpired, only) volume of this translation forced Charles III to make the first five volumes of the *Antichità* available for purchase. From 1789 Piroli began issuing comparatively inexpensive copies of the plates alone. Restrictions imposed by the Bourbon authorities on the making of any records at Herculaneum continued well after Dr. Burney encountered them in 1770. Lady Anne Miller, who saw the "Cabinet" at Portici, complained that "no person who visits [it] is permitted to take away any sketch, note or memorandum on the spot." Her account, published in 1776, is quoted by Raleigh Trevelyan, *The Shadow of Vesuvius* (London, 1976), 62–63.

27. Lomax 1983, 79. On 28 December 1776, Rebecca was paid for "the Paintings in the Salon & the three window curtains & the niches in the Dressing Room, £30-0-od." Thomas Moore was paid £84 for the circular carpet. The Red Drawing Room carpet at Syon is signed on the border "Thomas Moor, 1769." For the making of such a carpet from Adam's designs, see Stillman 1966, 107–108.

28. Eileen Harris and John Martin Robinson, "New Light on Fawley," *Architectural History* 27 (1984), 263–265; Croft-Murray 1970, 261.

29. Brian Fothergill, *Sir William Hamilton* (London, 1969); Jackson-Stops 1986, no. 362. Although vol. 1 of Hamilton's *Antiquities* was published in 1766 (vol. 2 in 1770, vols. 3, 4 in 1776), proof impressions of certain plates were circulated earlier to key figures such as Wedgwood and Piranesi, who exchanged with Hamilton trial plates of designs he would publish in *Diverse maniere d'adornare i cammini ed ogni altra parte degli edifizi desunte dall' architettura Egizia, Etrusca, e Greca* (Rome, 1769).

30. Harris and Robinson 1984, 264.

31. *A Catalogue of Cameos, Intaglios, Medals and Bas Reliefs . . . . Wedgwood and Bentley* (1773).

32. Harris and Robinson 1984, 265; *Catalogue Wedgwood and Bentley* 1773.

33. Thomas Dempster, *De Etruria regali* (Florence, 1723-1726); Anton Francesco Gori, *Museum Etruscum* (Florence, 1727-1743); Giovanni Battista Passeri, *Della pittura degli Etruschi* (Florence, 1755); Mario Guarnacci, *Delle origini Italiche o siano memorie istorico-Etrusche sopra l'antichissimo regno d'Italia, e sopra i di lei primi abitori* (Florence, 1767-1772). For a summary of the early history of Etruscanology see Robert Bloch, *The Etruscans* (London, 1958), and for more recent research, especially with respect to the Accademia Etrusca at Cortona, see Paola Barocchi and Daniela Gallo, eds., *L'accademia etrusca* [exh. cat., Palazzo Casali] (Cortona, 1985).

34. Piranesi's three plates appeared at the end of his polemical work, *Della introduzione e del progresso delle belle arti in Europa ne tempi antichi* (Rome, 1765).

35. Brinsley Ford, "James Byers; Principal Antiquarian for the English Visitors to Rome," *Apollo* 99 (June, 1974), 452.

36. Ford 1974, 452–453. Byers' plates, engraved by his partner, Christopher Norton, were eventually issued in 1842 by the painter Frank Howard in *Hypogaei or Supulchral Caverns of Tarquinia*, a supplement to Mrs. Hamilton, *Tour of the Sepulchres of Etruria*, of the same year.

37. *Transcript of the Correspondence of Father John Thorpe with the Eighth Earl of Arundell of Wardour*, 27 August 1774, p. 2. I am much indebted to Sir Brinsley Ford for this quotation as also for that relating to n. 39.

38. Sir William Hamilton, *Collection of Engravings from Ancient Vases Mostly of Pure Greek Workmanship Discovered in Sepulchres*

in the Kingdom of the Two Sicilies, 4 vols. (Naples, 1791-1795), 1:8–30.

39. Christopher Proudfoot and David Watkin, "A Pioneer of English Neo-classicism," *Country Life* (13/20 April 1972), 918–921.

40. Hamilton to Wedgwood, 23 May 1786, mss., Wedgwood Museum, Barlaston; quoted in Jackson-Stops 1986, 429.

41. *The Works in Architecture of Robert and James Adam,* 2 vols. (London, 1779) 2: preface.

42. *Works in Architecture* 1779, 2: preface. While naming far less direct sources, such as Bernard de Montfauçon, Anne Claude Philippe, Comte de Caylus, Passeri, and Gori "and the whole collection of antiquarians who have treated of these matters," the Adam brothers omit any reference to the crucial works of Hamilton and Piranesi.

43. Damie Stillman, "Robert Adam and Piranesi," in D. Fraser, ed., *Studies in Architecture Presented to Rudolf Wittkower* (London, 1967), 203. Besides those at Derby House and Osterley Park, other known Etruscan rooms included those at Home House, Cumberland House, "Mr. Adamson's Parlour" (The Adelphi?), a small room under the stairs of the garden facade at Osterley, and Harewood House and Byram Hall, both in Yorkshire.

44. Stillman 1967, 203. Of particular relevance to Robert Adam's design were the second and third etched wall compositions in Piranesi 1769.

45. John Wilton-Ely, *The Art and Mind of Piranesi* (London, 1978), 65–80. Piranesi's main polemical writings with their accompanying plates are reprinted in Wilton-Ely, ed., *Giovanni Battista Piranesi: The Polemical Works* (Farnborough, 1972).

46. John Wilton-Ely, "Vision and Design: Piranesi's 'fantasia' and the Graeco-Roman controversy," in Georges Brunel, ed., *Piranèse et les Français* (Rome, 1978), 529–544.

47. Piranesi 1769, 33 (English text).

48. Piranesi 1769, 9, pls. 1–3.

49. Caroline Lybbe-Powys, *Diaries*, ed. Emily J. Cleminson (London, 1899), 231.

50. Stillman 1966, 75–76; Maurice Tomlin, *Catalogue of Adam Period Furniture: Victoria and Albert Museum* (London, 1972) 75–82; John Hardy and Caroline Andrew, "The Essence of the Etruscan Style," *Connoisseur* 208 (November 1981), 225–227. I am currently preparing for publication a detailed analysis of the surviving designs for the Osterley Etruscan Room.

51. The attribution to Borgnis was first made by Croft-Murray 1970, on the basis of Caroline Lybbe-Powys' reference to "Berners" as the painter responsible. See also note 42.

52. Croft-Murray 1970, 173–174.

53. John Hardy, "Osterley Park House: a Temple of Flora," *The V and A Album*, Victoria and Albert Museum (London, 1984), 3:151–159.

54. Eileen Harris, *The Furniture of Robert Adam* (London, 1963), 95; Tomlin 1972, 77.

55. Horace Walpole to Reverend William Mason, 16 July 1778, Wilmarth Sheldon Lewis et al., eds., *The Yale Edition of Horace Walpole's Correspondence*, 48 vols. (New Haven, 1937–1983), 28:413–414.

56. Christopher Hussey, *English Country Houses: Mid Georgian, 1760–1800*, 2d ed. (London, 1963), 177–183. I am indebted to Miss Edith Clay for drawing my attention to another such scheme ornamenting the entrance hall at Newtimber Place, Sussex. Here the painted wall decorations, derived from Hamilton's vase paintings and attributed to Rebecca, are extended to

the embroidery of the furniture. See John Anthony Kiechler, "The Murals at Newtimber Place," *Sussex Archaeological Collections* 113 (1975), 175–181.

57. Croft-Murray 1970, 175, based his attribution to Borgnis on resemblances between the work at Woodhall and the Osterley Etruscan Room. For a discussion of the Print Room, see Francis Russell, "Microcosm of Eighteenth-century Taste: the Engravings Room at Woodhall Park," *Country Life* (6 October 1977), 924–926.

58. Edward Croft-Murray, "The Hotel Grimod de la Reynière: the Salon Decorations," *Apollo* 78 (November 1963), 377–383; Eriksen 1974, 66–67, 310–311, fig. 218, reproduces one of the drawings by Kamsetzer. For another, see Thomas J. McCormick, "Virginia's Gallic Godfather," *Arts in Virginia* 4 (1964), 10. McCormick, currently preparing a monograph on Clérisseau, has discovered that there were *two* such salon interiors in the antique taste produced for this patron.

59. Hussey 1963, 165–176; Croft-Murray 1970, 259.

60. For Adam's surviving designs for the Great Dining Room at Cumberland House (since destroyed), see Stillman 1966, 78, 82, 95, 106, pls. 56, 73, 112, 149.

61. Charles Cameron, *The Baths of the Romans: Explained and Illustrated, with the Restorations of Palladio Corrected and Improved* (London, 1772). Proposals for a subscription to the book were issued in London on 20 March 1770. See A. A. Tait, ed., *Charles Cameron c. 1740–1812* [exh. cat., Arts Council of Great Britain] (London, 1967), 10–14.

62. Franciszek Smuglewicz (1745–1807) and Vicenzo Brenna (1741–1820) produced watercolors of many of the paintings of the Domus Aurea Neronis for the *Vestaglia*. See Arts Council 1972, 736.

63. Ponce describes himself in this book as "graveur ordinaire du cabinet de M^{cr} Comte d'Artois, de l'Académie des Sciences, Belles Lettres & Arts de Rouen, Secrétaire Adjoint du Musée de Paris, etc."

64. Joan Evans, *A History of the Society of Antiquaries* (Oxford, 1956), 119–120, 153.

65. Evans 1956, 158–159.

66. "Account of the Discoveries at Pompeii, communicated by Sir William Hamilton," *Archaeologia, or Miscellaneous Tracts Relating to Antiquity* 4 (1786), section 14, 160–175.

67. Hamilton 1786, 170.

68. Hamilton 1786, 170.

69. Marcus Binney, "Packington Hall, Warwickshire," *Country Life* (9, 16, 23 July 1970), 102–106, 162–166, 226–229.

70. Croft-Murray 1970, 172–173.

71. The drawings for the Saloon and projected gallery are reproduced in Binney 1970, 165, figs. 8, 9; 227, figs. 4, 5.

72. Desmond Fitzgerald, "A Gallery after the Antique," *Connoisseur* 181 (September 1972), 2–13.

73. The Borgnis family connection apart, another indication of the essential continuity of these painted interiors brought about by the craftsmen involved is the fact that both Dominic Bartoli and Joseph Rose, Jr., had worked on the interiors at Kedleston and Heaton Hall.

74. Croft-Murray 1970, 268–269; William L. Pressly, ed., " 'Facts and Recollections of the XVIIIth Century in a Memoir of John Francis Rigaud Esq., R.A.' by Stephen Francis Dutilh Rigaud," *Walpole Society* 50 (1984), 20–21, 32, 74–75. According to Rigaud's son (Pressly 1984, 74–75) the Gallery at Packington "was painted in Encaustic, the water colours being used with merely a sufficient quantity of fine thin size [*sic*], made of glove leather, just strong enough to bind the colours to the stucco; and when the paintings were finished, they were sprinkled all over with melted wax, which being imbibed by the colours, was afterwards more equally diffused over the whole surface by a *salamander,* or heated iron being passed as near as possible to the pictures, without burning them. This gave additional richness and transparency to the colours, greatly increased the intense blackness of the ground upon which the figures were painted, and produced a magnificent effect; at the same time that it effectually preserves them from humidity or any other injury;—so that they will be as lasting as the stucco on which they are painted."

75. Marcus Binney, "A Pioneer Work of Neoclassicism: the Church at Great Packington in Warwickshire," *Country Life* (8 July 1971), 110–115.

76. Arts Council 1972, no. 1642.

77. For Hope's adaptation of antique furniture forms, see David Watkin, *Thomas Hope and the Neoclassical Idea* (London, 1968), 108–205. Figs. 10, 12 show such furniture in Watkin's London house on Duchess Street.

78. Rosenblum 1967, 135–137. Friedrich von Gartner designed the Pompeianum at Aschaffenburg (1841–1846) for Ludwig I in imitation of the House of Castor and Pollux at Pompeii. Prince Jérôme Napoléon's house on the avenue Montaigne, Paris (1854–1859), designed by Alfred Normand, was recorded in a painting by Louis Boulanger before its demolition in 1891. In England, meanwhile, Queen Victoria (who visited Pompeii in 1838) and the Prince Consort commissioned a garden pavilion (demolished in 1928) in the grounds of Buckingham Palace, including among other exotic interiors, a Pompeian Room by Agostino Aglio (1843–1845). A color lithograph of it from Anna Jameson and Ludwig Grüner, *Her Majesty's Pavilion in Buckingham Gardens* is reproduced in Trevelyan 1976, fig. 64. J. P. Crace's room of 1879 at Ickworth was directly based on the frescoes of Villa Negroni in Rome, a source of inspiration for Soane in his interior designs. The strength of Pompeian color particularly appealed to Soane, Hope, and their contemporaries. In 1828 the topographer Sir William Gell painted his own sitting room in Rome "in all the bright staring colours I could get, a sort of thing between Etruscan and Pompeii" (quoted in Watkin 1968, 69).

DAMIE STILLMAN

The Neo-Classical Transformation of the English Country House

During the half century from 1755 to 1805, the English country house underwent a fairly dramatic change.[1] This is not to say that its role at the center of upper- and even middle-class British life was challenged. Despite the fact that the aristocracy might spend more than half of the year in London,[2] the country house not only remained the focus of the economic, social, and political activities of the peers and gentry, but it also retained the symbolic function that it had long held. Its character, however, was altered in a number of ways.

First, the quantity of such buildings increased significantly. John Summerson has estimated that approximately 230 large country houses were erected between 1710 and 1759;[3] by his method of calculation, the number of country houses built in the ensuing forty years may have reached as high as 610.[4] Many of these dwellings, however, would certainly have been smaller than the typical examples of the preceding four decades; and many were not totally new houses, but properties that underwent substantial remodeling, addition, or alteration.[5]

Another indication of the continued significance of the country house as an architectural type at this time is furnished by the number of country-house designs shown at the annual exhibitions of the Society of Artists and the Free Society from 1760 to 1778 and of the Royal Academy from 1769 to 1799. These designs, many of which were only imaginary conceptions, total 324, as opposed, for example, to 81 designs for churches and 99 for various kinds of public buildings during that same period.[6]

Evidence of a tendency toward somewhat smaller houses is found in the rise of the villa, as distinct from the large mansion, also documented in the exhibition catalogues of the Society of Artists, Free Society, and Royal Academy. Generally smallish, secondary houses, situated either in the vicinity of London or in the country, as retreats, villas first appear in the 1720s and increase in popularity from the middle of the century on. Whereas only 6 of the 22 designs for country houses exhibited at the Society of Artists in the 1760s are specifically listed as villas, the number so described in the Royal Academy catalogues of the last three decades of the eighteenth century is 144, which is just over half of the total for all country seats shown.[7]

This development is confirmed by known examples, as well as by the increasing frequency with which the term *villa* appeared in architectural pattern books, even on their title pages.[8] As a corollary, one might note the tendency, toward the end of the century, to view the great house as a more old-fashioned edifice, as did James Peacock when he referred to such buildings as places of "melancholy magnificence."[9]

The great house—characterized by "magnificence and extensive range," according to Charles Middleton in a pattern book of 1793—the villa, which Middleton saw as manifesting "elegance, compactness, and convenience," and amalgamations of the two are the basic kinds of country house that dotted the English countryside during the last half of the eighteenth century.[10] But before examining the newly built versions of each, one should note again the substantial incidence of remodeling and redecoration which contributed to the neo-classical transformation of the English country house. A great many of Robert Adam's most important projects consisted of work of this kind, with vast sums of money expended on internal and external alterations at Syon House, Osterley Park, Kenwood, Newby Hall, and a host of other country seats. And Adam was not

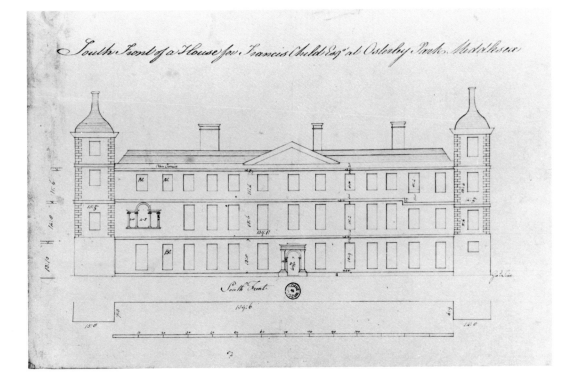

South Front of a House for Francis Child Esqr at Osterley Park. Middlesex

South Front

Fig. I.
Survey drawing of the south front of Osterley Park, Middlesex, 1761 (Sir John Soane's Museum)

alone in this. Sir William Chambers, James Wyatt, George Dance the Younger, Sir John Soane, and many of their contemporaries were often called upon to add to existing houses; carry out internal changes of great significance; and provide new ceilings, chimneypieces, and wall decoration.

Osterley is a particularly interesting example of this kind of transformation. A Tudor house with four corner turrets, it had been altered somewhat in the early eighteenth century and again in the late 1750s, when a new gallery and garden front were created, in this case apparently by the young William Chambers.[11] Its condition in 1761 can be seen in a drawing preserved in Sir John Soane's Museum, London (fig. 1).[12] When Adam was called in by Francis Child in 1761, Osterley's turrets, with their distinctive tops, were still in evidence, but the south side of the house had had a pediment added, and a Palladian motif had been installed near its west end, undoubtedly reflecting the gallery that had just been erected, presumably by Chambers. The drawing illustrates a fairly characteristic country-house composition of the mid-eighteenth century, rendered in familiar red brick, with emphasis on center and ends.

Adam's first thought was to tear down all but

the gallery wing and erect a similarly accented facade on the east, though with a fairly grand classical portico, end pavilions, and Palladian motifs within relieving arches, all derived from the style of Adam's Burlingtonian predecessors but handled with a bit more attenuation (fig. 2). This design of 1761, however, was left in abeyance, for Francis Child died two years later. In 1766 Child's brother Robert, who had inherited both Osterley and the banking house that provided the family fortune, again turned to Adam, who then created a totally different conception by inserting a dramatic open portico into the existing east end, regularizing and clothing the exterior, altering the tops of the towers, and covering over the old courtyard, thus raising the entrance to the level of the *piano nobile* (fig. 3).[13] The proportions and the detail are different, and the effect is indeed a transformation into what Horace Walpole called, on his visit to Osterley in 1773, "the palace of palaces!"[14] In part, of course, he was referring to the even more dramatic alteration inside, as seen in the entrance hall, reached by crossing the raised courtyard, or in the dining room, library, and drawing room, the last, in his words, "worthy of Eve before the Fall."[15]

Adam made even clearer his devices for effect-

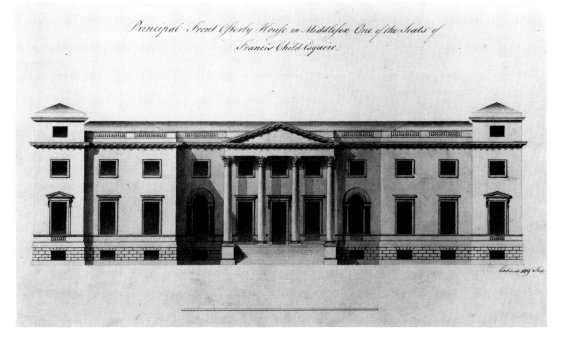

Fig. 2.
Unexecuted design for the east front
of Osterley Park, Middlesex, by
Robert Adam, 1761   (The Earl of Jersey)

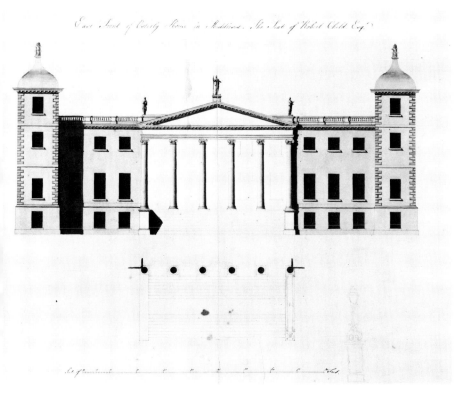

Fig. 3.
Design for the east front of Osterley
Park, Middlesex, by Robert Adam,
c. 1766   (The Earl of Jersey)

ing a neo-classical transformation of the exterior
of a country house in a drawing for Mistley Hall,
Essex (fig. 4),[16] which is a kind of before-and-
after illustration, prefiguring Humphry Re-

pton's Red Books of two decades later. At the
top is the fairly plain north front of the seat of
Richard Rigby, the Paymaster-General of Forces,
as it looked in 1777; beneath it is Adam's proposed remodeling of this earlier eighteenth-
century structure, complete with a rusticated
lower floor, elegant Ionic pilasters, and delicate
ornamentation in the form of a swag frieze, panels, and pedimental decoration, along with classical subject rondels. As at Osterley, both classical
antiquity and Burlingtonian Palladianism have
been made more elegant and refined and put at
the service of a new generation of architects and
patrons.

In part the emphasis on remodeling, decoration, and redecoration reflects the substantial
amount of major country-house construction in
the preceding half century, but it also indicates
the changes both in the pattern of life and in
artistic style that characterized the last half of the
eighteenth century, suggesting a perceived need
for modernization.

Before examining these changes, something
should be said about the patrons of this architecture. Although a great deal more work needs to
be done on a vast quantity of patrons, the source
of their income, and the nature of their housing
expenditures, to say nothing of the correlation
between house type and patron group, a few
tentative conclusions can be drawn. Established
landowners, primarily noblemen and gentry, still

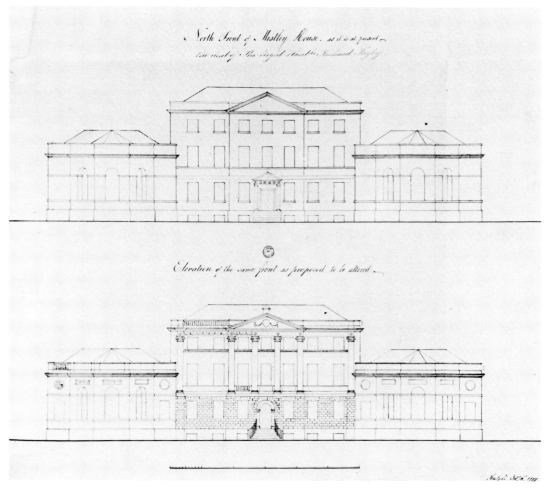

Fig. 4.
Survey drawing and proposed alterations for the north front of Mistley Hall, Essex, by Robert Adam, 1777 (Sir John Soane's Museum)

played a very important part in country-house construction, accounting, for example, for half of Adam's country-house commissions and for two-thirds of those of Chambers—indeed, for 77 percent of Chambers' commissions if one includes the royal family in that category. In Adam's case, all his country-house projects from established landowners in the first two decades of his career involved large houses, whereas slightly more than a third of his later commissions from that group of patrons were for villas or smaller houses. All of Chambers' country houses were concentrated in the 1758-to-1779 period. About one-third of his projects for peers and gentry were villas, though the figure jumps to 43.5 percent if those for George III and his family are included.[17]

Mercantile patrons—merchants, bankers, and others whose money came, either directly or through inheritance, from commerce, business, or such investment opportunities as the West Indies, the East India Company, or coal—account for 15 percent of Adam's country-house commissions and slightly more, 16.67 percent, of Chambers'. Again, a little over a third of these commissions were for villas, with 40 percent of Chambers' and 36 percent of Adam's mercantile clients requesting them, most of Adam's commissions for villas from mercantile patrons occurring in the latter part of his career. In contrast, Sir Robert Taylor, a City of London man himself, built most of his significant villas either for other City men or for those who had made their money themselves—or, at most, for those who had inherited their money from parents who were self-made.[18] This group of patrons would seem to have been responsible for an increasing number of country-house commissions as the century wore on, especially in the hands of those architects who were not at the very pinnacle of success.

Still other patrons came from the ranks of

politicians and government officials, military men, lawyers and doctors, churchmen, industrialists, and men of letters. Ten percent of Adam's country houses were commissioned by the first of these groups, 7 percent by the second; the other groups provided only limited patronage of this kind, much of which was for smaller houses. It is more difficult to arrive at such complete or accurate statistics for other architects, many of whom undoubtedly had a smaller number of titled patrons, but the figures we have give us some insight into country-house patronage, at least before 1792.

By the last two decades of the eighteenth century and the first decade and a half of the nineteenth, the role of the various groups of patrons had altered somewhat, with established landowners becoming a minority, albeit a still healthy one. Evidence for this can be found in Sandra Blutman's study of country houses during these thirty-five years, a period for which she was able to identify 257 people who commissioned such properties. Of these, 81 were from landowning families, 22 were bankers, 15 were merchants or businessmen, 9 were returned East Indian nabobs, and 5 owed their income to West Indian property. Of the remainder, only 7 of whose sources of income Blutman could not identify, 20 were distinguished military men and 11 each came from the ranks of the professions and the church.[19] Although Blutman did not specifically break down her study by house size, a few generalizations are possible on the basis of her lists. East Indian nabobs, not surprisingly, preferred larger houses, as on the whole did bankers, though the latter sometimes commissioned villas, especially if these were secondary homes.[20]

By 1800, not only the patronage profile but the general conception of the English country house had altered. Though many of the changes may be viewed as stylistic, they also reflect profound alterations in the nature of upper-class and well-to-do middle-class British life. The strict formality of seventeenth-century great houses and those of the first half of the eighteenth century, with their series of state apartments, began to give way, as Mark Girouard has effectively demonstrated,[21] to circuits or sequences of rooms more attuned to new modes of entertaining, in which a number of different activities—dancing, card playing, tea, supper, and polite conversation, for example—might take place either at the same time or in a more informal order.

Changes in both daytime and evening activi-

ties naturally affected the type, treatment, and arrangement of rooms. The events described above were usually undertaken in the evening following dinner, which would take place in the late afternoon and be served in the dining room—or eating parlour as it was still sometimes called—a room which became increasingly important. The ladies might retire from there to the drawing room, but both these rooms, plus a whole series of others, including the saloon, library, gallery, anterooms, and even possibly dressing rooms and bedrooms, would be employed for evening assemblies and parties, which often ended with a late supper. Many of these rooms would also, of course, be used for daytime activities, with the library, for example, being much frequented—and not just for reading—during the period between the late-morning breakfast and the late-afternoon dinner. Dressing rooms might also be used during that time for a variety of activities, as well as, perhaps, for breakfast, which was generally not a family meal but taken more or less individually. Sometimes specific breakfast rooms were included in houses, often on the east to take advantage of the morning sun, but they would be used also for sitting, reading, sewing, or conversation during the middle part of the day. Galleries, which might house books or pictures or statuary, would be very useful for rainy days, but they might also offer opportunities for various activities at other times.[22]

Increased informality is also reflected in the rising popularity of the villa, in which a whole series of apartments could be dispensed with. Often tighter and more compact in plan, these smaller houses were frequently arranged around central staircases, with the stairhall—as in the town residences and even in grander country seats—attracting a good deal of attention, both from the public and from architects. As was necessary in the generally more restricted space of houses in London, more than one floor of a villa might be used for entertaining; increasingly, however, the larger country houses began to feature the major reception rooms on the ground floor, with the bedrooms above them. A *piano nobile*, raised a full story above a rusticated level devoted to offices, cooking, storage, and informal activities and services, became more and more of an anachronism. In most country houses there was a movement away from multiple drawing rooms and the formal arrangement of suites of apartments on either side of a hall-

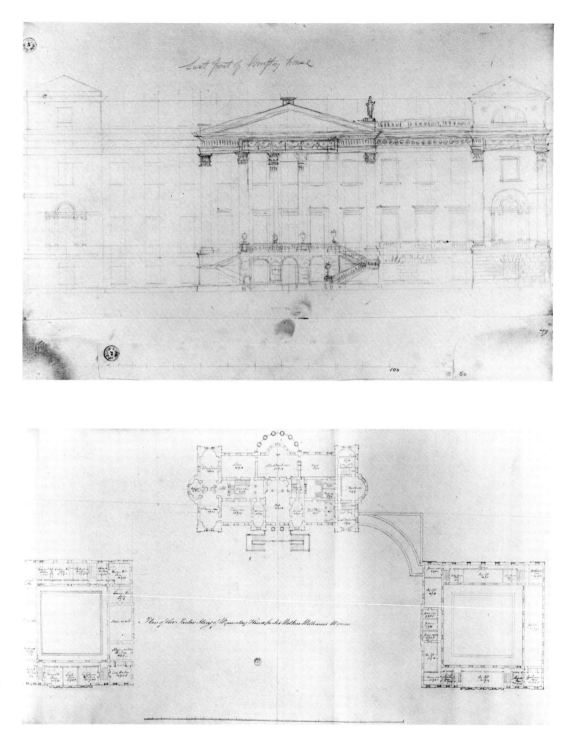

Fig. 5.
Detail of an unexecuted design for
the entrance front of Wynnstay,
Denbighshire, by Robert Adam,
c. 1768–1770   (Sir John Soane's Museum)

Fig. 6.
Unexecuted plan of the principal
floor for Wynnstay, Denbighshire,
by Robert Adam, c. 1768–1770
(Sir John Soane's Museum)

saloon axis, though this kind of great-house format continued during the period, at least on
paper and sometimes in stone or brick.

In between the large country house and the
villa was the contracted great house, which now
looked more like a villa, albeit sometimes a

rather large one, with wings. The plan of the
contracted great house, however, may or may
not reflect a relation to that of the villa. Descended, as Summerson has shown, from
Burlingtonian formats,[23] all three of these house
types were to be found during the last four dec-

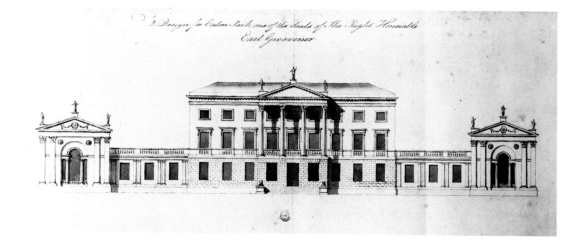

Fig. 7.
Unexecuted design for the entrance
front of Eaton Hall, Cheshire, by
Robert Adam, c. 1766–1768
(Sir John Soane's Museum)

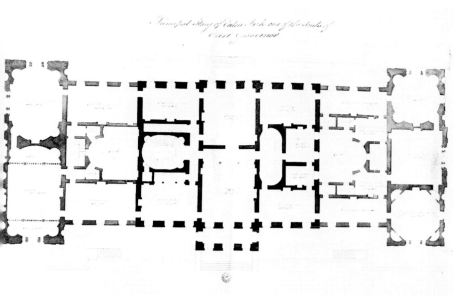

Fig. 8.
Unexecuted plan of the principal
floor for Eaton Hall, Cheshire, by
Robert Adam. c. 1766–1768
(Sir John Soane's Museum)

ades of the eighteenth century, but the degree to which they deviate from earlier prototypes and the frequency of the occurrence of each type indicate a changed situation at this time.

Thus, the traditional great house with its central hall-saloon axis, as at Colen Campbell's Wanstead House, designed between 1714 and 1720, is the least common. The frequent appearance of compressed plans and exterior expressions of the large villa with wings indicates a decided turn away from this grand formal model. Closer to Kent's Holkham Hall—which was begun about 1731—than to Wanstead, and utilizing attached wings in order to reduce the bulk of the main block, this format is represented in the last half of the century by Adam's

unexecuted designs for Wynnstay, Denbighshire, probably of about 1768 to 1770, for Sir Watkin Williams-Wynn (figs. 5, 6).[24] Although the basic format, thirteen-bay facade with central applied portico and end towers, and wings attached by quadrant links certainly recall the typical English Palladian formula, as at Houghton Hall or Holkham, the proportions, decorative treatment, and profusion of apses and unusual room shapes are characteristic of the neo-classical taste. On the exterior, the attenuated orders, with their capitals derived from the corner of the peristyle of the palace at Split, are the most obvious indication of the change that had occurred. Equally Adamesque are the Palladian motif within relieving arch and the Diocletian window on the right pavilion, but they, like the basic composition, are derived from Burlingtonian precedents such as on the garden facade of Chiswick, his Lordship's own villa begun about 1723. Similarly, the formal, almost symmetrical plan has been dramatically modified by the introduction of ovals, apses, a circle, and a columned screen, as well as by projecting exedrae, all evocative of the new ethos.

Another great-house format employed during this period was a still more compressed version of the Palladian formula, featuring a somewhat smaller central block of perhaps nine bays, one-story links, and story-and-a-half wings arranged in a straight line. It had the advantage of presenting a less grandiose image, while at the same time providing a large, more traditional plan belied by the exterior configuration. In his unexecuted designs of about 1766 to 1768 for Eaton Hall, Cheshire, for Earl Grosvenor (figs. 7, 8),[25] Adam demonstrated how he could recast this

composition in a more elegant neo-classical vein. Again, attenuated proportions and elegant detailing play important roles in this metamorphosis, as does the proliferation of varied room shapes, especially in the wings.

A more dramatic change in these formats could be effected by eliminating the rusticated bottom story and lowering the main rooms to ground level, as mentioned earlier. A characteristic example is furnished by Heaton Hall, Lancashire, of 1772, for the future first Earl of Wilton (fig. 9). Here James Wyatt not only dispensed with the lower level, but combined this treatment with links and wings in a straight line.[26] In addition to its increased horizontality and informality, as well as its neo-classical proportions and such appropriate details as Palladian motifs within relieving arches, classical subject panels, and delicate bucrania amidst a fluted frieze, Wyatt's building also employs a projecting domed exedra in the central block, octagonal wings, and significant variations in room shape. Because of a need for a series of elegant spaces, some of the principal rooms are actually located

in the links, thereby denying the concept of five separate parts as conveyed by the exterior.

Another modification of the centrally emphasized facade brought down to ground level can be seen in a design of 1797 by George Dance the Younger for a house in Cornwall for Sir Rose Price (fig. 10).[27] Gone are the delicate Adamesque details—except for the traceried fanlight above the doorway—and even the Palladian motifs. In their place is a starkness especially characteristic of Dance and Soane at the end of the century, as well as two square cupolas to provide, within, the kind of hidden lighting—"lumière mystérieuse," as Soane called it[28]—that both architects enjoyed.

A further development in the treatment of the neo-classical elevation was the complete elimination of a central emphasis. Two examples of this with quite different approaches to surface treatment and decoration are provided by Samuel Wyatt's Belmont Park, Kent, of 1787 to 1792, for General Lord Harris, and the proposed but unexecuted addition to Adderbury, Oxfordshire, of about 1768, by William Chambers for the

Fig. 9.
Garden front of Heaton Hall, Lancashire, begun in 1772 to designs by James Wyatt (City of Manchester Art Galleries)

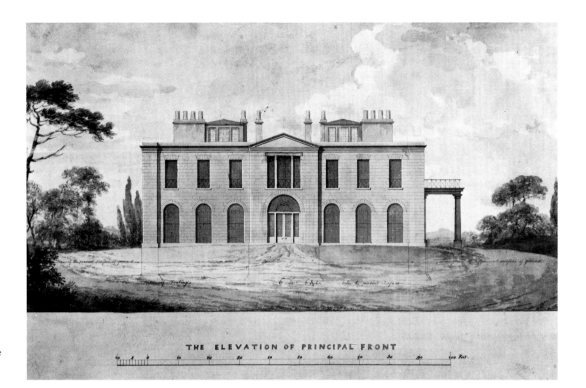

Fig. 10.
Design for the principal front of a
house in Cornwall by George Dance
the Younger for Sir Rose Price,
1797   (Sir John Soane's Museum)

Fig. 11.
Unexecuted design for an addition
to Adderbury, Oxfordshire, by Sir
William Chambers, c. 1768   (The
Duke of Buccleuch and Queensberry, KT)

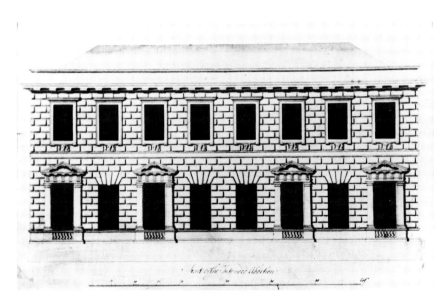

Duke of Buccleuch (figs. 12, 11).[29] In the former, an Adamesque variation of the nineties for a military man, two domed exedrae—a relatively unusual variation on a common theme of the period, which Pierre du Prey has dubbed the *bombé* facade[30]—frame the garden front, whose central section features three bays of attenuated ground-floor windows topped by delicate Coade stone panels, the middle one including an image of the house. In the design of the sixties for a scion of the aristocracy, there is not even a window in the center of the facade, which, with its heavy rustication, pronounced Doric enframents, and sculpted bucranium panels, clearly reflects Chambers' individual brand of neo-classicism.

Various facade compositions of the period balance an emphasis on the horizontal with some stress on the center, which is conveyed through the use of colonnades, small porches, or recession, with the character of these again quite different from those of the preceding era. Thus, at Rosneath, Dumbartonshire, built between 1803 and 1806 for the Duke of Argyll (fig. 13), Joseph Bonomi employed a giant five-column colonnade without a pediment as a porte-cochere to protect the arriving family or guests. This unusual number of columns, which is decidedly unclassical, was used out of necessity by Bonomi at an earlier house. He employed it here for effect between the similarly untypical three-column projections at either end of the building.[31] In contrast to the unclassical originality proclaimed by Bonomi at Rosneath, although equally stark, Soane's semicircular porch at Moggerhanger, Bedfordshire, erected between 1806 and 1811 for Stephen Thornton (fig. 14), illustrates the role of archae-

Fig. 12.
Belmont Park, Kent, from the southeast, by Samuel Wyatt, 1787–1792 (Photograph: Royal Commission on the Historical Monuments of England)

Fig. 13.
Design for the garden front of Rosneath, Dumbartonshire, by Joseph Bonomi, 1803–1806 (The British Architectural Library, RIBA, Drawings Collection)

Fig. 14.
Entrance portico at Moggerhanger,
Bedfordshire, by John Soane, 1806–
1811 (Photograph: author)

ology at the end of this fifty-year period. Basing his shape on a half tholos, Soane derived his Greek Doric columns with two-thirds fluting from an example found on Delos and published in the third volume of the *Antiquities of Athens* in 1794.[32] It was not that Soane was more derivative, but that his use of accurate archaeological details went hand-in-hand with his originality.

Despite the innovations and archaeological zeal of the neo-classical era, certain themes from the preceding generation continued to play an important part in the country houses of the half century after 1755. Especially interesting in this regard is the tripartite window arrangement, which remained popular throughout the eighteenth century. Composed of a taller and wider central-arched window flanked by abutting shorter rectangular units, known as a Venetian or Palladian motif but also as a Serliana, this form is one of the significant characteristics of Burlingtonian Palladian architecture. Used both alone and within a semicircular relieving arch, it can be seen not only at Houghton, Holkham, and Chiswick, but in scores of other examples. In the last half of the century, Adam was especially enamored of this motif within a relieving

arch, but he and others who followed modified it, attenuating its proportions in keeping with the new spirit and sometimes affixing to it more characteristic neo-classical decoration, such as a bell-flower ornamented velarium treatment for the surrounding frame, as in his Society of Arts of 1772 to 1774. Adam and his contemporaries also transformed this window arrangement, eliminating the taller central arch and substituting a blank tympanum, usually with a neo-classical motif set upon it, above the tripartite window. Adam could suggest such a treatment even on the same elevation as the more traditional overarched Serliana, as he did in one of his drawings of 1775, now in Sir John Soane's Museum,[33] for Combe Bank, Kent (fig. 15), designed for Lord Frederick Campbell, younger brother of the Duke of Argyll. Quickly adopted by others, this treatment could be further modified if the semicircular tympanum was converted into a segmental one, in keeping with later eighteenth-century tendencies. Both types were used together at Sledmere, Yorkshire, which was built between 1781 and 1788 and was probably designed by its owner, Sir Christopher Sykes.

Also developed by the Burlingtonians, the

villa was, if anything, even more transformed by the architects of the second half of the eighteenth century. Compact in plan and often expressed on the exterior by a three-bay portico, either applied or projecting, flanked by a single bay on either side, houses such as Stourhead in Wiltshire, Mereworth in Kent, and Lord Herbert's house in Whitehall, all by Colen Campbell, Burlington's Chiswick, and Marble Hill by Roger Morris and Lord Pembroke presented in the 1720s the paradigmatic illustration of this new, smaller, and essentially suburban type.[34] It gathered a few adherents in subsequent decades, flourished in the hands of Ware and others in the middle of the century,[35] and persisted, with modification, to century's end. One important change occurred in the 1750s with the introduction of canted and semicircular bays, evident particularly in the work of Sir Robert Taylor at, for example, Harleyford Manor, Buckinghamshire (fig. 16). Under construction in 1755, the house was designed for Sir William Clayton, the second baronet, whose family money came from commerce. Another change was the elimination of a high basement or rustic level. For this Chambers could claim some responsibility, as is demonstrated at Duddingston, near Edinburgh, built between 1762 and 1767 for the Earl of Abercorn, which also boasts an imposing portico.[36] Later in the century new types of exterior expression, such as arcaded facades, tall and narrower proportions, plainer surfaces, unusual shapes, and asymmetrical compositions appeared, as the villa became more pervasive and more informal. Another variation featured gabled end bays framing a slightly recessed center with a colonnaded loggia, as exemplified by Adam's design for Sunnyside, Midlothian, of 1786. Also present at Sunnyside is the ubiquitous Palladian motif within relieving arch, together with Adam's usual range of interesting room shapes, a projecting bow, and a T-shaped plan.[37]

Aside from the projecting bays, surfaces tended to become flatter. One method of organizing the facades was with a series of shallow relieving arches, either five or three, the latter being employed, for instance, in Robert Mylne's The Wick, Richmond, of 1775 for Lady St. Aubyn. Elegantly refined and planar, it has only the slightest vertical emphasis, achieved by the insertion of a low dormer window atop the central bay.[38]

Soane often arrived at such subtle verticality by means of an extra attic block placed above the

central bay, as in the garden facade of his own house, Pitzhanger, in Ealing, built 1800 to 1803, where the flatness of the surface is even more pronounced, articulated by piers fashioned from striated strips. The striations and indentations on this very flat facade are indications of a primitivism that appeared in and around the 1790s, going hand-in-hand with an enjoyment of the Greek Doric order.

Equally as significant as the exterior configuration of neo-classical villas are the villa plans, for

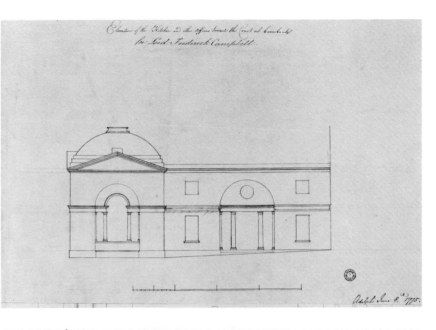

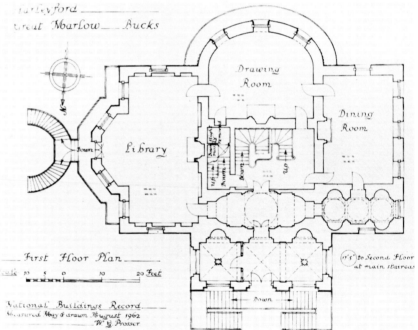

Fig. 15.
Design for a kitchen and office wing at Combe Bank, Kent, by Robert Adam, 1775 (Sir John Soane's Museum)

Fig. 16.
Plan for Harleyford Manor, Buckinghamshire, by Sir Robert Taylor, c. 1755 (Royal Commission on the Historical Monuments of England)

these tight, more compact structures often challenged architects to devise highly imaginative juxtapositions of varied room shapes, which increased the pleasure of circulating from room to room at the country-house parties of the last half of the eighteenth century. Thus, at Harleyford (fig. 16) Taylor created a plan in which each of the major main-floor rooms around the central rectangular stairhall and flanking service stairs is different. One could move from the library, with a polygonal bay in the center of one of its longer walls, to the drawing room, one long side of which is opened out into a semicircular apse, to the rectangular dining room. On the next floor, above the drawing room, are two oval spaces.[39]

Adam, whose accomplishments with spatial sleights-of-hand are evident in larger houses and more traditional formats, could produce equally impressive results with somewhat smaller compositions, as seen in one of his unexecuted designs for Great Saxham, Suffolk, of 1779, for Hutchison Mure, a London merchant. Here a whole series of rooms with curved walls—from a flattened ovoid breakfast room to a trefoil anteroom to a circular dressing room, separated by rectangular eating and drawing rooms with apses at one end—occupies the semicircular garden facade, detached from a group of more regular rooms on the entrance front by the oval main stairs and two subsidiary ovals.[40]

This kind of lively spatial play becomes extremely common during the latter part of the eighteenth century, though one could carry this sort of thing to excess, as Charles Middleton did in his *Architect and Builder's Miscellany* of 1799, in which one of his villas (fig. 17) includes not only a semicircular stairhall and pentagonal study, but hexagonal drawing room, rectangular dining room with one semicircular end, rectangular library with one polygonal end, and both a triangular closet and one of an even more unusual shape.[41]

A generation or two that took such evident delight in unusual room shapes and combinations could also be expected to respond to whole houses of unusual form, as, indeed, was the case. Although no great number of such houses were erected or even designed, both the variety and quantity of them are still significant. House designs in the shape of octagons, hexagons, trapezoids, triangles, semicircles, ovals, and circles are known, as are such variations as triangles with concave sides and at least one sixteen-sided house, A la Ronde, which was erected outside Exmouth, Devon, in about 1798 for two cousins, Jane and Mary Parmenter. Although its architect is not recorded and many of the other designs are by lesser-known figures, both Adam and Chambers produced such house plans, as did many of their significant colleagues.[42]

Of the more unusual polygonal geometric shapes, the triangle seems to have enjoyed the greatest favor. Designs for houses in this shape by Chambers, Adam, Dance, John Carr of York, and John Nash, as well as in the pattern books of John Carter and Richard Elsam, among others, are known; and some of these were carried out, including Adam's Walkinshaw House, Renfrewshire, built in 1791 for Dayhout Macdowell. Adroitly composed within a neo-classical exterior, Walkinshaw features octagonal rooms in each angle and rectangles with two apsed ends and a semicircular stairhall between them.[43]

Variations on the triangle were also employed, as in the concave-sided ones created on paper by S. Nelson in about 1790 and by James Malton in 1792[44] and in V-shaped houses arrived at by re-

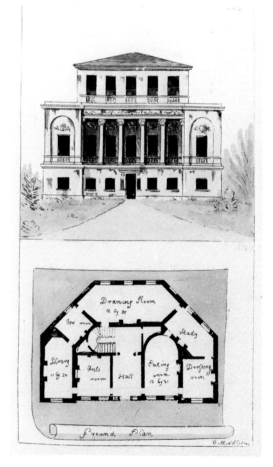

cessing the central portion of the triangle's base. Here again, as Alistair Rowan has effectively demonstrated, Adam provides a number of very interesting examples, none unfortunately executed, with skillful planning and dramatic castellar massing.[45] Among other V-shaped designs is Richard Elsam's published but unexecuted scheme for Finborough Hall, Suffolk (fig. 18), of about 1794 for Roger Pettiward, which uses octagons, circles, and apsed rooms galore.[46]

Circular and oval houses were yet another unusual form that especially appealed to architects and patrons of the neo-classical era. They can be considered together, since both shapes were often referred to as round. Although frequently found in small villas, the form could equally be used for huge, megalomaniacal conceptions. Typical of the former is Belle Isle, erected by John Plaw for Thomas English in 1774 on an island in Lake Windermere. Measuring fifty feet in diameter, it is an elegant neo-classical villa with an oval library and drawing and dining rooms with slightly convex outer walls, the latter with an apsed projection at one end.[47]

By contrast, Ballyscullion and Ickworth, erected during the last twelve years of the eighteenth century, were both very large, cylindrical houses, 350 and 600 feet long, respectively, including quadrant corridors and wings, with central oval units 84 by 74 and 120 by 106 feet.[48] Both were for the same patron, one of the most eccentric of the eighteenth century, the Bishop of Derry and Earl of Bristol. Ballyscullion, begun in 1787 on one of the Earl-Bishop's Irish estates, was based specifically on Belle Isle.[49] Partially completed by 1795, it was derelict within little more than a decade, its owner having died abroad without ever having lived in the completed house.[50]

While Ballyscullion was still under construction, the Earl-Bishop began an even grander project at Ickworth, his ancestral estate. In the summer of 1794 he wrote to his daughter from Siena that he hoped to lay the cornerstone the following year. In November he commissioned Charles Heathcote Tatham, who was then in Rome, to design "a Villa to be built in Suffolk, extending nearly 500 feet including Offices. The distribution of the Plan is very singular, the House being oval, according to his desire," as Tatham wrote to Henry Holland.[51] At some point, however, the Earl-Bishop consulted Tatham's Roman instructor, Mario Asprucci, and it was the latter's design that was followed, al-

beit in a somewhat modified fashion, by Francis Sandys, a young Irish architect who seems to have been in Rome in 1794 and whose brother Joseph was in charge of the actual construction.[52] Only completed in 1830, twenty-seven years after the death of its commissioner, who never even saw it, Ickworth (fig. 19) remains a dramatic testament to the appeal of circular and oval houses in late-eighteenth-century England.

In addition to the enjoyment of geometric shapes, an increasing addiction to flatness and austerity, and a heightened impulse toward archaeology, there were other tendencies in the 1790s that contributed to the change in architec-

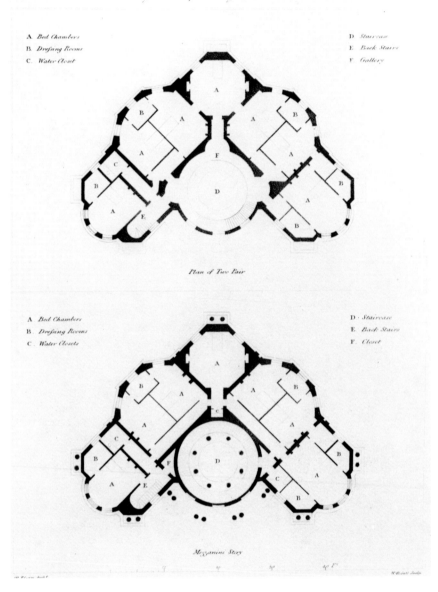

Fig. 18.
Unexecuted plan for Finborough Hall, Suffolk, by Richard Elsam, c. 1794, from his *An Essay on Rural Architecture,* c. 1803, plate 24

Fig. 19.
Garden front of Ickworth, Suffolk, by Mario Asprucci and Francis Sandys, built 1793–1830 (Photograph: author)

Fig. 20.
A side view of Castle Goring, Sussex, by J. B. Rebecca, c. 1790–1798, showing the junction between the two parts of the house (Photograph: author)

tural character. The efflorescence of the picturesque and the emergence of associationism encouraged the wide acceptance of a whole range of stylistic opportunities. Where a playful kind of gothic had been a viable, if rather low-keyed alternative to the classical approach during the preceding three or four decades, any number of possibilities were now available to the enterprising architect. Thus, in 1802, James Malton announced that "From his acquaintance with the various styles of architecture, Mr. Malton will alter any sound old building, to any particular style desired."[53] If a patron could not decide what he wanted, he could have a battlemented gothic on one front and an elegant example of classicism on the other, as J. B. Rebecca provided for Sir Bysshe Shelley, the poet's grandfather, at Castle Goring, Sussex (fig. 20), between 1790 and 1798.[54] Although the transition between the two parts—and styles—is not very elegant, it illustrates beautifully the theory of associationism propounded by Archibald Alison about the time that the house was begun.[55]

The triumph of the picturesque in the 1790s also made popular a variety of rustic cottages and irregular villas. Nash was, after the amateur Richard Payne Knight, one of the first to move consciously and decisively away from the general symmetry that marked almost all of the villas before 1800. At Luscombe, Devon, of 1800 to 1804, and at Cronkhill, on the Attingham estate in Shropshire, of about 1802 (fig. 21), Nash produced two determinedly asymmetrical villas, the

Fig. 21.
Cronkhill, Shropshire, by John
Nash, c. 1802 (Royal Commission on the
Historical Monuments of England)

first for a banker and the second for the steward to Lord Berwick, Nash's client at Attingham itself. Not surprisingly, neither was neo-classical in the conventional sense, Luscombe being gothic and Cronkhill Italianate, patterned more after the buildings in landscapes by Claude Lorrain than on specific Italian structures. Yet, despite the carefully placed off-center towers of two different projecting shapes, the irregular rooflines, and the dramatic play of light and shade at Cronkhill, all of which are enormously significant for the future development of English architecture, also present are such characteristics of late-eighteenth-century villas as plain surface, windows without moldings, attenuated proportions, horizontal oval lights, and, especially, the placement of the main floor at ground level.

Both the theory of the picturesque and that of association paved the way for even more exotic styles, such as the Indian or Hindoo, which was in evidence at Sezincote, Gloucestershire (fig. 22), designed about 1803 by S. P. Cockerell for his brother, a former East Indian nabob. Despite the Indian details, derived from drawings by Thomas Daniell, who had been to India, Sezincote is actually a symmetrical villa with a projecting exedra, akin in basic format to a host of conventional houses of the last half of the eighteenth century, such as Wyatt's Heaton Hall of 1772 (fig. 9).[56]

It is a long way from Duddingston, Wynnstay, or Heaton to Cronkhill, Pitzhanger, or Sezincote, but the development from the first group to the second constitutes one facet of the transformation of the country house in the second half of the eighteenth century. The other facet, as we have seen, is the more literal transformation of individual houses. Together they illustrate the impact of neo-classicism on a central feature of British life and architecture.

Fig. 22.
Sezincote, Gloucestershire, by S. P.
Cockerell, c. 1803, from a drawing
by John Martin   (British Museum)

NOTES

1. This paper is a reduced but significantly altered version, with additional material, of Damie Stillman, *English Neo-classical Architecture*, 2 vols. (London, 1988), chap. 5, to which the reader is referred for elaboration of certain points considered here.

2. Mark Girouard in various public lectures has, for example, cited the case of the Earl of Bristol, who, in the early eighteenth century, generally spent four months in the country (in his case at Ickworth), one in Bath, and seven in London.

3. John Summerson, "The Classical Country House in 18th-Century England," *Journal of the Royal Society of Arts* 107 (1959): 540.

4. This figure was arrived at by compiling a list of country houses with beginning dates between 1760 and 1799, entered under sixty significant architects in Howard Colvin, *A Biographical Dictionary of British Architects, 1600–1840* (London, 1978), supplemented by houses with uncertain or complicated authorship known from other sources. Summerson 1959, 552, n. 3, describes an analogous method. It must, however, be remembered that Summerson used the first edition of Colvin (*A Biographical Dictionary of English Architects, 1640–1840* [London, 1954]), whereas I have used the revised edition, which is much more extensive.

5. As Summerson 1959, 540, pointed out, deciding which houses to include is extremely difficult, since it depends on one's definition of size and on the degree of remodeling. To have excluded all remodelings would have meant the elimination, for example, of some of Adam's major works, resulting in a false picture. No house, however, was counted more than once, even if—as, for example, with Wormleybury—one architect (Mylne) built it and another (Adam) provided major interior decorations. The figures can only be used as a rough guide, allowing a healthy margin for error. A stricter interpretation discounting remodelings would produce significantly lower figures.

6. These figures have been compiled from the exhibition catalogues of the Society of Artists, the Free Society, and the Royal Academy.

7. These figures have been compiled from the exhibition catalogues of the Society of Artists and the Royal Academy.

8. Although this can be discerned from a detailed examination of these books, a statistical analysis by Pierre de la Ruffinière du Prey, *John Soane: The Making of an Architect* (Chicago, 1982), 381–382, n. 7, reveals that the word *villa* appears no more than three times in any book before 1765, and then in only one, but six to eight times in at least three different books of the 1766–1779 period. Carrying this study into the 1780s, one can find fourteen such references in John Plaw's *Rural Architecture* of 1785, and this is symptomatic of the outpouring of cottage books in the last fifteen years of the century. Similarly, Plaw's book is only one of a number that include the word *villa* in their subtitles.

9. Jose Mac Packe [pseud.], Οικιδια, or Nutshells, Being Ichnographic Distributions for Small Villas (London, 1785), 4. This evocative reference was first noted by Summerson 1959, 568.

10. Charles Middleton, *Picturesque and Architectural Views for Cottages, Farm Houses and Country Villas* (London, 1793), 9; quoted by Summerson 1959, 571.

11. For Chambers at Osterley, see John Harris, *Sir William Chambers* (London, 1970), 240; Helena Hayward and Pat Kirkham, *William and John Linnell: Eighteenth Century London Furniture Makers* (London and New York, 1980), 1:114–115.

12. Adam drawings, vol. 43, no. 94. Although labeled "South front of a House for Francis Child Esq.ʳ at Osterley Park Middlesex," it would appear to be a view of the house as existing in 1761, when Adam was first approached by Francis Child.

13. I am grateful to Lord Jersey for permission to reproduce both Adam's design of 1761 for the east front of Osterley and his new scheme of c. 1766.

14. Walpole to the Countess of Upper Ossory, 21 June 1773, Mrs. Paget Toynbee, ed., *The Letters of Horace Walpole*, 16 vols. (Oxford, 1903–1905), 8:291.

15. Toynbee 1903–1905, 8:291–292.

16. Sir John Soane's Museum, London, Adam drawings, vol. 41, no. 50.

17. The percentages in this and the following paragraphs have been arrived at through an analysis of Adam's and Chambers' country house patrons, using Colvin 1978; Arthur T. Bolton, *The Architecture of Robert and James Adam* (London, 1922); Harris 1970; and various other primary and secondary sources.

18. For these clients, see Marcus Binney, "The Villas of Sir Robert Taylor," *Country Life* (6, 13 July 1967), 17–21, 78–81; idem, *Sir Robert Taylor* (London, 1984), chaps. 2, 3.

19. Sandra Blutman, "English Country Houses, 1780–1815" (M. Phil. thesis, University of London, 1967), 1:11–12.

20. Blutman 1967, 1:47–51 (East Indian nabobs), 21–27 (bankers).

21. Mark Girouard, *Life in the English Country House* (New Haven, 1978), 194–201, discusses the changes in plans resulting from new types of entertaining.

22. A good discussion of these activities is provided by Girouard 1978, 201–206.

23. Summerson 1959, 554–583.

24. Sir John Soane's Museum, Adam drawings, vol. 10, no. 49; vol. 40, no. 63, which are also illustrated in Peter Howell and T. W. Pritchard, "Wynnstay, Denbighshire," *Country Life* (30 March 1972), 782. The drawings are not dated, but in November 1768, Sir Watkin Williams-Wynn wrote from Rome that he had not yet received Adam's plans (Howell and Pritchard 1972, 688). Unexecuted designs by James Byres are dated 1770 (Howell and Pritchard 1972, 688–689), as are Adam designs for ceilings in the existing house (Sir John Soane's Museum, Adam drawings, vol. 12, nos. 41–43).

25. Sir John Soane's Museum, Adam drawings, vol. 39, nos. 86–99, with the second design (nos. 93–99, of which 93 and 98 are illustrated here), being most indicative of this format. The drawings are not dated, though a design for a banqueting house for Eaton (vol. 19, no. 140) is dated 1766. Although they do not illustrate or discuss the designs, Guy Acloque and John Cornforth, "The Eternal Gothic of Eaton—1," *Country Life* (11 February 1971), 304, mention that "About 1768 Robert Adam made proposals for altering . . . [the existing seventeenth-century house], but they were abandoned probably because of the break-up of the 1st Lord Grosvenor's marriage and his case against the Duke of Cumberland in 1770."

26. See *Heaton Hall, Manchester, Bicentenary Exhibition, 1772–1972* (Manchester, 1972); Summerson 1959, 565–566.

27. Sir John Soane's Museum, Dance Cabinet.

28. This phrase was used by Soane not only in his Royal Academy lectures (e.g., Sir John Soane, *Lectures on Architecture*, ed. Arthur T. Bolton [London, 1929], 126), but also in his *Designs for Public and Private Buildings* (London, 1828), e.g., 25. David Watkin, "Soane and His Contemporaries," in John Summerson, David Watkin, and G.-Tilman Mellinghoff, *John Soane* (London and New York, 1983), 41, suggests that this use of the French phrase may reflect the influence of such French architects as Etienne-Louis Boullée and Nicolas Le Camus de Mézières. Although Boullée's concern with such a concept is well known, his writings were not actually published until the twentieth century (*Architecture, essai sur l'art*, ed. Helen Rosenau [London, 1953], e.g., 51). Le Camus, however, stated as early as 1780 in his *Le Génie de l'architecture* that light can make architecture "mystérieuse ou triste."

29. The Chambers drawing for Adderbury, preserved in the Muniment Room at Dalkeith Palace, is also illustrated in Harris 1970, pl. 72, with comment on 196. I am indebted to the Duke of Buccleuch for permission to reproduce this drawing and to John Harris for a photograph of it.

30. For this theme, see du Prey's article in the present volume. Extensive discussion of the use of a convex exedra on English country houses can also be found in Stillman 1988, 1: chap. 5, esp. 165–168.

31. The Rosneath drawing is preserved in the Drawings Collection, Royal Institute of British Architects. The five-column portico was suggested to Bonomi at Eastwell Park, Kent, 1793–1800, by necessity, for the decision to include the porte-cochere was made after construction had begun, and the central column opposite the doorway was required to support the long span of the lintel between the four columns placed in front of the piers between the windows (George Richardson, *The New Vitruvius Britannicus* [London, 1802–1808], 1:12). Having used the five-column portico at Eastwell, Bonomi returned to it at Rosneath, where, though not structurally dictated, it could help convey a balancing horizontality.

32. James Stuart and Nicholas Revett, *The Antiquities of Athens* (London, 1762–1816), 3: chap. 10, pls. 3–4; 3:58 identifies it as "the portico of Philip King of Macedon" on the island of Delos.

33. Adam drawings, vol. 42, no. 3.

34. For these houses, all designed and/or under construction between 1720 and 1724, and their significance, see Summerson 1959, 571–573.

35. Ware's significance—as demonstrated at Clifton Hill House in Bristol (1746–1750), Wrotham Park (c. 1754), and two houses in Scotland illustrated in Isaac Ware, *Complete Body of Architecture* (London, 1756), pls. 54–55, 56–57—is emphasized by Summerson 1959, 577–578. For the relatively few villas of the 1730s and 1740s, see Summerson 1959, 574–577.

36. For Chambers' early villas, see Harris 1970, 45–48; Stillman 1988, 1: 86–87. For the early villas of Taylor, see Binney 1967, 17–21.

37. For Sunnyside, see Sir John Soane's Museum, Adam drawings, vol. 48, nos. 90–91; Alistair Rowan, *Designs for Castles and Country Villas by Robert & James Adam* (New York, 1985), 78–79; idem, "Sunnyside and Rosebank: Suburban Villas by the Adam Brothers," *AA Files* 4 (1983): 29–39.

38. Still extant, this house is also shown in Mylne's drawing in the Richardson-Houfe Collection, Ampthill, Bedfordshire, no. 20.

39. The plan is also reproduced in Binney 1967, 17, as well as in Girouard 1978, 199, where there is a very good discussion of the plan and its relation to the country-house lifestyle.

40. Sir John Soane's Museum, Adam drawings, vol. 34, nos. 24–27. The design is reproduced in Rowan 1985, pl. 13, and in Stillman 1988, 1: pl. 88.

41. Various of these shapes, but in a different arrangement, also occur in Charles Middleton, *Architect and Builder's Miscellany,* pl. 21, reproduced in Stillman 1988, 1: pl. 87.

42. For A la Ronde, see Nikolaus Pevsner, *The Buildings of England: South Devon* (Harmonsworth, 1952), p. 167; for more on these unusual plans, see Stillman 1988, 1: 151–153.

43. For Walkinshaw, see Sir John Soane's Museum, Adam drawings, vol. 31, nos. 56–62. The design is reproduced in Rowan 1985, pl. 35, and in Stillman 1988, 1: pl. 89.

44. For Nelson's design for a gentleman's villa (The Metropolitan Museum of Art, 66.636), see John Harris, *A Catalogue of British Drawings for Architecture, Decoration, Sculpture, and Landscape Gardening, 1550–1900, in American Collections* (Upper Saddle River, N.J., 1971), 150, pl. 109; for Malton's design, which appears to be for a large garden building, see *Irish Georgian Society Quarterly Bulletin* 21, no. 3–4 (1978), back cover.

45. See Alistair Rowan, "After the Adelphi: Forgotten Years in the Adam Brothers' Practice," *Journal of the Royal Society of Arts* 122 (1974), 702–707. Adam's V-shaped designs for the following houses are preserved in Sir John Soane's Museum, Adam drawings, vol. 29, nos. 72, 75–79 (Barnton Castle, Midlothian, undated but c. 1791–1792); vol. 30, nos. 72–78 (Bewley Castle, Inverness-shire, 1777); vol. 37, nos. 51–58 (Barnbougle Castle, West Lothian, undated), 81–87 (villa at Harwich, Essex, for John Robinson, 1778). For these, see also Rowan 1985.

46. Richard Elsam, *An Essay on Rural Architecture* (1803), 2d ed. (London, 1805), pls. 22–25.

47. Illustrated in John Plaw, *Rural Architecture* (London, 1785), frontispiece and pls. 25–30.

48. For these dimensions, I have relied on Christopher Hussey, *English Country Houses: Mid-Georgian, 1760–1800* (London, 1956), 244.

49. Belle Isle was named as the source in an article in the *Belfast New-letter,* 14–18 September 1787, as was the Earl-Bishop's architect, Michael Shanaghan: "The general idea of the house was taken from a circular one in *Belleisle* Island, in the Windermeer lake: was immediately adopted and communicated to Mr. Michael Shanaghan, Architect, at Corke, who arranged the present building at Ballyscullin, and committed the inspection to Mr. D. Mc Blain." Quoted by Peter Rankin, *Irish Building Ventures of the Earl Bishop of Derry, 1730–1803* (Belfast, 1972), 50.

50. On the Earl-Bishop's death in 1803, Harry Bruce, who inherited his Irish estates, removed some objects from Ballyscullion to Downhill, auctioned the rest, and allowed the house to decay. Only the columns of its portico survive, having been reinstalled at St. George's Church, Belfast, in 1813 (Rankin 1972, 58). A good view of the house was published in G. V. Sampson, *Statistical Survey of the County of Londonderry* (Dublin, 1802), and is reproduced in Rankin 1972, 51, and in Hussey 1956, 241.

51. 19 November 1794 (Victoria and Albert Museum, D. 1479–1898, fol. 4). This and the letter from the Earl-Bishop to his daughter, Lady Erne, 10 August 1794, are quoted in William S. Childe-Pemberton, *The Earl Bishop* (London and New York, 1925), 2:465–466, 464, respectively. Tatham's relations with the Earl-Bishop were as fraught with problems and vicissitudes as had been Soane's fifteen years before, as can be judged from Tatham's pessimism in February, his renewed optimism in June, and his subsequent loss of the commission. For this, see his letters to Holland, 15 February and 7 June 1795 (Victoria and Albert Museum, D. 1479–1898, fols. 8, 13), and the rest of this paragraph.

52. Asprucci's designs are preserved in Cooper-Hewitt Museum, New York, 1938.88.7172, and at Chatsworth. For these, and a summary of the various contributors, see Pamela Tudor-Craig, "The Evolution of Ickworth," *Country Life* (17 May 1973), 1362–1365.

53. James Malton, *A Collection of Designs for Rural Retreats* (London, 1802), unpaginated.

54. For this house, see Sandra Blutman, "Castle Goring, Sussex," in Howard Colvin and John Harris, eds., *The Country Seat: Studies in the History of the British Country House Presented to Sir John Summerson* (London, 1970), 205–209.

55. Archibald Alison, *An Essay on the Nature and Principles of Taste* (Edinburgh, 1790). For a more detailed study of Alison's theories, see Walter J. Hipple, Jr., *The Beautiful, the Sublime & the Picturesque in Eighteenth-Century British Aesthetic Theory* (Carbondale, Ill., 1957).

56. For Sezincote and Daniell's contribution, see RIBA Drawings Collection, British Architectural Library, J5/16; David Verey, *The Buildings of England; Gloucestershire; the Cotswolds* (Harmondsworth, 1970), 392.

BRINSLEY FORD

Portraits of the English Abroad in Countries Other than Italy

In *The Treasure Houses of Britain* exhibition, all the portraits of the English, with one notable exception, were painted or sculpted either in England or in Italy. It therefore occurred to me to choose as my subject for this symposium those portraits that were painted in other countries. The attraction of this was that it was completely new to me. As I was only too aware of the omissions that were likely to occur when I attempted to cover so wide a field, I invited my audience to bring any deficiencies to my attention; this they have most generously done, with the result that this paper is not the one that I delivered, but a version enriched with the suggestions of my colleagues.

One of the earliest portraits of an Englishman painted abroad must be the fourteenth-century fresco of Sir John de Hawkwood on horseback by Paolo Uccello in the Duomo at Florence. This ruthless *condottiere* is in marked contrast to those young men whom Horace Walpole described five centuries later as "the staring boys that come [to Italy] in flocks, once a year like woodcocks."[1] By the second half of the eighteenth century it had become an established practice for the "staring boys" who went on the Grand Tour to have their portraits painted in Rome. In Anthony Clark's book on Pompeo Batoni, brilliantly edited by Edgar Peters Bowron, we learn that there are some two hundred portraits of English sitters by Batoni alone.[2]

In all other parts of the world except, perhaps, in India, there was something rather haphazard about the way the English came to be painted. Broadly speaking English sitters fell into six categories: first, there were the English envoys, or those sent on special missions to foreign powers; second, there were those who went into exile for political reasons, such as the cavaliers who left England during the Commonwealth or, later,

the Jacobites; third, there were soldiers campaigning abroad; fourth, members of organizations, such as officials of the East India Company; fifth, artists; and sixth, travelers and explorers.

America

It would be appropriate to start with portraits of the English done in America. I have not been able to find many portraits by America's most distinguished portrait painters, for Benjamin West and Gilbert Stuart both went to study in Europe when they were very young. Most of John Singleton Copley's splendid portraits, painted before he went to Europe, were of Bostonians. He did, however, paint the fine portrait of General Thomas Gage,[3] who was commander-in-chief in America from 1763 until 1772. This is now in the collection of Mr. Paul Mellon. Copley also painted the general's American-born wife, Margaret Kemble. On 6 November 1771 Copley wrote to his half-brother from New York, "I have done some of my best portraits here, particularly Mrs Gage's, which is gone to the exhibition. It is beyond compare the best lady's portrait I ever drew; but Mr Pratt says of it, it will be flesh and blood these 200 years to come, that every part and line in it is Butifull [*sic*] that I must get my Ideas from Heaven."[4] The portrait was exhibited in London at the Society of Artists in 1772. It remained at Firle Place, the home of the Gage family in Sussex, until recent years, when it was sold to the Timken Art Gallery in San Diego. Another fine Copley of an English soldier is that of Major John Montresor,[5] after whom the island in the vicinity of Hell Gate in New York is named. He served for many years in America and was present at the attack and capture of Long Island in 1776. This portrait belongs to the Detroit Institute of Arts.

One of Copley's most famous pictures, which was painted in London long after the event, illustrates the truly terrifying adventure that befell a young English boy in America. In 1749 Brook Watson, at the age of fourteen, was swimming in the harbor at Havana when he was attacked by a shark that bit off his leg. The painting, of which there are several versions, was commissioned by the victim who, despite his mutilation, was to have a successful career in the city that led to his becoming Lord Mayor of London and being created a baronet. Comparing this work with Benjamin West's *Death of Wolfe,* Sir Ellis Waterhouse has said that Copley's painting deserves, much more than that of West, "to be considered the pioneer work of a new age, for its like was not produced until the great days of the French romantics in the 1820s."[6]

Fig. 1.
Edward Grimston by Petrus Christus, 1446, oil on panel   (On loan to the National Gallery [reproduced by permission of the Earl of Verulam from the Gorhambury Collection])

Burgundy

The earliest surviving, fully documented portrait of an Englishman abroad in a country other than Italy is that of Edward Grimston (c. 1420–1478), one of the king's ambassadors to the court of Burgundy (fig. 1). The picture is signed by Petrus Christus (active 1442 [?], died 1472/1473), and dated 1446, a year in which Grimston is known to have been in Brussels. The picture belongs to Lord Verulam, the head of the Grimston family, and is on loan to the National Gallery in London.

Flanders

Some thirty years later, Hans Memling (active 1465, died 1494) painted in Bruges what is known as the *Donne Triptych* (fig. 2). It is so-called because the donor and his wife, Sir John and Lady Donne, are shown kneeling in front of the Virgin and Child and Saints. Sir John, who was knighted by Edward IV at the battle of Tewkesbury, and his wife are represented wearing the Yorkist collar of roses and suns with the king's's pendant, the Lion of March. It is not known how often Sir John Donne visited Bruges, but he was there in 1468 for the marriage of Margaret of York to Charles the Bold and returned to Flanders in 1477, so an exact

Fig. 2.
Detail of the *Donne Triptych,* by Hans Memling, c. 1477, oil on panel   (National Gallery)

date of execution is not deducible. The triptych, which belonged to the Duke of Devonshire, is now also in the National Gallery.[7]

When Sir John Donne was in Bruges in 1468, he would presumably have seen the decorative

Fig. 3.
Portrait of Alatheia Talbot, Countess of Arundel by Peter Paul Rubens, oil on canvas   (Alte Pinakothek, Munich)

music, had contributed generously. The head of Sir Edward Bonkil was, in the opinion of Sir Oliver Millar (from whose account of the panels all my information is taken), clearly painted from life in Flanders, and is much finer than those of the Scottish royal family. They were probably either executed from drawings taken to Flanders by Bonkil or inserted by a Scottish painter after the panels arrived in Edinburgh.[9]

In contrast to the gentle devotional character of the Memling and the van der Goes, which retain something of the spirit of the Middle Ages, my last example of a Flemish portrait of an English sitter is one of the most exuberantly flamboyant and baroque of Rubens' canvases. This is his picture of Lady Arundel and her attendants, in the collection of the Alte Pinakothek at Munich (fig. 3).[10] Born Alathea Talbot, the Countess of Arundel was the daughter of the 7th Earl of Shrewsbury and belonged to a family nearly as grand as the Howards. She had brought with her a considerable dowry when she married Thomas Howard, 2nd Earl of Arundel, in 1606. He was to become one of the greatest collectors of his age, and a loan exhibition has recently been held at the Ashmolean Museum, Oxford, to mark the four-hundredth anniversary of his birth. Lady Arundel sat for Rubens at Antwerp in 1620, when she was on her way to Venice. Everything about the picture is splendid, as befits so great a lady—everything from the standard richly embroidered with the Arundel arms to the red and gold attire of Robin the dwarf, from the Solomonic columns to the Turkey carpet. The figure standing on the right is the diplomat Sir Dudley Carleton, who is present in his capacity as ambassador to the United Provinces; he was an old friend of the Arundels and of Rubens. The full-length portraits by Daniel Mytens of Lord Arundel in his sculpture gallery and of Lady Arundel in the picture gallery at Arundel House in the Strand, which overlooked the River Thames, were in *The Treasure Houses of Britain* exhibition in Washington (THB nos. 49, 50).

Holland

Sir Dudley Carleton was one of several Englishmen to be painted by the Dutch artist Michiel van Miereveld (1567–1641). Others include Lord Vere of Tilbury and Edward Cecil, Viscount Wimbledon, both of whom took part

panels which Hugo van der Goes (active 1467, died 1482) painted for the wedding of Charles of Burgundy and Margaret of York. In about 1478 or 1479 van der Goes was commissioned by Sir Edward Bonkil and his brother, Alexander, who had become a naturalized citizen of Bruges, to paint the two votive panels, the *Holy Trinity Adored by Sir Edward Bonkil* and the *Royal Family of Scotland,* which are on loan from H. M. the Queen to the National Gallery of Scotland. Sir Edward Bonkil was the first provost of the Collegiate Church of Edinburgh, and his career illustrates the close mercantile and diplomatic links between Scotland and Flanders at this time. Formerly it was thought that the panels were the wings of a triptych of which the central element had been lost. However, M. J. Friedländer has advanced the now generally accepted theory[8] that the panels were painted as organ shutters that may have graced the celebrated organ of the Collegiate Church, made in Flanders between 1466 and 1467 under Sir Edward's auspices and to which James III, who took great delight in

in campaigns in the Netherlands. These three portraits were painted between 1628 and 1631. In the second half of the seventeenth century a number of Englishmen sat to distinguished Dutch artists. For instance, Caspar Netscher (1639–1684) painted the portrait of Sir William Temple when Temple was ambassador at The Hague in 1675 and busy fostering the match between William of Orange and Princess Mary, and in the next decade Nicholas Maes (1634–1693) painted the portraits of Archibald Campbell, 1st Duke of Argyll, and his brother, Colonel the Hon. Charles Campbell, when they joined William of Orange at The Hague before accompanying him to England.

Germany

From Germany I have only been able to produce two portraits of English sitters, though there must be many more. One, however, is of very considerable interest since, so far as is known, it is Dürer's only portrait of an Englishman (fig. 4). It is inscribed in the artist's hand, above his monogram, *heinrich morley aus engellant 1523.* Henry Parker, Lord Morley, a courtier and author, was sent in September 1523 on a diplomatic mission through the Low Countries and Germany to confer the Order of the Garter on the Archduke Ferdinand. On 19 November Lord Morley wrote to Cardinal Wolsey from Nuremberg: "Have waited One month and three days th[e coming] to Nuremburg of Donfurnando. Are assured that within six days of th[is letter] he will be here, and will be met by most of the gre[at] princes of Almayn to hold a great diet." On 8 December the Archduke himself wrote to Henry VIII to say that the order had been conferred on him the previous month by Henry, Lord Morley, the Archdeacon of Colchester, William Hussey, and Sir Thomas Wriothesley.[11] The drawing, which is in the British Museum, is difficult to reproduce as it is in leadpoint on green prepared paper.

The other, later portrait of an Englishman done in Germany is that of Sir Charles Hanbury-Williams, diplomatist, satirical writer, and friend of Frederick the Great. He sat for Raphael Mengs in 1751 or early in 1753, when he was English envoy at Dresden to Augustus III, elector of Saxony and king of Poland. I have been unable to trace the original painting, which once belonged to Hanbury-Williams' son-in-law,

Fig. 4.
Henry Parker, Lord Morley by Albrecht Dürer, 1523, leadpoint on green prepared paper (British Museum)

George, 5th Earl of Essex, and is only known to me through a poor engraving.

Denmark

The first Danish painting to enter the National Gallery, London, in 1963 was Jens Juel's portrait of Joseph Greenway (fig. 5), who was born at Stoke in Devonshire. Little is known about Greenway's career, but it must have been colorful since he amassed his fortune as a captain of a Danish East Indiaman. Under the protection of the Danish flag and Danish citizenship, which he acquired in 1785, he was able to carry out profitable trading activities which violated British acts and charters. However, his good fortunes did not last, for he died bankrupt in 1821. His portrait, which is dated 1788, is said to have been painted on an estate belonging to a friend, north of Copenhagen.[12] Jens Juel (1745–1802) was a fashionable portrait painter who traveled in Italy, France, and Germany, returning to Copenhagen in 1780. Although it is not recorded that he visited England, his portrait of Joseph Greenway is very English in feeling and recalls Gainsborough's early portrait of Mr. John Plampin in the National Gallery, London.

Fig. 5.
Joseph Greenway by Jens Juel, 1788,
oil on canvas (National Gallery)

Fig. 6.
John Cayley by Jean Voille, 1788, oil
on canvas (Alex Wengraf Ltd., London)

Russia

Dating to 1788, the same year as the Jens Juel
canvas, is the only portrait that I can produce
from Russia. It is entirely cosmopolitan in char-

acter, since it depicts an Englishman painted by a
Frenchman in St. Petersburg. John Cayley (fig.
6), the subject of this distinguished painting,
came from an old Yorkshire family. Born in 1730,
he was indentured to a Hull firm to learn the
Russian trade. He went as a young man to St.
Petersburg, as a junior partner to Thornton and
Cayley, an export/import firm. In 1787 he was
appointed English consul-general, and in October of that year he was presented at court and
kissed the hand of the Empress Catherine the
Great. It seems probable that this portrait was
painted to commemorate his appointment. In
May 1794 he was granted permission to return to
England on sick leave, and he died in Richmond,
Surrey, on 9 July of the following year.[13] Jean
Voille (1744–after 1802), the author of this portrait, studied under François-Hubert Drouais at
the Académie Royale in Paris. In 1770 or 1771 he
emigrated to Russia, where he was befriended by
the Grand Duke Pavel Petrovich, later Czar Paul
I, of whom he painted two portraits. He remained in St. Petersburg until 1793, when, due
to the hostility of Catherine the Great toward
the French Revolution, he was obliged to return
to France. He is recorded as living in Paris in
1795. As soon as circumstances permitted, he
returned to Russia, where he died at some time
after 1802.[14]

Poland

For Poland, I had drawn a blank until John Cornforth drew my attention to two portraits at
Scone Palace in Perthshire, belonging to the Earl
of Mansfield. They represent the 7th Viscount
Stormont and his first wife, a pretty widow,
Henrietta Frederica, Gräfin von Lunan, a Saxon
by birth who had been married to a Dane, Frederick Berregaard.[15] Lord Stormont had been appointed ambassador to Dresden in 1755, and
when Frederick the Great invaded Saxony, Lord
Stormont followed the elector when he retreated
to his Polish kingdom.

The two portraits were painted in Warsaw in
1759 soon after Lord Stormont's marriage. Although very French and rococo in character, they
were painted by an Italian artist, Marcello Bacciarelli. Born in Rome in 1731, Bacciarelli went
into the service of Augustus III in Dresden, followed him to Warsaw, and died there in 1818.

France

The search for English and Scottish subjects who sat for their portraits in France has resulted in a very mixed bag. First there is François Clouet's drawing of Mary Queen of Scots, which was formerly attributed to Holbein.[16] She is shown wearing the white garments of widowhood, which makes it possible to date the drawing to between the death of her husband, François II, in December 1560, and her return to Scotland in the following year. Sorrow seems to have aged her, for she was only nineteen when this drawing was made. It certainly does not do justice to her legendary beauty, which is said to have owed its enchantment more to brilliancy of complexion and grace of manner than to finely formed features.

Further research would probably produce a number of portraits of Englishmen at the court of Louis XIV, such as Hyacinthe Rigaud's portrait of Edward Villiers, 1st Earl of Jersey,[17] who was sent to Paris as ambassador extraordinary in 1698. This portrait was left to St. John's College, Cambridge, by Matthew Prior, who had served as secretary under Lord Jersey in Paris and subsequently held office under him in London. Prior also left to the college his own portrait by Alexis Simon Belle,[18] but by far the finest portrait of Matthew Prior is the marble bust (fig. 7) by Antoine Coysevox (1640–1720), which was commissioned by the French king and presented to Prior in gratitude for his services as English plenipotentiary. The bust is set in a niche in an elaborate monument designed by James Gibbs and executed by John Michael Rysbrack. It occupies a prominent place in Poets' Corner in Westminster Abbey.

As stated at the beginning of this paper, all the portraits in *The Treasure Houses of Britain* exhibition in Washington, with one notable exception, were painted either in England or in Italy. The exception (THB no. 148) was the splendid portrait by Nicolas de Largillière (1656–1746) of Sir Robert Throckmorton (fig. 8), which was painted in Paris in 1729. In its dazzling virtuosity, it represents the quintessence of the rococo style, which is also manifest in the marvellously carved Régence frame, in itself a work of art. Sir Robert belonged to an ancient Catholic family, which had been implicated in the so-called Throckmorton Plot of 1583, the object of which had been to depose Queen Elizabeth I. He may have come to Paris to escape the laws against

Fig. 7.
Matthew Prior by Antoine Coysevox,
c. 1711, marble   (Westminster Abbey;
photograph: National Monuments Record)

recusancy or, quite simply, he may have come to visit the three ladies of his family who had become members of the Order of Blue Nuns of the Augustinian Convent in Paris. He was no doubt responsible for commissioning Largillière to paint the ladies' portraits, which are as subtle and restrained as that of Sir Robert is flamboyant. Two of the portraits of the nuns have been sold in recent years, and only one still remains at Coughton Court, the family house in Warwickshire. One portrait has gone to Australia and the other, that of Sir Robert's sister, Elizabeth, is in the National Gallery of Art in Washington.

The splendor of the portrait of Sir Robert Throckmorton is perfectly matched by the frame, but there are occasions when the frame is more beautiful as a work of art than the picture it contains. An example of this is the spectacular carved and gilt frame that surrounds the portrait of the Hon. Richard Bateman by Robert Tournières Le Vrac (fig. 9). It was ordered by William, 1st Viscount Bateman in Paris in 1741, and was originally intended, being so magnificent, for his own portrait by Le Vrac. At a later date, however, it got transferred to the portrait of his brother. Lord Bateman had to leave England on account of his homosexual practices, and during his last years lived in Paris, where he

Fig. 8.
Sir Robert Throckmorton by Nicolas
de Largillière, 1729, oil on canvas
(The National Trust, Coughton Court)

who was also painted by Le Vrac. The frames were made by "Monyr Le Vasseur Tapissier." After settling the bill for his own and his brother's frame, Lord Bateman wrote on 23 October 1742, "The frame I have this Morn: paid for—it is excessive fine but most intolerably dear, it comes to 250 livres—mine because there are dragons at the corners, comes to L300—everybody says there never were 2 such frames made in Paris." The frame cost the same amount as Lord Bateman's portrait by Le Vrac.[19] A native of Caen, Le Vrac (1667–1752) had been a pupil of Bon de Boullogne. In style he was close to Jean-François de Troy, Rigaud, and Largillière, specializing in small, full-length portraits.

In the second half of the eighteenth century, with the ever increasing number of distinguished English portrait painters to choose from, there would have been no inducement to have one's portrait painted in Paris, with the additional risk of being made to look like a Frenchman. It is not known, for instance, how Henry Dawkins, in about 1750, came to sit for Maurice-Quentin de la Tour (1704–1788) for a brilliant pastel portrait (fig. 10), which is now in the National Gallery, London. Another fine portrait done by a French artist in Paris at this period is Jean-Baptiste Perronneau's painting of Francis Hastings, 10th Earl of Huntingdon. The police records show that this English milord was keeping a dancer, a Mlle Lang, who lived in the same street as Perronneau. The artist exhibited a pastel portrait of her at the Paris Salon in 1751. The portrait of Lord Huntingdon, which was exhibited at the Salon in 1753, is now in the Museum of Fine Arts, Boston.

Laurence Sterne, as the author of *Tristram Shandy*, was already a celebrity when he paid the first of several visits to Paris in 1762. He was welcomed into society and particularly into the circle of the Duke de Chartres, later the Duke d'Orleans, Philippe d'Egalité, who added Carmontelle's portrait of Sterne to his collection of "odd men." It was probably in this circle that Sterne met Carmontelle, who drew the delightful portraits of so many of his contemporaries. Carmontelle's drawing of Sterne, which is in the Musée Condé, Château de Chantilly,[20] shows the elegant figure that Sterne cut in Parisian society. Gone is the dingy clerical gown in which Reynolds had depicted him only two years earlier, and in its place he wears a velvet or satin costume showing that he had become very much *un homme du monde*. Both Carmontelle and Sterne

acted as agent for a number of English noblemen who wanted to purchase French furniture and furnishings. The correspondence and bills relating to the family pictures and frames have survived. In a letter to his brother, dated 13 October 1741, Lord Bateman wrote: "The frame is the prettiest & finest that ever was seen. Tournier & others say, there never was one made at Paris, si magnifique & de si bon gout—if it be to your taste, I shall be satisfied." This praise refers to the frame made for the portrait of his son, John,

were known as witty conversationalists, which must have made the sitting a sparkling occasion.

Jean-Baptiste Greuze (1725–1805) painted the portraits of at least two Englishmen in Paris, but on neither occasion does he appear to have given satisfaction. Frederick Howard, 5th Earl of Carlisle, sat for Greuze in November 1767 when, as a young man, he was setting out on the Grand Tour and passed through Paris on his way to Italy. In a letter to George Selwyn from Nice, dated 16 December 1767, he regretted that "Greuse has made me look like a Common-Councilman: it was not by my desire, for, you may be assured, had I aspired to the look of so much dignity, I should have paid you the compliment of looking as like an alderman of Gloucester as I could; but if the face is like, there will not be much trouble in altering the dress."[21] The allusion to Gloucester is explained by the fact that Selwyn represented that city in the House of Commons from 1754 until 1780. The dissatisfaction that Lord Carlisle felt over his portrait by Greuze must have been more than compensated for by the splendid full-length that Reynolds painted of him on his return from the Grand Tour in 1769. That picture was in *The Treasure Houses of Britain* exhibition (THB no. 482).

It is not clear why the 10th Earl of Pembroke was so insistent that his son, Lord Herbert, should be painted by Greuze wearing his regimentals when he was passing through Paris in May 1780 on his return from the Grand Tour, for Lord Herbert had already been painted in uniform by Pompeo Batoni in Rome. The portrait by Greuze is no longer at Wilton House, but when it arrived it was not a success. On 6 February 1781, Lord Pembroke added a note to his letter to Sir William Hamilton: "Pompeo's picture of George, & one still inferior by Kreuse, are indeed infinitely below our friend & Countryman Sir Joshua."[22]

I wish I could have begun the nineteenth century in France by including one of Ingres' wonderful drawings of Englishmen, especially as they were the subject of my first article, published half a century ago, but I have debarred myself from doing so because they were all done in Rome between the years 1806 and 1820, when this was Ingres' chief means of earning his livelihood. After such drudgery, Ingres resolved only to make portrait drawings of his friends, and unfortunately he did not count an Englishman among them.

Next I had hopes of including a drawing of

Fig. 9.
Richard Bateman by Robert Tournières Le Vrac, 1741, oil on canvas (Birmingham City Museum and Art Gallery)

Fig. 10.
Henry Dawkins by Maurice-Quentin de la Tour, c. 1750, pastel (National Gallery)

George Moore by Degas, but the work that passed as such proved of doubtful authenticity. Moore did, however, sit on more than one occasion for Manet. Moore had arrived in Paris in March 1873 with the intention of becoming a painter, but, about three years later, realizing that he had not the necessary gifts, he abandoned painting for literature. Moore has described in his *Modern Painting* (1898) his first meeting with Manet, and what a great event it was in his life when the artist spoke to him at the Café de la Nouvelle-Athène. He was invited to Manet's studio, which he describes, rather charmingly remarking that, as he was then a young man with a fresh complexion and fair hair, he was of a type most suited to Manet's palette and the artist invited him to sit for his portrait. Moore expressed his astonishment when Manet, after a few days, scratched out the painting he had begun and repeated the proceeding, each time making the canvas more luminous.[23] The portrait of George Moore, in The Metropolitan Museum of Art, New York, which probably dates to 1879, gives the impression of being painted with speed and spontaneity.

The Glasgow Art Gallery is fortunate in possessing one of the finest post-impressionist portraits. This is Vincent van Gogh's portrait of Alexander Reid (fig. 11). It was painted in 1887 when Van Gogh and Reid shared rooms in Paris. Reid was then working for the art dealers Boussod and Valadon, who also employed Vincent van Gogh's brother Theo. Alexander Reid, an art dealer of great vision, was instrumental in building up many of the collections of French nineteenth-century paintings in Scotland, which subsequently found their way into the Glasgow Art Gallery.

Rodin was in no need of an Alexander Reid to make his work known in England, where, from the 1880s onward, he began to have a following. Starting with the bust of the poet and journalist W. E. Henley, in 1886, he executed a number of portraits both in marble and in bronze of English sitters. These included George Wyndham, Lord Howard de Walden, Mrs. Charles Hunter, Lady Warwick, and Lady Sackville. All these busts were done in London. The only bust modeled in France was that of Bernard Shaw, which was commissioned by Shaw's wife in 1905. It was arranged that the dramatist should go to Paris for a sitting on 16 April 1906. From there, on the twentieth of that month, Shaw wrote in characteristic vein to Sydney Cockerell:

He [Rodin] is perfectly simple and quite devilishly skilful at his work—not the smallest whiff of professionalism about him—cares about nothing but getting the thing accurate and making it live. It is my solemn opinion that he is the biggest thing at present going—or likely to be going for a long time again—nobody in the running with him but Praxiteles & Michel Angelo, and both of them beaten in some points. Morris is the only man I ever met who made anything like the same impression on me. Imagine Morris without his temper, without the spoiling of the family income, and with an astonishing gift of shaping things into intense life, and you will get something like Rodin.[24]

Switzerland

It is satisfactory to be able to represent Switzerland by one of its most distinguished artists, Jean-Etienne Liotard (1702–1789), although it has proved impossible to photograph his portrait of Lord Mountstuart. The illustration shown is a photogravure of the engraving after the original, by J. R. Smith (fig. 12). In 1761 Lord Mountstuart, son of Lord Bute, the friend of George III and First Lord of the Treasury, was sent abroad at the age of seventeen on an extensive European tour, accompanied by his governor, Colonel Edmonstone. After studying in Holland he arrived in Switzerland in 1763, where he met Edward

Gibbon and Voltaire. In James Martin's journal of his Grand Tour is the entry dated [Geneva] 2 September 1763: "wt to Liotard's the Painter saw some very good Portraits of his own painting particularly one of Lord Monstewart [*sic*] very highly finished—He paints only in Crayons & expects to be very highly paid for his Labour. The picture above mentioned tho' not half so large as life was to cost 100 Guineas."[25] This was indeed a very considerable sum in view of the picture's size, and when one takes into account that in 1764 Reynolds was charging 30 guineas for a head, 50 for a Kit-cat, 70 for a half-length, and 150 for a whole length. One of the attractions of being painted by Batoni in Rome was that his prices were much lower than those of Reynolds. This would not have influenced Lord Mountstuart, who had extravagant tastes and cut a great figure in Italy, where he made friends with James Boswell and was painted by Batoni.[26] In the full-length by the latter, painted in 1767, Mountstuart is shown wearing a costume more richly embroidered than that of any other English traveler, and one wonders whether Batoni, who was very money minded, charged his sitter more than his customary fee of £25 for a full-length. Whatever he charged, his portrait is unlikely to have cost more than that by Liotard, which James Martin obviously thought very expensive.

Savoy

Next to Switzerland, on the south side of Lake Geneva, lay Savoy, and on its shores was the fashionable resort of Evian-les-Bains. It was there, in 1786, that Ludwig Guttenbrunn painted the delightful conversation-piece (fig. 13) belonging to Lord Wharncliffe, which shows a group of people, including members of his family, at a tea party. On the far left are the Princess and Prince of Piedmont. She was Madame Clothilde de France, the sister of Louis XVI, and her husband later became King Charles Emanuel of Sardinia. The hostess, seated at the table in her bedroom overlooking the lake, is Lady Erne, daughter of the eccentric Earl-Bishop of Bristol. With her is her daughter Lady Caroline Crichton, who was later to become the first Lady Wharncliffe. Standing on the right of the picture is Lady Erne's sister-in-law, Lady Hervey, and her daughter, Eliza. The cat, alas, remains anonymous.[27]

Ludwig Guttenbrunn (c. 1740–after 1810) was born at Krems, near Vienna, and met with some success as a portrait painter in Italy, Russia, and England.[28] The few reproductions of his work in the Witt Library of the Courtauld Institute, London, show nothing comparable in charm and accomplishment with this conversation piece. If he is to be judged as a history painter by his *Apollo and the Nine Muses*, dated 1785, all that can be said of that particular work is that it looks like a rather feeble derivation of Raphael Mengs' *Parnassus* in the Villa Albani in Rome.

Fig. 12.
Lord Mountstuart by Jean-Etienne Liotard, 1763, print (after pastel portrait in private collection)

Fig. 13.
A Tea Party at Evian by Ludwig
Guttenbrunn, 1786, oil on panel
(The Earl of Wharncliffe; photograph kindly
supplied by Robert Cecil)

Spain

Spain is represented by three portraits of Englishmen, those of a diplomat, a soldier, and a traveler. The portrait of Sir Arthur Hopton (fig. 14) in the Meadows Museum in Dallas, by an unknown Spanish artist, shows the subject seated at a table listening to some communication from a secretary. Sir Arthur had come to Spain in 1629 with Sir Francis Cottington, then English ambassador to the court of Philip IV. In Madrid Hopton was actively engaged in procuring paintings and works of art for Charles I and Lord Arundel. He remained there until 1636, when he returned to England for two years and was knighted at Whitehall on 2 February 1637. In April 1638 he was appointed ambassador to Madrid, and remained in that city until 1644. It seems most likely that he was painted on his second visit, when he would have been in his fifties. It has been suggested that the young man might be Christopher Windebank, son of Sir Francis Windebank, secretary to Charles I and in

constant correspondence with Hopton. Christopher stayed in Hopton's embassy in Madrid during 1638 and 1639; thus, if it is he who is represented, a near date for the painting could be established. It must, however, be admitted that the young man looks remarkably Spanish.[29]

It is open to argument to what extent a painter vests a foreign sitter with something of the look of his own compatriots. How true a likeness was Goya's portrait of the Duke of Wellington, when compared with that by Sir Thomas Lawrence, which is generally thought to be the best of the countless portraits done of the duke? Goya's portrait of Lord Wellington, as he then was, was painted during the general's first visit to Madrid in August 1812, after his victory over Auguste Marmont at the battle of Salamanca. The portrait, now in the National Gallery, London, corresponds with a drawing in the British Museum that was done at the same time and may have been used for the pose, but the liveliness and dynamism of the head in the painting, and the numerous pentimenti in the uniform, make it clear that the canvas was painted from life.[30]

At the risk of being thought rather presumptuous in following the portrait of the great duke with one of my own ancestor, I venture to introduce the watercolor by J. Becquer (1805–1844) of my great-grandfather, Richard Ford (fig. 15), author of the *Handbook for Spain* (1845). The drawing was done in Seville in 1832 and shows Ford in the dandyish dress that he wore as a *majo* at the *Feria de Mairena.* I own another drawing of him by Becquer, in which he is wearing the *zamarra,* or shepherd's jacket of undressed sheepskins, the attire he wore on his riding tours in Spain. During the three years that Richard Ford spent in the Peninsula, from 1830 to 1833, he produced over five hundred drawings of the places he visited. Since Spanish artists despised topographical drawings as an inferior branch of art, the sketches made by Richard Ford constitute an invaluable record of cities, such as Seville, where most of the Moorish walls and many of the monuments that he drew have since disappeared. Sketching in out-of-the way places was a hazardous pursuit, as there was always the danger of being mistaken for a spy. Indeed, on one occasion Richard Ford was marched off to a guardhouse for sketching a Roman ruin. As he says, once their suspicions were aroused, the "local Spanish 'Dogberries'" were "as deaf alike to the dictates of common sense or humanity as adders or Berbers."[31]

Dr. Johnson always regretted that his plan to go to Italy never materialized, and he said to Boswell, on meeting him at General Paoli's house in London on 11 April 1776: "A man who has not been in Italy is always conscious of an inferiority from his not having seen what it is expected a man should see. The grand object of travelling is to see the shores of the Mediterranean. On those shores were the four great empires of the world: the Assyrian, the Persian, the Grecian, and the Roman.—All our religion, almost all our law, almost all our arts, almost all that sets us above savages, has come to us from the shores of the Mediterranean."[32] Italy was, of course, the climax of the Grand Tour, and I tried to cover that subject in the essay that I contributed to *The Treasure Houses of Britain* exhibition catalogue.

Fig. 14.
Sir Arthur Hopton by an unknown artist, Spanish, 1638–1644, oil on canvas (Meadows Museum, Dallas)

Palmyra

It was largely due to the influence of the Society of Dilettanti, founded in 1732, and of which I have the honor to be the secretary, that Englishmen began to explore the farther shores of the Mediterranean in search of the famous

classical sites of antiquity. One of the earliest and most famous of these expeditions was that made by James Dawkins and Robert Wood, who set out from Athens in March 1751 for Palmyra and Baalbec. Their discovery of Palmyra was the subject of a large canvas (fig. 16) by Gavin Hamilton, who, as one of the leading protagonists of the neo-classical movement, has depicted them wearing togas. The print that was made of this picture added to their fame, as did the two volumes that Robert Wood produced on Palmyra and Baalbec.

The Levant

In 1764 the Society of Dilettanti decided to send an expedition to Asia Minor to record the ruins of the classical monuments that were to be found in those parts. Richard Chandler was appointed to lead the mission, with Nicholas Revett as architect, and William Pars as artist, to be his companions. During the year that they spent in western Turkey, they made Smyrna their headquarters, and from there they made several jour-

Fig. 15.
Richard Ford by J. Becquer, 1832, watercolor   (Sir Brinsley Ford)

Fig. 16.
The Discovery of Palmyra by Wood and Dawkins by Gavin Hamilton, 1758, oil on canvas   (C. J. Dawkins, on loan to the University of Glasgow, Hunterian Art Gallery)

neys to visit the classical sites. Of these William Pars made a number of beautiful watercolors, which the Society of Dilettanti later presented to the British Museum. In his *Travels in Asia Minor,* published in 1775, Chandler relates how they were ferried over the Meander, now called the Menderes river, on a triangular float with a rope. "The man was a black," Chandler wrote, "and his features strongly resembled a satyr." The incident was drawn by Pars. It shows the Theater at Miletus in the background. Chandler, in charge of the operation, is already firmly established on the craft, while Revett and Pars are about to maneuver their horses onto it.[33]

In the following century three of the most gifted Victorian artists visited Egypt and the Middle East. David Roberts' travels led to the publication, between 1842 and 1849, of *The Holy Land, Syria, Indumea, Arabia, Egypt, and Nubia* in six magnificent volumes consisting of 241 hand-colored lithographed plates made from his watercolors.

Sir David Wilkie set out for the Middle East in the autumn of 1840. He arrived in Constantinople in October and spent some time there before going by sea to Smyrna and then on to Beirut. There he recorded in his journal that the English consul, Mr. Niven Moore, asked him to do a painting of his wife. This he declined to do, but he agreed to make two drawings of her in the dress of a Bedouin lady—one for the consul and the other for himself. He began the first drawing on 12 February 1841, and completed both on the fifteenth. The consul had some difficulty in deciding which drawing of his wife he liked best, but finally chose the one on white paper, leaving Wilkie with the one on colored paper, which now belongs to the Fitzwilliam Museum in Cambridge.[34]

From Beirut Wilkie sailed to Jaffa, and traveled thence by land to Jerusalem, which he reached on 27 February. He was lent a house by Mr. Young, the English consul, and it was no doubt in return for this kindness that towards the end of March he made the beautiful drawing of Mrs. Young in Eastern costume (fig. 17), which is now in the Tate Gallery, London.[35] Wilkie embarked at Alexandria on 19 May for the homeward voyage, but was taken ill at Malta and died on the morning of 1 June 1841, shortly after leaving Gibraltar. His burial at sea was the subject of a famous picture by Turner and of a watercolor by Sir George Jones.

Fig. 17.
Mrs. Elizabeth Young in Eastern Costume by Sir David Wilkie, 1841, watercolor (Tate Gallery)

Egypt

The artist who became so enamored of the Middle East that he stayed there for over a decade, from 1840 until 1851, was John Frederick Lewis (1805–1876). After spending the best part of a year in and around Constantinople, he settled for the rest of the time in Cairo, where, as we know from Thackeray's entertaining account of him, he dressed and lived like a Turk.[36] The years that Lewis spent in Cairo provided him with subjects that he was to paint for the rest of his life. For instance, it was not until 1856, five years after his return to England, that he exhibited what is generally considered the masterpiece of his watercolors. Although it is signed and dated 1856, it is entitled *A Frank Encampment in the Desert of Mount Sinai, 1842.* The study illustrated here (fig. 18) represents the Englishman whose encampment it was. He has been identified by Rodney Searight[37] as Lord Castlereagh, and in the finished composition is shown reclining on cushions under a tent, surrounded by attendants. When the finished watercolor, which is now in the Yale Center for British Art, was exhibited at the Old Water-Colour Society in 1856, Ruskin,

Fig. 18.
Study for the Principal Englishman in the Frank Encampment by J. F. Lewis, 1842, watercolor   (Sir Brinsley Ford)

who was capable of saying some very silly things, declared that he had "no hesitation in ranking it amongst the most wonderful pictures in the world; nor do I believe that, since the death of Paul Veronese, anything has been painted comparable to it in its own way."[38]

The Middle East and Mesopotamia attracted not only many distinguished English travelers and archaeologists, such as Sir Richard Burton, Sir Charles Fellows, and Sir Henry Layard, to name only three, but also a number of adventurous and eccentric English ladies. One of the earliest to settle there was Lady Hester Stanhope, who, in 1814, established herself in the ruins of a convent among the half-savage tribes on the slopes of Mount Lebanon. She died in 1839, as she had lived, in proud isolation, and, as soon as she was dead her servants fled, stealing everything they could lay their hands on except the ornaments on her person. The only representation of her in oriental dress is an apparently posthumous lithograph by R. J. Hamerton, which is in the British Museum.

Lady Hester was followed by the beautiful Jane Digby who, after a highly romantic career, married a Bedouin sheikh and lived for many years in a camp in the desert near Damascus. In this century one can think of two intrepid lady travelers and explorers—Gertrude Bell, who ended her days at Bagdad, and Dame Freya Stark, who, I am glad to say, is still with us.

Turkey

Long before these indomitable ladies had fallen under the spell of the Moslem world, a woman with an equally strong and pronounced character, Lady Mary Wortley Montagu, had accompanied her husband when he was appointed ambassador to the Ottoman Court in Constantinople. During the year that they spent there, from 1717 to 1718, Lady Mary wrote a series of letters, which were subsequently published and which give a fascinating picture of life in the capital of the Ottoman Empire.[39] There are several portraits of Lady Mary in Turkish dress, but the only one that dates to her stay in Constantinople is attributed to Jean Baptiste Vanmour (1671–1737), who was living in that city from 1699 and became painter to the sultan in 1725. This picture (fig. 19), which is in the National Portrait Gallery, London, shows Lady Mary with her young son, Edward, on a carpeted dais on which a female attendant is seated playing the tambur (a Turkish lute), while on the right a Turkish messenger is presenting a letter. In the background there is a distant view of Constantinople. The young Edward grew up to become a remarkable eccentric, and ended his days in Venice, where, to use his own words, he became "a part of the polite education of any noble youth who comes to this place on the Grand Tour." It was in the spring of 1775, about a year before Edward Wortley Montagu's death in Padua—from an ortolan's bone stuck in his throat—that George Romney, during his stay in Venice, painted a portrait of him in full Turkish dress, which he later sold to Lord Warwick.[40]

The only artist of real distinction to paint the portraits of the English in Constantinople was Jean-Etienne Liotard, whom we have already met at a later date in Switzerland. He was in Italy in 1738, when the young Lord Sandwich arrived there and invited him to join a party—which included his friend William Ponsonby, later 1st Earl of Bessborough—on a cruise to the Levant, which lasted about six months. They sailed from Naples on 3 April 1738, and had returned to Leghorn by the beginning of October. Liotard was so enchanted by Constantinople that he left the party and remained there until toward the end of 1742. It was while they were together in Constantinople that Liotard painted the large full-length of Lord Sandwich in Turkish costume (fig. 20). It must have been at about the same time that Liotard also painted the portrait of the traveler Richard Pococke, which shows him full-length in Turkish costume on a terrace overlooking the Bosphorus.

It would be unfair to judge Liotard by these rather heavy-handed portraits, for it was as a pastelist that he excelled. I cannot resist including one of his most exquisite works in this medium. This is his pastel of Lady Coventry, one of the beautiful Gunning sisters. I am afraid this portrait is really inadmissible here for, although she is wearing Turkish dress, Lady Coventry never went to Constantinople. Liotard drew her when he came to London in 1754. Lady Coventry was more renowned for her beauty than for her tact, and when asked by George II if there was any whim of hers that he could gratify, she confessed that she had always longed to see a coronation.[41]

Greece

Another portrait that ought to be excluded from my paper, since it was painted in London, is Thomas Phillips' portrait of Lord Byron wearing the Albanian costume that he bought in the Epirus in 1809. But if Greece is to be represented by the portrait of an Englishman, Byron, with his romantic attachment to that country, must be the obvious, the only choice. The first version of the portrait, of which the version in the National Portrait Gallery, London, is a replica, was painted in London in 1813, when Byron was twenty-five and had become famous through the publication of *Childe Harold* in the previous year. Byron's contemporaries were divided as to whether it was a good likeness, but in our own day Sir David Piper, who retired as director of the National Portrait Gallery in 1967, has detected "a very unconvincing whiff of fancy-dress ball, or Hollywood spectacular, almost Errol Flynn playing Byron."[42]

Persia

For the third and I hope the last time I would like to break the rules that governed my choice of portraits (rules that excluded portraits of the English done either in England or Italy) by mentioning the beautiful portraits at Petworth House of Sir Robert Shirley and his Circassian wife in Persian dress, which were painted by the young Anthony van Dyck in Rome in 1622. Sir

Fig. 19.
Lady Wortley Montagu and Her Son Edward by Jean Baptiste Vanmour, 1717–1718, oil on canvas (National Portrait Gallery)

Fig. 20.
The Earl of Sandwich by Jean-Etienne Liotard, 1738, oil on canvas (Victor Montagu)

Robert Shirley spent most of his life in the service of the Shah of Persia, and, when sent on missions to European courts, he always wore his Persian attire. However, when presenting his credentials in Persian to James I, he breached the etiquette of his adopted country by removing his turban in the king's presence. Within a few years of his arrival in Persia, at the start of what was to prove an extraordinarily varied and eventful career that included attempts on his life both by gunpowder and poison, he married Teresia, a daughter of Ismael Khan, a Circassian of noble birth and of Christian faith, who was related to one of the Shah's Circassian wives.[43]

India

In addition to Italy, India is the only country where it became almost a tradition for the English to have their portraits painted. Although the subject is vast I shall only deal with it briefly, as it has been fully covered by Mildred Archer in her monumental and splendid book, *India and British Portraiture, 1770–1825,* which was published in 1979. And indeed, most of my information is taken straight from what she has written. In her first chapter, "The Lure of India," Dr. Archer gives the reasons why so many English artists were tempted to go to India; she tells us that in the years 1770 to 1825, the period covered by her book, some thirty British portrait painters in oil and at least twenty-eight miniaturists went to India "as a potent source of novel patronage."[44] I cannot do more than show you the work of three artists.

Dr. Archer points out that the first British portrait painter of any consequence to go to India was Tilly Kettle (1735–1786). He spent nearly seven years there, from 1769 to 1776, some two of them in Madras, where he painted the Nawab of Arcot, before moving north to Calcutta. There he was invited by Shuja-ud-daula, the Nawab of Oudh, to visit Faizabad to paint the Nawab's portrait. While he was there he made studies of the Nawab's son, Asaf-ud-daula, who succeeded his father in 1775, and of the Nawab's ministers. From these studies he painted in 1784, long after his return to England, the group that commemorated the appointment of Nathaniel Middleton as Resident of Lucknow; the Resident is shown with the Nawab and his ministers.

Johan Zoffany (1733–1810) was already fifty years old when he decided to go to India in 1783.

Through his portraits and conversation pieces he had achieved great success in England and had won the patronage of George III and Queen Charlotte, but he fell out of favor with the queen when, after a delay of some five years, he presented her with his picture of *The Tribuna,* which she had commissioned, and which met with her displeasure. Added to this, his long absence abroad had lost him his fashionable clientele. Arriving in Madras in July 1783, he had to wait five weeks before the ship sailed for Calcutta. During that time he painted several portraits, including that of the governor of Madras, Lord Macartney, who, when writing to a friend in Calcutta, described him as "without dispute the greatest Painter that ever visited India."[45]

In Calcutta Zoffany met with immediate success. He received commissions to paint the chief justice, Sir Elijah Impey, and Mrs. Warren Hastings, the wife of the governor-general. The vast portrait of Mrs. Hastings is conceived in the grand manner and vies in its majestic pose with Reynolds' portrait of Mrs. Siddons as *The Tragic Muse,* which was painted at about the same time. Zoffany also painted the charming picture of Mr. and Mrs. Warren Hastings at their country house at Alipore. The setting might be that of an English park, and but for the ayah holding her mistress's white-feathered hat, and the elephant in the distance, one would not be aware that the scene was set in India.

In 1784 Zoffany was invited to join Warren Hastings in Lucknow, the capital of Oudh, where Hastings had gone to put the Nawab's finances in order. During the two years that he spent in Lucknow, Zoffany made friends with two of the most civilized men in the service of the Nawab—Colonel Antoine Polier, a Swiss officer, and General Claud Martin, a French adventurer. Both collected Persian and Sanskrit manuscripts, and both bought Zoffany's paintings. Their friendship is commemorated in a lively conversation piece (fig. 21) in which Colonel Polier is shown on the left inspecting the vegetables brought by the gardener, and ordering the meal. Zoffany is in the center against one of his canvases, while on the right General Martin is showing a watercolor of his house on the river Gumti to his friend John Wombwell, the East India Company's accountant in Lucknow. John Wombwell played an important part in the life of the European community in Lucknow. He appears with other Englishmen in Zoffany's famous picture of *Colonel Mordaunt's Cock Match.*

Fig. 21.
Colonel Antoine Polier with His Friends Claud Martin, John Wombell and the Artist by Johan Zoffany, 1786 or 1787, oil on canvas (Victoria Museum, Calcutta; photograph kindly supplied by Dr. Mildred Archer)

He is also the subject of a delightful Indian miniature (fig. 22) by an unknown artist, which shows him in native attire smoking a hookah on a terrace overlooking a river, while an attendant holding a fly whisk stands behind him.[46]

The most elaborate of all Zoffany's conversation pieces, executed in Calcutta over a period of four years between 1783 and 1787, is that of the Auriol and Dashwood families. "This sumptuous picture," as Mary Webster has pointed out, "would be indistinguishable from one of Zoffany's English conversation-pieces were it not for the exoticism of the landscape and the presence of the Indian servants."[47] Zoffany also painted a charming picture of the chief justice, Sir Elijah Impey, and his family grouped together outside their Calcutta mansion listening to strolling musicians. Sir Elijah claps his hands while his little daughter, Marian, starts to dance in the Indian manner to the accompaniment of the players. Sir Elijah and his wife were both interested in the arts, and during their time in India, Lady Impey commissioned and supervised a series of natural-history pictures, which were painted for her by three artists who signed themselves as "of Patna," long a provincial center of the Mughal school. She also commissioned from an unknown Indian artist two enchanting pictures which evoke very vividly what her life in India must have been like, with an army of attendants. One painting shows the Impey children with their ayahs in their palatial, though very bare nursery, the principal feature of which is a semicircular recess with three doors leading out of it onto a colonnaded balcony. The other scene (fig. 23) depicts Lady Impey, surrounded by her household, being offered a hat. The majordomo is presumably the man in European dress, while in the foreground is the *mali* with his *dali* (the gardener with his daily offering of flowers and vegetables). The furniture is English and looks fine of its kind, while through a door can be seen the Impeys' four-poster bed.[48] Zoffany left India for England in January 1789, in bad health, but with his fortune made.

George Chinnery (1774–1852) spent twenty-three years, from 1802 to 1825, in India. "Of all British portrait painters who went East," Dr.

Fig. 22.
John Wombell by an unknown artist, Indian, c. 1790, miniature, gouache heightened with gold on paper (Institut Néerlandais, Fondation Custodia, Collection Frits Lugt)

Fig. 23.
Lady Impey Choosing a Hat by an unknown artist working at Calcutta, 1777–1783, opaque watercolor on paper (Photograph: Oliver Impey)

Archer writes, "Chinnery was the last of truly national calibre to settle in India."[49] He spent nearly five years in Madras, where his elder brother was a civil servant and where the family shipping firm was established. During that period he painted a number of portraits. Of these the most striking and attractive is that of William and Catherine Aurora (fig. 24), the children of Lieutenant Colonel James Achilles Kirkpatrick by his Indian wife, Khair-un-Nissa Begam, a great niece of the Prime Minister of Hyderabad. The two children are dressed in Indian clothes, and the boy seems to have inherited his mother's looks.

Chinnery spent the rest of his time in India in Bengal, staying three years in Dacca before settling in Calcutta. There he found ample employment in painting competent, if rather dull official portraits, but his real love, as Dr. Archer observes,[50] lay in sketching the countryside and its people. One of his more unusual drawings shows an Englishman being carried in a palanquin by four Indians. Chinnery was at his best when painting watercolors of ruined Indian temples. The colors of his exotic palette captured the haunting magic of the scene, which is usually enlivened by groups of figures. In 1822 Chinnery departed from Calcutta, leaving his unfortunate wife behind. He fled to the Danish settlement at Serampur to escape from his debts and, some said, from his wife. Three years later he quitted India forever, bound for the Portuguese settlement of Macao, near Canton, where we shall meet him again.

The Himalayas

I do not know when botanists first visited the Himalayas, but one of the most distinguished of them, Sir Joseph Hooker (1817–1911), was given a government grant to go there in 1847, when he explored part of eastern Nepal and Sikkim, and succeeded in introducing into cultivation through Kew Gardens the splendid rhododendrons that grew in the latter country. Sir Joseph's achievements in the Himalayas were commemorated in a painting by Frank Stone, of which there is an engraving by W. Walker.[51]

China

Lord Macartney, who as Governor of Madras had been painted by Zoffany in 1783, was appointed

Fig. 24.
Catherine and William Kirkpatrick by
George Chinnery, c. 1805, oil on
canvas   (The Hongkong and Shanghai Bank-
ing Corporation; photograph kindly supplied by
Dr. Mildred Archer)

Fig. 25.
*The Emperor Ch'ien Lung Presenting a
Purse to Master Staunton* by William
Alexander, c. 1792, watercolor
(The Henry E. Huntington Library and Art
Gallery, San Marino, California)

Fig. 26.
Mr. Dent's Veranda at Macao by
George Chinnery, 1841–1843, oil on
canvas   (Private collection)

in 1792 to lead an embassy to Peking, which was
sent to protest against the exactions and acts of
injustice perpetrated by the Chinese against English subjects. William Alexander (1767–1816),
who in 1808 was to become the first Keeper of
Prints and Drawings at the British Museum, was
chosen, at the age of twenty-five, to accompany
Lord Macartney's mission to China as junior
draftsman. But in view, it is stated, of the in-
competence of Alexander's nominal superior, all
the drawings illustrative of the expedition were
made by him. Alexander was a gifted draftsman
and produced a series of memorable watercolors
recording the notable events that took place during Lord Macartney's mission. One of the most
delightful of these watercolors shows the emperor Ch'ien lung presenting a purse to Master
George Thomas Staunton, one of Lord Macartney's pages, inside the imperial tent at Jehol (fig.
25). So impressed was the emperor with the
boy's mastery of the Chinese language that he

gave him a purse from his own belt as a mark of
great personal favor.[52]

Macao

Chinnery, it will be remembered, left India for
Macao in 1825, and there, with occasional visits
to Canton, he remained for the next twenty-
seven years until his death in 1852. At Macao he
was patronized by the leading merchants, such as
Dr. William Jardine and his partner, James
Matheson, the founders of the great trading
company. Next to Jardine and Matheson, Dent
and Company was the most important firm in
Macao. In his painting of Mr. Dent's veranda at
Macao (fig. 26), Chinnery has given us an evocative reminder of what life must have been like in
this Portuguese enclave. The men portrayed are
Mr. Durand, William Hunter, and Captain Hall.
William Hunter, who came to China in 1825,

was an American who worked for the firm of Russell and Company. Captain Hall, later Admiral Sir William Hutcheon Hall, was in China only between 1841 and 1843, during which time the picture must have been painted.[53] Chinnery must have made his living by portraiture, but he found delight, as he had done in India, in sketching the endless variety of scenes of local life, the junks in the harbor, the street vendors, the fishermens' tumbledown dwellings surrounded by goats and pigs. For these he developed an almost Canalettesque fluency and economy of line with his pen, which give to these sketches their brilliance.

Japan

Finally, there are the numerous portraits of unknown English people by Japanese nineteenth-century artists. One print shows a couple with an umbrella who appear to be on a sightseeing expedition, while in another an English merchant is examining a length of cloth. A print of an Englishman on horseback bears a not very illuminating description about England being a great island nation. And the interest to the Japanese of the woodcut of the ferocious-looking English soldier (fig. 27) would be focused—given the importance of the sword in Japan as an item of personal decoration—on the soldier's very long and clumsy-looking firearm, not unlike the archaic rifle issued to me in the last war. It must have seemed as strange to the Japanese as the soldier's hat and aquiline nose.[54]

Fig. 27.
An English Soldier by Ippōsai Yoshifusa, 1860, woodblock print (British Museum)

NOTES

I would like to head the list of my acknowledgments with the name of Francis Russell, who has greatly enriched my paper by putting at my disposal his extensive knowledge of the pictures in English country houses. I am also very grateful to the following, who have assisted me in many different ways with suggestions and answers to my queries: Mildred Archer, John Christian, Robert Cecil, John Cornforth, Judy Egerton, St. John Gore, Carlos van Hasselt, Oliver Impey, Stephen Jones, Ellen Miles, Sir Oliver Millar, Pierre du Prey, David Scrase, Rodney Searight, Damie Stillman, Gervase Jackson-Stops, Denys Sutton, Ross Waiser, Alex Wengraf, and the late Eric Young.

1. Walpole to Sir Horace Mann, 16 July 1751, *The Letters of Horace Walpole,* ed. Peter Cunningham, 9 vols. (London, 1891), 2:261.

2. Anthony M. Clark, *Pompeo Batoni,* ed. Edgar Peters Bowron (Oxford, 1985), 43.

3. Jules David Prown, *John Singleton Copley,* 2 vols. (Cambridge, Mass., 1966), 1:214.

4. Prown 1966, 1:79–80.

5. Prown 1966, 1:223.

6. Ellis Waterhouse, *Painting in Britain, 1530–1790* (Harmondsworth, 1953), 203.

7. Martin Davies, *Early Netherlandish School* (London, 1968), 125.

8. Max J. Friedländer, *Die altniederländische Malerei,* 14 vols. (Berlin and Leiden, 1924–1937), 4:43–46.

9. *Catalogue of Paintings and Sculpture,* National Gallery of Scotland, 51st ed. (Edinburgh, 1957), 106–107.

10. David Howarth, *Lord Arundel and His Circle* (New Haven, 1985), 152, pl. 3.

11. *The Graphic Work of Albrecht Dürer* [exh. cat., British Museum] (London, 1971), no. 282.

12. *The National Gallery of London Report, June 1962–December 1964* (London, 1965), 43.

13. I am most grateful to Alex Wengraf for allowing me to reproduce his picture by Jean Voille and for supplying me with information about the sitter.

14. Tinatine Taneyew, "Voille et Viollier," *Gazette des Beaux-Arts* (February 1959), 107–114.

15. John Cornforth, "Scone Palace, Perthshire—1," *Country Life* (11 August 1988), 94–95, figs. 7, 8.

16. In the Bibliothèque Nationale, Paris. Reproduced in *Chefs-d'oeuvre de l'art français* [exh. cat., Palais National des Arts] (Paris, 1937), pl. 92.

17. Reproduced in *Connoisseur* (December 1957). The portrait is a replica of the original in the possession of the Earl of Jersey.

18. There is a portrait in the National Portrait Gallery, London, of John Law of Lauriston by Alexis Simon Belle (1674–1734); St. John Gore has drawn my attention to two portraits by Belle at Sizergh Castle, Westmorland, of the Abbé Strickland and Roger Strickland; and Ross Waiser has likewise brought to my notice Belle's fine portrait of Sir Charles Haggerston in the National Gallery of Ireland.

19. Peter Cannon-Brookes and Robert Tournières, "Lord Bateman and Two Picture Frames," *The International Journal of Museum Management and Curatorship* 4 (1985), 141–145.

20. F. A. Gruyer, *Chantilly: les portraits de Carmontelle* (Paris, 1902), no. 414.

21. John Heneage Jesse, *George Selwyn and His Contemporaries,* 4 vols. (London, 1843–1844), 2:208. I am grateful to Francis Russell for giving me this reference.

22. *Pembroke Papers, 1780–1794,* ed. Lord Herbert (London, 1950), 88.

23. George Moore, *Modern Painting* (London, 1898).

24. George Bernard Shaw, *Collected Letters, 1898–1910,* ed. Dan H. Laurence (London, 1972), 618; Denys Sutton, "Rodin et l'Angleterre," *Rodin et la sculpture contemporain: compte-rendu du colloque organisé par le musée Rodin* (Paris, 1983), 94–96, fig. 26.

25. James Martin's journal of his Grand Tour, 1763–1765, 9 vols. Formerly in the possession of Mr. E. Holland-Martin. There is a study for this portrait of Lord Mountstuart, drawn in black chalk heightened with white on blue paper, in the Musée d'Art et d'Histoire, Geneva.

26. Clark 1985, pl. 285.

27. I am grateful to Robert Cecil for bringing this conversation-piece to my attention, for giving me a photograph of it, and for providing information about the sitters. Caroline Grosvenor and Charles Beilby, Lord Stuart of Wortley, *The First Lady Wharncliffe and Her Family (1779–1856),* 2 vols. (London, 1927), 1:14.

28. Ulrich Thieme and Felix Becker, *Allgemeines Lexicon der bildenden Künstler,* 36 vols. (Leipzig, 1907–1950), 15:360–361.

29. William B. Jordan, *The Meadows Museum* (Dallas, 1974), 28, fig. 9. Since this paper was completed, I have come across the portrait of another seventeenth-century English diplomat who was painted in Madrid. This is John Closterman's portrait at Chevening Park of the English Resident, the Hon. Alexander Stanhope. In a letter to his son, dated 2/12 November 1698, Stanhope says that he is being painted full-length "in Golilla" (Spanish court dress). See Malcolm Rogers, "John and John Baptist Closterman," *Walpole Society* 49 (1983), 229–230, pl. 54.

30. Neil Maclaren, *The Spanish School* (London, 1970), 16–23.

31. Richard Ford, *Gatherings from Spain* (1846; reprint ed., London, 1970), 295. Intro. by Brinsley Ford.

32. James Boswell, *The Life of Samuel Johnson. LL.D.,* 3 vols. (London, 1900), 2:248.

33. Richard Chandler, *Travels in Asia Minor, 1764–1765,* ed. and abridged Edith Clay, with an appreciation of William Pars by Andrew Wilton (London, 1971). The watercolor described is reproduced in color as the frontispiece.

34. Allan Cunningham, *Life of Sir David Wilkie,* 3 vols. (London, 1843), 3:396.

35. Cunningham 1843, 3:388.

36. William Makepiece Thackeray, *Notes of a Journey from Cornhill to Cairo* (London, 1846).

37. Rodney Searight, "Anonymous Traveller Rediscovered," *Country Life* (4 May 1978), 1259.

38. John Ruskin, "Notes on Some of the Principal Pictures Exhibited in the Rooms of the Society of Painters in Water-Colours, 1856," reprinted in *Old Water-Colour Society's Club* (1926), 1.

39. *The Complete Letters of Lady Mary Wortley Montagu,* ed. Robert Halsband, 3 vols. (Oxford, 1965).

40. G. S. Sykes, *Black Sheep* (London, 1982), 153–171.

41. François Fosca, *Liotard* (Paris, 1928), 54–55.

42. Richard Walker, *Regency Portraits* (London, 1985), 79–81.

43. *The Dictionary of National Biography,* 30 vols. (Oxford, 1938–1986), 18:136–137.

44. Mildred Archer, *India and British Portraiture 1770–1825* (London and New York, 1979), 36.

45. Archer 1979, 133–134.

46. *Miniatures Indiennes et Persanes de la Fondation Custodia (Coll. F. Lugt)* (Paris, 1986), 39.

47. Mary Webster, *Johan Zoffany* [exh. cat., National Portrait Gallery] (London, 1977), 75–76.

48. I am grateful to Oliver Impey for bringing these two delightful Indian miniatures to my attention. See *India: Art and Culture, 1300–1900* [exh. cat., The Metropolitan Museum of Art] (New York, 1985), nos. 281c, 281d.

49. Archer 1979, 357.

50. Archer 1979, 381.

51. John Gilmour, *British Botanists* (London, 1944), 38–40.

52. Susan Legouix, "Lord Macartney's Audience with the Emperor of China," *Connoisseur* (February 1979), 122.

53. *George Chinnery* [exh. cat., The Arts Council] (London, 1957), no. 48.

54. See *Great Japan Exhibition: Art of the Edo Period, 1600–1868* [exh. cat., Royal Academy of Arts] (London, 1981), nos. 129, 130, 131, 132.

ADDENDUM

GERMANY

Henry Voguell, a London merchant, painted when aged 65, c. 1746, by Antoine Pesne (1683–1757) (Gemäldegalerie, Berlin-Dahlem).

AUSTRIA

William Wickham (1761–1840) by Heinrich Füger (1751–1818). Wickham was envoy to the Austrian and Russian armies, 1799–1801. Oil on canvas, 45 x 35 in. (Lady Charlotte Bonham-Carter).

Major-General Sir Alexander Hope of Craighall (1769–1839) by Heinrich Füger (1751–1818). In 1800 Colonel Hope was appointed British Military Commissioner to the Imperial Army. Signed and dated 1801, oil on canvas, 43¹/₂ x 34¹/₂ in. (Hopetoun House, Linlithgow).

FRANCE

Alexander Campbell, 2nd Earl of Marchmont (1675–1740), by Maurice-Quentin de la Tour (1704–1788). In 1722 Campbell was nominated one of the British ambassadors to the Congress of Cambray, where the young La Tour drew his portrait. Pastel, 21 x 17 in. (Mr. Francis Russell). The other ambassador to the Congress of Cambray was Charles Whitworth, Baron Whitworth (1675–1725). His portrait, that of his wife, and also that of Robert Sutton, the secretary to the embassy, were drawn at Cambray by La Tour, and were sold in the same sale as the portrait of Campbell (Christie's, 11 December 1979; present location of the last-named three portraits unknown).

The 6th Earl of Coventry (1722–1809) by Maurice-Quentin de la Tour. Pastel, 27 x 22¹/₂ in. (Reproduced by Albert Besnard, *La Tour* [Paris, 1928], fig. 29; formerly Collection Cronier).

The Countess of Coventry by Maurice-Quentin de la Tour. Pastel, 25¹/₂ x 22¹/₂ in. (Reproduced by Besnard 1928, fig. 30.) Besnard merely refers to the sitters as Lord and Lady Coventry, but the latter was presumably Lord Coventry's first wife, the beautiful Maria Gunning. They were married in March 1752, and in the summer of that year they went to Paris.

Lady Amelia D'Arcy (1754–1784), daughter of the 4th Earl of Holdernesse, painted by François-Hubert Drouais (1727–1775) in April 1764. Oil on canvas, 27¹/₂ x 23¹/₂ in. (Formerly Collection of Lady Diana Pelham).

Isabella, Countess of Hertford (1726–1782) painted by Alexandre Roslin (1718–1793) in Paris in 1765, when her husband was British ambassador to France. Oil on canvas, 33³/₄ x 28³/₄ in. (Hunterian Art Gallery, University of Glasgow). The Hon. Campbell Scott, second son of Francis, Earl of Dalkeith, by Jean Baptiste Greuze (1725–1805). Oil on canvas, 25¹/₂ x 21¹/₂ in. (Lord Home of The Hirsel).

SWITZERLAND

William Windham II (1717–1761) by Barthélémy du Pan (1712–1763). This pastel was made either during Windham's first visit to Geneva in 1738, when he was on his way to Italy, or on his return to Geneva in 1739 or 1740 (The National Trust, Felbrigg Hall, Norfolk).

Lord Stanhope in the Uniform of the Geneva Volunteers by Jean Preudhomme (1732–1795). Despite the title of the portrait, there is no mention in the Dictionary of National Biography of either the 3rd or 5th earl having belonged to the Geneva Volunteers, so this may represent the 4th earl (Chevening Manor, Kent).

Douglas, 8th Duke of Hamilton, with his tutor, Dr. John Moore, and Ensign John Moore, the future hero of Corunna, by Jean Preudhomme (1732–1795). They are shown in an apartment at Geneva grouped around a table on which there is a globe; a view of mountains is seen through a window. Signed and dated 1774, oil on canvas, 37½ x 29 in. (Hamilton Palace sale, Christie's, 6–7 November 1919). The Duke and his companions were on the Grand Tour on their way to Rome, where they were painted (1775–1779) by Gavin Hamilton on a hill overlooking the Forum.

SPAIN

Sir Benjamin Keene (1697–1757) by Louis Michel van Loo (1707–1771). Professor Nigel Glendinning has drawn my attention to this portrait; it was probably painted on Keene's second visit to Madrid, when he returned as ambassador in 1748 (reproduced in *The Private Correspondence of Sir Benjamin Keene* [Cambridge, 1933]).

Sir Samuel Ford Whittingham (1772–1841). Attributed to Ascencio Juliá (before 1771–1816). After serving with great distinction in the Spanish army during the Peninsula War, Whittingham resided at Madrid, where this portrait was painted, until his appointment as lieutenant-governor of Dominica in 1819. Oil on canvas, 49½ x 41 in. (Meadows Museum, Dallas). I am grateful to Gervase Jackson-Stops for drawing my attention to this portrait.

Richard Ford (1796–1858) by José Gutierrez de la Vega (died 1865). Signed and dated Seville, 1831. Panel, 13¼ x 10½ in. (Sir Brinsley Ford).

Harriet Ford (1806–1837) by José Gutierrez de la Vega (died 1865). Signed and dated Seville, 1831. Panel, 13½ x 10 in. (Sir Brinsley Ford).

TURKEY

Richard Salwey (died 1775) by Andrea Soldi (c. 1703–after 1771). Richard Garnier has identified as a portrait of Richard Salwey, a merchant, the portrait of a man wearing Turkish costume that was sold at Christie's, 22 July 1988 (lot 85), and reproduced in the catalogue. Signed and dated 17[3?]3, oil on canvas, 36⅝ x 29⅜ in. According to John Ingamells ("Andrea Soldi—A Check-List of His Work," *Journal of the Walpole Society* 47 [1978–1980], 1) the artist "is first recorded painting portraits of British merchants of the Levant Company in Constantinople and Aleppo" before his arrival in England in 1736.

Old Masters at Petworth

The background to the inventories
recording the acquisitions of the 10th
Earl of Northumberland and of the 2nd
Earl of Egremont[1]

After visiting Petworth House in 1850, Gustav Friedrich Waagen wrote in his *Treasures of Art in Great Britain:* "The collection is in extent and value among the finest in the country."[2] Such an assessment requires no qualification, but in assuming that the collection had been largely formed by the late Earl of Egremont (that is, the 3rd Earl, who had died in 1837) and by his father (the 2nd Earl), Waagen neglected the role played in the seventeenth century by the 10th Earl of Northumberland.

The four volumes of Waagen's epistolary descriptions of British collections, the first in the great tradition of German catalogues of British art and architecture, must have been a revelation to the world when they first appeared in 1854 and 1857. Here was the earliest comprehensive published account of Petworth, as of so many other collections; and in view of the difficulties that Waagen had to face—of poor light, frequent inaccessibility, and varying degrees of hospitality—the lasting accuracy of so many of his judgements of over ten thousand works of art is altogether astonishing. It was largely as a result of his research that the staging of the famous *Treasures of Art* exhibition in Manchester in 1857 was possible. Waagen was appointed to the office of juror to the exhibition in 1851.

Given Waagen's opinion of the Petworth collection, it is a matter of speculation as to why no Petworth pictures were included in the Manchester exhibition. It is hardly credible that none was asked for; there was a great deal on which to draw. There were, and still are, some seven hundred paintings in the house, and together they form a broad conspectus of European painting. Most schools are represented, though there are no early Italian and few Spanish pictures. The explanation for these gaps is that before 1837 interest in these two schools was largely limited to specialists, and after 1837, the year of the death of the 3rd Earl of Egremont, collecting and patronage at Petworth came to a standstill.

The collection covers a span of three centuries, beginning with the acquisitions of the 10th Earl of Northumberland in the 1630s. The apparent inactivity during the late seventeenth and early eighteenth century comes as a surprise, given the lavish and ostentatious character of the 6th Duke of Somerset, who lived at Petworth during that period. However his successor, the 2nd Earl of Egremont, was a conspicuous buyer at London sales in the 1740s and 1750s, and the 3rd Earl, his son, was a figure who came to epitomize the character of Petworth as it appears today. Although he was to collect old masters sporadically throughout his life, the 3rd Lord Egremont came to fame primarily through his patronage of British artists. Patronage is outside the scope of this paper, but nonetheless it cannot pass unnoticed: Van Dyck, in the seventeenth century, and Turner, in the nineteenth, give to Petworth a position unrivaled by any other British collection.

From medieval times until the late seventeenth century, Petworth (fig. 1) had been the home of the Percy family, Earls of Northumberland. The founder of the collection was the 10th Earl (1602–1668), a man who, until the Civil War, when he was to declare for the Parliamentary cause, moved in the circle of the king and shared his sophisticated tastes. At his death the Earl left some 165 pictures reflecting in character, but nowhere near in quantity, the collection of the

king. Northumberland was an early patron of Van Dyck, but not, however, of Rubens.

The extent of the collection in the seventeenth century is disclosed by two documents. The first is the manuscript list made in 1652 by Richard Symonds, who was shown the pictures at Suffolk House (subsequently Northumberland House) in London by, he informs us, Mr. Stone, "who copys."[3] About fifty pictures are mentioned, including some that are not to be found in the second document, the much more comprehensive list of 1671. In June and July of that year an inventory and valuation was drawn up that recorded the Northumberland picture collection in three houses (Northumberland House, Petworth, and Syon House) following the early death abroad of the 11th Earl.[4] The "appraisal" was made by the Symon Stone who had showed Symonds the Suffolk House pictures in 1652 and who is known as a copyist of Van Dyck.

Only a small proportion of the pictures, valued at approximately £100, was housed at Syon. One would expect the major portion of the works to have been in the London house, which, from the valuation, would appear to have been the case: Northumberland House contained paintings worth roughly £4000, Petworth £750. But the disparity between the contents of the three houses is less great than the figures suggest. In London there were 67 paintings, in the

Fig. 2.
Unknown Man by Titian, oil on canvas (The National Trust; photograph: Jeremy Whitaker)

country 55. In London, however, there was one painting, described as the "Three Senators" by Titian, which alone was appraised, according to Stone, at £1000. This picture, today known as the *Vendramin Family,* was sold to the National Gallery, London, in 1929 by the Duke of Northumberland, in whose branch of the family the picture had remained.

The 10th Earl of Northumberland, like others among his peers, was an amateur of Titian. He owned thirteen works with which the artist's name was associated, seven of which were in 1671 acknowledged to be copies. The early portrait of an unknown man (fig. 2) is the only autograph work by Titian remaining at Petworth today. It cannot be precisely identified in the inventory of 1671—possibly it is one or other of the "Two Mens pictures done to the Wast, one by Jarjone, the other by Titian," together valued at £50. The portrait was recognized by Waagen as the work of Titian. Its identity was then lost until it was published by Antonio Morassi in 1956.[5]

Apart from the *Vendramin Family,* there were only two pictures whose value in 1671 exceeded £100: "A Womans head with naked Brests done by old Palma" (£200), which had belonged to the 1st Duke of Buckingham, and "A Piece of or lady and Christ and Joseph done by Coregio" (£150). Both are untraced. Among the small number estimated at £100 were two Titians, "A

naked Venus and a Satyr"—probably the picture of the subject at Petworth, which must, unless further research reveals otherwise, be regarded as a school production—and "The Duke of florence and Machiavil," that is, the *Georges d'Armagnac with Guillaume Philandrier,* previously the property of the 1st Duke of Buckingham, today owned by the Duke of Northumberland.[6] The Titian copies were valued at £10 to £15. By comparison, the Van Dyck three-quarter lengths were put at £30 (with his larger groups, such as that of the "10th Earl of Northumberland with his wife and daughter" [fig. 3], at £60), and the Lelys at £10 (with his group of the "Royal Children" at £40).

"Two Pictures (the story) of the Virgin Mary and Christ and other ffigures in them done by Andrea Dulcerto" were valued at £200 the pair.[7] Almost entirely overpainted, the features Victorianized, these works had for many years lain in the attics at Petworth. Damage to one of them led to its repair, and, subsequently, its cleaning, by John Brealey. It has now emerged, almost certainly, as the lost original of Andrea's often repeated composition of *The Madonna and Child and Angels,* painted for Alessandro Corsini, from whom it must have passed to the Duke of Buckingham. Northumberland would have known both it and its companion when, during the Civil War, he rented Buckingham's London residence, York House, by then forfeited to Parliament. His acquisition of the two pictures, the second of which is a good version of the *Madonna and Child with Saint John and Saint Elizabeth* in the Louvre, was not long delayed, for they feature in Symonds' list of 1652.

It should be axiomatic that in a collection of the mid-seventeenth century the emphasis will be on the Italian school, and that in it the Venetians are likely to predominate. The inventory of 1671 does not conflict with this broad assumption, but in fact the number of northern paintings is only marginally smaller. The names of Paulus Brill, Gerrit Dou, Frans Francken, Jan Davidsz. de Heem (three times) are to be found, and among the high valuations (£100) is "A rare Prospective done by Stenwick, the ffigures by Pullenburke" (untraced today), which is likely to have come from Buckingham's collection. The commerce between England and the Netherlands at this time, the fact that a number of Dutch artists were practicing in England, Hendrick van Steenwyck and Cornelis van Poelenburg among them, and the current taste for

small and exquisite paintings would all have encouraged an interest in the Dutch school.

Another painting to be valued at £100 was "A Mans Picture done by Holben," which may be the *Dirck Berck* sold from Petworth in 1927[8] and now in The Metropolitan Museum of Art, New York. Apart from Holbein, the only sixteenth-century northern painter to be represented is "Satto Cleeve," with a portrait valued at £15, perhaps one of the two Joos van Cleefs at Petworth today. Among other schools, "the Labouradore" (that is, the Spaniard Juan Fernandez) is represented by five still lifes. One of the earliest references to Claude Lorrain in England is a landscape by "Glaudilloraigne," valued at £30.[9] And it is to the 10th Earl that we owe the exquisite set of "Eight little pictures in one fframe by Elshammer," valued at £250, which came from the Duke of Buckingham's collection, was in 1671 at Northumberland House, and is now at Petworth (fig. 4 shows *Saint Thomas Aquinas* from the series).

In 1682 Elizabeth, daughter of the 10th Earl of Northumberland and heiress to the great Percy

estates, married the 6th Duke of Somerset, bringing to Petworth a dignitary of regal pretensions. The Proud Duke, as he was known, left his mark on the house by commissioning a French architect to remodel the old Elizabethan building,[10] employing a French artist, Louis Laguerre, to decorate the grand staircase, and buying a masterpiece of French painting, Claude's *Jacob and Laban*.[11] He appears to have added nothing notable to the collection apart from this one picture. He had himself painted by John Closterman, and to Michael Dahl, who acted as a sort of court painter, he entrusted an order for a series of portraits of beautiful women known today as the "Petworth Beauties." Such a commission may suggest further French influence, but in fact precedent is to be found not only with Sir Peter Lely's *Windsor Beauties,* but also at Petworth itself. The 10th Earl had acquired from Van Dyck the four countesses (of Bedford, Devonshire, Carlisle, and Sunderland). Since the late 1750s these have hung together in the beauti-

ful White and Gold Room (fig. 5), which Matthew Brettingham crated, with them in mind, for the 2nd Earl of Egremont.

The 2nd Earl, then Sir Charles Wyndham, succeeded to the title and to Petworth on the death of the 7th Duke of Somerset in 1750. It was at this juncture that the Percy inheritance was divided, Northumberland House, Syon House, and Alnwick Castle in Northumberland passing to the 7th Duke's daughter who married Sir Hugh Smithson, later to be created Duke of Northumberland, and Petworth and the Egremont title going to the 6th Duke's nephew, Sir Charles Wyndham. Sir Charles inherited with Petworth an income of twelve thousand pounds a year and was in a position to indulge himself.

His upbringing was conventional. He had made the Grand Tour in the late 1720s and if, as seems to have been the case, he returned from his travels empty handed, it was not long before he made up for this lack of acquisitiveness. His accounts, which are preserved from 1748 until his

Fig. 6.
Archduke Leopold's Gallery by David
Teniers, 1651, oil on canvas   (The
National Trust)

death in 1763, reveal prolific buying and the ac-
cumulation of a variety of paintings. His grand
Whig tastes and attitude are perhaps best demonstrated by the collection of classical antiquities
which were bought for him in Italy by his agents
Gavin Hamilton and Matthew Brettingham, and
which put Petworth among the foremost hold-
ings of Greek and Roman sculpture in England.[12] Insofar as paintings were concerned,
however, his approach was far from wedded to a
strict observance of the classical tradition.

Toward the middle of the century an interest
in Dutch paintings was beginning to manifest
itself and after 1740 Dutch landscapes became
increasingly popular among English collectors.[13]
It was an interest that strayed from the rigid
principles imposed in an age of almost academic
absolutism; and a surprisingly high proportion of
the 2nd Earl's purchases were Dutch and Flemish paintings.

Horace Walpole, whose critical views on
Dutch art are well known, objected to what he
regarded as the profligacy of Lord Egremont,
and in a letter of 1758 to Sir Horace Mann he
condemned Egremont for putting up prices by
the extravagance of his bids.[14] By far the most
expensive pictures that Lord Egremont ever
bought were the *Archduke Leopold's Gallery* by
David Teniers (fig. 6),[15] for which he paid £241
in 1756, and Carlo Maratta's *Martyrdom of Saint
Andrew*, which cost him £273 in 1758. However
Walpole, in his letter to Mann, was not referring
to these works, but to four lots purchased by
Lord Egremont at Sir Luke Schaub's sale in 1758:
Rembrandt's *Philosopher*, for £8; Eustache Le
Sueur's *Salutation*, for £32; and Guercino's *Saint
Peter* and *Saint Joseph*, for £32 and £22, respectively. If this does not seem culpably extravagant, it should be borne in mind that when the
pictures were sold thirty-six years later (included
in a two-day sale of 192 pictures sent to Christie's by the 3rd Lord Egremont in 1794), the
Rembrandt fetched £1 9s., the Le Sueur £3
13s.6d., and the two Guercinos together 8 guineas. Maratta's *Martyrdom of Saint Andrew* went
for £298.

Walpole, had he been alive, would have felt his censure confirmed, but he might still have appeared over severe in other instances. For £5 or less Lord Egremont bought, among others, pictures by Steenwyck, Jean-François Millet (a pair), Dou, and in 1753 Jean Barbault's *Lady with a Rosary*. For £10 or under he acquired works by Jan Miel, Jan Both, Gaspard Dughet, Jan van Goyen, Francesco Trevisani, Alexis Grimou, Giovanni Ghisolfi, Jan Wynants, and Orizonte; also Jacob van Ruisdael's *Waterfall* (fig. 7), and Salomon van Ruysdael's *River Scene* (fig. 8). For £20 or under there were paintings by Luca Giordano, Nicolaes Berchem, Meindert Hobbema (a pair), Francesco Solimena, Willem van der Velde, and Andrea Locatelli; Gerrit Horst's *Beggar Boys* for £21; and for £22 a pair of landscapes by Aelbert Cuyp (in fact by Abraham van Calraet). In 1760, what was probably the large view of a town on a river, then described as by Cuyp but again probably by Calraet (fig. 9), was bought for £24, and the same price was paid for Chardin's *Mère Laborieuse*—an uncommon purchase—in 1757.[16] These are but a few entries taken at random, but they reflect a range of prices for (where they can be identified) respectable paintings by the artists concerned.

Among the more expensive acquisitions were Sebastien Bourdon's *Selling of Joseph* for £99 in 1756 (fig. 10); Guercino's *Supper of Emmaus* for £105 in 1762 (untraced); "Laban's Departing by La Hire" for £186 in 1753 (untraced); and three

Fig. 7.
Waterfall by Jacob van Ruisdael, oil on canvas   (The National Trust)

Fig. 8.
River Scene by Salomon van Ruysdael, 1632, oil on canvas   (The National Trust)

Fig. 11.
Rocky Landscape by Paulus Brill, oil
on canvas   (The National Trust)

paintings sold in 1794, Bassano's *Money Changers* for £81, Valerio Castello's *Moses* for £86, and Giovanni Lanfranco's four Saints for £152. A landscape by Brill (fig. 11) cost £126 in 1754. There was only one early northern picture—in the account book it appears merely as "A Picture" by Quentin Massys (fig. 12). However, this is clarified in the sale catalogue of 1755, in which it is described as the "Artist and his Family at Cards."[17] Waagen was correct in identifying the artist as Jan rather than Quentin Massys. This was a far from conventional purchase in the eighteenth century, and perhaps expensive at £48. Another unusual entry is for two Murillos at £118.[18]

Although it is not necessarily apparent from this selection of artists, the Italian school was more extensively represented than that of any other country. As well as seventeenth-century masters, Lord Egremont bought the works of contemporary painters: Canaletto, Jacopo di Paolo Marieschi, Gianpaolo Pannini, Francesco Zuccarelli, and Antonio Joli; and there were

seven earlier paintings, all Venetian, apart from a Raphael-school history piece. In 1794, when the 3rd Earl came to sell his London house and the works of art that it contained, the majority of the pictures in the sale were Italian paintings collected by his father.

The 2nd Earl died in 1763. According to his account book, during the last fifteen years of his life he had bought a total, not counting commissioned portraits, of more than 150 pictures, acquisitions which, if they contained no masterpieces, reflected an impressionable eye and a catholic taste. The 10th Earl of Northumberland had at his death left the same number of works. The sale of 1794 saw a dispersal of 192 lots.

In the catalogue of 1920, over seven hundred items are listed. The figure is largely to be accounted for by the additions made to the collection by the 3rd Lord Egremont. However, as an examination of sale catalogues preceding 1748—the year of the first entry in the account book—reveals, some further pictures were bought by the 2nd Earl (fig. 13) in the London auction

rooms from the early 1740s onward, and still
others, apart from portrait commissions, may be
unrecorded purchases of the 6th Duke of Somerset. The Petworth collection, despite the loss of
the thirteen works that were sold in 1927,[19] remains today essentially as Waagen knew it, "in
extent and value among the finest in the country," a monument to three centuries of intensive
buying and munificent patronage.

Fig. 13.
The 2nd Earl of Egremont by William
Hoare, R.A., oil on canvas   (The
National Trust)

NOTES

First I wish to express my indebtedness to Lord Egremont for the interest that he has taken and for the unrestricted access he has given me to pictures in his own collection. I should make it clear that after Petworth was transferred to the National Trust in 1967, the contents of the showrooms were accepted by the Treasury in part-payment of death duties, and were later conveyed to the National Trust. The substantial part of the collection remaining in the private wing of the house is owned by Lord Egremont.

1. C. H. Collins Baker, *Catalogue of the Petworth Collection of Pictures in the Possession of Lord Leconfield* (London, 1920). For further remarks on the collection, see St. John Gore, "Three Centuries of Discrimination," *Apollo* 105 (May 1977), 346–357, in which the help of Frank Simpson was acknowledged.

2. Gustav Friedrich Waagen, *Treasures of Art in Great Britain,* 3 vols. (London, 1854), 3:31–43.

3. Egerton ms., 1636, British Museum, London, 92–94.

4. Ms. 107, collection of the Duke of Northumberland, Alnwick Castle, Northumberland.

5. Antonio Morassi, *Festschrift für W. Sas-Zaloziecky* (Graz, 1956), 126–128.

6. Michael Jaffé, "The Picture of the Secretary of Titian," *Burlington Magazine* 108 (1966), 114–126.

7. A third picture to which the name of Andrea del Sarto was attached was listed in 1671 as a copy valued at £15. Confusingly, the subject may be the same as the second of the two pictures referred to here. It is described as *O' Lady & Christ & Elizabeth.*

8. In 1927 thirteen outstanding pictures were sold from the collection by Lord Leconfield. In addition to the Holbein there were works by Rembrandt (four), Hals, and Watteau. A Bronzino portrait has in recent years been bought back by the family.

9. Possibly a version of *Liber Veritatis* 67; see Marcel Röthlisberger, *Claude Lorrain: The Paintings,* 2 vols. (New Haven, 1961), 1:210.

10. See Gervase Jackson-Stops, "Petworth and the Proud Duke," *Country Life* (28 June 1973), 1870–1874.

11. Sale, Banqueting House, London, 11 May 1686, lot 158.

12. Margaret Wyndham, *Catalogue of the Collection of Greek and Roman Antiquities in the Possession of Lord Leconfield* (London, 1915).

13. Frank Simpson, "Dutch Paintings in England before 1760," *Burlington Magazine* 95 (1953), 39–42.

14. Walpole to Sir Horace Mann. 10 February 1758, Mrs. Paget Toynbee, ed., *The Letters of Horace Walpole,* 16 vols. (Oxford, 1903–1905), 4:no. 557.

15. Prices fetched by Teniers were high: £15 each for two modest landscapes bought in 1751, and £48 in 1754 for a small picture, *Farmer and His Maid* (Lord Egremont collection, Petworth).

16. Sold in 1927 (see note 8); present whereabouts unknown.

17. Sir Robert Austin sale, 10 January 1755, lot 66.

18. Present whereabouts unknown.

19. See note 8.

FRANCIS RUSSELL

The Hanging and Display
of Pictures, 1700–1850

*T*he *Treasure Houses of Britain* exhibition offered an opportunity to focus attention on many facets of British taste that are in general neglected. Picture-hanging is a subject that remains surprisingly unexplored, despite a number of recent articles and such brave, if visually far from fully satisfactory ventures as the rearrangement of the Apsley House collection. In the space available it is only practical to concentrate on a relatively small number of houses and their collections, selected, where possible, from those represented in the exhibition. There are various obvious questions to consider. To what extent were certain categories of pictures thought suitable for rooms of specific kinds; how rigidly were such categorizations adhered to; what essential premises determined the deployment of such works; and how did changing fashions in architecture and decoration interact with those of picture-hanging. The evidence is tortuous, often contradictory, and I add a further disclaimer.

Except in the case of such decorative schemes as that represented by Sebastiano Ricci's canvases from the staircase at Burlington House, whose intended arrangement has now been plausibly explained by George Knox,[1] the arrangement of pictures was rarely devised with absolute precision. Great collectors generally altered the hang of their pictures as further acquisitions were made, and with major hereditary collections a similar process was inevitable. The picture hang of any great house was thus a compromise between the space available and the scale of the collection in question. Some collectors were keenly interested in the arrangement of their pictures, others would delegate this to agents or architects. But it is doubtful whether any of the major collections of the past were assembled with as precise a sense of the manner in which they would be disposed, as were the works selected for *The Treasure Houses of Britain* exhibition.

The origins of the collections of the great houses of Britain can be traced to two complementary but distinct processes. There are series of family portraits and allied topographical or sporting works that were built up over many generations—that of the Cecils at Hatfield is an obvious example—and there are collections of old masters or contemporary works formed by individual members of dynasties who had a particular appreciation of the arts or an understanding of the *réclame* associated with possessions of the kind. While long portrait sequences were an indispensable adjunct of any ancient seat, acquisitions of old masters or contemporary pictures could make an immediate impact on the character of a house, and there is, indeed, a fascinating correlation between the activities of great collectors and their architectural patronage.

Some collections of old masters were acquired for early houses. At Burghley, the 5th Earl of Exeter's acquisitions in Italy were quickly matched by an energetic program of internal redecoration, while at Wilton, two successive generations maintained the momentum given to the collection by the 4th Earl of Pembroke's patronage of Sir Anthony van Dyck and remodeling of the south front of the house.[2] At Petworth it was the grandson and great grandson of the builder of the present house who enlarged the collections of old master and English pictures, respectively, necessitating the construction of the North Gallery. With the early eighteenth century, an impressive sequence of great houses began to be built or greatly enlarged for men who were notable collectors as well as patrons in their own right: Blenheim, Chiswick House, and Burlington House; Wimpole, Houghton, Holkham, Kedleston, Luton Park, and Fonthill; and, in the early nineteenth century, Leigh Court and Somerley. The display of pictures was *ab initio* an important feature of such houses. In other cases, Lamport and Castle Howard, for example, it fell to the builder's son to form a worthy collection of pictures.

The Treasure Houses exhibition represented two more unusual situations. Having in 1746 acquired Uppark in Sussex, built some half a century earlier, Sir Matthew Fetherstonhaugh set out with great energy to fill his empty, ancestor-less walls with whole sets of pictures bought in Italy;[3] while Paul Methuen of Corsham Court commissioned Capability Brown to design the Gallery to display the collection he had inherited from his kinsman and namesake, Sir Paul Methuen of Grosvenor Street.

No eighteenth-century collection was more splendidly represented in the exhibition than that of the Dukes of Montagu, kept until the present century mainly at the family's London homes. At Boughton, their great house in Northamptonshire, there were only 17 pictures in 1683/1684, and 42 in 1722; by 1832 there were 269, but these were predominantly portraits and there were few old masters of distinction.[4] By contrast, at Montagu House, Whitehall, as an undated inventory on paper watermarked 1817 establishes, there were 395 pictures in the seven major rooms: 29, the majority old masters, in the Little Dining Room; 6 full-length portraits—including the 4 Van Dycks now at Bowhill which Gainsborough recommended that David Garrick study—in the Great Dining Room; 10 canvases by Jean-Baptiste Monnoyer and Jacques Rousseau from the earlier Montagu house in the Anteroom; 22 works, including Leonardo's largely autograph *Madonna of the Yarn Winder*, the small Mantegna, *Tarquin and the Sibyl*, now at the Cincinnati Art Museum, and Rubens' *Watering Place* now in the National Gallery, London, in the Breakfast Room; 70, including the series of panels connected with Van Dyck's *Iconographia*, in the Dressing Room; and no fewer than 210, among which were several cases of miniatures in groups of nine, in the Picture Closet. Many of the finest pictures in the collection, including Rembrandt's *An Old Woman Reading* in its splendid mid-eighteenth century English frame, lent to the exhibition by the Duke of Buccleuch, and Rembrandt's *Self-Portrait* now in the permanent collection of the National Gallery, were among the 48 pictures in the Drawing Room. The Rembrandts took their place in what was, without doubt, an elaborate hang, including such pictures as Murillo's *Saint John the Baptist* and El Greco's *Adoration of the Shepherds*, both now at Boughton. The wealth of the collection reflected the taste not only of the Duke but also of the Duchess of Montagu—one of relatively few eighteenth-century collectors of her sex—and of their son Lord Monthermer. Their acquisitions must have transformed the character of the interiors Henry Flitcroft had supplied for the Duchess' father, the Duke of Montagu, between 1731 and 1733.

In 1710, when the painter Louis Cheron helped prepare a valuation of the pictures in the former Montagu House in Bloomsbury, only 62 pictures were recorded, including the 37 "little pieces of Vandyck" now at Boughton.[5] These had been acquired by the 1st Duke of Montagu, and a fascinating insight into the presentation of his pictures is offered by the accounts of Thomas Pelletier, who worked at Montagu House, Bloomsbury, at Boughton, at Ditton, and at Whitehall from 1689 until 1708. "Picture Rings and nails" were supplied in 1691, and large numbers of frames of varying size were gilded. Some of these were specified as for flowerpieces by Monnoyer and landscapes by Rousseau, and it is likely that the "six large frames with corners and middles for the apartment at Whitehall," gilded at a total cost of £27, contained the four Van Dycks and two Lelys later placed in the Large Dining Room at Montagu House, Whitehall. Some frames were of elaborate design. One is cited "with two pilasters capitals and Bases" and was correspondingly expensive, while others, for sets of prints mounted on "stretching frames and clothes," were cheap. In 1700 "the Passion of Our Saviour painted by Luke Jourdan" called for two large carved gilt frames at £24, but the "cutting of twelve Ebony frames new black'd and polished for the small heads of Vandyke" cost only 15 shillings in 1701. In some instances the bills specify the intended destination of a picture. Thus, in 1706, £6 was paid "for carving and gilding a large frame for the picture of Susanna and the two Elders over my Lady Monthermers chimney." This was no doubt a suitable ornament for the bedroom of the Duke's daughter-in-law. As revealing of the temper of the period was the £4 paid at the same time for "a half length frame for the Venus in my Lord Monthermer's Dressing Room." Two bills of 1707 remind us that picture-hanging had also a political dimension. Twelve pounds was paid "for carving a large frame for the Queens Picture in the Room called the Salon at Ditton"—the picture was also relined—while £2 15s. was expended on "an oval three quarter frame embos'd

for the picture of Oliver Cromwell," whose treatment of Scotland must have seemed particularly significant in the year of the Act of Union.[6]

As the eighteenth century progressed, it is clear that certain kinds of pictures were perceived to be appropriate for rooms of particular types. The visitor to a great house might be confronted in the hall with portraits, or, as at Althorp, Badminton, and Longleat, with expressly painted sets of sporting pictures by John Wootton. Still lifes and fowl pieces might be thought suitable for a dining room, and collections of old masters, differentiated by size, might be divided between large apartments and cabinets. Portraits, particularly of literary sitters, were obviously appropriate for libraries; a well-known example is that of Lord Chesterfield's London house, first photographed in 1892 when the plaster frames contained pictures acquired by the 1st Lord Burton (fig. 1). In bedrooms there were often scattered pictures and also framed drawings or prints, and the seat of an ancient family might, of course, boast its gallery of early portraits, whose fate depended on the whim of the owner. Thus, at Hatfield House in the late eighteenth century, it was rumored that early por-

Fig. 2.
Projects for the Hall at Houghton
by William Kent, 1726 (Private collection, New York)

traits were being turned out; but as early as 1732 the formidable Sarah, Duchess of Marlborough, on visiting her granddaughter at Woburn Abbey, was struck by the very antiquity of the place: "I am sure, if it were my house, I would never pull it down. . . . The gallery has a great many pictures in it, which are valuable, as they belong to the family, and are in antique dresses. There is one of a countess of Bedford, that was quite charming—I mean her whom the father forbid his son from marrying."[7] Foreigners such as Pierre Jacques Fougeroux might not respond to pictures of this kind, but for English visitors like George Vertue and John Loveday, these were of paramount interest.

Sir Robert Walpole was not the first successful English politician to collect pictures, but none of his predecessors sought them out more systematically, and of his successors in the premiership only Lord Bute and Sir Robert Peel would be collectors of comparable determination. While Walpole was in office the bulk of his pictures remained in London, but the recent discovery of two drawings by William Kent for Houghton, dated 1726 (fig. 2), surely confirms that Houghton was always considered the ultimate destination of these works. The arrangement of the Houghton collection cannot be considered here, but the point should be made that Kent envisaged a grandly symmetrical display of the kind he would have seen in Rome, where the great patrician galleries offered obvious exempla for the ambitious sightseer.

It is not surprising that Kent, himself a practiced if unaccomplished painter, should seem to have had a pioneering role in the treatment of pictures—as opposed to murals—in an architectural context. Many of his patrons had experienced the same influences in Italy as he had, and thus the landscape section of the Colonna Gallery at Rome, still hung substantially as in the early eighteenth century, found English counterparts at Chiswick and at Holkham, where the State Dressing Room—now known as the Landscape Room—was one of the most striking features of the house.[8] Both Lord Burlington and Lord Leicester were connoisseurs of exceptional discrimination, and would have been quite capable of deploying their possessions without calling in professional advisors. As T. S. Rosoman has recently shown,[9] pictures played a paramount part in the decoration of Chiswick—there were thirty-four in the Red Closet and twenty-five in the Green Velvet Room—hung in tiers and

Fig. 3.
Detail of *The Cholmondeley Family*
by William Hogarth (The Marquess of
Cholmondeley, Houghton Hall)

placed not only over doors but above windows, as in the Red Velvet Room. Burlington's close friend the 2nd Duke of Devonshire, and his successor, had very similar tastes. Despite the Bachelor Duke's modifications at Devonshire House and his thinning out of the hang of several rooms,[10] some hint of the pictorial taste of the early eighteenth century is offered by late-nineteenth-century photographs of the ballroom and the Duchess' Boudoir at Devonshire House.

To judge from the account published by Matthew Brettingham in 1773,[11] the hang of the pictures at Holkham was more carefully thought out than that of any other English house of its

generation. Later acquisitions have displaced many of the 1st Earl of Leicester's pictures, but, with the exception of Titian's *Venus and the Lute Player*, now in The Metropolitan Museum of Art, New York, all the works remain in the house. The visitor ascended from the hall, with its antique sculptures, to the saloon, hung entirely with works of the Roman school, of which the larger were scenes from classical history and mythology. The drawing room—the north wall of which survives relatively unaltered[12]—followed with more varied works, large religious pictures by Pietro de' Pietri and Carlo Cignani, a Claude balanced by a Gaspard Dughet, Van Dyck's Duke of Arenberg, and others. Back through the saloon there followed the State Bedchamber Apartment with Rubens' *Flight into Egypt*, the Titian *Venus*, a large Guido, and other pictures. These set the mood for the State Dressing Room, with its great series of landscapes by Claude, Salvator Rosa, and others, and a single historical work, Luca Giordano's *Preaching of the Baptist*. The State Bedchamber itself was tapestried, but in the adjacent closet, hung against green satin, were a number of smaller pictures by Sebastiano Conca and others, and some two dozen watercolors and drawings. The closet to the North State Bedchamber was largely hung with small landscapes, including the *View of the Colosseum, with the Arch of Constantine* by Gaspare Vanvitelli (THB no. 184) over the door. There were further Italian pictures in the North State Bedchamber and the associated dressing room. Most of the portraits were in the family wing, but Lady Leicester's Dressing Room, with Canaletto's *Bucintoro at the Molo* over the mantel, contained further Italian works. The most exceptional of the smaller rooms was the Blue Satin Dressing Room, in which some fifty-five old master drawings were hung together with the Raphael cartoon for *La Belle Jardinière* and the well-known grisaille copy of Michelangelo's *Battle of Cascina*. No other major collection in England was arranged with such exacting precision, and there can be no doubt that Leicester himself was largely responsible for this.

One of Lord Leicester's later acquisitions was Dughet's *A Storm* (THB no. 313), which was placed in the State Bedchamber Apartment. This had previously been in the collection of George, 3rd Earl of Cholmondeley, Walpole's son-in-law. Pierre Jacques Fougeroux visited Cholmondeley, then Lord Malpas, in Arlington Street in 1728, and described the "jolie bibliothèque avec quel-ques bustes Antiques en Marbre."[13] It is scarcely a coincidence that in Hogarth's conversation piece of 1732 (THB no. 163), the Cholmondeley family is shown in such a library. In the background, pictures, some in modish, eared Kent frames, are ranged over a row of chairs (fig. 3), and above are awnings that were presumably intended to preserve Cholmondeley's treasures from the dirt of the metropolis. There is evidence of the use of such awnings in other houses, but Hogarth offers one of the few visual records of what may well have been a standard feature of major collections in London. None of the pictures in Hogarth's painting has been identified[14]—apart from the Dughet, few elements of the earl's collection can be traced—but nevertheless it is clear that Cholmondeley, who instructed Hogarth to adopt a very unusual iconographic program for the picture, wished his activity as a collector to be commemorated.

Cholmondeley's pictures were evidently crowded together, arranged in tiers with very little intervening space. Such arrangements differed only in their rigid symmetry from those recorded by David Teniers and other Flemish masters of the seventeenth century, whose views of picture galleries enjoyed a consistent popularity with English collectors. The preoccupation of the Palladian patron with patterned picture hangs, in which the spaces between works assumed a novel importance, is well illustrated in a series of drawings and papers formerly at Cholmondeley Castle, now at the Royal Institute of British Architects. These were almost certainly not assembled for the 3rd Earl; the papers in question are associated with a project by a Palladian architect of about 1750 for a house off Tyburn Lane. There are plans for the hang of a number of rooms, including an Octagon, a Blue Room, and a larger Drawing Room. Small sections of card (fig. 4), of which half a dozen survive, were cut and inscribed with artists' names and the dimensions of individual pictures, including the frames. These were then transcribed in the requisite order onto rough sheets, on which calculations of spacing, both vertical and horizontal, were carefully worked out. In the crowded arrangement of the Blue Room (fig. 5), a plan to leave only one foot eight inches of "spare room" in the upper tier of a wall measuring thirteen feet six inches was evidently considered unsatisfactory. Thus, in the definitive hang, the central element, a Rubens, displaced a

work in the center of the lower tier, leaving the vertical Rubens flanked by landscapes of equal height; the two large horizontal upper elements approximately matched the total width of the three pictures below. The calculations show that on a wall eleven feet high from dado level, it was considered adequate to have spaces of one foot between the dado and the bottom of the frames, and of six inches between the tiers of pictures and between the topmost frames and the cornice.

The hang of the drawing room in the house (fig. 6), which may be compared with the well-known scheme of 1764 for the Cabinet at Felbrigg Hall,[15] was particularly subtle, with its balance of horizontal and vertical elements, its

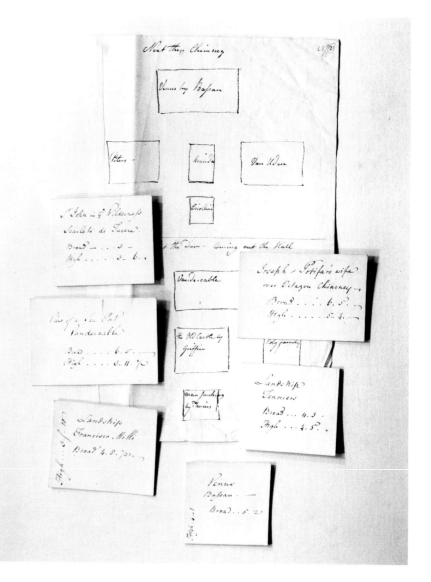

Fig. 4.
Cards prepared for a hanging plan, English School, c. 1750 (British Architectural Library, RIBA)

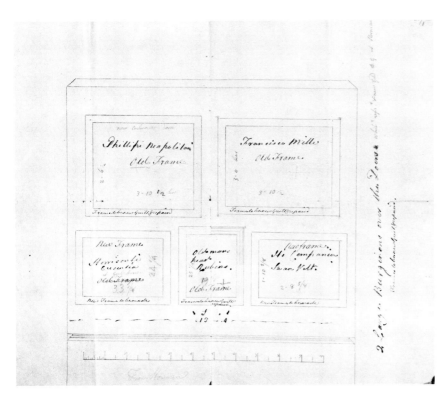

Fig. 5.
Hanging plan for the Blue Room in an unidentified London house, English School, c. 1750 (British Architectural Library, RIBA)

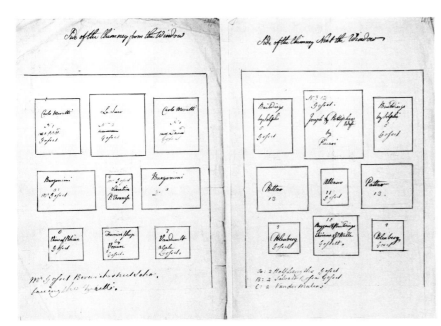

Fig. 6.
Hanging plans for two sections of the wall of a drawing room in an unidentified London house, English School, c. 1750 (British Architectural Library, RIBA)

gradual buildup of scale from the lower to the third and upper tier. Each section of wall was ten feet six inches wide, of which two feet eleven inches was to be left as vacant space. The walls were eleven feet nine inches high, and the plans show that the lower tier of paintings was an afterthought. One interesting feature of the drawings, which has already been noted by John Harris,[16] is that most of the pictures were marked to be sent to [Gideon] Gossett, the framemaker. As notes for pictures in the Blue Room establish, frames were variously to be replaced, "new built," or regilded, to achieve a suitably concerted effect.

It is in light of such drawings that one should consider the collection of Sir Paul Methuen, which was kept in his house in Grosvenor Street until it was progressively transferred to Corsham Court by Paul Methuen, his heir. The account of the collection in *London and Its Environs Described*, issued in 1761,[17] which was based in part on earlier material, is one of the few in which the specific position of each picture within a room is described. Only half the collection survives, and thus it is impossible to reconstruct the hang in its entirety, but certain specific observations may be made. The great pair of pictures by Gerard de Lairesse now in the hall at Corsham, were placed not as pendants, but one above the other opposite the windows in the hall of the Grosvenor Street house. Pictures were set above chimneys and doors, and the succession of parlors were hung two and three deep in descending order of size. Vertical works were usually placed in the center of these clustered groups, flanked by pictures of horizontal format. Pendants were often of very different character, and no attempt was made to distinguish Italian from Northern works or to make an iconographical selection.

Even in 1761 the hang at Grosvenor Street may have seemed rather outmoded. The most recent collection recorded in *London and Its Environs Described* was almost certainly that of a Jewish stockbroker of Portuguese extraction, Sampson Gideon, whose pictures at Belvedere near Erith in Kent, although not numerous, were of remarkably consistent caliber.[18] These were divided between the Long Parlour, the Lobby—where most of the smaller works were housed—and the Saloon, otherwise known as the Great Room (fig. 7). This last room was built, almost certainly to the design of Isaac Ware, in or after 1751. When it was photographed in 1960 before its destruction, only the less faded zones of the

Fig. 7.
The Saloon or Great Room at Belvedere prior to demolition   (National Monuments Record)

Fig. 8.
Project for a room in an unidentified house attributed to Thomas Paty   (Christie's [1982])

Fig. 9.
Project for an overmantel in a Red
Drawing Room by an associate of
Sambroke Freeman (Christie's [1983])

walls survived to tell of the room's purpose as the setting for the outstanding works in the collection: Murillo's *Immaculate Conception* and the pendant *Flight into Egypt*, respectively in the National Gallery of Victoria in Melbourne and The Toledo Museum of Art; Rubens' *Gerbier Family*, now in the National Gallery of Art, Washington; and works by Claude and Luca Giordano, below which hung the pair of gallery interiors by Teniers, of which one was included in *The Treasure Houses of Britain* exhibition (THB no. 291).

The collection at Belvedere was exceptional, but from the mid-eighteenth century there is clearer visual evidence of the importance architects and their patrons attached to pictures.[19] One can cite the example of a series of designs for an unidentified house associated with Thomas Paty (fig. 8), presumably intended for a Bristol merchant, in which pictures and furniture are indicated;[20] or the project for an overmantel frame intended for a large picture of Saint John the Baptist (fig. 9)—the size tempts one to suppose it a copy of the Raphael of the Pitti Palace—by an amateur associate of Sambroke

Freeman of Fawley Court.[21] In a complementary sphere one might point to the earliest of extant print rooms, that at Rokeby, the components of which leave little doubt that it was arranged in the lifetime of the last great amateur Palladian, Sir Thomas Robinson.

An architect who seems to have had a particularly clear comprehension of the role of pictures—as opposed to murals—in decorative schemes was James "Athenian" Stuart. In the early 1760s Stuart worked in two London houses which were intended to display major collections—Spencer House and Holderness House. The earliest project in which Stuart can be shown to have considered the role of pictures is that of 1757 for a saloon at Kedleston.[22] Stuart's drawings for the room reflect the brief he had been given by Sir Nathaniel Curzon, who, as Leslie Harris argues,[23] took Holkham, which had been inherited by a close friend and neighbor, as his *point de depart.* Stuart's scheme shows the great pair of canvases by Benedetto Luti and an outsize Giordano, which Curzon had recently purchased, and also a large portrait of Curzon and his wife, anticipating with remarkable prescience the picture Nathaniel Hone was to supply several years later.

We will return to Kedleston, but two other houses in which Stuart was involved should be mentioned: Lord Spencer's villa at Wimbledon, where Stuart's project for a room includes sketches of portraits in his patron's collection,[24] and Nuneham Park in Oxfordshire. As Giles Worsley has recently clarified,[25] Stuart had an important role in the decoration of Nuneham, which was begun in 1756 for an unusually discriminating patron, Simon, 1st Earl Harcourt. As early accounts of the collection show, the rooms were hung with careful attention to subject matter. There were early portraits leavened by two subject pictures in the Saloon, and further old masters in the anteroom. The Library (fig. 10) was hung with portraits of poets and other literary figures, and the Dining Room with Grand Tour views by Vanvitelli and Giovanni Paolo Pannini, game pieces by Jan Fyt and Frans Snyders, and other landscapes. The Octagon Drawing Room housed further old masters. The majority of the most celebrated works in the collection were in the Great Drawing Room, arguably the first neo-classical interior in England, to which Stuart made a significant contribution. Apart from four works—the Titian *Saint Margaret*, now in the Kisters Collec-

Fig. 10.
The Library at Nuneham Park, photographed in 1913   (*Country Life*)

Fig. 11.
The Great Drawing Room at Nuneham Park, photographed in 1913   (*Country Life*)

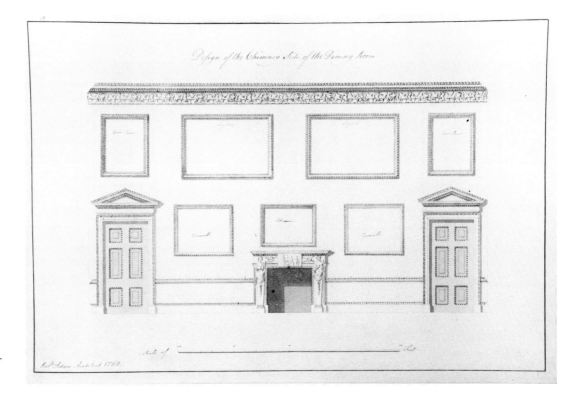

Fig. 12.
Project for the south wall of the dining room at Kedleston by Robert Adam, 1762 (The National Trust)

tion, Kreuzlingen, in which the saint is seen in a landscape of great grandeur; a *Holy Family* given to Eustache le Sueur in which there may well have been a landscape background; the Van de Velde of *The Yacht "Mary" and Other Vessels Under Sail Off Amsterdam* (THB no. 74); and the Adam Franz van der Meulen campaign scene paired with this—all the pictures in this room were landscapes, an arrangement almost completely lost by the time photographs were first taken (fig. 11). The accounts of John Adare, covering the years 1758 to 1763, establish that he was not only responsible for the joinery in the major rooms and for much of the furniture, but also for twenty-nine "Carlomarets" frames of varying width.[26] In some cases the relevant pictures are not specified, but those that can be identified with reasonable certainty include seven out of the seventeen in the Great Drawing Room. The frames in question were relatively inexpensive, but the conclusion is inescapable that patron and architect were concerned to achieve a strict uniformity in the presentation of the pictures.

Sir Nathaniel Curzon's great interest in pictures has already been mentioned in connection with Stuart's proposals for Kedleston. It was surely at Curzon's insistence that Stuart's successor, Robert Adam, prepared elevations of every wall in the state rooms, indicating how the pictures were to be placed. The scheme remains substantially intact. In the dining room, as projected in 1762 (fig. 12), the uniform picture frames are set into the walls, with large still lifes representing the fruits of the earth placed above landscapes by Francesco Zuccarelli and others, reflecting the Arcadian vistas over the park outside the windows. In other state rooms, some elements of the original hang have been sold and a number of the smaller pictures removed. In some rooms the subtlety of the original hang has been lost as a result of a failure to recognize what spacing was intended. Thus, in the drawing room, the pictures at either side of the chimney-piece should be centered on the sofas. The pictures have been moved less than a foot, and yet the harmony of the wall is awkwardly distorted.[27] If the main rooms at Kedleston were intended as a public demonstration of Curzon's taste, it was in the private wing, as at Holkham, that his discrimination could be experienced on a more intimate scale. His dressing room originally boasted a single work, a cartoon attributed to Carlo Maratta (fig. 13) of a suitably suggestive subject.

It was at Kedleston that Adam paid most attention to the hanging of pictures. Pictures would, however, have an important role in a whole series of houses he built. These included Lansdowne House, Berkeley Square, commissioned originally by Lord Bute, Bute's Luton Park, and, rather later, Udny House at Teddington, where a picture gallery was constructed for Robert Udny. Adam was also responsible for the redecoration of 19 Arlington Street for Sir Lawrence Dundas between 1763 and 1766. Johan Zoffany's celebrated view of the Arlington Street library (THB no. 281) does not record a specific picture hang, but suggests how carefully Dundas' exceptional collection of Dutch pictures was deployed and how crucial was the contribution of the frames. The painter also shows how the pictures were hung, with brass rings from nails, the latter supplied by the cabinetmaker William France in 1764. The elaborate French frames of the paintings by Teniers on the right (fig. 14), which contrast so strikingly with the more restrained English counterparts,[28] are reminders that the fashion for Dutch and Flemish pictures of this kind had been set in France, whence so many of these pictures had been imported.

Another Adam house that should be considered in this context is Saltram in Devon, remodeled between 1768 and 1779. Antonio Zucchi's inset pictures in the Dining Room were an integral component of Adam's decorative scheme, but Lord Boringdon's association with Reynolds clearly influenced the hanging of both the Velvet Drawing Room and the saloon. Boringdon was not only a persistent patron of Sir Joshua, but one of several collectors who were advised by him. It was normal for painters to act in this way, but Sir Joshua's influence, in this as in other spheres, was altogether unprecedented. Naturally his portraits were often intended for specific positions; he went to Blenheim in 1779 to supervise the hanging of the great Marlborough family group, only two days after it was delivered.[29]

Taste in picture-hanging inevitably influenced the treatment and formation of collections. The claims of symmetry placed a premium on sets and pairs. Individual works might be enlarged or reduced to serve as pendants. Examples may be cited in most old collections. At Knole, where, despite sales late in the last century, the collection is substantially intact, a number of portraits were enlarged to form pairs, including two ovals of

Fig. 13.
Venus and Putti by circle of Carlo Maratta, formerly at Kedleston
(Private collection, London)

Fig. 14.
Sir Lawrence Dundas and His Grandson in the Library at 19 Arlington Street by Johan Zoffany, 1769, oil on canvas   (The Marquess of Zetland)

the sixteenth and seventeenth centuries, which became rectangular. They were presumably treated in this way because such frames were less costly. Conversely, a feeble panel in the style of Adriaen Brouwer was cut down to supply two smaller elements for a picture hang.

What the Dukes of Dorset did on a grand scale at Knole, with the aid of their house carpenters, was echoed in the acquisitive policy of their Kentish neighbor John Warde, who inherited Squerryes Court in 1746 and over a period of some three decades spent just over £692 on some ninety-three pictures.[30] The catalogue of his purchases shows how sharp a watch he kept for possible pendants to works he already owned. He paired one landscape given to Ruysdael with another, and found a Cornelis van der Schalke to match a moonlight scene of similar dimension. To balance an old copy of a Willem van Mieris which he thought an original, he secured a copy after Mieris of a similar composition of identical dimensions by Jean Etienne Liotard. The pictures so paired were duly reframed, which, to judge from the variety of frames in the surviving portion of the collection, was not Warde's usual practice. Early nineteenth-century plans for hanging show how the family sought to ensure symmetry not only of pictures but of frames. Most of these were gilded, but some attempt was made to balance the few early black frames which had not been replaced. The hanging plans are not complete, but it would seem that Warde's old masters were kept separate from family portraits: the more substantial of them were in the drawing room and the upstairs gallery, but fifty-three of the smaller works, over half the collection, were in the small cabinet room, ranged in up to five tiers.

Knole and Squerryes have survived. Alas, this is not the case with other collections of their generation, and a survey of some of the early losses is revealing. Many complete houses were sold in the 1770s and 1780s and, where auctions were held in room sequence, the catalogues offer a fascinating insight into the role of pictures. On a modest scale one may take the example of Lord Vane's Easton Lodge, near Winchester, in 1774.[31] There were sets of prints in the breakfast parlor, eighteen Indian pictures and a small Flemish view in the dressing room, and two religious pictures and a painting by Pier Francesco Mola in the "Blue Strip'd Bed Chamber." A year later, in Lord Holland's sale at Holland House,[32] from which portraits were evidently held back, there were thirty-three pictures, including two Canalettos and two large history pictures in the White Damask Dining Room, and also prints and drawings in Lady Holland's Bedchamber.

Three sales of the period—those of Humphrey Hanmer's Hanmer Hall, Flintshire, in 1775;[33] of Sir Joshua Vanneck's Putney villa in 1778;[34] and of the 5th Earl of Scarbrough's Sandbeck Park in 1785[35]—offer a surprisingly consistent view of the way pictures were divided between rooms of particular character. The Hanmer collection was of some antiquity, begun by the Sir Thomas Hanmer who sat to Van Dyck (THB no. 63). There were miscellaneous old masters in many rooms, mixed with portraits in the dining parlor. In the breakfasting parlor were a Canaletto, two Dutch landscapes, and nine fowl pieces, while the most imposing works in the collection—a set of nine by Sebastiano Ricci—and twenty other pictures were in the "Room adjoining the Library," evidently the equivalent of a gallery. Sir Joshua Vanneck had been a particular connoisseur of Dutch pictures, and the sixty-five that were sold all seem to have been in the gallery of his villa, which James Wyatt had designed not long before Vanneck's death in 1777. The villa's other rooms were evidently hung more sparsely, with a set of Indian bird and flower watercolors in Vanneck's son's bedroom and fourteen prints after Giovanni Battista Piazzetta in the summer house.

At Sandbeck most of the one hundred old masters sent to London for sale are likely to have been in the great gallery above the ground floor, which is the centerpiece of the house James Paine constructed twenty years earlier for Lord Scarbrough's father. Three views of the house and a companion piece of Roche Abbey in the park were in the Eating Parlor, and an expensive Giordano was in the Brown Parlor. For posterity the almost simultaneous sale at Lumley Castle,[36] the original family seat, was more tragic. The portrait of Lord Lumley by Sir William Segar (THB no. 20) in the great hall, together with its sixteen companions of Lumley's ancestors, were bought in, but much of what remained of Lumley's collection was scattered, including fifteen more whole lengths from the Music Room, two dozen other early portraits and works by Jean Baptiste Monnoyer from two bedrooms, and, more surprisingly, the contemporary family portraits from the Blue Moreen Bedroom.

Many great houses, whether in London or in the country, were accessible to the tourist in the eighteenth century, but in default of any major public collection it was at exhibitions and salerooms that pictures were most readily viewed, and their influence on picture hanging should not be discounted. No private room could match the gallery of Somerset House in height, but the great symmetrical blocks of closely hung pictures there and the equally pragmatic hangs of the saleroom were echoed in some collections. Was it at Somerset House that Lord Egremont learned the advantage of tipping forward works in the upper tier of his gallery at Petworth?[37] Certainly, the advantages of top-lit galleries were visible both at Somerset House and in the auction room before they were adopted by Wyatt at Corsham Court and by Nash at Attingham Park. It is not without significance, either, that architects served on the small committees responsible for the hanging of the annual exhibitions at Somerset House: Thomas Sandby in 1775, 1781, 1782, and 1792; George Dance in 1778, 1784, and 1795; and James Wyatt in 1797. Dance was employed by two great collectors, Sir Francis Baring at Stratton Park and Sir George Beaumont at Coleorton, while Wyatt was keenly aware of the architectural role of pictures, as the inset landscapes of the Billiard Room at Heaton suggest. Wyatt's scheme for the Library at Castle Coole includes a series of five carefully spaced portraits that seem not to have been commissioned.[38]

Toward the end of the eighteenth century there is evidence of changing attitudes to the hanging of pictures. If the dining rooms of the past had been dominated by fowl pieces and landscapes or by portraits, there were now hints of the future dominance of sporting pictures—for example in the dining room of Peper Arden, designed by William Chambers, for which Stubbs supplied a series of overdoors. Moreover in some houses, notably at Luton Park, systematic attempts were being made to segregate pictures by school. In this Lord Bute may well have been a pioneer, for it was he who largely directed the taste of his erstwhile pupil King George III. A series of hanging plans for Buckingham House dating to the mid-1770s has recently come to light in the Royal Collection.[39] Both the library and a closet were entirely hung with Italian pictures. The rough design for the latter (fig. 15) is of particular interest as it is in the king's own hand; it was then copied by a professional draftsman (fig. 16). In other rooms, pictures were hung on cords with large bows above, while those in the lower tier were suspended from

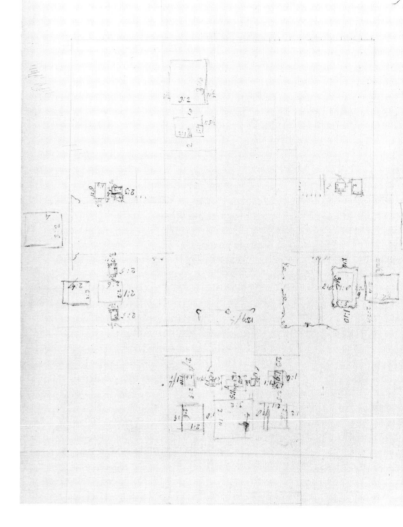

those above. Bute himself can have had no hand in the scheme, but it surely owed much to his influence nonetheless. In his long retirement from public life, he also took the unprecedented step of filling Robert Adam's low rooms at Highcliffe, perched on the Hampshire coast, with pictures of predominately naval subject matter.

Consideration of picture hanging in the early nineteenth century has concentrated, quite understandably, on the great galleries of the major town houses: Cleveland House, Grosvenor House, Apsley House, Stafford House, Bridgewater House, and Dorchester House, all top lit and each more opulent than its predecessor.[40] Of the collections in question, only that of Grosvenor House was represented in *The Treasure*

Fig. 15.
Design for the hanging plan in a closet at Buckingham House by King George III (The Royal Collection; reproduced by gracious permission of Her Majesty the Queen)

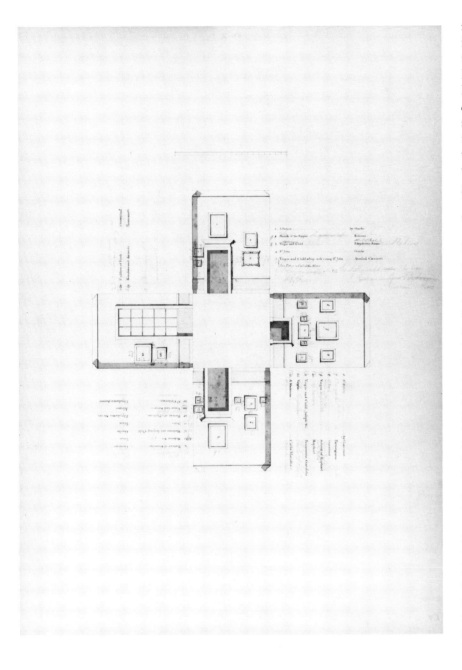

Houses of Britain exhibition. Charles Robert Leslie's portrait of the Grosvenor family of 1831 (THB no. 517) offers a fascinating insight into the way the Westminster collection was shown. Of the pictures, only the Velasquez *Don Baltasar Carlos: The Riding School* (THB no. 497) is hung flush with the wall; the others, including the vast Rubens cartoons whose acquisition in 1818 had precipitated the enlargement of the gallery, are tilted forward so as to be more readily seen. Presumably this was done with the approval of William Seguier, the dealer and restorer, who

received a retainer to attend to the collection. It is interesting to observe that pictures appear not to have been hung in this way at Cleveland House or Stafford House. Nonetheless, in 1838 Dr. Waagen was to complain in his *Works of Art and Artists in England* that only "a very feint and subdued light"[41] penetrated to the lower part of the room. Perhaps for this reason the pictures would be partly rearranged later in the century, when, as the progression seen in early photographs suggests, Reynolds' *Mrs. Siddons as the Tragic Muse* (fig. 17) was considered the culmination of the Westminster collection.

The gallery was an excellent setting for great baroque canvases; for Dutch pictures it was, of course, less satisfactory. There was no more discriminating collector in the latter sphere than the Prince Regent, who had distinct ideas about picture hanging. Rembrandt's *Portrait of a Shipbuilder and His Wife* was placed by itself on one wall in the Blue Velvet Room at Carlton House (fig. 18). In the Rose Satin Room pictures were hung in carefully selected groups on cords suspended from Henry Holland's decorative panels. It is revealing that the selection in the Rose Satin Room changed between 1817, the date of an engraving from Pyne's watercolor of the room, and 1819, when Pyne's *History of the Royal Residences* was published.[42] So selective was the regent's hanging that a substantial proportion of his extraordinary collection was always in store.

Contemporaries of the regent had individual ideas about the presentation of their collections, too. Lord Carlisle, who in 1772 wrote that he had "hung up all [his] ancestors"[43] in the Long Gallery of the west wing at Castle Howard, later commissioned Charles Heathcote Tatham to remodel the room, in which Carlisle was painted in about 1810 by John Jackson.[44] Lord de Tabley housed the more important of his modern English pictures not in the gallery at Tabley House, but in that of his house on Hill Street in London, where pictures were reported to be "hung in a perfectly novel style of elegance, suspended from chains by lions' heads splendidly gilt."[45] Both chains and lion masks survive at Tabley. The picture rail was a natural development from this, and, of course, made it much easier to rearrange collections. De Tabley's pictures were certainly hung in a more advanced way than those of his friend Thomas Parker of Browsholme, whose interest in contemporary English works so stimulated that of De Tabley.[46]

Written and visual evidence of picture-

hanging becomes very much fuller in the nineteenth century, and I will conclude with a brief
survey of some of the collections of old masters
formed at this time. No collector was more avid
than William Beckford, whose Grand Drawing
Room at Fonthill in Wiltshire suggests how he
liked to orchestrate his possessions.[47] His *Boy
with a Puzzle* by Bernardino Luini, then considered the work of Leonardo, was immediately on
the left of the chimneypiece (it is now at Elton
Hall); and Beckford evidently took care that the
more precious of his smaller pictures should be
readily visible.

The Fonthill interior is in revealing contrast to
the drawing room at Leigh Court, built for the
Bristol merchant Philip John Miles, whose great
collection included the two Claudes previously
owned by Prince Altieri (THB no. 309), which
William Beckford sold for such a spectacular
price in 1808. Waagen's praise of Leigh Court
was unstinting, and it is fascinating to see, in a
watercolor of the drawing room by Thomas Leeson Rowbotham (fig. 19), how fully integrated
the collections were—the way, for instance, the
central pictures in the lower tiers on either side
of the window were raised to accommodate the
antiquities on the consoles below. Another merchant collector, James Morrison, who acquired
much of Beckford's former estate at Fonthill,
had equally precise ideas about the deployment

of his possessions. Both in his London house, 57 Harley Street, and at Basildon Park in Berkshire, Morrison employed the architect John Papworth. Papworth's designs for the drawing room at Harley Street (fig. 20),[48] prepared in 1828 when the collection was far less extensive than it would later become, already contained pictures such as Constable's *The Lock* (THB no. 518).

Morrison's pictures were hung largely by school, as was to become increasingly common in the nineteenth century; already in 1835 Waagen felt that the failure to segregate the Italian pictures in the drawing room at Panshanger from those of the Northern schools was to their mutual disadvantage.[49] Some collectors were only interested in specific fields: Abraham Robarts, for instance, whose *Nieuwe Zijds Voorburgwal at Amsterdam* by Jan van der Heyden (THB no. 300) was in the Dutch Cabinet; or Sir Robert Peel, who, as Waagen records, placed his sixty or so Northern pictures, with two by Reynolds, in an "oblong appartment, with windows at the two ends" at Whitehall Gardens. The

Fig. 18.
The Blue Velvet Room at Carlton House by William Henry Pyne, 1817   (The Royal Collection; reproduced by gracious permission of Her Majesty the Queen)

Fig. 19.
The drawing room at Leigh Court by Thomas Leeson Rowbotham, watercolor   (Bristol City Art Gallery)

works were hung on red paper "in such a manner that they all have a bright side-light; most of them allow of a close inspection, and no one is hung so high as not to be seen well."[50]

Waagen looked at pictures as an art historian. Peel's most spirited critic, Disraeli, whose novels and letters offer such a comprehensive view of the many strands of contemporary taste in pictures, took a more social view of their function. "I do not approve," he wrote to Lady Bradford in 1874, "of prints in dining rooms. Essentially middle-classish and not in keeping with crimson footmen."[51] Disraeli's descriptions sometimes seem highly charged, but it is sobering to consider the scale of some mid-nineteenth-century collections.

After half a century of acquisition, Lord Northwick owned over two thousand pictures at Thirlestane House, Cheltenham. Almost every room had its mouth-watering quota. The English pictures were confined to the library and the Modern Gallery, and in many rooms Northwick's great collection of Italian works provided the dominant note.[52] Northwick was an eclectic collector of the old school, and despite a pioneering interest in primitives he would never have dreamed of limiting himself to these, as would his younger contemporary the Reverend Walter Davenport Bromley, whose drawing room at Wootton was given over entirely to his books and early Italian panels.[53] That both Northwick's and Bromley's pictures were sent for sale almost immediately after the death of each man suggests how difficult it was for normal families to absorb such maverick collections.

By way of conclusion I will glance at the gallery formed by another contemporary of Lord Northwick, the 2nd Earl of Normanton, who succeeded his father in 1809 at the age of thirty-one and lived until 1869. If his taste was less inspired than that of his uncle, Welbore Ellis Agar—represented in *The Treasure Houses of Britain* exhibition by the Westminster Claudes and Velasquez (THB nos. 310, 311, 497)—it was wider in range. The original arrangement of the gallery he created at Somerley was recorded with precision in two pictures by J. Walker (figs. 21, 22).

The hang of the pictures, which—unlike the late-nineteenth-century arrangements at Bridgewater House—were not rigidly aligned above or below, is interesting in several ways. Implicit claims are made for the status of English painting, and for Sir Joshua Reynolds in particular.

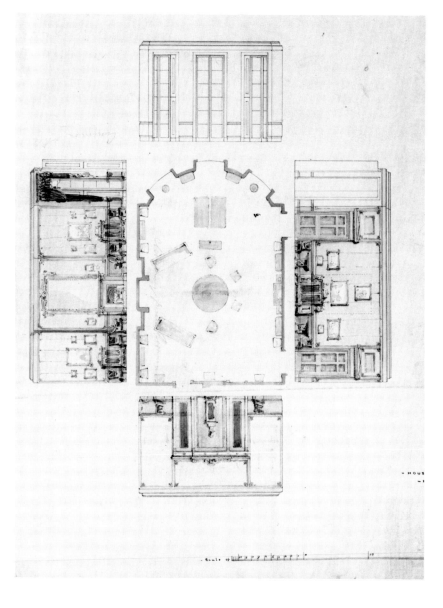

The end wall of the Gallery is dominated by William Beechey's portrait of King George III, which is flanked by family portraits: a Reynolds above the chimneypiece and, opposite, many of the large *modelli* for his great window at New College, Oxford, secured at Lady Thomond's sale. Normanton also bought with discernment works by contemporary painters: Sir David Wilkie, for instance, and Richard Parkes Bonington. But although the earl gave England the place of honor, he certainly prized his old masters. The arrangement was determined by symmetry. Religious pictures, whether Italian or

Fig. 20.
Design for the drawing room at 57 Harley Street by John Buonarotti Papworth (The British Architectural Library, RIBA)

Fig. 21.
The picture gallery at Somerley by
J. Walker (The Earl of Normanton,
Somerley)

Fig. 22.
The picture gallery at Somerley by
J. Walker (The Earl of Normanton,
Somerley)

by Sir Joshua, might be set beside Dutch land-scapes. Cabinet pictures were hung below. Other small but easily legible works, like the Madonna by Sassoferrato or the Holy Family by Carlo Maratta now at The Toledo Museum of Art, could be placed higher. The top line was reserved for larger "gallery" pictures, and the position there of the autograph version of Ti-tian's *Venus and Adonis* must explain why this work, admittedly a relatively inexpensive pur-chase, has been consistently underrated by most recent critics. Some echo of the pride Norman-ton felt in his collection may be sensed in the *Who's Who* entry of his descendant, the 5th Earl, who died in 1967: "owns about 7,000 acres; possesses picture gallery at Somerley." At a time when both acres and pictures are in so many cases under threat, it is salutary to remember the contribution personal taste and dynastic senti-ment have made to both the collecting and the display of pictures in British houses.

NOTES

I must thank Gervase Jackson-Stops for asking me to survey this sub-ject. Both John Cornforth and John Harris have helped me consider-ably; the former's paper explores the question of the color and materi-als against which pictures were hung, and I therefore touch on this only incidentally. I am particularly grateful to the Duke of Buccleuch and Miss Lorna MacEchern for enabling me to study the inventories and accounts for Montagu House and Boughton House. I am also in-debted to the researches of Miss Georgina Stonor, and, for information about individual collections and houses, to the Earl of Belmore, the Lady Burton, Mr. Peter Day, the Hon. Mrs. Gascoigne, Mr. Freder-ick Jolly, Sir Oliver Millar, the Hon. Mrs. Roberts, Mr. and Mrs. John Warde, and Mrs. Hugh Sackville West. Hugo Chapman has helped me with the proofs.

1. George Knox, "Sebastiano Ricci at Burlington House: a Venetian decoration 'alla Romana,'" *Burlington Magazine* 127 (1985), 601–609.

2. John Harris observes that the Van Dycks now at Wilton may have remained in London longer than is generally sup-posed.

3. It is, however, clear that by no means all the Grand Tour ac-quisitions now at Uppark were always intended for the house. The Batoni portraits constitute at least two series, and the Lacroix copies of some of the Vernets in the collection cannot have been intended for the same setting. The explanation must be that part of the extant collection was in Fetherstonhaugh's London house in Whitehall or in the possession of his brother-in-law Benjamin Lethuillier.

4. The inventories cited in this and the next paragraph are at Boughton.

5. Inventories, Boughton.

6. Framing bills inevitably crop up in many accounts for the fitting up of new or remodeled houses. Pelletier's Montagu ac-count is exceptional only in its scale and detail. So many frames have been replaced or regilded that we probably have a dis-torted impression of framing taste in the early eighteenth cen-tury. Thus, few examples of frames with simulated wood-graining now survive, though these were not uncommon.

7. Sarah, Duchess of Marlborough to Lady Russell, 5 July 1732. Quoted by J. H. Wiffen, *Historical Memoirs of the House of Rus-sell from the Time of the Norman Conquest* (London, 1833), 2:334.

8. John Cornforth and Leo Schmidt, "Holkham Hall, Nor-folk," *Country Life* (24, 31 January, 7, 14 February 1980), 214–217, 298–301, 359–362, 427–431.

9. T. S. Rosoman, "The Decoration and Use of the Principal Apartments of Chiswick House, 1727–1770," *Burlington Maga-zine* 127 (1985), 663–677.

10. A series of hanging plans now at Chatsworth, made for the Devonshire House collection in 1836, identify the pictures re-moved to Chatsworth by the 6th Duke.

11. Matthew Brettingham, *The Plans, Elevations, and Sections of Holkham in Norfolk, to which are added, the ceilings and chimney-pieces; . . . statues, pictures, and drawings, etc.* (London, 1773).

12. For a view in color, see Cornforth and Schmidt 1980, 361.

13. Pierre Jacques Fougeroux, "Voyage d'Angleterre d'Hol-lande et de Flandre, 1728," mss. Victoria and Albert Museum, London, fol. 83.

14. The pictures on the far wall are apparently a pair of histori-cal scenes with small figures in architectural settings. On the

wall on the right, in the upper tier, are a male portrait of seventeenth-century character and a large *Lamentation* to the right; below these, from the left, are a narrow upright *Assumption* (?) above a small reclining goddess, a *Holy Family with the Infant Baptist,* and another religious picture with a kneeling (?) woman, possibly an *Annunciation.*

15. John Fowler and John Cornforth, *English Decoration in the Eighteenth Century* (London, 1974), pl. 209. Mr. Gore informs me that evidence has come to light that this and the companion plans were drawn by an assistant of James Paine.

16. John Harris, *The Palladians* (London, 1982), no. 92. I am indebted to Mr. Harris for bringing this series of drawings to my notice. For architectural projects for the same house, see nos. 87–91.

17. *London and Its Environs Described* (London, 1761), 3:83–100.

18. *London* 1761, 1:271–273.

19. Another large collection listed in *London* 1761, 5:76–97, was in the townhouse of Charles Jennens. The catalogue is too telegraphic to give any clear idea of the arrangement of the collection, but the annotation of a drawing for Jennens' Leicestershire seat, Gopsall Hall, attributed to William and David Hiorne, is suggestive: "A Section of Dining Room Design'd for Charles Jennens Esqr. with the Pannels plain, being to be covered with Valuable Paintings." John Harris, *The Design of the English Country House* (Washington, 1985), no. 36.

20. One of a series of ten projects for a drawing room and a music room, sale, Christie's, 24 March 1982, lots 92–96; this drawing was lot 92.

21. One of a large series of drawings from the same source, this was sold at Christie's, 30 November 1983, as part of lot 163.

22. See John Hardy and Helena Haywood, "Kedleston Hall, Derbyshire," *Country Life* (2 February 1978), 264.

23. Leslie Harris, conversation with the author.

24. Harris 1985, no. 43.

25. Giles Worsley, "Nuneham Park Revisited," *Country Life* (3, 10 January 1985), 16–19, 64–67.

26. Harcourt mss., Bodleian Library, Oxford. Adair's account covers the period from 27 October 1758 to 28 May 1763.

27. Since this was written, the National Trust has reverted to the original arrangement in the room.

28. The Van de Cappelle is shown in its present frame, which is by the same craftsman as at least two others still at Aske. All the frames on the fireplace wall were English, and those of the Pynacker and the Cuyp, which are identical, were presumably made for Dundas when the pictures in question were paired.

29. I am indebted to Hugh Roberts for this observation.

30. Francis Russell, "Three and Four Deep," *Country Life* (4 June 1987), pp. 218–219. Warde's catalogue will be edited by the present writer in the *Burlington Magazine.*

31. Viscount Vane, Easton Lodge, near Winchester, sale, Christie's, 8 January 1774.

32. Stephen, Lord Holland, Holland House, London, sale, Christie's, 20 November 1775.

33. Humphrey Hanmer (d. 1773), Hanmer Hall, Flintshire, sale, Christie's, 31 July 1775.

34. Sir Joshua Vanneck (d. 1777), sale, Christie's, 2 November 1778.

35. The 5th Earl of Scarbrough, Sandbeck Park, Yorkshire, sale, Christie's, 11 August 1785.

36. The 5th Earl of Scarbrough, Lumley Castle, County Durham, sale, Christie's, 24 August 1785.

37. A watercolor by Mrs. Percy Wyndham, in the possession of Lord Egremont, is the most accurate record of the gallery at Petworth in the nineteenth century. See John Cornforth, *English Interiors 1790–1848: The Quest for Comfort* (London, 1978), pl. 20.

38. E. McParland, *Castle Coole* (London, 1980), 10.

39. The rediscovery of these drawings was generously communicated to me by the Hon. Mrs. Roberts shortly before my departure for Washington. For a full account, see Francis Russell, "King George III's Picture-Hang at Buckingham House," *Burlington Magazine* 129 (1987), 524–531.

40. For the most authoritative available account in this field, see John Cornforth, "Symmetry and Shapes, Patterns of Picture-Hanging—II," *Country Life* (11 June 1981), 1698–1699.

41. Gustav Friedrich Waagen, *Works of Art and Artists in England* (London, 1838), 2:303.

42. Pyne's watercolors prepared for his *History of the Royal Residences* (London, 1819), are in the Royal Collection at Windsor.

43. J. H. Jesse, *George Selwyn and His Contemporaries* (London, 1843–1844), 3:28.

44. Gervase Jackson-Stops, "Temples of the Arts," *The Treasure Houses of Britain* [exh. cat., National Gallery of Art] (Washington, 1985), fig. 3.

45. Quoted by W. T. Whitley, *Art in England, London, 1800–1820* (Cambridge, 1928), 106. For a view of the gallery at 24 Hill Street, see Cornforth 1978, pl. 166.

46. Peter Thornton, *Authentic Decor* (London, 1984), pl. 247, for Buckler's watercolor of 1808.

47. A view of the Grand Drawing Room at Fonthill was engraved by Stedman Whitwell after John Cleghorn for John Rutter, *Delineations of Fonthill and Its Abbey* (London, 1823), pl. 5.

48. See George McHardy, *Catalogue of the Drawings Collection of the Royal Institute of British Architects, Office of J. B. Papworth* (London, 1975), nos. 1–42, 178.

49. Waagen 1838, 3:11–12.

50. Waagen 1838, 2:3.

51. The Marquis of Zetland, ed., *The Letters of Disraeli to Lady Bradford and Lady Chesterfield* (London, 1929), 1:239.

52. The best-known view of the interior of Thirlestane House is the anonymous watercolor in the collection of the Knight of Glin; see Cornforth 1978, pl. 144.

53. A watercolor of the room, now at Capesthorne, by James Johnson is published by John Cornforth, "Family Histories in Watercolour, Capesthorne Hall, Cheshire—II, *Country Life* (8 September 1977), 607; for an account of the pictures, see Francis Russell, "Italian Art and the Clerical Collector," *Country Life* (5 December 1985), 1749–1750.

JOHN CORNFORTH

A Georgian Patchwork

At the new De Witt Wallace Decorative Arts Gallery at Colonial Williamsburg, eighteenth-century English and American artifacts are shown together against a neutral background, as a deliberate contrast to the arrangement in the buildings of the historic area. The aim is to concentrate the eye through the isolation of objects. In *The Treasure Houses of Britain* exhibition, on the other hand, the aim was to relate objects to their setting and to convey the mood of country-house interiors over the past four hundred years. I want to take this second approach a stage further, developing suggestions made in the decoration of two of the exhibition rooms focusing on the eighteenth century: the red room devoted to "Lord Burlington and the Palladian Revolution," and the blue "Souvenirs of the Grand Tour" room. In both of them pictures were hung against a bold damask pattern based on original Georgian wallpapers and textiles.

What follows is almost a first attempt to deal with this subject, and I should explain that I came to make it as a result of Gervase Jackson-Stops' persuasion. He said he wanted something on textiles and patterns, and I realized that I had quite a lot of scraps of information, perhaps enough to make a patchwork. That, at least, gave me a title. However, I am not a textile expert but a squirrel who likes seemingly useless pieces of information to do with attitudes to patterns, the applications of patterns, materials, colors, and so on—often tiny fragments that may come in useful at some time.

Once I began to make a pile of my scraps, I realized not only how broad the subject was, but how elusive. I also realized that people today are much less used to looking at pattern and ornament than they must have been in the eighteenth century. This is partly because of the antiornament bias of the modern movement, but also because few people today have the chance to buy elaborately patterned materials. Most choose their clothes off the peg rather than visit the descendant of the silk mercer and the woollen draper, where they might train their eye.

If one considers English taste in the eighteenth century, what is so striking is the way that patrons strove for unity—in their houses, their gardens, and their landscapes, in plans, decoration, and furnishing. Inevitably they did not always succeed in this, and what has survived is only a small part of what they did achieve. However, as we find out more about the century we become increasingly aware of how the fine and applied arts and the spirit of technical enterprise all interlocked in the service of unity. It is here that pattern comes in, not least because it is often the combination of pattern and texture that holds a room together. When the hangings are taken down from the walls of an eighteenth-century room and not replaced, the chances are that the room, the pictures, and the furniture will all fall apart.

A few scholars have worked in specialized related fields, among them Peter Thornton on baroque silks, Natalie Rothstein on Spitalfields silk, and Florence Montgomery on printed cotton, but there is very little general literature to start one off. Thus, to give an idea of some of the patterns found in eighteenth-century English houses and how they were used—particularly in relation to the kind of pictures and furniture seen in the eighteenth-century rooms in *The Treasure Houses of Britain* exhibition—I want to concentrate on materials in big pieces and on some wallpapers. This is not easy, particularly because there are so few contemporary views of rooms. Conversation pieces are seldom wholly satisfactory evidence, for even the rooms that appear entirely convincing, like that in Johan Zoffany's picture of Sir Lawrence Dundas and his grandson at 19 Arlington Street (THB no. 281), is a composition made specially for the picture. I know of no accurate series of interiors earlier than those of Strawberry Hill,[1] most of which are now in the Lewis Walpole Library at Farmington, Connecticut, and I have not come across many others until the early nineteenth century.

I must stress that the survival rate of patterns is very uneven. There is a preponderance of grand materials and flock wallpapers from the first seventy years of the eighteenth century, but there is much less from the last thirty years, when more use was made of lighter materials, and wallpapers tended to be stuck straight onto the plaster, no longer treated as printed hangings and mounted on scrim and battens.

I had hoped that what would emerge from the sorting of my scraps was some fairly broad but clear picture of the way patterns developed in relation to architectural style during the course of the eighteenth century, with pattern responding to the dictates of architecture. But I soon came to realize that it was naive of me to expect this, because the histories of architecture and ornament have not necessarily been in step. Ornament and pattern have a life of their own, distinct from architecture and influenced by a whole range of nonarchitectural considerations. Thus, while there are obviously rococo patterns in materials and wallpapers, the few known wall hangings associated with the Palladian period cannot really be described as Palladian; they are Italian. And, where one expects to find English neo-classical patterns of the kind made familiar by the silks associated with Philippe de la Salle and the wallpapers of Reveillon, there appears to be an unexpected gap in the 1760s and 1770s. The wallpaper in the Palladio Room at Clandon Park, Surrey,[2] and the hangings in the White Drawing Room at Houghton Hall, Norfolk,[3] dating to the 1780s and 1790s, are exceptions, but also great rarities. The patterns that are usually said to be Adam are much more often "Adam Revival" of the 1880s and 1890s.

So, rather than attempt to make my patchwork go in stripes, decade by decade through the century, I thought that I would try to suggest some of the factors that appeared to affect the choices of pattern, color, and material, looking first at some of the grand designs that were fashionable until about 1770, and then, more briefly, at the impact on textile and wallpaper design of developments in printing. For lack of space I have omitted tapestry, Chinese wallpapers, and Indian chintzes, and their influence.

Fortunately there are fascinating letters from the opening years of the eighteenth century that immediately plunge us into detailed accounts of rich patrons ordering fine materials.[4] In 1707 the

Earl of Manchester, Vanbrugh's patron at Kimbolton Castle in Huntingdonshire and at that time ambassador to the Low Countries, was sent on an embassy to Venice. There he immediately became active on behalf of the Duchess of Marlborough, who wanted advice about huge orders of materials for Blenheim Palace in Oxfordshire, where building was underway. What is striking about the correspondence is the importance that such patrons attached to materials used in a great house, what they were prepared to spend on

Fig. 1.
A corner of the State Bedchamber at Kimbolton Castle, Huntingdonshire, 1911 (*Country Life*)

them in terms of money and effort, and also the extent to which the choice was theirs. In Lord Manchester's case, the cut velvet used in the old state bedroom at Kimbolton (fig. 1) is markedly richer than the room itself, for none of the moldings of the cornice or of the dado were carved, as might be expected in a room of parade. Unfortunately the room can only be judged from old photographs; Kimbolton was sold after the Second World War and is now a school.

On 6 July 1708 Lord Manchester wrote to the duchess an immensely long letter in which he said:

It is always best to have rather more than less [of what] you shall want, for in the measuring of the rooms they may be mistaken. Besides, there must be chairs, window curtains, and for the doors, according to the manner in Italy, which looks very handsome, and is as cheap as anything, I think, as can be made of silk. The height of the hangings for the rooms I must know; else there will be a great loss when they come to be cut to make the figures join right, for they can be made to what height you please.[5]

The duchess was duly grateful for this advice. She said his directions were so exact that it would be her fault if there were any mistakes, and that she would keep the information carefully until the duke "takes a resolution to furnish Woodstock."[6] The ambassador also sent someone to Genoa to ask about damasks and velvets for the duchess. He discovered, to his surprise, that there was no quantity of either ready made. "Whatever is sent from Genoa is bespoke, and [in] about four months time the quantity may be had by employing so many more. My Lord Rivers has two pieces making of yellow damask. He sent the pattern from England drawn upon paper."[7]

In one letter the Duchess said she wanted 1300 yards of green damask, 600 of yellow, 600 of crimson, 200 yards of both scarlet and blue velvet, 100 yards of scarlet damask, and 200 yards of scarlet satin and blue satin to match the velvets.[8] Lord Manchester made a note that he had bought for her 4,755 1/4 Venetian yards of damasks and velvets, which was 3,300 English yards, and that including the cost of transport to England the total came to £2,139 19s. The idea was to send it on a man-of-war and so avoid paying customs duties.

I do not believe that any of the duchess' materials survive in the state rooms at Blenheim today, and I need hardly say that no house in England has survived absolutely intact. However, the nearest thing to a complete interior is the Nostell dolls house (THB no. 590), which is a microcosm of a country house in about 1740.[9] It gives a clear picture of the grading of different parts of the house: the combination of economy and practicality on the ground floor or "rustic," in such details as the leather seats on the chairs in the parlor; the demonstration of rich dignity on the *piano nobile* above; and the nice distinctions between the treatment of these rooms of state and the family rooms on the attic floor above, with crimson velvet giving way to exotic and light printed or painted cotton. Indeed, the dolls house confirms all the evidence of such gradations that I have come across in houses and documents.

Here it is necessary to remember the distinction between what Sir John Summerson has called the greater country house, with its rooms of parade, and the villa.[10] In the first fifty or sixty years of the century the greater house represented the ideal, and dominated attitudes toward decoration and furnishing; but during the late 1750s and early 1760s the concept of the greater house went out of fashion and the villa became the dominant form, bringing with it rather different approaches to life, different requirements of decoration and furnishing, and thus different materials and patterns, too.

It is interesting to see how old houses, as well, were replanned, redecorated, and refurnished in the third quarter of the century. Two houses that are revealing in this respect are Hatfield House in Hertfordshire[11] and Dalkeith Palace near Edinburgh.[12] Surviving documents give a strong sense of the way the owners and their wives altered the character of their houses in order to bring them into line with the lighter feeling and the less formal way of dressing and living that was expressed in contemporary villas. The elaborately worked materials that had survived at Dalkeith from the beginning of the century gave way to chintz and painted furniture in the 1770s, just as the formal setting of the house had been swept away in 1769 and replaced by a "picturesque" landscape. The way of life had changed too. In 1781 Lady Carlow wrote to Lady Louisa Stuart: "There is a perfect ease reigns here, which you must know makes all places pleasant, and particularly so for people that are lazy, as they live in their riding habits even on public days, so there's very little time spent on the toilet."[13] Two years earlier Lady Louisa had written of Archerfield near North Berwick: "It wants nothing but more furniture for the middle

Fig. 2.
Engraved cross section of Holkham Hall, Norfolk, from Matthew Brettingham, *Plans and Elevations of the late Earl of Leicester's House at Holkham*, 1761 (The British Architectural Library, RIBA, Drawings Collection)

of rooms, I mean all is set out in order, no comfortable tables to write or read at; it looks like a fine London house prepared for company; quite a contrast to the delightful gallery at Dalkeith, where you can settle yourself in any corner."[14]

These remarks are particularly revealing because they hint at two things that tend to get forgotten. First, the difference in fashion, mood, and style between country houses and houses in London, which probably developed quite markedly in the course of the century, and second, the fact that the modern idea of country clothes, at least for men, was by that time established. François de la Rochefoucauld noted in 1784, after staying with the Duke of Grafton: "In the morning you come down in riding boots and a shabby coat, you sit where you like, you behave exactly as if you were by yourself, no one takes any notice of you, and it is all extremely comfortable." On the other hand, in the evening "unless you have just arrived, you must be well washed and well groomed. The standard of politeness is uncomfortably high."[15]

The changing quality of light in English rooms should also be borne in mind, though I am not aware of contemporary references to it. If, however, one thinks about changes in window design in the eighteenth century, it is obvious that the level of light in many rooms increased. As people grew more appreciative of light and sunlight, they would naturally have reacted against the light-absorbing textures of tapestry, velvet, and damask, expressing enthusiasm for the light-reflecting qualities of wallpaper and for airy, open patterns. Similarly, the appeal of plain wallpapers, which began to be used in the third quarter of the century, lay partly in

their simple, clear colors, partly in the way they threw up pictures, but surely also in the way light bounced off them, particularly if they were slightly glazed.

All this may be general, but it helps to put into context what Isaac Ware had to say about daylight and night light in his *A Complete Body of Architecture,* published in 1756, given that the cost of candles was always a consideration. Ware pointed out that a wainscotted room that was painted was the lightest, after that came stucco, and hung rooms were the darkest. All this, he said, affected the number of candles required: six for a wainscotted room, eight for a stucco room, and ten for a hung room.[16] It is interesting to compare Ware's statements with a story told by William Cole of Lord and Lady Hardwicke at Wimpole Hall in Cambridgeshire in the mid-eighteenth century. Cole describes them "discussing the painting of the room they usually sit in . . . my Lord was for having it an ash or olive colour as being cheaper and more durable. But my Lady objected that, though more expensive, the fashionable French white would be cheaper in the end" since it enabled the room to be lit by two instead of four candles.[17]

What makes the overall picture harder to grasp is that the place that provides the fullest evidence of materials used in a greater house of the first half of the century—Holkham Hall in Norfolk[18]—was only finished in the late 1750s and early 1760s. However, Holkham is fortunately complemented to some extent by its slightly earlier neighbor, Houghton.

Although William Kent had a major hand in the conception of Holkham and had an undoubted feeling for decorating and furnishing a great house, the rooms on the south front (fig.

Fig. 3.
Detail of the caffoy wall hangings in the saloon at Holkham   (*Country Life*)

Fig. 4.
The West Drawing Room at Holkham   (*Country Life*)

2) were not actually designed by him and they were fitted up after his death; indeed, it was largely thanks to the determination of Lady Leicester that they were finally finished during her widowhood. The key to their furnishing lies in the enormous mercers bill of 1755, when Robert Carr was paid no less than £3,166 13s. Luckily, much of the material listed in the bill is still in situ at Holkham, giving one an idea of the progression of textiles through the state rooms. The double doors at the head of the stairs in the apse of the great hall lead into the saloon, which is hung with a material usually described today as cut velvet but referred to by an early visitor, the Duchess of Northumberland as "caffoy" (fig. 3):[19] a mixture of crimson silk and wool. The two rooms flanking the saloon are hung with silk cut velvet, also crimson but of a much finer

texture and a more delicate pattern. In the West Drawing Room to the left of the saloon (fig. 4), where the pictures on the chimneypiece wall are in their original positions, the velvet has been rewoven, but the original material survives in the balancing drawing room on the east (fig. 5). The Landscape Room, beyond the East Drawing Room, was originally the state dressing room, and was hung with crimson damask. Thus there was a unity of color but a progression of patterns and textures in these rooms. The state bedroom was hung with tapestry, as was the usual practice, and the bed was hung with a three-color cut velvet (fig. 6), which by an odd coincidence is of the same pattern as the bed designed by John Vardy now at Hardwick Hall, Derbyshire (figs. 7, 8). The caffoy cost about 16s. a yard, the crimson cut velvet above £1 18s., and the three-color velvet about £3 9s.

It is interesting to be able to compare the materials at Holkham with what is known about those at Houghton, where inventories were taken on Sir Robert Walpole's death in 1745 and on his son Horace's inheritance in 1792. Again, a stone hall leads through to the saloon hung with caffoy, as John Loveday described it in 1731.[20] The rest of the great apartment was hung with green velvet, even though there are variations in the patterns of the chairs. Bearing in mind Lady Burlington's observation to her husband that "in any velvet that is much used, there will be always the print of people's sitting,"[21] it was an obvious extravagance, quite apart from the association of green with Venus and with sleep, which were the themes of the state bedroom. The family drawing room to the left of the saloon, where there was no architectural gilding, was done with yellow caffoy hangings and yellow upholstery on walnut furniture; it may be that the furniture now in the library, which looks like old gold cut velvet, is part of that suite. The damask hangings with a huge sunflower pattern now in the drawing room were copied in the 1920s from a bedspread at Houghton by Lord and Lady Cholmondeley, and in 1745 there was a yellow damask bedroom on the second floor; the same pattern was used on a bed at Leeds Castle and is now in the Victoria and Albert Museum.[22] One refinement that I have not seen in any other house is that the backs of the saloon chairs are covered in a red moreen impressed with the same pattern as that of the caffoy.

It is likely that similar ideas about the progres-

Fig. 5.
Detail of the velvet wall hangings in the West Drawing Room at Holkham   (*Country Life*)

Fig. 6.
Detail of the three-color velvet in the State Bedroom at Holkham
(*Country Life*)

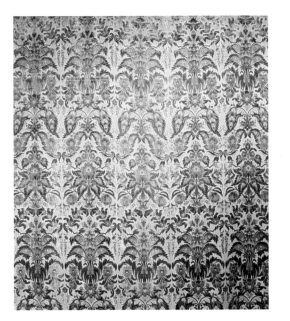

sion of materials were found in other houses furnished in the second quarter of the eighteenth century. One place where this happened was at Erddig in North Wales, in the 1720s. John Loveday noted in 1732 "ye apartments handsome, & furnished in ye grandest manner, & after ye newest fashion. They are furnished with Mohair, Coffoy Damasks etc"[23] (fig. 9).

Houghton, Holkham, and Erddig lead us in several directions, posing a number of questions. How long did the idea of a progression of stuffs last? When did the idea of hanging all the rooms of an apartment in the same stuff come in? And who did the choosing of the stuffs: the patron, the architect, or the upholsterer?

As far as the first of these questions is concerned, I suspect that Holkham was almost old fashioned by the time it was finished, although the details of its design continued to evolve right up to the moment of Lord Leicester's death in 1759. By the late 1750s there was another way of treating state rooms, as could be seen at Woburn Abbey in Bedfordshire. In 1756 the Duke of Bedford paid Robert Swann the mercer £500 for blue damask for the state rooms, and the material was put up in 1760.[24] Horace Walpole describes how "the whole apartment is hung with blue damask; and the pictures in the Dressing Room are too small for state rooms.[25] But the gallery at Woburn was hung with paper, as if there was a distinction between history pictures and landscapes in state rooms and a range of family portraits in a gallery.

In light of the uniformity of Woburn, it is worth remembering the treatment of the principal rooms at Norfolk House, Saint James's Square, which belonged to the Duke of Norfolk and his francophile wife. William Farington went to the opening of the Grand Apartment in February 1756, and afterward wrote: "there were in all eleven rooms Open, three below, the rest above, every room was furnish'd with a different colour, which used to be reckon'd absurd, but this I Suppose is to be the Standard."[26] On the first floor (fig. 10) at the head of the stairs, guests went first into the anteroom and then into three rooms overlooking the square: the paneled Music Room (removed to the Victoria and Albert Museum when the house was demolished in the 1930s); the Green Damask Room; and the Flowered Red Velvet Room, presumably decorated with a material like that at Holkham. Behind these lay the Great Drawing Room or Tapestry Room, hung with a set of

Fig. 9.
Pair of chairs with caffoy covers at Erddig Park, Clwyd, North Wales, one shown before, and the other after restoration *(Country Life)*

Gobelins *Les Nouvelles Indes.* Then, at the back, lay the state bedroom, hung with what Farington described as blue velour; the dressing room with Chinese painted taffeta or satin; and the china closet with taffeta painted with flowers. There seems to have been a surprising amount of painted materials in the mid-eighteenth century, but little survives except in a bedroom on the second floor at Houghton[27] and on a bed at Osterley Park, Middlesex.[28]

The variety within a succession of rooms found at Norfolk House does not seem to have caught on, and it is interesting to see how Robert Adam combined uniformity with variety at Osterley, when he took over there in 1766.[29] The series of richly decorated rooms contrast with each other, but they also lead on from one to another, being linked through the use of green. In the gallery, pea-green paper and green damask upholstery were introduced in 1767; the drawing room was hung with pale green damask in 1772 and the dado was painted green; in the ante room, for which Gobelins tapestries were or-dered in 1772, the skirting was painted green; and in the adjoining bedroom, where the bed was designed between 1775 and 1776 and the carpet in 1778, the walls were described by Horace Walpole as being hung with light-green plain velvet.[30] This kind of control through color, involving an architect, seems to have been fairly new, and it is illuminating to compare Adam's drawings with those of James Stuart,[31] William Chambers, and Chambers' followers. In 1757 Stuart started to show works of art and pieces of furniture in his drawings of rooms, with some indication of colors, and in about 1759 Chambers produced a sectional design for York House in Pall Mall, London,[32] that not only shows the architectural decoration in detail but also indicates colors and patterns for walls. This idea was taken up in drawings by Edward Stevens (fig. 11)[33] in 1763 and then by John Yenn (fig. 12).[34]

In engraved sections of houses it was still un-usual to suggest the treatment of walls—other than stucco, of course—and except for one or

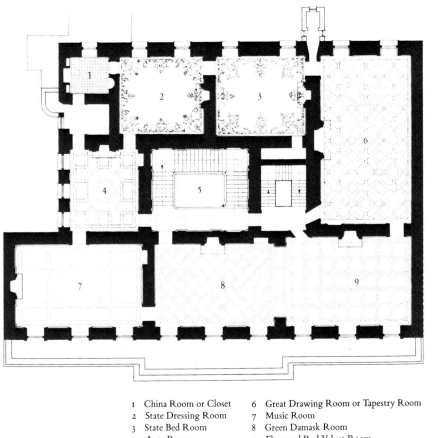

1 China Room or Closet   6 Great Drawing Room or Tapestry Room
2 State Dressing Room   7 Music Room
3 State Bed Room   8 Green Damask Room
4 Ante Room   9 Flowered Red Velvet Room
5 Great Staircase

Fig. 10.
Plan of the first floor of Norfolk House, Saint James's Square, London. The names of the rooms are taken from an inventory of about 1756 (Reproduced from *Survey of London*)

two plates in Thomas Chippendale's *The Director* of 1754, few engraved designs for furniture before those of George Hepplewhite in 1787 and of Thomas Sheraton between 1791 and 1793 show patterns for upholstery. John Linnell suggests damask on some of the seat furniture in his drawings, but without any attempt to show patterns accurately. Only in some of Adam's drawings for seat furniture, such as in those for Audley End, does one see materials that correspond with what was actually used.[35]

Changes in the furnishing trades were to have a profound effect on the kinds of patterns and materials used, and on who supplied them. In the late seventeenth and early eighteenth century it was the upholsterer, not the cabinetmaker, who was the dominant figure in the furnishing trades, and, as Karen Walton has pointed out,[36] in the Duke of Chandos' household at Canons in

Middlesex the upholsterer dined in the main dining room with the senior members of the household, while the cabinetmaker was relegated to the servants' quarters. In about 1750, however, the balance between these two tradespeople began to change, particularly as a result of the growing fashion for lighter, more portable chairs with splat backs, and for showing the frames of beds. Chippendale's *The Director* makes the point particularly clearly, for the publication is called *The Gentleman and Cabinet Makers Director*. Not only did the cabinetmaker start to win against the upholsterer in the middle of the century, but the mercer, too, seems to have lost some of his prominence. The mercer is now a more-or-less forgotten figure in the history of the eighteenth-century interior, and while a great deal of research has been done on furniture makers, even the names of the leading mercers are unfamiliar, except to textile experts. Theirs, however, was a trade that required a great deal of capital. R. Campbell in his *London Tradesman* of 1747 said:

He deals in silks, velvets, brocades and an innumerable Train of expensive Trifles, for the Ornament of the Fair Sex . . . must have a great deal of the Frenchman in his Manners, as well as a large Parcel of French goods in his Shop; he ought to keep close Intelligence with the Fashion-Office at Paris, and supply himself with the newest Patterns of that most changeable People. . . . The Business of a Mercer requires a very considerable Stock; Ten thousand pounds, without a great deal of prudent Management, makes but a small Figure in their Way.[37]

He reckoned a banker needed a minimum of twenty thousand pounds to set up as a master in his trade, a brewer two thousand to ten thousand, a factor of coals one to ten thousand, and a laceman, a mercer, a wool stapler, and a woollen draper one to ten thousand pounds. Compared with this, an upholsterer only needed between one hundred and one thousand pounds, a carver from fifty to one or two hundred pounds, a cabinetmaker from two hundred to two thousand pounds, and a paper-hanging printer from one to two hundred.

To what extent owners discussed materials with upholsterers I do not know, but Chambers liked to be consulted, and so did Adam. In 1768, for instance, Lady Shelburne noted: "The morning I spent as usual and got some patterns of silk for Furniture of Buck and Swann. Mr. Adams dined here . . . with the latter I consulted on the furniture of our painted Anti Chamber & determined that it should be pea green satin spotted with white and trimmed with a pink and white

Fig. 11.
Cross section of a town house designed by Edward Stevens, signed and dated 1763, watercolor (The British Architectural Library, RIBA, Drawings Collection)

Fig. 12.
Cross section of a house designed by John Yenn, c. 1785, watercolor (Royal Academy of Arts)

fringe. . . . It was originally my own thought & met with his entire approbation."[38] She then went on to say that she had ordered one hundred yards of spotted satin from Buck and Swann.

Sometimes the upholsterer would supply the material himself, as happened at Hopetoun House, near Edinburgh, in 1766. James Cullen the upholsterer wrote to his client that he had an opportunity to get eight hundred yards of damask at 13s.6d. a yard, which a nobleman had brought from abroad but not used because he was going abroad again.[39]

On a surprising number of occasions an owner seems to have obtained his material from abroad, often with the help of a friend or contact. Diplomats were particularly useful, as in the case of Lord Manchester and the Duchess of Marlborough, but the Duke of Chandos got damask and velvet from Genoa,[40] the Duke of Bedford got scarlet damask from Genoa,[41] and Horace Mann, the British consul in Florence, evidently helped several friends, including Horace Walpole.[42] When John Parker, later 1st Lord Boringdon, enlarged Saltram in Devon, he built on a great saloon to Adam's design and bought a carpet for it made by Thomas Whitty of Axminster. On 17

September 1769 Mrs. Parker wrote to her brother, Frederick Robinson: "We must further trouble you to send some patterns of Blue Damask, as we shall soon write to Genoa and wish to fix upon the best Blue for setting off the Pictures.[43] The material cost three hundred pounds the following year.

Again and again in the eighteenth century, the choice of material and color was made primarily to suit pictures, and it is quite clear that cut velvet of a single color, plain velvet, or damask were considered the richest and most handsome background for subject pictures. Crimson was the most expensive color and was thought the grandest and most suitable for pictures, looking splendid both in damask and cut velvet, particularly with gilding. As Sarah, Duchess of Marlborough wrote to her granddaughter, an earlier Lady Diana Spencer, in 1732: "Though several people have larger rooms, what you have is as much as is of any real use to anybody, and the white painting with so much red damask looks mightily handsome."[44]

On occasion owners quite deliberately chose a color other than crimson, as was the case at Longford Castle, near Salisbury, where the 1st

Fig. 13.
The Round Drawing Room at
Longford Castle, Wiltshire
(*Country Life*)

Viscount Folkestone used green damask in the gallery and green velvet in the Round Drawing Room (fig. 13).[45] The damask cost £170 and the velvet £1 5s. a yard and £150 in all, and Lord Folkestone bought it through a Mr. Hoare in Leghorn. The Duchess of Northumberland approved, and in her journal noted: "Taste in the Apartments dressed with Green, of which there are several furnish'd with different manufacture & various hues of this pleasing colour."[46] It is worth noting how the velvet is carefully cut to suit the backs and seats of the chairs, so that the pattern still reads symmetrically. Surprisingly little stamped wool velvet has survived in English houses, perhaps because of the delicate nature of wool pile. The only complete room of it known to me is at Knole.[47] The stamping of the wool velvet gives a two-tone effect, but without the contrast and cost of cut velvet.

A taste for striped materials as a ground for pictures did not develop until about 1770. Mrs. Lybbe Powys' reference in 1771 to the drawing room at Fawley Court in Buckinghamshire "being fitted up with every possible elegance of the present taste, hung with crimson strip'd damask, on which are to be pictures"[48] is an early example of this. Another was in the Green Velvet Drawing Room at Houghton Hall. After Sir Robert Walpole's pictures were sold to Catherine the Great in 1778, it was no doubt necessary to take down the original plain velvet, which would have been badly marked by the frames; it was replaced by green striped hangings that are mentioned in the Houghton inventory of 1792.[49]

The relationship between damask and flock paper is also interesting, because there are cases where one might expect damask but finds flock paper—as at Wilton House, Wiltshire (fig. 14) and at Uppark in Sussex. The owners of these properties were much richer than Mrs. Delany, but doubtless they would have agreed with her in 1742 when she noted "——is quite angry that I would not let my room be hung with mohair instead of paper, which I absolutely would not; it would have been ridiculous when I desire to cover it with pictures."[50] However, our expectation of the different uses of damask and flock may be slightly misguided, given the tendency to enrich wall decoration in the late eighteenth and early nineteenth century. There are two examples of this at Clandon Park in Surrey. When, in 1970, the state bed was taken out of the Green Drawing Room and the damask hangings were

taken down, a complete wallpaper of about 1730 was found behind them. No doubt the wallpaper seemed too crude to a later generation; and the same thing happened upstairs in the Prince Regent's Room.[51] Sometimes the process of enriching happened quite quickly, as was evidently the case at Felbrigg in Norfolk[52] and at Corsham Court in Wiltshire.[53] The accounts at Felbrigg mention a rich flowered paper being bought for the drawing room and Cabinet in the 1740s, but whereas the drawing room was hung with a damask of about 1824 with a thirty-inch repeat, the Cabinet has a mixed damask with an eight-foot repeat that cannot be nineteenth century

Fig. 14.
The Little Ante Room, Wilton House, Salisbury, Wiltshire (The Earl of Pembroke)

and must represent a change of mind on the part of William Windham in the 1750s or 1760s. The same thing happened at Corsham. The gallery formed in about 1761 was originally hung with a flock paper, but in 1769 it was rehung with damask supplied by Morris and Young at 13s.6d. a yard.

It is usually assumed that eighteenth-century collectors liked to hang fine pictures against material, and frequently material with a bold pattern. We ought, however, to be cautious about this, particularly after the mid-1760s, because quite apart from flock papers, which after all were intended to imitate damask, there was a considerable fashion for plain papers of the kind suggested in Johan Zoffany's painting of Sir Lawrence Dundas and described at Osterley and at Luton Hoo in Bedfordshire.[54] One of the earliest examples of this kind of paper that I have come across was in the Duchess of Portland's closet at Bulstrode in Buckinghamshire in 1758.[55]

If most wall hangings were chosen in relation to pictures, the converse must also be borne in mind, for there were patterns that were never intended to be covered with pictures. Some of the most interesting damask patterns were used in bedrooms, on beds where they could be "read" or on walls where there would be few pictures. This is true of the design found on the state bed at Hatfield House,[56] which has been identified as close to a damask designed by James Leman in about 1710, and to the cut velvet on the Londesborough bed at Hardwick Hall. Also there are, or rather were, a group of rooms at Audley End hung with what the Duchess of Northumberland called a "three colour damask."[57] What appears to be the original material in the Great Drawing Room can be seen in *Country Life* photographs taken in 1926, when the room contained the state bed (fig. 15).[58] Unfortunately the room was rehung in the 1960s with a poor copy of the original hangings. It was never intended that pictures should hang there, except over the chimneypiece. Indeed, there seems to have been a distinct fashion at one moment for having no pictures, just large, expensive pier glasses of French origin for which customs duties might or might not have been paid.

In 1764 Lady Caroline Fox, who was just back from Paris, wrote:

I am out of conceit with India paper, and am all for the magnificent style of single velvet damask etc. I have three immense looking glasses to put in my drawing room and propose hanging it with a damask or brocatelle of two or three colours. I am rather changeable to be sure in these things; but tho' whims and fripperies may have a run, one always returns to what is really handsome and noble and plain.[59]

Surely this was the idea in the Red Drawing Room at Syon House, Middlesex, where I suspect that the hangings are a nineteenth-century repeat because they appear on the dado (not a usual eighteenth-century practice) and on a Morel and Hughes settee in the Victoria and Albert Museum. Probably the most beautiful of such large-scale damasks was the one seen in old photographs of the Saloon at Brocket Hall in Hertforshire.[60] There appears to be a very complex pattern with the garlands linking up and the pattern "dropped."

The connection between color and pictures is also mentioned in Horace Walpole's letters to Horace Mann. In 1760, for instance, Walpole wrote: "I shall some time hence trouble you for some patterns of brocadella of two or three col-ours: it is to furnish a round tower that I am adding, with a gallery to my castle; the quantity I shall want will be pretty large, it is to be a bedchamber entirely hung, bed and eight arm chairs."[61] After a good deal more correspondence on the subject, he then wrote: "I don't approve damask at all, for as there will be no pictures in the chamber, nothing is more *triste* than a single colour." Horace Walpole's friend John Chute bought brocatelle of two different patterns in Italy in 1760 at a cost of 18s.6d. a yard,[62] and this still survives in three rooms at The Vyne in Hampshire (fig. 16). The only other house in which I have encountered this material as an eighteenth-century hanging is in the visitors' wing at Holkham Hall.

It would be interesting to know how early wallpapers were copied from textiles. One day at Christie's I happened to see an early eighteenth-century chair (fig. 17) and the pattern of the velvet or possibly caffoy seemed familiar; I ran it to earth as a flock in the Victoria and Albert Museum,[63] where it is combined with stamped leather (fig. 18), and described as the earliest known English flock paper in that collection. I also found it in the early eighteenth-century trade card of the Blew Paper Warehouse (fig. 19).[64]

Fig. 17.
Chair covered in velvet or caffoy, early 18th century   (Christie's, London)

Fig. 18.
Pattern of the earliest-known English flock paper   (Victoria and Albert Museum)

Fig. 19.
Advertisement of the Blue-Paper Warehouse, Aldermanbury, London, c. 1720. The pattern of the wallpaper displayed on the far left should be compared with figs. 17 and 18
(Gough Collection, Bodleian Library, Oxford)

The grand materials and patterns mentioned so far are only part of the total picture, and I must end by at least suggesting the impact of printed materials, examining them in the light of developments in printing in the second quarter of the eighteenth century. One important factor was the expansion of the print market, which led to such ventures as John Boydell's "Gallery" and other celebrated series of engravings. Another influence on wallpaper designs was the reproduction of works by the Old Masters. In the 1720s Elisha Kirkall, who was inspired by chiaroscuro woodcuts, worked in different colors of mezzotint and combined mezzotint, etching, and woodblocks; and in the 1730s Arthur Pond and George Knapton produced a series of small prints after Old Master drawings in English collections. In the late 1730s and early 1740s John Baptist Jackson produced wood engravings in color after Venetian pictures that are triumphs of printing, before going on to make designs for calico and then wallpaper in the late 1740s.

This kind of cross fertilization was important in the world of china, too. The Chelsea and Bow factories both started in 1745, and it is interesting to find that Thomas Craft, a painter at Bow, owned a considerable calico printing business. Similarly Thomas Frye, who was one of the founders of Bow, had started in Ireland as a portrait painter and made some of the most exciting mezzotints of the century. Thus it is possible to find the same engraving after Charles-

Fig. 20.
The Peter the Great Room, Blickling Hall, Norfolk   (The National Trust)

Nicolas Cochin the younger, published by Francis Vivares, used as a source of decoration both on a Bow plate of about 1756 and as a wallpaper at Doddington Hall, probably supplied in about 1762.[65] In the field of textiles, the great advance was Francis Nixon's invention of printing from large copper plates, which was first advertised in Ireland in 1752. On October 3 of that year *Faulkner's Journal,* published in Dublin, carried an advertisement for Drumcondra printed linens "Done from Metal Plates (a Method never before practised) with all the Advantages of Light and Shade, in the strongest and most lasting Colours."[66] Within a short time Mrs. Delany went to see them and pronounced them "excessively pretty."[67] Four years later Francis Nixon, the inventor of this printing method, sold the secret to George Amyand and speedily joined him in Surrey. As a result Drumcondra closed in 1757, but soon there were a number of imitators in England and Ireland. Robert Jones, who did the finest of all prints, started work in 1761."[68]

I have come across few good early descriptions of printed cotton in country houses and, of course, they do not usually say whether the cotton was printed from woodblocks or from copper plates. In 1766, for instance, the Duchess of Northumberland wrote of Etal in Northumberland: "William Carr Esq has a seat here which he built himself it is a very good one, & proper for a Man of his Fortune which is about 1400£ a year. There is a very good Hall Drawing Room & Eating Room & Upstairs very neat Lodging rooms furnish'd with printed cotton Bed Hangings etc."[69] The following year, in a description of William Cole's house at Bletchley in Buckinghamshire, there are references to a bed of "a beautiful stained cotton with Birds & Trees & Flowers" and to another bedroom with red and white paper and a bed of "a most beautiful stained cotton of crimson & white by a Copper Plate, having Parrots, & Baskets of Flowers etc."[70]

Each of the different aspects of printing has attracted specialist attention, but also worth exploring is how the aspects relate to each other and to contemporary views of patronage. The need to promote art and industry emerged in Ireland in 1745, when the Dublin Society, anxious to improve the drawing of patterns for printed linens, offered prizes to children for the best patterns. This idea was taken up by the Royal Society of Arts in London, which offered

its prizes in the late 1750s. William Shipley was the moving spirit here; his pupils won several of the prizes and he also proposed members for the society, among them Sir Edward Astley, a patron of Arthur Pond, and Astley's brothers-in-law, one of whom, Sir John Hussey-Delaval, was the owner of Doddington Hall. This last bought a series of interesting wallpapers for the house in about 1764, one of which is of special relevance in America because it also occurs in the Lady Pepperell House at Kittery in Maine.[71] Owners like Sir John were interested not only in decoration, but also in technical processes that raised the standards of the applied arts. This is particularly apparent in the case of Thomas Anson, the brother of the admiral who sailed around the world. Thomas was a patron of James Stuart, a supporter of canal building, and an early patron of Josiah Wedgwood. Wedgwood was represented in *The Treasure Houses of Britain* exhibition by a covered dish that he made for Catherine the Great (THB no. 429). On the dish appears a view of the Arch of Hadrian in Thomas Anson's park at Shugborough in Staffordshire, which was designed by Stuart. Inside Shugborough there are a series of paintings of the house and park by Michael Dahl, and a series of watercolors by Moses Griffiths. They both show the property as a rococo landscape of linked scenes, and it is not difficult to see how such views could be broken up into subjects for copper plates—just as one of Chambers' views of Kew was made into a printed cotton by John Collins of Woolmers[72] in 1766. Thus a love of gardens, flowers, and landscapes, of country life and classical and gothick architecture, the taste for ruins, the inventive spirit, and good economy could all be brought together in printed cottons.

By the early 1770s the old grand look was fast going out of fashion. When Mrs. Lybbe Powys went to Wanstead in Essex in 1781, she described the principal rooms as "most furnish'd and fitted up in the ancient taste, with Brussels tapestry in Flanders and cut velvet."[73] When François de la Rochefoucauld went to Houghton Hall in 1778, he wrote: "this magnificence, which has now passed out of fashion, has such an overwhelming effect that, while I was compelled to admire it, I should have preferred to be at a distance from it."[74]

The result of this change of mood can be seen at Blickling Hall in Norfolk, where in the late 1770s the Earl of Buckinghamshire formed a new state apartment to complete the quadrangle of

the house and to show off the relics of his career as an ambassador.[75] The tapestry of Peter the Great given to him by the Empress Catherine demanded a huge room (fig. 20), and yet the earl was decidedly short of suitable large pictures to go with it; there must always have been some sense of strain in the room. To make the task more difficult, a big patterned damask was by then out of fashion, so a worsted damask was chosen in what appears today as an odd combination of ivory and orange, with a small pattern based on two sprays of flowers and a loose stripe formed from a vertical garland (fig. 21). The material reads as a slight texture rather than as a pattern, and the sheen of the ground probably came into its own by candlelight which, after all, was how the room was generally seen. The original material has been replaced three times, and the National Trust has just had it copied yet again.

Finally, a fragment of wallpaper on the stairs at Boston Manor, Middlesex (fig. 22), is included here, because it takes us back to the taste for classical architecture and ruins, and because it is yet another paper that used to survive in the Lady Pepperell House at Kittery. It is instructive to see it alongside the painting of the Corbally family in their Irish house, which shows a complete architectural paper (fig. 23). The picture reminds one of an advertisement in *Faulkner's Journal,* published in Dublin on 13 April 1762, placed by John Gordon, who produced wallpapers "and others consisting principally of Gothic or Grecian Architecture, in due Perspective, and

proportioned agreable to their respective Orders."[76] Sadly no rooms like that of the Corbally family survive in the British Isles today, and we have to come to America if we really want to see eighteenth-century English printed cottons and wallpapers.

Fig. 21.
Detail of the silk wall hangings from the Peter the Great Room, as recently rewoven by Richard Humphries (The National Trust)

Fig. 22.
Early wallpaper fragments on the staircase at Boston Manor, Brentford, Middlesex (*Country Life*)

Fig. 23.
Philip Hussey, *A Family Group (traditionally the Corbally Family),* oil on canvas   (National Gallery of Ireland, Dublin)

NOTES

1. J. Mordaunt Crook, "Strawberry Hill Revisited—I," *Country Life* (7 June 1973), 1598–1602; John Cornforth, *English Interiors 1790–1848; the Quest for Comfort* (London, 1978), 105–108.

2. John Cornforth, "Clandon Park Revisited—II," *Country Life* (11 December 1969), 1584.

3. John Fowler and John Cornforth, *English Decoration in the Eighteenth Century* (London, 1974), pls. XVII, XXIV.

4. *Royal Commission on Historical Manuscripts, Eighth Report* (London, 1881), Appendix II, Duke of Manchester's mss., I.

5. *Royal Commission,* 100.

6. *Royal Commission,* 101.

7. *Royal Commission,* 102.

8. 7th Duke of Manchester, *Court and Society from Elizabeth to Anne* (London, 1864), 2:387.

9. John Cornforth, "The Nostell Priory Doll's House," *Country Life* (28 November 1985), 1692–1697.

10. John Summerson, "The Classical Country House in the 18th Century," *Journal of the Royal Society of Arts* (July 1959), 539–587.

11. John Cornforth, "Hatfield House Revisited—I–IV," *Country Life* (1, 8, 15, 22 December 1983), 1575–1578, 1712–1715, 1786–1789, 1850–1853.

12. John Dunbar and John Cornforth, "Dalkeith House, Lothian—I–III," *Country Life* (19, 26 April, 3 May 1984), 1062–1065, 1158–1161, 1230–1233.

13. Lady Louisa Stuart, *Gleanings from an Old Portfolio,* 3 vols. (London, 1895–1898), 1:129.

14. Stuart 1895–1898, 2:280.

15. J. Marchand, ed., *A Frenchman in England in 1784: The Mélanges sur L'Angleterre of La Rochefoucauld* (Cambridge, 1933), 28.

16. Isaac Ware, *A Complete Body of Architecture* (London, 1756), 469.

17. Gervase Jackson-Stops, *Wimpole Hall* (London, 1982), 56–57.

18. John Cornforth and Leo Schmidt, "Holkham Hall, Norfolk—III, IV," *Country Life* (7, 14 February 1980), 359–362, 427–431.

19. Journal of the Duchess of Northumberland, ms., Alnwick Castle, Northumberland.

20. Sarah Markham, *John Loveday of Caversham 1711–1780: The Life and Tours of an Eighteenth-Century Onlooker* (Wilton, 1984), 88.

21. James Lees-Milne, *Earls of Creation* (London, 1962), 132.

22. Karen Walton, *English Furniture Upholstery 1660–1840* [exh. cat., Temple Newsam] (Leeds, 1973), pl. 35.

23. John Loveday, *Diary of a Tour in 1732* (London, 1890), 80.

24. Gladys Scott Thomson, *Family Background* (London, 1949), 78, 79.

25. Paget Toynbee, ed., "Horace Walpole's Journals of Visits to Country Seats," *Walpole Society* 16 (1927–1928), 17.

26. Desmond Fitz-Gerald, *The Norfolk House Music Room* (London, 1973), 48.

27. Fowler and Cornforth 1974, fig. 117.

28. John Hardy and Maurice Tomlin, *Osterley Park House* (London, 1985), 53.

29. Hardy and Tomlin 1985, 103–104.

30. Hardy and Tomlin 1985, 106–107.

31. David Watkin, *Athenian Stuart: Pioneer of the Greek Revival* (London, 1982), pls. 20, 21, 22, 23, 28.

32. Fowler and Cornforth 1974, pl. 1.

33. Fowler and Cornforth 1974, pls. 11, 12.

34. Marcus Binney, "A Forgotten Pupil of Chambers: John Yenn at the RIBA Drawings Collection," *Country Life* (14 September 1973), 713.

35. J. D. Williams, *Audley End; the Restoration of 1762–1797* (London, 1966), pl. 12.

36. Walton 1973, iv.

37. R. Campbell, *The London Tradesman* (London, 1747), 197.

38. Ms. at Bowood.

39. Anthony Coleridge, *Chippendale Furniture* (London, 1968), 167.

40. C. H. Baker and M. I. Collins, *The Life and Circumstances of James Brydges, First Duke of Chandos* (London, 1949), 65.

41. Scott Thomson 1949, 78, 79.

42. Wilmarth Sheldon Lewis et al., eds., *The Yale Edition of Horace Walpole's Correspondence*, 48 vols. (New Haven, 1937–1983), 21:447.

43. Dudley Dodd, *Saltram* (London, 1981), 52.

44. Sarah, Duchess of Marlborough, *Letters of a Grandmother 1732–35*, ed. Gladys Scott Thomson (London, 1943), 76.

45. Christopher Hussey, "Furniture at Longford Castle—I, II," *Country Life* (12, 26 December 1931), 680, 715.

46. Victoria Percy and Gervase Jackson-Stops, "Exquisite Taste and Tawdry Ornament; the Travel Journals of the 1st Duchess of Northumberland—II," *Country Life* (7 February 1974), 252.

47. Fowler and Cornforth 1974, pl. xix.

48. Emily J. Climenson, ed., *Passages from the Diaries of Mrs Philip Lybbe Powys* (London, 1899), 146.

49. Houghton inventory, ms., Houghton Hall.

50. Lady Llanover, ed., *The Autobiography and Correspondence of Mary Granville, Mrs Delany*, series I, 3 vols. (London, 1861), 2:204.

51. Cornforth 1969, 1583, 1585.

52. Gervase Jackson-Stops, *Felbrigg Hall* (London, 1985), 13.

53. Frederick J. Ladd, *Architects at Corsham Court* (London, 1978), 59.

54. Lady Llanover, ed., *The Autobiography and Correspondence of Mary Granville, Mrs Delany*, series II, 3 vols. (London, 1862), 2:33; Hardy and Tomlin 1985, 25.

55. Llanover 1861, 3:477.

56. Cornforth 1983, 1852, fig. 7.

57. Journal of the Duchess of Northumberland.

58. H. Avray Tipping, "Audley End—IV," *Country Life* (24 July 1926), 131.

59. Brian Fitzgerald, ed., *The Correspondence of Emily Duchess of Leinster* (London, 1949), 1:425.

60. H. Avray Tipping, "Brocket Hall—III," *Country Life* (18 July 1925), 96–103.

61. Lewis 1937–1983, 21:420, 458.

62. James Lees-Milne, *The Vyne* (1959; rev. ed., London, 1985), 8.

63. Charles C. Oman and Jean Hamilton, *Wallpapers: A History and Illustrated Catalogue of the Collection in the Victoria and Albert Museum* (London, 1982), 92–93.

64. E. A. Entwisle, *A Literary History of Wallpaper* (London, 1960), pl. 20.

65. *Rococo: Art and Design in Hogarth's England* [exh. cat., Victoria and Albert Museum] (London, 1984), 250, fig. O18.

66. A. K. Longfield, "Early Irish Printed Fabric," *Country Life* (7 December 1972), 1578.

67. Llanover 1861, 3:180.

68. Ada Longfield (Mrs. Leask), "History of the Irish Linen and Cotton Printing Industry in the 18th Century," *Journal of the Royal Society of Antiquaries of Ireland* 67 (1937).

69. Journal of the Duchess of Northumberland.

70. F. G. Stokes, ed., *Cole's Bletchley Diary 1765–67* (London, 1931), 235–270.

71. Richard C. Nylander, Elizabeth Redmond, and Penny J. Sander, *Wallpaper in New England* (New York, 1986), 51–52.

72. Victoria and Albert Museum, no. 492-1894.

73. Climenson 1899, 205.

74. Marchand 1933, 224.

75. Christopher Hussey, "Blickling Hall—III," *Country Life* (28 June 1930), 936.

76. Ada Longfield (Mrs. Leask), "History of the Dublin Wallpaper Industry," *Journal of the Royal Society of Antiquaries of Ireland* 77 (1947), 101.

OLIVER IMPEY

Eastern Trade and the Furnishing of the British Country House

This paper discusses the use in British country houses of four of the most prominently displayed categories of goods imported from the East: carpets, porcelain, lacquer, and wallpaper. Of the huge quantities of exotic oriental things imported during the sixteenth, seventeenth, and eighteenth centuries these made by far the most lasting impression on English houses both by their own presence and by the imitations and pastiches that they engendered. Only silk and cotton (the ancestors of wallpaper) and tea can be considered to have had anything approaching the same importance; these will be discussed, but in lesser detail, while other imports will barely be mentioned. The question asked here is: what did the owners of country houses do with their Turkish, Indian, and Persian carpets, their Chinese and Japanese porcelain, and their Japanese and Chinese lacquer? To answer this question I cannot, and do not wish to avoid some discussion of the origins of these things, and the way their manufacture was influenced by the preferences of the customers for whom they were intended.

Carpets

That Near-Eastern carpets, particularly from Turkey, were reaching Italy and the rest of Europe in the Renaissance is easy to confirm by reference to Renaissance paintings in any picture gallery.[1] Today we even classify some Turkish carpets by the names of painters in whose works they appear; Holbein carpets and Lotto carpets are the most obvious examples. But when did they come to Britain? And how were they used?

Among the first Eastern carpets to be found in Britain were the sixty—presumably Turkish—carpets sent to Cardinal Wolsey from Venice in October 1520.[2] In the list of the property of Henry VIII taken at his death in 1547[3] there were, in his twelve houses and in the garderobes of his three children, a total of 801 carpets, some 66 of which traveled with him on his royal progresses from one house to another. The majority of these were "of turquey making" and very few were "foote carpets," that is, carpets for the floor. Most carpets were used on tables, cupboards, and window seats, and for hanging. In the inventory of Hardwick Hall of 1601 there are only five "foote carpetes," three of them in Bess of Hardwick's bedchamber: "three foote turkie Carpetes the grounds of them white, to laye about the bed." The other two were "of turkie-worke."[4]

Of course, carpets can sometimes be seen on the floor in portraits,[5] included as a mark of status, of grandeur. Much more commonly in pictures they can be seen on tables, often in contexts that demonstrate the high esteem in which they were held (fig. 1).[6]

In the sixteenth century most carpets in paintings came from Turkey; a few survive in English country houses. At Boughton House there is a mid-sixteenth-century Lotto carpet and a slightly later Lotto rug.[7] The great Ushak carpets at Hardwick Hall (fig. 2) may well have been purchased in 1610, though this is not certain.[8] In the seventeenth century, Persian and Indian carpets appeared. The best Persian carpets, probably from Kashan, were of silk. A hunting carpet, probably made in the 1570s and thought to have been in the possession of the Dukes of Holstein-Gottorp by 1637, is described in the Swedish royal inventory of 1656 as a "tapetz bordtechte," a tapestry tablecloth.[9] Indian carpets could be ordered from Agra and Lahore; Sir Thomas Roe, James I's ambassador to the Mughal emperor Jahangir from 1615 to 1619, ordered for himself

Fig. 1.
Holbein carpet, already old, in use on a table for an important state occasion. *The Somerset House Conference* by an unknown artist, 1604, oil on canvas   (National Portrait Gallery)

"a great carpet with my arms thereon."[10] The Girdlers' Carpet, woven in 1631 in Lahore for the Girdlers' Hall, London, was made to an exact size for the table on which it was to be placed.[11]

In Holland in the seventeenth and early eighteenth centuries—and indeed still today—carpets for tables never seem to have gone out of fashion, and thus they can be seen in paintings, in still-lifes, and in domestic interiors.[12] After the 1670s they can more often be seen on the floor.

It is much more difficult to understand what happened to carpets in England in the eighteenth century. In the first half of the century oriental carpets were used on the floor, but almost never on tables, if one judges by the evidence of painting.[13] Although we know that carpets continued to be imported from Turkey throughout the century, we rarely see one in a painting, and it is difficult to imagine how they would have been used in the formal arrangements of rooms then in fashion. It must be assumed that they were used mostly in bedrooms. If this is the case, and I can only suggest it, then it is greatly at variance

with the fate of porcelain and lacquer, which we will soon discuss.

In inventories of the seventeenth century, the term Turkey carpet usually referred to an oriental carpet, but not always. In the dining room of Northampton House in 1614 there was: "a longe Turkie carpett of Englishe worke with the Earle of Northampton his armes, being 5 yeardes and 3 quarters longe," which presumably was placed on the "longe table of walnuttree," which stood in the same room.[14] Such English carpets were highly prized. At Boughton there are two English copies of variant star Ushak rugs, bearing the arms of Sir Edward Montagu and dated 1584 and 1585 (fig. 3).[15] Normally such carpets would probably have come under the generic term *turkey work,* which meant any form of imitation of the oriental, from fine to very coarse. Sometimes these would have been foot carpets, such as the one in the Northampton House dining room, "a foote carpett of Turky worke, the ground redd and yelowe," but every piece of furniture also had its carpet or cupboard cloth. In the same

room there was "a cupboord of walnuttree with a Turkie carpett, the ground redd."[16] Inventories of the seventeenth century therefore usually list great numbers of textiles, many of which would have been quite small, and many of which would have been imitations of imported oriental rugs—turkey work.

Even before the end of the sixteenth century, the writers of inventories were interested in the differences between Turkish and Persian carpets. At Kenilworth in 1588 Robert Dudley, Earl of Leicester, had not only "A Turquoy carpett of Norwich work, in length ij. yards, in breadth j.yard quarter," but also "a fine Turquoy carpett, wrought with orient colours; in length iiij. yards 3 quarters, breadth ij. yards quarter."[17] At Hatfield House in 1611, among many "Turkie" and "Percian" carpets, there was "one other Carpitt of Chyna work imbrothered with silver and gould," and in 1629 "I Cubberd Carpit of silke of India work lyned with buckrome;" and

by 1685 Hatfield even had, in the Wardrobe, "I large Smerna Carpet."[18]

The importation, treatment of, and imitation of oriental carpets typifies the Western attitude to imported exotic rarities. We shall follow the same line with porcelain and with lacquer.

Porcelain

In the National Gallery of Art in Washington, there hangs a great picture begun by Giovanni Bellini and finished by Titian in 1514, entitled *The Feast of the Gods.*[19] Generations of orientalists have delighted in the fact that the gods here eat not off gold or silver gilt, but off Chinese blue and white porcelain of the fifteenth century. This implicit comment on the status of porcelain in Europe is borne out by its rarity at that time, by inventories such as that of Cosimo di Medici[20] taken in 1553, and by the practice of mounting porcelain vessels, as if they were precious hard-stone carvings, in silver-gilt mounts.[21]

Only in the second half of the sixteenth century were the Portuguese able to import sufficient quantities of Chinese porcelain, by the new sea routes, to enable porcelain to come out of the cabinet of curiosities onto the cup-board.[22] At the beginning of the seventeenth century, with the trade falling more and more into the hands of the Dutch, Chinese porcelain became common enough for actual use.[23] Nearly all of it was blue and white; a certain amount of the green glazed ware we call celadon was still available,[24] and a small quantity of white porcelain and colored enameled porcelain, but this was exceptional.

After the fall of the Ming dynasty in 1644, the porcelain trade with China was seriously disrupted for nearly twenty-five years.[25] To keep up its supplies the Dutch East India Company turned to Japan, and by 1661 Japanese porcelain was being shipped to Europe in quantity.[26] Much of this Japanese porcelain was colored with overglaze enamels; brightly colored porcelain thus became widely available for the first time. These were the wares that were to lead to the somewhat brash Imari and the more refined Kakiemon styles.[27] By the 1670s China was competing with the Japanese, exporting mostly blue and white, white wares (*blanc-de-Chine*), *famille verte* enameled pieces, and brown stonewares (Yixing). In the early eighteenth century the Chinese made their own version of Imari (Chinese Imari), and also white wares and *famille rose*. Price wars resulted in the Chinese winning back the European market in the 1730s or 1740s, and throughout the eighteenth century enormous quantities of Chinese porcelain flooded into Europe, much of it very poor stuff.[28]

Just as the Delft potters had imitated first blue and white and then colored wares,[29] so the new porcelain factories of eighteenth-century Europe imitated this great range of oriental porcelain. And, of course, imitation led to pastiche—chinoiserie.[30]

Porcelain was clearly uncommon in England until the mid-sixteenth century. Possibly the earliest documented piece in England is the fourteenth-century celadon bowl mounted in silver gilt given to New College, Oxford, by Archbishop Warham in 1532.[31] In 1597 Sir Walter Raleigh, in his will, left to "my Right Honorable good Frinde Sir Robert Cecill . . . one suite of Porcellane sett in silver and gylt."[32] It is just possible that this "suite" corresponds to the

three (possibly four) Wanli pieces with fine English silver-gilt mounts that were sold from Burghley House in 1888 and are now in The Metropolitan Museum of Art, New York.[33] At Hatfield House in 1629 there were "in the Chamber over the Porters Lodge . . . XXVI China dishes to sett out a banquett."[34] In the "Inventory of all the parcels of porselin, glasses

Fig. 3.
English rug, possibly made in Norwich, bearing the arms of Sir Edward Montagu, 1585. Imitation of a variant star Ushak Turkish Lotto rug (Duke of Buccleuch and Queensbury, KT, Boughton House)

and other goods now remayning in the Pranket-
ing Roome at Tart Hall" taken on 8 November
1641, the porcelain included "3 white little porselin figures, the first a man and a woeman; the
second a dolphine" and "a lyon on a pedestall of
white porselin,"[35] which, as Peter Thornton
points out, were surely *blanc-de-Chine.*

The architect Daniel Marot is credited with
the introduction into Britain, in the 1690s, of the
orderly arrangement of porcelains (fig. 4; see
Somers Cocks, 196),[36] though even before this it
must have been a practice not unusual in England. The Burghley House inventory of 1688
includes, in "My Lords Dressing Roome," a
subheading "China over ye Chimney;" this
comprised: "2 Doggs, 2 Lyons, 2 Staggs, 2 blue
& wt Birds/1 heathan Godd with many Armes/2
figures with Juggs att their backs" (fig. 5).[37]
Some of these figures are quite large and they
must have made an impressive display. Clearly
there were so many porcelains in some collections that there was no alternative to a massed
display. The inventory of Kensington Palace of
1697 describes the exact position of each of the
154 pieces of Chinese and Japanese porcelain in
the gallery by such rubrics as "Over the dressing
roome door" and "Upon ye cabbanett next ye
closet," even stating in which row each piece
stood.[38] However, there seem to have been few
English equivalents of the great pyramids of porcelain to be seen at the Oranienburg Palace,
Berlin,[39] the Palace of the Stadholder at Leeuwarden in the Netherlands, or at Arkhangelskoye
Palace near Leningrad; no equivalent of the Mirror Room at the Residenz in Munich;[40] and perhaps only one English example—at Hampton
Court[41]—of a *Porzellanzimmer* such as can still be
seen at the Charlottenburg Palace in Berlin.[42]

In the eighteenth century there was some actual collecting of oriental porcelains that were
even then "antique," in the sense that they were
not straight off the ship. We know, for instance,
of keen competition between Margaret, 2nd
Duchess of Portland, and Elizabeth, Countess of
Ilchester, for a Japanese blue and white plate.[43]

Porcelain could be misused or adapted for decorative purposes, just as could lacquer. Vases
could be mounted in ormolu as jugs, or covered
bowls as potpourri containers.[44] In the collection
at Dresden of Augustus the Strong, king of Poland and elector of Saxony, some pieces of Japanese porcelain were fitted together to form candlesticks; at Rosenborg Castle Chinese and
Japanese porcelains were combined to form an

étagère. This was not common in England, though occasionally, as at the Vyne and Warwick Castle, very large Imari plates of the early eighteenth century were used as table tops. They must have been very inconvenient. In all countries small pieces seem to have been considered suitable for mounting together in ormolu, either as clocks, for which they often had Vincennes flowers added, as ink stands, for which they were frequently combined with lacquer, or simply as ornaments. No one thought twice about the mixing of Chinese, Japanese, and European things.

Lacquer

Japanese lacquer was first imported into Europe in the late sixteenth century.[45] At Schloss Ambras in Austria there is a Japanese cabinet inventoried in 1596. Such lacquer is always in shapes made to European order, usually coffers and cabinets, but also in pieces such as shrines and bible rests made for the Society of Jesus. The style is the so-called *namban* style, which has pearl-shell inlays in dark, coarse lacquer overpainted with gold lacquer. The cabinets usually have fall-fronts and so can be called scriptors; the coffers have domed, half cylindrical lids. The cabinets take their shape from *varguenos*, the coffers from iron-bound chests. By about 1630 this style was changing: cabinets now had two doors opening sideways, and the small painted areas of the *namban* pieces became bigger and more important. The interiors became simpler (as if they were scarcely meant to be opened), the borders smaller, and little pearl shell was now used, as the decoration was in gold lacquer or in shades of gold and silver lacquer on a glossy black ground. By the 1670s the borders had disappeared altogether and the picture asymmetrically covered both doors or the whole of the front of a coffer. Coffers now tended to have flat or nearly flat tops. This was true of the typical export wares. There were, of course, intermediate stages of development, and also better quality pieces that were out of the ordinary category of export wares and may have been made to special orders.[46]

Japanese lacquer, even that made for export, was recognized as superior in the seventeenth century. William Dampier, writing of his visit to Tonkin in 1688, states: "The lackered ware that is made here is not inferior to any but that of *Japan* only, which is esteemed the best in the world."[47] Engelbert Kaempfer wrote in 1690 of the Japanese: "All their varnish or japanned household goods are surprizingly fine. The Chinese and Tonquinese, with all their care and industry, never came up to that skill and dexterity, which the Japanese have in the composition of their varnish, as well as in the laying of it on."[48] But by the 1670s Japanese lacquer was expensive, and, as so often happened, the Chinese copied the Japanese styles and shapes (which we have seen were already European) in cheaper material, undercutting the Japanese. By 1693 the Dutch East India Company stopped buying Japanese cabinets and bought the cheaper Chinese version.[49]

For the English, it was even more advantageous to buy Chinese and Tonkinese lacquer, for all Japanese lacquer had had to be bought through an intermediary; now the English could buy directly from the maker. This, of course, influenced what was ordered. As early as 1684 the East India Company had sent pieces of furniture to Tonkin to be lacquered. On 26 September a letter to "The Chief and Factors at Tonquin" states:

> You will see by the Invoice y* we have sent you (to help fill up ye ship) some quantity of Joyners ware to be lackered there, w*ch we have done upon conference with Capt. Knox and Mr. James, who both assure us that you may with care and circumspeccon procure them to be bett* lackered and painted than ordinary wherein we can give you no particular directions, they being things of Fancy, but we would have them all well done and substantiall that may hold for many yeares and with as much variety as may be, some plain black, but most to be adorned with birds, fflowers or Imagery such as you shall with the advice of Mr. Clyve Purser of the Dragon, think may be most acceptable in England, the said Mr. Clyve was formerly a Cabinet maker, and kept a great shop of such wares in this City, and by his former profession and his observacon now, he should probably be able to make the best judgment w* sort of workes may be most in request here . . . and direct the workmen you shall employ in the lackring of those joyners wares in the most comly and agreeable manner to the humour of this place.[50]

William Dampier wrote of Tonkin in 1688:

> The joyners in this Country may not compare their work with that which the Europeans make: and in laying on the lack upon good or fine joyned work they frequently spoil the joynts, edges or corners of Drawers of Cabinets; Besides, our fashions of Utensils differ mightily from theirs, and for that reason Captain Poole, in his second Voyage to the Country, brought an ingenious Joyner with him, to make fashionable Commodities to be lackered here, as also

Deal-boards, which are much better than the Pone-wood of this Country.[51]

But Captain Poole returned from Tonkin in 1691, when the goods "turn'd to a very discouraging Acc[t]. and [the] lacquered ware especially is of little or no value not worth the freight being abundantly outdone by what we receive from China."[52]

Clearly by 1691 the East India Company did not agree with Dampier's opinion of the quality of Tonkinese lacquer, preferring to buy that of Amoy in China. Thus, many of the lacquer cabinets in English country houses are Chinese or Tonkinese imitations of the Japanese, sometimes on an English carcass. They are always of lesser quality, both in the lacquer material and in pictorial design.

Japanese cabinets were being copied in Europe by 1612.[53] In 1641 some cases of "brass hinges" were imported into England from China (though it is not known if they were of Chinese or Japanese origin), presumably to be fitted to japanned cabinets in the name of verisimilitude.[54] Japanning became not only a professional occupation, but also a genteel pastime for ladies, particularly after the publication of Stalker and Parker's *Treatise of Japanning and Varnishing* in 1688.[55]

In the late seventeenth century the Chinese began to make the so-called Coromandel lacquer, in which the pictorial parts are cut into the solid wood and the shallow cavity thus formed is filled with colored pigments. This was usually imported as large screens which were easy to cut up to be used as paneling or wainscot. On 23 July 1697 the merchants on the ship *Nassau* were ordered by the East India Company to buy at Amoy:

Two hundred Lacker'd Boards finely lackered on both sides for screens or panelling rooms and any sort of lackered ware that will lye close, and you think will pay the ffreight and all other charges, one third of them all richly double gilt wth Gold. The boards must be dry wood, and to that end we have sent with you 100 Deals dry and the fittest we think for this purpose to be lackered rough or smooth as shall be found best.[56]

On 27 October 1697 it is specified that these boards were "of a sufficient thickness 3/4 of an inch or thereabouts."[57] Almost certainly the "very large high india Japann sckreen twelve leaves which was in two but the Queen had it putt together" in the Queen's New Bedchamber in Kensington Palace[58] was one of these screens.

Sometime in the early eighteenth century the Chinese began to make lacquered screens in another style. These screens were painted in shades of gold lacquer on a black ground, imitating, as it were, the effect of the Japanese lacquer cabinets. These were often cut up to make furniture,[59] so that it was possible to have the look of lacquer upon fashionably up-to-date furniture. In fact, as we shall see, lacquer was scarcely out of fashion during the eighteenth century.

In the inventory of Hardwick Hall of 1601[60] there is no mention of China-work, Japan, or japanning. In 1611 in an inventory of Hatfield House there is mention of "One Chyna Table of black gilded and painted" and "1 high Chaire . . . the frame guilt China worke."[61] It seems possible that in the first decade of the seventeenth century lacquer and its imitations were first to be seen in English country houses. The "china guilt cabonette upon a frame" (a stand, made in Europe to fit the cabinet) belonging to the Earl of Northampton in 1614[62] would almost certainly have been one of the *namban* fall-front scriptors with pearl-shell inlay. One such piece still at Hatfield is known as "Queen Elizabeth's chest," and although there seems to be no firm evidence for this provenance at least the date is possible (fig. 6).

Captain John Saris, returning from Japan in the *Clove* in 1614 had written: "some Iapan wares, as ritch Scritoiries: Trunckes, Beoubes [*byobu*, the Japanese word for screen], Cupps and Dishes of all sorts, and of a most excellent varnish, I have in the ship; But tell sale be made I cann give you no great Incouradgement to deale therein"[63]—which presumably means they were uncommon enough for the value not to be known (in fact, two of these "small trunckes or chests of Japan stuff guilded and set with mother of pearle" sold for £4 5s. and £5.[64]

The "2 great China Chests . . . in the Lobbie to the upper Chapple" and the "one large China Chest . . . in the Wardropp" of Salisbury House in 1629[65] were probably great Japanese coffers much like those in the Danish Royal Collection,[66] rather than the pearl-shell inlaid type (*namban*) like those at Corsham Court,[67] while the "1 Cabinet of China worke blacke and guilt" also "in the Wardropp" was probably a cabinet with two doors.

The pictorial style of chest with doors, usually decorated without pearl shell, was certainly appearing in England by the 1660s. In 1661 Samuel

Pepys saw in the Duke of York's closet "two very fine chests covered with gold and Indian varnish, given him by the East India Company of Holland"[68] and in 1662 John Evelyn wrote that "the *Queene* brought over with her from Portugal, such *Indian Cabinets* and large truncks of laccar as had never before ben seene here."[69] In 1679 Evelyn was still commenting on such things, though they must by now have been relatively common; at the house of the Portuguese ambassador he saw "rich *Jopon Cabinets* of which I think there were a dosen."[70]

Cabinets such as these were later sometimes cut up and made into different pieces of furniture. At Ham House the "fine Japan cabinet"[71] of about 1670 which stood in the Long Gallery (in 1679 it was still called Indian) had its top removed in 1730 by the cabinetmaker George Nix to make a table top (fig. 7); fortunately the cabinet was relatively unharmed and the top is, after all, above eye level.

Suites of tables, mirrors, and candlestands made up from lacquer cabinets were not uncommon in the late sixteenth century. There was one in the Archbishop of Canterbury's lodgings in Kensington Palace in 1679.[72] One survives at Ham,[73] while another from Spencer House (or Althorp) was made up of several disparate pieces of lacquer of widely differing date (fig. 8).[74] With French furniture, which often used lacquer panels simply as inlay, much as *pietra dura* panels had been used earlier, old lacquer would be reused as its host article went out of date. If it was drastically cut (as with the Spencer pieces) or bent, as it often was in the mid-eighteenth century in France, then it could not be reused. Some of the pieces thus bent into serpentine and *bombé* shapes were already nearly one hundred years old.

Cabinets and coffers and their like were not, as we have already seen, the only lacquers imported. In the late seventeenth century in England a new fashion arose for lacquer rooms, parallel to that in France and Holland.

In 1692 John Evelyn visited his neighbor Christopher Bohun, "a rich Spanish merchant . . . whose whole house is a Cabinet of all elegancies, especially *Indian,* and the contrivance of the *Jopan* Skreenes instead of wainscot in the *Hall,* where an excellent *Pendule*-clock inclosed in the curious flower-work of Mr. *Gibbons* in the midst of the *Vestibule* is very remarkable."[75] Because Japanese lacquer was of better quality than Chinese, lacquer was usually described as Japa-

Fig. 6.
Scriptor in *namban* style, similar to "Queen Elizabeth's chest" at Hatfield House and probably of the type described as a "china guilt cabonette" in 1614. Japanese export lacquer inlaid with pearl shell, c. 1600 (Private collection, England)

Fig. 7.
The "fine Japan cabinet" in the Long Gallery of Ham House, 1679. The top was removed in 1730. Japanese export lacquer, c. 1670 (Victoria and Albert Museum, Ham House)

Fig. 8.
Mirror, table, and candlestands formerly at Spencer House (or Althorp), mainly Japanese lacquer, 17th century (Victoria and Albert Museum)

nese, or as japann. In fact the pieces used for wainscot were usually of the so-called Coromandel lacquer of China, which in England was usually called "hollow burnt Japan." In 1683 Gerrit Jensen was employed at Chatsworth for "framing, moulding and cutting of the Japan, and joyning it into panels."[76] The room on which he worked pleased Celia Fiennes in 1697: "The Duchess's Closet is wainscoated with hollow burnt japan and at each corner are peers of looking-glass."[77] She had also recently admired "My Ladyes Closet" at Burghley: "very fine the wanscoate of the best Japan and cushons very rich work."[78]

Probably the only surviving lacquer room of

the seventeenth century furnished with oriental lacquer is that of the former Stadholder's Court in Leeuwarden (fig. 9).[79] This was constructed for the Frisian Stadholder Henry Casimir II and his wife Henrietta Amalia of Anhalt-Dessau in 1695. The walls of this cabinet are preserved in the Rijksmuseum, Amsterdam. At first glance one wall seems to be made up from a twelve-panel screen, as is the later one at Burton Agnes Hall in Yorkshire, but on closer examination it is clearly made up from pieces. This cutting up of lacquer provoked the famous letter of Constantijn Huygens to Queen Mary, in which he pretended to be an outraged Chinese who had heard that:

a certain publiq peece of proof and demonstration of their national skill and industry in gilt and painted lackwork, in form of a royal skreen, having had the great happiness to fall into Your Royal Highness noble hands, to their inconsolable greef and mor[t]ification, they have lately been told, how some most ignorant, barbarous and malitious people, mooved only by mere envie and jalousie of our ancient oriental China honour, should have so farre prevailled with your Highn. renowned sweet, mild and gracious disposition, as to persuade her to lett the same illustrious monument [be] sawed, divided, cut, clift and slit asunder and reduced to a heap of monstrous shivers and splinters, and all this desolation to no higher purpose then to see the wals of some miserable cabinet decked and adorned forsooth with our unhappy ruines.[80]

In fact, the Leeuwarden "paneling" is beautifully put together so that the main picture makes sense—it is the border that betrays it. Most wainscoting was assembled much more ruthlessly than this, and often there was no attempt at matching the pictures at all. It was as if odds and ends of lacquer had to be used up somehow.

Screens could be cut up for furniture, too. Cabinets and commodes made up from Coromandel lacquer are not uncommon; there is a fine cabinet at Chatsworth whose sides clearly show this piecing together of remnants. Later in the eighteenth century it was the black and gold type of screen that was cut up and used for furniture. Two commodes of this type can be seen at Osterley, one in the State Bedroom, one in the Etruscan Room; a japanned commode formerly at Harewood House is made of English japann imitation of this sort of lacquer.[81] The placing of lacquer furniture in neo-classical settings—particularly in an Etruscan room—is not as aberrant as it may at first seem. The scenes from the lacquer screens used for this furniture were of buildings and gardens, thus fitting in

well with the planning of the scheme of decoration.[82]

Lacquer remained in fashion throughout the eighteenth century. In Bedford House, London, in 1771 there was in the Red Drawing Room, "A Cabinet of the old Japan, with brass hinges and corner pieces, on a carved and gilt frame," and also "a table under (a pier glass) of the old

Japan on a partly gilt frame."[83] This latter may have been a reused top of a lacquer cabinet, like the one at Ham House[84] and like another at Belton House, Lincolnshire, or it may have been of lacquer taken from a screen; the tables with lacquer tops in the Long Gallery at Osterley, which were used for the display of porcelain and of mother-of-pearl pagodas (of which there are

Fig. 9.
The lacquer room from the Stadholder's Court at Leeuwarden, 1695, cleverly made up from various Coromandel screens   (Rijksmuseum)

two at Burghley), seem not to have been brought into the room until later; they may have come from a dismantled chinoiserie tea house in the park.[85]

The Bedford House reference to "old Japan" is interesting. Culpepper Tanner in the inventory of 1688 of Burghley House refers to "Right Japan,"[86] which may be a quality judgement, but may simply mean oriental. "Fine Japan,"[87] in the Ham House inventory of 1683, is certainly a comment on quality. "Old Japan" may also simply mean oriental (as opposed to japanning), but it is worth noting that at Bedford House, in 1771, there was in Her Grace's Dressing Room, "a dressing box of the rare old Japan and a leather cover to ditto."[88] Could it be that this was of the especially good quality of the famous lacquer box bearing the name of Maria van Diemen, the wife of the governor general of the Dutch East Indies, made probably between 1636 and 1639, which was once in the collection of William Beckford at Fonthill Abbey and is now in the Victoria and Albert Museum?[89] Such pieces are very uncommon, though Beckford had two. The second one, inscribed with the name Pieternellae Buys, he had dismembered and made into two secretaires by Justin Vulliamy, which are now at Elton. A variation of this type can be seen at Burghley,[90] and one of lesser quality is at Belton. It is interesting, too, that the Duchess of Bedford's dressing box had a leather cover; in the late seventeenth century some of the lacquer at Ham House was protected thus, too.[91]

Were these cabinets only for show or were they also useful? We know what people kept *on* these cabinets—china—but we know remarkably little about what they kept *in* them—possibly merely the typical muddle of a large house. In June 1629 in "the Wardropp" of Salisbury House there was:

1 Cabinet of China worke blacke and guilt and in it
1 bason and Ewer of porselin ye Ewer bound with silver.
1 Castinge bottle for sweet water of silver, set with diamonds and other stones and Caesar's head in the midst.
1 other small Castinge bottle for sweet water of silver set with stones.
3 little Cupps or dishes of Christall spotted and painted in divers colours.
1 houre glasse of Ibonie broken, in a Case of Red velvett.
1 little earthen Jugge with a Cover.[92]

In 1638 the Viscountess Dorchester kept:

In the Cabinet in the roome next my Ladies Chamber
2 amber cupps, 2 candle sticks of amber, 1 amber spoone, 2 amber dishes and divers odd things
1 looking glass sett in gold, 1 silver bottle, 1 little cabinet of gold and silver, 1 little looking glass imbroydred, 11 purses
3 silver boxes of counters—1 box: 31, another 36, and the other box 29
1 diall case of silver and a few other small things
6 hoodes of curle

and:

In the black Ebony Cabinett
1 imbroydred prayer booke, 6 paire of gloves imbroydred with gold
12 paires of plaine gloves
3 ymbroydred capps of gold and 3 plain capps
3 little silver bottles, 1 little silver cupp, and some other things of silver
4 combe case baggs
6 purses
1 paire of slippers imbroydred, 1 imbroydred cushion and 1 imbroydred table booke.[93]

Queen Charlotte Amalie of Denmark (d. 1714) kept an assortment of curiosities in her lacquer cabinet. This was a fine Japanese cabinet of about 1670, certainly in Denmark before 1699. A list of 1731 describes some of the contents. Seashells (many of which must have been imported from the East) occupied the top drawer and two deep bottom ones; most of the contents of one of the middle drawers have recently been rediscovered at Rosenborg Castle (fig. 10). In 1731 this drawer contained:

A dried bird of paradise
A dry lizard
A small dry fish
A dry fruit, another filled with cotton
A small basket of palm leaves
Two small paper dolls
A stalk of cloves
Two shells painted within

Fig. 10.
Some contents of Queen Charlotte Amalie of Denmark's Japanese lacquer cabinet, as listed in 1731: a "small wooden comb," one of "two shells painted within," and "an oyster shell, carved with in and mounted with small shells" (Danish Royal Chronological Collections, Rosenborg Castle)

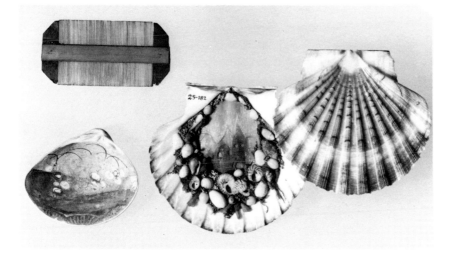

*An oyster shell, carved within and mounted with small
shells
A small wooden comb
A rectangular cardboard box with some Indian coins on two
strings, and some loose ones
A tree in the shape of a fan
Two Indian drawings*[94]

For this discussion the most important of these
typical *Wunderkammer* objects are the "shells
painted within" (only one survives) from the
Japanese *kaiawase* game.[95] The paper dolls are
Chinese.

This use of Chinese or Japanese lacquers or
their European counterparts to hold cabinets of
curiosities was not at all unusual. The four great
chinoiserie cabinets made by Gerard Dagly before 1696 for the *Kunstkammer* of the Elector
Friedrich III of Brandenburg in Berlin were specifically intended to hold curiosities.[96]

We do not know what shape the Duchess of
Bedford's "dressing box of the rare old Japan"
was, but it must surely have been used.

Silk, Cotton, and Wallpaper

In 1586 Filippo Sassetti bought in Cochin for the
Grand Duke Francesco of Tuscany "a canopy of
white sarsenet with a blue tuft, embroidered like
the coverlets from China (where this too was
made) but of much greater richness, and so well
worked that the things embroidered there seem
worthier to be prized than the reality of
them."[97] This was very expensive; together with
a bedcover, valances, a case for a bolster, and two
for two small pillows, it cost "a thousand of the
angels of these parts, and its bed-frame of gilded
wood, eighty." The comparative prices are remarkable. Such exotic and expensive oriental
items must have been very rare in England, but
as early as 1611 there was "in the Ante Chamber
at the westende of the Kings Withdrawing
Chamber" at Hatfield House a "Tester, Val-
launce, 5 Curtins and headecloth of white taffata
imbrothered all over with China silke and
gould," and in the wardrobe "One fyne Chena
Cannapie of Nedleworke with Tester vallance
and headcloth with a traine sutable to it,"[98]
among other obviously Chinese textiles.

Such silks were embroidered, as Francesco
Carletti wrote in 1598, "with sewing threads of
all the colours that can be imagined, both light
and dark . . . [with] work . . . of divers fantastic
figures of animals and birds never before seen,

and flowers, also extravagant, in which that land
[China] abounds . . . also adorned with leaves,
all very natural-looking."[99] In other words, they
were markedly different from the more ancient
Chinese silks that had had such a profound effect
upon Lucchese silk and Genoese velvet, and that
were themselves represented by their distant descendants as wallhangings in every great house in
Europe.[100]

Fig. 11.
Chinese needlework embroidery on
the bed hangings, state bed at Calke
Abbey, before 1734 (The National
Trust; photograph: Mark Fiennes)

Fig. 12.
Painted and dyed cotton hanging from Ashburnham House, West India, late 17th or early 18th century (Victoria and Albert Museum)

In all probability these late-sixteenth-century silks looked much like those on the great state bed from Calke Abbey (THB no. 375), which were probably made before 1734 (fig. 11). When these bed hangings were discovered they had with them, en suite, some panels which suggest that the walls may well have been hung with the same embroidery. In the late eighteenth century such a room would more likely have been hung with Chinese floral wallpaper.

Chinese wallpaper was a cheap substitute for cotton, just as cotton itself was, at least in part, a cheap substitute for silk. Painted, and later printed, cotton had been ordered from India in the early seventeenth century.[101] By the mid-seventeenth century European demand very strongly influenced the styles of export cotton, just as we have seen in the case of porcelain and lacquer. Such cottons were called "palampores" or, more generally, "chintz." On 5 September 1663 Pepys went with his wife "to Cornhill and after many tryalls bought my wife a Chinke; that is a paynted Indian Callico for to line her new Study, which is very pretty."[102] Most early chintz was patterned after the "tree-of-life" pattern, related to crewelwork patterns, in which a sinuous leafy tree grows from some form of

rocky ground (fig. 12). In the eighteenth century Chinese wallpapers were ordered to conform to this taste and were often painted or printed on a pale green background. When they were actually hung in a room, it was not uncommon for extra birds or flowers to be added, either painted in or applied as cutouts from other panels. Some other wallpapers depicted landscapes, sometimes nonrepeating, and yet others showed scenes such as the manufacture of tea.

Wallpapers of these types were much used in the more intimate rooms of houses: bedchambers, dressing rooms, or private sitting rooms. Many of the smaller bedchambers at Chatsworth are hung with Chinese wallpapers; many of the rooms at Osterley used to be.

In such bedrooms the bed curtains could be silk or cotton; at Osterley Mr. and Mrs. Child's bed was hung with embroidered Indian cotton, while in the Yellow Taffeta Bedroom (the principal guest bedroom) the bed is hung in Chinese yellow taffeta which is painted with flowers and foliage.[103] So much were these materials considered alike that it was not incongruous for the latter bed to have an Indian embroidered cotton counterpane. Much of the furniture, too, would have reflected the Orient—Chinese or Japanese lacquer cabinets and, in Mrs. Child's dressing room, an overmantel mirror of about 1765 by John Linnell with stands for porcelain. "The lodging rooms are in the atticks," wrote Lady Beauchamp Proctor in 1772, "and are furnished with the finest Chintzes, painted Taffatys, India paper and decker work, and such a profusion of rich China and Japan, that I could almost fancy myself in Peking."[104]

Of course many of the "oriental" things could be chinoiserie; in the State Bedchamber at Nostell Priory, Thomas Chippendale supplied the Chinese wallpaper as well as the famous suite of green japanned furniture.[105]

We have been discussing the use in British country houses of four types of oriental imports into the West. Almost all these imports from the East were heavily influenced by Western demand, and are thus often barely representative of the true arts of their origin. The carpets with coats of arms, the lacquer in Western shapes, the porcelain *garnitures de cheminée,* and above all the wallpaper, that splendid amalgam of European, Chinese, and Indian styles, were all demanded in styles and shapes useful in a Western setting; no

one in Europe was really having to adapt to a new idea.

Perhaps the exception to this is tea. It would be absurd to talk of the use of Eastern imports in English country houses without mentioning tea. A novelty in the mid-seventeenth century—Samuel Pepys first tasted it on 25 September 1660[106]—by the mid-eighteenth century it took more space in ships from the East and brought in more revenue than any other cargo.[107] The effect that the drinking of tea had upon the furniture, the arrangement of rooms, on ceramics, and on silver in Europe cannot be overemphasized, not to mention its effect on the daily habits of millions of western people (fig. 13).

Fig. 13.
A very lively tea party; drawing by Louis-Philippe Boitard, active in England c. 1735–1760 (The Visitors of the Ashmolean Museum, Oxford)

NOTES

1. For a discussion of carpets depicted in paintings, see Donald King and David Sylvester, *The Eastern Carpet in the Western World* [exh. cat., Hayward Gallery] (London, 1983).

2. John Mills, "The Coming of the Carpet to the West," in King and Sylvester 1983, 11–23.

3. Donald King, "The Inventories of the Carpets of King Henry VIII," *Hali* 5 (1983), 293–302.

4. Lindsay Boynton, "The Hardwick Hall Inventory of 1601," *Furniture History* 7 (1971), 1–40.

5. Gervase Jackson-Stops, ed., *The Treasure Houses of Britain: Five Hundred Years of Private Patronage and Art Collecting* [exh. cat., National Gallery of Art] (Washington, 1985), nos. 49, 50, 53, 54.

6. King and Sylvester 1983, pl. 1; see also Peter Thornton, *Seventeenth Century Interior Decoration in England, France and Holland* (New Haven and London, 1978).

7. May H. Beattie, "Antique Rugs at Hardwick Hall," *Oriental Art* 5 (1959), 52–61.

8. Beattie 1959, 60–61.

9. King and Sylvester 1983, no. 65; see also Gudrun Ekstrand, ed., *Islamic Treasures in the Royal Collection* [exh. cat., Royal Palace] (Stockholm, 1985), no. 1.

10. For an account of this trade, see John Irwin and P. R. Schwarz, *Studies in Indo-European Textile History* (Ahmedabad, 1966), 20–22.

11. John Irwin, *The Girdlers' Carpet* (London, 1962).

12. See, for instance, King and Sylvester 1983, pl. 24.

13. Peter Thornton, *Authentic Decor: The Domestic Interior 1620–1820* (New Haven, 1985).

14. Evelyn Philip Shirley, "An Inventory of the Effects of Henry Howard, K.G., Earl of Northampton, Taken on His Death in 1614," *Archaeologia* 42 (1869), 347–378.

15. C. E. C. Tattersall and S. Reed, *A History of British Carpets* (Leigh on Sea, 1966), 27–28.

16. Shirley 1869.

17. J. O. Halliwell [Phillipps], *Ancient Inventories of Furniture, Pictures, Tapestry, Plate etc. illustrative of the Domestic Manners of the English in the Sixteenth and Seventeenth Centuries* (London, 1834).

18. Inventory of Hatfield House, 1611, Hatfield House. Information kindly given to me by Robin Harcourt Williams.

19. Arthur Spriggs, "Oriental Porcelain in Western Paintings 1450–1700," *Transactions of the Oriental Ceramic Society* 36 (1965), 73–87, figs. 59a, b.

20. R. W. Lightbown, "Oriental Art and the Orient in Late Renaissance and Baroque Italy," *Journal of the Warburg and Courtauld Institutes* 32 (1969), 230–280; see also Marco Spallanzani, *Ceramiche Orientale a Firenze nel Rinascimento* (Florence, 1978).

21. D. F. Lunsingh Scheurleer, *Chinesisches und japanisches Porzellan in europäischen Fassungen* (Brunswick, 1980); Francis Watson, *Chinese Porcelains in European Mounts* [exh. cat., China House Gallery] (New York, 1980).

22. John Ayers, "The Early China Trade," in Oliver Impey and Arthur MacGregor, eds., *The Origins of Museums: The Cabinet of Curiosities in Sixteenth and Seventeenth Century Europe* (Oxford, 1985), 259–266.

23. T. Volker, "Porcelain and the Dutch East India Company," *Medelingen van het Rijksmuseum voor Volkenkunde, Leiden* 11 (1954), 1–243.

24. Chinese celadon had been imported into Europe from Turkey and from Egypt. Few celadons were carried by either the Portuguese or the Dutch.

25. Volker 1954, 109.

26. Oliver Impey, "Japan; Trade and Collecting in Seventeenth Century Europe," in Impey and MacGregor 1985, 267–273.

27. Oliver Impey, "Porcelain for the West," *Connoisseur* 203 (1981), 196–199.

28. C. J. A. Jörg, *Porcelain and the Dutch China Trade* (The Hague, 1982).

29. C. J. A. Jörg, *Oosters porselein Delfts aardewerk; Wisselwerkingen* [exh. cat., Groninger Museum] (Groningen, 1983).

30. Hugh Honour, *Chinoiserie; the Vision of Cathay* (London, 1961); Oliver Impey, *Chinoiserie; the Impact of Oriental Styles on Western Art and Decoration* (Oxford and New York, 1977).

31. Impey and MacGregor 1985, 262.

32. Will of Sir Walter Raleigh, July 1597, Sherborne Castle. Information kindly given to me by George Wingfield Digby.

33. Louise Avery, "Chinese Porcelain in English Mounts," *The Metropolitan Museum of Art Bulletin* 2 (1944), 266.

34. Inventory of Hatfield House, 1629, Hatfield House.

35. Thornton 1978, 249, 383, n. 22.

36. Thornton 1978, 63–67, 249–252.

37. Culpepper Tanner, "An Inventory of the Goods in Burghley House belonging to the Right Hon[ble] John Earl of Exeter and Anne Countess of Exeter Taken August 21 1688," Burghley House.

38. T. H. Lunsingh Scheurleer, "Documents on the Furnishing of Kensington House," *Journal of the Walpole Society* 38 (1960–1962), 15–58; see also Linda Shulsky, "Queen Mary's Collection of Porcelain and Delft and Its Display at Kensington Palace," (M.A. thesis, Cooper-Hewitt Museum and Parson's School of Design, 1985).

39. The Oranienburg pyramids can be seen in a print by J. B. Broebes, 1733. At least one still exists in the Charlottenburg Palace. Information kindly given to me by Dr. Winfried Baer.

40. Mirror glass was frequently used with the display of porcelain, however, even on the ceiling, as at Het Loo Palace, the Netherlands.

41. See the prints by Daniel Marot, *Nouveaux Lievre de Cheminées à la Hollandoise,* c. 1690. There seems to be no pictorial record of the rooms at Hampton Court. See also Thornton 1978, 66, 250.

42. See the prints by Eosander von Göthe in M. Merian, *Theatrum Europaei* 16 (1717), 17 (1718).

43. Soame Jenyns, *Japanese Porcelain* (London, 1965), 7.

44. Watson 1980.

45. For a chronology of Japanese export lacquer, see Oliver Impey, "Japanese Export Lacquer of the 17th Century," in William Watson, ed., *Lacquerwork in Asia and Beyond,* Percival David Foundation Colloquy on Art and Archaeology in Asia, no. 11 (London, 1981), 124–158.

46. Joe Earle, "Genji meets Yang Guifei: a Group of Japanese Export Lacquers," *Transactions of the Oriental Ceramic Society* 47 (1984), 45–76.

47. William Dampier, *A New Voyage Round the World* (London, 1699), 2:60.

48. Engelbert Kaempfer, *The History of Japan* (London, 1727).

49. C. J. A. Jörg, "Japanese Lacquerwork Decorated After European Prints," in *Collection of Essays in Commemoration of the 30th Anniversary of the Institute of Oriental and Occidental Studies, Kansai University* (Osaka, 1981), 57–80.

50. Quoted in Robert W. Symonds, "Furniture from the Indies," *Connoisseur* 93 (1934), 283–289.

51. Dampier 1699, 2:62.

52. Quoted in Robert W. Symonds, "Furniture from the Indies II," *Connoisseur* 94 (1934), 38–44.

53. Hans Huth, *Lacquer of the West; the History of a Craft and an Industry 1550–1950* (Chicago and London, 1971), 14.

54. Symonds 1934, 284.

55. John Stalker and George Parker, *A Treatise of Japanning and Varnishing* (London, 1688).

56. Symonds 1934, part 2, 40.

57. Symonds 1934, part 2, 40.

58. Lunsingh Scheurleer 1960–1962, 35.

59. Oliver Impey, "Lacquer and Japann in European Furniture," in *Summer Exhibition Catalogue* [Partridge Fine Arts] (London, 1984), 20–24.

60. Boynton 1971.

61. Inventory of Hatfield House, 1611.

62. Shirley 1869, 354.

63. Ernest M. Satow, *The Voyage of Captain John Saris to Japan 1613* (London, 1900).

64. John Irwin, "A Jacobean Vogue for Oriental Lacquer Ware," *Burlington Magazine* 95 (1953), 193–194.

65. Inventory of Salisbury House, 1629, Hatfield House. Information kindly given to me by Robin Harcourt Williams.

66. Joan Hornby, "Japan," in Bente Dam-Mikkelsen and Torben Lundbaek, eds., *Ethnographical Objects in the Danish Royal Kunstkammer 1650–1800* (Copenhagen, 1980), 221–252.

67. William Watson, ed., *The Great Japan Exhibition: Art of the Edo Period 1600–1868* [exh. cat., Royal Academy of Arts] (London, 1981), no. 155.

68. Samuel Pepys, *The Diary of Samuel Pepys,* ed. Robert Latham and William Matthews, 11 vols. (London, 1970), 2: 79.

69. John Evelyn, *The Diary of John Evelyn,* ed. E. S. de Beer, 6 vols. (Oxford, 1955), 3: 324.

70. Evelyn 1955, 4:190.

71. Peter Thornton and Maurice Tomlin, "The Furnishing and Decoration of Ham House," *Furniture History* 16 (1980), 134, 181.

72. Lunsingh Scheurleer 1960–1962.

73. Thornton and Tomlin 1980, 114.

74. Now in the Victoria and Albert Museum.

75. Evelyn 1955, 4:288.

76. Ralph Edwards, *The Dictionary of English Furniture,* 2d ed. (London, 1954), II, 271.

77. Celia Fiennes, *The Journey of Celia Fiennes,* ed. Christopher Morris (London, 1949), 100.

78. Celia Fiennes 1949, 69.

79. T. H. Lunsingh Scheurleer, "Stadhouderlijke Lakkabinetten," in *Opstellen voor H. van der Waal* (Amsterdam and Leiden, 1970).

80. Quoted in full in J. A. Worp, "De Briefwisseling van Constantijn Huygens (1608–1687)," *Rijks Geschiedkundige Publikaties* 6 (1917), 456. I am grateful to Dr. A. M. L. E. Erkelens for drawing my attention to this publication.

81. Sale, Christie's, London, 29 November 1984, lot 109.

82. I am grateful to John Hardy for clarifying this point for me.

83. Gladys Scott Thomson, *The Russells in Bloomsbury (1669–1771)* (Oxford, 1940), 344.

84. Thornton and Tomlin 1980, 114.

85. Information kindly given to me by John Hardy.

86. Culpepper Tanner 1688.

87. Thornton and Tomlin 1980, 134.

88. Thomson 1940, 342.

89. Earle 1984, 46–75.

90. For an illustration of such a lacquer in a painting by Simon Renard de Saint-André (1613–1677), see Thornton 1978, pl. 239.

91. Thornton and Tomlin 1980, 134. It seems that the protection of the better pieces of furniture with leather covers was not uncommon.

92. Inventory of Salisbury House, 1629.

93. Francis W. Steer, "The Inventory of Anne, Viscountess Dorchester," *Notes and Queries* 198 (1953), 469–473.

94. Mogens Bencard, "Dronning Charlotte Amalies Kunstkab," in Gunilla Eriksson, ed., *Neptuns Kabinett* (Lund, 1985), 22–42.

95. For the set in the Danish Royal Collection, see Hornby 1980, 239, 240.

96. Christian Theuerkauff, "The Brandenburg *Kunstkammer* in Berlin," in Impey and MacGregor 1985, 110–114.

97. Lightbown 1969, 237.

98. Inventory of Hatfield House, 1611.

99. Lightbown 1969, 237.

100. Impey 1977, 63–65.

101. John Irwin and Katherine B. Brett, *The Origin of Chintz* (London, 1970).

102. Pepys 1970, 4:299.

103. John Hardy and Maurice Tomlin, *Osterley Park House (London,* 1985), 50–55.

104. Quoted by Hardy and Tomlin 1985, 105–106, from a letter written by Lady Beauchamp Proctor in 1772.

105. Lindsay Boynton and Nicholas Goodison, "Thomas Chippendale at Nostell Priory," *Furniture History* 4 (1968), 10–61. One "sheet fine India paper" seems to have cost about the same as one yard of chintz.

106. Pepys 1970, 1:253.

107. Jörg 1982, appendix 8, 217–220.

ANNA SOMERS COCKS

The Nonfunctional Use of Ceramics in the English Country House During the Eighteenth Century

The rising popularity and increased availability of china in the later seventeenth century has been analyzed by Oliver Impey elsewhere in this volume. This paper sets out to describe what was done with that china—the oriental porcelain—and the other types of ceramics that were acquired by the English gentry and nobility. It deliberately leaves out tablewares, whose use is bound up with issues—such as changes in gastronomic fashion and in table manners—separate from interior design.

"For use and ornament" is a recurring phrase in eighteenth-century advertisements, and it is the ornamental aspect that is considered here. This also has to do with ceramic collecting and with what was considered rare and fine at any given period. In 1700 only two sorts of ceramics would normally have been considered important enough for display in the state rooms of a nobleman's house: oriental porcelain—whether Chinese, Japanese, or the one imitating the other—and Delftware, the tin-glazed earthenware often made in imitation of oriental porcelain, but also manufactured in elaborate baroque forms which owed little to the East and more to the designs of Daniel Marot, court architect to William and Mary. This Delftware tended to be found in households in which the family had had some formal attachment to the monarchs, such as at Dyrham Park, Avon, where the builder of the house, William Blathwayt, served on an embassy to the Hague and subsequently became an important court official. The very small number of purely ornamental pieces made of English "Delftware" suggests that it did not rank as highly as Dutch, although it was bought by the lesser gentry, as shown by certain armorial examples.

In the late seventeenth century the fashion for what might be called the architectural use of ceramics had been established; the heavy moldings of a baroque room—the cornices, overdoors and large mantelpieces—were ideal places for china. The amount displayed was often very great as porcelain began to be imported in large quantities. It was still an exciting novelty, but no longer as rare as it had been when it received the attentions of still-life painters such as Willem Kalf (1622-1693). The court of the House of Orange, with its easy access to the imports of the Dutch East India Company, seems to have been the origin of the integrated decorative use of porcelain in rooms designed for that purpose. Mary's apartments in The Hague and at Honsselarsdijk, her country house nearby, both included porcelain rooms. In 1687 her audience chamber at the latter was "very richly furnished with Chinese work and pictures. The ceiling was covered with mirrors which showed the room afresh, so that, with the most beautiful effect imaginable, the more one gazed into the reflections, the more endlessly extended the perspectives. The chimney-piece was full of precious porcelain, part standing half inside it and so fitted together that one piece supported another" (fig. 1).[1]

From 1689, after her move to England, Mary decorated the old Water Gallery at Hampton Court as her temporary dwelling place, while Christopher Wren's more ambitious plans for the southeast range of the vast building were being executed. Daniel Defoe described her apartments with extreme admiration: "Here, as if she had been conscious that she had but a few years to enjoy it [Mary died in 1694] the Queen order'd all the little neat curious Things to be done, which suited her Convenience, and made it the pleasantest little Thing within Doors that could possibly be made, tho' its Situation being such as it could not be allowed to stand after the Great Building was finished; we now see no remains of it. The Queen had here her Gallery of Beauties, being the Pictures, at full length, of the principal Ladies attending upon her Majesty. . . . And here was also her Majesty's fine Collection of *Delft* Ware, which indeed was very large and fine; and here was also a vast stock of fine *China* ware, the like whereof was not then to be seen in *England;* the long Gallery, as above, was fill'd with this China and every Place, where it could be placed, with Advantage."[2] As Defoe says, the Water Gallery no longer survives, but we do have an engraving by Daniel Marot which may represent the Gallery of Beauties, and the Office of Works Accounts gives hints of how it was fitted out, with a lot of routine moldings and ten brackets, "half boy and foliage," which may well have been for china shelves.[3] The general effect to which she aspired must also be reflected in the series of drawings executed for her by Grinling Gibbons of projects both for Kensington Palace and Hampton Court. Although it is almost certain that none was executed *in toto,* they show the queen's "Custom or Humour," as Defoe put it, "of furnishing Houses with *China*-ware, which spread to lesser mortals and increased to a strange degree afterwards, piling their *China* upon the tops of Cabinets, Scrutores, and every Chymney-Piece, to the Tops of the Ceilings and even setting up Shelves for their China-Ware, where they wanted such Places, till it became a grievance in the Expence of it and even injurious to their Families and Estates."[4] Whether this last censorious comment was justified we do not know, but the queen's personal influence on how porcelain was displayed must have been reinforced by the circulation of Daniel Marot's engravings, and there is no doubt that the style was quickly picked up by those in close contact with the court.

At Petworth in Sussex, which was much rebuilt in the grand baroque manner at the end of the seventeenth century by the 6th Duke of Somerset, the arrangement of the porcelain is recorded in the inventory made in 1749 after the duke's death at the age of eighty-three.[5] The arrangement described was almost certainly fashionable in the early part of the century, rather than at the date of writing. The ceramics are all referred to as "China" and it is clear that porcelain is intended by this, as the small amount of

Delftware in the house is always described as such; "China," until the very end of the eighteenth century, always meant porcelain of oriental origin. Occasionally, in the inventory of 1749, a piece is called "Japan china," which shows that there was an understanding of the differences between Japanese and Chinese porcelain at the time, but whether the difference between the Japanese, and the Japanese in the Chinese manner, was perceived is uncertain. Occasionally colors, such as "blue and white" or "red and white," are specified.

The inventory shows that there was a great deal of porcelain in most of the state rooms including the bedrooms, but not in the dining

Fig. 1.
Engraving of a late seventeenth-century porcelain room, possibly in the Dutch royal house of Honsselarsdijk, by Daniel Marot (c. 1663–1752), from *Opera D. Marot Architecti Gulielmi III Regis Magna Britanniae,* The Hague, 1703 (Victoria and Albert Museum)

Fig. 2.
Consoles for porcelain, 1730s, part
of the plasterwork in the dining
room at Easton Neston   (*Country
Life*)

room, vestibule, or on the staircase. For example, in the King of Spain's Bedchamber, so called because the future Emperor Charles VI had stayed there early in the century, there was one large blue and white china jar over the chimney together with eleven pieces of "different sorts of China upon the same place." There was porcelain over the doors in the South Gallery and in the Closet to the Duchess's Bedchamber, where a device reminiscent of the mirrored ceiling at Honsselarsdijk was used. A looking-glass panel was introduced over the door and the chimney, "both ornamented with carved work and 45 pieces of China."

The same disposition of china can be found at Drayton House in Northamptonshire, another residence with baroque additions from the time of William and Mary by Sir John Germain, an Anglo-Dutch soldier of fortune. Described by Horace Walpole in 1763 as, "Covered in portraits, crammed with old China, furnished richly, not a rag in it under forty, fifty or a thousand years old,"[6] the house was inventoried in 1710.[7] Most of the porcelain remaining there today is Kangxi (1662–1722), and includes *famille verte*, celadon, and *blanc-de-chine* figures. In the Great Parlour "at the foot of the Walnut Staircase" there were nine pieces of chinaware over each door and twenty-two pieces of "China ware" over the chimney. In the state bedroom there were "two little blue and white rollwagons [a cylindrical-bodied vase current in the mid-seventeenth century in Kangxi porcelain], two China bottles, two little blue and gold rollwagons, two flowerpots with three feet and one little blue and white Jarr on a door cornice," while in a special adjoining lacquer china closet (a small intimate room, not a cupboard) the corner shelf supported sixty-eight pieces of china.

Some gilt étagères, now of great rarity, were made to enable porcelain to be hung on the walls at Drayton: one has the arms of the Duchess of Norfolk, Sir John Germain's first wife and collector of most of the china, who died in 1705, and three bear the arms of Lady Betty Germain, his second wife. These are movable equivalents to the wall consoles shown in Daniel Marot's engraving (fig. 1), a necessary invention as furnishings in the seventeenth and throughout the eighteenth century remained sparse and confined to the edges of the rooms, so that the area available to show objects of any kind was strictly limited. Such consoles are part of a broad overall design at Easton Neston in Northamptonshire (fig. 2), which William Kent remodeled in the 1730s. They are suspended from plasterwork swags on either side of the chimneypiece in the dining room (now a drawing room), and were clearly intended to take large vases. The rococo carved overmantel from Berkeley House in Gloucestershire (fig. 3) is a mass of little shelves for porcelain, and Mrs. Child's bedroom at Osterley Park, Middlesex, has a delicate gilt overmantel mirror designed by John Linnell about 1765, which also has three shelves for china. The rococo descendants of the Drayton étagères are the designs (fig. 4) published in 1756 by Thomas Johnson (fl. c. 1755–1766). These closely resemble the equally light and airy gilt rococo wall sconces of the period, while others by George

Edwards (fl. c. 1750–1778) and Matthias Darley (fl. c. 1741–c. 1771), published in 1754, are in the fanciful Chinese manner of contemporary china cabinets.

Neither as part of the fabric, nor in their movable form, do such shelves and consoles occur in grand neo-classical interiors, nor indeed in lesser interiors, until the invention, in the early nineteenth century, of light, hanging wall shelves. However, the mantelshelf and door cornice (where wide enough) continued throughout the eighteenth and into the early nineteenth century to be the basic places where ceramics could be displayed. Queen Charlotte, wife of George III, was a noted collector of porcelain and a constant

Fig. 3.
Rococo carved overmantel with shelves for porcelain, Berkeley House, Wootton-under-Edge, Gloucestershire, c. 1760 (Victoria and Albert Museum)

admirer of oriental art in all materials; her breakfast room at Buckingham House, illustrated in a
lithograph of 1819 (fig. 5)[8] shows both these surfaces (although in the case of the mantelshelf it is
a secondary one) covered with Imari porcelain
against lacquered panels on the walls.

The tall beakers and vases over the door on the
left-hand side are a classic set or "garniture" of
the kind imitated by western factories. Such a
combination of vases or jars and beakers or bottles was not oriental in origin, since the only
truly oriental garniture was one made for altars,
consisting of a perfume burner, two vases, and
two candlesticks. Garnitures became fashionable
first in the Netherlands in the last third of the
seventeenth century. Initially they were free
combinations of types, but they settled down
into the typical five-piece or seven-piece group-
ing that the Chinese then began to make specifically as a set for the export market.[9] Western
imitations in a variety of materials started to
appear from the 1670s onward. There are two
pairs of silver bottles and beakers with the London hallmark for 1677 at Belvoir Castle in Rut-
land, and a pair of beakers and a silver jar, un-
marked but of similar date, at Knole in Kent.
Delft was producing large numbers in lead-
glazed earthenware, the set being called a "Kast-

stel," something which stood on a cupboard ("Kasten").[10] Meissen was making them in porcelain from the factory's first decade of production, between 1710 and 1720; Chelsea ones are mentioned by name in the advertisements from 1755 onward,[11] but may have been in production earlier; Bow produced them as of 1758, and other factories followed suit.

The fireplace was another area that remained a constant site for ceramics throughout the eighteenth and into the nineteenth century. It was thought to look undressed without a fire in it, and so was either covered with a painted chimney board or concealed behind a large vase. The inventories of Dyrham dated 1703 and 1710 repeatedly record Delftware "flowerpots" in the fireplaces of the principal rooms.[12] Vases can be seen in Daniel Marot's engraving of a porcelain room (fig. 1), and in Arthur Devis's painting of Mr. and Mrs. William Atherton (fig. 6), which depicts a room furnished in the typically sparse manner of the eighteenth century, with an oriental covered vase in the fireplace. Sometimes an urn was put there, containing an orange, myrtle, or bay tree moved in from the greenhouse; sometimes that position was taken up with a large open pot in which greenery and blossoms were arranged. As fireplaces were filled up with hob or dog grates from the 1760s onward, the demand for pots to go in them may have slackened. The tall Delftware pyramids, which survive at Dyrham, Chatsworth, and elsewhere, were used for flowers, but they were probably not intended for the hearth as their nozzles project in all four directions, an unnecessary feature if only the front can be seen.[13] Josiah Wedgwood, writing to Thomas Bentley on 25 July 1772, sums up contemporary usage and some of the confusions that had occurred: "This morning I have had an opportunity of consulting with Lady Gower and Lady Teignham and their two Lords (who have been at the works here and bo! some flower pots) upon the subject of Bough pots, and find that they prefer those things with the spouts, such as the old Delft ones and they say that sort keep the flowers distinct and clever. Vases are furniture for a chimney-piece—Bough pots for a hearth, under a Slab or Marble Table; I think they can never be used one instead of the other, and I apprehend one reason why we have not made our *dressing* flowerpots to please has been adapting them for Chimney pieces where I think they do not place any pots dress'd with flowers. If I am wrong in this idea I should be glad to be set

right as it is of consequence in forming these articles to know where to put them."[14]

No doubt Wedgwood was correct, writing as he was when the austerities of neo-classicism were influencing taste, but twenty years earlier, when rococo and the naturalism intrinsic to that style were all the rage, flowers were certainly seen on mantelpieces. There are beaker-shaped vases full of them in Hogarth's *The Lady's Last Stake* of 1759 (Albright-Knox Art Gallery, Buffalo), and Chelsea in 1755 advertised "a set for a chimney-piece or a cabinet consisting of seven JARS and BEAKERS, *beautifully enamelled with flowers,* and the beakers filled with flowers *after nature.*"[15]

The enduring place for flowers was the window embrasure. Queen Charlotte's Green Pavilion at Frogmore in Berkshire, depicted in a lithograph of 1819 (fig. 7), has flowerpots on small, easily movable tables, and at Osterley Park, Middlesex, there still survive plain mahogany tables of the 1760s, for the same purpose.

Like the fireplace, the corners of rooms were considered to be in need of adornment. A satire in *The Spectator* of 12 February 1712 involves a City of London gentleman who has married the

Fig. 6.
Mr. and Mrs. Atherton by Arthur Devis (1763–1822), c. 1740, oil on canvas (Walker Art Gallery, Liverpool)

Fig. 7.
Lithograph of the Green Pavilion,
Frogmore, 1819 (Victoria and Albert
Museum)

uppity and condescending daughter of a peer and complains that his wife has "set herself to reform every Room of my House, having glazed every chimney-piece with Looking-glass, and planted every corner with such Heaps of China that I am obliged to move about my own house with the greatest Caution and Circumspection."[16] Obviously one must allow for exaggeration here, but at Petworth in 1749 there were eight vases in the corners of the rooms. By the time the next inventory was made in 1763,[17] these corner vases had increased in number to fourteen, and the most up-to-date room in the house, the rococo White and Gold Room dating to between 1754 and 1755, had very large china jars with covers, three feet four inches high, in two of its corners. As the earlier inventory is less precise in its descriptions and does not give measurements, one cannot tell whether these entered the house at the time of the 6th Duke, who died in 1748, or were acquired by his successors, the 7th Duke, who died in 1749, and the 2nd Earl of Egremont, who lived until 1763. Drayton in 1710 also had

"two very large China Jars and Covers" in the King's Dining Room,[18] presumably standing on the floor, where they can still be seen.

Three different kinds of carved stands for vases, dating to the 1690s, survive at Petworth, and at Hampton Court there are some similar ones. It may be that Drayton also had something like them, as the "Long Gallery at ye Top of ye Great Stairs" had "Two Delf flower potts upon Black pedistals."[19] A Delftware flower vase that survives at Drayton, shaped like a circular tureen with a flattish lid out of which stick fish heads with open mouths to hold flowers, may be one of these. There are two neo-classical vase pedestals at Erddig in Wales, and there are stands by Thomas Chippendale for large, almost circular pots at Harewood House (THB no. 366). Chippendale also published designs for stands (fig. 8) in *The Gentleman and Cabinet Makers Director* of 1754, whose purpose was to give jars of merely middling height more prominence.

Great eighteenth-century houses, both in town and in the country, were often furnished

Stands for China Jarrs

Fig. 8.
Engraved design for stands by
Thomas Chippendale in *The Gentleman and Cabinet Makers Director*,
1754

with giant vases, extraordinary achievements of
the potter's craft. At Corsham Court in Wiltshire five vast Chinese covered blue and white
jars still stand in the windows and on either side
of the end door in the picture gallery, a triple-
cube room built by Paul Methuen in about 1770
and hung with crimson damask. The jars had
come to Methuen, together with other substantial pieces of oriental porcelain, from the Grosvenor Street house of his cousin and godfather,
Sir Paul Methuen, the diplomat, traveler, and
collector of porcelain and antiquities.[20] Captain
Henry Napier, writing of the childhood of his
mother, the beautiful Lady Sarah Lennox, says
that she was often taken to see King George II
(1683–1760) in Kensington Palace, and in the
1750s, "on one occasion, after a romp with my
mother he suddenly snatched her up in his arms,
and after depositing her in a large china jar, shut
down the cover to prove her courage: but soon
released her when he found that the only effect
was to make her with a merry voice begin sing-
ing the French song of 'Malbruk', with which
he was quite delighted."[21]

Considering the range of furniture on which
ceramics might be displayed, and comparing it
with that of the nineteenth or twentieth century,
one realizes how limited the choice was, even in
a great house. From the 1660s onward the classic
piece was the cabinet on a stand, itself often of
oriental origin. One can be seen in the painting
by Arthur Devis (fig. 6), and one was at Drayton in 1710, in Lady Betty Germain's drawing
room, where there were, "One China jarr, four
Bottles, two wherof has gold Tips, Two blew
and gold coloured rollwagons All upon ye Indian
Cabinet."[22] In 1749, at Petworth, every cabinet
was covered with china; for example, there were
eleven pieces each on the two cabinets in the
King of Spain's Drawing Room. Pieces were
also put under cabinets, between the legs of the
stands, and at Drayton there are still a pair of
Chinese black and gold lacquer cabinets at either
end of the Green Drawing Room on unusually
elaborate carved and gilded stands, made in England in the 1690s, each with nine separate plat-
forms on their stretchers to take vases or jars.
Porcelain was not, however, placed on the pieces
of furniture that traditionally stood against the
window piers—that is, on commodes or pier
tables—as is implicit in Wedgwood's remarks
quoted earlier. In the Drayton inventories of 1710

and 1749 and in the Petworth inventories of 1763, china is recorded in this position only once. A pier table would either have borne a candelabrum (fig. 5), if there were no candlestands flanking it, or, as in the case of the grand marble-topped tables in the state rooms at Petworth in 1763, some other kind of item considered more worthy of display there: a marble bust, for example, in the Carved Room, and a small marble sleeping Hermaphrodite in the Tapestry Room. Porcelain vases were placed under the pier and side tables, however—an extension of the idea that the space between the legs of a cabinet should be filled.

Around 1800 some new types of furniture evolved to clothe the walls that had hitherto been lined with chairs or settees: the low cabinet or bookcase, often incorporating old boulle or lacquer panels, or the table placed against an internal wall (fig. 7). These provided new areas that could be decorated with porcelain. William H. Pyne, in his *History of the Royal Residences* published in 1819,[23] shows a low-level bookcase, its top supporting a Sèvres garniture and two candelabra, to the right of the fireplace in the Golden Drawing Room of Carlton House, the Prince Regent's London palace. A circular center table, which was the focus of activity in a room, became a common feature, and this was often ornamented with a large vase, usually containing flowers.

In the eighteenth century there would not have been a table permanently placed in the center of any room, with only one exception: both the Drayton inventory of 1710 and the Petworth one of 1749 record tea tables or occasionally, in the case of Drayton, a tray, permanently laid out with teapot, cups, and other vessels in the grander bedrooms and even in the state rooms. Thus, at Drayton in the "King's Dining Room" there was "one eight-Cornered inlaid tea table with blew and white Cups and Sawcers A large bason and a sugar pott A Brown Tea Pott;" in the Blue Drawing Room on the upper floor, "A Cain tea table with six blue and white old Chaney tea Cups and Sawcers A dish for the tea pot a new tea Pot and a Sugar Box and a Bason and 6 silver Spoons and a Little Shovel A milk jug and a sugar dish 4 Bath [?] mettal spoons A Japan Box under the table 2 Handkerchers to cover the tea tables . . . Six coffee cups with Handles & sawcers upon the table with one foot." And there was more in a dressing room, the long gallery, and the drawing room to the

"Spangled bedroom."[24] At Petworth in the King of Spain's bedchamber, there was "A Japan tea table $\frac{w}{th}$ 6 tea cups and 7 sawcers 2 Sugar dishes and one tea pot in a large sawcer," and one each in the dressing room to the Crimson Damask Bedchamber and in the Tapestry Room.[25] This, like the early eighteenth-century English portraits of families having tea, presumably reflected the fashionable display of a still relatively novel (and expensive) pastime. By 1763, however, it had become commonplace, and so the tea tables disappeared from the rooms at Petworth.

By the 1760s the quantity and range of available ceramics had greatly increased. The shipments of oriental porcelain must have risen enormously if the English East Indies trade was at all comparable with that of the Dutch East India Company, which imported more between 1729 and 1734 than in the whole period between 1602 and 1682.[26] The European and English manufactories were also now in operation. The wares of Meissen, the first factory in Europe to discover the secret of hard-paste porcelain, were being imported into England from the 1740s onward. The other manufactories on the Continent, with the exception of Vincennes and Sèvres, are rarely mentioned by name in contemporary advertisements, leading one to wonder whether only a few connoisseurs like Horace Walpole took an interest in them. The factories at Chelsea and Bow were in production from 1745 and 1747 respectively, Lund's Bristol between 1749 and 1752, Worcester from 1751, and Derby from about 1750. Much of this ceramic ware was sold at well-publicized auctions, and visiting the salerooms became part of fashionable life from the mid-eighteenth century onward. Meissen porcelain (perhaps cheerful commedia dell'arte figures and shepherds and shepherdesses) was even being sold at night in May 1749 in shops around the amphitheater at Ranelagh pleasure gardens, which were visited by Horace Walpole.[27] James Christie, who began his career as an auctioneer in 1763, furthered the connection between porcelain and high society, and whenever an important collection was to be sold his great room would be lit up and a reception held, with an official from the opera to prevent the riffraff from entering.[28] Of course porcelain was only one of the things to be sold at these auctions, but it must have helped make the mere act of buying chic. The excitement stimulated by the choice now available also made the third quarter of the eighteenth century a heyday for upper-class interest in ceramics.

It is no coincidence that the china cabinet as a piece of freestanding furniture first appears in the 1750s. Thomas Chippendale published a number of designs for these in *The Gentleman and Cabinet Makers Director* of 1754 and in subsequent editions. One design (fig. 9), which he actually executed for Milton Abbey in Dorset, is now in the Olaf Hambro collection in Denmark. Such a cabinet is the descendant of the expensive ebony, ivory, marquetry, lacquer, or japanned cabinets which, after the bed, were traditionally the most important furnishing of a bedchamber and in which small, expensive *Kunstkammer*-type objects were kept, to be brought out and admired among friends. A Flemish ivory-veneered cabinet is still in the Queen's Bedchamber at Ham House, Middlesex, and there was a large Japan cabinet in the Countess of Devonshire's bedchamber at Chatsworth in 1690.[29] The emergence of the china cabinet implies that china was viewed as not merely ornamental, but collectable and worthy of safe but easily accessible housing in a specially designed piece of furniture. (It should be noted that glazed bookcases and bureau-bookcases were not used for displaying ceramics, as they so often are today. Such a confusion of categories would be quite atypical of the eighteenth century.)

Nearly all surviving examples of eighteenth-century china cabinets (and they do not appear to be a very common type) are in the Chinese style, a tribute to the origins of the porcelain displayed in them. They were undoubtedly made for bedrooms or closets, since the Chinese style was used almost exclusively for those apartments—as at Erddig in North Wales, Nostell Priory in Yorkshire, and Osterley Park in Middlesex. There was a strong tendency, also, for these rooms to be the women's quarters, and this brings up an essential point about the collecting of china in the eighteenth century: it was largely, although not exclusively, a feminine occupation. Queen Mary, the Duchesses of Portland, Norfolk, and Somerset, and the Countess of Devonshire were all great collectors at the end of the seventeenth century. The complaint quoted earlier, by the city gentleman about his wife's china buying, is typical. Hogarth's painting of the Countess' dressing room in the series Mariage à la Mode, painted about 1743, shows her at the dressing table while a dealer offers her all manner of oddities and ceramics of a caricatured oriental

China Case.

appearance. The *Birmingham Gazette* of 5 March 1753, summarizing David Garrick's play *Lethe,* describes the amusements of the heroine, the "Fine Lady," thus: "She lies in bed all morning, rattles about all day, and sits up all night . . . ridicules her friends, coquets with her lovers, sets 'em together by the ears, tells fibs, makes mischief, buys china, cheats at cards, keeps a pug-dog and hates the parsons."[30] In 1762 Horace Walpole wrote of Melbury, home of the Earl of Ilchester, as being furnished, "with the finest old China and Japan collected by Mrs Horner,"[31] the mother-in-law of the earl.

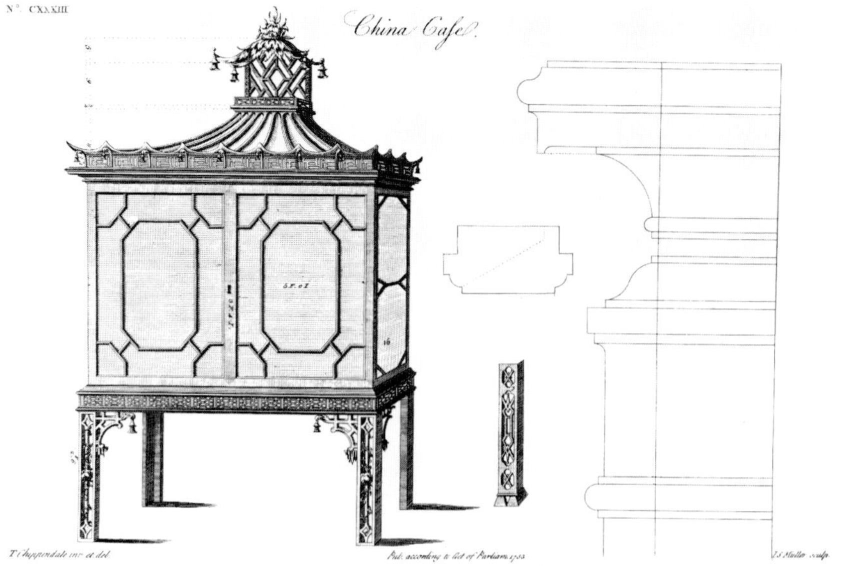

Women had a powerful voice in the ceramics market, a fact that is implicit in a satirical article (often the most revealing form of journalism) in *The Adventurer* of 20 November 1753. It describes an imaginary visit to Bedlam where "You wonder to see that cell beautified with Chinese vases and urns. It is inhabited by that famous virtuoso Lady Harriet Brittle, whose opinion was formerly decisive at all auctions, where she was usually appealed to about the genuineness of porcelain. She purchased at an exorbitant price a Mandarin and a Jos that were the envy of the female connoisseurship and were allowed to be inestimable. They were placed at the upper end of a little rock-work temple of Chinese architecture, in which neither propriety, proportion nor true beauty were considered, and were carefully

Fig. 9.
Engraved design of a china cabinet by Thomas Chippendale, in *The Gentleman and Cabinet Makers Director,* 1754

packed up in different boxes; but the brutish waggoner happening to overturn the carriage, they were crushed to pieces. The poor lady's understanding could not survive so irreparable a loss; and her relatives, to soothe her passion, had provided those Chelsea urns with which she decorated her chamber, and which she believes to be the true Nanqin.''[32] (This, incidentally, shows that the writer still thought oriental porcelain to be superior to English wares.)

Women were not only important buyers of ceramics; they also sold it. Much of the porcelain bought for Petworth by the 6th Duke of Somerset in the 1690s was from a Mrs. Harrison,[33] and Horace Walpole, under the pseudonym of Adam Fitzadam, mentioned perhaps the most famous china woman of all in *The World* of 8 February 1753, when he castigated society for decorating its dessert tables with Meissen figurines: "Toymen and china-shops were the only fashionable purveyors of polite entertainment. Women of the first quality came home from Chenevix's laden with dolls and babies, not for their children but for their housekeepers.''[34] Mrs. Chenevix was the widow of the goldsmith and toyman Paul Daniel Chenevix (died 1742), and the phe-

nomenon of women china sellers may well be analogous with the well-established one of widow goldsmiths carrying on their husband's profession after his death. An engraving of 1750 (fig. 10) is probably an accurate depiction of Chenevix's shop front in Charing Cross, the bow windows full of vases and pagods.[35]

The great force represented by women in the ceramic markets was recognized by that consummate retailer Josiah Wedgwood, who told Capability Brown that his [Wedgwood's] life, "was devoted to the service of the Ladys, as his [Brown's] was to that of the Noblemen and Gent[n];''[36] and his efforts to attract female customers by elegant showrooms, judicious display, and not-so-subtle appeals to the snobbish instincts of the majority are well recorded and analyzed.[37]

Information on what kinds of porcelain women bought for their apartments, and what they did with it there, is patchy. There is the occasional reference in contemporary writing, the occasional representation in paintings (fig. 11), and for the rest one has to extrapolate from the advertisements of the day and the objects themselves.

Further confirmation that, at least in the early days of the factories, the products of Bow and Chelsea were considered lowlier than imports from the Orient can be found in Elizabeth Montagu's letter to a friend, dated 1750: "I saw our friend Cotes the other day before I left town, she is very well and in good spirits, and seems determined to keep her freedom and enter no more into wedlock's bonds. She has only a small lodging, and I think that with her economy she might furnish it in the present fashion, of some cheap paper and ornaments or Chelsea China or the manufacture of Bow, which makes a room look neat and furnished. They are not so sumptuous as my mighty Pagodas of China or nodding Mandarins."[38]

By the later 1750s, however, when the Chelsea factory began to experiment with the rich overall colors and extensive gilding of the kind evolved at Vincennes and Sèvres—the "rare," "rich," "curious inimitable" (to quote contemporary epithets) crimson and mazarine blue—Chelsea porcelain had become worthy of noble and indeed royal patronage. The Duke of Cumberland, whose secretary, Sir Everard Fawkener, had an interest in the factory probably until 1757, hung a Chelsea chandelier, worth £500 according to Mrs. Lybbe Powys,[39] in his tower outside Windsor, and George III and Queen Charlotte had a service made at Chelsea, reputed to have cost £1,150, for presentation to Charlotte's brother, Duke Adolphus Frederick IV of Mecklenburg-Strelitz. Queen Charlotte herself, who had a large collection of predominantly oriental, Meissen, and Sèvres porcelain, owned many more pieces from Chelsea than from any other English manufactory.[40]

In other words, without any direct royal involvement in it, such as there would have been in France or at one of the German princely courts, Chelsea was the most prestigious factory in England. And just as Wedgwood, in the next two decades, discovered that to maintain the interest of the quality market there was no point in being cheap, so Chelsea did not sell at low prices. The Christie's sale of Chelsea in 1770 shows that at the top end of the price range a pair of "large fable candlesticks, with an ox, ass etc," cost £3, "a very large and curious group representing the Roman charity, on a pea-green and gold pedestal," £6 16s. 6d., two small blue and gold vases of "the royal pattern" (presumably like the Mecklenburg service) "curiously enamelled in flowers, £6 5s.;" and "one picturesque beaker of

the mazarine blue and gold, curiously enamell'd in figures upon a gold ground, £16 16s."[41] Such prices are not so far away from the cost of silverware by two of the smartest goldsmiths in town, John Parker and Edward Wakelin: a pair of forty-seven-ounce pillar candlesticks and nozzles cost £13 13s. 1d. and a twenty-six-ounce chamberpot £10 5s. 4d. (1771); a small twenty-seven-ounce gadrooned tea kettle £7 18s. 5d. (1770); and a pair of twenty-four-ounce Gothic pillar candlesticks £7 2s. 7d. (1772).[42]

Obviously vases and garnitures still went on mantelpieces, and potpourri vases could be put there as well; figures might be for the dessert table but also for wall brackets: "single figures for brackets" were described in an auction announcement in the *Public Advertiser* for 19 March–12 April 1759.[43] Many figures are, in any case, too large and too frontal in design to have been intended for a dinner table; instead they were probably the equivalent in a lady's apartments of the small bronzes after the antique by Giacomo Zoffoli that a man would have on his mantelpiece, as in Johan Zoffany's portrait of 1769 of Sir Lawrence Dundas (THB no. 281). Throughout the century there was a strong feeling that the decoration of a room, from the themes represented in the plasterwork on the walls to the subject matter of the paintings to the ornaments, should be appropriate to the function of that room and its ranking in the hierarchy of grandeur within the house. With this in mind it is impossible to imagine floral rococo porcelain in place of the sober bronzes in Sir Lawrence's own very masculine interior, with its seascapes on the walls.

The announcement in the *Public Advertiser* of 1759 also included one of the first references to "Cabinet two-handled cups and covers," that is, pieces of functional form but of such fineness that, from the first, they were intended for the recently invented China cabinets rather than for use. If this reference meant shallow, covered bowls with two handles (there is a mazarine-blue example in the Victoria and Albert Museum), then it was yet another instance of the contemporary admiration for Sèvres,[44] for the *écuelle* form was frequently made in the Sèvres factory before 1759. The deep, allover ground colors such as mazarine blue were also imitating Sèvres porcelain.

An interesting insight into how porcelain colors might be integrated into a decorative scheme is given in a letter from Lady Sarah Bunbury (née Lennox, who as a little girl had been put in the jar by George II) to the Duchess of Leinster on 10 September 1775, advising her how to decorate her drawing room at Carton, County Kildare:

The trumeau [chimney breast] *over the mantelpiece is to be covered with small pictures, china, Wedgwood's imitations of antiques, in short in the style of the dressing room at Holland House. If the hangings are white their plainness must be broken by your pretty blue and green Sèvres china vases, on pretty brackets; and then all the trumeaux must be green and the little wainscot that appears. If you have coloured hangings, of course the wainscot must be white and the biscuit china figures (of which there are some most beautiful of eighteen inches high now made) on the grey or green hangings; or by the by, on damask couleur de rose tendre, which I never saw a room done with, but which I fancy would be beautiful if it was the real French yellowish pink.*[45]

Indeed the colors of the porcelain did not exist in isolation but in conjunction with contemporary paint and textile hues, sometimes leading, sometimes following them. The Sèvres *rose*, a color never before seen in any medium, must be imagined in the context of the deep pinks being used by the Gobelins tapestry factory from the 1760s onward (as seen, for instance, in the Tapestry

Room at Osterley Park). Similarly, some Derby colors, such as the vivid sky blue of the 1770s, were clearly from the same palette as that used by Robert Adam for his polychrome decorations (figs. 12, 13).

It was Josiah Wedgwood who brought ceramics out of the women's rooms and into the state apartments again. From the later 1760s onward he adopted more architecturally or archaeologically inspired forms, gradually eschewing enamel colors and gilding in favor of monochrome or bicolored effects, which gave his work the necessary *gravitas.* The *goût grec,* which was imported from France and which permeated British taste throughout the 1760s, was reinforced by the publication in England of studies of classical antiquity, of which William Chambers' *Treatise on Civil Architecture,* published in 1759, and James Stuart's and Nicholas Revett's *Antiquities of Athens,* 1762, were early and influential examples. Crucial to a reassessment of the ceramic arts in particular was Sir William Hamilton's collection of red- and black-figure vases, published between 1766 and 1767,[46] which Wedgwood made haste to imitate with his black basalt decorated with "encaustic."

An important reason why Wedgwood was so successful with the nobility, who were furnishing newly built or decorated rooms, was that the neo-classical interior was a more integrated design than ever before, the wall decorations and furnishings all being of a piece. It is true that architects had designed furniture at an earlier date, but never in such a thorough way as did the neo-classical architect Robert Adam, for example; no alien styles or colors could be allowed to creep into his rooms, and Wedgwood's productions, drawing on the same sources as the architects themselves, were eminently suited to the apartments they designed.

Wedgwood's correspondence with Thomas Bentley from 1768 onward chronicles his response to the new style, and the way in which his various clients greeted it. In December 1768 he says that he has been turning two or three sorts of faithful copies from Etruscan vases and is surprised both at the beauty of their forms and the difficulty of making them;[47] on 6 February 1769 he describes a visit from Lord Bessborough:

a very fine old Gentleman, admires our vases and manufactures prodigiously, says, he sees we shall exceed the Antients, that friezes and many other things may be made, that I am a very ingenious man (theres for you now, did I not tell you what a fine Gent^n he was) and that he will do

me every service in his power. He has given me four Guineas for three vases, one of them the large blue wch. I ment^d. Mr Cox had not sold one of, the other two Etruscans at a Guinea each. I hope he will set these large blue ones a going.[48]

He sees the chance to replace bronzes of the type made by Zoffoli: in September 1769 he begins the modeling of "Terra Cotta figures with a sphynx, Lion and Triton" and says, "They wo^d. have the appearance of Models, and make an agreeable variety with the black, both figures and Vases."[49] The same month he banishes encrusted floral decoration on the grounds that ele-

gant simplicity is the goal and, "*Flowers being allways stuck in the wrong place . . .*—no more flowers—was one of my first ord^{rs}. when I came home, and have converted Dame Flora into a spoutmaker."[50] In April 1772 he decides that gilding is offensive and must be reduced, if not eliminated, at the suggestion of Sir William Hamilton:

I am not without some little pain for our Nobility and Gentry themselves, for what with the fine things in Gold, Silver and Steel from Soho, the almost miraculous magnificence of Mr Coxes Exhibition, and the Glare of the Derby and other China shews—What heads or Eyes could stand all

Fig. 12.
Ceiling decoration from 6 Adelphi Terrace, London, designed by Robert Adam, c. 1770. Compare the magenta red and sky blue with the vases in fig. 13   (Victoria and Albert Museum)

Fig. 13.
Two pairs of vases and a single bottle, Derby, c. 1770, displayed on the mantelpiece of a room from 6 Adelphi Terrace, London (Victoria and Albert Museum)

this dazzling profusion of riches and ornament if something was not provided for their relief, to give them at proper intervals a little relaxation, and repose. Under this humble idea then, I have some hopes for our black, Etruscan and Grecian vases still.[51]

In his assumption that the contrast of his wares with the porcelain produced by the other factories would be welcome, Wedgwood was right. In September 1769 he attended upon Sir William Bagot at Blithfield House, Staffordshire, to take orders for large vases to stand in the niches of a room that he had just built, and he intended also to wait upon Mr. Anson, "Who wants, and says he will have, some black Vases with White Festoons; he has some excellent Figures and other Antiques very suitable for our purposes which I intend to signify my longings after." The following day Sir Harry Mainwaring came into the showrooms in London to order a set of Etruscan vases for a large room, at £13 4s.[52] In 1774 Lord George Germain bought five black basalt vases (fig. 14) from Wedgwood and Thomas Bentley, at a cost of £8 6s. 6d., for the mantelpiece in his dining room at Drayton House, Northamptonshire, which he had just completed remodeling, probably after William Chambers' designs.[53] Another new neo-classical interior to be furnished with Wedgwood vases was Nuneham Court, Oxfordshire, designed by Capability Brown for Lord Denbigh. Wedgwood visited the house in June 1776 and remarked: "The Grand drawing room is magnificent. It is full of Family pieces by Vandyke, and the Chimney piece is elegantly furnish'd with a fine set of Vases by Wedgwood and Bentley."[54] And then in April 1778 Wedgwood was visited at the Etruria factory by Sir Lawrence Dundas, (who had earlier been depicted with the Zoffoli bronzes by Zoffany) and sold him "Our set of Greek vases at abo.[t] 25 Gs," as well as one of the relief tablets—a sacrifice to Flora—which were made to be set into chimneypieces or into stucco decoration.[55]

Other new rivals of the pretty, brightly colored porcelain vases were the chimneypiece ornaments in ormolu which began to be produced from 1768 onward at Matthew Boulton's factory. In 1770 Boulton wrote to his wife: "then the Queen [Charlotte] sent for me into her bedchamber, shewed me her chyney [*sic*] piece and asked my opinion how many vases it would take to furnish it. For, she says, all that china shall be taken away."[56] Both she and George III bought pieces from Boulton.

Fig. 14.
Dining room at Drayton with five black basalt vases bought for its chimneypiece from Wedgwood in 1774 *(Country Life)*

Queen Charlotte did not by any means banish all china (see figs. 5, 7), but the garniture beneath the upper shelf of porcelain in the Queen's Breakfast Room is indeed of ormolu and is probably all by Boulton. Similarly, Osterley Park, a house rebuilt and furnished by Robert Adam for the banker Robert Child with a lavishness that astonished contemporaries, had Boulton ormolu and blue-john vases on the drawing-room chimneypiece, and three more with two obelisks in the Breakfast Room, but no ceramics of any sort in the state rooms when they were inventoried in 1782.[57] Thus, while the nobility, principally its women, were still buying both decorative and useful porcelain at the Christie's sale of Derby porcelain in 1785,[58] the heyday for European porcelain as an exciting novelty was over, and in its decorative role it could be replaced by objects in other materials.

According to Sir Joseph Banks, the great naturalist, who in 1807 wrote a very informative essay on his wife's collection of "old China and Japan wares," oriental china also fell into neglect, through having simply become too cheap and common, and, "had it not been Mr Spalding's taste for collecting it, and the whim of ornamenting Dairies with it, which the ladies have lately adopted interfering in its favour, the whole stock of it might have been entirely broken or destroyed before it was again call'd into notice."[59]

Dairies were, of course, natural places for ceramics, as they were generally tiled and they needed numerous vessels for the cream and the curds and whey. They were also the women's special preserve, and it is therefore not surprising that, like Marie Antoinette's Hameau at Versailles, they were sometimes elevated out of the rustic into the genteel class. For example, in 1771 Mrs. Lybbe Powys records that Mrs. Freeman of Fawley Court, Buckinghamshire, had "a pretty menagerie and most elegant dairy in the garden ornamented with a profusion of fine old china."[60] Lady Banks' dairy was therefore a conflation of the display china closet, with which a number of country houses were provided, and the gentrified dairy.

The lacquer china closet created in the late seventeenth century at Drayton has already been mentioned; at Narford Hall, Norfolk, home of Sir Andrew Fountaine, there were two rooms in which ceramics were kept, of completely different status in the household and containing quite different things. One was through the kitchen and, according to Lord Oxford, who was shown it by the owner in 1732, "a most wretched place, set out upon shelves like a shop, no old china, a mere baby room."[61] However, Fountaine's own and highly valued collection of maiolica, acquired on his travels in Italy, was kept in a closet off the drawing room. Sir Andrew was probably unique in England at this time in having a large collection of maiolica, which would have ranked highly because of its supposed association with the great Raphael. The room which he built for it was octagonal, like the Tribune in the Uffizi, which he knew well; the ceiling was painted with a round picture in the middle, and there was a glass door into the room, which was kept locked. George Vertue, the antiquary, was much impressed with it when he visited Narford in 1739:

A most rare Cabinet of Earthen ware painted, guilded and adorned, with great beauty and variety, of ancient Italian designs and painting from Raphael, Jul. Romano. del Sarto and other famous masters of that Age, being Vases of beautiful shapes and colours, cesterns, dishes, plates cupps vessels of many formes, all these are in a room ranged in the most elegant and delightfull order possibly can be imagind . . . this collection has been seen by the Royal Family who wanted to purchase it if they coud (or woud spare money but allow tis the most compleat collection of the kind in this part of Europe yet,) he has another room adornd with a great variety of china Ware for all necessary uses— and ornament only Blew and White.[62]

Lady Burlington, wife of the great architect and 3rd Earl, kept her personal ceramics in a (now destroyed) closet (fig. 15) off the Garden Room at Chiswick House, in the link building between the old and new houses. This she furnished lavishly at her own expense, and it was her inner sanctum, where she read and painted and doubtless enjoyed her collection of oriental and Meissen porcelain.[63]

Another vanished china closet was at Kirtlington Park, Oxfordshire, its owner one of those alarming collectors who felt obliged to test her visitors. Mrs. Lybbe Powys describes it thus in 1778:

Lady Dashwood's china room, the most elegant I ever saw. 'Tis under the flight of stairs going into the garden; it's ornamented with the finest pieces of the oldest china, and the recesses and shelves painted pea-green and white, the edges being green in a mosaic pattern. Her Ladyship said she must try my judgement in china, as she ever did all her visitors of that closet, as there was one piece there so much superior to the others. I thought myself fortunate that a prodigious fine old Japan dish almost at once struck my eye.[64]

Visiting the china closet must have been one of the entertainments of a country house, and doubtless that is why Robert Adam called the little lobed room which he designed at one end of the Long Gallery at Syon House, Middlesex, a porcelain closet.[65] This Long Gallery had become a withdrawing room, with Etruscan vases set into the niches, and Horace Walpole said that it was "Converting into a museum in the style of a columbarium [a chamber with niches in the walls for funerary urns], according to an idea that I proposed to Lord Northumberland."[66] At the opposite end of the gallery, another little room was intended to take the miniatures, and the whole suite was supposed to be full of visual and antiquarian delights. Perhaps, however, because the Percy family lacked a true spirit of antiquarianism, neither little room was used as originally intended.

In contrast, Horace Walpole's own famous collection of ceramics at Strawberry Hill certainly was part of the pleasure of dining with him. After a tour of the whole house, Mary Hamilton, who visited it in 1784, sat down to a very elegant dinner, "incomparably well served," but they did not delay over it, rising, men and women together, to go to his china closet, "filled with modern and old china. After we had amused ourselves there for some time we went upstairs and spent the remainder of our time after coffee and tea in very agreeable converse."[67]

This is not the place to discuss Walpole's collection of ceramics in detail, for he was an original, and both his collection and Strawberry Hill itself were atypical; but it is worth describing his china closet, as this must have shared characteristics with other, less famous ones. It was a rectangular room, lined with shelves, measuring twelve feet by nine feet nine inches; like Fountaine's maiolica room, it was close to the principal rooms of the house—in this case, off the Waiting Room which preceded the Great Parlour. There is only one illustration of it, an engraving in *A Description of the Villa of Mr Horace Walpole . . . at Strawberry Hill near Twickenham*, published in London in 1784. It shows the mantelpiece, evocative, like others in the house, of a medieval wall tomb, but still incorporating some more conventional features, such as the blue and white oriental vase in the hearth, and on the chimney breast, for ceramics, little ledges that have merely been gothicized (fig. 16). Untypical of the day (and not shown in the engraving) were the two medieval tiles in the hearth, and other tiles that Walpole set into the floor of the China Room. He was a pioneer in this area of collecting.

The spirit of romantic antiquarianism emanates from Walpole's collection, embracing a far wider range of artefacts of all sorts than merely an aristocratic taste—with its liking for the ex-

pensive, the finely finished, the novel, the rare and exotic—would have considered. Such a spirit broadened the scope of collecting and, correspondingly, of what was considered worthy of display. The dining room at Cotehele in Cornwall, shown in a lithograph of about 1840 (fig. 17), is another example of antiquarian taste. The Reverend Arundell, author of the book on this

Fig. 15.
Lady Burlington's china closet at Chiswick House, c. 1785. Photographed c. 1948 before its destruction (English Heritage)

Fig. 16.
Engraving of the chimneypiece in Horace Walpole's china closet, c. 1784   (Victoria and Albert Museum)

late medieval house, called Cotehele "the ancient mansion of an old English Knight,"[68] and the general belief was that the house had remained untouched since the seventeenth century, its contents intact. The lithograph, however, makes one suspicious, for the pots arranged so prominently are far too heterogeneous to be the natural contents of an old Cornish house. There is English Delft, German stoneware, Italian maiolica probably of the eighteenth century, and a sixteenth-century Nuremberg brass dish. Enough of these pieces survive at the house for one to be sure that they were not merely the artist's invention. One discovers that the late-eighteenth-century owner of Cotehele was a Fellow of the Society of Antiquaries, and his brother, Richard Edgcumbe, was a close friend of Horace Walpole—all of which makes one's suspicions greater. The ancient house was probably given an even more ancient allure than it possessed, perhaps just before George III visited it in 1789. "Here are drinking vessels of all

Fig. 17.
Lithograph of the dining room at Cotehele, Cornwall, by Nicholas Condy, c. 1840   (Victoria and Albert Museum)

shapes and capacities, for sack and malmsey, metheglin and October," writes the Reverend Arundell. The obsolete words roll off his pen and the poetry of them elevates the originally humble items to the status of relics, if not works of art. It is the beginning of a new stage in the history of ceramic collecting and display.

Thus, china collecting began as a woman's hobby in the late seventeenth century, and women remained a major force in the market throughout the next century. Oriental porcelain, both blue and white and enameled, and some pieces of very large size, can be found in most houses for which purchases were made at any time in the eighteenth century, and, until the 1770s, can be found in any of the important rooms. But oriental porcelain and chinoiserie interior decorations were natural allies, and hence the first pieces of furniture specifically designed for ceramics were in the chinoiserie manner. This was also the style for bedroom apartments and women's apartments in particular.

The third quarter of the eighteenth century was the heyday for English society's interest in all kinds of porcelain, whether oriental or, increasingly, European and English. The feminine emphasis continued, and I have not found any evidence that European rococo porcelain stood in the main state rooms or in men's apartments of British country houses. Josiah Wedgwood, however, made ceramics worthy of masculine interest, and there is plenty of evidence of noblemen buying directly from Wedgwood for their new neo-classical rooms. The china closet for the dense display of especially cherished pieces, as a place to show off to friends and in which to entertain them, remained a feature of a number of houses throughout the century.

NOTES

This being my first venture into print on a subject to do with ceramics, I must begin by thanking everyone who has been so helpful to me: John Mallet, Michael Archer, John Hardy, John Cornforth, Clive Wainwright, Rose Kerr, Craig Clunas, and Gervase Jackson-Stops.

1. Nicodemus Tessin, the Swedish architect, quoted by Robert J. Charleston, "Porcelain as Room Decoration in Eighteenth-Century England," *Antiques* 96 (1969), 894.

2. Daniel Defoe, *A Tour thro' the Whole Island of Great Britain,* ed. G. D. H. Cole, 2 vols. (London, 1968), 1:175.

3. David Green, *Grinling Gibbons: His Work as a Carver and Statuary, 1648–1721* (London, 1964), 69.

4. Defoe 1968, 1:166.

5. "Inventory of the Household Goods of the Late Duke of Somerset, March 1749," Petworth House archives, ms. 6263.

6. Quoted by Gervase Jackson-Stops, *Drayton House, Northamptonshire* (London, 1978), 5.

7. "An Inventory of Goods at Drayton made 14 Sept 1710," Drayton House archives. I am most grateful to Mr. Lionel Stopford Sackville for allowing me to quote from this.

8. William H. Pyne, *The History of the Royal Residences of Windsor Castle, St. James's Palace, Carlton House, Kensington Palace, Hampton Court, Buckingham House and Frogmore,* 3 vols. (London, 1819), 2:21.

9. For example, the Kangxi (1662–1722) *famille verte* garniture in the Victoria and Albert Museum.

10. Theodoor Herman Lunsingh Scheurleer, *Delft, Niederländische Fayence* (Munich, 1984), 81–85.

11. In March 1755 a sale of the previous year's production at Chelsea was held by Mr. Ford at his Great Room in the Haymarket; the sale catalogue is published in full in William King, *Chelsea Porcelain* (London, 1922), 69–130.

12. Quoted by Michael Archer, "Delftware at Dyrham," *National Trust Yearbook* (London, 1975), 12–18.

13. Michael Archer, "Pyramids and Pagodas for Flowers," *Country Life* 159 (1976), 166–169.

14. Lady Farrar, ed., *Letters of Josiah Wedgwood,* 3 vols. (Manchester, 1973), 2:84.

15. King 1922, 108.

16. *The Spectator* 299 (12 February 1712).

17. "An Inventory of Furniture belonging to the Rt Hnble the Earl of Egremont in Sussex 1763," Petworth House archives, ms. 6266.

18. "Inventory," Drayton House.

19. "Inventory," Drayton House.

20. "List of China Jars in the Possession of Sir Paul Methuen at His House in Grosvenor Street," drawn up in 1757, probably after his death. Corsham Court archives, ms. 6613.

21. Captain Henry Napier, "Memoir of Lady Sarah's Early Life," in *The Life and Letters of Lady Sarah Lennox 1745–1826,* ed. Countess of Ilchester and Lord Staverdale (London, 1901), 1:87.

22. "Inventory," Drayton House.

23. Pyne 1819, 3:56.

24. "Inventory," Drayton House.

25. "Inventory," Petworth House.

26. From 1602 to 1682, 3.2 million pieces of Chinese and Japanese porcelain were shipped into Europe by the Dutch East India Company; T. Volker, *Porcelain and the Dutch East India Company 1602–82* (Leyden, 1954), 59, 172, 227. From 1729 to 1734 the Company imported nearly 4.5 million pieces, and from 1730 to 1789, about 4.5 million pieces; C. J. A. Jörg, *Porcelain and the Dutch China Trade* (The Hague, 1982), 149. Unfortunately comparative figures for the English trade are not yet available.

27. Wilmarth Sheldon Lewis et al., eds., *The Yale Edition of Horace Walpole's Correspondence,* 48 vols. (New Haven, 1937–1983), 4:46–47.

28. James E. Nightingale, *Contributions towards the History of Early English Porcelain from Contemporary Sources* (Salisbury, 1881), xc–xcii.

29. Bequeathed with all her *objets de vertu* (many still extant) to her daughter, the Countess of Exeter, in the "Conveyance and Schedule of Gift 18 April 1690," Burghley House archives, Ex 41/82.

30. Nightingale 1881, xliv.

31. Lewis 1937–1983, 4:47.

32. Nightingale 1881, xc.

33. Gervase Jackson-Stops, "Furniture at Petworth," *Apollo* 105 (May 1977), 361–362.

34. The inventory of 1771 of Sir Lester Holte's house, Aston Hall, in Warwickshire (Warwick Record Office), records dessert-table decorations packed away among the glassware: "3 looking Dessert glasses with artificial flowers China figures and in 2 Boxes. A Salver with artificial flowers in a square box 14 salvers sizes 1 cover . . . 22 pieces of cut glassware for a Desert 52 small glass stands for Flowers." In the China Closet there was a "Piece of rock and shell work for a Desert, gilt edge."

35. The publication of this print was announced in the *General Advertiser,* 18 January 1751. It depicts the occasion of a lady's coach blocking the footway in front of the toyshop and the rabble's reaction to it; *The Quiet Conquest* [exh. cat., Museum of London] (London, 1985), no. 382.

36. Wedgwood to Thomas Bentley, 23 May 1767, Farrar 1973, 1:143.

37. See the excellent article by Neil McKendrick, "Josiah Wedgwood: an Eighteenth Century Salesman," *Proceedings of the Wedgwood Society* 4 (1961), 161–208.

38. Montagu to Sarah Robinson, 3 January 1750, in E. J. Climenson, *Elizabeth Montagu, the Queen of the Blue-stockings: Her Correspondence from 1720 to 1761,* 2 vols. (London, 1906), 1:271.

39. E. J. Climenson, *Passages from the Diaries of Mrs Philip Lybbe Powys of Harwick House, Oxon., 1756–1808* (London, 1919), 114.

40. *Catalogue of the Sale of Queen Charlotte's Oriental Curiosities and Porcelain,* Christie's, London, 7, 8, 9, 10 May 1819.

41. Sale catalogue quoted in full in Nightingale 1881, 1–14.

42. Parker & Wakelin Ledgers 1770–1776, Victoria and Albert Museum, Department of Metalwork, 4:21v, 20v, 14v, respectively.

43. Nightingale 1881, xvii.

44. See Geoffrey de Bellaigue, "The Royal Taste for Sèvres," *House & Garden* (January 1986), 121–122, 172–174; Brian Fitzgerald, ed., *The Correspondence of Emily Duchess of Leinster 1731–1814* (Dublin, 1949), 383, 432. Lady Holland to the Marchioness of Kildare, 15 July 1763: "I am delighted your taste for pretty things continues for I have sent you a *petit-déjeuner* I do think you'll admire; it goes to England by a Mr Rutter and

consists of a china plate upon which are a cup, saucer, milk-pot and sugar-dish; the china is new and particular. . . . By the French ambassador's things I have sent you two of the biscuit china figures, which I admire vastly." Holland to Kildare, 16 July 1765: "I sent to Mr Foley [from Paris] some time ago two green vases and a little *plateau* with little cups for drams of a blue and white and gold china, which I think pretty enough; these are presents. Then in obedience to your commands sent me by Sally or Louisa I sent two square blue *celeste* orange tubs to the Folly's, just before I came away." These items can only have been Sèvres.

45. Fitzgerald 1949, 2:153–154.

46. Sir William Hamilton and Philippe d'Hancarville, *Antiquités Etrusques, Grecques et Romaines,* 4 vols., 2d ed. (Naples, 1800–1808).

47. Farrar 1973, 1:237.

48. Farrar 1973, 1:244.

49. Farrar 1973, 1:272.

50. Farrar 1973, 1:273.

51. Farrar 1973, 2:67–69.

52. Farrar 1973, 1:278.

53. Jackson-Stops 1978, 16.

54. Farrar 1973, 2:292.

55. Farrar 1973, 2:419.

56. Nicholas Goodison, *Ormolu, the Work of Matthew Boulton* (London, 1974), 158.

57. "An Inventory of All the Household Goods Plate, Pictures, Prints and Books at Osterley House Compiled on the death of Robert Child 1782," Victoria and Albert Museum, Department of Furniture and Interior Design.

58. Nightingale 1881, appendix, 86–92.

59. Sir Joseph Banks, "Collections on the Subject of Old China and Japan Wares with Some Remarks on These Interesting Manufactures Made in Lady Banks' Dairy at Spring Grove 1807," Kent Archives Office, Maidstone, Knatchbull & Banks ms. 11951. I am most grateful to Lord Brabourne for allowing me to quote from this manuscript.

60. Climenson 1919, 148.

61. Quoted in Andrew Moore, *Norfolk and the Grand Tour* [exh. cat.] (Norfolk, 1985), no. 23.

62. Moore 1985, no. 23.

63. The Chiswick House Inventory of 1770 in the Chatsworth House archives is published by Treve S. Rosoman in the *Journal of the Furniture History Society* 22 (1986), 81–106. See also Treve S. Rosoman, "The Decoration and Use of the Principal Apartments of Chiswick House 1727–1770," *Burlington Magazine* 127 (1985), 663–677.

64. Climenson 1919, 198.

65. "The little closets or cabinets, the one circular one for china, and the other square for miniatures, at each end of the gallery, serve only for additional amusement;" Robert Adam and John Adam, *The Works in Architecture* (London, 1900), 1:9.

66. Lewis 1937–1983, 38:429.

67. Lewis 1937–1983, 38:216.

68. The Reverend F. V. J. Arundell, *Cothele on the Banks of the Tamar, the Ancient Seat of the Rt Hon.ble the Earl of Mountedgcumbe,* with lithographs by Nicholas Condy (London, n.d.).

A British Parnassus: Mythology and the Country House

The theme of classical mythology, present in so many of the works of art in *The Treasure Houses of Britain* exhibition, is worth exploring in greater depth, both for the way it relates the objects to the rooms from which they come and for what it tells us about the character, the colors, even the uses of such rooms.

In Britain as in other northern European countries, it was the influence of the Italian Renaissance that brought the gods and goddesses and heroes and heroines of antiquity to the forefront. In Lucas de Heere's *The Family of Henry VIII: An Allegory of the Tudor Succession* from Sudeley Castle (THB no. 2), Mars, the god of war, accompanies Mary and Philip of Spain on the left, while Peace leads in Elizabeth on the right, accompanied by Ceres, the goddess of plenty. Elizabeth's own identification with Astraea, the just virgin of the golden age, described in Ovid's *Metamorphoses* and Virgil's *Eclogues,* is clear both in *Elizabeth I: The Rainbow Portrait* from Hatfield House (THB no. 48), attributed to Marcus Gheeraerts the younger, and in the marvellous procession from Sherborne Castle, *Eliza Triumphans* (THB fig. 1), attributed to Robert Peake.[1] In post-Reformation England such images replaced the religious subject matter that had been the staple diet of painters throughout the Middle Ages. Hans Eworth's jolly portrait of Sir John Luttrell of Dunster (fig. 1) shows him as a triton riding the storm, unarmed by Peace with her olive branch, while in the background Venus curbs the snorting horse of Mars. Juno, on the left, with her peacock, holds two money bags—thought to refer to the Treaty of Boulogne in 1550, by which France undertook to pay England in two cash installments for the surrender of the town.[2]

In the early seventeenth century the application of mythology to one's personal circumstances could be discreet—as in Sir Anthony van Dyck's portrait of the Earl and Countess of Arundel with a bust of Minerva from the Arundel Marbles symbolizing the earl's learning[3]—or flamboyant—as in Rubens' equestrian *Duke of Buckingham,* formerly at Osterley Park, in which Neptune and Amphitrite greet the Lord High Admiral.[4] But after the Restoration such ostentation, fatally associated with absolutism and the propagandist art of central Europe, was to be replaced by a gentler, more lighthearted use of mythology, typified by John Michael Wright's portrait of the Cecil children (THB no. 85), the girl with Proserpine's pomegranate and flowers, the boy with a cameo of Cupid in his hat, the shells and pistol respectively referring to Cupid's parents, Venus and Mars.

Almost a century later, in 1751, Pompeo Batoni's portraits at Uppark of Sir Matthew and Lady Fetherstonhaugh dressed as Endymion and Diana (figs. 2, 3), have the same feeling of fancy dress wonderfully appropriate for a country squire and his wife.[5] But Allan Ramsay's *Macleod of Macleod* in the pose of the Apollo Belvedere,[6] and Sir Joshua Reynolds' *Lady Elizabeth Keppel* (THB no. 481) are more serious, attempting to find a new nobility of expression based on classical formulae, which would raise portraiture to the level of the old masters. Lady Elizabeth is shown in the bridesmaid's dress she wore for the wedding of George III and Queen Charlotte in 1761. She garlands a statue that bears an inscription from Catullus: "Crown the temples [of Hymen] with sweet-smelling marjoram, may you be present to help, O God of Marriage." The actress Mrs. Musters was surely still more flattered to be represented by Reynolds as Hebe, goddess of youth (fig. 4), pouring a libation for Jupiter in the form of an eagle.[7] This portrait—like Reynolds' painting of David Garrick as

Hercules[8]—underlines the close relations between artistic and dramatic iconography in the eighteenth century. The divinities we are to see in plaster, ormolu, needlework, and porcelain, tumbling from ceilings or rising through clouds, can be exactly matched in the operas of Handel and Haydn and the poetry of Alexander Pope and James Thomson.

Examples of the many different mediums to which mythology could be applied include needlework panels, like the one of 1574 from Hardwick Hall depicting the Judgment of Paris (fig. 5),[9] or Julia, Lady Calverley's screen at Wallington Hall, embroidered in 1727 with scenes from Virgil taken, in turn, from much earlier engravings by Wenceslaus Hollar.[10] Book illustrations were used as patterns well into the eighteenth century. Tapestries from the Mortlake workshop, like *The Story of Vulcan and Venus,* formerly at Glemham Hall (THB no. 128), symbolize, in the same way, the endless series of such hangings used as wallpaper in withdrawing rooms, bedchambers, and dressing rooms during the baroque period (and used in *The Treasure Houses of Britain* exhibition as wallpaper behind the Knole silver furniture). The chairs from Stoneleigh Abbey (THB no. 133), with embroidered covers from Ovid's *Metamorphoses,* show pairs of famous lovers, including Venus and Vul-

Fig. 1.
Sir John Luttrell by Hans Eworth, 1550, oil on panel   (Courtauld Institute)

Figs. 2, 3.
Sir Matthew and Lady Fetherstonhaugh by Pompeo Batoni, 1751, oil on canvas   (The National Trust; photograph: Courtauld Institute)

Fig. 4.
Mrs. Musters as Hebe by Joshua Reynolds, 1785, oil on canvas (The Iveagh Bequest, Kenwood; photograph: English Heritage)

can once again, Paris and Helen, and Leda and the Swan, while a pair of gilt rococo brackets from the Cabinet at Felbrigg Hall in Norfolk, attributed to John Cheere, represent Apollo and Daphne.[11] The chimeras of the sixteenth-century Hardwick sea-dog table (THB no. 32) also find an early nineteenth-century equivalent in the pair of Italian tables from Burton Constable by Giuseppe Leonardi and Giacomo Rafaelli (THB no. 528), whose winged harpies must have been attracted by the glitter of the specimen marble table tops.

Suitability is, as always, the key to the casket of mythology. The appearance of the three Graces on Paul Storr's candelabrum centerpiece at Attingham Park (THB no. 463) is no accident; as embodiments of the threefold aspect of generosity—the giving, the receiving, and the returning of gifts—they must have immediately struck guests at Lord Berwick's table as ideal ornaments for an ambassador's banquet. In the same way, the nineteenth-century viewer, steeped in a classical education, would instantly have identified the goldsmith in John Flaxman's *Shield of Achilles* (THB no. 529) with the lame god Hephaestus, forging his great targe for a modern warrior-prince, the Duke of Wellington.

Fig. 5.
Needlework table-carpet showing the Judgment of Paris, 1574 (The National Trust; photograph: Victoria and Albert Museum)

Fig. 6.
Chelsea porcelain figures of Apollo
and the nine Muses, c. 1765   (The
National Trust)

It would have been in character for the Chelsea potters to produce gold-anchor figures of Apollo and the Muses—like the set at Upton House (fig. 6)[12]—perhaps for the garniture of a music-room mantelpiece; but even the Chinese, to whom the world of Greece and Rome must have seemed very remote, were forced to copy western engravings of mythological subjects for the export market, like the *Choice of Hercules* plates, mostly dating to the 1740s,[13] or a charming blue and white teapot of 1671 (fig. 7), based on an engraving by Sebastien le Clerc illustrating the rarely told story of Dircée, a hapless nymph who was turned into a mermaid and fell in love with a carp.[14]

How far did such individual objects fall within the mythological scheme of a whole room? And did the treatment of different rooms in a British country house ever add up to a wholly consistent program of classical iconography? In an attempt to answer these questions, it is worth embarking on a brief tour of country-house interiors, considering the rooms in the same order in which they might have been approached in the seventeenth or eighteenth century.

The hall, the obvious place to start, had, since the Middle Ages, been the place where arms and armor were hung, for this was where the household gathered to resist attack. There is thus a direct link between the great hall at Cotehele in Cornwall, with its walls decked in arms and armor (fig. 8), and Robert Adam's military trophies in plasterwork in the entrance hall at Os-

Fig. 7.
Chinese porcelain teapot with decoration depicting the story of the nymph Dircée, based on an engraving by Sebastien le Clerc, 1671
(Heirloom and Howard, London;
photograph: Prudence Cuming Associates)

terley Park (fig. 9), over three hundred years later. Masculinity prevails here, but, as we shall see, the transition from masculine to feminine—feats of arms overcome by the power of love—is the overall theme of the rooms that follow.

Plaster statues of the nine Worthies—that curious mixture of pagan and Christian mythological and historical heroes—were set high on the walls of the Jacobean great hall at Blickling Hall in Norfolk, until the 2nd Earl of Buckinghamshire's alterations at the end of the eighteenth century; and a similar series, dating to between 1616 and 1630, can still be found at Aston Hall near Birmingham.[15] The Worthies consisted of Hector, Alexander, and Julius Caesar represent-

ing the Gentiles; Joshua, David, and Judas Mac-
cabeus representing the Jews; and Arthur,
Charlemagne, and Godfrey de Bouillon representing the Christians.

The baroque scene painters of the later seventeenth century were interested in mythology not
so much for its display of abstract virtues as for
the political messages it could convey. In the

Painted Hall at Chatsworth, Louis Laguerre's murals (fig. 10) have always been described as the Triumph of Julius Caesar, but the real hero of the story is Brutus,[16] and the relish with which Death throws her poisoned spear at the emperor leaves no doubt that the 1st Duke of Devonshire, one of the chief architects of the Glorious Revolution, saw himself as the Brutus to James II's Caesar. At Boughton House in Northamptonshire, another of William III's main supporters, Ralph Montagu, commissioned Louis Chéron to paint the ceiling of the hall—in preparation for the king's visit in 1695—with a marriage of Hercules and Hebe,[17] undoubtedly intended to symbolize the marriage of William and Mary. As Child of State in Holland, William had been depicted as the infant Hercules strangling the serpent, and Hercules was always his favorite mythological persona; Hebe, the daughter of Jupiter and Juno, however, underlined Mary's status as the legitimate heir.

In the hall at Blenheim Palace, James Thornhill was able to depict the great Duke of Marlborough in 1716 as a hero being received on Parnassus, explaining the plan of the battle to the assembled gods.[18] But later, in the new climate of the Whig supremacy, such personal self-gratification was frowned upon, and a return

Fig. 9.
Trophies of arms and armor in the hall at Osterley Park, Middlesex, designed by Robert Adam, 1767, and executed by Joseph Rose the Younger (The National Trust)

Fig. 10.
The Painted Hall at Chatsworth, Derbyshire, with ceiling and murals by Louis Laguerre, 1697 (Country Life)

Fig. 11.
The Hall at Clandon Park, Surrey, designed by Giacomo Leoni with plasterwork attributed to Giovanni Battista Artari and Giovanni Bagutti, c. 1731   (The National Trust)

Fig. 12.
One of the chimneypieces in the Hall at Clandon Park by John Michael Rysbrack, c. 1731   (The National Trust)

was made to purer use of Greek and Roman myth. Mars, the god of war, was too much associated with unjust causes to be a popular persona, and Minerva, though on the side of right, was too feminine. So Hercules remained the most popular guardian of the hall, with Jupiter often dominating the saloon beyond—the senior hero preceding the senior god, the human giving way to the divine. This is the plan at Clandon Park in Surrey, conceived by the Palladian architect Giacomo Leoni and carried out by the plasterers Giovanni Battista Artari and Giovanni Bagutti and the sculptor John Michael Rysbrack.[19] To go with the cast of the Farnese Hercules and the ceiling with its central scene of Hercules and Omphale, Rysbrack's two marble overmantels in the hall (fig. 11) show Hercules sacrificing to Diana after killing the Erymanthian boar, and sacrificing to Bacchus after killing the

Cretan bull (fig. 12). The hall at Ditchley House, Oxfordshire, by William Kent and Henry Flitcroft, has the same program, and its famous side tables, carved by Matthias Lock to Flitcroft's design (see THB no. 155), display Hercules clothed in the lion pelt that he often used as a headdress.

At Kedleston Hall, Apollo and the huntsman Meleager, who slew the Calydonian boar, together occupy pride of place in the Marble Hall, flanking the door to the Saloon (fig. 13) and accompanied by casts of antique statues representing many of the other inhabitants of Olympus. Adam's aim in recreating the Roman atrium with its statues of ancestors was to take the Curzon family's already distinguished Norman lineage still further back in time, suggesting that as harbingers of a new Augustan age they themselves descended from the antique gods.[20]

The bas-relief scenes from Homer above are paralleled in the Saloon by scenes from British history—involving the Black Prince, Queen Eleanor, and Lady Jane Grey—linking the antique and modern worlds still more firmly. The overmantels in the hall, designed by Adam's chief draftsman, George Richardson,[21] contain roundels representing Apollo and Hyacinthus after Domenichino, and Diana and Arethusa (not Ceres and Arethusa as previously identified) after Hubert Gravelot. These are of particular interest, for they illustrate the creation of the landscape through which the visitor has traveled to reach the hall—a highly architectural room that was always supposed to act as a transition from exterior to interior. Hyacinthus was the Spartan

the ground floor, and thus the staircase usually succeeded the hall. The newel posts here were often carved with heraldic beasts, like the leopards at Knole, taken from the Sackville family's coat-of-arms, but the very form of the stairs encouraged their use as a demonstration of genealogy rather than mythology. Horace Walpole was later to call a staircase at Boughton, its treads emblazoned with different quarterings, "the descent of the Montagus."[22]

In the baroque period, however, the staircase gave painters a heaven-sent opportunity to represent the approach to Parnassus, with men or heroes round the walls aspiring to reach the gods above. Antonio Verrio's staircase at Hampton Court has a complicated iconography based on Julian the Apostate's *Satire of the Caesars*: Romulus and Hercules (again a personification of William III) press the rival claims of Alexander the Great and the twelve Caesars to be invited to the heavenly banquet of the Saturnalia, shown in the ceiling above[23]—a daunting allegory for those bidden to dine at the king's table in the state rooms on the upper floor. On the staircase walls at Boughton, trompe l'oeil bas-reliefs of Romans capturing Barbarians are like an earthly miasma contrasting with the vivid colors of another heavenly banquet in the ceiling, where Discord throws the apple among the gods.[24]

As a prelude to the great chamber or saloon, where dinners for huge numbers of people would be served, the Great Staircase at Chatsworth was decorated by Verrio with triumphs of Ceres and Cybele, who first taught men to cultivate the earth, and of Bacchus, from whom they learned to cultivate the vine.[25] As in the hall, such wall paintings could convey very specific messages. At Petworth, Laguerre's story of Prometheus, who stole fire from the gods, very probably alludes to a fire which destroyed that part of the house the year before, in 1714.[26] The Petworth staircase is also rare in showing an owner personified as a goddess: the Duchess of Somerset (the heiress of the Percy family) rides as Juno in her chariot, accompanied by her very English-looking spaniel (fig. 14), while one of the Muses on the upper landing (their home being on the slopes of Mount Olympus) holds the plan of the house. In the same way Gerard Lanscroon's staircase at Powis Castle is thought to include portraits of the 2nd Marquess of Powis' daughters as Venus watching Vulcan forge the arms of Achilles, and as Amphitrite in the seashell chariot of Neptune.[27]

prince loved by Apollo but killed by a discus, hyacinth flowers sprouting from the place where his blood fell. Arethusa was rescued by Diana from Alpheus, but only at the cost of being turned into a stream.

Just as the family coat-of-arms predominated in the Elizabethan great hall, informing the visitor from the outset of the owner's lineage, so in the entrance hall at Syon House, the bust of the 1st Duke of Northumberland by Joseph Wilton was placed next to those of Julius Caesar and Homer in a room dominated by Wilton's copy of the Apollo Belvedere, proclaiming for the owner a much more distinguished ancestry than rows of Smythson and Percy portraits, relegated to an adjoining corridor.

In the sixteenth and seventeenth century, the principal rooms in the house lay one flight above

A still more literal and political point was made by Thornhill on the staircase at Hanbury Hall in Worcestershire. Once again the walls are decorated with the story of Achilles, a hero whose exploits recalled the Norman ancestors of the Vernon family, owners of Hanbury; the gods are assembled in the ceiling, and Mercury, the messenger between gods and men, flies happily through the cornice (as seen in Thornhill's original sketch at the Cooper-Hewitt Museum, New York). In 1710, however, between the making of Thornhill's original sketch and the painting of the ceiling, Edward Vernon, a prominent Whig, was outraged by what he regarded as the treasonable sermon preached by the Tory Dr. Sacheverell in Saint Paul's Cathedral, in which he criticized those who supported Marlborough's wars. To celebrate Sacheverell's impeachment, Thornhill gave Mercury an engraving of the doctor, about to be burnt to ashes by the torches of the Furies (fig. 15).[28]

The idea of the *piano nobile,* adopted for the later Palladian villas of the Whig aristocracy, reduced the importance of the staircase, and only in rare cases was mythology summoned to the aid of the decorator. One example is the staircase off the hall at West Wycombe Park, with its rare depiction of Angerona, the Roman goddess of silence, with her finger to her lips, encouraging those who ascend not to disturb the occupants of the bedrooms above, or—knowing Sir Francis Dashwood's proclivities—not to reveal the nocturnal perambulations they may chance to discover.[29] Giuseppe Maria Borgnis' paintings, also including biblical scenes after Carlo Maratta and the Carracci, date to the 1750s.

If ever there was a fitting habitation for the gods it was the great chamber or saloon that often lay at the head of the main stairs. At Hardwick, as befits a Renaissance hunting lodge in the tradition of Chambord or Caprarola, Diana and her maidens sport in an enchanted forest that runs along the plasterwork frieze (fig. 16), while in the bay window Flora as Spring and Ceres as Summer welcome the light.[30] Perhaps we can even imagine the scattered flowers embroidered on the farthingale chairs below as posies that they have thrown down. Yet again, humans are represented on the walls in tapestries that tell the story of Ulysses, while the gods, larger than life size, appear above.

At Wilton House in the 1630s, the Double Cube Room ceiling by Emmanuel de Critz had scenes from the story of Perseus, the embodi-

ment of honor and integrity, accompanying Van Dyck's portraits of the noble Herberts;[31] this theme was not forgotten in the eighteenth century, when side tables were made for the room featuring the heads of Minerva and Andromeda, the two leading actresses in the Perseus drama.

A pantheon of family portraits on a much smaller scale, the Saloon at Sudbury Hall in Derbyshire, dating to the 1670s, has a painted ceiling added in the 1690s by Laguerre, which invokes prosperity on the house of Vernon (another branch of the family already encountered at Han-

Fig. 15.
Staircase at Hanbury Hall, Worcestershire, with wall paintings by Sir James Thornhill, c. 1710 (The National Trust)

bury).[32] The seasons, represented by Ceres, Flora, Bacchus, and Vulcan, show how the riches and pastimes of a county family were based above all on land, and it was here, at tables brought in on occasion, that the fruits of that land were enjoyed.

Verrio's ceiling in the State Dining Room (originally the Great Chamber) at Chatsworth, painted in 1691, is a much more elaborate affair, representing the battle between *Ratio* or Reason, supported by Apollo, Diana, and Mercury, and *Libido* or the Passions, supported by Cupid, Venus, Vulcan, and others. Few ceilings come nearer to justifying Pope's gibes about the "sprawling saints of Verrio and Laguerre,"[33] though there are amusing moments even here, such as the artist's depiction of Mrs. Hacket the housekeeper (whom he detested) as the most hideous of the Furies, wielding the "abhorred shears" (fig. 17).

Another room at Chatsworth, at the head of the West Staircase, also counts as a saloon, though long since known as the Sabine Bedroom.[34] Far from being the scene of the 1st Duke of Devonshire's amours, as Thornhill's saucy rape scenes might suggest, the room was the first in another sequence of state apartments, and celebrated a serious political event, namely the union of England and Scotland achieved in 1707—hence the statue of Concord above the chimneypiece. The intermarrying of two races and its peaceful result evidently counted for more than the initial scenes of violence.

In the Palladian period the saloon was used to house large-scale old masters more often than family portraits, and, following Italian fashion, red was the color usually preferred as a background. There may be a particular reason why the saloon—so often dedicated to the sun-god Apollo—should have been covered with crimson damask or velvet, as can still be seen at Houghton or Holkham Hall. In his *Academy of Armory,* published at Chester in 1688, the antiquary Randle Holme writes: "This colour Vermilion, or Red, is the chief amongst Colours, for as much as it representeth the Fire, which of all the other Elements is the most lightsome, and approaches nearest to the quality of the Sun."[35] He goes on to associate green with Venus (representing Felicity and Pleasure), and purple with Mercury (representing Honor and Dignity).

Though Apollo does appear in the ceiling of the Saloon at Houghton (fig. 18), watching Phaeton drive the chariot of the sun, the room is

also dominated by Neptune, who can be seen in William Kent's painted cove, and whose shells appear on the famous chairs (THB no. 153) and pier tables, and on the elaborate frame for a great Van de Velde seascape on the wall opposite the chimneypiece.[36] As Prime Minister, Sir Robert Walpole had built his career on the expansion of commerce overseas, so the theme of Neptune may again be an intentional reference. Despite the fact that separate dining rooms began to be made in the early eighteenth century, saloons continued to be used as banqueting rooms on great occasions. Thus Borgnis' *Banquet of the*

Fig. 18.
The Saloon at Houghton Hall, Norfolk, with ceiling paintings by William Kent, c. 1726 (*Country Life*)

Fig. 19.
Detail of the ceiling of the Long Gallery at Blickling, with plasterwork by Edward Stanyan, 1620 (The National Trust)

Gods at West Wycombe (after Raphael's decorative scheme at the Villa Farnesina),[37] and Francis Wheatley's Ganymede, the cup-bearer of the gods, in the center of the saloon ceiling at Brocket Hall,[38] are eminently appropriate.

Long galleries in the sixteenth and seventeenth centuries were places both to exercise the body and improve the mind, but it was more common to find extensive series of family portraits in them than mythological pictures like the full-length Sybils described in the gallery at Erddig in 1732.[39] In the Long Gallery at Hardwick alabaster statues of Justice and Mercy over the fireplaces show that this was where Bess of Hardwick presided as magistrate over her tenants and household, but the embroidered cushion covers provided for each window bay included subjects like the Death of Actaeon and Europa and the Bull.[40] Emblems and devices, dear to the Elizabethan mind, can still be seen in the ceiling of the Long Gallery at Blickling, executed by the plasterer Edward Stanyan. Most of these are taken from Henry Peacham's *Minerva Britanna,* published in 1612,[41] including a wonderfully naive rendering of Athena being drawn from the axe-cleft head of Zeus (fig. 19).

George Vernon of Sudbury, builder of the long gallery at Sudbury in the 1670s (extraordinarily old-fashioned for its date) commissioned the plasterers Robert Bradbury and James Pettifer to supply a long series of Roman emperors' heads in the frieze running parallel with the iconography of family portraits on the walls below.[42] In the eighteenth century, however, when the long gallery became the home for antique statues bought on the Grand Tour—as at Holkham and Newby Hall—the heads seem to have been arranged purely for decorative effect, rather than to fulfill any philosophical program. The Temple of the Graces, built at one end of the Woburn Sculpture Gallery to contain Antonio Canova's famous group of the Three Graces (THB no. 480), contrasts with a temple of modern worthies at the other end of the gallery, dedicated to the Duke of Bedford's political heroes, the circle of Charles James Fox.[43] But the crowded display of sarcophagi, urns, statues, and pedestals between the two were there to be admired in their own right, not to convey any special message.

Dining rooms, by contrast, presented one of the most obvious fields for mythological treatment, and the Bacchic theme was to become almost a cliché in eighteenth-century country houses. It can already be found in the 1690s, in Chéron's ceiling of the so-called Egyptian Hall at Boughton,[44] apparently used as a smaller dining parlor in preference to the great hall which it adjoins. But Kent's decoration of the dining room at Houghton fully exploited the Bacchic theme for the first time.[45] Kent also had a hand in remodeling the dining room (now used as a drawing room) at Easton Neston in 1732.[46] A large series of boar and stag hunts by Frans Snyders were fitted into plasterwork frames and complemented by a version of Titian's *Venus and Adonis* in the ceiling (fig. 20), probably by Charles Stanley, with the goddess vainly trying to prevent the young shepherd from leaving for the chase.

James Paine's dining room at Felbrigg is a typical example of Bacchic decoration without the actual presence of figures. Trophies of the chase are everywhere, with the four seasons in the corners offering different kinds of fruit and game, and even Grand Tour bronzes (a satyr, for instance, carrying a goatskin) joining in.[47] At Burton Constable a full-size statue of Bacchus surveys the proceedings (fig. 21), the wine cooler below carved with his pinecone thyrsus and other attributes. William Collins' plasterwork overmantel shows Bacchus carrying Ariadne away on the back of a tiger (taken from a cameo owned by Baron Stosch), while a large oval at the other end of the room has the three Graces

Fig. 20.
Ceiling of the dining room at Easton Neston, Northamptonshire, with plasterwork attributed to Charles Stanley, c. 1735 (*Country Life*)

Fig. 21.
Dining room at Burton Constable, Humberside, by Timothy Lightoler, c. 1767 (*Country Life*)

Fig. 22.
One of the patchwork hangings of the Virtues and their Contraries at Hardwick Hall, c. 1575 (The National Trust)

dancing before Pan, Flora embracing a shepherd and an extremely drunken cupid.[48] Not even the Society of Dilettanti could ask for a better setting for its revels.

Robert Adam's dining rooms brought a politer, more serious mode of decoration, as in Giovanni Battista Cipriani's overmantel at Osterley representing maidens offering sacrifices to Ceres,[49] but Bacchic nymphs, like those supporting Pierre-Philippe Thomire's candelabra in the dining room at Woburn Abbey,[50] show that Bacchic imagery was to be found in furniture, metalwork, and ceramics long after the rooms themselves had succumbed to the chaste and abstracted Louis XVI style.

The threshold of the withdrawing room represents an entrance into female territory, particularly in the eighteenth century, when the custom first began for the ladies to withdraw from the dining room before the men. Bess of Hardwick's withdrawing room was lined with patchwork hangings of the Virtues and their Contraries (fig. 22)[51]—such as Penelope representing Constancy and Artemesia Fidelity—all of them ladies, while the sea-dog table in the center of the room (THB no. 32) represented the chimera which Bellerophon slew, the fastest creature in the world placed here on the back of the slowest, the tortoise. The relief of Apollo and the Muses above the chimneypiece came from Elizabethan Chatsworth,[52] but it is a reminder that withdrawing rooms were often to be used for the making of music, and foreshadows the roundels of Antonio Zucchi and Angelica Kauffmann in a later age. Withdrawing rooms were usually hung with tapestries, and these were likely to tell mythological histories as a kind of strip-cartoon. Their subject sometimes even gave its name to the room, as with the Diogenes Room at Dyrham Park, showing the philosopher who made his home in a tub, being visited by Alexander the Great.[53]

At Chatsworth, the cove of the withdrawing room was painted by Laguerre with the story of Venus, Mars, and Vulcan: a favorite theme for this room, appearing, for instance, at the same

point in the state apartments at Boughton. Perhaps its mixture of male and female protagonists
and its message, the conquest of strife by love,
were thought appropriate as one approached the
bedchamber beyond.

Sometimes a mythological treatment could be
suggested by the pictures or tapestries with
which the room was to be hung. The drawing
room at Hagley Hall in Worcestershire (fig. 23)
was made to contain an outstanding series of
Soho tapestries of the 1720s, already owned by
Lord Lyttleton, who wrote in 1758 that "Athenian" Stuart "has engaged to paint me a Flora
and four pretty little Zephyrs, in my drawing
room ceiling,"[54] Francesco Vassalli's plasterwork
garlands continuing the idea of a floral bower.
At Harewood House in West Yorkshire, Adam's
Music Room (in effect a withdrawing room) has
a Zucchi ceiling of Midas presiding over the musical contest between Apollo and Marsyas—
strings versus woodwind; there are roundels of
Minerva and the nine Muses painted by Biagio
Rebecca, and even the peasants and brigands in
the ruin pieces play pipes or dance (fig. 24).[55]

The finishing touch is the portrait by Reynolds
over the chimneypiece, depicting Edwin Las-
celles' cousin Mrs. Hale as Euphrosyne.

At Osterley the theme in the drawing room is
the difference between sacred and profane love;
the former is represented by Diana and the latter
by Venus and Cupid, in the marquetry panels of
the two commodes between the windows (THB
no. 257).[56] This provides an interesting comparison with the commode by Chippendale at Harewood (THB no. 265), on which Minerva and
Diana represent spiritual and physical love, respectively. A copy of Antonio Canova's Venus,
and his bust of a dancer, in the drawing room at
Attingham, show how drawing rooms became
still more feminine in character in the early nineteenth century.

In the bedroom, of course, love predominates.
The state bedchamber at Blair Castle in Scotland
was made to contain a splendid series of
seventeenth-century Brussels tapestries representing the story of Atalanta and Meleager. That
athletic couple's combination of hunting and
love must have seemed especially appropriate for

this Highland setting, particularly their pursuit
of the Calydonian boar. The baroque scene painters also enjoyed depicting nighttime views, as in
the State Bedroom at Chatsworth, where Laguerre shows Diana as goddess of the moon, or
at Boughton, where Chéron shows Arcas restrained by Jupiter from shooting at his mother,
the bear Callisto (among other stars and signs of
the Zodiac), while in the next-door dressing
room Aurora brings the dawn.[57] Kent's Embroidered Bedchamber at Houghton, completed by
1730, is also strictly "after dark," displaying Diana and Endymion accompanied by owls, bats,
and other nocturnal creatures.[58]

In the State Bedchamber at Houghton (fig.
25), created in 1732, the tapestries represent the
story of Venus. The scallop shells of Kent's famous bed refer to her birth, presided over by
Aurora in the ceiling, while the green velvet
reminds us that green was always Venus' color.
The goddess was, of course, born of the sea,
from the foam produced when the genitals of the
castrated Saturn were cast upon the waters, and
this, perhaps, is the inspiration for the prodigious use of silver fringes and braids.[59]

At Osterley (fig. 26), the state bed was again
conceived as a temple to Venus, hence its architectural character, almost like a garden pavilion,

Fig. 25.
The State Bedroom at Houghton Hall, Norfolk, with ceiling paintings by William Kent, after 1726 (*Country Life*)

and the fact that green is the predominant color. A medallion of Venus being garlanded by nymphs appears on the headboard, and the outer valances are embroidered with poppy heads (to induce sleep) alternating with the eagle and serpent crest of the Child family.[60] In the ceiling Venus' attendant nymph Aglaia is being enslaved by love—a discreet bondage scene that is well above Zucchi's usual insipidity.

Dressing rooms, at the very end of the baroque progression of state apartments, were usually too crammed with porcelain, small cabinet pictures, or rich hangings, to receive the full mythological treatment, though the dressing room at Chatsworth has an amusing Laguerre ceiling of Juno, Minerva, and Venus dispatching Mercury with the apple of Discord[61]—surely a reference to the gossip among the fairer sex that was a hallmark of such rooms. Pairs of famous lovers were another popular motif, however, best illustrated by the famous Boucher tapestry room at Osterley (fig. 27), really a dressing room

though it precedes the state bedchamber.[62] The rose, as the flower sacred to Venus, is supposed to have been always white until Venus, while hastening to help the dying Adonis, pierced her foot on a thorn and stained the rose's petals red. Against a rose-color background, therefore, among garlands of flowers, are the Elements, personified as the loves of the gods: Fire is represented by Vulcan with Venus herself, Air by Cephalus and Aurora, Earth by Vertumnus and Pomona, and Water, rather jokingly, by the huge mirror between the windows. The overmantel of Cupid and Psyche completes the series.

It would be wrong to end this survey of country-house interiors without reference to one other room—the library. Here, from the bookshelves of classical literature, the obsession with the myths and legends of Greece and Rome originated, and it was here that classicism and patriotism met. Above the chimneypiece at Nostell Priory Zucchi's oval of 1766 shows Minerva presenting the Arts of Painting, Sculpture, and Architecture to Britannia (fig. 28),[63] while at Osterley the panel over the door, also by Zucchi, has Britannia encouraging the Arts and Sciences,

Fig. 26.
The State Bedroom at Osterley Park, Middlesex, by Robert Adam, 1775–1776   (The National Trust)

Fig. 27.
The Tapestry Room at Osterley by Robert Adam, 1772, hung with Gobelins tapestries ordered in the same year   (The National Trust)

flanked by plaster medallions of the Greek authors Homer and Hesiod and the Romans Horace and Cicero.[64] Over one chimneypiece Anacreon sacrifices to the Graces, and over the other Sappho writes the Odes dictated by Love. The famous "lyre-back" chairs (THB no. 256) again invoke the celestial music of Apollo, the origin of lyric poetry.

Minerva and her owl appear time and again in eighteenth-century book rooms, as in the Old Library at Harewood, where they are painted by Rebecca above a trompe l'oeil bas-relief of the *Triumph of Homer*.[65] Busts of philosophers crown the bookcases, and the other inset paintings have subjects such as the *Education of Pliny's Daughter*—enough to inspire the keenest governess. The library designed by the high-minded Sir Richard Colt Hoare at Stourhead in Wiltshire (fig. 29) has scenes from Raphael's *Parnassus*

painted in the lunette at one end by the Reverend Samuel Woodforde, and this is balanced at the other end by Francis Eginton's stained-glass *School of Athens*.[66] And, lest this seem dull and bookish, beyond the French windows the gods and goddesses also preside over a truly Elysian landscape: the Temple of Hercules, representing the labors by which the gardens at Stourhead were made; the Temple of the sun-god, Apollo, whose light and heat cause plants to grow; the Temple of Flora, the goddess who scatters the spring and summer flowers; and the dark grotto, where Neptune strikes the rock with his trident, causing the waters to flow and the lakes to fill.[67]

A dream of Arcadia, a search for a rural Parnassus, is—we should not forget—what the country house is all about.

Fig. 28.
The Library at Nostell Priory, West Yorkshire, by Robert Adam, 1766   (The National Trust)

Fig. 29.
The Library at Stourhead, Wiltshire, by Sir Richard Colt Hoare, 1792 (The National Trust)

NOTES

1. Roy Strong, *Portraits of Queen Elizabeth I* (Oxford, 1963), 86–87.

2. Frances A. Yates, "The Allegorical Portraits of Sir John Luttrell," *Essays in the History of Art Presented to Rudolph Wittkower* (London, 1967), 149–160.

3. Oliver Millar, *Van Dyck in England* [exh. cat., National Portrait Gallery] (London, 1982), no. 59.

4. F. Huemer, *Corpus Rubensianum Ludwig Burchard—Portraits,* 2 vols. (Brussels, 1977), 1:57–59.

5. Anthony M. Clark, *Pompeo Batoni* (Oxford, 1985), nos. 154–155, pls. 144–145.

6. David and Francina Irwin, *Scottish Painters at Home and Abroad: 1700–1900* (London, 1975), 54.

7. Nicholas Penny, ed., *Reynolds* [exh. cat., National Gallery] (London, 1986), 50, fig. 35.

8. Penny 1986, 205, fig. 42.

9. Mark Girouard, *Hardwick Hall, Derbyshire: A History and a Guide* (London, 1976), 106–107.

10. John Cornforth, "Wallington Hall, Northumberland—II," *Country Life* (23 April 1970), 922–926, fig. 5.

11. Michael Snodin, ed., *Rococo: Art and Design in Hogarth's England,* no. S55; the figure of Daphne is misidentified as a winged Victory.

12. J. V. G. Mallett, *Upton House, the Bearsted Collection: Porcelain* (London, 1964), no. 23.

13. David Howard and John Ayres, *China for the West* (London, 1978), 333, pl. 329.

14. François Hervouet, Nicole Hervouet, and Yves Bruneau, *La Porcelaine des Companies des Indes* (Paris, 1987), 309.

15. John Maddison, ed., *Blickling Hall* (London, 1984), 19.

16. I am indebted to John Hardy for this new interpretation of the Painted Hall murals.

17. Edward Croft-Murray, *Decorative Painting in England 1537–1837*, 2 vols. (London, 1962–1970), 1:244; I am indebted to Tessa Murdoch, who is making a particular study of Chéron's work at Boughton, for confirming my views as to the symbolism of this ceiling.

18. David Green, *Blenheim Palace* (London, 1951), 306–308.

19. Geoffrey Beard, *Decorative Plasterwork in Great Britain* (London, 1975), 202, 204, pl. 67.

20. Leslie Harris, *Robert Adam and Kedleston: The Making of a Neo-Classical Masterpiece* (London, 1987), no. 43.

21. Harris 1987, nos. 46, 49.

22. Paget Toynbee, ed., "Horace Walpole's Journals of Visits to Country Seats," *Walpole Society* 16 (1927–1928), 54.

23. Edgar Wind, "Julian the Apostate at Hampton Court," *Journal of the Warburg and Courtauld Institutes* 3 (1939–1940), 127–137.

24. Croft-Murray 1962–1970, 1:244.

25. Francis Thompson, *History of Chatsworth* (London, 1949), 123–124.

26. Gervase Jackson-Stops, "The Building of Petworth," *Apollo* 163 (May 1977), 329.

27. Christopher Rowell, *Powis Castle, Powys* (London, 1987), 30.

28. Croft-Murray 1962–1970, 1:270.

29. Gervase Jackson-Stops, *West Wycombe Park, Buckinghamshire* (London, 1981), 15.

30. Girouard 1976, 65–69.

31. Croft-Murray 1962–1970, 1:198.

32. John Cornforth, *Sudbury Hall, Derbyshire* (London, 1982), 16–17.

33. Alexander Pope, *Epistle to the Right Honourable Richard, Earl of Burlington* (London, 1731), ll. 145–146.

34. Thompson 1949, 189–190.

35. Randle Holme, *The Academy of Armory*, 2 vols. (Chester, 1688), 1:12.

36. Illustrated in Francis Russell's paper in this volume, fig. 2; see also Christopher Hussey, *English Country Houses: Early Georgian, 1715–1760* (London, 1955), 80–81, figs. 105, 107.

37. Jackson-Stops 1981, 23.

38. Croft-Murray 1962–1970, 2:246, 292.

39. John Loveday, *Diary of a Tour in 1732* (London, 1890), 80.

40. Girouard 1976, 61, 75.

41. Maddison 1984, 21–22.

42. Cornforth 1982, 24–25.

43. Denys Sutton, "A Noble Heritage," *Apollo* 82 (December 1965), 437–441.

44. Croft-Murray 1962–1970, 1:244.

45. Gervase Jackson-Stops and James Pipkin, *The English Country House—a Grand Tour* (London and New York, 1985), 122–123.

46. Victoria Percy and Gervase Jackson-Stops, "The Travel Journals of the 1st Duchess of Northumberland—II," *Country Life* (7 February 1974), 250; Christopher Hussey, "Easton Neston, Northamptonshire—II," *Country Life* (27 August 1927), 300–302, figs. 7–9.

47. Jackson-Stops and Pipkin 1985, 125–126.

48. Ivan Hall, "William Constable and Burton Constable—IV," *Country Life* (13 May 1982), 1358–1361.

49. John Hardy and Maurice Tomlin, *Osterley Park House* (London, 1985), 30–32.

50. Jackson-Stops and Pipkin 1985, 137.

51. Girouard 1976, 54–56.

52. Girouard 1976, 90–91.

53. Anthony Mitchell, ed., *Dyrham Park, Gloucestershire* (London, 1985), 25–26.

54. Quoted by Croft-Murray 1962–1970, 2:284.

55. Croft-Murray 1962–1970, 2:259.

56. Hardy and Tomlin 1985, 61, 65.

57. Croft-Murray 1962–1970, 1:244.

58. Jackson-Stops and Pipkin 1985, 166–167.

59. Jackson-Stops and Pipkin 1985, 170–171.

60. Hardy and Tomlin 1985, 78–81.

61. Croft-Murray 1962–1970, 1:251.

62. Hardy and Tomlin 1985, 67–77.

63. Gervase Jackson-Stops, *Nostell Priory, Yorkshire* (London, 1978), 11.

64. Hardy and Tomlin 1985, 38–43.

65. Richard Buckle, *Harewood House, Yorkshire*, rev. ed. (Leeds, 1983), 11–12.

66. Dudley Dodd, *Stourhead, Wiltshire* (London, 1981), 15–16.

67. Kenneth Woodbridge, *The Stourhead Landscape* (London, 1986), 18–19.

ALASTAIR LAING

The Eighteenth-Century English Chimneypiece

In 1759 William Chambers devoted a complete chapter of his *Treatise on Civil Architecture* to chimneypieces. That he did so was no longer unusual—Isaac Ware had dedicated a whole book of his *Complete Body of Architecture* to chimneypieces only three years before—but the terms in which Chambers spoke of them were exceptional, in that he elevated them into a peculiarly English art form:

Neither the Italians nor the French have excelled greatly in compositions of Chimney-Pieces. I believe we may justly consider Inigo Jones as the first who arrived at any great degree of perfection, in this material branch of the Art. Others of our Architects, since his time, have wrought upon his ideas; and some of them, particularly the late Mr. Kent, have furnished good inventions of their own. England is at present possess'd of many able sculptors, whose chief employment being to execute magnificent Chimney-Pieces, now happily much in vogue, it may be said that, in this particular, we surpass all other nations; not only in point of expence, but likewise in taste of Design, and goodness of Workmanship. Scamozzi mentions a Chimney-Piece in one of the Public Buildings at Venice, executed from his Designs, as a most uncommon piece of magnificence, having cost upwards of a thousand crowns. In this country a much larger expence is very frequent, and many private houses are furnished with Chimneys, at least as valuable.[1]

Chambers here encapsulates many, but not all of the distinguishing characteristics of the eighteenth-century English chimneypiece: its form, deriving—or at least thought to derive—from Inigo Jones;[2] the fact that it was not only sculpted but a major branch of the sculptor's art; and its often quite prodigious cost. He does not, as Isaac Ware had done,[3] specify the distinguishing characteristic of its most distinctive, fully arrayed form: that it continues as an entity up to, or almost up to the ceiling, and that this continuation generally incorporates an overmantel painting or relief. He can therefore hardly be reproached for not commenting on what we, with art-historical hindsight, may regard as its

lack of a most significant adjunct: the overmantel mirror, a *sine qua non* of French chimneypieces of the period,[4] and the most usual feature of substantial chimneypieces in England in the last third of the eighteenth century and for most of the nineteenth. After all, was it not by climbing onto the mantelpiece that Alice passed through the looking glass (fig. 1)?

Successive editions of Chambers' book, entitled from the third edition onward, in the absence of the intended sequel on structures, *A Treatise on the Decorative Part of Civil Architecture*, yield useful insights into the subsequent evolution of the chimneypiece in Britain.

The second edition of 1768 is little more than a reprint of the first. More surprisingly, even the third edition of 1791 only makes a few editorial changes to the portion of the text dealing with chimneypieces; the reference, for instance, to William Kent, by then outmoded, was excised. However, among the additional plates at the end of the book was an engraving showing chimneypieces executed in the 1770s at Windsor Castle and Melbourne House. Of somewhat *retardataire* form even at the time they were executed, they are not very different in character from the designs of chimneypieces illustrating the first edition of 1759. Those designs had been somewhat at variance with the text of the first edition, in any case; none of them was of the "continued" type, so that they in fact abandoned the very Inigo Jonesian exemplars that the text implicitly commended. In 1759 little was laid down explicitly about the form—as opposed to the placing and execution—of chimneypieces, so it was perfectly possible to retain the original text unaltered in 1791. Nevertheless, by the time of the so-called fourth edition in 1826, the editor, John Buonarotti Papworth, the son of a stuccador much employed by Chambers, felt compelled to add the following footnote:

Since the publication of this treatise by Chambers, the fashion in chimney-pieces has undergone a complete revolution, for they are now treated rather as pieces of furniture than as integral portions of the edifice. . . . Immense looking-glasses, with gilt frames, have superseded the carved and painted superstructure of the fireplace, and the chimney-piece is now reduced from its late magnificence, to the duty of supporting clocks, girandoles, vases, and bijoutry.[5]

Curiously, by the time of the last edition of Chambers' *Treatise,* W. H. Leeds' revision of 1862 of Joseph Gwilt's edition of 1825, the pendulum had swung back to the kind of ornate chimneypiece of which Chambers seemed to approve but which he failed adequately to illustrate. Thus, while counseling that "the examples shown by Chambers are not now to be recommended as faultless and unimproveable," Leeds made it clear that this was not because he held with the chasteness implicitly commended by Papworth:

A chimney-piece ought not to be the least striking feature in a room—rather the contrary. . . . Yet, if it be made, as is sometimes done, of black or dark-colored marble, a chimney-piece shows only as a dismal blot in the room. . . . Another more common, but hardly less offensive, solecism is that of putting a plain marble chimney-piece, without any carved mouldings at all, into a room that makes a pretentious show by its elaborate cornice and other stuccatura work. . . . So much depends upon a chimney-piece that particular attention ought to be given to it. Tasteless furniture can be changed, chimney-pieces are fixtures, and once put up must remain.[6]

Sadly, as we know from such a flourishing business as Crowther's of Syon Lodge in our own day, such a statement is by no means true, and chimneypieces have been ripped out and replaced,[7] making the study of executed examples particularly difficult. This is perhaps one of the reasons why a serious, comprehensive study of so important a feature of the eighteenth-century interior seems never to have been undertaken.[8] There is obviously not the space to attempt it here, but it may be worth exploring the distinctive form that the English eighteenth-century chimneypiece took, and to investigate some of the reasons for this form.

In the great continental divide between those nations that adopted the fireplace and those that preferred the stove, the British chose the open hearth. Social attitudes as well as practical considerations were partly responsible for this. The choice is perhaps best expressed by Nathaniel Wraxall, who approved of the installation of chimneypieces rather than the more usual

"Dutch" (that is, German) stoves by the francophile Frederick the Great at his summer residence, Sans Souci:

Frederic . . . has discovered that nothing can compensate for the cheerful and vivifying influence of a fire. The body may indeed be completely warmed by the equal diffusion of heat from a stove; but the mind, the temper, and the fancy, receive animation as well as heat from the sight of a blazing hearth. . . . It is one of the many proofs that might be adduced, how superior he is, in little, as well as in greater things, to the generality of German Princes, who never see a fire, and are satisfied with feeling its operation.[9]

This "cheerful and vivifying influence" was eminently social in its operation. A fire, particularly in a drafty house, requires people to draw up to it to enjoy its effects, and this brings them together. However, it is evident from the repeated complaints about men openly warming their bottoms before a fire that women, being much more circumscribed by notions of propriety, were at a disadvantage in such matters.[10] The social implications of the fireplace can be deduced from the fact that the Duke of Somerset was installing lavish chimneypieces in the new apartments of Northumberland House between 1748 and 1750, but decided on a stove in the new chapel.[11]

Inasmuch as the English were at one with the

Fig. 2.
Engraving by Jacques-François Blondel of the chimneypiece designed by Jean-Baptiste Pineau for the architect Jean-Baptiste Le Roux, executed in the gallery added to the Hôtel de Villars, Paris, 1731–1733 (Bibliothèque Nationale, Paris)

Fig. 3.
A Couple Taking Tea in Front of a Fireplace, signed J. Poitvin In.ᵛᵗ, English, c. 1710 (National Galleries of Scotland)

French in opting for fireplaces rather than stoves, it is all the more striking that they rejected one of the classic elements of the French eighteenth-century interior, the kind of chimneypiece that was so much a product of French invention and design that it was known as the *cheminée à la française*.[12] The essential features of such chimneypieces were a marble surround or *chambranle*—generally curvilinear—ormolu mounts and appurtenances, and above all an overmantel mirror in a gilt frame extending almost up to the cove of the ceiling (fig. 2).

It was the mirror that was the stumbling block to the adoption of similar chimneypieces in England. For although the overmantel mirrors that were first adopted by the French in the 1680s were oblong panels or roundels, like those found in England in the following decades (fig. 3), what really led to the vogue for overmantel mirrors in France was the technique of casting vast plates of glass, which was perfected by Bernard Perrot and by Abraham Thévart and his associates between 1687 and 1688.[13] Not that such plate-glass mirrors were by any means cheap. For many years they were the preserve of the royal palaces—hence the name *cheminées à la royale* given to one of Pierre Lepautre's sets of prints (fig. 4), which misled Fiske Kimball into extending this name to the whole type[14]—and of the *financiers* who profited so conspicuously from the king's wars. Even Louis XIV sometimes shrank from the expense of these mirrors, and then the vast area of glass might be composed of a grid of separate panes. This latter practice is what we find imitated in an overmantel mirror of 1691 in Kensington Palace.[15]

At first it appeared as if the English might emulate the ability of the French *Manufacture Royale des Glaces* to cast large sheets of plate glass. In 1691 Robert Hookes and Christopher Dodsworth obtained a patent for a new method of casting glass, "particularly looking glass plates, much larger than ever was blowne in England or any foreigne parts," and an advertisement of 1702 claimed that these plates could be made up to ninety inches in length.[16] Hookes' and Dodsworth's claim was not strictly true, for by this date the French could produce sheets measuring one hundred *pouces* by sixty,[17] and the *pouce* was marginally longer than the inch. Even so, it was impressive, or would have been if plates of such size had ever been produced and used in England. The considerable problems involved were never ironed out, however, so that although cast plate glass was certainly made on a small scale in England in the eighteenth century, by 1773 a descendant of one of the original proprietors of the Southwark works claimed that the factory's apparatus for doing so had long since been destroyed.

Until 1773 and even after that, sizeable mirrors in England were either made up of several plates or were imported from France. The one kind of chimneypiece that made regular use of overmantel mirrors was, appropriately, the rococo type, whether in the so-called ''French'' or ''Gothick'' taste; in both styles the busy mesh of curvilinear ornament functioned as a useful disguise for the number of separate plates of native glass needed. The combination of glass and *rocaille,* a form of ornament also particularly associated with France, seems more than mere coincidence. Huge single plates of looking glass were not cheap in France, but when they were imported into England a duty of 75 percent *ad valorem* was payable as well. James Christie, the auctioneer and one of the major importers of mirrors, knew of plates that had cost as much as one thousand pounds apiece, and thus most of such glass was smuggled or illicitly imported under cover of diplomatic immunity.[18]

The year 1773 should have been the turning point in the manufacture of English plate glass, for that was when the British Cast Plate Glass Manufacturers, ancestors of the Pilkington works at St. Helen's, were incorporated at Ravenhead in Lancashire. We even know from a letter written by Lady Mary Coke in September 1774 that Adam made designs for Luton Hoo counting on the forthcoming production from these works: ''Fine glasses there are only in one of the drawing rooms; the rest are to be bought here, as soon as the new project for casting larger plates than they do at Paris is brought to perfection.''[19] Luton Hoo must have had an unfinished look—or have made do with pieced-together or smuggled plates of looking glass—for a long time, since it was only when Robert Sherbourne took over the Ravenhead works in 1792 that technical problems were overcome, and large-scale manufacture could begin.

It is thus clear that for most of the century large overmantel mirrors were difficult to come by. The fact that they were expensive and incurred heavy import duties would not necessarily have been a deterrent to their use, for circumstances were much the same for other items of French furniture and tapestry, and even for ma-

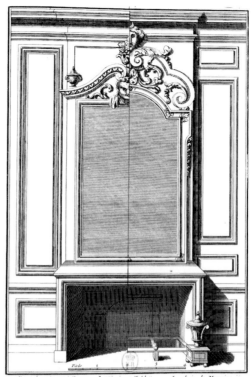

Fig. 4.
Engraving of a *cheminée à la royale*
by Pierre Lepautre, c. 1698
(Bibliothèque Nationale, Paris)

hogany. The crucial factor was probably the strong possibility of breakage during transport. It was one thing to pay large sums for items of conspicuous consumption—though the Duke of Northumberland was prepared to resort to smuggling in an attempt to reduce the real, as opposed to the apparent cost of the celebrated Glass Drawing Room at Northumberland House[20]—but quite another to disburse large sums for something just as likely to end up in fragments. The Glass Drawing Room was actually designed in 1773, and the Duke of Northumberland may thus, like Lord Bute, have intended to obtain his glass plates from Ravenhead, particularly since he was one of its shareholders.[21] If so, he would only have been driven to import his mirrors by the teething problems of the manufactory.

There were also those who voiced objections to the use of overmantel mirrors on aesthetic and social grounds. It is evident from the comments of English visitors to Paris that most of them—like many academic and moralizing critics in France—were shocked by the two features of French interiors that seemed to exemplify mean-

ingless profusion and expense for expense's sake: mirrors and gilding.[22] Samuel Johnson and Mrs. Thrale repeatedly commented on the proliferation of "gold and glass" on their journey to Paris in 1775.[23] Though careful not to express any admiration, they may nonetheless have been more than a little dazzled by it. Horace Walpole, by contrast, who was familiar with real magnificence at his father's house, Houghton Hall, found such interiors simply monotonous. As he wrote to Ann Pitt from Paris in 1765: "I have seen but one idea in all the houses here; the rooms are white and gold, or white; a lustre, a vast glass over the chimney, and another opposite, and generally a third over against the windows compose their rooms universally;"[24] he added in his letter to Lady Suffolk: "I never know one from another."[25]

English chimneypieces were, of course, every bit as expensive as those of the French; the expense was simply incurred by different objects: the sculpture of the fireplace surround and the overmantel. Rather than a looking glass there was generally an—admittedly cheaper—painted overmantel in an elaborate tectonic frame continuous with the chimney breast.[26] This painted overmantel might be a portrait, a figural subject (fig. 5), or most often, despite Gérard de Lairesse's disapproval of their illogicality,[27] a landscape or a ruinscape. Gracile representations of mythology or putto-pictures as overdoors and overmirrors, against which French artists protested,[28] were almost unknown.

When the architecture required it, especially in a stone hall, the overmantel might be a relief of stone or marble. This had been completely out of fashion in France since the days of Louis XIV, but in England it was evidently one of the elements that was thought to contribute most to the *romanitas* of the Palladian interior. Such reliefs were almost invariably of classical subjects, often of antique sacrifices.[29] They seem particularly to have been a product of the collaboration between William Kent and John Michael Rysbrack, some of the earliest being those designed for Houghton around 1726. Another very early example that may also have been carved by a Fleming is the relief of *Mercury Bringing a Message to Zeus* at 4 Saint James's Square in London (fig. 6). This house, which belonged to the Duke of Kent, was burnt down in 1725 and rebuilt between 1725 and 1728. The duke's account with Hoare's bank, opened specifically for the redecoration of the house, contains payments to a surprisingly large number of sculptors who can only have been working on the chimneypieces and overmantel reliefs admired by Horace Walpole some years later.[30] They were Henry Cheere, Laurent Delvaux, John Nost, Rysbrack, and Henry Scheemakers—every one but the first Flemings. Of all of them, either Delvaux or Scheemakers seems the likeliest author of the Mercury relief.

What was even more singular about the English fireplace, however, was the sculpture lavished on its surround. As Chambers makes claim in the quoted passage from his *Complete Body of Architecture*, chimneypieces (next only to funeral monuments) were indeed the "chief employment" of sculptors in England. This too was in contrast to France, where the marble *chambranle* was relatively simple and usually devoid of figurative sculpture. There, however, it was the province of the *marbrier*, or marble mason, and guild demarcations no doubt conspired both to keep it so and to prevent the marble mason from diverging into sculpture. In England sculptors succeeded in making chimneypieces—like monuments—one of their recognized spheres of activity, partly because they claimed special expertise in working the imported material of marble—and, as in the case of Francis Bird and Joseph Wilton, were sometimes themselves wholesale importers of it—and partly to compensate for the fact that, again unlike France, the idea of commissioning or collecting any freestanding sculpture other than an antique or a bust was painfully slow to take root. Baron de Pollnitz claimed in 1732 that in England: "Sculpture is of all Arts the least cultivated."[31] and twenty years later Horace Mann could still write from Florence to Horace Walpole concerning England: "But is there really any taste for sculpture there above that of a looking-glass-polished chimney-piece?"[32]

In England the difference of opinion over chimneypieces was between sculptors and architects on the one hand and joiners and carpenters on the other. Was the chimneypiece an architectural element of the interior, as Ware and Chambers were clearly maintaining, or was it a piece of furniture, as the designs in publications by Matthias Lock, Thomas Chippendale, and William Ince and John Mayhew evidently implied?[33] Yet instead of proposing different types of chimneypieces, both the carpenter-cum-carver and marble sculptor essentially rivaled one another in the use of the same forms. Both had an interest in maintaining the enlarged chimneypiece as the broadest field for the deployment of their art, and once it was abandoned both lost or found considerably less work in a lucrative branch of activity.

Some of the most characteristic ornaments of the English chimney breast were life-size figures in the round: caryatids, Persians, and even nude atlantes, though Isaac Ware thought that these last were going too far: "Modern sculptors are fond of nudities; but in a chimney-piece they would be abominable. . . . Let no statuary here object that the great excellence of his art is withheld. . . . We banish anatomy from the parlour of the polite gentleman: that is all."[34] Tessa Murdoch, inspired by the bearded term on the chimneypiece in Goldsmith's Hall, traditionally attributed to Louis François Roubiliac and implausibly said to come from Canons,[35] is making a special study of telamonic chimneypieces, so I do not want to trespass upon the field of her researches here. I should only like to make a couple of observations about chimneypieces with whole figures. Such figures, which seem to have first been used in the 1750s, demonstrate (as Ware's caveat implies) the frustrated urge of sculptors in England to make freestanding figure sculpture. They were not simply a spontaneous invention of the sculptors, but a result of the thought architects had given to the chimneypiece. For the latter the chimneypiece, like the staircase, afforded one of the best opportunities for inventiveness, untrammeled by any rules or precedents from antiquity.

Terms (figs. 5, 7) had formed part of the repertoire of chimneypiece ornament since the earliest designs by Kent (and before that, in Elizabethan and continental examples). As Isaac Ware pronounced, referring to them as *termini*: "We set out with observing, that fancy was to be freely indulged in the construction of chimney-pieces: these are, of all the figures that can be introduced, the most fantastical; and it will be no where so proper to introduce them."[36] It might seem a natural progression to have introduced steadily more of the human body into the carving of these terms, but the advance to the whole figure nonetheless required architectural sanction. This it received by virtue of the fact that, since they took the place of columns, caryatids and Persians could be regarded as distinct architectural orders. They are referred to as such by both Kent and Chambers, and, what is more, they drew their authority as orders from Inigo Jones's use of them in his designs for the circular

court of the projected palace of Whitehall. Isaac Ware thought that caryatids were best suited to chimneypieces with no superstructure (fig. 8), which is how they are generally employed, though Robert Adam's reasoning was that: "for a Drawing Room the woman is surely the propperest,"[37] regardless of type. Ware also considered Persians suitable for chimneypieces of the continued kind, and is quite explicit about their role:

When we speak of these male and female figures under the name of Persian and Caryatick orders, we do not consider them as simple statues, but as parts of an order of architecture. They supply the place of a shaft of a column; and they support an entablature.[38]

Robert Adam may only have been using his draftsman to correct an original design by Rysbrack for the chimneypiece with caryatid terms at Hopetoun House (fig. 9), but we now know that he and his brother John studied the propriety of the design thoroughly at the Earl of

Hopetoun's behest, and that he also took advice from Joseph Wilton when he was in Florence.[39] I should also be inclined to attribute to Adam the design of the chimneypiece with caryatids formerly at Moor Park, which was always mistakenly said to have come from the Borghese Palace in Rome—a confusion with the frieze, copied from the *Borghese Dancers,* which, with its lapis lazuli ground, may well have been sent back from Rome. It also seems highly probable that Chambers was consulted about the design of the two great chimneypieces with "Persians," attributed to Wilton, in the gallery of Northumberland House (figs. 10, 11), one of which is now in the Victoria and Albert Museum and the other at Syon House.[40] Not only were the two friends in Florence together, but also Chambers approved in his *Treatise on Civil Architecture* the use of Persians and caryatids on chimneypieces and provided a whole plate of potential models for them (fig. 12), taken from paintings and sculpture that he had drawn in Italy.[41]

Most intriguingly of all, in their separate treatises Ware and Chambers explain the legendary origin of caryatids and Persians, seeing them as a perpetuation of the memory of the captives taken by the victorious Greeks. The authors seem to hint that an unconscious memory of this origin is one of the reasons for the adoption of such figures in England. They appeared, after all, during the very years in which the foundations of the British Empire were being laid in a series of victories over the French. There is even an overt evocation of the British Empire and of the parallel between it and the ancient Greeks in the substitution of Indian women for caryatids in the splendid chimneypiece that Thomas Banks carved for Warren Hastings at Daylesford House, Gloucestershire, in 1792 (fig. 13).

One of the first blows to the continued chimneypiece was the virtual abandonment of relief sculpture in the overmantel after the 1750s. Rysbrack's *Sacrifice to Diana* at Woburn Abbey, made in 1755, which was a copy of a piece executed for Houghton Hall almost thirty years before, and a *Sacrifice to Apollo,* also a repetition, are among the last instances of this kind of chimneypiece adornment.[42] Another blow was the devaluation of overmantel pictures, as picture collecting became an autonomous activity in Britain.

There is a significant episode in *The Memoirs of Thomas Jones,* at 1764, of "a friend, who after keeping my Expectations afloat from some weeks, with the idea of painting a picture for his

Fig. 8.
Design for a "Chimney-Piece of the Caryatick order" by Isaac Ware, engraved by Charles Grignion for *A Complete Body of Architecture, 1756,* plate 88, and a variant of the chimneypiece executed in the Great Drawing Room at Chesterfield House, London, c. 1750

Fig. 9.
Design for a chimneypiece with caryatid terms by John Michael Rysbrack (Victoria and Albert Museum)

Fig. 10.
Design with alternatives for the chimneypieces in the Gallery at Northumberland House, London, by Benjamin Carter, with a "Persian" as a whole figure on the left and as a term on the right, and female terms in the continuation (Victoria and Albert Museum)

Fig. 11.
Chimneypiece by Benjamin Carter from the Gallery at Northumberland House, delivered 1767 (Victoria and Albert Museum)

Chimney piece, at length very cooly told me, that on Reflection, he could purchase a piece of *India Paper* [that is, Chinese Wallpaper] for a few Shillings which would be prettier, and more fashionable."[43] This ties in with Joseph Collyer's observations in *The Parent's and Guardian's Directory* of 1761, that "Paper Hangings Makers . . . now make landscapes, ruins, and sea-pieces, as the ornaments of chimney-pieces."[44]

Such a devaluation of the content of overmantels clearly presaged the abandonment of them altogether. As Isaac Ware reiterated, "continued chimney-pieces" were anyway only appropriate to rooms decorated tectonically, or at least with stucco, whereas plain chimneypieces were adequate to rooms hung with paper. The steady encroachment of wallpaper thus itself brought with it the abandonment of continuous over-

mantels. There may even have been feminine influences at work here, since the renunciation of overmantels was considered to increase the intimacy of the interior. Emily, Marchioness of Kildare (the future Duchess of Leinster), wrote to her husband in 1762 about the installation of his portrait at Kildare House: "It shall hang in my new mohair dressing-room here, upon the hangings, not to be made up as part of the chimney; for a lady's room that is not pretty."[45]

As we have seen, Chambers' *Treatise* of 1759 failed to illustrate any designs for chimneypieces of the continued type, even if the author implicitly approved them. Pattern books, however, went on proposing them as models for a little time yet: William Pain included different designs for continued Palladian chimneypieces, as well as four designs for gothick chimneypieces,[46] in the three editions of his *Builder's Companion and Workman's General Assistant* in 1758, 1765, and 1769, and he still included a plate of a continued Palladian chimneypiece in his *Practical Builder* of 1774. There were superstructures of every kind—Kentian, rococo, and gothick—in the first volume of Robert Baldwin's *The Chimney-Piecemaker's Daily Assistant,* published in 1766, but Baldwin included no continued chimneypieces in his second volume of 1769. And there were no examples of chimneypieces with a superstructure in N. Wallis' *Complete Modern Joiner* of 1772, or in William Pain's *Carpenter's and Joiner's Repository* of 1778. This cannot have been because these publications were repertories of designs by and for carpenters and joiners rather than for architects and sculptors, since it was the former who had the most to lose by the abandonment of overmantel superstructures.

Sculptors, nevertheless, continued to gain considerable employment from the demand for richly sculpted mantelpieces. Joseph Nollekens executed few himself, but made a rich living by subcontracting them to the masons of the New Road, London.[47] Wilton was especially favored with the execution of Chambers' designs, but also made several "on spec."[48] John Deare actually began his career carving ornaments for the son of one of the major specialists in chimneypieces from the previous generation, Thomas Carter the younger, but also continued to execute chimneypieces for British clients when he was in Rome.[49] In this he found himself in good company, since Piranesi was the most celebrated of the Italians to carve or make up chimneypieces for dispatch to Britain.[50] It was in one of the leading provincial centers for the production of chimneypieces "in the Egyptian, Grecian, Gothic and modern taste," the statuaries Messrs. Franceys of Liverpool, that John Gibson served his apprenticeship.[51]

Gibson, however, stood at the tail end of a tradition. For it was at about the time that he served his apprenticeship, in the early years of the nineteenth century, that most chimneypieces became markedly plainer, requiring only the skills of the mason and not those of the sculptor. It can scarcely have been a coincidence that these were also the years in which the production of large cast looking glasses became routine, since tall overmantel mirrors with plain reeded frames of the kind recommended by Thomas Sheraton[52] naturally called for plainer chimney breasts to match.

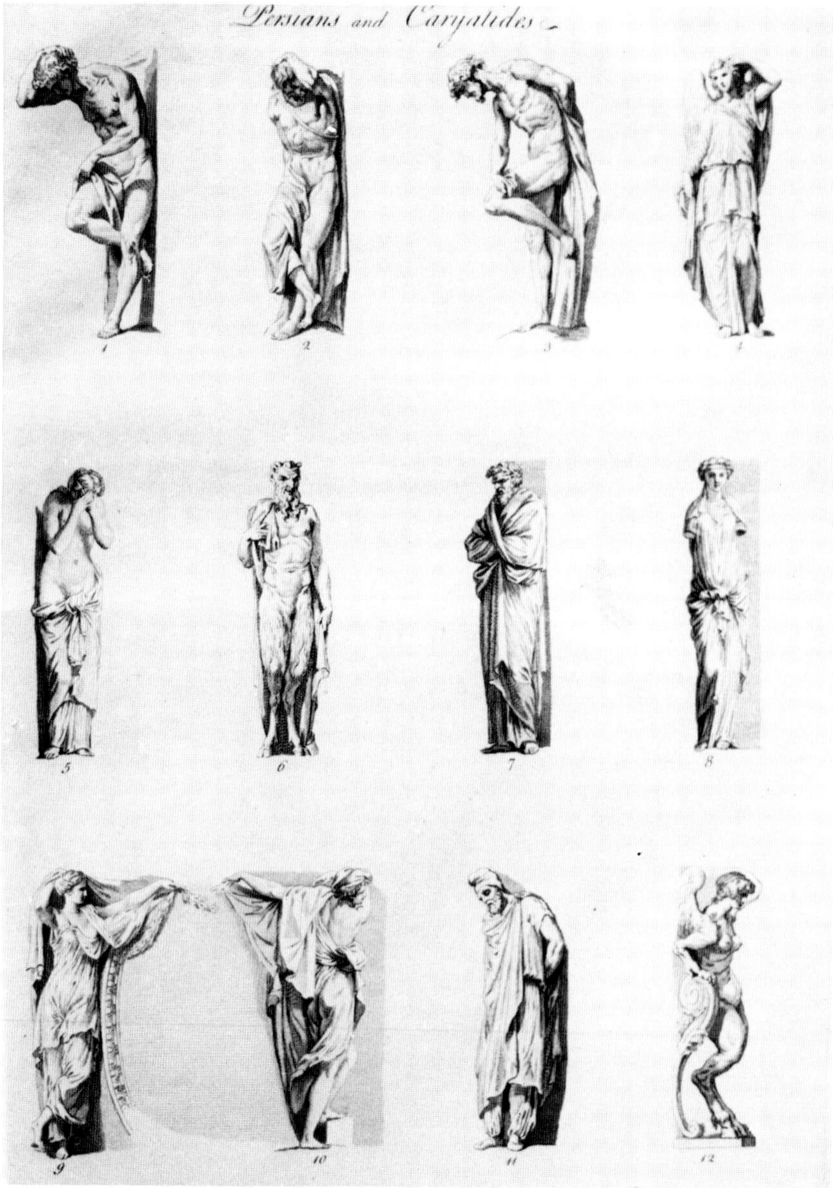

Persians and Caryatides

Architects played their part in this evolution too, recommending the chaster interiors and largely planar ornament of the Greek Revival. There was indeed one particular architect who received the blame for taking the bread out of sculptors' mouths. Joseph Farington recorded a visit in his diary on 28 May 1815:

Rossi called. He complained of Architects having made such a change in their designs for Chimney pieces, leaving out ornaments and making them so plain that they could now be executed for from four pounds to fifteen, while formerly a Chimney piece would have cost fifty or sixty

Fig. 12.
Engraving by Charles Grignion after drawings by Giovanni Battista Cipriani of figures taken from paintings and sculpture in Italy, assembled as models of Persians and caryatids for William Chambers' *Treatise on Civil Architecture,* 1759

Fig. 13.
Chimneypiece with Indian caryatids in the small drawing room at Daylesford House, Gloucestershire, by Thomas Banks, 1792 (National Monuments Record)

Fig. 14.
Chimneypiece from the Dining Room at Dorchester House, London, by Alfred Stevens, 1859–1875 (Victoria and Albert Museum)

pounds. This branch of business to the Sculptors, he said, had greatly suffered by this alteration, which he said was calculated to lessen the expense of building and finishing houses. I asked him who had introduced this change, & he mentioned Robert Smirke as being the leader of it.[53]

There were, of course, sculpted or ornamented chimneypieces after 1815, especially following the rococo revival, but continuity had been broken and by the time there was a demand for them again the sculptor's view of his own calling had changed. Henceforward chimneypieces would be the preserve of monumental masons, and sculptors would mostly be restricted to executing parts or embellishments of them. It took the unique genius of Alfred Stevens, for whom all art was subordinate to design, to create a chimneypiece for Dorchester House between 1859 and 1875 (fig. 14) that was not only a vehicle for a completely fresh conception of the caryatid, but a piece of sculpture in its own right.[54]

1. William Chambers, *A Treatise on Civil Architecture* (London, 1759), 77–78.

2. Aside from the fact that such 'Jonesian' models as the chimneypieces at Wilton or Gunnersbury were in fact designed by John Webb, it has long been known that Jones' own designs were indebted to French models: not only to such engraved designs as those by Pierre Collot (1631 and 1633) and Jean Barbet (1632), but also to drawings apparently transmitted via the French ambassador to London in 1636; see John Harris, "Inigo Jones and His French Sources," *The Metropolitan Museum of Art Bulletin* (May 1961), 253–264.

3. Isaac Ware, *A Complete Body of Architecture* (London, 1756), book VI: "Of Chimney-Pieces," esp. chap. 2: "Of simple and continued chimney-pieces," 555–556.

4. See Alastair Laing, "Die Entwicklung der *Cheminée à la française* und seine Dekoration," in Hans Ottomeyer and Peter Pröschel, *Vergoldete Bronzen: Die Bronzearbeiten des Spätbarock und Klassizismus* (Munich, 1986), 2:443–458.

5. Sir William Chambers, *A Treatise on the Decorative Part of Civil Architecture*, ed. John Buonarotti Papworth (London, 1826), 146. Curiously, though styling itself the fourth edition, this was in fact the fifth, having been preceded by Joseph Gwilt's edition (1825).

6. Sir William Chambers, *A Treatise on the Decorative Part of Civil Architecture*, ed. W. H. Leeds (London, 1862).

7. How chimneypieces could shift about even within one building is very well illustrated by a single house, Temple Newsam, in Christopher Gilbert and Anthony Wells-Cole, *The Fashionable Fire Place* [exh. cat., Leeds City Art Galleries] (Leeds, 1985), 13–20. That even lesser mortals shifted chimneypieces is exemplified by Margaret Jourdain and Ivy Compton Burnet, who removed an Adam chimneypiece from Linden Gardens to Braemar Mansions (Hilary Spurling, *Secrets of a Woman's Heart* [London, 1984], 61).

8. The one substantial study in English treating of chimneypieces, Walter Bernan, *On the History and Art of Warming and Ventilating Rooms and Buildings*, 2 vols. (London, 1845), is, as its title makes clear, primarily concerned with technique rather than adornment. Lawrence Wright, *Home Fires Burning* (London, 1964), and Eileen Harris, *Keeping Warm* (London, 1983), range over all the functions and parts of apparatuses for generating heat. Even such stylistic guides as L. A. Shuffrey, *The English Fireplace* (London, 1912), and Alison Kelly, *The Book of English Fireplaces* (London, 1968), are disappointingly cursory in their treatment of the eighteenth-century chimneypiece. Gilbert and Wells-Cole 1985, an excellent exhibition catalogue, is chiefly devoted to fire furniture.

9. N. William Wraxall, *Memoirs of the Courts of Berlin, Dresden, Warsaw, and Vienna, in the Years 1777, 1778 and 1779*, 3d rev. ed. (London, 1806), 1:262–263. Exactly the same spirit is found in Sébastian Mercier in *Tableau de Paris* (Amsterdam, 1782–1788), 10:303, at a time when stoves were very much the vogue in France: "Quelle distance entre un poële & une cheminée! La vue d'un poële éteint mon imagination, m'attriste & me rend mélancolique: j'aime mieux le froid le plus vif que cette chaleur fade, tiède, invisible. . . . l'on tisonne; c'est ainsi que j'ai fait presque tous mes livres: mes pensées riantes [se] font au bout des pincettes, & je regarde comme un cachot toute chambre à poële."

10. Mercier 1782–1788, 1:69–70, 10:309–310, has two passages on the indecency of men warming their bottoms before the fire and shutting the heat off from women. There is an amusing story of Edward Lear being repeatedly invited to see something on the far side of the room by a Lord-in-Waiting, to prevent him from warming himself in the presence of Queen Victoria (Vivien Noakes, *Edward Lear: The Life of a Wanderer* [London, 1968], 72).

11. [Thomas] Hull, *Select Letters Between the Late Duchess of Somerset . . ., William Shenstone Esq., and Others* (London, 1778), 1:98. Compare with this Parson Woodforde's disapproval of the fireplaces installed in niches in the Octagon Church in Milsom Street, Bath: "It is a handsome building, but not like a place of worship, there being fireplaces in it, especially on each side of the Altar, which I cannot think at all decent, it is not liked" (Parson Woodforde, *The Diary of a Country Parson*, ed. John Beresford [London, 1924], 1:83).

12. Laing 1986, 2:443–458.

13. Elphège Frémy, *Histoire de la manufacture royale des glaces de France au XVIIe et au XVIIIe siècle* (Paris, 1909), 52–101, 262–269; James Barrelet, *La verrerie en France* (Paris, 1954), 75–84.

14. Fiske Kimball, "The Development of the '*Cheminée à la royale*,'" *Metropolitan Museum Studies* 5 (1934–1936), 259–280.

15. For an example of Louis XIV's use of a grid of mirror panes after the manufacture of large sheets of looking glass had become feasible (although the reasons may have been as much a desire to harmonize with other rooms as economy), see *Collections de Louis XIV*, [exh. cat., Musée de l'Orangerie] (Paris, 1977–1978), no. 269. An example of this treatment survives in Queen Mary's Gallery at Kensington Palace; see Percy Macquoid and Ralph Edwards, *The Dictionary of English Furniture* (London, 1924), 2:323, fig. 36.

16. Robert W. Symonds, "Early English Mirrors," *Connoisseur* 96 (1935), 315–321; 97 (1936), 243–248; 98 (1936), 9–15; T. C. Barker, *Pilkington Brothers and the Glass Industry* (London, 1960), 43–48.

17. Frémy 1909, 197, 205–206.

18. See Geoffrey Wills, "Furniture-Smuggling in Eighteenth-Century London," *Apollo* (August 1965), 112–117; William Rieder, "Furniture-Smuggling for a Duke," *Apollo* (September 1970), 206–209.

19. *The Letters and Journals of Lady Mary Coke* (Edinburgh, 1896), 4:389. Macquoid and Edwards 1924, 336, mistranscribed the crucial word "bought" as "brought."

20. David Owsley and William Rieder, *The Glass Drawing Room from Northumberland House* (London, 1974), 15.

21. Owsley and Rieder 1974, 14.

22. A reaction like that of the Reverend William Cole to the Galerie des Glaces at Versailles: "all too glaring & gaudy" (*A Journal of My Journey to Paris in the Year 1765*, ed. F. G. Stokes, [London, 1931], 237) was surely not untypical. Comments on private houses are rarer, because most English tourists had little or no access to them. Samuel Johnson and Hester Thrale were more fortunate in this regard, thanks more to her connections than to his fame; see Moses Tyson and Henry Guppy, eds., *The French Journals of Mrs. Thrale and Dr. Johnson* (Manchester, 1932).

23. *The Yale Edition of Samuel Johnson* (New Haven, 1958), 1:230–233, 242–243, 249; Tyson and Guppy 1932, 112, 116, 117.

24. Wilmarth Sheldon Lewis et al., eds., *The Yale Edition of Horace Walpole's Correspondence*, 48 vols. (New Haven, 1937–1983) 31:87.

25. Lewis 1937–1983, 31: 49.

26. See esp. William Kent's designs in *The Designs of Inigo Jones* (London, 1727); Isaac Ware's designs in *Designs of Inigo*

Jones and Others (London, c. 1733), and John Vardy's designs in *Some Designs of Mr. Inigo Jones and Mr. William Kent* (London, 1746).

27. Gérard de Lairesse, *The Art of Painting in All Its Branches*, trans. J. F. Fritsch (London, 1738), 292.

28. See esp. [La Font de Saint Yenne], *Reflexions sur quelques causes de l'état présent de la peinture en France* (The Hague, 1747), 16–17:

La s[c]ience du Pinceau a donc été forcée de céder à l'éclat du verre; la facilité méchanique de sa perfection, & son abondance ont exilé des appartemens le plus beau des Arts, à qui l'on n'a laissé pour azile que quelques misérables places à remplir, des dessus de portes, des couronnemens de cheminées & ceux de quelques trumeaux de Glace raccourcis par oeconomie. Là, resserrée par le défaut d'espace à de petits sujets mesquins hors de la portée de l'oeil, la Peinture est réduite dans ces grandes Pièces à des représentations froides, insipides & nullement intéressantes: les quatre Elemens, les Saisons, les Sens, les Arts, les Muses, & autres lieux communs triomphes du Peintre plagiaire, & ouvrier.

29. As John Hardy has kindly pointed out to me, the depiction of sacrifices made a witty connection between the sacrificial flame and the fire in the hearth.

30. *Survey of London: The Parish of St. James, Westminster: Part One: South of Piccadilly* (London, 1960), 29:89–90, and inserted addendum; "Horace Walpole's Journals of Visits to Country Seats," ed. Paget Toynbee, *Walpole Society* 16 (1927–1928), 39–40. The composition of this Homeric relief is based on the engraving of an antique relief in Pietro Santo Bartoli, *Admiranda Romanarum Antiquitatum* (1693), fig. 27. This was later also to be drawn on by Francis Hayman for a grisaille overdoor in the Library at Blickling Hall (c. 1745), and by an anonymous artist for one of the attic paintings in the Marble Hall of Kedleston Hall (c. 1765).

31. *The Memoirs of the Baron de Pollnitz*, 2d rev. ed. (London, 1739), 2:434.

32. Mann to Horace Walpole, 9 November 1753, Lewis 1937–1983, 20:398.

33. Designs for chimneypieces appear to be almost evenly divided between the publications of architects and surveyors on the one hand—e.g., Kent's designs in *Inigo Jones* 1727, and those in James Gibbs, *A Book of Architecture* (London, 1728); William Jones, *The Gentlemens or Builders Companion* (London, 1739), though these designs were originally appended to James Smith, *Specimen of Antient Carpentry* (London, 1736); Batty Langley, *The City and Country Builder's and Workman's Treasury of Designs* (London, 1740); idem, *Ancient Architecture Restored* (London, 1742); Robert Morris, *The Architectural Remembrancer* (London, 1751); Ware 1756; William Chambers, *A Treatise on Civil Architecture* (London, 1759); Thomas Milton, John Crunden, and Placido Columbani, *The Chimney-Piecemaker's Daily Assistant* 1 (London, 1766); Robert Baldwin, *The Chimney-Piecemaker's Daily Assistant* 2 (London, 1769); Giambattista Piranesi, *Divers Manners of Ornamenting Chimneys* (London, 1769); George Richardson, *A New Collection of Chimney-Pieces* (London, 1781); G. Cooper, *Designs for Decorative Architecture* (London, 1807)—and those of carpenters, carvers, joiners, and (latterly) cabinetmakers, on the other—e.g., Abraham Swan, *The British Architect* (London, 1745); Matthias Lock, *A New Book of Ornaments* (London, 1752); idem, *A New Book of Ornaments for Looking Glass Frames, Chimney Pieces &c, &c* (London, n.d.); William Pain, *The Builder's Companion* (London, 1758), 2d ed. (London, 1765), 3d ed. (London, 1769); Thomas Johnson, designs published in parts without a title in 1756 and 1757, and together but without a title in 1758; republished as *One Hundred and Fifty New Designs* (London, 1761);

William Ince and John Mayhew, *The Universal System of Household Furniture* (1759–1760; London, 1762); *Household Furniture in Genteel Taste for the Year 1760. By a Society of Upholsterers, Cabinet Makers, etc* (London, 1760); Thomas Chippendale, *The Gentleman and Cabinet-Makers Director*, 3d ed. (London, 1762); N. Wallis, *The Complete Modern Joiner* (1772; London, 1792); William Pain, *The Practical Builder, or Workman's General Assistant* (London, 1774); idem, *The Carpenter's and Joiner's Repository* (London, 1778); idem, *Pain's British Palladio* (London, 1786).

34. Ware 1756, 574. Ware's admonitions do not appear to have been heeded by James Lovell in the chimneypiece that he carved for the hall at Hagley Hall around 1758; see Christopher Hussey, *English Country Houses: Early Georgian, 1715–1760* (London, 1955), 200, fig. 361.

35. Nikolaus Pevsner, *The Buildings of England: London*, 3d rev. ed. (Harmondsworth, 1973), 1:242. Tessa Murdoch has found documents showing that Henry Cheere carved this perfectly conventional chimneypiece between 1734 and 1735, when Roubiliac may have been working for him. Roubiliac's later readiness to carve such chimneypiece sculpture is firmly suggested by two passages in a letter from Robert Adam to Lord Hopetoun, Rome, 3 May 1755: "One Brittinghame [i.e., Matthew Brettingham] . . . Two years ago carried a Dozen of Marble Chimney pieces to England: But they were so generally condemned and found so defective that Rysbrack & Rubiliack had to correct the Sculpture and their men to help the Carving & polishing . . . if Your Lordship employs Rubiliack or Rysbrack You are sure they will be much better done than anyone here can do them." See Brian Allen, "Joseph Wilton, Francis Hayman and the Chimney-pieces from Northumberland House," *Burlington Magazine* (April 1983), 201. I am indebted to Mr. Allen for sending me a photocopy of the rest of the letter.

36. Ware 1756, 582.

37. Brian Allen 1983, 202, n. 61.

38. Ware 1756, 571.

39. Adam to Lord Hopetoun, 3 May 1755. Adam begins the second paragraph of his letter by saying: "Wilton's Letter confirms strongly my own opinion both concerning the Design of the Chimney, & the Execution of it. He says that taking it altogether it will have a very good Effect if executed well & entirely of Statuary Marble. Only he objects to some of the Ornaments, says the Therms may be improved, That the Festoons in the Recesses on each side of the Block wou'd do better if confined to those Spaces than to return with an Angle, Join the Shoulder of the Therm & then hang down, which wou'd both look ill at the Bend, & be difficult to execute." This makes it clear not only that Adam was commenting on a preexisting design (no doubt by Rysbrack) sent out by Lord Hopetoun, but that this design already included terms (a word which in Adam's and Rysbrack's usage clearly extended to half-caryatids). From the wholly English configuration both of the executed chimneypiece at Hopetoun (fig. 11) and of the drawing for it (fig. 10) obtained by Adam from his draftsman in Rome (whom the indications in the letter identify almost certainly as Laurent Pecheux), as well as from Adam's description of how he set about improving the design, it is clear that Adam's amendments were restricted to making the details more classical. Nevertheless, it is still not wholly clear whether the drawing by Rysbrack (fig. 9) preserved in the Victoria and Albert Museum (see Damie Stillman, *The Decorative Work of Robert Adam* [London, 1966], fig. 95) represents another version of Rysbrack's original design, or an adjustment to take account of Wilton's and Adam's suggestions. The chimneypiece as executed employs half-caryatids in a pose found in Rysbrack's and Adam's drawings, but turned diagonally as Adam had done in

his alternative proposal for a male half-atlantes. Ware and an unknown sculptor had done the same with the caryatids on the chimneypiece in the Great Drawing Room of Chesterfield House (fig. 8) in about 1750 (see James Parker, "Designed in the Most Elegant Manner and Wrought in the Best Marbles," *The Metropolitan Museum of Art Bulletin* [February 1963], 202–213; engraved in variant form in Ware 1756, pl. 88). The half-caryatids on the chimneypiece in the dining room at Moor Park were probably designed by Adam and perhaps carved by Rysbrack. The frieze employs the sphinx-and-candelabrum motif (from the Temple of Antoninus and Faustina) found in another Rysbrack design in the Victoria and Albert Museum (Stillman 1966, fig. 96), but turned inward as in the Adam drawing. The tablet, on the other hand, combines the imitation of half of a Duquesnoy relief known in *His* several guises with a variation of the naiad and putto carved by Rysbrack for another chimneypiece at Woburn Abbey at exactly the same epoch (see Geoffrey Beard, *Craftsmen and Interior Decoration in England 1660–1820* [Edinburgh, 1981], fig. 142, mislabeled as in the Saloon rather than in the Blue Drawing Room).

40. Allen 1983. Though impressed by, and indebted to much of the evidence that Allen adduces for his identification of Joseph Wilton and his family as the subjects of Hayman's conversation piece, I am puzzled by certain features of the case. The first is that the whole tenor of the picture suggests that it portrays the executant rather than only the designer of the Northumberland House chimneypieces, and we know the supplier to have been the chimneypiece specialist, Benjamin Carter. The female term on the right of the picture similarly bespeaks a chimneypiece carver rather than a sculptor with the aspirations of Wilton. The variant design for the chimneypiece in the print room of the Victoria and Albert Museum (fig. 13) is likewise surely from the hand of a specialist chimneypiece designer rather than the work of Wilton—all of which leaves the latter little role in the affair, unless it was to transmit to his fellow sculptor his friend William Chambers' partiality for "Persians" as possible chimneypiece adornments.

41. Chambers 1759, 36–38.

42. M. I. Webb, *Michael Rysbrack, Sculptor* (London, 1954), 128–30, figs. 55, 56. Isolated commissions for such overmantel reliefs continued to be given, however, e.g., that by John Penn in 1793 for John Deare's *Caesar Checked in His Invasion of Britain* at Stoke Park (see Alastair Laing, "Clubhouse Neo-Classicism," *Country Life* [1983], 187, fig. 4), and the belated completion of the Great Hall at Wentworth Woodhouse with John Gibson's *The Hours Leading Forth the Horses of the Sun* and *Phaethon Driving the Chariot of the Sun* in 1826 (see Hussey 1955, figs. 253, 260; Rupert Gunnis, *Dictionary of British Sculptors 1660–1851*, rev. ed. [London, 1968], 173).

43. "The Memoirs of Thomas Jones," *Walpole Society* 22 (1951), 10.

44. Joseph Collyer, *The Parent's and Guardian's Directory, and the Youth's Guide, in the Choice of a Profession or Trade* (London, 1761), 207. Isaac Ware's arguments against employing a continued chimneypiece in a room with hung or papered walls (Ware 1756, 589) had evidently lost their force: "a light ornament continued from the lower work of the chimney will, where there is paper or silk, have the aspect of a frame; and these will appear as pictures in it. All know how poor this must look; since, in the reality, what could be so mean as the thought of framing a piece of the hanging?"

45. Brian Fitzgerald, ed., *Correspondence of Emily, Duchess of Leinster (1731–1814)* (Dublin, 1949), 1:158.

46. The full range of possibilities of both simple and continued chimneypieces open to a designer in the mid-century is beautifully shown in a sheet of designs by William Newton in the Royal Institute of British Architects (see John Harris, *The Design of the English Country House 1620–1920* [London, 1985], 172).

47. John Thomas Smith, *Nollekens and His Times*, 2 vols. (1828; London, 1829), 2:17.

48. Smith 1828 and 1829, 2:113–115.

49. Smith 1828 and 1829, 2:236–253. See also note 43.

50. William Rieder, "Piranesi at Gorhambury," *Burlington Magazine* (September 1975), 582–591; Damie Stillman, "Chimneypieces for the English Market: a Thriving Business in Later Eighteenth-Century Rome," *Art Bulletin* (March 1977), 85–94.

51. Gunnis 1968, 156, 171; T. Matthews, *The Biography of John Gibson, R.A., Sculptor, Rome* (London, 1911), 11–12, 30; John Physick, *Designs for English Sculpture 1680–1860* (London, 1969), no. 140.

52. T[homas] Sheraton, *The Cabinet Dictionary* (London, 1803), 150.

53. Kenneth Garlick, Angus MacIntyre, and Kathryn Cave, eds., *The Diary of Joseph Farington* (New Haven and London, 1978–1984), 13:4633.

54. Christopher Hussey, "Dorchester House—II," *Country Life* 63 (1928), 684–689; Susan Beattie, *Catalogue of the Drawings Collection of the Royal Institute of British Architects: Alfred Stevens* (Farnborough, 1975), 36–43, cat. nos. 35.12–35.29, figs. 94–100. Quite remarkable for the nineteenth, or indeed any century, is the exchange between Stevens and the client for the work, R. S. Holford, as reported by the latter to Hugh Stannus (Beattie 1975, 42): "When I first had negotiations with him, I told him plainly that I was not prepared to embark on a system of decoration to be charged as fine art. He answered, very fairly, that he proposed to charge his work as decorative work and not as high art." Stevens' high-minded craftsmanly integrity is not compromised by the fact that given his relentless pursuit of perfection, the sculptor's work at Holford House was far from complete at his death after sixteen years, and had cost between seven thousand and eight thousand pounds. There were other sculpted chimneypieces in the house, e.g., that designed by Robert (Richard?) Westmacott and carved by J. S. Whitehead in 1860 (Hussey 1955, 689, fig. 12), but this latter division of labor is typical of the ordinary Victorian sculptor's self-distancing from this kind of job, and the result is convincing neither as sculpture nor as a chimneypiece (albeit not dissimilar to others designed by Richard Westmacott the younger).

Introduction

To the Symposium Papers
Presented at The Folger Institute

7 February 1986

When we concentrate our attention on country-house buildings and their grounds, or on their furnishings, art works, and libraries, we generally find ourselves regarding country houses and their contents in aesthetic and curatorial terms. We tend in fact to treat them as if they had always been museums of some sort. Correspondingly, if the historical owners of the great estates assume any personae for us at all, they do so as connoisseurs and patrons of the arts. We appreciate, admire, and perhaps envy the taste, energy, and wealth they devoted to encouraging the arts, to sustaining the British country houses, and to preserving both as our material legacy.

As a result, however, we may lose sight of other irreducibly human components and consequences of country-house life. Overwhelmed by the splendor of these estates, we all too easily forget that the country houses were once centers of social life as well as the loci of power and authority for their surrounding communities. They were places where people lived, gathered together, and—of most significance here—talked and wrote. Much of what was discussed was important in ways that went far beyond the walls of the estate itself; country-house occupants concerned themselves with politics and order, with money and business, and with arts and letters. There was what might be called a "country-house culture," which, like any powerful and dominant culture, defined much of British life in its period. The period with which we are here concerned is that before urban industrialization, and for much of what we understand about it we are indebted to the thoughts recorded by country-house occupants.

Country-house culture cannot be characterized without reference to the environment it constructed and the possessions it amassed, displayed, used, and gloried in; but it neither sprang from nor was encapsulated in them. The relationship was much more dynamic and, for us, elusive than that. On the one hand, the possessions were not always the artifacts of the culture that preserved them; many of them were alien objects gathered from other societies and cultures and were more exemplary of the fashions and tastes of preindustrial Britain than they were of its essential nature. On the other hand, neither were the architectural achievements, handsome gardens, art collections, musical performances, and fine-book libraries merely a backdrop for an ongoing life, or simply objects to be admired by the owners and their guests. They reflected their owners' aspirations and embodied their values, in particular those related to continuity and community.

Our aim in the group of papers that follows is to explore the country-house culture, to complement the other essays in this volume that engage the material legacy. What went on in the country house? What was the relationship between the country-house environment and the activities it hosted and fostered? What did the country house signify to those who enjoyed, observed, and represented it? What other kinds of life and aspects of British culture impinged upon it? The issues raised are far too complex to be settled in this brief forum, but they are at the least opened up here.

The contributions by William McClung and Barbara Lewalski consider the role and representation of the country house itself, its "arcadian" and natural setting, and its inhabitants in sixteenth- and seventeenth-century literature. It seems perfectly obvious to us that the literature generated by and within the country-house culture should sometimes take that setting for its subject, but had that culture readily been taken for granted, reflections upon its character and function would not have been necessary. While it is true that the exigencies of patronage may have played some role in the development of the genre known as the country-house poem, for example, there was something more profound at work as well. Implicit in the works drawn upon in both the McClung and Lewalski papers is a sense that the whole of country-house life was somehow threatened and therefore in need of articulation, defense, and intercession. The threat was perceptible but largely undefined. As it turned out, the enemy was the future, which would eventually replace the arcadian world of the country house with social and economic change and urban industrialization.

Some country-house dwellers clearly recognized that their way of life was in jeopardy; how else can the impulse to idealize that life be explained? In the literature of the time, the country house is identified with "nature" and all the good and valuable things it is understood to stand for, however vague and numerous and perhaps even contradictory they are. They sustain and rejuvenate; they provide a standard and comfort; they are the links with Britain's past and the sources of her continuing and future vitality; they are the font of true virtue. When, in the next century, there was a sense that all this had been lost, nature was conventionally restored and recreated in fashionably rusticated walls and the distinctive English garden.

Michael Mendle and Richard Tuck raise a different aspect of country-house culture: its contribution to politics and political thought. Because they concentrate on the circle of writers, philosophers, and religious and political leaders who were gathered at the single estate of Great Tew, their conclusions are perhaps less definitive and certainly less easily generalized than those of Mc-Clung and Lewalski. In effect, they have provided separate parts of a single "case-study" that reveals much about the cohesiveness as well as the subsequent divisions in one very important community. Before the Civil War, Tew was host to Edward Hyde, the future Lord Clarendon and Restoration chancellor, as well as to the philosopher Thomas Hobbes. What apparently united the circle at Great Tew was an adherence to traditional Anglican values rather than a specifically royalist ideology. In the end, when Hobbes

was accused of atheism, he lost the support of his former associates. Mendle and Tuck have illustrated some ways in which we can go about rediscovering the internal dynamics of the Tew circle, as well as of groups that gathered at other estates, in order to understand their individual and collective impact upon British politics and thought.

The final paper in this section is concerned with the country house in what might be identified as the beginning period of its decline. Mark Girouard considers the varied and changing relationships between the life of the older and traditional "country town," as he calls it, and that of its neighboring and historically dominating great house. As he demonstrates, two institutions that had previously provided much service and sustenance were, by the eighteenth century, starting to go their independent ways. Among the causes for this phenomenon were the importance of London and its attractions for the nobility—who seem to have grown indifferent to and neglectful of rural pleasures and responsibilities—and the growth and increasing independence of the towns themselves. This, perhaps, was a tangible manifestation of that modern threat to "nature" that had troubled the glorifiers of country-house life in earlier years.

GORDON J. SCHOCHET and
LENA COWEN ORLIN

BARBARA K. LEWALSKI

The Lady of the Country-House Poem

In some ways my topic might be thought a bit perverse, since English country-house poems commonly focus upon the estate and its lord, not the lady. This is eminently true in the earlier seventeenth century, the period when the genre flourished.[1] It will come as no surprise, of course, that these estate poems embody the patriarchal values and social structures of the seventeenth-century family and society, as social historians such as Lawrence Stone and Philippe Ariès have described them.[2] Focusing on the relevant literary texts, Raymond Williams, James Turner, Don Wayne, and others have explored some ways in which occasional poems about country estates and landscapes may at once register and help to shape the ideology of an age.[3] But even poems such as these, which are so manifestly products of patronage relationships, need not simply respond to contemporary society. As products of the imagination they may also call upon the resources of myth to set forth more complex visions of human and social relationships.

I mean to focus here upon those English estate poems in which the lady (the wife or daughter of the house) plays a prominent role. Pre-Restoration England produced four important poems of this kind: they include the two admitted masterpieces of the genre, Ben Jonson's "To Penshurst" and Andrew Marvell's "Upon Appleton House;" the first estate poem written by a woman, Aemilia Lanyer's "The Description of Cooke-ham;" and Richard Lovelace's Cavalier estate poem, "Amyntor's Grove."[4] Given the strong influence of Jonson's poem on subsequent examples of the genre, we might expect a passage on the lady to become a standard *topos*, but this is not the case. As we shall see, such passages occur only when the woman in question is of some special importance to her husband or family, or in her own right. These four estate poems respond to the actual social roles enacted by cer-

tain seventeenth-century ladies, but they also recast those roles in mythic terms, relating these ladies in various and complex ways to nature and to culture.[5]

First, though, a few words about the genre of the country-house or estate poem, to distinguish it from certain near neighbors which have contributed something to the mix of elements that comprise the kind. One such strand includes classical (and Renaissance) poems praising a happy rural retirement from city business or courtly corruption—the "beatus ille" tradition which began with Horace's Epode II and Martial's Epigram III.58 on the Baian villa, and continued in such seventeenth-century poems as Robert Herrick's "A Country life: To His Brother Master Thomas Herrick," Thomas Randolph's "An Ode to Mr. Anthony Stafford to Hasten Him into the Country," and Katherine Phillips' "A Country Life."[6] Another strand comprises Horatian and especially Juvenalian satire on waste, ostentation, or miserliness; English examples include Joseph Hall's *Virgidemiarum* V. 2 and Pope's moral essays III and IV, to Bathurst and Burlington. Still another strand contains landscape or topographical descriptive poetry, such as Michael Drayton's *Polyolbion,* John Denham's "Coopers' Hill," Charles Cotton's *Wonders of the Peake* (which ends with an embedded country-house poem on Chatsworth), and Pope's *Windsor Forest.* More generally, estate poems owe something to classical and Renaissance pastoral and golden age poetry, and even more to the georgic tradition emanating from Virgil and Hesiod.[7]

But despite many shared characteristics, country-house or estate poems differ from all these related kinds, and are properly approached as a distinct kind, a thematic genre defined by subject matter and specific topics rather than by form or mode.[8] As a thematic genre, estate poems may employ a variety of structural patterns, may contain several modes (satiric, pastoral, georgic, panegyric) mixed in various proportions, and may take various generic forms—epigram, encomium, ode, verse epistle, valediction. Jonson's ode "To Penshurst" is commonly used as the standard by which the topics, characteristics, and moral values pertaining to the genre are defined, but this normative approach discounts generic changes throughout the century that not only reflect changing social conditions but also changing myths about the place of the aristocracy and gentry in society. Later country-house poems treat topics other than Jonson's and project different ideals.

Despite these changes, a few common topics characterize poems in the genre during the period 1600 to 1660. These include: (1) description of the house and the topographical features of the estate as some kind of *locus amoenus,* and the course of life on the estate as the good life; (2) use of a negative formula contrasting the civility and good order of the house and the life of the estate with what is outside; (3) praise of the landholder's values and virtues as these are manifested in the estate; (4) concern with family history and continuity; (5) examination of the human relation to nature, usually through some fusion of pastoral and georgic elements; (6) some description of familial and social roles—lord of the manor, lady, children, host, guests, servants, tenants.[9]

Ben Jonson's "To Penshurst," published in 1616 but certainly written before November 1612,[10] is cast in the form of an ode celebrating the estate of Sir Robert Sidney as a *locus amoenus* harmonizing pastoral and providential abundance with georgic cultivation. Robert Sidney, younger brother of Sir Philip Sidney and the Countess of Pembroke, became head of the family at his brother's death in 1586. Like his brother, he also fought in the Low Countries, served as governor of the English stronghold in Flushing, and wrote poetry.[11] A prominent courtier in the reign of James I, he was created Baron Sidney of Penshurst and Lord Chamberlain to Queen Anne in 1603, Viscount Lisle in 1605, and Earl of Leicester in 1618.

Jonson's poem begins by contrasting the house at Penshurst with more recent and much more ostentatious "prodigy" houses (like Knole or Longleat) built especially for show. He then describes the estate and its life: the woods inhabited by nature gods; the fish, fowl, and beasts eagerly offering themselves to the lord's table;

the tenants tendering their produce out of love rather than need; the generous and egalitarian hospitality of the hall (which the poet describes from his own experience). Next he praises the "high huswifery" of Barbara Sidney, notable even during her absence when King James and Prince Henry paid an unexpected visit to Penshurst; he also praises her virtue and fruitfulness, which assure a worthy and religious progeny. Jonson concludes by identifying the lord, Sir Robert Sidney, as the moral presence that gives order and stability to the entire estate and social community.

By associating the course of life at Penshurst with the permanence and stability of nature itself, Jonson finesses the fact that the Sidneys' occupancy of Penshurst dates only to the 1550s. And, as Raymond Williams observes, the poem's Edenic images of profusion and natural abundance—fruit ready to hand, fish leaping into nets, game gladly offering itself to the table—disguise the harsher realities of arduous rural labor and landowners' power and greed.[12] Yet the social ideals projected by the poem are clear: a benevolent and virtuous patriarchal governor; a house characterized by simplicity and usefulness; a large extended family with lord, lady, children, servants, and retainers all fulfilling their specific, useful functions and coming together for prayer and for dinner in the Great Hall; the harmony of man and nature; a working agricultural community of interdependent classes linked together in harmony, generosity, and love; ready hospitality to guests of all stations, from poets to kings; and stability ensured by the religion and virtue passed on from lord and lady to their progeny. Jonson presents Penshurst as an integral part of the larger society as well as an idealized microcosm of it.

Jonson's extended praise of Lady Barbara Sidney focuses on her role as helpmeet, housewife, and mother; the special circumstance motivating such praise was no doubt Jonson's awareness that Robert Sidney was deeply devoted to his wife and relied on her to manage family, household, and estate during his frequent and prolonged absences while on the continent or attending the king. The marriage of Robert and Barbara Sidney seems to have embodied the Protestant matrimonial ideal articulated in numerous contemporary marriage manuals and advice books,[13] and also to have combined elements of the various family structures that Lawrence Stone describes as overlapping in the early modern period. The couple were part of the extended kinship network of the Sidneys (Stone's "open lineage" family); they exhibited several features of the "restricted patriarchal nuclear family" dominant in the period; but they displayed as well the domestic intimacy, the conjugal affection, and the cherishing of children characteristic of the domesticated nuclear family emerging in the later seventeenth century.

Lady Sidney's importance to her husband and his estate began with the large fortune she brought him at their marriage on 23 September 1584, when she was twenty-two and he a year or so younger. After her father's death on 8 September, Barbara Gamage's marriage to Robert Sidney was hastily arranged by her guardians, to subvert designs by other kinsfolk and suitors to gain control of the Welsh heiress and her wealth. There is no hard evidence for P. J. Croft's romantic suggestion that this was a love match,[14] but Robert's many letters to her—more than 320 are extant—testify to a marriage marked by enduring affection, tenderness, and domestic happiness. Barbara Sidney's side of the correspondence does not, apparently, survive: the Penshurst papers contain only a few lines to him in her hand.[15]

Robert Sidney's letters project a portrait of Barbara as a highly valued domestic helpmeet, manager of the estate and its hospitality, and mother of his children. His characteristic intimacy and tenderness is evident in a letter of 3 June 1594, apparently accompanying a gift: "Sweet heart. I would not for anything that the il husbands at the court should know how fond I am growne to send you on this fashion the first dainties I can come by: least they should think I were quite mad."[16] His letters continually complain of his enforced absences from her and from Penshurst, and regularly discuss when she will join him at Flushing or for the season in London. That she usually postponed such ventures from home as long as possible is evident from the repeated pleas in Robert's letters, and also from a letter of Rowland Whyte (the steward) on 3 November 1599: "I had much a doe to persuade my Lady to come up [to London], she being soe farre in love with sweet Penshurst."[17] Many letters speak of improvements to the estate: in May 1594 Robert writes in reference to various minor building operations, "I need not send to know how my buildings goe forward, for I ame sure you are so good a housewyfe you may be trusted with them;" and he also wrote frequently from

Flushing about plans for the gardens.[18] Very many letters over several years refer to baskets of peaches, apricots, and grapes sent from the estate to the king and queen and many friends at court: in a letter of September 1609 he complains humorously, "I thank you for letter and peaches, but you send me such store as I have not frends enow to bestow them upon."[19]

Sidney also shared his mounting financial difficulties with his wife, and sought her advice and help in coping with them. The financial situation seems to have become especially threatening in 1607, as a letter of November 10 indicates:

Before you come from Penshurst I pray you conferr at large with Golding and take his opinion what is to be done. For I never was in that case in my lyfe as I ame now. . . . The howshold debts and many of them to poor and clamorsom persons come to a thousand pound: a sum that I thinck you did not imagine. . . . I should be extreemly ashamed if I were not to you and to Golding to discover the greatnes and indeed the foulnes of my wants. As I have sayd, I have not mony to pay the interest [which] growes due nor to buy necessary clothes for this winter nor to pay for man's meate or horsemeate. . . . so I feare I shall not be able in a manner to show my head if I make not present sale of something till somewhat may come in from the King which I have no reason to doubt of, though perhaps it will require some time. . . . So as, to conclude, I ame at my wits ends what to doo. . . . Thinck of these things I pray you: for you see how I acquaint you with the depth of all and do desyre your advise.[20]

On 29 September 1609 he wrote to her regarding her proposal of one Thomas Morgan as steward; the letter shows an affectionate concern for her place and authority in the household, and for preserving their good reputation for hospitality despite the needful retrenchment of expenses:

Touching Morgan, for whom you have written to me and to Mr. Whyte . . . it is a steward indeed that I want as I have often times told you. For it is not the expense of the kitchen alone but of all the house that is out of order, and cannot be remedied but by the care of a good steward. Whether Th. Morgan be sufficient for that place is the question. . . . The steward of a mans hous of my quality must have both the spyrit and knowledg to commaund and experience of all things that belong to a hous both within doores and without. . . . Besydes hee must know how to give entertainment to strangers according to theyr qualities, which is not easily found in one that is not bredd where such courses are used. Truly I was exceeding sory to see you so greeved as you were at my coming from you; as I would have given better token if I had had any time to stay. It is not my desyre that you should undertake the charge of the hous, to be a greef unto you. . . . Never trouble yourself with what is past; if the hous bee in debt I must pay it and will. But this wee must at the last resolve, to keep such a hous as wee may, not as we would: and our 'frends' must beare with us: for wee must not bee undon. . . . and whatever blame may bee of it I will take upon mee: and you shall be free: neyther is it anyway my meaning to take any authoritie of the hous from you; but all things shall still be commaunded by you: only the steward shall take directions from you and yeald accounts to you, and doe those things which indeed is unfitt for you to trouble yourself withall. For I would have you be mistress and not put yourself to those things which indeed belong to servants.[21]

The other consistent theme of the letters concerns Barbara's love and devotion to the children: she bore twelve in all, eight girls and four boys, of whom two sons died in infancy. Robert praises her highly for her devotion, continually urging her to "make much of" the children for him, but, as J.C.A. Rathmell notes, he expostulates with her often for her tendency to hold the boys too close to her apron strings.[22] A letter of 22 August 1597 concerning arrangements for the family's visit to him in Flushing includes an early formulation of this persistent motif:

It is trew that in the former of my long letters I wrote that I would have you leave some of your children behind you: but in the later I left it to yourself, as I do stil, since I see you will not bee otherwise pleased. For the girls I kan not mislike the care you take of them: but for the boies you must resolve to let me have my wil. For I know better what belongs to a man then you do. Indeed, I will have him [the elder son, William] ly from his maide for it is time, and now no more to bee in the nurcery among women.[23]

The theme continues through several letters concerning choice of a tutor for the boys, and later, amusingly, in annual epistolary wrangles about William and Robert's return to Oxford at the beginning of term—for Barbara seemed always to delay their departure date as long as possible.

The portrait of Lady Sidney and six of her children by Marcus Gheeraerts, ca. 1596 (fig. 1), emphasizes the family and gender roles implied in the letters—and also in Jonson's poem. Robert is conspicuously absent and, as Don E. Wayne notes, Barbara's hands rest on her two sons, betokening her special care of them as the vessels of family continuity.[24] The central figure is the presumptive heir, William, though in fact William's early death made the second son, Robert, the heir. The daughters are arranged in two pairs, with the mother's nurturing gesture replicated by the elder of each pair—almost a textbook illustration of Nancy Chodorow's theory about how girls learn to identify with and replicate the mother's role.[25] Gheeraerts' portrait

of Barbara Sidney as fruitful, fostering mother underscores the public and dynastic implications of that role, while also hinting at familial affection and intimacy.

In Jonson's "To Penshurst" Lady Sidney is portrayed in very similar terms, though there are no references to quotidian domestic arrangements or financial difficulties. Jonson also gives Barbara Sidney mythic significance as embodying the estate's ideal fusion of nature and culture. Along with the classical nature gods (Pan, Bacchus, dryads, satyrs, fauns) who inhabit Penshurst, and the Sidney memorials such as the tree marking Philip Sidney's birth, several signs of Barbara's life and lineage are inscribed in the estate, identifying her closely with its superabundant natural fruitfulness. A copse where she fed deer is "named of Gamage;" a tree where she began labor with one of her children is called "My Ladies oke;" and the ripe peasant daughters whose offerings of fruit to the estate are "an embleme of themselves, in plum, or peare" must seem a reprise of her well-known penchant for sending fruitbaskets to court.[26] More important, she both embodies and maintains the cultivated life of Penshurst. The ready and liberal hospitality of the hall is founded upon her "high huswifery," while her chastity and careful religious education of her children serve as guarantors that the culture of Penshurst will be transmitted to a noble progeny:

>   *what praise was heap'd*
>   *On thy good lady, then who, therein, reap'd*
> *The just reward of her high huswifery;*
>   *To have her linnen, plate, and all things nigh,*
> *When shee was farre: and not a roome, but drest,*
>   *As if it had expected such a guest*
> *These, PENSHURST, are thy praise, and yet not all.*
>   *Thy lady's noble, fruitfull, chaste withall,*
> *His children thy great lord may call his owne:*
>   *A fortune, in this age, but rarely knowne.*
> *They are, and have been taught religion: Thence*
>   *Their gentler spirits have suck'd innocence.*
> *Each morne, and even, they are taught to pray,*
>   *With the whole household, and may, every day,*
> *Reade, in their vertuous parents noble parts,*
>   *The mysteries of manners, armes, and arts.*
> *Now, PENSHURST, they that will proportion thee*
>   *With other edifices, when they see*
> *Those proud, ambitious heaps, and nothing else,*
>   *May say, their lords have built, but thy lord dwells.*
>   (83–102)

In the perfect balance of nature and art, of providential abundance and human cultivation that is

Jonson's idealized Penshurst, Lord Robert Sidney, who "dwells" at Penshurst, is the virtuous force that sustains its enduring values. His lady is the highest manifestation of the estate's natural fruitfulness, and also the principal agent through which its good is dispensed to present and future generations.

Aemilia Lanyer's little known country-house poem, "The Description of Cooke-ham," was published in 1611 in a volume bearing the title of Lanyer's long religious poem, *Salve Deus Rex Judaeorum*.[27] Evidently written in 1609 or 1610, "Cooke-ham" may well predate "Penshurst" and was certainly published first.[28] The poem focuses on three women residing together at Cookham at some period during the 1590s or 1600s, but certainly before 1609. The lady chiefly celebrated is Margaret Clifford, Countess of Cumberland (fig. 2), estranged wife (and in 1605 widow) of the 3rd Earl, George Clifford, the dashing Elizabethan sea adventurer, flamboyant courtier, and notorious womanizer. With her is

her as yet unmarried daughter Anne Clifford, who was to become mistress of Knole by her marriage in 1609 to Richard Sackville, Earl of Dorset, and still later mistress of Wilton House by her marriage in 1630 to Phillip Herbert, Earl of Pembroke and Montgomery. Lanyer herself, as the sometime protegée of Margaret Clifford, is the third woman. The manor house at Cookham no longer exists: the manor belonged to the crown from before the Conquest until 1818, and was annexed to Windsor Castle in 1540; it was occupied off and on in the 1590s and 1600s by members of Margaret Clifford's own family (the Russells), and the Countess evidently spent some time there during her troubles with her husband, and perhaps in the early months of her widowhood.[29] Located a few miles from Maidenhead in Berkshire, the area is still a beauty spot, with extensive frontage on the Thames, rich woodlands, lush meadows, picturesque scattered hamlets, and high hills.

The specific social circumstances of these three women are all inscribed in the poem, and dictate its unusual form as a valediction, an elegiac fare-well to Cookham, rather than a celebration of presence. First, for Aemilia herself: born in 1569 the daughter of a court musician, she was or-phaned early in life, became paramour to Queen Elizabeth's Lord Chamberlain, Lord Hunsdon, bore him an illegitimate son, and was promptly married off in 1592 to another musician, Captain Alphonso Lanier; she found little scope for her ambition and talent at the Jacobean court, and was hard pressed for money both before and after she was widowed in 1613. She died in 1645 at the age of 76.[30] Her book of poems is a transparent bid for patronage from the several noble ladies to whom it is addressed, but Margaret Clifford is its principal dedicatee: Lanyer claims (evidently with some truth, else the bid for renewed pa-tronage would be doomed) that the countess urged her to write about Cookham and that she owes both her religious conversion and her per-ception of herself as a poet to a period of resi-dence there with the countess and her daugh-ter.[31]

Margaret Russell married George Clifford (her father's ward) in 1577 in a splendid wedding with the queen in attendance; he was nearly nineteen, she not yet seventeen.[32] The dashing adventurer soon cast his affections elsewhere, and his melancholy wife found such solace as she could in religion, literature, literary patronage, her own kin, and her children. Her two sons, however, died in 1590 and 1591, leaving her daughter, Anne, born in 1590, as the only surviv-ing child. Lacking a male heir, George Clifford settled his estates upon his younger brother, Francis, who would inherit the Cumberland ti-tle, with a reversion to Anne in the event of the failure of male heirs. In doing so he ignored a deed from the reign of Edward II entailing those estates upon his *child*, regardless of sex. Margaret Clifford and later Anne engaged in continual litigation and court appeals over Anne's right to those estates, taking on the combined force of law courts, powerful courtiers, the Lord Cham-berlain, the Archbishop of Canterbury, their own husbands, and even the king himself. That struggle against the male establishment devel-oped in both women a very strong sense of fam-ily, self-worth, and female solidarity, evidenced especially in Anne's memoirs of her father and mother and of her girlhood, and in the diaries she kept throughout most of her long life.[33] Of her mother she wrote:

Presently after her husband's death there arose great suits in law between her and her brother-in-law Francis, Earl of Cumberland, for the maintenance of the right of her only daughter the Lady Anne Clifford to the antient lands of her father's inheritance; in which suit she met with great oppositions, even from King James himself, who then reigned, and professed himself to be against her, and from some of the greatest men of power of that time in the king-dom; in which business she shewed she had a spirit too great to yield to fortune or opposition, further than necessity com-pelled her to it; and so much constancy, wisdom and resolu-tion did she shew in that business, that the like can hardly be parallelled by any woman.[34]

Fig. 2.
Margaret Russell Clifford, Countess of Cumberland by an unknown artist, 1585 (National Portrait Gallery)

Anne might have said, and indeed did say, the same of herself as she detailed her own long struggle against her husband, Dorset, who pressured her continually to give over her suits and come to a composition for money, which he badly needed. She held out despite his exiling her to the country, cutting off her allowances, and even taking away for a time her beloved only daughter. She held out even against the king, who proposed himself as peacemaker. But the long struggle of mother and daughter only achieved its goal when the death of Sir Francis Clifford's son in 1643 gave Anne the titles, authority, and large powers which pertained to those northern estates.[35] She exercised her powers as Baroness Clifford, Westmoreland, and Vessey, Lady of the Honor of Skipton in Craven, and High Sheriffess of the County of Westmoreland for more than thirty years, until her death in 1676.

Lanyer deals with Margaret Clifford's anomalous situation as estranged wife or widow (rather than lady of her husband's estate) by celebrating her as "mistress" of a manor belonging to the crown, a place which she—like anyone else—could only possess on a temporary basis. Also, Lanyer structures the poem as an elegiac valediction, a last farewell to the estate—perhaps in specific reference to the countess's removal to those residences she would occupy as a widow. The elegiac tone is established in the opening lines—"Farewell, sweet Cooke-ham"—and it is reinforced throughout by a pastoral pathetic fallacy whereby the entire estate responds to the arrival and departure of its mistress in terms of the seasonal round. The house itself is barely mentioned, but the estate is depicted as a *locus amoenus* as each part decks itself out in all its spring and summer loveliness for her arrival:

The Walkes put on their summer Liveries,
And all things else did hold like similes:
The Trees with leaves, with fruits, with flowers clad,
Embrac'd each other, seeming to be glad,
Turning themselves to beauteous Canopies,
To shade the bright Sunne from your brighter eies:
The cristall Streames with silver spangles graced,
While by the glorious Sunne they were embraced:
The little Birds in chirping notes did sing,
To entertain both You and that sweet Spring.

(21–30)

Though her tenure is temporary, Margaret Clifford is the ordering presence of the estate while she is at Cookham. All aspects of nature greet her with an obsequiousness reminiscent of the Penshurst fish and game: the hills descend humbly for her tread, the river banks deliver their fish to her, birds and animals sport before her, vales and woods salute her. But Lanyer's poem gives no hint of any interaction between Cookham and the larger society, nor yet of the larger household within the estate; we see only the three women. The countess spends happy hours meditating on the creatures and on the scriptures, and Lanyer takes part in the young Anne's sports. The discrepancies of rank and age (Lanyer was twenty years older than Anne) which make such intimate association unlikely are all happily dissolved in this idyll of a classless, ageless enclave of female friends.

Lanyer next describes Cookham's grief at the countess's preparations for departure, attributing to that grief the seasonal change from autumn to winter—again, the pathetic fallacy. The imagery of the final passage echoes that of the opening, as all the beauties of the *locus amoenus* wither in desolation:

And those sweet Brookes that ranne so faire and cleare,
With griefe and trouble wrinckled did appeare.
Those pretty Birds that wonted were to sing,
Now neither sing, nor chirp, nor use their wing;
But with their tender feet on some bare spray,
Warble forth sorrow, and their owne dismay.
Faire Philomela *leaves her mournefull Ditty,*
Drownd in dead sleepe, yet can procure no pittie:
Each arbour, banke, each seate, each stately tree,
Lookes bare and desolate now for want of thee;
Turning greene tresses into frostie gray,
While in cold griefe they wither all away.
The Sunne grew weake, his beames no comfort gave,
While all greene things did make the earth their grave:
Each brier, each bramble, when you went away,
Caught fast your clothes, thinking to make you stay:
Delightfull Eccho wonted to reply
To our last words, did now for sorrow die:
The house cast off each garment that might grace it,
Putting on Dust and Cobwebs to deface it.
All desolation then there did appeare,
When you were going whom they held so deare.

(182–204)

In mythic terms, Margaret Clifford is so closely associated with aspects of nature at Cookham that she seems virtually a Persephone whose arrivals and departures bring the seasons and their changes. But the primary myth presents Cookham as a female paradise whose natural beauty and religious values inhere in and are sustained by its lady, in sharp contrast to Penshurst, whose values have their ultimate source in its lord. However, Cookham is from the outset a lost Eden: Penshurst's lord "dwells" permanently in his estate, whereas Cookham takes on the appearance of a ravaged Eden when its lady departs. Like the first human couple expelled from Eden, here a female pair—or rather trio—is forced by the social structures of a patriarchal society to abandon it: the countess is called away by the "occasions" attending her situation as an estranged and embattled wife or widow; the virgin daughter goes forth to make a brilliant but not very happy marriage; Lanyer's destiny is social decline. Lanyer's estate poem is a long lament for the loss of this happy garden state in which women lived without mates but found contentment and delight in nature, God, and female companionship.

Other major country-house poems of the period pay scant attention to the lady. Jonson's verse epistle "To Sir Robert Wroth" (written circa 1612 and published in 1616) on Durrants in Middlesex gives a bare three lines to Wroth's "noblest spouse," Robert Sidney's daughter Mary, who was herself a writer and the subject of Jonson's praises in other poems. Jonson's reticence here probably reflects the fact that the Wroths shared few interests, domestic or otherwise, and were thought to be unhappily wed.[36] The lady is an even more nebulous figure in most Cavalier estate poems: Robert Herrick's "Panegyrick to Sir Lewis Pemberton" on Rushden in Northamptonshire, and his "The Country Life" to Endymion Porter on Aston-Sub-Edge in Gloucester; Thomas Carew's "To Saxham" on Saxham Parva in Suffolk, the estate of Sir John Crofts, and his "To G. N. from Wrest" on Wrest Park, the estate of Henry de Grey, Earl of Kent.[37]

Changing social conditions and social ideals over the next decades go far to explain this phenomenon. Increasingly the aristocracy resided in London, seeking status and fortune through court office rather than estate management—a situation prompting several royal proclamations during the years between 1614 and 1629 ordering gentlemen to return to their estates to "keepe hospitality" and the king's peace. Inflation was making agriculture a precarious enterprise, and the maintenance of a large household and open hospitality was now prodigiously expensive. Country estates were becoming detached from the surrounding community, rather like islands of refined aristocratic privilege and power securing themselves against external threat. And new ideals of individualism, privacy, and familial af-

fection in a nuclear family were displacing older, communal values.[38] Cavalier poets Herrick and Carew did not come to terms with the role of the lady in this new ethos, but Richard Lovelace did.

Lovelace probably wrote "Amyntor's Grove, His Chloris, Arigo, and Gratiana" (1649) in late 1641; it honors Endymion Porter, his family, and Woodhall, the country estate in Hertfordshire inherited by Porter's wife.[39] As a member of the Duke of Buckingham's household, Porter took part in Prince Charles's madcap visit to Spain to woo the Spanish Infanta, as well as in several more sedate diplomatic missions. He became Groom of the Bedchamber to Prince and later King Charles, held control of several profitable wardships and commercial monopolies, and played a primary role in directing Charles's extensive art patronage and collecting. His wife, Olivia Boteler, was the high-spirited and independent daughter of Buckingham's favorite sister; she became one of Queen Henrietta Maria's most prominent Catholic converts and was notoriously active in converting others. Of her twelve children, five sons and two daughters survived infancy.[40] When war broke out in 1642, Porter accompanied the king to Oxford; three years later he joined the court in exile in Paris, and Olivia followed; he returned to England shortly before his death in 1649.

Lovelace's poem (labelled an "elogie") participates in the decorative pastoral mode so popular at the court of Charles and Henrietta; it identifies the estate and the personages only by pastoral names, eschewing the specificities of locale and history usual in this genre. Indeed, despite the title ("Amyntor's Grove"), and the pastoral imagery of fruit, flowers, and scents, only interior scenes are described: the "curious ordering/ Of every room" redolent of rich perfumes; the paintings from Porter's extensive private collection—"Titian, Raphael, Georgone"—which cover the walls almost as a tapestry; an intimate dinner party with wine and many toasts to the lady; the sudden appearance of two of Porter's children, the boy five (probably Thomas), the "nymph" either Mary (twelve) or Lettice (ten).

Lovelace's poem portrays Olivia Porter as the focal point of an intimate and affectionate domestic circle of family and close friends. The circumstance accounting for the lady's prominence in this poem seems to be the general perception that Endymion and Olivia were united in their in-

Fig. 3.
Family of Endymion Porter (Olivia
Boteler Porter with Endymion
Porter and three of their sons) by Sir
Anthony van Dyck, c. 1633   (Private
collection)

tense love for each other and in their devoted service to the king and queen. This perception is confirmed by Endymion's letters over many years (and the few extant from Olivia), though they also testify to Olivia's jealousy and to strains and quarrels exacerbated by long absence.[41] Endymion's letter of 10 March 1623 from Madrid is typical in its protestations of love and fond inquiries about his children:

My sweetest Love—Although I have so much employment here at Madrid, that I have scarce time to dress myself, yet if I should not watch and lose my sleep to write to thee, I were unworthy of such a wife and could not deserve the smallest part of thy inestimable love to me. Oh, that you did but know how great a grief it is for me to live without you, for then you would believe that nothing but you could give me content, nor any but the want of you cause sorrow in me. . . . [There follows a newsy account of his activities.] Dear Olive, all these things I thought fit to acquaint you withal, that you may not say I never tell you anything, but all these things, compared to the desire I have to see thee, are nothing but vanity, that is the real felicity only which makes me breathe, and God Almighty grant me leave that it may be quickly, and His blessing light on you and George and Charles, and I pray you send me word how you do, and which is the prettiest boy.[42]

Several letters seek to allay her propensity (whether warranted or not) for jealousy: "As I hope for mercy at God's hands I neither kist nor touched any woman since I left you, and for the innkeeper's daughter at Boulogne, I was so far from kissing her that as I hope to be saved I cannot remember that I saw any such woman."[43] The tenderness persists: in January 1642 as he follows the king's flight out of London to Windsor, he writes:

My Dearest Love . . . I could wish you and your children in a safe place, but why Woodhall should not be so I cannot yet tell. . . . I pray you have a care of yourself, and make much of your children, and I presume we shall be merry and enjoy one another long. . . . I will give you leave to kisse Mrs. Marie [his daughter] for me; I wish sweet Tom [then six] with me, for the King and Queen are forced to lie with their children now, and I envy their happiness . . . and so Goodnight sweet Noll.[44]

The fine though somewhat damaged family portrait by Van Dyck (1633) contrasts markedly with the Sidney family portrait by Gheeraerts, even as Olivia's role contrasts with Barbara Sidney's (fig. 3). This is an intimate family picture, exhibiting many characteristics of Stone's domesticated nuclear family. Olivia dominates it, placed in the center and holding the hand of her youngest son, Philip; the two older boys, George and Charles, stand close to her on the other side, but no special attention is given to the heir. Her two daughters (then aged four and two) are not shown. Endymion is part of the family group (as Robert Sidney was not); he stands to one side, gazing fondly upon his wife and resting his arm on her chair in a gesture of protection.

In Lovelace's Cavalier estate poem the country house has become a private, domestic "Paradice," an interior hideaway affording some temporary respite from what it terms the "wide Jawes of our feares" without. The society enclosed here is a small, intimate circle of family and friends, held together by affection and love, and at its center the lady, gracing an intimate dinner party, which has taken the place of the extended hospitality of the Hall. As Mary Ann McGuire notes, in these interior spaces art triumphs entirely over nature: the paintings are said to perfect what "weake Nature" intended, and to mend "what *She* wrought, and *Her*."[45]

Curiously enough, however, in Lovelace's literary myth the lady who presides over all this art is virtually identified with nature, almost as if she is made its surrogate in this domestic enclosure. The poem begins with a Petrarchan blazon of her as Chloris—gentlest shepherdess, goddess of spring—in whom all the external beauties of the estate are reflected:

It was Amyntor's *Grove, that* Chloris
For ever Ecchoes and her Glories;
Chloris, *the gentlest Sheapherdesse,*
That ever Lawnes and Lambes did blesse;
Her Breath like to the whispering winde,
Was calme as thought, sweet as her Minde;
Her Lips like coral-gates kept in
The perfume and the pearle within;
Her eyes a double-flaming torch
That always shine, and never scorch;
Her selfe the Heav'n in which did meet
The All of bright, of faire and sweet.[46]

She is identified with the fiery Phoenix by reason of her great love for Endymion. And her children are represented as the flowers and fruits of the estate. The daughter "nymph" has the expected Petrarchan coloring of carnation mixed with snow; and both children—"Blooming boy and blossoming maid"—are tender flowers to be protected from harsh winter storms until they ripen and bear the fruit of posterity. This poem

subsumes into the lady and her progeny the *locus amoenus* which other country-house poems identify with the several regions of the estate.

Andrew Marvell's "Upon Appleton House" (written circa 1650 to 1652 and published in 1681) again locates us in a particular place and time. Marvell describes an estate whose static, mythic features are caught up in the movement of history and the conflicts of contemporary society. The poem identifies as its point of departure the retirement in 1650 of the parliamentary general Sir Thomas Fairfax to his estate at Nunappleton in Yorkshire, profoundly dismayed by the regicide and the impending invasion of Scotland. Marvell lived at Nunappleton between 1650 and 1652 as tutor to Fairfax's daughter Mary, twelve years old at the time of Marvell's arrival. His very long country-house poem has something of epic scope, assimilating the topographical features of the Fairfax estate, the myth of origin of the Fairfax family, and the experience of the speaker who is making a progress around the estate, with the course of providential history, biblical and contemporary; it concludes with a long panegyric to Mary. The lady of this poem is daughter rather than wife, and, again, special circumstances account for her prominent role.

The speaker begins with the expected comparison between the modesty and humility of this house—whether the present brick edifice or the remodeled stone nunnery, as John Newman thinks[47]—and the proud palaces designed by others. Nunappleton, like Penshurst, carries some adumbrations of Eden, but it is clearly much less idyllic and stable. In Marvell's poem the house is too small for its lord and groans to accommodate him. Also, unlike Penshurst, where the lord "dwells"—permanently it seems—this house is only a temporary habitation, a house of pilgrimage, built "Only as for a *Mark of Grace*/ And for an *Inn* to entertain/ Its *Lord* a while, but not remain."[48]

The speaker pauses in his circuit of the estate to recount the largely fictional founding legend of the Fairfax family, according to which the fair and lovely virgin heiress, Isabel Thwaites, was enticed by wily, deceiving nuns to break faith with her intended bridegroom (Sir William Fairfax) and enter a convent characterized by perversions of sexuality and of religion. Sir William then stormed the convent, rescued his bride, demolished the nunnery, and founded his own family in that place which, the poet observes, was "no *Religious House* till now."[49] This founding

tions emblematize not only the Christian warfare needed to till the garden of the soul but also the garden state to which Fairfax might have restored England; they thereby question the rightness of his retirement. The meadows present a kaleidoscope of harvest scenes emblematic of the bloody events of the English Civil War—harvesting, destruction, pillaging, leveling, flooding; these events also recapitulate the Exodus story of sinful and embattled Israel in the wilderness, as well as the biblical flood. The forests provide the speaker refuge from all this in a "green, yet growing Ark;" he finds in its birds and trees emblems of an uncorrupted natural order and by utter passivity attempts to become one with that nature. Moving to the river (the fourth region) he maintains that passivity, fishing lazily in contented irresponsibility.[50]

It is upon this scene that the young lady of the poem bursts, all brisk movement and dynamic energy; she startles the speaker from his passivity and impels nature to better order. This lengthy and altogether remarkable treatment of young Mary Fairfax reflects her very special social situation as the only child of the lord general and his wife Ann (the "Starry Vere" of the poem). Fairfax sought to assure his daughter a brilliant marriage by cutting off the entail on his estates at Nunappleton and Bolton Percy to give to her in dowry—causing much consternation to members of his family.[51] (Interestingly enough, Fairfax's arrangements precisely reverse those of George Clifford for his only child, Anne.) In the event, the plan could hardly have turned out worse: the daughter of the upright parliamentary general married George Villiers, 2nd Duke of Buckingham, who became a dissolute philanderer and the very epitome of the Restoration rake.[52] And, ironically, Mary died childless in 1704.

But in the early 1650s Marvell could predict none of that: he makes his young pupil the embodiment of the values and hopes of her family, and presents their effort to found a new house and line in the daughter as a reprise of the old legend—"To find a Fairfax for our Thwaites" (fig. 4).[53] In the poem's literary myth Mary Fairfax becomes Maria—an embodiment of Nature, passive and active, but also of the human power that orders and transforms both nature and society. As emblem of fruitful nature she is a sacred plant to be cut off and regrafted in the ritual sacrifice of marriage:

Fig. 4.
Mary Fairfax Villiers, Countess of Buckingham by an unknown artist (Leeds Castle Foundation, Leeds Castle, Kent)

legend recapitulates and fuses the events of mankind's first fall through the seduction of Eve by the serpent and her (our) rescue by the bridegroom, the second Adam, as well as the corruption of nature and religion in the English nation by popery and their restoration through the Protestant Reformation. It also foreshadows the marriage of Mary Fairfax.

The estate itself continually reflects the larger world. The gardens laid out in martial forma-

Hence She *with Graces more divine*
Supplies beyond her Sex *the* Line;
And like a sprig of Mistleto,
On the Fairfacian Oak *does grow;*
Whence, for some universal good,
The Priest shall cut the sacred Bud;
While her glad Parents *most rejoice,*
And make their Destiny *their* Choice.

(737–744)

But she is also a terrifying force of nature, a "new born Comet" drawing a flame through the sky. More remarkable still, this young woman exercises the role given to Adam at the creation in that she exercises dominion over nature, restoring it to something like the Edenic state:

Tis She *that to these Gardens gave*
That wondrous Beauty which they have;
She *streightness on the Woods bestows;*
To Her *the Meadow sweetness owes;*
Nothing could make the River be
So Chrystal-pure but only She;
She *yet more Pure, Sweet, Streight, and Fair,*
Then Gardens, Woods, Meads, Rivers are.

(689–696)

As she walks forth, "loose" nature, responding to that dominion, "recollects" itself from its disposition to carelessness and disorder and takes on its highest perfection; the sun goes more carefully to bed; the halcyon comes forth; the air and stream and fishes are "vitrified" by her presence and power.

As Maria learns her languages, staves off the advances of wanton suitors, and awaits the unfolding of her marital destiny, Marvell shows the daughter assuming the responsibility her retired father has given over—to order nature and society. In claiming that her marriage is "for some universal good," Marvell intimates that she may be able to extend the virtues her family represents into the public realm. But the restoration of England to its Edenic garden state is not in prospect. Rather, the final stanzas contrast the disordered outside world in its chaotic, fallen condition with the Fairfax estate, "Paradice's only Map." The last stanza places in jeopardy even that map, Nunappleton, and its epitome, Maria. The coming of evening gives the world over to the "dark *hemisphere,*" reminding us how tenuously held and continuously threatened are all such visions of human order.

As we have seen, the ladies of these country-houses poems exhibit some of the actual social roles enacted by women during the first half of the seventeenth century. Barbara Sidney exemplifies the Reformation ideal of the wife as helpmeet in all domestic affairs, but at Penshurst that role still had the communal and public dimension pertaining to the mistresses of great estates since medieval times. Lady Sidney had primary responsibility for maintaining the harmony and orderly functioning of the extended society that was Penshurst, and also for assuring the preservation of the family, the estate, and the Sidney values by producing and nurturing a virtuous progeny. Margaret Clifford occupied the vulnerable, displaced, and isolated position of estranged wife and widow, without husband or sons to define and secure her place in the social order; yet she is represented at Cookham enjoying the freedom and power which that independent status sometimes brought, especially to widows. Olivia Porter is portrayed as the domestic wife whose chief function is to warm an enclosed circle of family and friends with her beauty, charm, and affection, as they take refuge from a society threatened by disintegration and chaos. Mary Fairfax, as the only child of aspiring parents and the sole hope of her family's perpetuation, is cast in the remarkable role (for a woman) of founder of a new dynastic line. The role assigned to Mary does not reflect any notable undermining of patriarchal assumptions and arrangements in society, but it is consonant with the somewhat expanded scope of women's activities after the Restoration—especially in the arts.

Even more significant is the mythic dimension with which the poems invest these social roles. The Lady of Penshurst is identified both with nature and culture in a quasi-Edenic community. She embodies in herself the abundant natural fruitfulness of Penshurst, but she is also the primary agent for her lord in ordering the estate, dispensing its hospitality, nurturing its young, and transmitting its values. The (temporary) mistress of Cookham is, while there, the locus of human virtue and worth to whom all nature pays tribute, taking on the role Robert Sidney plays at Penshurst; she is also a Persephone figure whose presence or absence controls the seasons. The three women together are represented as a guiltless trio cast forth from the Edenic female paradise of Cookham by the social arrangements of a patriarchal society. Chloris in *Amyntors Grove* is at once a pastoral shepherdess, the vernal deity Flora, and a goddess of the domestic hearth: her physical attributes manifest the beauties of nature to her enclosed circle of family and friends even as she enacts the role of gracious hostess appropriate to the artful, interior setting. Maria in *Appleton House* is at once a terrifying, transformative force of nature (a comet) and an active human power ordering nature and society. She does not merely sustain and elicit tribute from the stable and flourishing natural and social orders, as the lord of Pembroke does permanently and the lady of Cookham does temporarily, but has power beyond theirs to reorder and transform both realms.

These four poems, written within a fifty year period, develop different myths carrying different implications about female nature, female roles, and family relationships. They suggest how literature's power to transmute fact into myth may inscribe given social norms more deeply in the culture. But they also suggest how the imaginative power of such literary myths may promote the development of other norms, founded upon more expansive concepts of womens' familial and societal roles.

NOTES

1. The Restoration period and the earlier eighteenth century produced some estate poems, but the genre was largely superseded by topographical poems such as John Denham's *Cooper's Hill*, Charles Cotton's *Wonders of the Peake*, and Pope's *Windsor Forest*. For a discussion of some continuities, see Virginia C. Kenny, *The Country House Ethos in English Literature, 1688-1750* (Brighton and New York, 1984).

2. Lawrence Stone, *The Crisis of the Aristocracy, 1558-1641* (Oxford, 1965); idem, *The Family, Sex, and Marriage in England, 1500-1800* (New York, 1977); Philippe Ariès, *Centuries of Childhood: A Social History of Family Life,* trans. Robert Baldick (New York, 1962).

3. Raymond Williams, *The Country and the City* (London and New York, 1973); James Turner, *The Politics of Landscape: Rural Society in English Poetry, 1630-1660* (Cambridge, Mass., 1979); Don E. Wayne, *Penshurst: The Semiotics of Place and the Poetics of History* (Madison, Wis., 1984).

4. Edmund Waller's two poems entitled "At Pens-hurst" center on a woman, Lady Dorothy Sidney, but these are quasi-Petrarchan poems of courtship for which the estate simply provides the setting. Almost a century after Lanyer, Anne Finch, Countess of Winchilsea, wrote another estate poem (of sorts), "Upon my Lord Winchilsea's Converting the Mount in His Garden to a Terras" (London, 1713). Alastair Fowler calls attention to a Scottish estate poem of the Restoration era celebrating a woman, Sir George MacKenzie's "Caelia's Countryhouse and Closet" (written in 1667/1668), in James Watson, *Choice Collection of Comic and Serious Scots Poems* (Glasgow, 1869), part 2, 67-93. See also Alastair Fowler, "Country-House Poems: The Politics of a Genre," *The Seventeenth Century* 1 (1986), 1-14.

5. For a suggestive discussion in anthropological terms of the problematic situation of woman see Sherry B. Ortner, "Is Female to Male as Nature to Culture," in *Woman, Culture, and Society,* ed. Michelle Zimbalist Ranaldo and Louise Lamphere (Stanford, 1974), 67-87.

6. For a study of this tradition, see Maren-Sofie Rostvig, *The Happy Man: Studies in the Metamorphoses of a Classical Ideal,* vol. 1: *1600-1700,* vol. 2: *1700-1760* (Oslo, 1962-1971).

7. Fowler argues, in "Country House Poem," that the georgic mode is a defining element of the estate poem, but he undervalues, I think, the mix of pastoral and satiric modes in many of these poems.

8. The habit of distinguishing some kinds essentially by content or subject harks back to rhetorical genres in ancient literature. See Francis Cairns, *Generic Composition in Greek and Roman Poetry* (Edinburgh, 1972); Rosalie Colie, *The Resources of Kind: Genre-Theory in the Renaissance* (Berkeley, 1973), 15-17.

9. For discussion of these and other topics common to most estate poems of the period, see G. R. Hibbard, "The Country House Poem of the Seventeenth Century," *Journal of the Warburg and Courtauld Institutes* 19 (1956), 159-177; Charles Molesworth, "Property and Virtue: The Genre of the Country-House Poem in the Seventeenth Century," *Genre* 1 (1968), 141-157; William A. McClung, *The Country House in English Renaissance Poetry,* (Berkeley, 1977); Heather Dubrow, "The Country-House Poem: A Study in Generic Development," *Genre* 12 (1977), 153-179; Mary Ann C. McGuire, "The Cavalier Country-House Poem: Mutations on a Jonsonian Tradition," *Studies in English Literature* 19 (1979), 93-108.

10. Jonson's poem, published in the collection entitled *The Forest* in the folio edition of Jonson's *Works* in 1616, refers (line 77) to the visit to Penshurst of King James and the Prince of Wales, Henry Frederick; the prince died of typhoid on 6 November 1612, at the age of eighteen.

11. See the introduction in P. J. Croft, ed., *The Poems of Robert Sidney,* (Oxford, 1984).

12. Williams 1973, 26-34.

13. See the discussion and the bibliography of marriage books in Suzanne W. Hull, *Chaste, Silent & Obedient: English Books for Women, 1475-1640* (San Marino, Calif., 1982).

14. Croft 1984, 69-73.

15. Croft's explanation is that Barbara could not write (beyond signing her name) and probably could not read well enough to read Robert's letters to her without assistance. This speculation gains plausibility from research confirming high rates of illiteracy among women of all classes; Margaret Spufford, *Small Books and Pleasant Histories: Popular Fiction and Its Readership in Seventeenth-Century England* (Atlanta, 1982) estimates that in the period 1580-1700 only 11 percent of women could sign their name. Still, in Robert Sidney's and Rowland Whyte's letters there are several references to letters from Barbara Sidney, and without the texts we cannot assume, with Croft, that they were written by an amanuensis and that Robert destroyed them to hide evidence of her illiteracy. A man of affairs who often traveled on missions abroad and followed the court from place to place might well see no reason to save letters from his wife which were no doubt concerned chiefly with quotidian domestic news.

16. Robert Sidney to Barbara Sidney, 3 June 1594, Penshurst Papers, U 1475, C 81/41, Kent County Archives Office, Maidstone, Kent.

17. *Historical MSS Commission, 77, Report on the MSS of Lord De L'Isle and Dudley,* 6 vols. (London, 1925-1966), 2:409.

18. *Historical Commission 77,* 2:153. See other letters relating to improvements to the house and gardens cited and discussed in J. C. A. Rathmell, "Jonson, Lord Lisle, and Penshurst," *English Literary Renaissance* 1 (1971), 250-260.

19. *Historical Commission 77,* 4:161.

20. Robert Sidney to Barbara Sidney, 10 November 1607, Penshurst Papers, U 1475, C 81/158.

21. Robert Sidney to Barbara Sidney, 29 September 1609, Penshurst Papers, U 1475, C 81/192.

22. Rathmell 1971, 253-254.

23. Robert Sidney to Barbara Sidney, 22 August 1597, Penshurst Papers, U 1475, C 81/98.

24. My discussion of the picture is indebted to Wayne 1984, 73-75.

25. Nancy Chodorow, *The Reproduction of Mothering: Psychoanalysis and the Sociology of Gender,* (Berkeley, 1978).

26. Suggested by Wayne 1984, 68. Quotations from the poem are from C.H. Herford, Percy Simpson, and Evelyn Simpson, eds., *Ben Jonson,* 11 vols. (Oxford, 1925-1952), 8:93-96.

27. The STC (1976) lists only eight extant copies of the edition; all citations are from the Huntington Library copy of the very rare first issue (STC 15227).

28. See note 10. Lanyer's poem was written sometime after Anne Clifford's marriage to Richard Sackville on 25 February 1609, since she is referred to as Dorset, the title her husband inherited two days after the marriage; *terminus ante quem* is the date the volume was registered with the Stationer, 2 October 1610. If Jonson's poem was written first, Lanyer might possibly have seen it in manuscript, but there are no obvious allusions and no probable channels for such transmission.

29. I have not found evidence indicating the specific periods of the countess's residence at Cookham. Anne Clifford's diary records a visit to Cookham (occupied at that time by her Russell uncle, Sir William Russell of Thornhaugh, and his family) in 1603, but unfortunately there are no entries from 1604 to 1616; see Vita Sackville-West, ed., *The Diary of the Lady Anne Clifford* (London, 1923), 15. The Survey of the Manor of Cookham in 6 James I (1609) also indicates Russell occupancy of some part of the estate (PRO L.R.2, vol. 198, fol. 102).

30. For the known biographical facts about Lanyer, see A. L. Rowse, ed., *The Poems of Shakespeare's Dark Lady* (London, 1978), introduction; for an analysis of the poems and a critique of Rowse's case for Lanyer as "dark lady," see Barbara K. Lewalski, "Of God and Good Women: The Poems of Aemilia Lanyer," in *Silent but for the Word: Tudor Women as Patrons, Translators, and Writers of Religious Works,* ed. Margaret P. Hannay (Kent, Ohio, 1985), 203–224.

31. "The Description of Cooke-ham," lines 1–12. It is not clear when or for how long Lanyer was at Cookham.

32. For the lives of the Cliffords, see George C. Williamson, *George, Third Earl of Cumberland (1558–1605): His Life and Voyages* (Cambridge, 1920); idem, *Lady Anne Clifford, Countess of Dorset, Pembroke and Montgomery 1590–1676* (Kendal, 1922); see also Martin Holmes, *Proud Northern Lady* (London, 1975).

33. See J. P. Gilson, ed., *Diary of Lady Anne Clifford, and Lives of Lady Anne Clifford Countess of Dorset, Pembroke and Montgomery (1590–1676) and of Her Parents, Summarized by Herself* (London, 1916).

34. J. P. Gilson, ed., *A Summary of Records and also a Memorial of That Religious and Blessed Lady, Margaret Russell, Countess of Cumberland* (London, 1916), 26.

35. Gilson 1916 (*Diary*), 25–78.

36. Jonson addressed items 103 and 105 in *Epigrammes* to Lady Mary Wroth, as well as a sonnet, item 30 in *Under-wood.* He also dedicated *The Alchemist* to her. Lady Wroth is the author of a long prose romance, *The Countesse of Mountgomeries Urania (London,* 1621), to which is appended her sonnet sequence, *Pamphilia to Amphilanthus.* Domestic troubles between the Wroths began early, as Sir Robert Sidney's letter of 10 October 1604 indicates (Penshurst Papers, U 1475, C 81/117). See also Josephine Roberts, ed., *The Poems of Lady Mary Wroth* (Baton Rouge, La., 1983), introduction.

37. In the Restoration the lady received similar short shrift. The most notable example, the embedded country-house poem on Chatsworth in Charles Cotton's *The Wonders of the Peake,* praises the Countess of Devonshire very briefly for adorning the house in the modern style.

38. See McGuire 1979, 93–96; Stone 1965, 187–188.

39. The poem cannot be dated precisely, but several facts suggest late 1641. The poem mentions a son aged five and a daughter somewhat older. Porter's daughters Mary and Lettice were not born until 1629 and 1631 and so were aged twelve and ten, respectively, in 1641. Thomas, five years old in 1641, is the only Porter son of that age at a period conceivable for the poem, and the only one who, like the son in the poem, is described as notably precocious in contemporary accounts. Porter returned with the king from Scotland in November 1641, and followed him to Oxford early the next year. The tone of the poem suggests the imminence, but not the actual onset, of war in England. The house celebrated must be Woodhall rather than Porter's own estate at Aston-sub-Edge, Gloucestershire, because his collection of paintings, so prominently described in the poem, was chiefly housed there and in London; the collection was confiscated and dispersed in June 1643. Woodhall itself does not survive. See the discussions in Gervas Huxley, *Endymion Porter: The Life of a Courtier, 1587–1649* (London, 1959), 224–229, 267–271; Dorothea Townshend, *Life and Letters of Mr. Endymion Porter* (London, 1897), 193–202.

40. See Huxley 1959, 41–44, 227, 235–237.

41. Townshend 1897, esp. 17–19, 59–61, 74–78, 82–83.

42. Townshend 1897, 48–49.

43. Townshend 1897, 50.

44. Townshend 1897, 199–200.

45. McGuire 1979, 104–105.

46. All quotations are from C. H. Wilkinson, ed., *The Poems of Richard Lovelace* (Oxford, 1930), 71–74.

47. John Newman, "Marvell's Appleton House," *Times Literary Supplement,* 28 January 1972, 99.

48. Lines 70–72. All quotations are from H. M. Margouliouth, ed., *Poems and Letters of Andrew Marvell,* 2 vols. (Oxford, 1971), 1:62–86.

49. See the discussion of this myth, based on Marvell's poem, in Clements H. Markham, *The Life of the Great Lord Fairfax* (London, 1870), 3–4; and an argument for its dubious authenticity in Lee Erickson, "Marvell's *Upon Appleton House* and the Fairfax Family," *English Literary Renaissance* 9 (1979), 158–168.

50. For further analysis, see Rosalie L. Colie, *My Ecchoing Song: Andrew Marvell's Poetry of Criticism* (Princeton, 1970), 181–294; Barbara K. Lewalski, *Donne's Anniversaries and the Poetry of Praise: The Creation of a Symbolic Mode* (Princeton, 1973), 337–370.

51. Erickson 1979, 161, quotes the complaints recorded by Fairfax's uncle Charles in the *Analecta Fairfaxiana,* to the effect that Thomas Fairfax by reason of his pride and desire to rise above his rank would "destroy his house." Erickson also argues that the present brick mansion at Nunappleton was built for Mary Fairfax as part of her dowry.

52. For the circumstances of the meeting, courtship, and wedding of Villiers and Mary (then aged nineteen), see M. A. Gibbs, *The Lord General: A Life of Thomas Fairfax* (London, 1938), 236–241; Hester W. Chapman, *Great Villiers: A Study of George Villiers, Second Duke of Buckingham, 1628–1687* (London, 1949), 93–102. Fairfax was in possession of part of Villiers' estate, confiscated during the interregnum.

53. This picture obviously postdates Marvell's poem by several years.

WILLIAM A. McCLUNG

The Country-House
Arcadia

At this moment of celebration of the glories of the British country house, it is worth remarking that response to *The Treasure Houses of Britain* exhibition was by no means altogether approving; specifically, both the *Times Literary Supplement* and the *New York Review of Books* ran hostile essays, assailing the exhibit as a propaganda machine for perpetuating genteel and aristocratic privilege.[1] Leaving aside the obvious though unremarked point that such propaganda would be better addressed to the British than to the American electorate, one appreciates Tzvetlan Todorov's recent contention that where judgments of ethics and value are allowed, contemporary criticism tolerates only a Marxist analysis.[2] In the examination of country-house literature as well as of its parent phenomenon, the disinterested modern modes of structuralism and deconstruction commonly are displaced by strongly evaluative historical criticism grounded in Marxist theory. Consequently, both the country house and country-house literature have in recent years been chastised as the perpetuators and products of dishonest cultural mythologies. It should be no surprise that the *TLS* reviewer called the Washington exhibition "elitist and ultimately mischievous in its rationale."[3]

The best new writers in this vein, like Don Wayne, in *Penshurst: The Semiotics of Place and the Poetics of History* (1984), acknowledge as their inspiration Raymond Williams, who in *The Country and the City* (1973) briefly and forcefully characterized seventeenth-century country-house poetry as dishonest because the factor essential for the well-being of each estate, the tenants' labor, was gracefully erased from the literary equation, leaving a Tory fantasy of frictionless social relationships. Alistair Duckworth wrote a clearly reasoned demolition of Williams' literary criticism in 1975,[4] but it has not altered the course; in 1985 Harold Toliver offered a subtle

defense of the country house on historical grounds, arguing that both Renaissance country-house life and its reflection in literature are part of an emerging anti-heroic ethic, a system of values grounded in familial and intimate social relations that largely govern later, and present, notions of right and happy living.[5] It is in this vein, and not in that one exploited so effectively but to such negative effect by Williams, that the reader of the country-house poetry of the seventeenth and eighteenth centuries and of the prose fiction that continues its central preoccupations, will find an analysis ethically adequate to the aesthetic satisfaction afforded by the works themselves. The same approach will serve the student of the estates. It can be called the identification of the country house as an evolving type of Arcadia, a partially realized equivalent or reconstitution of a system of physical and metaphysical relationships understood or felt in some sense as prior to and authoritative over culture, and therefore "natural."

"Arcadia" is a complicated notion. As a literary figure it first appears charged with irony, being actually and as described by the Greek historian Polybius a rough and unproductive stretch of the Peloponnese, whose inhabitants supposedly cultivated the art of song as a distraction from their toil.[6] The frustrated lover Gallus of Virgil's tenth *Eclogue* retreats to a dreamscape called Arcadia, a paradise of gratification that compensates subjectively for the wild and barren emotional landscape of unsatisfied love. As such Arcadia is a state of wish fulfillment, where nature and psychology cooperate, an image of the ideal but also, like the objects of nostalgia, of the unattainable. In the fifteenth century Jacopo Sannazaro made of this subdivision of Virgil's complex bucolic landscape an entire world, his *Arcadia*. Within the tradition Sannazaro established and Sir Philip Sidney and others continued, Arcadian literature is distinct from pastoral, having place rather than occupation as its ground of being, and specifically a replete place, complex and beautiful in its phenomena and adequate to many possibilities of love and other activities. Rich in mythological and classical inhabitants and allusions, Arcadia becomes an equivalent of the idea of the world, uniting the pristine to the perfected as the setting and mechanism for the fullest possible life.

The conceptual antagonist of Arcadia is Utopia, the world to be created rather than the world to be discovered. As John Outram argues, the architecture of Arcadia reconstitutes the primary natural relationships of the world and is largely verbal and pictorial, whereas that of Utopia reifies abstractions into exemplary models and is found in numbers and constructions.[7] One makes an idea of the world, the other the world of an idea. In this opposition lies the root of the quarrel over the country house and its products, understood either as codes containing the components of the natural order of things or as programs limited by the contingencies of their time. Historical criticism of the country house judges it by Utopian standards, as an idea representing itself as the world.

On these terms any institution short of New Jerusalem will be consigned to the dustbin of history, despite the counterweight of at least a century of dystopian fables of the futility or evil of utopian programs. But as an Arcadia the country house has been significant in the maintenance and definition of broad cultural options: privacy over publicity, shelter against accessibility, comedy instead of tragedy. Psychologically as well as topographically, country houses imply the limits of the possible and discourage Faustian aspirations; they are strongly defined by boundaries and by the juxtaposition and balancing of their different elements: buildings, gardens, cultivated and uncultivated properties, and the kinds of people centered in each. The estates of country-house literature are essentially narratives, even fables: they actualize the order of natural, human, and artificial relationships both as the timeless constant underlying appearances and as the historical moment that validates or betrays that order. So the method of country-house literature is both emblematic and narrative, restating one story, that of Arcadia, while meshing it with others, those of the place and the moment.

A sequence of such constructions or fables proceeds typologically from Milton's Paradise through the landscape of Sannazaro's and Sidney's Arcadias to country-house literature, mainly the sequence of poems stretching from Ben Jonson's "To Penshurst" of 1612 to Alexander Pope's Epistles to Burlington (1731) and to Bathurst (1733), including to a limited extent celebrations of and meditations and attacks upon rural life and conditions, and continuing in eighteenth-, nineteenth-, and twentieth-century fiction. Those works dealing with estate life itself look to the architecture, grounds, and domestic economy as achieved, failed, or perverted types of a natural order of relationships, first among men, second between men and the rest of created nature, and third between men and their artifacts. A threat is characteristically present, essentially the threat of history, that is, of time that attacks rather than renews the order of things. The historical sequence of events that began with Lucifer's rebellion in *Paradise Lost* eventually unravels the self-sustaining fabric of Adam and Eve's bower and garden; Virgil's *georgoi* live to the side but in the shadow of civil war; Arcadias are threatened and (as in the *Faerie Queene*, book 6) sometimes destroyed by outsiders; and country houses may violate their contracts with Nature by adopting the ostentation and exploitative behavior of the city. The country house in English literature contains the timeless but registers the effects of time: Andrew Marvell's "Upon Appleton House" of about 1652, for example, while affirming Lord Fairfax's Yorkshire estate as a paradigm of paradise, narrates the contingencies of its strife-torn past, its problematic present, and its hard-won status as a nursery of magical virtue. Like other country houses in literature, Appleton House is a dynamic as well as an emblematic figure, a manifestation of becoming as well as of being.

Colen Campbell's *Vitruvius Britannicus* of 1715–1717 was "the first British collection of designs devoted primarily to dwellings, and the first anywhere in which domestic designs were tied to a program of architectural reform."[8] In recommending the country house as the vehicle for returning the nation to authoritative principles of architecture, Campbell implicitly recognized the centrality of the country house, a fact of several centuries of British history and a necessary factor of the estates' claim to be models of Arcadia. Neither retreat nor nostalgia are Arcadian properties, and they are inconsistent with the claim to be in various senses essential and

prior to historical contingencies. The power, wealth, and respect invested in the country house find their imaginative equivalent in the representation of those houses as central rather than peripheral, a representation dependent in literature upon rhetorical strategies like, for example, the definition of the architecture of the house as conformable or identical with nature rather than as superficial or idiosyncratic. This centrality is ultimately mythic, a localization of Paradise: "The True design then of such Places of Pleasure and Retreat," writes Timothy Nourse in 1700, "is to sweeten the Fatigues both of the Body and of the Mind, and to recover us to our former Bent of Duty, which is but in some measure to restore Man to his lost Station." Cultivation and gardening on an estate are activities that "may most properly be called a Recreation, not only from the Refreshment it gives to the Mind, but from the Restauration of Nature, which may be lookt upon as a New Creation of things; when from Nothing, or from something next to Nothing, we become the Instruments of producing, or of restoring them in such Perfection" (fig. 1).[9]

Nourse's text, *Campania Foelix,* attempts to transfer from city to country the quality of the essential in civilization. Nourse dwells on the agricultural preoccupations of the ancients and the link with civic virtue and heroic behavior in men like David and Cincinnatus, and he argues for the metaphysical significance of building: "it looks great in a Man, and carries something of a divine Character stampt upon it, to be able to frame a Building after the Idea he has within himself; that is, to be able to give a durable Existence to something which was not before."[10] This is a reduction to the simplest terms of country-house values: the reconstitution of paradise and the identity of man both with the nature he improves and with the artifacts he fashions (fig. 2). It embraces the sequence of types—paradisal, arcadian, georgic, country-house—that are properly centers rather than escapes. Such organizations of men and nature become escapist only when the sense of the natural relationship of things breaks down. It is then, when it seems too late to find the proper order of things, that literary Arcadias and the settings or institutions upon which they depend become the creatures and victims of nostalgia. But as actual—or at least possible—institutions, each of these types is not so much a reproach to the city, or to the unsatisfactory state of historical time, as

Fig. 1.
Frontispiece to Timothy Nourse,
Campania Foelix, London, 1700
(William Andrews Clark Memorial
Library, University of California, Los Angeles)

a model for it, a code of relationships from which the larger polity derives value and nourishment, and on which it might pattern itself. Pope, for example, seems to be recommending an identity rather than a dichotomy of civilizations in his use of a natural setting, Windsor Forest, as emblematic of the identity of court and nation, and, in his assigning the products of Lord Burlington's estate to the ends of the nation: prosperity and empire.[11]

Country-house literature reflects changes in the idea of what is good about country-house life. Jonson's poem of 1612 marks not only a formal beginning of a genre, the seventeenth-century country-house poem, but an elevation of a new value that ultimately came to undermine the claim of the estates to be central, that is, Arcadian, models of completeness. The literature of country-house complaint from William Langland to Tobias Smollett insists on the central role of hospitality in country-house life, and therefore on the estates as models of the nation.[12] Properly managed, the estates are inclusive rather than exclusive, offering, like Chaucer's Franklin, a daily open house, and, in "To Penshurst," including the entire hierarchy of society from king to clown. But Jonson attributes the continuing fruitfulness and largesse of Penshurst in part to values bred within the inner family of the Sidneys themselves. The family as cultural icon is consistent with the anti-heroic ethic of the Arcadian ideal and the country-house poem, but it inhibits the greater communality, just as private dining in the parlor, complained of in *Piers Plowman,* disestablishes the hall of its function.

The complaint structure of country-house literature depicts the estates as arenas of an eternal struggle between timelessness and history. The rhetorical strategy accommodates all kinds of factors in its dialectic: the hall against the parlor, undressed stone against the orders, asymmetry against symmetry, Chiswick against Blenheim—elements on one side of the equation may have little or nothing in common, but their tension with their contraries is equivalent from pair to pair. The emergence of the family as the central value of country-house life, however, undermines the dichotomy because it draws an inner boundary, interrupting the flow of characters across the Arcadian landscape and the vision of interchange and identity implicit in the spontaneous cooperation of all components of the ideal estate. Jonson's family of Sidneys appear in the poem as a strong and confident lot in physical

and spiritual contact with those above and beneath them, but Marvell's Lord Fairfax and his daughter Maria are isolated figures in their poem and on their grounds, in contact with nature but not with men, not even with each other or with the absent Lady Fairfax. Though eulogized, the family is never assembled; saints or goddesses, they barely touch the earth. Their estate, though rationalized by argument and analogy into a fi-

Fig. 2.
A bucolic ideal of labor in an ordered landscape centered on an idealized manor house, from the *Georgics,* in *Publii Vergilii Maronis Opera,* London, 1663 (William Andrews Clark Memorial Library, University of California, Los Angeles)

gure of paradise, is a retreat and a kindergarten. In locating significance and virtue in the family, country-house literature undercuts the dichotomy of the natural and the unnatural by finding virtue on the wrong side of the equation, in that which protects and preserves not others but itself. The cult of the family means the limitation of possibilities where once was space for all activities legitimate to men, and it means the exclusion of discordant elements rather than their sublimation. Increasingly in eighteenth-century literature the "good" country house is a point of departure and an image of childhood. Tom Jones, for example, cannot become himself until he leaves it. As such the house is an object of nostalgia, devalued as a container of renewable values. It becomes the prisoner of the past.

The conflict of values is apparent in the understanding of the country house in history. An 1833 account of sixteenth- and seventeenth-century domestic architecture restates the complaint about the growth, in tandem, of architectural luxury and complexity and inhospitable and wasteful behavior, but it inconsistently applauds the new security and comfort of building as supportive of domestic tranquility.[13] The myth of the erosion of natural character is set against the newer myth of quintessential English charm: big, new glass windows are bad because "the buildings began to assume an appearance of lightness and insecurity" and because the windows unnaturally penetrate the interior with floods of light; yet they are good because they are suitable to the English atmosphere and because the Elizabethan style is particularly appropriate to country life.[14] The author admires Penshurst, on the one hand, for maintaining a central hearth and so stating its identity with humble farmhouses; elsewhere, however, he admires the removal of fireplaces to end walls in the interests not only of comfort but also of elegance.[15] The consequence of a close identification of country-house life with the charms and comforts of domesticity is an imaginative distancing of the institution from the real business of life. Its architecture, for example, should be Elizabethan, because—in the words of a writer in 1837—those "quaint," "fantastic," "intricate," and "grotesque" architectural features "connect themselves intimately with surrounding scenery:"[16] that is, Elizabethan architecture is "natural" in the restricted modern sense, like organic growth, and not in the comprehensive earlier sense, as an equivalent of reality. By no

means, however, should "the complex purposes of modern civic architecture" depart from classicism.[17] For this writer the oriel window is an experiential touchstone, offering a balance of society and withdrawal—a kind of synecdoche for the country house itself.[18] This no doubt is an idyllic state, but as a code of civilized values it is incomplete.

Joseph Nash joined history, medieval and Renaissance domestic architecture, the cult of the family, and the distancing mechanism of nostalgia in four volumes of plates published between 1839 and 1849 (figs. 3, 4, 8).[19] Here, charming scenes of domestic life alternate with archetypal ceremonies and celebrations in a rhythm of inoffensive pleasures and pleasant duties: old men help toddlers walk; young men compete at archery and bowls; there is much intimate conversation and many meals (figs. 5, 6). These rooms are replete: their inhabitants extend and complete their architectural and decorative presence, and they are anachronistically old, with surfaces rendered as the nineteenth rather than the sixteenth or seventeenth century would see them (fig. 7). The effect is that of an old photograph of a young person. The country-house Arcadia here is a hopeless vision of disconnected, dreamlike icons, inaccessible except to reverie (fig. 9).

That reverie extends to the nation at large, as a yardstick for defining the English "moment," the moment when social life and architecture united to sum up "Englishness." Many histories of the country house return to this idea. In 1910 P. A. Ditchfield, for example, celebrates the blend of stateliness and homeliness in the smaller Tudor manors while decrying the prodigy houses.[20] Garner and Stratton's monumental survey of Tudor domestic architecture, issued in 1910 and revised in 1929, identifies its subjects as the true national type, vessels of medieval humanism and of the essentially literary (rather than visual and plastic) genius of the English Renaissance. "House building," they argue, "is indigenous to the soil. It is as national as the name with which it is stamped; it breathes the restful yet vigorous spirit of the time that gave it birth, and withal is characterised by a self-contained homeliness, redolent of the life and customs of the Englishman of the day, and impossible to be either originated or imitated by his continental contemporaries." Great Chalfield in Wiltshire of the mid-fifteenth century is somewhat surprisingly identified as typical of the fully developed English manor, beyond the need for

Fig. 3.
The cult of the family joined to nostalgia for the manorial past: the Long Gallery at Haddon Hall, Derbyshire, from Joseph Nash, *The Mansions of England in the Olden Time*, 1839, vol. I (The Henry E. Huntington Library and Art Gallery, San Marino, California)

fortification but before the taint of foreign innovation.[21]

The Arcadian vision here is defensive, acknowledging the passing of the conditions that made possible such an epitome of the national spirit. The customary twentieth-century complaint for the loss of the country house owes much to this isolation and idealization of one period of history at the expense of others, a conceptual framework that is itself a development of the ancient argument against innovation of any sort. Although country houses continue to flourish, as the architect John Martin Robinson has argued in his recent study of well over two hundred new or substantially reconstructed ones, all built since the Second World War and all the seats of agricultural enterprises,[22] their demise is authoritatively noted at least every decade. That this is so may be due to the continuing function of the institution as a container of values, so much so that many country houses—and in the extreme cases all since the close of some ideal past era—simply do not qualify, and are invisible. A century and a half of cultural nostalgia has made the loss of the country house more acceptable than its mutation, which may appear to be a betrayal.

Henry James, as a child, fed on that nostalgia; he was a fan of Nash's seductive pictures.[23] Yet it is perhaps he who most thoroughly appreciated the country house as a mechanism for infusing the present with the past, diachronically repeating and renewing the systems of relationships that in the guise of changing centuries remain constant. His special emphasis is by no means on the family, but on the individual, and the gift of the country house is not security or shelter, but freedom, where "every provision is made for the convenience of people bent on a liberal freedom of intercourse."[24] As an "envelope of circumstances," in a phrase from *The Portrait of a Lady*, the house acts both as an extension of the self and as an accommodating medium for interchange between the self and the past, a past contained both in the phenomena of the place and in the consciousness of its inhabitants. To this kind of transference the reviewers from the *Times Literary Supplement* and the *New York Review of Books*, both of whom recommend the permanent removal of country-house artifacts to museums, are either skeptical or indifferent. The past, it should be stressed, is by no means an idyll, as an extreme example of James's work, *The Turn of the Screw*, makes obvious, and as the complicated

ethical problems of the major novels suggest as well; the freedom of the country house is Arcadian in the complete sense: circumstances, literally in the sense of surroundings, are ideal, so that action for good or evil may proceed without contingency. In the fullness of Arcadia even Death is present.

James's ultimate or limiting vision of the country-house Arcadia is found in a short story, "The Great Good Place."[25] In it a distinguished man of letters, on the point of nervous collapse, appears to be miraculously transported to a beau-

Fig. 7.
Tranquil daily life in the hall at Ockwells, Berkshire, from Joseph Nash, *The Mansions of England in the Olden Time*, 1839, vol. 1 (The Henry E. Huntington Library and Art Gallery, San Marino, California)

Fig. 8.
Sweet and pensive solitude in the porches and corridors of Ockwells, Berkshire, from Joseph Nash, *The Mansions of England in the Olden Time*, 1839, vol. I (The Henry E. Huntington Library and Art Gallery, San Marino, California)

There is here no narrative structure of history or myth; good and bad, health and sickness, are felt rather than understood. In the torture chamber of his study he reacts to the vehicles of his obligations:

the bristling hedge of letters planted by the early post an hour before and already on the customary table by the chimney piece, formally rounded and squared . . . newspapers, each with its hand on the neck of the other, so that the row of their bodiless heads was like a series of decapitations . . . other journals . . . made a huddled mound that had been growing for several days and of which he had been wearily, helplessly aware. . . . It was the old rising tide, and it rose and rose even under a minute's watching. It had been up to his shoulders last night; it was up to his chin now.

A threatening formal garden, shackled and beheaded prisoners, the grave, a killer sea—the progression toward shapelessness is topped by ironic agricultural imagery: "he must reap as he had sown." In this system of phenomenal relationships the natural and the artificial bring out the worst in each other. Their contrary is the physical presence of the Great Good Place, "an easy bench," "a high clear portico," the "wide far-reaching garden where the things that most showed in the greenness were the surface of still water and the white note of old statues." In pondering the mystery of these healing powers, the convalescent man acknowledges a likeness to a sequence of historically related institutions and building types, including the monastery, the hospital, the hotel, and the club. The country house, lying midway in this sequence, in this instance gathers their advantages while dispensing with their faults, ultimately in an image both of maternity and of connoisseurship: "the large simple idea of a general refuge—an image of embracing arms, of liberal accommodation . . . the poetisation by perfect taste of a type common enough."

James is both daring and cautious in generating his archetype of civil architecture from minute particulars, matters closely observed and carefully pieced together by the wondering but appraising guest. From the data of sensory experience he constructs the grand formula that the Great Good Place defines an ideal state of being in terms of elemental relationships between men, nature, and artifacts, while making those relationships possible within the historical and psychological context of its occupants. Though the state of being at the Great Good Place is inclusive of all significant experience, and though the conversation is angelic, having the present state of

tiful place in the English countryside, where the mere state of being restores his spiritual and physical health. As though waking from a dream he returns to his study and to himself, to a paradisal "lost Station" of psychic integration.

His experience both of the world that is tearing him down and of the Great Good Place is not narrated or explained but conveyed experientially, through his interaction with phenomena.

being as its only subject, still the place lies at the most immediate, the most modern end of the country-house spectrum in its alignment of the grand universals of the human condition with the requirements of culture and history. The key to this is money, the fact that the guests pay, and that they are served by paid though nearly invisible help. Money is both the substance and symbol of the localization of this Arcadia in the year 1900; through its neutral medium all debts are discharged, and the guests enjoy absolute freedom. James's words for the conditions of the place are "calculation" and "generosity." They take their place in the sequence of particular value systems adequate to the realization of the Arcadian ideal of frictionless interchange within a comprehensive order of things, and in the instance of a James character they liberate the vivi-

fying qualities of the Great Good Place from psychological identification with the past, whether parent or place, and from a religious obligation enforced by charity and expressed in humility. Freedom is purchased, and the guests of the house are its masters.

Freedom from the past characterizes the Great Good Place itself, as well as its clients. James' model should point up the folly of searching for, and the danger in locating, a historical Arcadia, which can only validate the dismissal of the country house as Utopian and an anachronism. The displacement of narration by experience in "The Great Good Place" suggests that phenomenology provides a better approach to understanding. "The existential purpose of building [or] architecture," writes Christian Norberg-Schulz, "is . . . to make a site become a place,

Fig. 9.
Merriment at Moreton Hall, Cheshire, from Joseph Nash, *The Mansions of England in the Olden Time*, 1849, vol. 4 (The Henry E. Huntington Library and Art Gallery, San Marino, California)

that is, to uncover the meanings potentially present in the given environment."[26] Through a variety of rhetorical strategies, country-house literature narrates architecture and landscape; its natural ally is the discipline that discovers essences "within" or "behind" phenomena, holding that they are a priori and that they yield objective and universally valid insights into the hidden structures and meanings behind the phenomenal world.[27] To intuit them is to grasp the universal within the particular, the object of Arcadian literature. In Heidegger's formula, "the thing things the world,"[28] or the built, inhabited, and bounded community reifies the immanent order of things. The aim of such analysis is not to affirm or deny the ethical status of any particular system of estate life at any particular time, but to corroborate James' imagination of country houses as experientially active and significant presences, and to justify a definition of the country house as a system of relationships striving for an equivalence with "nature" in its full sense, an immutable though ineffable order of things. As country houses in Britain again find architects like Quinlan Terry, who have returned to classical theories of the identity of nature and craft, it is time less for ideological sparring than for a deepening of the conceptual grounds of the institution itself.

NOTES

1. Linda Colley, "The Cult of the Country House," *Times Literary Supplement,* 15 November 1985, 1293; David Cannadine, "Brideshead Re-Revisited," *New York Review of Books,* 19 December 1985, 17–23.

2. Tzvetlan Todorov, review of *Textual Power: Literary Theory and the Teaching of English* by Robert Scholes, *Times Literary Supplement,* 4 October 1985, 1093–1094.

3. Colley 1985, 1293.

4. Alistair M. Duckworth, "Raymond Williams and Literary History," *Papers on Language and Literature* II (1975), 420–441.

5. Harold Toliver, " 'Householding' and the Poet's Vocation: Jonson and After," *English Studies* 66 (April 1985), 113–122.

6. Eleanor Winsor Leach, "Parthenian Caverns: Remapping of an Imaginative Topography," *Journal of the History of Ideas* 39 (October–December 1978), 540. I am indebted to this article for details of this paragraph.

7. John Outram, "Uses and Abuses of Arcadia," *Architectural Review* 175 (June 1984), 76–80.

8. John Archer, *The Literature of British Domestic Architecture 1715–1842* (Cambridge, Mass., 1985), 35.

9. Timothy Nourse, *Campania Foelix, Or, A Discourse of The Benefits and Improvements of Husbandry, Containing Directions for all manner of Tillage, Pasturage, and Plantations . . . To which are added Two Essays: I. Of A Country House . . .* (London, 1700), 3.

10. Nourse 1700, 341.

11. See Isabel Rivers, *The Poetry of Conservatism, 1600–1745: A Study of Poets and Public Affairs from Jonson to Pope* (Cambridge, 1973), 178–179.

12. References are to William Langland, *The Vision of William Concerning Piers the Plowman,* ed. W. W. Skeat (Oxford, 1886), I:292, text B, passus X, and to Tobias Smollett, *The Expedition of Humphry Clinker,* ed. Lewis M. Knapp (London, 1966), esp. 292.

13. *The Domestic Architecture of the Reigns of Queen Elizabeth and James the First, Illustrated by a Series of Views of English Mansions, with Brief Historical and Descriptive Accounts of Each Subject. By T. H. Clarke, Architect* (London, 1833).

14. Clarke 1833, iii, x.

15. Clarke 1833, ix.

16. Charles James Richardson, *Observations on the Architecture of England during the Reigns of Queen Elizabeth and King James I. &. &.* (London, 1837), 8.

17. Richardson 1837, 8.

18. Richardson 1837, 9–10.

19. Joseph Nash, *The Mansions of England in the Olden Time,* 4 vols. (London, 1839–1849).

20. P. A. Ditchfield, *The Manor Houses of England* (London, 1910), 4.

21. Thomas Garner and Arthur Stratton, *The Domestic Architecture of England During the Tudor Period,* 2d ed. (London, 1929), I: 1, 6, 9–10.

22. John Martin Robinson, *The Latest Country Houses* (London, 1984), 6–8.

23. *Henry James: Autobiography,* ed. Frederic W. Daper (New York, 1956), 13, cited in Richard Gill, *Happy Rural Seat: The English Country House and the Literary Imagination* (New Haven, 1972), 21, 267n.

24. Joseph Warren Beach, *The Method of Henry James* (Philadelphia, 1954), 122–123, cited in Gill 1972, 24.

25. Citations from "The Great Good Place" are from the *New York Edition of the Works of Henry James* (New York, 1909), vol. 16.

26. Christian Norberg-Schulz, *Genius Loci: Towards a Phenomenology of Architecture* (New York, 1979), 18.

27. See Max Scheler, *Man's Place in Nature,* trans. Hans Meyerhoff (New York, 1981), xvi.

28. Norberg-Schulz 1979, 10.

MICHAEL MENDLE

The *Convivium Philosophicum* and the Civil War: A Country House and Its Politics

Great Tew, eighteen miles north of Oxford, was the principal seat of Sir Lucius Cary, the 2nd Viscount Falkland. Tew—one presumes—exerted considerable influence in its vicinity as a source of employment, as a leasor of land and a collector of rents, and as a point of contact of the local and national cultures. In this Tew functioned like the houses of other of the ranking gentry and peerage of early seventeenth-century England.

But Tew was also unlike its fellows. Most importantly, Tew was in its own right a contributor to the national culture, and a contributor not in direct relation to the wealth and power of its owner, but according to other, and for its time, idiosyncratic principles. Tew's reputation flowed outward because a group of friends gathered there at the urging of its owner, rather than because it was the center of a great family or connection. And while the men who came to Tew were all gentlemen by education, and most by birth as well, in the mid-1630s few of them laid claim to such grand establishments.

Great Tew as a cultural institution was a creation of its owner, and to understand his house we must turn to that remarkable man. Lucius Cary was born in 1610, the son of Sir Henry Cary. Sir Henry received his Scottish viscountcy in 1620, and became the Lord Deputy of Ireland in 1622, both the peerage and the office owing much to the patronage of the Duke of Buckingham. At Sir Henry's death in 1633, the title passed to his son Lucius. Four years earlier, in 1629, the nineteen-year-old Cary had inherited Tew and Burford Priory, worth about £2000 a year, by virtue of the will of his maternal grandfather, Sir Lawrence Tanfield. Lucius' good for-

tune came at a time when his father's finances were desperate, and was the consequence of Tanfield's disapproval of his son-in-law's profligacy. Young Lucius took advantage of his new-found wealth to go his own way in the world: to marry for love, to sojourn in London amongst the coterie associated with Ben Jonson, and briefly to seek military glory in the Netherlands.[1] By 1632, Lucius had begun to develop his scheme to transform Great Tew into "a college in a purer air, a university bound in a lesser volume."[2]

The young owner of Tew was aristocratic; but his sense of the purpose of his house, and indeed of life, was not that shared by the gentry of his day. Thomas Triplett, a lesser member of the Tew circle, reminisced:

How often have I heard him pity those hawking and hunting gentlemen, who if unseasonable weather for their sports had betrayed them to keep house, without a worse exercise within doors, could not have told how to have spent their time.

Falkland, so Triplett went on, kept busy with his books, such company "as being bidden, are ready, uninvited intrude not, that bite no man's meat or reputation . . . candidly communicating themselves to us without betraying our secrets committed to them." To these friends Falkland resorted while "others studied the heraldry of horses, of dogs, or at the best their own."[3]

The bookish young man sought out kindred spirits to share with him the delights of Tew. Clarendon tells us that apart from a few friends chosen "for the agreeableness of their natures," the circle at Tew was selected "by other rules than were prescribed to young nobility of that time."[4] One steady guest was a neighbor, Sir Francis Wenman. Others were visitors from the London days, some very occasional; but one, the young Edward Hyde himself, was also a "regular." The rest were Oxford-trained and largely Oxford-resident divines.

Of the entire company only one member was significantly younger than Falkland: this was Abraham Cowley, an occasional guest down from London and at that time regarded primarily as a child prodigy. A few others were contemporaries of Falkland: Hyde, Sidney Godolphin, and—an odd man out in this company—Sir John Suckling. But most were older. William Chillingworth was eight years Falkland's senior; John Earle, nine; Triplett, seven; Henry Hammond, five; Edmund Waller, four. Some leading guests were older still. George Morley was twelve years Falkland's senior, Gilbert Sheldon thirteen. Of a different generation altogether were George Sandys, born in 1578, John Hales and John Selden, born in 1584, Thomas Hobbes, born in the year of the Armada, and Robert Sanderson and Endymion Porter, born the year before Hobbes.[5]

As these names indicate, Falkland brought to Tew a few poets and a large number of scholars, some with literary ambitions, most of them (unlike their host) established, older men. One might make bold and style them aristocratic intellectuals;[6] Hyde described the large contingent from Oxford as "the most polite and accurate men of the university."[7] Their manner more nearly resembled Falkland's books than the ways of "those hawking and hunting gentlemen," and the deliberate informality of the routine at Tew must have done much to commend the house to the scholars. When in residence, they devoted their days to study and writing (Chillingworth's *Religion of Protestants* was written there), making use of Falkland's ample library. In the evening they joined together for meals and conversation. Hyde's panegyric on Falkland speaks of the viscount's "whole conversation" as "one continued *convivium philosophicum* or *convivium theologicum;*"[8] but this is a figure, like Triplett's play upon books and houseguests, drawn from Hyde's memories of gatherings at meals (a *convivium*, of course, is a banquet) and the general texture of life at Tew, where the master artfully provided for the alternation of the scholar's solitude with the good talk of sophisticated and discreet company. This was Hyde's own experience of the king's peace, of the idyll before the rage of faction, tumult, and war. Hyde's remark that England at this time "enjoyed . . . the fullest measure of felicity" of "any people in any age for so long time together" puzzles many historians, but it reflects, perhaps embarassingly so, his own circumstances.[9] In this connection one notes that among Hyde's evidence of England's flourishing was the publication of *The Religion of Protestants*.[10]

To fit all these men into a single mold would be foolish. The conversation would never have captivated such vigorous minds, had they but parroted one another. Moreover, leading members of the Tew circle actively encouraged intellectual openness and the free play of responsible reason. And yet one may speak of ethic if not of dogma. For example, one might be able to bring the name of Arminius into a discussion of Tew without suggesting that Arminianism was "a Tew doctrine" or that whole systems were accepted by men who had the strength or inclination to give assent to a part. The figures of special interest to the men at Tew were Erasmus, Grotius (Dr. Tuck's special interest), and Jean Daillé (whose importance to the Tew circle has been demonstrated by Brian Wormald). If the historical Socinus and true or doctrinal Socinianism cannot be said to have been part of Tew culture, the more general significance of Socinianism as a sort of highminded Christian freethought ought to be allowed.[11]

Not without reason, then, given these intellectual guides, has Tew been characterized as an outpost of Christian enlightenment. Certainly, the challenge faced by Tew's rational, latitudinarian, ethically oriented Christianity can be viewed in Enlightenment-derived categories. Especially helpful is the pair of terms recently reviewed by Professor Pocock in a discussion of the religious outlook of Hume and Gibbon.[12] These two distinct and separate opponents threatened the ethos that flourished at Tew. On the one hand was Superstition: iconodulic, hierocratic, and uncritical in its acceptance of authority and tradition; on the other was Enthusiasm: bibliolatrous, demotic, and antinomian. The likelihood that resistance to Superstition would encourage Enthusiasm, and vice versa, imperiled rational religion; at the same time it also delineated the need for it.

Of course this dilemma was not unique to the Enlightenment, Christian or otherwise: Hume and Gibbon had come to these categories through the study of religious history. In a recognizably cognate form, the dual threat of Superstition and Enthusiasm was an element of considerable tension in Erasmus and other humanist reformers and their critics: in fleeing Münster one risked a mugging at Trent. And closer to home, an intellectually respectable course between Superstition and Enthusiasm had been charted by Richard Hooker (in no mean regard at Tew) and was congenial with and perhaps essential to the whole adiaphorist tradition of late sixteenth- and early seventeenth-century Anglicanism.

In the 1630s Tew was a living repository of that tradition; responses found there to Laud's brand of Arminianism and to Puritanism can be seen as continuous with Elizabethan and early Jacobean establishment Protestantism. The men of Tew, like other mainline Anglicans, were puzzled by both movements. Laudian Arminianism, radical and reactionary at the same time, on the one hand, and the Anglican respect for "authority" on the other, prevented Tew from making an unequivocal response to Laudianism. Falkland and Morley had little use either for Laud or for his ways.[13] By contrast, Hales, Selden, and Hyde were in varying degrees inclined to put a charitable construction on his aims, though not to the point of endorsing his churchmanship.[14] In this respect, Falkland's scathing indictment of the Laudians could have been uttered by any of the men of Tew: the Laudians "brought in superstition . . . under the titles of reverence and decency," and had "labored to bring in . . . a blind dependance of the people upon the clergy, and of the clergy upon themselves."[15]

On the other side were the ambiguities of Puritanism. At a given moment, Puritanism might be near the doctrinal center of late sixteenth- and early seventeenth-century Anglicanism, the locus of the educational and homiletic impulses scarcely separable from Christianity itself, and, nevertheless and most disturbingly, the matrix of both Superstition ("new presbyter, old priest," "godly discipline") and Enthusiasm ("no bishop, no king," "tender consciences"). The Anglican response to such a chameleon usually waited upon events, but when Puritanism betokened irrationality and instability, the response of Tew—like that of earlier English churchmen (notably Whitgift and Bancroft) to Puritanism and that of Catholic humanists before them to kindred threats—was to seek protection from the authorities (if not from Authority) and comfort and legitimacy from continuity (if not from Tradition). In peace, all manner of high-minded thoughts could breeze about, and the enlightened approach to the milder sorts of Puritan deviance was to affect a charitable, latitudinarian, and reasonable posture calculated to charm or shame dissidents into nearer conformity. In the whirlwind, the liberal window slammed shut. So Erasmus, so Thomas More, so Hooker, so Grotius.

So, too, the men of Tew. Members of the Tew circle are commonly said to have belonged to the broad reform coalition that greeted Charles so coldly at the beginning of the Long Parliament in November 1640. The problem for most commentators has been how then to explain Falkland's and Hyde's subsequent defection to the king's service (and also to explain why Selden, so much their colleague, decided to remain behind). In the variant, eccentric formulation of Brian Wormald, the task is to explain how Hyde managed to serve the king without leaving the parliamentarians.[16] But there is no problem, for the truth is that Hyde and Falkland were on the outer edges of the reform coalition, sharing attitudes that would prevent them from ever moving toward its leadership. On the church issue, possibly they were not part of the coalition at all. Though they disagreed seriously on how best to preserve episcopacy as well as on the degree of reform appropriate to the dismantling of Laud's *iure divino* hierocracy, from the first moments of the Long Parliament Falkland and Hyde worked to avert the total (or, as it was then put, root-and-branch) abolition of episcopacy. By contrast, John Pym, neither friend nor foe of episcopacy per se, merely wished to avoid the divisiveness that root-and-branch might bring. When that could no longer be done, he went with the party most useful to him. It was not Tew, whose drift toward the king was inevitable: on the one hand, Hyde's and Falkland's efforts to divert the anti-episcopal juggernaut ceased to be tolerated by the opposition leadership, which excluded them from their own schemes to obtain office; on the other, the interests and principles of Falkland and Hyde coincided with those of a Laud-less Charles to a degree that could not be ignored, by Charles least of all.

The precise position of Falkland and Hyde at the beginning of the Long Parliament has been a matter of supposition and extrapolation. Curiosity is inevitable; George Morley—a member of the Tew circle, whose cooperation with Hyde would extend into the era of the Restoration—delivered one of the four Fast Sermons that marked the beginning of the parliament. Though he was thanked for his sermon by the House, and given permission to print it if he wished, Morley's sermon was not published, unlike those of the two Puritans, Stephen Marshall and Cornelius Burgess, and that of John Gauden, who seems to have stood for an Anglicanism more accommodating to Presbyterianism than anything advocated by Falkland, Hyde, or Morley. Trevor-Roper supposed that Morley's sermon was left unprinted because it displeased some opposition chiefs.[17] Notes on Morley's sermon, taken by an unidentified member of the House of Commons, lend support to Trevor-Roper's intuition. Like Falkland, Morley held no brief for the Laudians, and his sermon noted certain liturgical "prophanations." But Morley's text, 1 Corinthians 12:27 (along with the succeeding several verses, upon which Morley also drew), was a favorite for ecclesiastical law-and-order homilies, and Morley used it to pursue standard Anglican themes: the supremacy of the king under God, and the due place of the bishops (along with the nobility and commonalty) under the king. The report closes on a surprising note of cultural atavism: "The priest prays for all[,] the soldier fights for all."[18] Whether this statement directly quoted Morley's sermon, or whether it was a gloss or reflection of Morley's auditor, remains unclear. If, however, this was Morley, he could count himself in the company of Hyde and Selden in asserting the importance of the traditional, medieval estates for the maintenance of the existing constitution.[19] Another clue to the attitudes of Hyde and Falkland is to be found in Hyde's correspondence. Letters to him from Triplett and other members of the Tew circle in the early days of the Long Parliament reveal substantial anti-Puritan animus that Hyde's correspondents assume he shared;[20] one friend and correspondent, William Aylesbury, took it for granted that Hyde could muster sympathy for the self-exiled courtier, Sir Francis Windebanke.[21] Even before the fate of episcopacy was placed formally on the table, Tew seems to have been drifting toward a posture of defense.

But the members of the Tew circle defended Hooker's church, not Laud's. Falkland, going further, believed that the removal of the bishops from the House of Lords was an acceptable, even desirable, reform and a retreat from an indefensible salient. In this the lord of Tew clashed with Hyde and Selden, who thought the exclusion of the bishops the prelude to their extinction.[22] And in the reforming spirit Selden, almost certainly, Morley, Hales, and Falkland probably, and perhaps even Hyde, were tempted by schemes, Elizabethan in origin and Anglican in contemporary revival, to leaven episcopacy with a measure of presbyterianism.[23]

But the basic hostility of the men of Tew to root-and-branch abolition of episcopacy was widely recognized. The Scottish Presbyterian Robert Baillie called Selden "the avowed proctor for the bishops."[24] Hyde, Falkland, and Selden made their views clear in the preliminary debates concerning root-and-branch in the winter of 1640 to 1641.[25] In late February 1641, Hyde and some pro-episcopacy men in the Commons successfully raised a loan for Parliament from similarly inclined merchants in London, a direct challenge to the "governing party," as Hyde later called them, and one that brought Alderman Pennington, a root-and-branch man, to compare Hyde's success to coloquintida, a poisonous cathartic.[26] When the opposition leadership formally identified itself with root-and-branch at the introduction of the root-and-branch bill on 27 May 1641, Falkland and Hyde were the first to speak against it.[27] Wormald's account notwithstanding, Hyde was generally perceived as a key opponent of the root-and-branchers. Hyde's explanation in the *History* that he was made chairman of the committee of the whole house to debate the root-and-branch bill in order to exclude him from the debate is supported by an entry in D'Ewes's diary, just as his continuing, if ever critical friendship with Laud is attested to in Laud's own memoranda.[28]

In the summer of 1641, when root-and-branch became the focus of new-found but growing impatience of many moderates with the opposition leadership, Falkland and Hyde were still months away from engaging straightforwardly in the service of the king; the pair's discomfort with the parliamentary leadership had not yet ripened into resistance. Still, there are signs that the interests of Hyde, Selden, and Falkland had begun to spill into other areas. Selden attempted to protect the Army Plotters through a strained argument that they were pardoned by the Act of Pacification with the Scots. Later he showed himself opposed to the first steps of the radicals toward governance by ordinance.[29] Falkland tried to protect a fellow partisan of the bishops,

Sir Thomas Aston, from Puritan fury.[30] Hyde and Falkland, the latter protesting against the "rude multitude," both tried to get the Commons to move against civil disorders in the Lincolnshire Fens, activity suggestive both of *peur sociale* and a desire to be useful to the court since, as a landlord on the short end of his rents, Charles was directly affected by the outcome of the land disputes in the Fens.[31]

It should be clear that Clarendon's account of his conduct in the first year of the Long Parliament, before he joined the king, was not a fabrication after the fact. This is not to deny that Hyde's account in the *History* was self-serving. It was, but Hyde's goal was not to affect a more intimate connection between himself and Laud from 1640 to 1641 than was the case, or to make himself out to be a committed episcopal partisan when he was not. Hyde's aim, rather, was to use his *History* to make a case in the intra-royalist disputes of 1646 to 1648; in his recounting, the events of 1640 to 1642 were an implicit argument against the propriety of Charles accepting a Presbyterian settlement, then a prospect hotly debated by royalists. As Hyde saw it, this possibility amounted to a remake, featuring a nearly identical cast, of an earlier script involving bishops' exclusion. Earlier, Henrietta Maria and Culpeper had supported the acceptance of bishops' exclusion (and had manipulated the gullible Falkland into agreeing with them). Now they would accept Presbyterianism. Hyde, sternly against acquiescence in both periods, was desperately concerned that Charles, who had caved in on bishops' exclusion, would falter once again. The symmetry of the events of 1640 to 1642 and those of 1646 to 1648 is revealed by virtually identical language in the account of 1640 to 1642 in the *History* and in Hyde's correspondence between 1646 and 1648. In both cases the bishops were cast as "landmarks" and "foundations" that could not be removed without grave damage to church and state.[32] Equally revealing is Hyde's startling and petulant statement that he might burn his manuscript (about the past) if Charles deviated from the course that he wished him to take (in the present).[33] As he wrote to Secretary Nicholas in March 1647, Charles "should sadly apply himself to the part he is to act, that is to suffer resolutely, and to have no tricks," as if Hyde were insisting that Charles conform to the role Hyde had assigned to him in his *History*.[34]

The interplay of the circumstances of Hyde's retirement in Jersey and his memory of the past also animated Hyde's treatment in the *History* of Tew, Falkland, and himself.

Tew had been peace; Tew had been leisure. Hyde's self-exile from the prince, the queen, and from active politics—in Jersey between 1646 and 1648—was a recovery of both. Hyde needed the break, and knew it; Virgil's line, "Deus nobis haec otia fecit," which much later he had graven in the pediment of his house at Cornbury, corresponded to moods that came to him at intervals throughout his life.[35] In July 1646 Hyde wrote to Sir John Berkeley that Jersey was a "very pleasant secure place;" Hyde would use it to "refresh and strengthen" his "mind and spirit" with "sitting still, and revolving past omissions and mistakes." In November he shared a fantasy with Secretary Nicholas: "our honest friends of the clergy . . . must erect a college here in Jersey"—Tew *redivivus*. The *convivium* at Tew had fed the belly as well as the soul; it is not surprising that in the same letter, Hyde announces with some satisfaction that "we make one very good meal a day."[36] In another letter of the same day, he promised to write to Lord Cottington as unfailingly as he used to attend another *convivium*, "at Oriel College, when there was a pasty of venison."[37] In Jersey Hyde became all but a proselytizer for the contemplative life, trying (against all reasonable hope) to convince the hyperactive Lord Digby that a spell of quiet would be "as cheerful and pleasant a part of your life as ever you enjoyed."[38]

His leisure in Jersey gave Hyde the opportunity to reflect not only upon the flurry of events of 1640 to 1642, but also upon the nature of the friend whose loss had been so cruel. In the *History*, Falkland emerges as Machiavelli's tragic protagonist, a man whose character, so admirable in the abstract, so suited to the king's peace, was overwhelmed by events. Hyde's bitterness is double: obviously he is angry at the world that destroyed Falkland, but he is also angry at Falkland, who, had he been less himself, might have been himself longer. Falkland was "too much a contemner of those arts which must be indulged in the transaction of human affairs."[39] He hoped to fight a war by the rules of peacetime civility, without employing spies or opening other people's mail. He was fooled by Hampden; fooled by those who said that the bishops' exclusion from the House of Lords was the cornerstone of their preservation in the church; and fooled by Culpeper, whom Hyde blamed for the serious error of making the king an estate of the realm in Charles's *Answer to the XIX Propositions.* According to Hyde, Falkland also sacrificed ordinary social courtesies and petty hypocrisies on the altar of his integrity. On one occasion Falkland's rudeness to the king caused remark.[40] There followed the moment in the House of Commons when the members were to tip their hats to one of their number who had done a special service (possibly Goring in his revealing of the Army Plot), and Falkland, not content with merely registering his protest by simple noncompliance, clamped both hands upon his hat and "held it close down to his head."[41] Falkland, Clarendon said more than once, acted as if he lived "in republica Platonis non in faece Romuli."[42]

Falkland would not live in the dregs of Romulus. As the civil war dragged on, his personality disintegrated. The affable and dandyish host at Tew became morose, uncivil, and unkempt as the hopes of peace faded. He recovered his former cheerfulness only when he courted death. Hyde could not bring himself to say outright what his account and others imply, that his friend died looking for a bullet.[43]

But Clarendon was, as we say, a survivor, equipped with the skills and the temperament appropriate to the world that was the inverse of Tew, the world of *negotium* (un-leisure) or as Clarendon called it again and again, of "business."[44] And here Hyde's precise relation to Tew and Falkland, loving but ultimately ambivalent, emerges. From the beginning, Hyde's connection with Falkland, with Tew, with *otium,* was both intimate and discontinuous, a romance rather than a marriage. His entire life had been punctuated by the succession or alternation of *otium* and *negotium.* When, as a young man, Hyde had become a lawyer, Ben Jonson had resented it: the poet "had for many years an extraordinary kindness for Mr. Hyde, till he found he betook himself to business."[45] Hyde came to Tew from London, not Oxford, to escape the business that soon enough reclaimed him. Indeed, judging from the early correspondence, Hyde served his friends at Tew and clerical friends elsewhere as their lawyer, the agent, so to speak, of the republica Platonis.[46] He relished the role. In 1645, momentarily forgetting his friend Falkland, Hyde complained to Jermyn of "the unaptness of most men for business" and of the "envy" of "those few, who are compelled to transact that business." Describing him in the *History,* Hyde portrayed Falkland, the future Secretary of State, as "totally unacquainted with business."[47] Hyde never forgot that the joys of *otium* were fleeting; leisure was only a lull in the action, a restorative to business.[48]

So Hyde's quarrel with Falkland was a quarrel with himself as well. Between 1646 and 1647 that quarrel took shape as a dialectic of letters on the subject of compounding with the Parliament.[49] The king's defeat made all but die-hard royalists lose heart; many acted upon what even more contemplated, a financial settlement (or composition) with the victors that would allow compromised ("delinquent") royalists to resume at least a facsimile of normal life. Hyde had found a measure of peace in Jersey, away from king, queen, prince, council, court, and business, and he himself was enough tempted by the prospect of a return to England to need to talk himself and his staunchly royalist correspondents out of compounding. Conscience was always motive to Hyde, and this is all he needed to have said. But it was not all he did say. A letter to John Earle is painfully incisive. To compound with Parliament was to give in to nostalgia for the lost *convivium.* But nostalgia would not work.

Is it possible that you can think that . . . the mere living in England with your friends could restore you to the old delight and comfort in those friends you have formerly enjoyed . . . and for your life in the parsonage of Bishopstone, . . . can you believe the company and presence of your friends . . . would have the same relish it used to have?

Hyde's thought-experiment in the sociology of compounding found the worst of it in the terror. The "saucy insolence" of inferiors was the start of a scenario of escalating demands ("every day some new ill thing required") and of constant fear. "How could you and I live in any tolerable degree of happiness in a place, where all conversation must be snares, and all commerce reproaches?"[50] Writing a few weeks later to Nicholas, Hyde said that if he could not afford the freedom of exile, he would take jail in England "rather than skulk up and down with the agony of being taken." "A gaol is a quiet place," he went on, and his friends at least would "know where to find him."[51] This, for Hyde, was all that remained of the *convivium philosophicum* in England.

It is usually supposed that reflections such as these emerged only with Hyde's return to leisure in Jersey. According to this line of thought, stated most forcefully by Brian Wormald, Hyde's account of the period before the war in the *History,* full of distress at the "defeat of civility" (in Irene Coltman's phrase), was a retrospective creation, and did not accurately portray Hyde's attitudes between 1640 and 1642.[52] Once this assumption is made, it is tempting to try to arrive at an Ur-text of Hyde's earlier position by discounting the later distortions and bitterness. The 'real' Hyde who materializes out of the smoke of this critical alchemy is an earnest reformer, only partially disenchanted with Pym and his friends, who joined with the king to get him to accept parliament's just demands. The view that Pym and his associates had engaged in a plot to destroy the king's government, that they would stop at nothing to get their way, that before the war they so threatened civility that a war was necessary to stop them—all these are seen to be the harvest of later years, of other seeds in different soil.[53]

Unfortunately, the method, which bears a resemblance to biblical higher criticism, cannot survive exposure to the actual evidence it seeks so cleverly to deduce. For example, the most magnificent of Hyde's contemporary testimonies to his reading of events in 1640 to 1642 has been quite ignored by modern scholarship, with the result that the *History* is credited with an originality it simply does not possess. Graham Roebuck, whose Clarendon bibliography goes furthest to set the record straight, correctly points to the king's declaration of 12 August 1642, which Hyde wrote, as the embryo of the pre-war part of the *History.*[54] In this declaration, Hyde fairly exploded with all the horrors, including the personal torments, that to this time he had not openly acknowledged. Their recounting make clear where and when Hyde developed his understanding of the perils of compounding.

The declaration attempted to show the connection between "the wicked and damnable combinations and conspiracies" against the king and the threat to the subject's "peace and security."[55] Amid a masterly recital of the plot's unfolding, Hyde revealed that from the beginning he had serious doubts about "the faction" as well as a certain respect, both born of fear of the "mischievousness and indefatigable industry of that malignant party." By the time of the Grand Remonstrance the pattern was all too evident. It is particularly significant for all Hyde scholarship that Hyde objected in 1642 to the Grand Remonstrance as a slander upon England's peace and

prosperity, its "blessed condition . . . to the envy of Christendom" in the years before the war.[56]

The faction destroyed that peace. For Hyde, two things were unforgettable and unforgiveable. One was the tumults. These, Hyde was convinced on the basis of reports delivered to him by Edward Kirton, had been fomented by the London chieftains of the faction, particularly Captain John Venn, who with his wife's assistance had called out his "myrmidons" as needed.[57] Nothing is more common or consistent in all of Hyde's writings on this period— whether they date to 1642 or to 1646 or after— than his insistence that the opposition bore full responsibility for the riots and the menacing petitions of December 1641 and January 1642. The perpetrators of the tumults, though themselves substantial men, had not respected the tacit understandings among men of property. They had "exposed" some of their own social rank "to be torn in pieces by the People."[58]

Horrible as the street disturbances were (and doubtless they were worse in Hyde's imagination than in fact), the tumults never touched Hyde directly. His second indictment of the faction, however, was so patently autobiographical that its presence in a declaration purportedly by the king is jarring. The faction's ruthlessness toward those "whose opinions ran not with the Torrent"[59] led them to use their power in the House of Commons and its committees to terrify their opponents into compliance. Anyone who dared to disagree risked "an Inquisition into his whole life" in order to prepare "something against him, for matter of which their Favourers were equally guilty."[60] Even more pernicious were the invasions of privacy, which Hyde called violations of the "Laws of Society and civill Conversation" and the "Laws of Hospitality and Civility."[61] The faction had sent spies to "the tables of Persons of Honour and Qualitie," had sought to "examine the discourses passed at meals and entertainments" as well as "whispers in gardens and walks." Such "monstrous things" would "render life it self unpleasant" by destroying "freedome and libertie of Conversation (the pleasure and delight of life)."[62] To make "every Room and Table a bait to betray men, and to bring them to ruine and destruction" was to declare war on the *convivium* Hyde cherished as the quintessence of cultivated life.[63] In these words, therefore, Hyde did not describe the origins of Charles' civil war, or John Pym's; rather, he defined his own.

NOTES

1. Kurt Weber, *Lucius Cary, Second Viscount Falkland* (New York, 1940). Despite the appearance of important new work on Tew, Weber's account remains useful. Since the presentation of this essay, two valuable accounts of Tew culture have appeared: Hugh Trevor-Roper, "The Great Tew Circle," in *Catholics, Anglicans, and Puritans* (London, 1987), 166–230; Richard Ollard, *Clarendon and His Friends* (London, 1987). While I have found no reason to change the substance of what I presented in February 1986, I have brought these new studies to bear on the annotation.

2. Edward Hyde, Earl of Clarendon, *History of the Rebellion and Civil Wars in England,* ed. by W. Dunn Macray, 6 vols. (Oxford, 1888), 3:180.

3. Lucius Cary, Viscount Falkland, *Sir Lucius Cary, Late Lord Viscount of Falkland, His Discourse of Infallibility* (London, 1651), "To the Right Honourable, Henry, Lord Viscount of Falkland," unpaginated, inconsistently signed.

4. Hyde 1888, 3:179.

5. The list of members of the Tew circle is adapted from Weber 1940, 82; I have not used every name in the list, but only those most important to the group. In arriving at the age differences, I have simply subtracted from the year of Falkland's birth (1610, so it is believed) the birth years of the others. Of course, this procedure can introduce errors of up to a year, but for the present, essentially statistical purpose, it is adequate. In any event Trevor-Roper is incorrect (Trevor-Roper 1987, 166) to assert that the members of the Tew circle were "all young men."

6. Compare Irene Coltman, *Private Men and Public Causes: Philosophy and Politics in the English Civil War* (London, 1962), 143.

7. Hyde 1888, 3:180.

8. Edward Hyde, Earl of Clarendon, *The History of the Rebellion . . . Also, His Life,* 2 vols. (Oxford, 1843), 2:926.

9. Hyde 1888, 1:93.

10. Hyde 1888, 1:95.

11. The culture of Tew is discussed by Weber 1940; Brian H. G. Wormald, *Clarendon: Politics, History, and Religion* (Cambridge, 1952); Coltman 1962; Hugh R. Trevor-Roper, *Edward Hyde, Earl of Clarendon* (Oxford, 1975); idem, "Clarendon and the Practice of History," in French R. Fogle and Hugh R. Trevor-Roper, *Milton and Clarendon* (Los Angles, 1965), 43–48; Trevor-Roper 1987 (especially 186–192 on Tew's adherence to Socinianism in a "wide" sense); Thomas H. Robinson, "Lord Clarendon's Moral Thought," *Huntington Library Quarterly* 43 (1979–1980), 37–59; Richard Tuck, *Natural Rights Theories: Their Origin and Development* (Cambridge, 1974), 101–118; Ollard 1987, 29–41, 335–337.

12. J. G. A. Pocock, "Superstition and Enthusiasm in Gibbon's History of Religion," *Eighteenth-Century Life* 8 (1982), 83–94; see also Hugh R. Trevor-Roper, "Religious Origins of the Enlightenment," *Religion, the Reformation, and Social Change* (London, 1967), 216–226.

13. For Falkland, see Hyde 1888, 3:186; Wormald 1952, 277–280; Lucius Cary, Viscount Falkland, *A Speech Made to the House of Commons Concerning Episcopacy* (London, 1641) [British Library, Thomason Collection, E. 196 (36)]. This speech taken as a whole and in its political context is a defense of episcopacy. It was made to prevent a root-and-branch petition from being further considered by the House of Commons; see Sir Simonds D'Ewes, *The Journal of Sir Simonds D'Ewes from the Be-*

ginning of the Long Parliament to the Opening of the Trial of the Earl of Strafford, ed. Wallace Notestein (New Haven, 1923), 335, n.9, 336. For Morley, see his famous quip about the Arminians (cited by Trevor-Roper 1967, 216) and a tract possibly by Morley, *A Modest Advertisement* (London, 1641). Thomason attributes this tract to Morley. Against this stands Morley's statement in 1661 in *A Sermon Preached at the Magnificent Coronation of . . . Charles the IId . . . the 23d of April, . . . 1661* (London, 1661), A2: "I am now past my great climacterical, and this is the first time that ever I appeared in print." See also Trevor Roper 1987, 199, 207–208, 299; Ollard 1987, 32, 37, 43.

14. [John Hales], *A Tract Concerning Schism and Schismatiques* (Oxford, 1642); on this and the connection with Laud, see the *Dictionary of National Biography,* q.v. Hales, John. Selden and Hyde were friends of the archbishop and members of his wider circle, though not uncritical or slavish followers. For Selden, see Richard Tuck, "'The Ancient Law of Freedom': John Selden and the Civil War," in *Reactions to the English Civil War 1642–1649,* ed. John Morrill (New York, 1982), 137–162.

15. Falkland 1641, 3–4, 7. The Laudians are attacked as "some bishops and their adherents."

16. Wormald 1952, x, 13, 45, 84, 93.

17. *Commons Journal,* 2:40; Trevor-Roper 1967, 300: "Fast Sermons of the Long Parliament." Morley was thanked on 1 December 1640; Trevor-Roper is in error on this point.

18. Cornwall Record Office, Carew Pole Ms. BO/25/59, 30–34. These notes do not identify the sermon as Morley's; they are part of a series of notes on the other fast sermons. This ms. is cited with the permission of its owner, Sir John Gawen Carew Pole, Bart., d.s.o., t.d., to whom I am grateful.

19. Michael Mendle, *Dangerous Positions: Mixed Government, the Estates of the Realm, and the Making of the Answer to the XIX Propositions* (Alabama, 1985), 7–9, 19–20, 148–150.

20. Henry Octavius Coxe and Sir Charles Firth, eds., *Calendar of the Clarendon State Papers Preserved in the Bodleian Library,* 5 vols. (Oxford, 1864–1970), 1:1447, 1460, 1470, 1476, 1481, 1503, 1506, 1513, 1530.

21. Richard Scrope and Thomas Monkhouse, eds., *State Papers Collected by Edward, Earl of Clarendon,* 3 vols. (Oxford, 1767–1786), 2:133–134.

22. Hyde 1888, 1:311; Mendle 1985, 148–150.

23. Mendle 1985, 141–147, esp. 144.

24. Robert Baillie, *Letters and Journals,* ed. David Laing, 3 vols. (Edinburgh, 1841–1842), 1:303.

25. D'Ewes 1923, 138–141, 335, 337 n., 341.

26. D'Ewes 1923, 420–421; *Commons Journal,* 2:91; Hyde 1888, 1:284–285.

27. British Library, Harleian ms. 163, fol. 238; BL Harl. ms. 477, fol. 107a.

28. BL Harl. ms. 163, fol. 190a: this testifies to the motivation, not the date; compare the implication of D'Ewes' casual remarks about Hyde's attitudes in BL Harl. ms. 163, fols. 336b, 381a. William Laud, *The Works of the Most Reverend Father in God, William Laud, D. D. Sometime Lord Archbishop of Canterbury,* ed. William Scott and James Bliss, 7 vols. (1847–1860; reprint New York, 1975), 3:244.

29. BL Harl. ms. 164, fols. 61a, 70a.

30. BL Harl. ms. 163, fol. 69a.

31. BL Harl. ms. 479, fols. 14a, 164a; for Falkland's social attitudes, BL Harl. ms. 163, fol. 284a. On the fenland disturbances, Keith Lindley, *Fenland Riots and the English Revolution* (London, 1982); on an aspect of their constitutional signifi-

cance, Michael Mendle and Maija Jansson, "Sauce for the Gander: Charles I's Claim of Parliamentary Privilege," *Parliamentary History* 7 (1988), 122–129.

32. Hyde 1888, 1:311, 357, 406, 568; Hyde 1843, 2:941, 953; Coxe and Firth 1864–1970, 2:326, 332–333, 338, 379.

33. Coxe and Firth 1864-1970, 2:326–327.

34. Coxe and Firth 1864-1970, 2:346.

35. Trevor-Roper 1975, 22.

36. Coxe and Firth 1864-1970, 2:241, 288–289.

37. Coxe and Firth 1864-1970, 2:290.

38. Coxe and Firth 1864-1970, 2:330-331.

39. Hyde 1888, 3:181.

40. Hyde 1888, 3:182-183.

41. Hyde 1888, 3:188-189.

42. Hyde 1888, 3:189; Hyde 1843, 2:297.

43. Hyde 1888, 3:187–189. David Nichol Smith, ed., *Characters from the Histories and Memoirs of the Seventeenth Century* (1918; reprint Oxford, 1967), 278.

44. *Negotium* and *otium* are explored in Quentin Skinner, *The Foundations of Modern Political Thought,* 2 vols. (Cambridge, 1978), 1:108, 115–116, 217–218, 276; see also idem, "Sir Thomas More's *Utopia* and the Language of Renaissance Humanism," in Anthony Pagden, ed., *The Language of Political Theory in Early-Modern Europe* (Cambridge, 1987), 123–157.

45. Hyde 1843, 2:923.

46. See note 20. Coxe and Firth 1864-1970, 2:360.

47. Coxe and Firth 1864-1970, 2:204; Hyde 1888, 1:458.

48. Coxe and Firth 1864-1970, 2:288, 331; Ollard 1987, 82–83.

49. Coxe and Firth 1864-1970, 2:284-285, 309-310, 315-317, 348-349, 363-364.

50. Coxe and Firth 1864-1970, 2:348-349.

51. Coxe and Firth 1864-1970, 2:364.

52. Coltman 1962, 36; Wormald 1952, xi.

53. Wormald 1952, 152-154, 159-160.

54. Graham Roebuck, *Clarendon and Cultural Continuity: A Bibliographical Study* (New York, 1981), 43–46. Though Roebuck implies that the declaration was not directly quoted in the *History,* it was paraphrased at length in a passage cut from the final text (Hyde 1888, 2:277–281).

55. *His Majesties Declaration to All His Loving Subjects of August 12 1642* (Cambridge, 1642) [BL E. 115 (11)], 1. Thomas H. Robinson, "Lord Clarendon's Conspiracy Theory," *Albion* 13 (1981), 96–116, recognizes that Clarendon's first conspiracy theory was rooted in 1640-1642 (97, 110–111), but Robinson does not utilize or mention this declaration. Close textual analysis of Hyde's earlier declarations would establish that Hyde had arrived at a belief in an opposition plot by stages; curiously, Wormald 1952, 93-100, begins this task.

56. *His Majesties Declaration,* 20, 24.

57. *His Majesties Declaration,* 17, 29-32, 40. Coxe and Firth 1864–1970, 1:221.

58. *His Majesties Declaration,* 48; of course, in a literal sense no member of either house suffered this fate during the tumults.

59. *His Majesties Declaration,* 71.

60. *His Majesties Declaration,* 47.

61. *His Majesties Declaration,* 45, 71.

62. *His Majesties Declaration,* 44, 45, 71.

63. *His Majesties Declaration,* 45.

RICHARD TUCK

Philosophy at the Country House: The Ideas of the Tew Circle

It is easy to forget, when talking about the owners of English country houses, that there were often spectacular differences in wealth and standing among them. Even fellow members of the peerage could differ greatly in their resources, and be fully conscious of the gap between them; the gap could be signaled by various conventions, such as, most obviously, the different titles that were bestowed (there was rarely a poor duke, and there are few even today). The wealthiest peers in the early seventeenth century had immense sums at their disposal: the earls of Devonshire, for example, may have had an annual income of some £15,000, at a time when a day laborer would earn in a good year about £15 (multiplying by 750 gives the laborer the modern income of £11,250 and the earl £11.25 million). We can put this sum in another perspective by recalling that the ordinary revenue of the government in 1600 was only about £300,000 per annum. With sums of money of this magnitude available to them, it is hardly surprising that the great peers were able to amass the kinds of riches collected in the *Treasure Houses of Britain* exhibition; but it is also not surprising that they could provide a livelihood for many interesting writers and artists who for one reason or another were not catered to by the conventional career structures.

If we consider the lives of the three most interesting English political theorists of the seventeenth century—Hobbes, Selden, and Locke—it is a remarkable and hugely important fact about all of them that they relied for their income on the patronage of one of these wealthy peers. All were themselves from relatively poor backgrounds (Selden's father was a yeoman worth £20 per annum according to Aubrey, Hobbes' was a parish clerk, and even Locke's was much

poorer than is sometimes thought); all avoided the orthodox careers open to bright, poor boys—the Church or the law. (Selden, though a practicing lawyer, never relied on this for his livelihood.) Instead, their bills were paid by noble families: Hobbes lived in the household of the earls of Devonshire from the time he left Oxford until his death, Locke lived with and greatly depended on the Earl of Shaftesbury at a crucial period in his life, and Selden lived in the houses of the Earl and Countess of Kent on Fleet Street and at Wrest in Bedfordshire, where a chamber described as "Mr Selden's room" was always kept ready for him. This last case was actually one of dependence not on the peer but on the peeress: the earls of Kent were among the poorest of the aristocracy, but Elizabeth Countess of Kent was one of the coheirs of the prodigiously wealthy Gilbert Talbot, Earl of Shrewsbury, and therefore controlled a vast fortune in her own right.

In return, such men provided their patrons with specific services. In general, these were the services with which humanists had provided patrons ever since the Renaissance (for we must not forget that they were all first and foremost trained in the *studia humanitatis*): the education of the children, secretarial assistance, and political advice. Selden, in addition, was able to provide technical legal guidance for all the heirs of the Talbot estate; coarse-minded contemporaries conjectured that he provided other services for his patroness, a piece of gossip that is related to an important issue—the fact that all of these writers were bachelors, for whom subsistence in a noble household was a complete substitute for orthodox family life. Their dissociation from the traditional professions and the orthodox family carried with it ideological messages: it is no accident that all three eventually became deeply hostile to the established Church (and Hobbes was of course equally hostile to the profession of the law), nor that they were also hostile to any kind of patriarchal political theory.

While the great country houses could foster this alternative life, potentially radically at odds with the norms of lesser society, this was not so likely to happen in smaller houses with fewer resources to exempt their occupants from the pressures of the outside world. The houses of Lord Falkland at Burford and Great Tew are a good example of what would happen at this rather lower level of society. Falkland was quite different from the great patrons we have been considering: his title was about as low an honor as one could have, being a new creation in the Scottish peerage for an Englishman, his father, a follower of the Duke of Buckingham. The family had no Scottish lands, and therefore no real interest in Scottish politics; but they were not entitled to sit in the English House of Lords. Their life-style and finances were indistinguishable from those of ordinary country gentlemen: the 1st Viscount sat as a county member in the Commons of 1620, and the 2nd did not even do that, sitting instead in the Parliaments of 1640 for the borough of Newport (Isle of Wight), a seat effectively in the gift of the Earl of Portland. Money was always a problem for the 1st Viscount, and his son's income was estimated by Edward Hyde, Earl of Clarendon, as only some £2,000, which would have put him among the poorest of the English peerage (though still giving him in modern terms an income of £1 million). By comparison, the poet Edmund Waller, a frequent visitor at Falkland's houses, is said to have had an estate worth £3,000.

Falkland could thus not act as a patron of intellectuals in the manner of the Cavendishes; what he could do was act as a host, in the style memorably recorded by Clarendon (the most striking little vignette being his description of how Falkland would not know who was visiting his house until dinner in the evening, when all would meet). The relationship between host and guests was much more one of equals than the relationship between a patron and a client could be, and it is perhaps this aspect of the life at Tew that has made it peculiarly attractive to modern eyes. It is also perhaps what made it attractive to Clarendon, who recorded with some transparency his own edgy feelings about relationships of social dominance, and how in his early life "he

was conversant with a rank of men (how worthy soever) above his quality, and engaged in an expense above his fortune, if the extraordinary accidents of his life had not supplied him for those excesses. . . . He had ambition enough to keep him from being satisfied with his own condition, and to raise his spirits to great designs of raising himself. . . . [but] he was never suspected to flatter the greatest man."[1] Both Clarendon and Falkland in fact owed their social position in the 1630s to their earlier relationship of deference to the great figure of the Duke of Buckingham, who had plucked Falkland's father from relative obscurity into the peerage, into whose family Clarendon married in 1629, and into whose former political circle the latter remarried in 1634.

As Clarendon testifies, Falkland acted as host to two kinds of men. One was a group of people of whom many had had experience of court politics under Buckingham, and who were conversant with the modern analyses of such politics. The other was a group of clergymen, men such as Sheldon, Morley, Chillingworth, Earles, Hales, and Hammond. Again, there is a certain incongruity in this mixture: court and Church were often opposed or estranged circles, and part of Tew's special character was that it bridged this divide. But the divide was bridged in a particular way: what the meetings at Falkland's houses represented was the emergence of a common culture that married reason of state to the defense of the Anglican order, and in which a political theory was to be judged by the success with which it vindicated the Anglican system of church government.

The Tew writers did not believe that theology on its own was going to vindicate the system; they were always pretty cautious, for example, about *iure divino* theories of episcopacy. But they did believe, profoundly and unshakably, that a correct understanding of political realities implied the necessity of episcopacy in England. What Clarendon wrote when in exile in 1672 would, I think, have been true for him forty years earlier:

Ill Temper of Mind and Understanding proceeds from no Cause so much, as from the Want of Knowledge or Consideration, how much of the Religion in all National Churches is of the Religion of State, nor hath any other Foundation than in Reason of State; nor is it the less Obligatory for that. . . . All Jurisdictions and Precedencies are of the Grant and Authority of Princes, and consequently Matters of State. . . . All Ceremonies, Festivals, Fasts, and

Lent *itself, (all which make up the Bulk of the* Roman *Religion) are so many Constitutions of State.*[2]

Something like this has been observed about the Tew writers before (for example by Brian Wormald), but the non-theological character of their episcopalianism has usually been presented as in some way compromising its fervor. What I want to argue is that the fact that it was a political and not a theological commitment served in no way to make them less devout—or, in the end, less self-sacrificing—Anglicans than the *iure divino* theorists.

The political writings that emanated from Tew all had this in common: they put one or other of the two principal modern accounts of politics to the service of the Church of England. These two accounts were the reason-of-state analysis provided by writers from the 1590s onward, and the natural law theories of Hugo Grotius and his followers. Although in some ways very different, these approaches both drew on the skeptical writers of the late sixteenth century to argue that conventional (Aristotelian) moral theories were clearly false, and that the principle of self-preservation was the only truly universal principle of human action. Grotius measured his own theory primarily against that of the skeptic, and a certain sympathy with skepticism remained a hallmark of the tradition that he founded. At Tew, we find all this replicated: Falkland expressed great admiration for the modern skeptics, and Chillingworth used their arguments to great effect in his *Religion of Protestants.* Clarendon himself, in his earliest work, revealed his familiarity with the reason-of-state literature: this was in an essay criticizing Sir Henry Wotton's "Parallel" between the Earl of Essex and the Duke of Buckingham, which Clarendon composed about 1634. (The date and contents of this have been overlooked by almost all writers on Clarendon.)[3] In this "Disparity," Clarendon advocated the manipulation of court factions, and provided an analysis of Buckingham very much in line with contemporary European accounts of how a king's chief minister should behave; the work constitutes an eloquent defense of Buckingham, and an attack on the "busie querulous froward time" in which he fell, which foreshadows his similar attack on the unreasonable conduct of the parliamentary leaders of the 1640s.

As I stated, within the Tew circle these ways of talking about politics had always to be di-rected to a common end, the defense of the Church of England. If they veered away, then the men responsible would be dropped, in circumstances of some savagery and rancor, even though their fundamental political ideas might have remained unaltered. One example of this which I would like to consider in some detail is both instructive and historically very important in its own right: it is the unhappy relationship of Thomas Hobbes and the Tew writers.[4] Clarendon's account of the people who visited Falkland makes no mention of Hobbes, and yet there is abundant evidence that Falkland's friends were also Hobbes': Waller, Chillingworth, Sidney Godolphin, and Gilbert Sheldon are the most obvious. Falkland himself was said by Aubrey to have been Hobbes's "great friend and admirer," while as late as 1647 Clarendon was still regarding himself as an "old acquaintance" of Hobbes, with no hint of hostility. Clarendon clearly omitted Hobbes's name from the list (and insinuated in his critique of *Leviathan* of 1676 that Hobbes was morose and unsociable—against all the other evidence) with a particular purpose: to dissociate himself and his idealized picture of Tew from what Hobbes had come to represent.

Insofar as there is a conventional explanation for this, it is that while the Tew writers found Hobbes' ideas congenial before the Civil War, they were alarmed by Hobbes' defense of the new regime in *Leviathan*—that is, the alteration in his political theory. The fact that Hobbes was an associate of theirs before 1640 is then used as evidence of the rationalistic and modern character of the philosophy that they favored, and the extent to which they could be sympathetic to ideas potentially at variance with Anglicanism. But the story of Hobbes' relationship with Tew in fact illustrates the priority over all else of the defense of the Church of England. It was because Hobbes' particular extension of the Grotian ideas seemed to provide a defense of Anglicanism that he was taken up before the Civil War; it was because he abandoned the Anglican cause (rather than simply the royalist one) that he was dropped.

This might seem a surprising claim, given the standard view that Hobbes' extreme Erastianism was always a vital part of his political theory, as adumbrated in the *Elements of Law* (1640) and *De Cive* (1642), as well as in *Leviathan.* Hobbes, according to this conventional view, always believed that the sovereign had absolute power to determine the religious life of his state, and that no particular ecclesiastical regime had anything other than certain pragmatic advantages (advantages which in *Leviathan* are firmly declared to be on the side of Independency in church government). How could such a philosophy be regarded as of any special service in the struggle to defend a specifically Anglican system?

Before answering this question, I want to document the fact that it was seen in this way, and that the break in 1651 came over Hobbes' new ecclesiastical rather than political views. A close associate of Sheldon, Hammond, and Morley was another Oxford don, Robert Payne; in the 1630s he was also particularly close to Hobbes, being the chaplain of William Cavendish, Earl of Newcastle at Welbeck, and a correspondent of Hobbes while the philosopher traveled on the Continent with the earl's son. In 1635 he expressed gratitude for favors from Clarendon, so he belonged in every respect to the Tew intellectual circles.[5] His letters to Sheldon during the late 1640s and early 1650s survive, and in them he reports to Sheldon on the correspondence which he has at the same time with Hobbes in Paris. In May 1650 Payne heard that an unauthorized English translation of *De Cive* was about to appear; he wrote to Hobbes "and desired him to prevent that translation by one of his own, but he sends me word he hath another trifle on hand, which is Politique in English, of which he hath finished thirty-seven chapters (intending about fifty in the whole), which are translated into French by a learned Frenchman of good quality, as fast as he finishes them." This "trifle" was, of course, *Leviathan*.[6]

Payne's enthusiasm for an authorized translation of *De Cive* (which never appeared, the one usually ascribed to Hobbes being the unauthorized one, translated by "C.C.") illustrates the fact that the Tew writers and their associates were not at all worried by the arguments in that work; indeed, Payne obviously regarded it as a statement of his own royalist and Anglican position. So, it should be said, did "C.C.," who arranged for his translation to be published adorned with royalist iconography and dedicated to a leading royalist lady. But when Payne got into correspondence with Hobbes over the contents of the new work, he received a nasty shock. There is no suggestion in his letters to Sheldon that it was the political theory of *Leviathan* that disturbed him: as we know, it was in its essentials the same as that of *De Cive,* and Hobbes had not yet composed the wounding "Review and Conclusion" at the end of *Leviathan.* Instead, it was Hobbes's new repudiation of the "tribe" of bishops:

I have written to my friend abroad again and again since I writ to you last, and heard from him; he assures me he hath no particular quarrel to that tribe, only this position he shall set down and confirm, that the Civil sovereign (whether one or more) is chief pastor, and may settle what kind of Church government he shall think fit for the people's salvation; which will be enough to justify those who have cassierd Bishops already, and may tempt others who have not, to follow their example. The truth is, I fear, he is engaged too far already to retreat, and therefore I have small hopes to prevail, yet in my last I commended this consideration to him, that all truths are not fit to be told at all times, and if the argument he had undertaken did necessarily require that he should publish it, yet I should expect even for the antiquity's sake of that order. . . . it should not be so indifferent with him, but that it should find at least as much favour with him in regard of Presbyterians and Independents, as monarchy had done in respect of Democr. and Aristoc.[7]

Once one is alerted to the fact that Hobbes' theory of church government in *Leviathan* came as a surprise to men whose knowledge of his views was based on *De Cive* or the *Elements of Law* (a manuscript copy of which, incidentally, Payne possessed), then one can read those earlier works in a different light, and see that they do indeed contain a very obvious and rather plausible apologia for a specifically Anglican system. During the time of his association with the Tew writers, Hobbes (like them) was an Anglican apologist:

*There are two kindes of controversies, the one about spiri-*tuall matters, *that is to say, questions of faith, the truth whereof cannot be searcht into by naturall reason; such are the questions concerning* the nature and office of Christ, of rewards and punishments to come, of the Sacraments, of outward worship, *and the like: the other, about questions of humane science. . . . Seeing to the end we may attaine aeternal salvation, we are oblig'd to a supernatural Doctrine, & which therefore it is impossible for us to understand; to be left so destitute, as that we can be deceiv'd in necessary points, is repugnant to aequity. This infallibility our Savior* Christ promis'd (in those things which are necessary to Salvation) to his Apostles untill the day of judgement; that is to say, *to the Apostles, and Pastors succeeding the Apostles who were to be consecrated by the imposition of hands. He therefore who hath the Soveraigne power in the City, is oblig'd as a Christian, where there is any question concerning* the Mysteries of Faith, *to interpret the Holy Scriptures by* Clergy-men lawfully ordain'd.[8]

Much could be said about the way in which this passage illustrates fundamental features of the Tew outlook—for example, the argument that the infallibility of the Church relates only to those things necessary for faith was the central doctrine of both Chillingworth and Falkland in their writings on infallibility. The point I want to stress, however, is that in 1642 Hobbes used his general political theory to underpin Anglicanism; in 1650 (for reasons which are not yet entirely clear) he abandoned this bit of his enterprise, and his old friends from Tew refused ever to associate with him again. Hammond denounced *Leviathan* in 1652 as "a farrago of Christian atheism,"[9] and Clarendon, of course, wrote a full-scale attack on the book; Hobbes after 1666 even feared that he might be tried for heresy by a Church now headed by Sheldon. The men of Tew were open minded, modern and liberal, when being so helped the cause of their Church; when it did not, they had no more time for modern ideas than the most obscurantist royalist. It was in the great country houses such as Hardwick, the home of the earls of Devonshire and of Hobbes, that genuinely new ideas could flourish: perhaps, in the end, the culture of Tew and Burford was not so different from that of the houses of the royalist squires from among whom Falkland's father had been plucked by Buckingham.

NOTES

1. Edward Hyde, Earl of Clarendon, *The History of the Rebellion . . . Also, His Life,* 2 vols. (Oxford, 1843), 933.

2. Edward Hyde, Earl of Clarendon, *A Collection of Several Tracts* (London, 1727), 262.

3. "The Difference and Disparity between the Estate and Condition of George, Duke of Buckingham, and Robert, Earl of Essex," in Sir Henry Wotton, *Reliquiae Wottoniae* (London, 1685), 185. The date of this work is provided by Sir John Bramston, *Autobiography,* Camden Society 6 (1845), 255.

4. The relationship between Hobbes and Tew is depicted in Gilbert Sheldon's correspondence with Robert Payne and Henry Hammond, in "Illustrations of the State of the Church during the Great Rebellion," *The Theologian and Ecclesiastic* 6 (1848), 161–174, 212–226.

5. Payne's relationship with Clarendon may be deduced from a letter in J. Halliwell, *A Collection of Letters Illustrative of the Progress of Science* (London, 1841), 69.

6. Payne's letters are touched on in Thomas Hobbes, *De Cive* (Latin version), ed. Howard Warrender (Oxford, 1983), 14; Richard Tuck, "Warrender's *De Cive,*" *Political Studies* 33 (1985), 308–315, also deals with the question of the translation of *De Cive* into English.

7. "Illustrations of the State of the Church," 173.

8. Thomas Hobbes, *De Cive* (English version), ed. Howard Warrender (Oxford, 1983), 248–249.

9. "Illustrations of the State of the Church during the Great Rebellion," *The Theologian and Ecclesiastic* 9 (1850), 294.

MARK GIROUARD

The Country House and the Country Town

This paper derives from my work in progress on a study of the English town. It is concerned with the relationship between country towns and country houses, and in particular with the effect that this relationship had on the planning and contents of the latter.

Perhaps I had better start by defining what I mean by *country town*. I mean towns other than London, other than the new resort towns of the eighteenth century, such as Bath and Brighton, and other than the new manufacturing or trading towns that sprang up in the course of the century, notably Birmingham and Liverpool. I am concerned with the towns that had been the centers of their local areas for several hundred years.

The relationship that these towns had with the country-house owners who lived within their catchment area was complex. There were many different connections that on the whole worked or could work to mutual advantage. The business patronage of country-house owners brought trade and employment to the country town. Charities, hospitals, and schools received generous donations from the country-house aristocracy and gentry. Town bridges, as in the case of the great eighteenth-century bridge at Shrewsbury, were often paid for in whole or part by the country-house owners of the neighborhood. And country towns also benefited from the protection and support that any country-house owner who was powerful in London could give to them. It was for this reason that, from the sixteenth century onward, one finds country towns beginning to choose country-house owners rather than the town merchants, manufacturers, or professional people as their Members of Parliament.

Country-house owners, in their turn, relied on the local town for a wide variety of services, and quite often lived there for a portion of the year. Above all, in the course of the eighteenth century, as Parliament grew in importance, the fact that so many country towns sent two members to Parliament became more and more relevant to country-house owners seeking to increase their power and status. With a little work an ambitious family could build up an interest in a town, and to a greater or lesser extent control who was elected its Members of Parliament. The way in which the country-house owners muscled in on country towns politically, and the different methods by which they took over or managed their parliamentary representation, is a fascinating study. It is also a very complex one, and there are all sorts of variations that I cannot go into. But it is worthwhile looking at a few examples.

There were some country towns that were almost totally dominated by one powerful local family. The town hall of Buckingham stands at the end of the main street of the little town, and floating above it, on top of the cupola, one can still see the swan (fig. 1) that was one of the crests of the dukes of Buckingham, who lived up the road at Stowe (fig. 2). They were an extremely powerful family on a national scale, but they also owned considerable property in and around the town, and dominated it politically and socially. The two Members of Parliament for Buckingham were for all intents and purposes actually appointed by the dukes of Buckingham and their predecessors at Stowe, and were very often members of the Stowe family. In a paper given at this symposium, William McClung discusses the country house as Arcadia. This aspect is much in evidence at Stowe, but Stowe also functioned as a power center. Its Arcadian character derives from its temples, lakes, and magically beautiful glades and vistas; its power is almost brutally symbolized by the dead-straight, four-mile-long avenue that connects it to the town and is angled on the spire of Buckingham

church at one end and the great central portico of Stowe at the other.

In spite of this overawing power, the Stowe family observed the proprieties, and probably could only keep absolute control by doing so. Thus they fostered what was called their "interest." Interest was a vital eighteenth-century concept, which was of the greatest importance to country-house families. A family's interest was based on its possession of land or town property, but was increased by the superstructure of good will that derived from getting jobs for people, bringing business to them, and entertaining at all levels of society. In order to help maintain the powerful family interest in Buckingham, every now and then the whole town corporation was trundled up that immensely long avenue and entertained with meals at Stowe. In 1775 Mrs. Lybbe Powys, the great eighteenth-century traveler, complained bitterly of the discomfort and squalor of the little inn at one of the main en-

Fig. 1.
The swan, crest of the dukes of Buckingham, on Buckingham town hall   (Photograph: author)

Fig. 2.
The south front of Stowe House, Buckinghamshire   (Photograph: author)

trances to Stowe, but relented when she realized that the Stowe family could not improve it without taking business from the inns in Buckingham itself. "Interest," she wrote, "must be kept at such places."[1]

There were many places that needed more complex management than towns such as Buckingham, because, for various reasons, control was harder to achieve; the town might be larger, the voters more numerous or independent, or the family less powerful. Such towns needed continuous nursing. An interesting example is the relationship between Bury St. Edmunds and the Hervey family, earls of Bristol, who lived just outside Bury at Ickworth. The Herveys were well-established courtiers, but were much less rich and powerful than the great family at Stowe, and Bury was a bigger town than Buckingham. Ickworth, before its grand neo-classical remodeling between 1796 and 1830, was quite a modest house, but the Herveys also built a handsome town house on the main square in Bury St. Edmunds (fig. 3). At both houses they sedulously buttered up the town council, who were the electoral body in Bury, as is described in the Hervey family diaries and papers.[2] As a result of

careful feeding of their interest by this and other means (such as canvassing in London for donations to Bury Grammar School), they managed to control one of the two parliamentary seats belonging to Bury St. Edmunds, and fill it either with a member of the Hervey family or with a friend or nominee. The other seat was left, by mutual agreement, to the control of another powerful local family, the dukes of Grafton. Such deals were a commonplace in the eighteenth century.

Many country towns were politically important to country-house owners because they were also county towns, the local administrative centers of their respective counties. The counties had been run since the sixteenth century by local Justices of the Peace. In the eighteenth century these were drawn from landed gentry and Church of England clergy, who were often related to the gentry. They ran the county from the buildings variously known as sessions houses, county halls, shire halls, and assize courts, which were in part local courts of law but also centers of local government. County matters were decided by the justices either by the procedure known as "presentment" in the pu-

Fig. 3.
The Earl of Bristol's town house, Bury St. Edmunds, Suffolk   *(Country Life)*

Fig. 4.
The shire hall and county jail,
Warwick   (Photograph: author)

Fig. 5.
One of the court rooms in the shire
hall, Warwick   (*Country Life*)

Fig. 6.
The assize courts, York   (Royal Commission on Historical Monuments)

blic courts or upon retiring at the end of the court session into a room known as the grand jury room. Here they met together privately and, according to their critics, fixed rather too much business away from the public eye.

The county hall in Warwick is one of the first and finest of an impressive series of eighteenth-century county buildings. It was built between 1753 and 1758 to the design of Sanderson Miller, a country-house owner and an amateur architect; an almost equally impressive county jail was built next door between 1779 and 1782 (fig. 4). The county hall contains the actual hall, off of which are two octagonal court rooms, to either side of

the grand jury room (fig. 5). The hall was used for the county meetings, which were another important aspect of political life in county towns. The freeholders of the county, who included and were completely dominated by the country-house owners, met either to discuss who was going to be elected as Member of Parliament for the county or to send up remonstrances or messages to Parliament in London. One of the most exquisite of eighteenth-century county buildings is the assize courts at York, designed by the York architect John Carr between 1773 and 1775 to contain octagonal courts to either side of a grand county room or hall (figs. 6, 7). Another fine collection of county buildings survives at Lancaster Castle, which was the center of county government in Lancashire. Its shire hall was used both for the sessions of the assizes when the judges came on circuit and for county meetings (fig. 8); it and adjacent rooms, including a grand jury room, were designed by Thomas Harrison from 1788 onward, all in the gothic style, as part of his remodeling of the medieval castle.

Very often the choice of a county Member of Parliament was fixed at a county meeting so that there was no need for an actual election. Elections took place only when there was a clear disagreement between the freeholders who turned up at the county meeting. On occasion the contests could be very bitter, both in county and town elections. Hogarth's famous picture

Chairing the Member (Sir John Soane's Museum) shows what was a common custom at the end of a disputed election when everyone on the electoral roll had been well bribed and boozed. The successful member was carried around the town by often extremely drunken supporters who at intervals would toss him up in the air, an experience that plumper or less intrepid new Members of Parliament could find alarming. The handsome chair used in elections at Norwich actually survived until recently.

The services that country towns offered increased in number and sophistication throughout the eighteenth century, and were another inducement to country-house owners to come into town. Apart from the services of doctors, lawyers, and other professional men, a whole series of what can be described as services of an artistic nature were on offer, involving architects, painters, sculptors, woodcarvers, furniture-makers, and silversmiths. There were more and more of these people producing, on the whole, better and better work throughout the century. Much has been published on this in recent years, and increasingly it has been established exactly what was available in these country towns, to what extent they provided an alternative service to London, and what high quality many of them achieved. I will take a quick look at some examples, starting with York.

Fig. 7.
One of the court rooms of the assize courts, York (Royal Commission on Historical Monuments)

Fig. 8.
The shire hall, Lancaster (*Country Life*)

In the eighteenth century York was one of the most important and successful provincial centers from a social point of view, although in terms of manufacture and commerce it was in decline. It offered a complex array of services,[3] including the work of several architects of whom the most famous and successful was the redoubtable Carr of York. Carr started as little more than a builder and ended with a great fortune of over one hundred thousand pounds. He designed buildings of all sorts all over the north of England, including a great many country houses and a number of public buildings, such as the York Assize Courts. He established a high-powered body of craftsmen to serve him. Fairfax House in York, which he remodeled for Lord Fairfax between 1760 and 1763, has exquisite plasterwork that was probably done by the Italian stuccador Cortese (fig. 9). Carr later established a native York school of plasterers, including the Roses, who were to become one of the main eighteenth-century plastering dynasties in England. A traveling Italian painter, Andrea Soldi, was in York for a few years in the early eighteenth century, and painted numerous portraits of local country-house families, notably a whole series of the Fauconberg family of Newburgh Priory. Phillippe Mercier was a French painter who failed to make the grade in London and settled in York from about 1739 to 1751, with more success. He painted both the local gentry and their children, and families such as the Fothergills, who were mainly resident in York (fig. 10). Both Mercier and Soldi were competent and charming artists. York also acquired a whole range of shops providing luxury goods from behind elegant facades in the style of the most advanced London shops of the period; a number of these still survive.

But it isn't only in York that one finds this kind of development; one can find it in country towns all over England. In Shrewsbury, for instance, Thomas Farnolls Pritchard has been put on the map by the research of John Harris.[4] Pritchard was a combined builder, sculptor, and furniture designer, living in Shrewsbury, who designed numerous country houses in the area and could run up interior designs for anyone who wanted them. He had his own little group of sculptors and woodcarvers. A number of his designs for houses in the Shrewsbury area, such as Croft Castle, Condover Hall, and Bitterley Court, survive. Very often, written on the drawings, are estimates of the cost and the names of the craftsmen who were going to do the work.

A table at Burghley House in Lincolnshire (fig. 11) carries the label of the Stamford craftsman, Henry Tatam.[5] He had worked for Cobb, one of the most fashionable of London furniture-makers, and so put "From Mr. Cobb's, London" at the top of his label (fig. 12). Tatam moved up from London to the busy and prosperous little town of Stamford, where he became a successful maker of furniture. He did a good deal of work for the family of the earls of Exeter at Burghley, which is just outside Stamford. He settled in Stamford in 1772, and by 1797 was able to build himself an elegant little house on Barn Hill, which was one of the two most select

Fig. 10.
The Fothergill Family by Philippe Mercier, oil on canvas (York City Art Gallery)

Fig. 11.
A table at Burghley House, Stamford, made by Henry Tatam (*Country Life*)

streets in Stamford; amusingly enough, the house is detailed more like a cabinet than a masonry building (fig. 13). Another country house that contains local furniture is Burton Constable in Yorkshire. The research of Dr. Ivan Hall has shown how very heavily William Constable,

who remodeled Burton Constable in the mid-eighteenth century, relied on local craftsmen.[6] Among them, Jeremiah Hargrave, who was originally from Beverley and then moved on to Hull, was responsible for furniture of very high quality in the dining room. There was a whole group of these Yorkshire furniture-makers in York, Beverley, and Hull.

One also finds numerous painters settled in towns all over England. In Norwich, for instance, Thomas Bardwell advertised in the local paper on 10 June 1738, to announce that he was prepared to provide "Historys, Land-skips, Signs, Shewboards, Window-Blinds, Flower-Pots for Chimneys, and House-Painting in imitation of all sorts of Wood, Stone and Mahogany." In short, he would do anything for a country-

Fig. 12.
Henry Tatam's business label   *(Country Life)*

Fig. 13.
Tatam's house in Barn Hill, Stamford   (Royal Commission on Historical Monuments)

house owner from decorating his drawing room to painting a view of his house. A number of the latter views survive, and very charming they are. In his way Bardwell is a minor master, but sometimes one finds a major master working in a country town, usually an artist born locally who spends an initial period in his neighborhood town. This was the case with Thomas Hudson at Exeter, with Joshua Reynolds at Plymouth, and with Thomas Gainsborough. Gainsborough set up as an artist in his birthplace, the little Suffolk town of Sudbury, worked for a time in Ipswich, moved on to Bath, and ended up in London. Each move was a step upward in terms of his career, but in the opinion of many people, myself included, his Ipswich pictures are as good as anything that he ever did.

Country-house owners also lived in country towns, as well as using their services. It has become something of a cliché to say of the Georgian houses in any attractive town that they were the houses of the local country-house owners who came into the town for the winter. This did happen, but has been much exaggerated. It was a feature of a few towns, of which York is the most important example, but on the whole the fine domestic architecture in country towns was the product of the town establishment rather than of country-house owners.

The grander families only had a house in a country town if for some reason this was important for their political patronage. For instance, the earls of Bradford had a house in Shrewsbury, which they used as a base for their control of parliamentary elections in Shrewsbury, in much the same way that the earls of Bristol used their house in Bury St. Edmunds. But on the whole such families had their town house in London, spent the winter and spring there, and came into their local country town relatively seldom, to county meetings or to a week or two of festivities in the summer. In York, for instance, the local grandees, such as the Earl of Carlisle at Castle Howard, the Marquis of Rockingham at Wentworth Woodhouse, and the Earl of Burlington at Londesborough, did not have town houses. When they came into York they rented a house or prestigious lodgings for a week or more, but it was not worth their while to maintain a permanent house.

York was especially notable for town houses belonging to local landowners who were middling and lesser country-house owners, a rank below the grandees. Their favorite place of residence in York was Micklegate. What is now 86 Micklegate, for instance, was for a time the town house of a Yorkshire landowner with the pleasing name of Abstrupus Danby, who owned a charming but modest country house called Swinton Hall. The neighboring and more elegant house in Micklegate was designed by Carr of York and finished in 1752 for John Bourchier, one of the most important country-house owners with a house in York. He lived at

Beningbrough Hall, a rather grand, though not enormous baroque house not very far from York (fig. 14).

Fairfax House, which has already been referred to, belonged to Lord Fairfax, whose country seat was at Gilling Castle, about twenty miles out of York. Lord Fairfax was, I think, the only peer who had a permanent house in York in the eighteenth century. He had previously, like other lords, spent the winter and spring seasons in London, but was in increasing financial difficulty and finally decided to move to the cheaper ambience of York. He acquired what became Fairfax House, in Castlegate, and got Carr to remodel it for him. Grand though the house was, his move to York was essentially a confession that he, like the painter Mercier (if for different reasons), had failed to make it in London.[7]

But even in York, where country-house owners figured so prominently among the residents, one must never forget what can be called the town gentry. These were a mixture of people with private incomes (including widows and cadet branches of country-house families), lawyers, doctors, clergymen, and the more prosperous merchants and manufacturers, who often profited financially from dealing with country-house families, to a certain extent mixed with them socially, but who lived primarily in the towns. Just across the road from Fairfax House, for instance, is an equally imposing house also designed by Carr of York, in this case not for a country-house owner but for Peter Johnson, the Recorder of York, the main legal official in the town government (fig. 15). York also contains examples of another situation found in many towns, that of the successful town family which made enough money to acquire a country house. A nice little house on Duncombe Place was built in about 1700 by Sir William Robinson, who was a Member of Parliament for York, Lord Mayor in 1700, and belonged to an old York merchant family. About twenty years after building the town house, he acquired a country estate at Newby, near Ripton, and there built a small but much more elegant country house to the designs of the Palladian architect Colen Campbell.

If one looks at Shrewsbury, one finds the same mixture of houses belonging to country and town gentry. The Shrewsbury house of the Newports, earls of Bradford, who effectively controlled the parliamentary representation of Shrewsbury in the late seventeenth and early eighteenth centuries, has already been referred to. But it is worth noting that when the parliamentary interest of the Newports was taken over by the Pulteney family (under circumstances that provide one of the great horror stories of eighteenth-century town life),[8] the latter did not feel it necessary to have a house in the town. The grandest of the surviving eighteenth-century houses in Shrewsbury was designed by Thomas Pritchard, built at the expense of William Pulteney, Earl of Bath, but lived in by the attorney Charles Bolas, Pulteney's political agent in the town (fig. 16).

In many towns one finds impressive houses that were built or occupied by people who lacked even this kind of connection with country-house owners. The grandest house surviving in the town of Warwick, for instance, was built by Job Lee, a prosperous baker who was mayor in the early eighteenth century. His house, which is on the market place, was built to the designs of his son-in-law Francis Smith, one of the most interesting of the many architects (or builders turned architects) whose practice was based in a country town. Another interesting type of house ownership is represented in Warwick by the structure now known as Landor House. This was originally built by a successful doctor in the late seventeenth century, and then, in the mid-eighteenth century, was acquired by Dr. Landor, the father of the poet Walter Savage Landor. Dr. Landor owned land in several counties and a country house not very far from Warwick, but his estates seem to have been either small, or mortgaged, or both. His country house had been largely demolished, and his country residence was a patched-up and not very attractive building converted out of the stable block. Landor's main activity was his medical practice in Warwick and he seems only to have spent the summers, or to have camped out occasionally, on his property in the country. Many of these town-gentry families owned some form of country property or summer retreat, but their main residence was still in the town.

It is worth taking a look at Norwich, which contains many fine eighteenth-century houses, and used to contain even more. Norwich was the main textile center in England until the end of the eighteenth century, when the industry was finally overtaken by the Yorkshire wool towns. Many of the best Norwich houses were built by families that had made their money in textiles. Its clothiers and manufacturers were an interesting and enlightened set of people. Perhaps the

Fig. 16.
Swan Hill Court House, Shrewsbury (Photograph: author)

Fig. 15.
Castlegate House, Castlegate, York (Photograph: author)

finest house to survive (which is on Surrey Street) was not built by a country-house owner, but by a man called John Patteson who made a sizeable fortune in the textile trade; he had this house designed for him in 1764 by Robert Mylne, a good London architect. John Patteson's son (also called John) went on the Grand Tour as a young man, met up with John Soane, traveled in Italy with him, and became one of Soane's patrons and his lifelong friend, as has been discussed and described by Pierre du Prey.[9] An especially elegant house on All Saints' Plain was built by John Morse, a Norwich brewer with sporting interests. He was one of a group of gentlemanly Norwich citizens who ran the local Carrow Abbey Hunt, and hunted the surrounding countryside; but Morse, as far as I know, did not own a country house. As far as I can establish, very few country-house families had houses in Norwich in the eighteenth century.

Country gentry and town gentry between them generated what can be called a polite society in each country town. A full social life grew up to cater to this society. It was based on two seasons: a long and less prestigious winter season, which in most towns ran from late October until March, and a shorter but much more glamorous summer season, which was usually geared to the two weeks of the summer assizes, when visiting judges came from London to the country town, and to the week of the summer race meet-

ing. The visit of judges to a country town became a great social event partly because the Grand Jury sat for the assizes and was made up of local justices of the peace, that is, of local country-house owners, rather than of the more modest middle-class people who sat on ordinary juries. The families involved in sitting on the Grand Jury, as well as all of the country gentry and often the local aristocracy, came into the town to participate in a whole series of social events that took place in addition to the actual assizes. The judges were escorted into the town in a procession, headed by the sheriff, who was always a local country-house owner, and by his guard of javelin carriers; riding behind the judge himself there was usually a large assortment of local country gentry.

One finds the same kind of social activities taking place during race week. The grand families, who in winter were away in London, were in their country houses for the summer and came into town for the races. Race meetings varied in size and glamour according to the neighborhood. Families would often drive onto the course in coaches from which they watched the races. Sometimes rather crude little stands were built as well, but the more successful race meetings acquired elaborate and fanciful grandstands built specifically for local country-house owners. At York, which had the most prestigious of all race meetings in the eighteenth century, a very

Fig. 17.
The racestand, York (York City Art Gallery)

elegant grandstand (fig. 17) was built in 1754 by John Carr of York at the expense of a great local magnate, the Marquis of Rockingham; the commission was the starting point of Carr's successful career as an architect. Eighteenth-century grandstands took the form of a big room at ground level for refreshment and entertainment, and terraces above, covered or open or both, for viewing the races. A charming but pathetic example of the type exists in ruins outside Stamford. It was built in 1766 for a race meeting long ago abandoned. It is sad that it has not been maintained, because it is a unique survival; at some stage it was turned into a barn, but it is now no longer even used as such and is in full decay.

Another important event that almost inevitably occurred at both race week and assize week was the arrival of a good touring company for a week or more of theatrical performances. Theaters were part of the central round of social life in country towns, reaching their peak of activity in race or assize weeks, but also visited by touring companies in the winter months. The theaters were nearly always modest buildings with few architectural pretensions. An unusually elegant one survives at Bury St. Edmunds, designed for the corporation by Robert Adam between 1775 and 1780, above a covered market. It, like the theater at Stamford (1766–1768; fig. 18), has lost its interior. Complete eighteenth- or early nineteenth-century theaters survive in a later example at Bury St. Edmunds, and at Bristol and Richmond in Yorkshire. An amusing engraving of a very thin house in a provincial theater, in Pierce Egan's *Life of an Actor* (1825), makes the point that whereas in race and assize weeks any theater could rely on a good audience, in the much less frequented winter season it was often hard to fill the house. Nearly all of these country-town theaters were in a greater or lesser state of financial crisis.

The most important center of social life in all country towns was the assembly room or rooms. Assemblies first appeared in England early in the eighteenth century; the fact that the first English examples were often referred to as *assemblées* suggest that they originated in France. Assemblies in private houses and in public rooms developed rather differently from each other. Public assemblies consisted of groups of subscribers meeting together, mainly to dance but also to play cards, take tea or refreshments, or to just talk and gossip. They became extremely popular. To begin

Fig. 18.
The theater, Stamford   (Royal Commission on Historical Monuments)

with, they took place in any large room that was available. Hogarth's picture of a country dance, from his *Marriage à la Mode* series (fig. 19), appears to show dancing at a provincial assembly held in a pre-eighteenth century building with latticed glazing; the fact that there is what looks like a royal coat of arms over the window suggests that the location may be the big room of a courthouse. It is worth noticing the full moon shining through the window in the picture; the significance of this is that assemblies were usually held at or close to the time of a full moon, so that in addition to people living in the town, local country-house owners could drive in to at-

tend and then drive back by the light of the moon. The catchment area seems to have included any house within about a ten-mile radius.

The frequency of assemblies varied from town to town, depending on their importance. York Assembly Rooms had a weekly dancing assembly, a weekly concert, and a weekly card assembly. In most towns dancing assemblies took place once every two weeks or once a month, card assemblies perhaps more frequently. Dancing assemblies, which drew more people and took up more room, offered both cards and dancing. Tea and perhaps light refreshments were served; provision of supper seems to have been a rarity at early eighteenth-century assemblies, but grew more common later.

In the course of the eighteenth century many newly built town halls and county halls were also designed to provide rooms for assemblies. The splendid Great Room in Carr of York's town hall at Newark (1776) is a fine example. In the building known as the court house (but in effect built as a town hall) at Warwick, which was designed by Francis Smith in 1725, the big room on the first floor was used both by the town corporation for its banquets, and for winter assemblies that were, according to an early nineteenth-century description, "graced with all the beauty and fashion of the county."[10] Sometimes theater and assembly rooms were combined in one building, as in the charming example that survives in Truro. But many new buildings were erected just for assemblies. The grandest and best known example is at York, and was designed by the Earl of Burlington between 1731 and 1732. It has an enormous columned hall (renowned among architectural historians as an attempt to reconstruct an Egyptian hall as described by Vitruvius) and lower and smaller rooms to either side. The great room was only used in race and assize weeks, when there were enough people to fill it. In winter the dancing assemblies took place in the smaller rooms.

Assembly rooms in general, and the York ones in particular, are usually thought of as the creation of local country-house owners, but as far as I can discover from my research to date, this was seldom the case. Those that I have been able to document were mainly the creation of the town gentry, although their promoters inevitably aimed at bringing in the country aristocracy and gentry as well, because both their subscriptions and their prestige were needed. Francis Drake, in a history of York published in 1736, says of the York Assembly Rooms that "the design was first set on foot by a set of public spirited gentlemen for the most part resident in the city." The list of those who subscribed to the cost of buying the site and building the rooms contains large numbers of the aristocracy and country gentry, but also a selection of the York gentry of all sorts, including, for instance, a draper, an apothecary, a surgeon, a wine merchant, an attorney, and a grocer. The steering committee that was responsible for getting the scheme under way does seem to bear out Drake's statement that building the assembly rooms was mostly the idea of the town gentry, for the three most active people on the committee were a York attorney and two members of well-known York merchant families.

In fact the town gentry in York, including the members of the corporation, were very conscious of the advantages of bringing country-house owners to live in York. The textile industry, which had been of great importance in York, was for various reasons in total decline by the beginning of the eighteenth century, so the city was in need of a separate source of income. As Drake puts it, "our races and the residence of the gentry amongst us, in our present decay of trade, seems to be the chief support of the city. Our magistrates take great care that families of this sort should be encouraged to live here by allowing of all innocent diversions, making of public walks for their entertainment, etc."[11] Promenading on a public walk was an essential part of the social life of polite society in all country towns. The promenade at York was known as the New Walk, and ran along the river on the edge of the city (fig. 20). The man who laid it out was an apothecary called John Marsden, a member of the town council (which paid for its construction in the 1730s) and also one of the original subscribers to the assembly rooms. A similar example of a town council promoting "innocent diversions" can be found a decade or so later at Doncaster. The new mansion house there was built partly for mayoral entertainments, but perhaps even more for winter assemblies and assemblies at the Doncaster race meeting, which the corporation of Doncaster was trying to promote for much the same reasons as was the corporation of York. Accordingly, in 1744, its members commissioned James Paine to design this magnificent building and its series of rooms.

A similar story lies behind the assembly house in Norwich, which was built in 1754. An anony-

Fig. 19.
Detail of *The Happy Marriage* by William Hogarth, oil on canvas (National Gallery)

mous diarist, writing in 1753, made a note of "great designs on foot by several gentlemen of the city for purchasing ground in order to build a grand fabric both for an assembly room and playhouse." One can verify his statement about gentlemen of the city being responsible, since copies of the original deeds survive.[12] The site was acquired from a local country-house owner, the Earl of Buckinghamshire, by a group of seven people in the city, six of whom were members of the corporation, and nearly all of whom were involved in one way or another in the local textile trade. They brought in twenty more people to form with them a group of "proprietors," who put up the money and took whatever profits there were. In the end this group was made up of sixteen town gentry and eleven country gentry. The country gentry included the Earl of Buckinghamshire, who was also the ground landlord, his son Lord Hobart, two baronets, Sir William Harbord and Sir Randal Ward, and a selection of local country gentlemen. The town gentry included, in addition to the ones already mentioned, a worsted weaver, a wool merchant, the town clerk, a silversmith, a dyer, and a grocer. One must not think of a grocer in contemporary terms as a man behind a counter; he was

likely to have had a substantial wholesale as well as retail trade. In fact, the town proprietors were all among the richest and most established citizens of Norwich, but they had clearly brought in country-house owners as proprietors in order to give prestige to the whole operation. James Burrough, the Cambridge amateur architect, was commissioned to design the interior and possibly the exterior of the new building, which in the end contained assembly rooms but no theater. It included what had become the requisites for all assembly rooms of any pretensions: a room for dancing, a room for playing cards, and a room for taking tea or supper. At one stage of the evening the dancing would stop, everyone would go in to tea or supper, and then go back to dancing.

The Norwich rooms were decorated with considerable elegance and richness, but were not quite as splendid as the assembly rooms in Derby, which went up between 1763 and 1764. These followed the plan of the York rooms, with a great central hall running from end to end and lower rooms to either side. The exterior was the work of a Derby architect, Joseph Pickford, but the magnificent interior was by Robert Adam. Alas, the building was completely destroyed by

Fig. 21.
The assembly room in the Lion Hotel, Shrewsbury   (B. T. Batsford, Ltd.)

fire some years ago. Among the best surviving assembly rooms is the more modest but delicately decorated one built onto the back of the Lion Hotel in Shrewsbury; numerous assembly rooms in country towns were attached to a hotel or inn in this way. The entrepreneur responsible was John Ashby, a Shrewsbury attorney who was in with all the local gentry, managed their affairs, had his finger in every sort of pie, and in the end acquired a country estate. In addition to a lot of other property in the town, he owned the Lion, and at one stage lived next door to it.[13] The elegant plasterwork in the assembly room (fig. 21) was probably designed by Thomas Pritchard; certainly the charming lion that surmounts the end of the room externally was carved by Nelson, who was one of Pritchard's carvers.

What were the effects and purposes of all these assembly rooms? There is no doubt that one of their most useful and popular functions was as a marriage market. As early as 1722, John Macky wrote, "these assemblies are very convenient for young people; for formerly the country ladies were stewed up in their father's old mansion houses and seldom saw company but at an assize, a horse race or a fair. But by the means of these assemblies, matches are struck up, and officers of the army have had pretty good success, where ladies are at their own disposal; as I know several instances about Worcester, Shrewsbury, Chester, Derby, or York."[14] One can actually observe this marriage market in operation in an undated letter from Lady Mary Wortley Montagu. It refers to none less than the great architect John Vanbrugh, who was currently working at Castle Howard and therefore attending the assemblies in York. These were held in what had been a private house in the town, as Burlington's Rooms had not yet been built. Lady Mary describes how "for those that don't regard worldly muck," by which she means the fortunes of women with their own money, "there's extraordinary good choice indeed. I believe last Monday there were 200 pieces of women's flesh, fat and lean. But you know Van's taste was always odd, his inclination to ruins has given him a fancy for Mrs. Yarborough. He sighs and ogles that it would do your heart good to see him, and she is not a little pleased. In so small a proportion of men among such a number of women, a whole man should fall to her share."[15] And indeed, in January 1719, he married Mrs. Yarborough, who came from Heslington Hall, a country house just outside York.

Apart from this function as a marriage market, country assemblies played an important role in civilizing both the town gentry and the lesser country gentry. Lady Mary Wortley Montagu was aware of this aspect too: "The frequency of assemblies," she wrote, "has introduced a more enlarged way of thinking; it is a kind of public education, which I have always thought as necessary for girls as for boys."[16] Take a look, for instance, at the assembly room at Stamford. As far as I know this is the earliest surviving purpose-built assembly room in England, for it was constructed slightly before the York one, in about 1727. It was built on property belonging to the Earl of Exeter by Askew Kirk, who had run a school in Stamford but then handed the school over to his wife in order to specialize as a dancing master. It was impossible to attend an assembly room with any pleasure or profit without knowing how to dance, and how to converse and behave with that "politeness, elegance and ease" (as Oliver Goldsmith phrased it)[17] that was so much admired in the eighteenth century. Literature and letters of the seventeenth and early eighteenth century contain all sorts of references to clumsy, oafish local gentlemen, of the type that Pope made fun of in his "Epistle to Miss Blount on her leaving the town after the coronation:"

Some squire, perhaps, you take delight to rack;
Whose game is whisk, whose treat a toast in sack. . .
Or with his hound comes hallooing from the stable,
Makes love with nods, and knees beneath a table;
Whose laughs are hearty, though his jests are coarse,
And loves you best of all things—but his horse.

And similarly there are many references in letters, and even more in literature, to hoydenish country-house daughters who have no idea how to behave in terms of polite London life. Such local country-house families, which were not rich enough to have a house in London, benefited in terms of social behavior both from going to the assembly rooms and from going to plays, where they could watch London actors portraying fashionable London life. Through these they would learn the ways of dressing and behavior dealt with in contemporary courtesy books, such as Nivelon's charming *Rudiments of Gentle Behaviour*, published in 1727. This gives engravings of different positions, for both men and women, for "the courtsey," "giving or receiving anything," "walking and dancing," "giving a hand in a minuet," "giving both hands in a minuet," "walking and saluting," "passing by," "the bow," "the compliment," "retiring," "to offer or receive," and "dancing the minuet" (fig. 22). Collectively these are described as "accomplishments which will distinguish the polite gentleman from the rude rustic."

This is an appropriate point at which to turn to the country houses themselves to try to determine what differences, if any, in their planning and arrangement were brought about by assembly rooms and the social life that centered on them. The hypothesis can at least be put forward that these did have a considerable effect, that not

Fig. 22.
Two plates from *The Rudiments of Gentle Behaviour* by François Nivelon, 1727 *(Country Life)*

only did the lesser country-house owners learn from them how to behave, but that the owners were encouraged to put on in their own houses, if on a smaller scale, the kind of entertainments that they had become accustomed to. It is further arguable that an increase of sophistication in country neighborhoods also encouraged the grander families to alter their houses. One of the most noticeable changes in the course of the eighteenth century, in country houses of all sizes, is a change in the disposition and often the number of larger rooms. In the early eighteenth century the entrance hall and a saloon or dining room leading off it—or sometimes on the floor above it—were usually the largest rooms; to both sides of these were apartments designed either for the family or for guests, each consisting of a series of quite small rooms. This kind of plan did not work for a ball on the assembly-room model, which required a room for dancing and a room for supper. The hall could not be used for either activity because of its placement.

A good example of the problems caused by the wrong type of plan is revealed in Mrs. Lybbe Powys' description of a ball given at Fawley Court in Oxfordshire in 1777. Fawley was a late seventeenth-century house which had the arrangement just described, of a hall and a saloon opening off it. The ball required a big room for dancing and a big room for supper, but to set out supper in the hall, which was the room by which everyone normally entered, wearing their outdoor clothes, was neither civilized nor conven-

ient. The way round this at Fawley was to serve supper in the hall, but to keep it closed from the company until the time of supper by knocking a temporary door into another room and using this as the entrance hall for the evening.

Mrs. Lybbe Powys' account is also interesting because it reveals who actually came to the ball. The guests were the same as those who had been invited two days before to a play put on by Lord Villiers and an amateur cast at a house a few miles from Fawley, just outside Henley-on-Thames. The list starts with an impressive series of grand titled people, many of whom were not local, but ends with a roll-call of the local squirearchy: "The families of Onslow, Churchill, Conways, Rivers; John Pitts and General Pitts; Howes, Pratts, Claytons, Freemans, Prices, Tufnells, Vanderstegens, Jennings, Eliots, Rices, Mortons, Stonors, Tilsons, Englefields, Norths, Monsons, Winfords, Herberts, etc., etc." All these families clearly knew how to behave at a ball. Mrs. Lybbe Powys described how the guests went around the house exclaiming "Fine Assembly," "Magnificent house," "Sure we are in London." Some of the local families no doubt had London connections and experience, but their basic school of behavior must have been the assemblies that were held at the Bell at Henley-on-Thames all through the winter months, as at other towns throughout England. Mrs. Lybbe Powys comments in another place that these were "always attended by the whole agreeable neighbourhood."[18]

It is worth comparing the plans of two country houses of modest size. Burrow Hall in Lancashire (figs. 23, 24, 25) was built in about 1738 by Robert Fenwick, a local lawyer who had made an independent fortune in Lancaster. Bottisham Hall near Cambridge (figs. 26, 27) was built in 1797 for a "squarson" (a man who was both squire and local parson) called the Reverend G. L. Jennings, probably to the design of Charles Humphrey. Both are of about the same size, but their interior organization is quite different. At Burrow, the only sizeable rooms—and those are not very large—are the entrance hall and a room above the hall. To either side are pretty, elaborately decorated, but very small rooms, about fifteen feet square. The house would not have served for a dance in London or assembly-room style. At Bottisham one finds what had become the standard arrangement in even quite modest country houses by the late eighteenth century. There was a small entrance hall, a very much

Fig. 23.
The plan of Burrow Hall, Lancashire (*Country Life*)

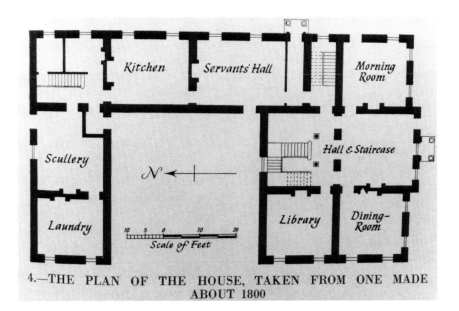

4.—THE PLAN OF THE HOUSE, TAKEN FROM ONE MADE ABOUT 1800

Fig. 24.
The exterior of Burrow Hall, Lancashire (*Country Life*)

bigger drawing room and dining room to either side, and a smaller living room off the drawing room, giving the necessary requisites for a ball: a room for dancing, a room for supper, and a smaller room for playing cards.

Bottisham must have formed part of a Cambridgeshire "agreeable neighbourhood" of socially sophisticated families such as also existed in the area around Fawley and Henley. Such neighborhoods scarcely existed in country areas of England in the early eighteenth century, as is exemplified by the plan and arrangement of Houghton, the great house built by Sir Robert Walpole between 1721 and 1730. The main reception and living areas of Houghton were divided between two floors: one at ground level in what tended to be called at the time the "rustic," the other on the *piano nobile* above it. The splendid rooms on the latter level had essentially been designed for the entertainment of a single important visitor, such as the Duke of Lorraine, who came to Houghton in the 1720s, was put up in style in one of the state apartments off the saloon, and entertained to a great dinner. Quite different from this kind of event at Houghton were the regular occasions on which Sir Robert Walpole came down from London to entertain the local squires. They were the basis of his political power and it was very much in his interest to entertain them, but it seems never to have occurred to him to allow them up onto the *piano nobile*. They (husbands only, the wives do not

Fig. 25.
The saloon at Burrow Hall, Lancashire (*Country Life*)

Fig. 26.
Bottisham Hall, Cambridgeshire
(Royal Commission on Historical Monuments)

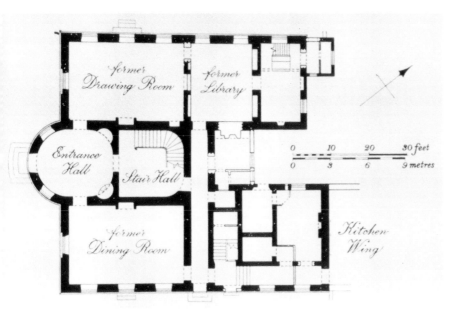

Fig. 27.
Plan of Bottisham Hall,
Cambridgeshire   (Royal Commission on
Historical Monuments)

seem to have been invited) were accommodated in the low-ceilinged and not at all grand rooms down in the "rustic." Here they were vividly described in 1731 as living "up to the chin in beef, venison, geese, turkeys, etc. and generally over the chin in claret, strong beer and punch."[19]

By the second half of the eighteenth century the local gentry would no longer put up with this kind of entertainment. They expected to be with their wives up on the *piano nobile*. It is worth suggesting that the need to entertain such families in a more sophisticated way was one

reason for the formation or addition of suites of large rooms to many bigger country houses in the later eighteenth century. A good example is at Crichel in Dorset, which was much enlarged by Humphrey Sturt in the 1770s, partly to the designs of James Wyatt. Sturt was extremely wealthy and was the Member of Parliament for the county. Entertaining the local gentry was part of the basis of his "interest." To one side of Crichel he added a series of splendid rooms that have very much the same sequence as in the assembly house in Norwich (fig. 28). A smaller, but by no means small, central room could be used for cards, and two huge and superbly decorated rooms, one to either side, were ideal for dancing and for supper.

Carr of York formed similar suites of rooms at two Yorkshire houses: Farnley Hall in about 1786, and Ribston Hall in about 1773. Ribston was a late seventeenth-century house originally divided up into a series of small rooms, possibly with a saloon in the middle. Carr was brought in to convert it for modern needs, and by knocking rooms together created a big dining room and a new and very large saloon. The rooms were partly formed for the display of his pictures, but must also have been intended for entertaining on a large scale. The saloon epitomizes the sophistication, gaiety, and elegance of social life at its best in country houses in the late eighteenth century, and is a glamorous country-house version of one of the big assembly rooms in the country towns, or of one of the great reception rooms in London houses.

Fig. 28.
The saloon at Crichel *(Country Life)*

NOTES

1. British Library, Additional ms. 42167 fol. 5. The relevant passage is omitted in the published diaries (for which, see note 18).

2. Especially in the *Diary and Letter-Books of John Hervey, First Earl of Bristol*, ed. S. H. A. Hervey (Wells, 1894).

3. See, e.g., John Ingamells, "Art in 18th-Century York," *Country Life* (10 June 1971), 1412–1414, (17 June 1971), 1530–1532.

4. John Harris, "Pritchard Redivivus," *Architectural History: Journal of the Society of Architectural Historians of Great Britain* 11 (1968), 17–24.

5. Eric Till, "A Stamford Cabinet-maker at Burghley," *Country Life* (3 May 1973), 1236–1238.

6. Ivan Hall "Furniture at Burton Constable," *Country Life* (3 June 1976), 1476–1480, (17 June 1976), 1622–1624.

7. York Civic Trust, *Annual Report 1983–1984*, 10–15.

8. Sir L. Namier and John Brooke, eds. *The History of Parliament* (New York, 1964–), *The House of Commons, 1715–1754*, ed. Romney Sedgewick (1970), 2:294.

9. Pierre de la Ruffinière du Prey, *John Soane: The Making of an Architect* (Chicago, 1982), 112–114, 123.

10. William Field, *An historical and descriptive account of the town and castle of Warwick . . .* (1815), 81.

11. Francis Drake, *Eboracum: or the History and Antiquities of York* (1736), 241.

12. Bond-Cabell deeds, Norfolk County Records Office, Norwich.

13. J. D. Nichol, "Social and Political Stability in 18th-Century Provincial Life. A Study of the Career of John Ashby of Shrewsbury," *Shropshire Archaeological Society* 59 (1969–1970), 53–62.

14. John Macky, *A Journey through England* (London, 1722), 2:41–42.

15. Lord Wharncliffe, ed., *The Letters and Works of Lady Mary Wortley Montagu* (1893), 1:206–207.

16. Quoted in Lawrence Stone, *The Family, Sex and Marriage in England, 1500–1800* (London, 1977), 402.

17. Oliver Goldsmith, *The Life of Richard Nash, Esq.* (1762).

18. Emily J. Climenson, ed., *Passages from the Diaries of Mrs. Philip Lybbe Powys of Hardwick House, Oxon* (London, 1899), 181–182, 185–186, 246.

19. Quoted in Robert Halsband, *Lord Hervey: Eighteenth-Century Courtier* (Oxford, 1973), 121.

Introduction

To the Symposium Papers
Presented at Dumbarton Oaks

8 February 1986

The symposium theme at Dumbarton Oaks was country house gardens. Since, however, there has been so much study of the actual gardens, their design, plantings, and use, and even of the influence of literature on gardens, we reversed the usual focus and solicited talks on the role played by gardens in literature.

Gardens can be, and have been used, not just as passive settings for the action taking place in novels but as an active factor to create and enhance the emotional climate of a scene, to serve as the vehicle for social comment and criticism, or as a means of indicating status and character. One need only think of Pope's description of Timon's villa in his "Epistle to Richard Boyle, Earl of Burlington" (1731) or Francis Coventry's satire of Squire Mushroom's villa in an essay in *The World* to see how the images of the two gardens are used to mock the social pretensions of their owners.[1]

Time of day, heat or cold, storm or sudden silence in the garden, even the degree of formality of its design or the state of its upkeep can be used to create a mood or characterize the protagonists and their roles in life.

John Dixon Hunt and A. A. Tait participated in the first session of the day, titled "Travel and the Garden." Hunt discusses how descriptions of Italy, derived from visits abroad by aristocrats and artists, played a role in the formation of the seventeenth-century Italianate garden style in England. Tait publishes Joseph Spence's journals recording his journeys in Scotland in the eighteenth century.

From the second session, which was titled "The Writer's Idea of the Garden," Michel Baridon's paper shows that changing ideas of history and its concomitant myths were an influence on the role of the garden in the social and intellectual life of England from 1700 to 1760. Alistair Duckworth, in a wide chronological span from the seventeenth to the twentieth century, examines the social and political uses of the garden in English fiction.

ELISABETH BLAIR MacDOUGALL

---

1. The two texts appear in John Dixon Hunt and Peter Willis, eds., *The Genius of the Place: The English Landscape Garden 1620–1820* (New York, 1975), 212, 275–276.

JOHN DIXON HUNT

The British Garden and the Grand Tour

In 1741 George Vertue described the gardens at Rousham in Oxfordshire, which William Kent had recently redesigned, as "finely disposed adornd with statues arcades Temples cascades, vistos various views of a fine River a lawn and distant prospects of various kinds—a Noble Triumphal Arch the utmost point of view."[1] His sense of English ground colonized by classical imagery—a triumphal arch being the "utmost" in emphasis as well as in distance—is clearly registered and expressed. The unpunctuated list of garden architectural features has strong Italian color, an Italianism that is classical as well as modern. The same view was taken by Horace Walpole in a letter of 1760 that emphasized that Rousham was "Daphne in little; the sweetest little groves, streams, glades, porticoes, cascades and river, imaginable; all the scenes are perfectly classic;"[2] while in his *History of the Modern Taste in Gardening* he was even more emphatic: "The whole is as elegant and antique as if the emperor Julian had selected the most pleasing solitude about Daphne to enjoy a philosophical retirement."[3] Some years earlier, in 1751, Walpole had made similar remarks about Stowe in Buckinghamshire: "I do like that Albano glut of buildings, let them be ever so much condemned."[4] The thrust of these descriptions is to highlight the concentration in one place of many reminiscences of the Grand Tour. Some of the allusions are specific; often the aim and effect is more general but nonetheless forceful. Collections of such imagery in a garden ensured for those able to respond to them continuing recollections of an Italy visited perhaps only briefly years before.

Gardens were a prominent and exciting feature of the Italian segment of a Grand Tour during the seventeenth and early eighteenth centuries; yet clearly they were not transportable, let alone portable souvenirs, even if an Italian virtuoso complained to Edward Wright that "were our Amphitheatre portable, the ENGLISH would carry it off."[5] Many tourists did at least carry off guidebooks that illustrated reconstructions of long-lost classical gardens or engravings of modern ones; some drew garden scenes or copied engravings; some visitors were perhaps lucky enough to purchase antique fragments or modern copies of classical statuary, which they could believe were garden ornaments. By such means certainly gardens could be recollected in tranquillity.[6] But other travelers were more ambitious. John Raymond records in his travel book, *Il Mercurio Italico,* that he decided while at the Villa D'Este in Tivoli, "This shall be my patterne for a Countrey seat,"[7] though presumably he might have encountered some economic difficulties in realizing this ambitious project. Notwithstanding, his urge to reconstitute fine Italian garden art back home in England was shared by many travelers. A more modest as well as much earlier attempt seems to be recorded in the diary of Sir Thomas Hoby, translator of Baldassare Castiglione's *Book of the Courtier.* In Italy in the late 1540s Hoby frequently admires what on one occasion he calls "sumptious palaces, delicious gardines." Back home, he is building "new lodgings" in 1561, planting "the garden and orchard" the following year, and in 1563 decorates the garden with a fountain.[8] He is typical of many who during the next two hundred years would use their Italian experience to learn (as their guide books advised) how to make a fine house and garden.[9]

I propose to look closely at three visitors to Italy—Lord Arundel, John Evelyn, and William Kent—who in different ways established gardens, just as much as the interiors of mansions, as prime locations for treasure trove, the garden itself being often the most prized item. Arundel is typical of wealthy, aristocratic collectors, while Evelyn was of the more modest English gentry who were unable to compete on the scale of the Arundels but were nonetheless dedicated to creating around themselves serviceable allusions to Italy; Kent provides an example both of agents based in the field—he spent nearly ten years in Italy—acquiring treasures for English patrons who were not themselves able to stay abroad indefinitely, and of those artists who helped to create images of Italy for similar patrons at their English country estates. I have chosen these three also because they suggest some of the important developments that occurred in the organization of gardens as treasure houses between the early seventeenth and early eighteenth century.

Gardens do not get created independently of contemporary ideas and conventions. They express, perhaps even more eloquently and fully than do other art forms, certain of the prevailing assumptions and habits of mind of their owners and creators. Three such mental structures will be of particular consequence in my discussion, and therefore it seems worth isolating and explaining them at the start. They are the Renaissance notion of representation in art, the affinities of gardens with cabinets of curiosity during the sixteenth and seventeenth centuries, and systems and techniques for memorizing elaborated during the Renaissance from classical texts and maintained as educational tools well into the eighteenth century.

Throughout the period with which I shall be dealing it was axiomatic that art was mimetic, that it represented—held the mirror up to nature, to use Hamlet's famous phrase. Whether a stage play, a poem, a painting, or a statue, the work of art was expected to offer an image of the world, miniaturized perhaps and certainly purged of the dross and casual exigencies of real life, but re-presented and so representative. Audiences, for example, at Shakespeare's Globe Theatre were specifically encouraged by the very decoration of the playhouse to expect that they would see on the stage an image of the world in its fullness. Now these expectations were also held of gardens, the more so as garden art aspired to be one of the fine arts; indeed, it was precisely this claim to be a mimetic art that was challenged by skeptics, such as Samuel Johnson, of the status of landscape gardening in the eighteenth century.

Early English visitors to Italian gardens declare how forcibly they were struck by the representations of events in such places. Their experience of

these gardens in turn dictated garden design in Britain: from being oases of flowers and plants set out in simple patterns, gardens came to be regarded as inadequate without imagery that reproduced in the garden a whole range of mythological, political, dynastic, meteorological, scientific, or historical events. A manuscript in the Bodleian Library, which narrates an unknown man's Italian travels in 1648, tells of his visit (very common, of course) to the Medici villa at Pratolino. There he saw "a man playing on organs, another givin water to beasts[,] a smith working, a woman [? drawing] water and diverse such like all made to goe by ye water."[10] Robert Bargrave of Canterbury, in another manuscript, also noted how Pratolino "excells for waterworks; such as give Statues motion, making a Satyre sound a fluit, a Nymph dance, an Angel sound a Trumpett; bringing out a chorus of birds which sing their several Notes."[11] The grottoes at Pratolino, with their hydraulic wonders, were of course designed like theaters, and therefore were readily understood as representing various mythological or human events in the way that was expected of the stage or a painting; one such representation—of Pegasus striking his hoof against Mount Helicon with the Muses playing—even had an amphitheater provided for the audience (fig. 1). But garden imagery did not need these quasitheatrical formats to draw the attention of English visitors to what it represented. Ellis Veryard writes of fountains at the Villa D'Este representing rainbows or a storm, of "a Representation of Old Rome in Perspective" (fig. 2), and at the Villa Aldobrandini at Frascati he reported the representation of a "Stair-case of Water" and of "an artifical Tempest."[12] I must insist that Veryard (as other tourists) was not saying he saw a tempest or a staircase of water, but that he saw it represented; it was performed by art, not in this case by actors or painted shapes upon a canvas, but by the varied forms of garden imagery. The consequences of this way of viewing gardens were, as we shall see, fundamental.

The affinities of gardens with cabinets of curiosity are easier to demonstrate. I have written elsewhere of the ways in which gardens functioned both as spillovers for collections and, with their botanical riches, engineering wonders, and statuary became a valued part of the cabinet itself.[13] Again, continental travels often afforded opportunities for Englishmen to see these *Kunstundwunderkammern* for the first time:

Fig. 1.
Drawing of Parnassus at Pratolino
by Giovanni Guerra, c. 1600
(Graphische Sammlung Albertina, Vienna)

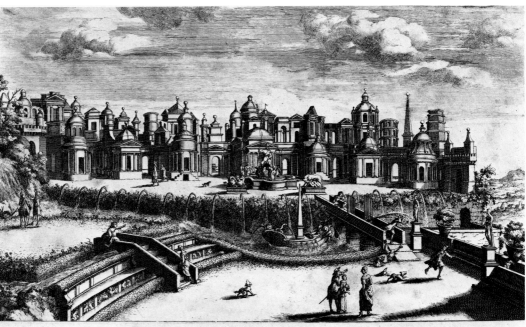

Fig. 2.
Engraving of the Fountain of Rome
at the Villa D'Este, from G. B.
Falda, *Le Fontane di Roma* (Photo-
graph: The Garden Library, Dumbarton Oaks,
Washington, D.C.)

at Pisa the young Sir Percy Cust admired "all manner of rare flowers" and diversity of trees in the Botanical Garden, and he added that "By this garden also is a fine gallery adornd with many naturall curiosities"[14] (we know it also contained some paintings). But inevitably Rome was the climax, and Evelyn summarized his stay in that city by writing that "[Rome] justly art term'd the *Worlds sole Cabinet*."[15] He had seen at least seven cabinets, visited twice as many gardens, and noted how in some of these collections rarities were intermingled; but his praise of the city as the "world's sole cabinet" was a hyperbolic claim for the collection within one place of images of the world's fullness. Indeed, there was a time in the seventeenth century when virtuosi thought that it was within their power to encompass within a museum or a botanical garden, or both, specimens of all artistic and natural events.[16] Peter Mundy visited one of the earliest such gardens-cum-museums in England, owned by the Tradescants in Lambeth, and his comment in 1634 was that he was "almost perswaded a Man might in one day behold and collect into one place more Curiosities than hee should see if he spent all his life in Travell."[17] The Tradescant collections were, in fact, increasing at an enormous rate, and would have burst the seams of even the most capacious site.[18] But this did not prevent others from espousing similar schemes. In his huge manuscript compilation, "Elysium Britannicum," Evelyn devised a garden where plants from different habitats would be properly accommodated (fig. 3). He incorporated features he had seen in Paris, Leyden, and Pisa, and the garden, if created, would have received plants from all over the world.

It was no accident that such a conspectus or complete collection came to be called a theater, as in the title of John Parkinson's *Theatrum Botanicum. The Theater of Plants. Or An Universall and Complete Herball.* Nor was it an accident that the word *garden* was also used to signal a complete collection, as in Henry Peacham's emblem book subtitled *A Garden of Heroicall Devises* . . .[19] Gardens, especially those that concentrated upon botanical specimens, were theaters in the double sense that they incorporated the whole world in miniature and that they were a stage upon which that world was represented. This is all expressed on Parkinson's title page (fig. 4) with the four continents at the corners and then, upon a stagelike platform across the middle, Adam the first gardener and Solomon, to repre-

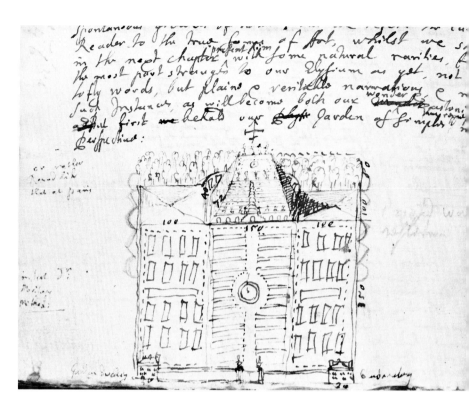

Fig. 3.
Drawing of a universal garden by John Evelyn, from his "Elysium Britannicum" (Christ Church College, Oxford)

Fig. 4.
Title page of John Parkinson's *Theatrum Botanicum*, 1640 (Photograph: The Garden Library, Dumbarton Oaks, Washington, D.C.)

sent the skill or wisdom needed now to recover the natural, prelapsarian world. Even though this confidence in gathering all the world into one place—"A World of wonders in one closet shut"[20]—was undermined almost completely during the seventeenth century, it continued to have repercussions for the gardens.

If gardens were designed in part to recall the world in its natural and artificial fullness, then that imagery in its turn functioned as a device to remind visitors of that plenitude beyond the garden wall. Iconographical programs in the gardens of the Villa D'Este at Tivoli, the Villa Lante at Bagnaia, or the Medici villa at Castello were designed to trigger certain responses in visitors, release specific ideas and themes stored previously in the memory.[21] Isolated items, independent of programs, achieved the same effect. Again, it was clearly during their Italian visit that the British registered how gardens functioned in this way. Raymond in the seventeenth century writes of "marbles, which speak Roman history more palpably then any Author,"[22] while in the eighteenth century Edward Wright observes of statuary of Roman emperors that "standing (as it were) in their own Persons before us, gives a Man a Cast of almost two thousand years backwards, and mixes the past ages with the present."[23] All this, as Elisabeth Blair MacDougall has pointed out about earlier Italian sculpture gardens, bears "a striking resemblance" to contemporary theories of memory and memory systems.[24] We know from Frances Yates' fascinating study how arcane these systems became in the Renaissance,[25] but as far as gardens are concerned I think we need bother only with the more everyday manifestations of those theories and practices. Drawing upon classical rhetoricians, notably Quintilian, Renaissance speakers, whether professional orators or grammar-school boys, were encouraged to store their ideas in some sequence arranged throughout an imaginary or real building that they would revisit as their speech unfolded, taking up the ideas previously stored there. As we shall see, it was a popular educational mode of developing the memory and makes one important intervention in mid-eighteenth-century garden history.

Such are the three contemporary assumptions and habits of mind that my discussions of British garden design will need to invoke; their application to the proper understanding of the garden's relationship to the Grand Tour will become clearer as we proceed.

Of Lord Arundel's various gardens we know tantalizingly little. But sufficient documents survive to enable us both to recognize his gardens' vital place in his larger cabinet of curiosities and to register their role as a theater or collection of antiquity. Arundel was by no means the first English collector, but his and his countess' direct, enthusiastic experience of Italy and their clear determination to fashion a universal model of that country's cultural history are of prime importance. As Sir Edward Walker, one of Arundel's secretaries, expressed it, his master "was the only great subject of the northern parts who set a value upon that country."[26] And as we know that the Arundels bought cloth in Milan for their Highgate house and held feasts at Highgate "after the Italian manner,"[27] it is clear that their emulation of Italy must have extended to all aspects of their life and habitat. John Smythson recorded their "newe Italyan gate" at Arundel House.[28]

The portraits of the earl and countess by Daniel Mytens (figs. 5, 6) show them among their treasures of sculpture and painting, respectively. What concerns us is that in both cases— apparently with a deliberate distortion of the facts—views of the garden are incorporated. Given what we know of Arundel's and his wife's character, it is likely that those fictitious exterior views were incorporated at their explicit request. Despite what the catalogue of *The Treasure Houses of Britain* implies,[29] exterior views of Arundel House showing mullioned and transomed windows rather than open arches, and a flat-roofed gallery rather than a barrel vault, together with a remark about the display of sculpture that I shall quote later, reveal that Mytens is inaccurate in showing an elegant open archway one level above the ground floor behind the earl; and we must therefore also be skeptical about the accuracy of the background of the countess' portrait. Arundel's recent biographer suggests that the pairs of portraits are capriccios and speculates that they were comissioned to make Sir Dudley Carlton, from whom in 1616 the earl was trying to buy a major collection, believe that the Arundel galleries were much more up-to-date and modish than in fact they were.[30] But there are other explanations, not least that Arundel planned to extend the piecemeal modernizations that Inigo Jones had begun—classicizing some window frames and fireplaces inside, adding two gateways outside—and that the portraits anticipated those plans. What is crucial, I believe, is

Fig. 5.
Thomas Howard, 2nd Earl of Arundel and Surrey by Daniel Mytens, c. 1618, oil on canvas   (National Portrait Gallery)

Fig. 6.
Alatheia Talbot, Countess of Arundel by Daniel Mytens, c. 1618, oil on canvas   (National Portrait Gallery)

that in giving such prominence to layouts and designs that did not exist, Mytens was guided by the *idea* that sustained the whole enterprise of Arundel's sculpture garden.

The garden was designed first as a homage to Italy and those Italian sculpture gardens that the Arundels had seen during their five months in Rome, and then as an example to Arundel's own countrymen. Just as Jones' gateways[31] were a tribute to Sebastiano Serlio's book of archways, the gardens were contrived, as much as the existing site allowed, according to the models of Italian gardens: vistas out from the immediate garden—Arundel's biographer suggests that he even had large sculptural items as eyecatchers[32] on the opposite bank of the Thames, which Mytens actually shows—and intricate spatial experiences that Sir Henry Wotton counted among the highlights of an "incomparable" Italian garden.[33] Behind the countess our eye is taken through a classical doorcase into a fountain court, while beyond an arbor (in the modish pan-European mannerist style of Hans Vredeman de Vries, which Mytens could be expected to know well, yet a style not without Italian precedents) a further garden can be seen. The invitation to explore what is glimpsed is a prime Italian experience, as many travelers besides Wotton testified. And the one precious contemporary description we have of the layout of the sculpture garden reveals that Arundel knew exactly how to contrive such garden experiences: the "fine head of Jupiter" given to Arundel by Sir Dudley Carleton was positioned in "his utmost garden, so opposite the Gallery dores, as being open as soon as you enter into the front Garden you have the head in your eie all the way."[34]

Arundel's virtuosity was widely acknowledged, and so equally clearly was the garden's place in his cabinet of curiosities. Sending him some coral for his collections, Sir Thomas Roe remarked that it might "affect you for fountains, your Lordship's curiosity being unlimited."[35] "Unlimited" was undoubtedly the word. The sculptures and pictures that Mytens shows were the high points but by no means all of the Arundel collection, which came to include precious stones, notably amber and tortoiseshell, folios of beautifully colored birds, inscriptions, etchings, woodcuts, reliefs, drawings, books on topography and architecture—including many views of classical and modern Rome—*pietre dure* furniture, and coins.[36] That Arundel himself saw gardens as simply an element of this universal hoard may be judged both from his own casual remarks and from publications by his associates and employees. In a letter to his wife he talks in the same breath of Sir Thomas Roe's "antiquities, Gods, vases, inscriptions, medals or such like" and the expertise in flowers of one "Mistress Smith, whose garden we saw at Moor Fields."[37] The tutor to the earl's children, Henry Peacham, is much more explicit about the connection of gardens and cabinets in *The Compleat Gentleman,* dedicated in 1622 to the eldest Howard boy. The second edition of 1634 contains a new chapter "Of Antiquities," in which Arundel House is celebrated among the "Gardens and Galleries of great men."[38]

But Peacham is far more interesting on the ambition of the Arundel collection to be a microcosm of world history: it was designed, he writes, "to transplant old Greece into England" in such a fashion as "to perswade a man, that he now seeth two thousand yeares agoe."[39] What Arundel House attempted was no less than to reanimate beside the English Thames that classical tradition of sculpture garden that Roman literature frequently invoked and that the Renaissance city beside the Tiber had first attempted in modern times, and in such a sculpture garden to provide a conspectus of history.[40] Arundel had participated in one important stage of this process when he excavated in the Forum for classical remains (carefully "planted" beforehand by Vincenzo Giustiniani). Such searches for antiquities amid Rome's surviving ruins, and their reuse or reanimation in contemporary settings, is a major theme of the Renaissance. Its significance for England was frequently articulated in literary terms as the progress of poetry: it was the fashion to chart the progress of poetry or of any art from its classical beginnings, through its recovery and renaissance in modern Italy, to its arrival across space and time in the British Isles. The arts "sought," in the words of

Thomas Gray, "oh Albion! next thy sea-encircled coast."[41] That Arundel saw himself as occupying, or creating for himself, a crucial role in the progress of the arts to Britain may be judged from the inscription which he caused William Camden to devise for the sculpture gallery: it announced that Arundel was continuing the work of his fathers by having the venerable monuments of antiquity carried from the ruins of Rome to the palace of the Arundel Howards.[42]

That Arundel House, but especially its garden and gallery, constituted a memory theater is clear from various testimony: Peacham himself wrote that "you shall find the walls of the house inlaid with [marbles] and speaking Greek and Latin to you."[43] Sir Francis Bacon is reported to have exclaimed to Arundel upon his first sight of the collections, "My Lord, I see the Resurrection is upon us."[44] And Christopher Arnold, later professor of history at Nuremberg, saw the already decaying Arundel property in 1651 and remarked upon "certain gardens on the Thames, where there are rare Greek and Roman inscriptions, stones, marbles: the reading of which is actually like viewing Greece and Italy at once within the bounds of Great Britain."[45]

In 1645 and again in 1646, during the last weeks of his life, Arundel, exiled in Italy, met and talked with John Evelyn, another refugee from civil war at home. They visited various sites and the older man provided the young tourist with an account of the major items to be seen. Significantly Evelyn referred to this as the earl's "Remembrances."[46] Evelyn was to realize other remembrances of Italy in gardens that he created back home, the most intriguing of which was in Arundel's own Albury.

English visitors to Italy were often concerned as to how they could recall and reconstitute memories of that country once they were back home. One simple means was by writing up their journals of the *giro d'Italia,* or by poring over the engravings and other portable souvenirs that then, as now, tourists purchased.[47] But it was also clearly possible to envisage creating for oneself an environment of house and garden where those memories could be even more tangibly realized. Not every landowner had Arundel's means (and even he went bankrupt), but many less wealthy people shared his wish to represent Italy on their own English land. The Evelyn

family estate at Wotton or—to take another example in Wales—Mutton Davies' property at Llanerch in Denbighshire, were modest by the standard of Arundel's or of the Earl of Pembroke's extensive and emphatically Italianate gardens at Wilton; but it seems evident that both Wotton and Llanerch served their owners well as "remembrances" of Italian travel.

Upon his return from Italy Mutton Davies "made [gardens] . . . in the foreign taste, with images and water tricks;"[48] another generation added a cabinet of curiosities. What is striking about Llanerch (fig. 7) is that, though the site apparently did not allow a modern garden axially aligned on the house, its structures and its "im-

ages" are Italianate: terraces or "hanging gardens" were identified by the British as Italian, so were the split stairways, the grottoes (perhaps containing "water tricks") which we must surely imagine in the openings between the staircase arms, and the round pool that recalls (as did a similar feature at Evelyn's Sayes Court) both the Isolotto at the Boboli Gardens and the so-called Maritime Theater at Hadrian's Villa; furthermore, in exact emulation of Italian villas, where *boschetti* were juxtaposed with more regular garden layouts, Llanerch's descending terraces give, via a bridge, into a grove.

The Evelyn gardens and groves at Wotton were drawn by John Aubrey (fig. 8) in the late

Fig. 7.
Garden at Llanerch, Denbighshire, British School, 1662, oil on canvas (Yale Center for British Art, Paul Mellon Collection)

seventeenth century as part of his researches into the English "way of Italian gardens."[49] This watercolor shows that once the old-fashioned moat around the manor house was removed and a quartered garden with a fountain in its center was established, John Evelyn could persuade his brother to create both a terraced hillside after the fashion of many he had admired in Italy and a grotto with temple front. But these effects and earlier additions and rearrangements at Wotton, which furnished it with what Evelyn told Aubrey were "all the Amoenities of a villa and Garden, after the Italian manner,"[50] were slight compared to what Evelyn was about to achieve a few miles away at Albury.

This Surrey seat of the Arundel family had become the earl's favorite: he wrote to Evelyn in 1646 that he would "have sold any Estate he had in *England,* (*Arundel* excepted) before he would have parted with this Darling Villa."[51] From his Italian exile Arundel commissioned Wenceslaus Hollar to do a set of twelve engravings of Albury, and in one of these (fig. 9) we can see that the hillside was terraced in vineyards and adorned with a fine classical portico. It was Arundel's grandson, Henry Howard, who commissioned Evelyn to transform that hillside, cre-

ating in effect a complex series of allusions to Italy.

Evelyn recorded in his diary "the Designe & plot I had made [for Albury], with the Crypta through the mountaine in the parke, which is 30 pearches in length, such a *Pausilippe* is no where in England besides."[52] The reference is to what was known as the Grotta di Posilippo near Naples, which Evelyn had visited in February 1645. It was a favorite tourist attraction, much written about and illustrated. The Italian original cuts through the promontory between Naples and Pozzuoli (fig. 10); Evelyn's goes through the Surrey hillside and leads nowhere in particular (fig. 11). So by itself it seems rather an odd representation of an Italian feature, however famous. But the *grotta* at Naples was associated with Virgil, whose magical powers were supposed to have cut the tunnel through the hill and who is equally supposed to have been buried in a tomb immediately above his *grotta*; it was a tomb that John Raymond visited and found to be in a garden.[53] It had a square base, but the higher part of the structure was circular, a shape that is perhaps echoed by Evelyn in the exedra from which the Albury *Pausilippe* leads.

The specific allusion to Italy—gardenist gener-

Fig. 9.
Engraving of vineyards and casino or grottoes "bey [by] Albury" by Wenceslas Hollar (Victoria and Albert Museum)

ally both in its association with Virgil and its invocation of the garden surrounding his "tomb"—is enhanced by others. The exedra is a hemicycle, with niches and a sunken pool; its prototype could have been seen in innumerable Italian gardens like that at the Villa Mondragone at Frascati which Evelyn had admired and called a "theater for pastimes."[54] Below the Albury

Fig. 10.
Engraving of the tunnel at Posilippo, Naples, from P. A. Paoli, *Antiquità di Pozzuoli*, 1768 (Photograph: The British Library)

Fig. 11.
The Exedra at Albury, Surrey (Photograph: Douglas Chambers)

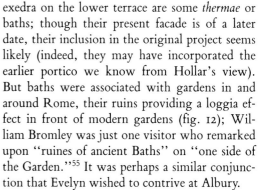

Fig. 12.
Remains of Roman baths with modern gardens, from A. Donati, *Roma Vetus ac Recens utriusque Aedificiis Illustrata,* Amsterdam, 1694
(Photograph: Bibliotheca Hertziana)

THERMARVM NOVATII RELIQVIAE

exedra on the lower terrace are some *thermae* or baths; though their present facade is of a later date, their inclusion in the original project seems likely (indeed, they may have incorporated the earlier portico we know from Hollar's view). But baths were associated with gardens in and around Rome, their ruins providing a loggia effect in front of modern gardens (fig. 12); William Bromley was just one visitor who remarked upon "ruines of ancient Baths" on "one side of the Garden."[55] It was perhaps a similar conjunction that Evelyn wished to contrive at Albury.

His final gesture toward Italy was the terraces themselves, at the center of which were the exedra and baths. Such a cluster of shapes and spaces echoes any number of reconstructions of classical gardens as well as modern structures in Italy, known to English visitors from maps, engravings, and actual sightings. But the Albury terraces are extremely long *grass* walks, and their length is emphasized by the fact that the only access from one level to another is by the split stairway in the center (with the *thermae* situated in place of a grotto) and by gentle ramps at the extremities (fig. 13). As terraces they are cer-

Fig. 13.
Aerial view of Albury, Surrey
(Photograph: Cambridge University Committee for Aerial Photography)

tainly Italianate, but their length and the method of joining them suggests a more precise reference—to the remains of the Temple of Fortune at Palestrina (fig. 14), the classical Praeneste, which played such a significant part in determining the form of Italian Renaissance gardens. In the context of Evelyn's other allusions, a reference to Praeneste and the ruined terraces of the classical temple would not be out of place (as we shall see, a similar gesture was made by William Kent at Rousham in the next century). That these Albury terraces were grassed perhaps suggests that they were deliberately naturalized, or Englished.

It was perfectly proper that Evelyn's gardens for Henry Howard at Albury should be a small memory theater, designed to recall sites visited on both families' Italian journeys. After all, as we have seen, it was the 3rd Earl who advised Evelyn as to what to visit in Italy, his recommendations including the Giusti Gardens in Verona where the walks were "cutt out of the maine rocke."[56] And to focus the gardens around a poetic *grotta* or *crypta* was apt: we know Arundel had had a grotto on the site "wherein he delighted to sit and discourse," and we know that his contemporaries considered grottoes "do contribute to contemplative and philosophicall enthusiasme."[57] So to sit beside the spring that filled the exedral pool and to gaze down to the vineyards, a feature on which Virgil's *Georgics* had discoursed, must have been as potent a recollection of Italy as any.

It is also worth noting at this point that some landowners who did not manage to get to Italy were nonetheless impelled to create gardens that have every appearance of being calculated references to a whole congeries of Italian motifs. John Aubrey was one such landowner. Always frustrated in his ambition to make the Grand Tour, he dedicated himself (perhaps as a poor best substitute) to charting the "way of Italian gardens" in England—yet another of the projects he left unrealized upon his death.[58] He also planned to make his own house and grounds at Easton-Piercy in Wiltshire wholly Italianate. In 1669 he prepared two manuscripts on his villa project, of which only the one with drawings has survived in the Bodleian Library, Oxford; but even without the corresponding and explanatory text, we can judge his ambition. The cartouche of his title page surrounds the Latin and Italian word *villa* (a usage that antedates by many years the one first

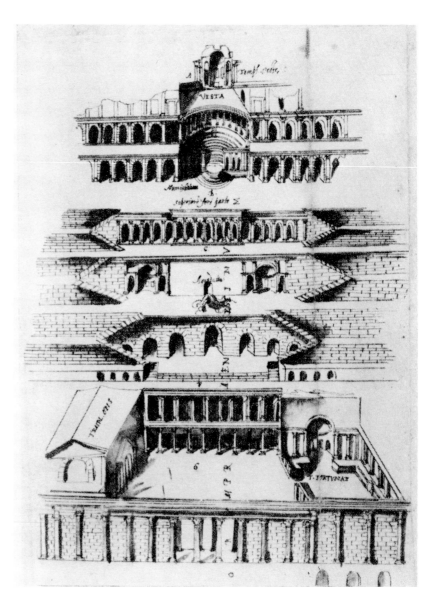

recorded in the Oxford English Dictionary) with quotations from Ovid and Horace that celebrate the countryside and its numinous potential; further references to grottoes and two quotations from the *Georgics* are written on the facing page and its verso, respectively. The folios that follow are visual attempts by Aubrey to project his idea of an Italianate villa: one drawing shows descending terraces, a fountain, and a grotto, and a note signals the "grove where the jetto is."[59]

A later garden enthusiast who sought to create a garden full of reminiscences and allusions to

Fig. 14.
Reconstruction of the Temple of Fortune at Praeneste, the modern Palestrina, by Pirro Ligorio
(Biblioteca Apostolica Vaticano)

growing interest in Britain's own cultural history and a corresponding skepticism about whether classical Greece and Rome were applicable to contemporary life and times undermined efforts to represent Italy on English country estates. Thus Joshua Childrey's *Britannia Baconica* had already claimed that "as Italy hath Virgils Grott, and the Sybils Cave by Puteoli; so England hath Okeyhole by Wells."[61] The reasons for these inevitable changes are complex and cannot detain us on this occasion, but their repercussions for English garden design are important, and can be tracked most visibly in the work of William Kent.

William Kent spent nearly ten years in Italy, mainly collecting or copying treasures for the country houses of his English patrons.[62] His intention was to become a painter, with of course the contemporary insistence upon the centrality of some mythological or historical event; his skills did not, alas, match his ambition, but this initial dedication to history painting can be seen to determine his garden designs when he eventually took up that branch of work. While in Rome he also seems to have initiated his career as a stage designer, which he continued together with his painting once he returned to England. We have precious little information about the theatrical aspects of his work, but one design survives at Chatsworth, bound at the end of a volume of Burlington's theater collection;[63] it suggests that, not only should we perhaps see even more of Kent's surviving drawings as stage sets rather than landscape sketches, but that his garden work has strong theatrical overtones. Besides the influence of his training as a history painter and of his work for the theater, his landscape designs also reflect his (often amusing) enthusiasm for all things Italian. His involvement in Lord Burlington's Palladian ambitions gave him ample opportunity to realize his taste for Italian remembrances, but his versatile and energetic imagination was also attracted to the gothick, first perhaps because of its formal opportunities, but also because it represented an indigenous, British style.

Two drawings can perhaps focus some of these intricate and as yet largely unexplored themes in Kent's garden work. The first (fig. 15), a proposal for a new hillside at Chatsworth, is an anthology of Italian reminiscences: the temple near the top of the ridge recalls the so-called Sybil's Temple above the Aniene Cascades at

classical and modern Italy was Alexander Pope. But, as I have argued elsewhere,[60] his attempt introduces us to a striking alteration in the way the English wished to imitate or represent Rome. For various attitudes had changed by Pope's time. Neither the confidence in the potential of a cabinet of curiosities to contain the whole world in miniature, nor the absolute faith in Italian culture as a model to be imitated by the British survived beyond the seventeenth century. Both specialization and an overabundance of materials preempted the virtuoso and his cabinet. A

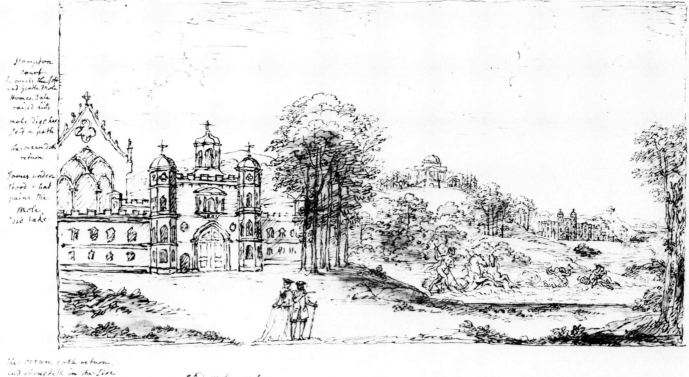

Tivoli, the waterfalls allude to the structures on the hillside of the Villa Aldobrandini at Frascati, while the flanking pavilions are an eclectic concoction of famous Roman ruins.[64] It is possible to see this design as the translation into garden art of Kent's history painting and theater designs. He represents the arrival upon Derbyshire soil of the traditions of antique gardening, mediated by Italian Renaissance versions of them; the event becomes a theater, not simply in its conspectus of memorable items, but in its enactment before a group of spectators whose appreciation of the transformation of their native hillside is an essential part of its meaning.

The second drawing (fig. 16) is of a river scene with classical and gothick buildings and with modern and classical figures. Neither Kent's recent biographer, who thinks the verses in the margin are Kent's, nor the catalogue of the Kent exhibition at Hull in 1985 pinpoint the significance of the scene or its gloss.[65] In fact, Kent has illustrated some lines on the meeting of the rivers Thames and Mole from Michael Drayton's early seventeenth-century poem, *Poly-Olbion*. Its Greek title means "having many blessings," and the poem, consisting of thirty songs on the beauties of the English countryside and its legends, is in fact a meditation on the progress of the arts, whereby England was hailed as the ultimate destination of ancient culture, transferred across space and time to the British Isles. Kent offers to some contemporary spectators a pageant of a classical river-god sailing past both gothick buildings upon which Kent himself had worked—Hampton Court to the left and Esher in the distant right—and a Palladian temple. Each element of the scene recalls memories of the various heritages upon which England can rely and expand, and these flow together like the rivers Mole and Thames. It all suggests Kent's own acknowledgment of the central issue of transferring, establishing, and naturalizing classical imagery in the English countryside.

We have one surviving garden in which we

Fig. 16.
Illustration of lines from Michael Drayton's *Poly-Olbion* by William Kent (British Museum)

can plot Kent's actual realization or representation of these themes: Rousham.[66] Kent was called there in 1739 to remodel the grounds that Charles Bridgeman had laid out in the 1720s. Kent gave the house battlements, ogee niches and mullioned windows, English touches, and some fine interior decoration, classical ceilings, and grotesque work *all'antica*. A similar scheme faces visitors who enter the gardens, not via the house, but direct from the road, where, emerging through a classical gateway, they are confronted by a gothick seat also decked with battlements. Such eclecticism is not simply a play with forms, but as George Clarke and Michel Baridon have argued, it signals cultural and political messages.[67]

Italy, classical and modern, is recalled frequently at Rousham, but it is also treated sceptically and juxtaposed with imagery that is local, indigenous, British. Proceeding from the house, visitors see a copy of Peter Scheemaker's statue, *Lion Attacking a Horse* (fig. 17), one of the many pieces in his patron's collection that it was Kent's task to display. Kent was therefore creating a sculpture garden in the classical, Renaissance, and (if we think of Arundel's) English traditions. The Scheemaker recalls an identical piece in the Fountain of Rome at the Villa D'Este (fig. 2), from which one could look out across the Campagna toward the modern city. But here in Oxfordshire, there is simply a wide expanse of rural scenery; if Rome is present, it is by omission.

A similar suggestion is made a little farther along the garden route. Here Kent introduced the arcaded terrace (fig. 18), called Praeneste in a description of Rousham by a former gardener;[68] it therefore is intended to recall the Temple of Fortune (fig. 14), which Evelyn had also probably represented at Albury. Kent, however, miniaturizes it—an effect Walpole was aware of throughout the gardens when he called them "Daphne in little."[69] Praeneste Terrace performs the same function as its larger, classical model: it is a platform from which to view the surrounding countryside, and it is a landmark that can be seen from a distance—either from the Campagna, or from the spot at which a copy of the Vatican Belvedere Antinous marks the line of sight at Rousham (fig. 19). But Kent has reduced his structure to one elegant line of arched openings—such are the exigencies of translating the classical world into the modern. Upon the top of his Praeneste Kent installed one of the many imitations of famous classical sculptures, the Dying Gaul, which was originally designed with a sarcophagus base.[70]

If the copies of classical statues recall the antique world, there were others that recalled modern items, like Giambologna's Mercury, then at the Villa Medici in Rome, a smaller version of which Kent placed in Charles Bridgeman's theater, now naturalized as a glade with views across the river Cherwell. And the classical structures represented in the gardens were matched also by modern ones: the Vale of Venus (fig. 20) derives its cascades from the Villa Aldobrandini, which Kent had also invoked at Chatsworth.[71] This quotation of a modern Italian garden underlies the theme of the progress of the arts, for Aldobrandini exemplified the revival of classical garden art in the modern Tusculum, and therefore one stage in the passage of that art to English estates. Suitably, the Vale is presided over by a modern copy of the Medici Venus, the Roman goddess of gardens.

But the views outward from the Vale of Venus, as from everywhere in this exquisite garden,

Fig. 17.
Copy of *Lion Attacking a Horse* by Peter Scheemaker, Rousham Park, Oxfordshire   (Photograph: author)

Fig. 18.
The Praeneste Terrace, Rousham
Park   (Photograph: author)

Fig. 19.
Distant view of the Praeneste Terrace, Rousham Park, down the elm
walk   (Photograph: author)

are an integral part of its message.[72] To underline
this Kent established his eyecatcher on a distant
ridge and his Temple of the Mill closer by: the
former is gothick, but was seen by contemporaries as a triumphal arch and therefore Roman;
the latter was a local cottage provided with a
temple front in the battlemented and therefore
British style.[73] Heyford Bridge with its busy
country traffic was brought into view at the end
of the garden by moving the road, while the
fields across the river—the spectacle to be
watched from the woody theater—were always
alive with flocks and herds, classical traditions of
agriculture naturalized.

Kent's garden designs were quickly inter-
preted by garden historians like Walpole as a
Whiggish progress from artificial to natural gardens; they continue to be misread in that way
today.[74] But for Kent nature and what was natural in the form of British views and British architecture were as much part of the subjects represented in his gardens and parks as were classical
items. As was the case with translations of poetry for Pope, a friend of Kent's from whom I

Fig. 20.
Design for the Vale of Venus,
Rousham Park, by William
Kent (Rousham Park, Oxfordshire)

suspect he derived some of these ideas, translations into English of classical and modern Italian garden art were subject to much debate. If successful, like Pope's Horation imitations, they had to speak such "good English"[75] as to pass for English statements.

Translation of classical literature, architecture, or garden imagery was not accomplished without difficulty, and not without some skepticism about the aptness or intelligibility of the past for the present. This was a theme of Joseph Spence's book, *Polymetis,* published in 1747, the year before Kent's death. Spence was concerned that his contemporaries no longer recognized and distinguished the Roman divinities ("a perfect mob of deities"), so he proposed a vast memory theater, utilizing an English landscaped park ("rather wild than regular") which he dotted with temples, in each of which were represented statues of particular kinds of gods and goddesses together with inscriptions, reliefs, or engravings relevant to each of them.[76] This compendium of Roman

mythology became a school textbook in 1764 and went into six editions. So the need and the desire to remember classical lore was very much alive in Britain. Yet in the gardens that Spence himself was designing, such imagery played a smaller and smaller part.[77] Gardens no longer worked as memory theaters; no longer could they represent Italy in its glory, ruin, and revival. True, this could be faked after an empty fashion, as Robert Lloyd noted in 1757:

And now from Hyde-Park Corner come
The gods of Athens and of Rome.
Here squabby Cupids take their places
With Venus and the clumsy Graces:
Apollo there with aim so clever,
Stretches his leaden bow for ever;
And there, without the pow'r to fly,
Stands fix'd a tip-toe Mercury.[78]

But such wan and ersatz images seemed less acceptable. After Kent's death British gardens under the direction of Capability Brown seemed to be all nature. Though the majority of their visitors may have regarded them as simply natural, they were, in fact, the supreme climax of the progress of gardens—a representation of *la belle nature,* the epitome of English nature refined by art, a collection of native beauties, a theater of recollections.

NOTES

1. Quoted by John Fleming, "William Kent at Rousham: an Eighteenth-Century Elysium," *Connoisseur* 153 (1963), 159.

2. Wilmarth Sheldon Lewis et al, eds., *The Yale Edition of Horace Walpole's Correspondence,* 48 vols. (New Haven, 1937–1983), 9:290.

3. I. W. W. Chase, ed., *Horace Walpole: Gardenist; an Edition of Walpole's "The History of the Modern Taste in Gardening . . ."* (Princeton, 1943), 29.

4. Lewis 1937–1983, 9:122.

5. Edward Wright, *Some Observations Made in Travelling Through France, Italy . . . in the Years 1720, 1721 and 1722,* 2 vols. (London, 1730), 1: vii.

6. The English experience and re-creation of Italian garden art is the subject of John Dixon Hunt, *Garden and Grove. The Italian Renaissance Garden in the English Imagination 1600–1750* (Princeton, 1986), to which readers are referred for a much fuller discussion of matters raised in this essay. Much of the material used here is also used in my book, though occasionally with somewhat different emphases.

7. John Raymond, *Il Mercurio Italico* (London, 1648), 167.

8. Edgar Powell, ed., "The Travels and Life of Sir Thomas Hoby," *Camden Miscellany* 10 (1902), 28, 129.

9. See, for example, Henry Cogan, *A Direction for Such as Shall Travell unto Rome* (London, 1654), preface, 2; James Howell, *Instructions and Directions for Forren Travell* (London, 1650), 58.

10. Bodleian Library, Oxford, ms. Rawl. D 120, fols. 19–20.

11. Bodleian Library, Oxford. ms. Rawl. C 799, fol. 8.

12. Ellis Veryard, *An Account of Divers Choice Remarks . . . Taken in a Journey . . .* (London, 1701), 205–206, 207.

13. John Dixon Hunt, " 'Curiosities to adorn Cabinets and Gardens'," in *The Origins of Museums,* ed. Oliver Impey and Arthur MacGregor (Oxford, 1985), 193–203.

14. Lady Elizabeth Cust, ed., *Records of the Cust Family* (London, 1898), 193–203.

15. E. S. de Beer, ed., *The Diary of John Evelyn,* 5 vols. (Oxford, 1955), 2: 405.

16. This theme is set out in John Prest, *The Garden of Eden; the Botanic Garden and the Re-creation of Paradise* (New Haven and London, 1981).

17. Sir R. C. Temple, ed., *The Travels of Peter Mundy,* 5 vols. (London, 1907–1925), 3: 1–2.

18. See Arthur MacGregor, ed., *Tradescant's Rarities* (Oxford, 1983); Keith Thomas, *Man and the Natural World* (London, 1983), esp. 226–227.

19. Henry Peacham, *Minerva Britannia* (London, 1612); Parkinson's *Theatrum Botanicum* was published in London in 1640.

20. This is the inscription on the Tradescants' tomb in London.

21. These three gardens have been the subject of detailed iconographical study. See David R. Coffin, *The Villa D'Este at Tivoli* (Princeton, 1960); Claudia Lazzaro Bruno, "The Villa Lante at Bagnaia," *Art Bulletin* 59 (1977), 553–60; L. Châtelet-Lange, "The Grotto of the Unicorn and the Garden of the Villa di Castello," *Art Bulletin* 50 (1968), 51–58.

22. Raymond 1648, 78.

23. Wright 1730, 343.

24. Elisabeth Blair MacDougall, "Imitation and Invention:

Language and Decoration in Roman Renaissance Gardens,'' *Journal of Garden History* 5 (1985), 131.

25. Frances Yates, *The Art of Memory* (London, 1966).

26. Quoted in David Howarth, *Lord Arundel and His Circle* (New Haven and London, 1985), 33.

27. Howarth 1985, 35, 86.

28. Mark Girouard, ''The Smythson Collection of the R.I.B.A.,'' *Architectural History* 5 (1962), 53.

29. Gervase Jackson-Stops, ed., *The Treasure Houses of Britain* [exh. cat., National Gallery of Art] (Washington, 1985), nos. 49, 50.

30. Howarth 1985, 58.

31. See, for instance, Roy Strong, *The Renaissance Garden in England* (London, 1979), fig. III; Howarth 1985, figs. 37, 38.

32. Howarth 1985, 113.

33. Sir Henry Wotton, *Elements of Architecture* (London, 1624), 109–110.

34. Quoted by Mary F. S. Hervey, *The Life, Correspondence and Collections of Thomas Howard, Earl of Arundel* (Cambridge, 1921), 101–102.

35. Howarth 1985, 149.

36. On Arundel's collections, see Howarth 1985, 184.

37. Howarth 1985, 95.

38. Henry Peacham, *The Compleat Gentleman*, 2d. ed. (London 1634), ''Of Antiquities.'' (There is a modern edition of *The Compleat Gentleman*, ed. Virgil B. Heltzel [Ithaca, N.Y., 1962].)

39. Peacham 1634, 104–106.

40. See Howarth 1985, 71.

41. Thomas Gray, ''The Progress of Poetry. A Pindaric Ode,'' line 82.

42. ''Thomas Howardus Comes Arundelia: Philippi F./ Thomae Ducus Norf. summus N. venerandae/ Antiquitatis admirator hanc porticum antiquis/ quae Italian collegit monumentis dicavit.'' Quoted in Howarth 1985, 241, n. 12.

43. Peacham 1634, 124–125.

44. Thomas Tenison, *Baconiana* (London, 1679), 57.

45. Quoted by David Masson, *Life of Milton,* 7 vols. (London, 1881), 4: 350.

46. The ''Remembrances'' are published in Hervey 1921, 450–453.

47. I have discussed these matters at more length in Hunt 1986, esp. chap. 1.

48. C. A. Usher, *Gwysaney and Owston* (Denbigh, 1964), 82, 87.

49. Bodleian Library, Oxford, Aubrey ms. 2, fol. 53r.

50. Bodleian Library, Oxford, Aubrey ms. 4, fols. 28–29.

51. John Aubrey, *Natural History of Surrey,* 5 vols. (London, 1718–1719), 4:66.

52. De Beer 1955, 3:393.

53. Raymond 1648, 146.

54. De Beer 1955, 2:393.

55. [William Bromley], *Remarks in the Grand Tour* (London, 1705), 183.

56. De Beer 1955, 2:487.

57. Douglas Chambers, ''The Tomb in the Landscape,'' *Journal of Garden History* 1 (1981), 40, 50.

58. See Bodleian Library, Oxford, Aubrey ms. 2 for scraps of Aubrey's history.

59. See Hunt 1986, 153–157, for further discussion and reproductions of these pages.

60. John Dixon Hunt, ''Pope's Twickenham Revisited,'' *British and American Gardens in the Eighteenth Century,* ed. Robert P. MacCubbin and Peter Martin (Williamsburg, 1984), 26–35.

61. Joshua Childrey, *Britannia Baconica: the Natural Rarities of England, Scotland and Wales* (London, 1661), sig. B₁I.

62. This section draws upon John Dixon Hunt, *William Kent, Landscape Garden Designer; an Assessment and Catalogue of His Designs* (London, 1987).

63. Hunt 1987, no. 47.

64. Hunt 1987, no. 18..

65. Hunt 1987, no. 62; see also Michael I. Wilson, *William Kent* (London, 1984), 154.

66. A good standard discussion of Rousham Park is by Christopher Hussey, *English Gardens and Landscapes 1700–1750* (London, 1967); see also Mavis Batey, ''The Way to View Rousham by Kent's Gardener,'' *Garden History* 11 (1983), 130.

67. George Clarke, ''Grecian Taste and Gothic Virtue: Lord Cobham's Gardening Programme and Its Iconography,'' *Apollo* 97 (1973), 566–571; Michel Baridon, ''Ruins as Mental Construct,'' *Journal of Garden History* 5 (1985), 84–96.

68. Batey 1983, 130.

69. Lewis 1937–1983, 10:72.

70. Hunt 1987, no. 42.

71. Hunt 1987, no. 105.

72. See Hal Moggridge, ''Notes on Kent's Garden at Rousham,'' *Journal of Garden History* 6 (1986), figs. 12, 13.

73. Hunt 1987, no. 106.

74. On this Whiggish history, see Richard E. Quaintance, ''Walpole's Whig Version of Landscaping History,'' *Studies in Eighteenth-Century Culture* 9 (1979), 285–300; see also, for a fuller analysis of Kent's stance, Hunt 1987.

75. The phrase is Sir William Trumbull's, from a letter urging the poet onward with his translation of Homer; see George Sherburn, ed., *The Correspondence of Pope,* 5 vols. (Oxford, 1956), 1:45–46.

76. Joseph Spence, *Polymetis* (London, 1741), 1–3; the whole passage is quoted and discussed in Hunt 1986, 221–222.

77. See R. W. King, ''Joseph Spence of Byfleet,'' *Garden History* 6 (1978), 38–64; 7 (1979), 29–48; 8 (1980), 44–65, 77–114.

78. Quoted by Fleming, 1963, 163.

A. A. TAIT

The View from the Road: Joseph Spence's Picturesque Tour

It was as well that Joseph Spence liked to travel, for he was condemned to it. As an impecunious scholar and clergyman, he made his career as the wandering tutor to the Earl of Lincoln, nephew of the Prime Minister Henry Pelham. In return for his pains and on returning from Italy, he acquired a house in Surrey, a rectory in Oxfordshire, and a prebendary of Durham Cathedral—not bad for eighteenth-century plurality.[1] To develop his fortune he had to travel, and unlike many of his contemporaries his journeys were vertical, that is to say, to the north. As befitted an Oxford professor of poetry, let alone professor of modern history, he saw in travel both intellectual and practical ends quite apart from the mundane business of moving from A to B. For Spence, the view from the road required observation, thought, and action, whereby the serenity of nature could become part of the human experience. Not only was pointing out prospects and discussing the pleasures of gardening held out as a cure for the lovesick, like Lord Lincoln, or the infirm, like the publisher Robert Dodsley, but they could also inspire a critical language evaluating both pleasure and prospects.[2] To listen to Spence was to judge a landscape as well as to make one.

Since his death in 1768, Spence's reputation has remained modest.[3] Perhaps that is the way it should be, for he was, as Horace Walpole said, "a good-natured harmless little soul, but more like a silver penny than a genius. It was a neat fiddle-faddle bit of sterling, that had read good books and kept good company, but was too trifling for use, and fit only to please a child."[4] Unkind and dismissive though Walpole was, Spence undoubtedly did try throughout his life to please, and this was the basic aim of the often contrived and labored accounts of his travels

written, it must be admitted, for a pretty sophisticated child.

Such sweet concern for others was equally true of his improvement plans sketched out for gardens encountered on the way. His approach was simple. "To please in laying out a friends grounds," he wrote "one must not mind what the place requires so much, as to how to adapt the parts as well as one can to what he wants."[5] Such a disingenuous spirit is alive in the gardening letters, written in 1755, to the Earl of Darlington about Raby Castle.[6] They catch well Spence's tactful, perhaps unctuous, almost oriental style of self-effacement, remarkable even in the mid-eighteenth century. Spence had a sympathetic ear in the 1st Earl of Darlington, an improver dedicated to undoing the task begun by his spiteful father who had despoiled the entailed estate and partially demolished the patriarchal castle (fig. 1).[7] Lord Darlington was only relatively successful in these restorations, and Spence was one of several wiseacres to whom he turned for advice. A surviving plan of 1749 shows the state of play more or less when Spence arrived on the scene (fig. 2).[8] The problem was a familiar eighteenth-century one: how best to close the public road and remove the village, both of which are shown as ghostly dots on the plan. For such a timid and courtly soul, Spence's suggestions were surprisingly bold, though couched, as might be expected, in the familiar discreet style.

Spence began in his predictable, ambulating manner. "Here are the thoughts that naturally rise in my mind," he wrote, "on seeing the delicious place that they may be ready for your consideration, at any time, when you have a few minutes to spare; or, if you find nothing worthy of considering among them, this paper may easily be flung into the fire or thrown away." He

Fig. 1.
Entrance of Raby Castle, County
Durham   (Massingbred mss., Lincolnshire
Record Office; photograph: author)

Fig. 2.
Plan of Raby Castle with part of the
park, 1749   (Monument Room, Raby
Castle)

then gently moved to the point. "I find Raby
much more beautiful than I expected. I saw
thousands of instances of what your Lordship has
already done to improve it, but very little in
comparison that wants to be done to complete
it." He then flatteringly suggested that Lord
Darlington was "acting something like those
few heroically generous men who are so engaged
in doing good to their neighbours all round that
they neglect themselves," and that keeping the
village at Raby was such an instance. "Should,"
he asked rhetorically, "one wish for a very ugly
village so intimately in one's neighbourhood and
to pass always through the terrible length of
it?"[9] It was a common improver's dilemma, of
course, the results of which can be seen in the
contemporary removed villages of Nuneham
Courtenay or Middleton Stoney,[10] and more
emotionally in Oliver Goldsmith's *The Deserted
Village.* Spence's ultimate solution for Raby was
to make a driveway through the park in between

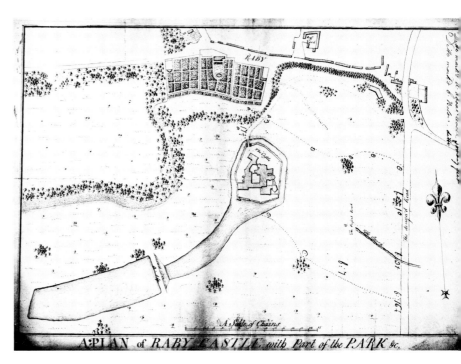

Fig. 3.
View of the park between the two
lakes (Photograph: author)

the two waters to the corner of the Terrace (that is, the wood on the left in fig. 2) and so to the castle (fig. 3). He wrote that "through this means the village (with a little planting) might be quite concealed and that the kitchen garden and offices would stand at the back of your house."[11]

Most of the improvements were carried out in a gradual manner and were completed before the next set of major reforms that were under consideration—that is, those of the landscape gardener Thomas White in 1774.[12] A picturesque view of Raby in 1827 (fig. 4) shows the restored and gothicized castle unfettered by public road and hidden from the prying eyes of the estate village. It stands in a deer park as a bastion of peace and privilege. Spence would have been delighted: a victory for good literary manners. He might have been less pleased to know that his (practical and theoretical) contributions to such an idyll had been forgotten, but he would have been cheered to see that his northern tours and the punishment of such bad food and uncomfortable inns had not been in vain, and that he had established a taste and language on which bolder spirits relied, and which they exploited.

The accounts of the two Scottish tours and some fragments of a similar undertaking have survived with Spence's papers in the Osborn Collection (Beinecke Library, Yale University; see Appendix). They are a mixed bag in which several of the tours, particularly the Scottish one of 1760, exist in rough and unpublished draft. Whether they were ever intended for the press is doubtful, for Spence was shy of print; and so unpublished they have remained. Related to them are straightforward accounts of particular gardens like Stourhead or Piercefield, and a series of small notebooks that Spence called his "road remarks," which deal with anything of interest encountered on his journeys up and down to Durham.[13] They range from the hazards of travel—the cost of dinner at Grantham—to an account of the Leeds man who claimed, dubiously, to be 108 years old.

It is perhaps as well to recall how fresh and new the northern landscape was in 1758 when Spence and Dodsley set off for Scotland. William Gilpin's tour of the Highlands and Lake District in 1776 was still to come, and even Thomas Gray's highland jaunt to Glamis was only undertaken in 1765.[14] Both of these were decisive events in the history of aesthetic taste, and dwarfed the more conventional and historical opinions, of which Thomas Pennant's was the most distinguished.[15] Spence, however, was distinct. He was not a subjective recorder of impressions and feelings like Gilpin and Gray, nor was he an animal, vegetable, and mineral historian like Pennant; he was the polite, industrious

Fig. 4.
View of Raby Castle by Joseph
Miller, 1827   (Photograph: author)

cicerone, preparing his notes as though with some perpetual pupil just over his shoulder who had to be humored and instructed. The habits learnt in France and Italy in the 1730s as a walking topographical dictionary died hard, if at all.

Certainly Spence's reaction to whatever romantic scenery he came across was tame, and measured in broad, not necessarily British terms. At Yew Scar he compared the water running between the winding openings of the mountains with the Rhone at Lake Geneva, and his comparative vocabulary relied strongly on general terms such as "rude" and "alpine."[16] With a similar lack of adventure he turned down the opportunity to visit Eagles Cliff at Lake Ullswater because the day was not fine and the paths "rough," obstacles that would surely have inspired rather than discouraged the true picturesque tourist satirized by William Combe in the adventures of Dr. Syntax.

However, over and above such timidity, Spence's view of the landscape and its relation-ship to gardening was essentially literate. It was, of course, almost rudimentary when compared with that of the professional wanderer like William Gilpin some eighteen years later. With Gilpin the response was set and the vocabulary established, to the extent that it was satirized:

I'll ride and write, and sketch and print,
And thus create a real mint;
I'll prose it here, I'll verse it there
And Picturesque it ev'ry where.[17]

And such writing was just as easily ridiculed visually, in a print by Thomas Rowlandson (fig. 5). As I have suggested, Spence's concept of the traveler's world was that of a diligent bear leader, who looked at his journal with an editorial eye and saw the rural landscape as a text to be made sense of within the literary tradition of the mid-eighteenth century. Nothing makes such attitudes plainer than the tour of 1758, whose purpose was a pursuit not of the picturesque, like Gray's, but of a shy and difficult Scottish poet,

Thomas Blacklock, with the publisher Robert Dodsley.[18]

The point of departure for all of Spence's northern journeys was Durham and his prebendal priory of Finchale. It was to the latter that Spence removed himself in high summer and there that he had rooms in the small farmhouse adjoining the ruins that can be seen in a contemporary print of about 1760 (fig. 6).[19] It was an attractive spot, with river and woods forming a dramatic bank on one side and Spence's new and small garden on the other. Finchale still remains, though rather muddy and the worse for twentieth-century wear. The priory had the added attraction for the antiquarian that it had been the home of Saint Goderic the hermit, whose torments fascinated and appalled the eighteenth century.[20] Saint Goderic is still remembered; Spence, alas, forgotten.

The point of return for both of Spence's Scottish tours was Edinburgh. The route of his journey can be traced on an eighteenth-century map of the southern half of Scotland (fig. 7). The tour of 1758 was virtually a square, across the top of England from Durham to the Lake District, then up the west coast to Dumfries, eastward through lowland Scotland to Edinburgh, and then down the coast again to Durham. In 1760 it was Durham to Edinburgh with an excursion to Glasgow in the west.[21] Such journeys gave Spence a fair scenic range and allowed him to see, in perspective as it were, the progress of the landscape movement in a very conservative part of the kingdom. It was probably this concern with landscape rather than with scenery that discouraged him from extending his tour farther

Fig. 6.
Finchale Priory, from Thomas Pennant's *A Tour in Scotland*

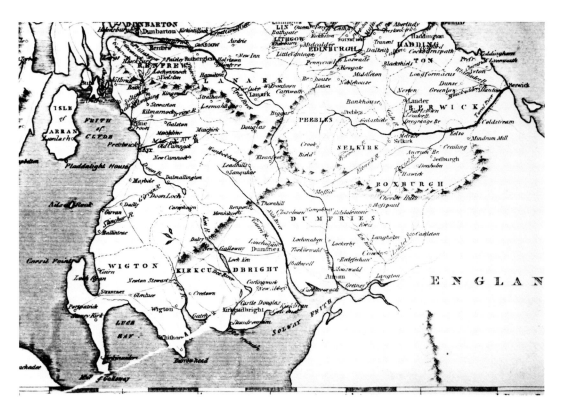

Fig. 7.
Map of Scotland, c. 1770

Fig. 8.
The Annandale Hills, from Sir Robert Jardine's *Inchology of Annandale*

VIEW AND SECTION ACROSS THE VALLEY OF THE ANNAN FROM EAST TO WEST.

PLATE XII.

Fig. 9.
The Moffat Hills   (Photograph: author)

fries, is *Criffel Hill"* (fig. 8). From Dumfries he began his journey eastward across Scotland to Edinburgh and traveled through some of the bleakest of all Scottish landscape, more welcoming in a modern photograph than it would then have been (fig. 9). After Moffat he was almost continuously among the hills till the edges of Edinburgh. "As soon as you begin rising up that mountain," he wrote, "everything grows quite barren about you" and "on the right, was the Grey Mare's Tail; the mountain that had appeared before us all day, with clouds on its top & sometimes a good way down." Beyond these mountains Spence came upon the moorland center of Scotland, and here his editorial guard slipped and the guide despaired at the grim repetition of the endless waste. He noted balefully, "On, on, on, without a leaf or blade of corn to be seen.—Heath and rushes ye highest things that grew; except 3 or 4 little shrubs on the sides of our bank" (see Appendix, pp. 367, 368). The view from the road was distinctly bleak. Between Moffat and Broughton he had seen only two minor country houses and the gardener and landscape critic in Spence was appalled by the "badness of the land." So dead was Spence's critical response that at West Linton, to the southwest of Edinburgh, he confused a statue of Lady Gifford and her five children with the Virgin Mary—and that in Presbyterian Scotland (fig. 10)![23]

In the account of this journey, and to a lesser extent in the shorter account of his travels of 1760, Spence regularly used a distinct vocabulary of his own fashioning. It had a range, and dealt in types as well as in smaller descriptive declensions. Most were straightforward, like "Shenstone fall," "champaine country," "Fontainbleau rocky" or "Fontainbleau—Picture," and "grovettes," all of whose sources may be pinned down fairly easily. "Shenstone fall" was derived from one of the waterfalls at William Shenstone's garden, The Leasowes, which Spence had visited for the first time on his way north in 1758 and where an oak had been named after him (fig. 11).[24] Spence's phrase "champaine country" was taken from the *Essay on Landscape Gardening* of the 1750s by the Scottish theorist Sir John Dalrymple.[25] It meant for Spence nice countryside, well cultivated, populated, and cheerful, and was associated by him with the landscapes of William Kent. "Grovettes" were small clumps of trees that Spence described in his "Letter about Gardening" of 1751 and showed

north to the Scottish Highlands. It may well be that he found the empty hills and moorlands of the Scottish border and the lakes and mountains of the Lake District indulged and absorbed all his exploratory zeal. Spence may well have been in Gray's sights when Gray explained that he gave "not a fig for your Poet, Painter, Gardener and Handyman, that have not been among them [the Highland mountains:] their imagination can be made up of nothing but bowling-greens, flowering shrubs, horse-ponds, Fleet-ditches, shell-grottoes and chineé-rails."[22]

Spence had come to Scotland along the edge of the Lake District. Unlike Gray, he was daunted and possibly depressed by high mountains. He observed them with a conscientiously wary eye: "a waving line of newly cultivated hills" and in their midst rises "*Birrenswark,* with a more mountanous & dark aspect. The dark high one to the west that runs into the sea beyond Dum-

there in a little pen sketch (fig. 12).[26] They were again an essential element in any Kent landscape. "Fountainbleau rocky" was derived from the sixteenth-century Grotte des Pins at Fontainebleau, which Spence had seen in his tutoring days and to which he referred in his letter of 1747 to the *General Advertiser* (fig. 13).[27]

Spence's landscape types were predictable. "Pretty" and "alpine" were two of his standard and categorical adjectives, which he employed in the conventional way—alpine hills and pretty view. More interesting was his term "new Taste," by which he meant the informal style of gardening that he and the circle around Alexander Pope approved and practiced. Sir Thomas Hay's house at Alderston (seen on the way back from Edinburgh to Durham) was accurately described by Spence as having "the prettiest gardens (3 quarters in ye new-taste)" that he saw in Scotland (see Appendix, p. 370).[28] The meaning of the term was made clear by Spence's description of Prestonfield House, the home of his Scottish host Sir Alexander Dick, as in the "old style of le Notre."[29] A similar example of this style was at Hopetoun House, where the "large stiff scale" of the formal garden can be glimpsed still in an aerial view of Hopetoun in drought (fig. 14). It was a style that Spence detested; for the formal garden and all its trappings he held a "mortal Aversion" and that, for Spence, was very strong language.[30]

Fig. 10.
Carved figure at West Linton, Peeblesshire (Royal Commission on the Ancient and Historical Monuments of Scotland)

Fig. 11.
View of the waterfalls at The Leasowes, from Paul Sandby's *Virtuosi's Museum* (Glasgow University Library)

At Prestonfield Spence made his most obvious attempt to suppress the old style in Scotland. Like all zealots he gave himself wholeheartedly to the business, and returned there in 1760 and possibly in 1762.[31] At about this time he had a survey made and from it produced a general scheme of improvement, probably now lost. By 1760 he had got rid of the box edging of the parterres, had a pavilion built where he suggested, but failed to have the "hateful yew" (its owner's expression) cut down.[32] In the parkland to the south and east of the house he had several of his grovettes planted. One of them survived at least into the nineteenth century; it appears on an ordnance survey sheet of about 1855 (fig. 15). Spence admired Prestonfield House and its setting for having a "Verdure as soft and Plantations as light-some as the Rock [the Edinburgh landmark of Arthur's Seat] is huge and horrid". A just, but unsympathetic judgment, as present photographic views clearly show (fig. 16). Certainly Prestonfield was a less grand commission than Raby, and Spence's improvements there modest—more a gentle bending of fashion than any sharper change of the stylistic guard. And, paradoxically, here lies much of Spence's importance. As both a traveling and gardening pundit he accurately reflected the shift in attitude toward landscape, scenery, and Scotland in the mid-eighteenth century. The very modesty of his views and the caution of his opinions emphasize their acceptability and importance.

In this account of Joseph Spence as a reluctant tourist of the picturesque I have consistently emphasized the qualities of discretion and modesty. I have, perhaps unkindly, seen Spence as a perpetual cicerone or bear-leader and have likened him

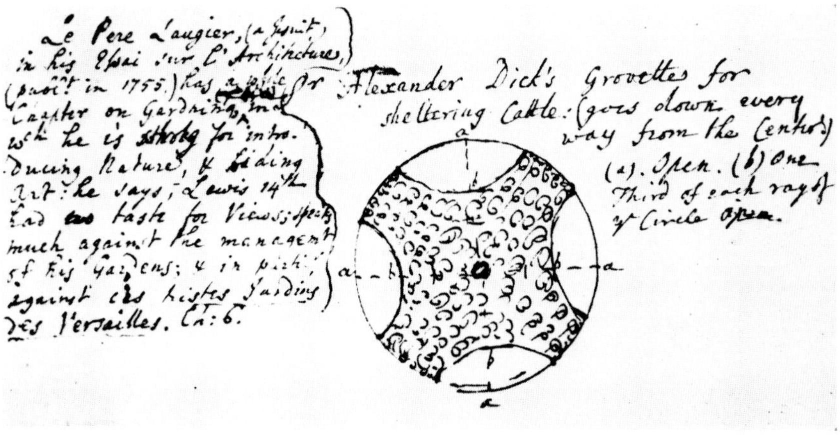

Fig. 12.
Sketch of "grovettes," by Joseph Spence (Osborn Collection, Yale University)

Fig. 13.
The Grotte des Pins at the Château de Fontainebleau (Photograph: The Garden Library, Dumbarton Oaks, Washington, D.C.)

to a walking topographical dictionary and also a copy editor. I have called him disingenuous with an occasionally slippery nature and an almost oriental cast of mind. I have not been friendly. At the same time I have shown his wholehearted devotion to the new style of landscape gardening, and how he went subtly about his business

of suggesting improvements and making sure that they were taken up. In his northern tours to the English lakes and lowland Scotland Spence grappled conscientiously with the difficult matter of adjusting language to scenery and keeping a sort of standard vocabulary. None of these are high aims, all are modest. He epitomized chang-

Fig. 14.
Aerial view of Hopetoun House, West Lothian District (Royal Commission on the Ancient and Historical Monuments of Scotland)

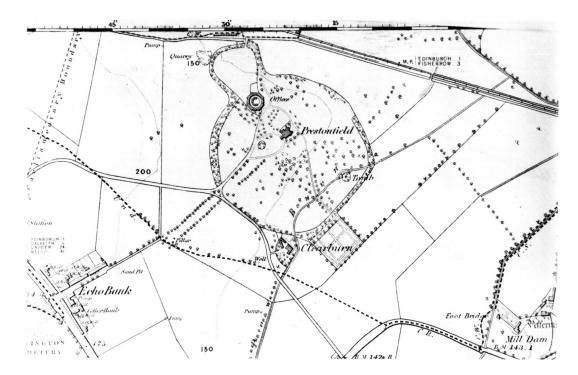

Fig. 15.
Detail of the ordnance survey plans of Edinburghshire, 1855 (Glasgow University Library)

Fig. 16.
View of Prestonfield House, Edinburgh (Royal Commission on the Ancient and Historical Monuments of Scotland)

ing opinion—not at grass roots (he was intellectually and socially above that), not in fashionable society like Walpole's, not among the philosophers of nature, but in the heartlands of sensible, informed, and comfortable opinion. For Spence there is no niche in the hall of fame, but there is a modest alcove in the more congenial anteroom of the famous.

NOTES

1. For an account of Spence's career, see Joseph Spence, *Observations, Anecdotes and Characters of Books and Men,* ed. James Osborn, 2 vols. (Oxford, 1966), 17–37; for a more general account of his life, see Austin Wright, *Joseph Spence* (Chicago, 1950).

2. Spence had been the traveling tutor to the Earl of Lincoln during the earl's Grand Tour of 1739–1741, and Lincoln remained Spence's principal patron. He was a significant benefactor both as the future 2nd Duke of Newcastle and as nephew of the Prime Minister Henry Pelham. In 1751 Spence wrote to Lord Lincoln that he had had the satisfaction of steering him away from "a match which you seem'd thoroughly inclined to" and "leading you into an inclination for Planting and Gardening" (Osborn Collection, Beinecke Library, Yale University). Robert Dodsley had accompanied Spence on his Scottish tour of 1758 and Spence hoped he would accompany him on his journey of 1764: "I hope the air and exercise may give a new will to him." In fact the reverse was true, and Dodsley died as Spence's guest at Durham in 1764; see Ralph Straus, *Robert Dodsley* (London, 1910), 300.

3. See Wright 1950, 1. In 1950, Wright wrote of Spence "the position he occupies today in the history of English literature is not a lofty one. Nevertheless, that position, though humble, is honourable and secure."

4. Wilmarth Sheldon Lewis, ed., *The Yale Edition of Horace Walpole's Correspondence,* 48 vols. (New Haven, 1937–1983), 2:216–217.

5. Spence 1966, 1:419.

6. There are two reports by Spence on Raby, both of 1755; one in a letter to the Earl of Lincoln, 15 July 1755, which paraphrases parts of Spence's earlier report to the Earl of Darlington, 7 July 1755. The draft of the latter is in the Osborn Collection, Beinecke Library, Yale University. Spence's diary for 1755 shows that he was at Raby on 11 June, 2 July, 4 August, 11 August (letter, 15 July 1755, Osborn Collection).

7. For an account of Raby, see Alistair Rowan, "Gothic Restoration at Raby Castle," *Architectural History* 15 (1972), 23–50.

8. This unsigned map is captioned "A Plan of Raby Castle with Part of the Park;" Rowan, 1972, 50.

9. Spence to Lord Darlington, 7 July 1755, Osborn Collection, Beinecke Library, Yale University.

10. For a succinct account of these two removals, see Jennifer Sherwood and Nikolaus Pevsner, *The Buildings of England. Oxfordshire* (Harmondsworth, 1974), 703, 725; and more fully in Stephen Butler et al., *Of Oxfordshire Gardens* (Oxford, 1982), 51-76.

11. Spence to Lord Darlington, 7 July 1755, fol. 4, Osborn Collection, Beinecke Library, Yale University.

12. Rowan 1972, 50. For the career of Thomas White, see A. A. Tait, *The Landscape Garden in Scotland* (Edinburgh, 1980), 146–173.

13. Some of the individual accounts or reports have been published in R. W. King, "Joseph Spence of Byfleet," *Garden History* 6 (1978), 38–64; 7 (1979), 29–48; 8 (1980), 44–65, 77–114.

14. Gilpin's tour was published as *Observation, relates chiefly to picturesque beauty . . . Highlands of Scotland,* 2 vols. (London, 1789); Gray's account appears in P. Toynbee and L. Whimbley, eds., *Correspondence of Thomas Gray,* 3 vols. (London, 1935), vol. 2.

15. Thomas Pennant, *A Tour in Scotland* (Chester, 1771).

16. See Appendix, pp. 366.

17. William Combe, *The First Tour of Doctor Syntax,* 3 vols. (London, n.d.), 1:5.

18. Blacklock lived in Dumfries, where Spence and Dodsley visited him in 1758. See Appendix. For an account of Blacklock and Spence, see Spence 1966, 428–431.

19. For Spence at Finchale, see Wright 1950, 147–148; Spence 1966, 1:422. The priory was described by Pennant, who visited it in 1769: "the view towards the ruins of *Finchal-Abbey* is remarkably great; and the walk beneath the cliffs was a magnificant solemnity, a fit retreat for its monastic inhabitants" (Pennant 1771, 28). For Spence's possible improvements in the garden there, see King 1980, 58.

20. There is an account of Saint Goderic at Finchale in Pennant 1771; during the saint's sixty-three years at Finchale, his "austerities" were seen as "the most senseless extravagance." He died in 1170.

21. The manuscript for this is in the Osborn Collection, Beinecke Library, Yale University; it is captioned: "Set out from Durham; September 5 1760." It is incomplete and made up from several different drafts. It ends with Spence's return from Glasgow to Sir Alexander Dick at Prestonfield House. The last document is a charge for the hire of a chaise with two horses with which the journey was accomplished.

22. Toynbee and Whimbley 1935, 2:899.

23. See Appendix, 368. The monument survives in part, and is dated 1666; see *Royal Commission on the Ancient and Historical Monuments of Scotland: Peebleshire,* 2 vols. (Edinburgh, 1967), 2:340.

24. For Spence's visit to Shenstone, see Wright 1950, 160; Marjorie Williams, *The Letters of William Shenstone* (Oxford, 1939), 496; for Spence's own description of The Leasowes, see King 1980, 63–64.

25. See Tait 1980, 45. Among Dalrymple's four categories of landscape, his "third situation" was that of "a champaine rich country, full of gentle equalities" (Sir John Dalrymple, *An Essay on Landscape Gardening,* ed. Boton Corney [London, 1823], 17).

26. Rule 14 in Spence, "Letter about Gardening," 1751, Osborn Collection, Beinecke Library, Yale University, maintained the need to intersperse "different sorts of trees in each Grovette. Mr. Kent was always us'd to stake out his Grovettes before they planted."

27. Spence 1966, 1: 409.

28. Alderston, East Lothian, was laid out before 1752 by the landscape gardener James Bowie for Sir Thomas Hay (Tait 1980, 64).

29. For a succinct account of Prestonfield House, now a hotel, see Colin McWilliam, *Buildings of Scotland: Edinburgh* (Harmondsworth, 1984), 638–640.

30. Spence 1751, 3; Spence wrote: "I have such a mental aversion to them, that was I to chose a Motto for myself, as a Pretender to Gardening, it shd be, Mutat quadrata rotundis."

31. Sir Alexander Dick, Spence's Edinburgh host, wrote in September 1762: "I have a thousand new things to tell you. My Nieces the Miss Leiths are here & will be of our Circle when you come" (Henry E. Huntington Library and Art Gallery, San Marino, California, Newcastle ms. 466). In 1765 Spence and Dick planned to meet at Durham in the following July, 1766 (Henry E. Huntington Library and Art Gallery, San Marino, California, Newcastle ms. 470).

32. Sir Alexander Dick wrote to Spence in 1762: "some works that are going on in the garden, particularly a new, neat little house, in the very spot where you fixd it and some road work on the north side of the house" (Newcastle ms. 460). Later Dick wrote again: "the hateful yew with its Bushy top and ugly waste still remains to stare me in the face; and give opportunities to James to exclaim every day against it in your name" (Henry E. Huntington Library and Art Gallery, San Marino, California, Newcastle ms. 464).

APPENDIX

In the following text, Spence's "Tour in Scotland," I have adjusted the spelling of names and places, the use of capital letters, and the numbering of footnotes. The punctuation, abbreviations, paragraphs, and content of the footnotes are as in the original.

At Penrith saw the Skiddaw, from the old ruin'd Castle; (now belonging to the D of Portld:) several old pieces of antiquities in the Churchyard, (said to belong to Owen Caesareus—went thro an arbor-lane; & by Mr. Hassel's) to the Ullswater Lake. It opens to the view, just beyond a very pretty hill, almost wholy cover'd wth trees; except where they have cut the walk all up & down again on the other side, strip'd on each hand with 5 or 6 rows of firs. The Lake is more like a wide serpentine river than a lake; tho there is no very great bending till toward the end. We pass'd 7 or 8 miles on the right (or N) side of it; sometimes thorough arbor-road; sometimes woody, & at others quite open. Went beyond the Fine Rock,[1] that very well deserves a print of it; (they call it, Yew-Scar,) & saw where the water comes in, between the winding openings of the mountains, (very much like the passage for the Rhosne to the Lake of Geneva). The water begins about three miles higher. As we advanc'd a pretty hill, this mountain grew more & more rude & alpine; & saw the clouds beneath the tops of several of them, all the morning. The man, at whose house we dined, had caught trouts of above 20 pound weight there; & speaks of them as excellently good. These are also Charr there, etc, etc. The side on wch we pass'd is Gowbarrow Park, belonging to Mr. Howard; the other side is Martindale Park, Mr. Hassel's (The pretty hill is call'd Dunmollard.) Pass'd almost half way from Penrith thro' a mixture of down & heath; uncultivated, tho' said to be very fit for cultivation: (six endow'd schools within less than ten mile of Penrith) with a line of fields to the left; & the Black Hills we pass'd between to Ullswater appearing behind them, as there was another line of barren hills, at a distance, beyond ye heath on the right.—Then, village with cultivated grounds, hedges, & some trees.—From the rising after this, appear'd the view of a more extended & better looking country, wth Carlisle, about the middle of it, & back'd again with hills. We saw clouds again under the tops of some of these hills, (and particularly, the middle one in the Opening to Ullswater,) tho' the day was quite clear & sunshiny.—Carlisle is neither large nor handsome; the walk on the ramparts too narrow to walk with pleasure; & the view thence hardly pays for any trouble.

Very soon after we left Carlisle, we pass'd two considerable stone-bridges; both over the River Eden, & very near each other.—Soon after Mr. Paterson's, with large plantations of firs a good way on before it.—About 4 miles on, came by the side of the Eden, & saw people crossing it. (horseman first; man, 2 cows: man: boys) & afterwards drove thorough that river, the Esk & the Sark: on the other side of which we were in Scotland.

With the Solway Firth all along to ye left, we came on thorough a poor looking & too naked country; & with three or four sheds of dirt wall'd cottages, & saw scarce anything pleasing, but the good stocks of firing laid in at each of them, (piles of turf & peat) against the winter for ab't 10 miles to Annan. Here we saw more distinctly the ridge of hills, several of which had appear'd wt others first rising tw'd Carlisle. (Behind Mrs. Blair's house to the north are two brown ones near Woodcock Hill to the left, & the Brown Moor to the right;) farther off is a waving line of newly cultivated hills, from one of these to the other, call'd *Cowdens:* & in the midst behind that, rises *Birrenswark,* with a more mountanous & dark aspect. The dark high one to the west that runs into the sea beyond Dumfries, is *Criffel Hill.* The chief street at Annan is broad; & is terminated by the town house & kirk adjoining to the farther end of it; & a little way on, is a very good bridge, on which att 1/3 on you pass under an arch, built abt 70 year ago; & both very good work & in the old Roman stile; partly the Arch: much above par with the town. Here we saw a salmon leap; & bought one that had been caught, but a little before, of 6 1/2 pd weight for a shilling (The usual prices for salmon there fro' 3 halfpence to 2 pence & halfpenny). Bank new planted with firs just beyond their garden. Poor women even in the streets, without shoes and stockings; (Master Spearman with ruffles & naked legs) and the eagerness visible in the boys, for your halfpenny at ye gates.) The close wheels ceas'd at Penrith; but appear'd again in the poorer parts of the road: & were the common ones when we got into Scotland. The rocky appearances, first near Lancaster, continu'd on here & there on the road sides quite into Scotland. There is no supply of Post Horses at Annan; & we were forced to send on for some to Dumfries, to get thither.

Soon after leaving the bridge, we got into heaths & barren country again; with the Solway Firth to the left, & sometimes along parts of it: yet more like the Lincolnshire Washes. Before we were got half way, we saw some fir woods (Ld. Stormont's seat) to the right & then pass'd thorough Ruthwell, (pronounc'd Revel) a length of dirt-built cottages, the sight of which gave you concern for inhabitants & call'd at Mr. Lothian's, at the end of the Town, very near the Firth again:

& came the nearest of any part we were in to *Crif-felhill;* from which extends a nearer and lower line of hill, of good cultivation; which with *Bankend,* the town at the extremity of it, has all along a very good appearance. Then the ground grows naked & barren again, till you come in sight of Dumfries.

There are a great many good new houses in Dumfries; particularly in the High Street; (had lately a great trade in Tabacco which is now quite broke down by the additional Duties on that commodity) The old houses were much in ye Flemish stile. The Town House (one of the old & irregular buildings) has St. Michael drest like a Bishop, (Wingd with Mitre & Crosier) & treading on a serpent, in mezzo relievo, on the front of it: 'tis the arms of the place & appears (only better done) on our Patents for the Freedom of the Town. The Trades-Hall by, built about 50 year ago, but indifferent too; has a Lyon with this Motto round it, GOD BLESS THE QUEEN AND CRAFT, & on the side a bad relivo of two women with their hair loose & fighting over a measure not full, & head of a Devil grinning or gaping over them.

There are two Kirks; & Mr. Jameson's very pretty Chapel; (Octagon with venetian window for eastend; not half a circle, but adapted to the Octagon stile.)—The river Nith runs by the town; & about 6 miles S'ly of it, falls into the Solway Firth. There is a bridge with 9 arches over it & the walks on the bank of it are pretty. The path ye S., is prettily terminated at each end; & goes more in sight of the river that to the N looks farther, but not so pretty at first but when you rise upon the high bank it exceeds it for prettiness a good deal: (the walk there sd be 3 or 4 times as broad as it is, & be carryd on thro' the pleasing wood below). It was from this, that we saw Queensberry-Hill (that gives the ducal title) before us, & Terregles, Ld. Nithsdale's seat, to the S. (In going to it, we passd by the Well, where Mr. Blacklock was in so much danger; as the high bank itself is at what he describes as a Promentory, in his Pastoral to Eventhe).—When you are two thirds over the bridges, you go under an arch & step into Galloway.—(The woman treading linnen in a tub by the waterside &, at times, showing her backside)—Above 5000 inhabitants.

The morning we set out from Dumfries was overcast & gloomy with faint dashes of sun-shine (sometimes) here & there; & the face of the Country, for the 5 or 6 miles, was not unlike it: the greatest part of what we pass'd being Heathy; with darkish hills in the distant view; but houses, woody, & corn fields; sprinkled on their sides & about the middle ground. Pass'd, the first line of cultivated land; about a mile over—Then barren again; with green hills, on each side for a little way; & then a stream of cultivated vale[2] close along the road on the right, (& 2 or 3 cornfields on the left) for about 3 mile. Crossed the River A; & then 2d line of half-cultivated vale for about half a mile—barren again for a mile—crossed 3d line of quarter cultivated; above 2 mile?—Barren again for a mile? Threequarters cultivated corn & fallow fields: not long—strip of barren: little dale, thorough cultivated; with the Kinnel running thro' it: Pass'd that river (Then all barren near; went on, for a considerable way, on a high bank; to ye right of the Kinnel; the opposite bank, all the way, more or less pleasing; pieces of rocks & now and then a hollow in, tufted with woody. A little corn-field & another fallow, down in the bed of the River.— Come into a longish dale, terminated with moderate hills, cultivated above & wooded below; on each side the Kinnel wch is still by you. The rising of that hill you pass is somewhat equivocal;[3] the latter part of the descent barren on each side, near Birrenswark, with lines of quite wild mountains before you—[4] Descends into the great vale, encircled with hills, sprinkled here & there with cottages; and mostly cultivated; (as far as the badness of the ground will allow it.) Pass'd the River Evan wch runs in a Shenstone sort of Fall, to the bridge—(The ruin, on ye right Evan-Castle)—The houses all the way hither from Dumfries poor but built with stone & covered with Turf or Clods of Earth. Got soon after to Moffat.

The street at Moffat is so broad that the Marquis of Annandale, (who lives but 3 miles off), has a good Bowling-green in the midst of it; for the benefit of the place: it has been much improved in its buildings since; t'was before only a (Cot-Town or) Town of Cottages.—As soon as you leave, the plain grows narrower & the hills less cultivated, except in one or two little widenings, especially that a little before you come to the foot of *Erickstane—brae.* As soon as you begin rising up that mountain, every thing grows quite barren about you: (I mean as to any sort of corn; for the sheep were feeding in good numbers round the very highest point of it). From the top, you see the banks of the Evan which we pass'd in the morning; & quite into England, particularly the great Table Hill by Cockermouth.[5] Tis from this mountain that the Tweed, Clyde & Annan have their sources. On the right, was the Grey Mare's Tail; the mountain that had appeared before us all day, with clouds on its top & sometimes a good way down. When we began to descend, the hills appeard still more alpine (from the frequent mosses there on;) & a little way down, we stopd at the Great Hollow on ye right hand, (visible long in front too, as we came toward Moffat,) which is call'd the Marquis of Annandale's Beeftub.[6] On the first step on this side the Mount, (& often after) water running in the road; (from the mosses). On the first piece of ground, anything like a plain, a house with 3 or 4 fields, chiefly grassfields; crossd a little rivulet; all uncultivated again. Then, Head of the Tweed to ye right.

Soon after a House (Tweed-brae-Foot) with a grass field or two & 3 spots of garden stuff (including potatoes etc.) Not a tree or blade of corn to be seen between the former and this—one or two houses by[7] the young Tweed, some time after in ye Valley; & a stream running down from our side to join him: (does not do it soon & a little after the narrow Vale looks broken entirely by their different windings). There are several streams that run down to him from the same side after, but he does not look anything like a river till we came toward The Crook.—A mile on, 2 or 3 houses, & 2 or 3 fields.—On, on, on without a leaf or blade of corn to be seen.—Heath and rushes ye highest things that grew; except 3 or 4 little shrubs on the sides of our bank, like sallows. A house between the hills to ye left with a potatoe bed—First tree, ditto; abt a mile & a half before you come to the Crook—A line of cultivated soon after, to the right, with scattering houses, quite to the Village (Tweeds-Muir) little church on odd rising that concealed two thirds of it; some trees & a bit of a hedge. On our side, opposite to it a Gentleman's House; with a grovette and line of firs etc.—Fontainbleau-Rocky on our side & on the other, the round steep Hill, with sheep moving along the sides in such strait lines; one above another; & some confusedly out of the lines. All this road of uncultivated ground lies between green hills, like downs; very fit for sheep & sometimes with flocks feeding upon them: & some parts, you have cattle grazing, esp'ly low and the latter end of it.

Fontainbleau rocky & ruder hills, when you leave the Crook. The house to the right (full planted round with fir walks etc.) is Broughton where Murray was taken. Hanging fields on beyond it for a good way & a (shrub) Wood. Another such wood on farther, on our side; (they might both be oaks, for the trees are extremely stunted) with very good cornfields, walks of trees: & a round-fenced plantation of firs a little beyond it. Turn'd off to the left from the Tweed a little after, as the Tweed too turns off to the right for Peebles, on the elbowing ground where it goes off, the ruins of an old Castle, which they call'd Drummelzier—After the turn thro' a vale for a good way full cultivated.—At about 8 miles, *Mr. Murrays* own house; with a grove, walks & wood running along the foot of the Hill. After, passed a vale less cultivated (the badness of the land) and coasted it on riding to ye right hand of it, till we lost sight of it in mounting *Broughton Hill.* There was then a vale again to our right; worse ground & much less cultivated: (not their fault, from the *very little* slips which they catch where they can.) Nothing but uncultivated visible to us, in some parts fm toward the top of that Hill.[8] From the

highest points of it, you see Errickstane Brae, W'ly—Tweedsmuir Hills,—Tinto Hills, (each cap't with clouds)—Lauder Hills, Pentland Hills;[9] opening where our road for Edinb: (all the round beside, hilly)—When you begin to descend you have a full cultivated vale to the left; which rises all over your spur of the hill, in the latter parts of it.—

Then full cultivated rising grounds & hills mostly ditto.—The Gimelli; (or two springs) just before Blyth Bridge. Pasd that: went on thro' little cultiv'd to quite uncult'd for a step: soon well cult'd to ye right again.—Then the former heath widens, on each hand; & you have not cult'd ground on each again, till a little before you come to West Linton; on entering which, I was at first very much surpriz'd to see a Statue of the Virgin Mary, standing erect on ye basis in the midst of the Market place; but on enquiry; found it was a Lady Giffard, formerly of that town. Her husband, it seems, was a very good man & very fond of Statuary; he made this figure of his wife; & 5 of her children: one for each corner of the base & another *stood* on her head: (there are but 3 of them remain'g) tis said, he had adorned all windows & chimney-pieces, with figures relating to the same; (tis a pity his art, was not equal to his affection. The odd feathered fire-skreens that they all hold down before their aprons—like Priests in cowls; button'd over the breast & flowr'd behind.)

We had been told every where, & by every body that the road from Linton to Edinburgh was all thro' a plain; but I suppose in Scotl'd they call that ground flat, which we call hilly in the southern counties of England. It was almost all misted over, different spurs of the Pass at Pentland-Hills, or waves from them. The former half of the way generally lookd wild & barren;[10] afterwards the view grew better & better, & at last quite enlarged & fine.

Long line of rising ground (Water of Leith) with several pieces of wood to the right.—After we turn'd on the left & coasted the farther side of the Pentland-Hills, there are 2 or 3 large houses, with woods & plantations about them; & then part of our road planted on each side with pleasing-looking trees,[11] a thing we had not been usd to for a great while: & after the woody, you came at once into a quite open cultivated Champain: to the right.—on the rising before us a neat Summer House;[12] in an opening between two lines of woody.—The next eminence had a long line of rocky before us,[13] to ye right & when the Pentland Hills cease to interfere, a charming long view opened on the left; flanked (next on) by 3 or 4 strangely-pleasing swellings or hills,[14] with very pretty white-houses, or villas; as the ground on again from them to the Firth is think studded with other generally red ones.[15]

When you first come up to the Rocky Line, you see the Castle on the right, the town in the middle & (too much of) a high black dreary rock on ye left.[16] The Firth appears in a length to the right & in greater breadth to the left. And also behind all is a chain of hills & mountains of a vast length; which closes the scene in a great & pleasing manner.

The castle is built all on rock. One fine view (on the opening of the Pentland Hills) W; Highland hills, very indistinct then, NW-Leith, a mile from Edinburgh.[17] On the seaside, their port 9 or 10 th'd inhabitants in it. Range of Hills called Montis Ocelli by Buchanan—NE—The Bass a vast squarish rock, E'ly—The pointed mountain (we saw so far off as by itself) North Berwick-Law, E— (pass'd the two cannons that point to the Weigh-House) Arthur's Seat S.E.—Herriots Hospital more S.—The Meadows; (pleasure-walks of a mile) S—(& the Wright's House of James (6th & 1st.).—The Blackford Hill & Braid Hills S.W. We came in, between the Braid Hill & the Pentland-Hills. The Firth goes into the land 20 miles to the left & tis 40 (open fr. 15 on at ye sea: its greatest breadth) to the main sea on the right.[18]

The Great Street begins from the Weigh House & goes on to Holyrood House; it was the former which was beat about the Rebels ears in '45, by 2 Canons (pointed a little differently from what they are now,) without hurting a single house in the very *narrow street* that goes to it from the Castle-Hill. In that street ye house for water brought (in leaden-pipes) from about Moreton (2 or 4 miles); to a cistern there, that holds 260 tun of water.

We lodg'd (at Mrs. Thomsons over the old Coffee House,) opposite to the Royal-Exchange, wch will be a good handsome building when finisht. The ground which it stands on & incloses, cost 12th^d pound, tho' not large; (wch, by the way, will account for their building houses so high in Edinburgh; (how put up?) & the middle row of houses which blocks up the great street so much, cost the same sum.

We went thorough the Netherbow,[19] to Holyrood House. The front looks not ill; & the square-court within, very well; (Arcade, with Doric pillars & ye two stories above, Ionic, & Corinthian.) Parts of the pallace are granted out; (to the D of Argyle, & 1 or 2 other noblemen:) & the State-Rooms, that are not so, look naked & dirty. First ye Guard Room; then ye Antechamber & then ye Presence Chamber. In 2 of these? is Le Bruns design of Alexander's Battles, (for ye K.L. of France's tapestry) colour'd by Dewit. In a long Gallery are bad pictures of all their Kings, fro 330 years before Christ to Ch: 2nd; who is call'd the 110th (they are all number'd, but not hung in any order) This Gallery is 147 f long in all (there's a wooden partition that takes off a pretty well pro-

portioned room from ye end of it, lately put up) 28 f broad & 18 high. The Pallace was built in 1671.

The Royal Infirmary is a (better &) neater building than Heriot Hospital[20] & may be call'd an *Universal Infirmary,* for they take in any of his Majesty's subjects, from any of our Colonies as well as from the 3 Kingdoms. There's a good operation-room, (like that of Leyden) & very well contriv'd Hot (& Cold) Baths. From the top of it, you have a good view of the City: you see ye houses go down and then *up* again to ye High Street, (& they do the same on the other side.) Mr. Hamilton's printing office is a very good one: tis there they have printed the pretty Terence; the Anacreon etc.

The length of the City from the Castle to the Pallace[21] is a large mile without the gate, half a mile large (wide?)—The Parliament Close houses, 14 story high; (including one under ground:) there are many others of 10 or 11—The number of souls by the last computation, 53000; but it was reckon'd too large: it may be 50000—The Chief Trade & Manufactures are fine linnen, tan'd leather, iron work, course woolen & a small quantity of fine[22]—In the Low Countries the publick inclination, is in favour of the Government, excepting in the City of Edinburgh, where the inhabitants being made up from all the different parts of Scotland it must be more mixt.—In the Highlands of Scotland, they are more generally disaffected to the Government, but it is not so general, but that there are many exceptions. The most northerly countries are well-affected. The Commonalty follow the opinions of their Chiefs: & now that the Forfeited Estates are annext to the Crown, & put into Commission, 'tis imagin'd that in a few years all disaffection may be rooted out.

The two first Posts (to & fm Dunbar) from Edinburgh we pass'd thorough a very good & cultivated country; sprinkled, here & there with Gentlemen's seats & plantations. Got soon to the seaside; (or the Firth of Forth.) Tis a nobel Bason; & the greatest part of it looks land-lockt: (by East Lothian on ye right, and ye shire of Fife to ye left.) Before the 4th milestone, you have woods coming down from the right toward the shore, & I was very glad to find on enquiry that they were Sr David Dalrymple's: for tis a very pleasing place; (and only wants a few openings to catch the sea oftener in ye walks & in intermix light among the shades,) & a few scattered clump & little touches in the more modern way.) The House very good; & the Library particularly so, both as to its proportions & furniture.[23]—Soon after we pass'd thorough Musselburgh[24] by the sea-side again.— Turn'd to ye right & left Preston-pans a little before us on the sea-side.—Stoppd when higher on the rising of the road, to view the field of Battle (or rather at the begin'g of the flight of our men.) About a quarter of a mile below, was poor Col:

Gardner's, with the two summer houses & gardens towards us; then the walks, woods, and house, of Ld Preston-Grange:[25] backt, with Prestonpans; as that by the sea. (Gladsmure, by wch the rebels lovd to call that battle in regard to some old *prophecy,* is 2 mile off.)—About a mile after, & 9 from Edinburgh, we went thro' Tranent; a little Village, where ye rebels lay the night after their easy victory—Sr Thomas Hay's on the left a little before Haddington is a very odd up & down house, with rooms elegantly furnisht; & the prettiest gardens, (3 quarters in ye new-taste,) that we saw in Scotland.

Sr Thomas loaded us with kindness, talk & strawberries—Mr. Charteris' principal house & woods afterwards to ye right; & abt in a mile or 2 on, to ye left: & plantations on each side the road.—Came to the seaside again, abt 4 miles beyond Haddington: at 5th look'd back on our Pointed Hill.—Ld Haddington's (to the left too,) with large woods on each side of the house.— Light-House & Dunbar by the seaside. D. of Roxburgh just beyond the town; with his odious deadwall, that kept us so long from seeing the sea—between 6th & 7th m'st. Sr John Hall's to the right, with woods & plantations, break in the shore; pass'd Dunglas-Bridge; & lookd down on a Fontainbleau-Picture, to the right, & thorough a rocky opening to the sea on the left; (Point, at a distance before us, St. Abbs-head;) A house down in each: We afterwards came to an ugly quick descent, with (as bad) a steep rising; that whole hill is call'd The Peese as the moor hill is call'd The Resting Bell. We saw full sea for four miles before we came to Berwick & a long line on of the English shore. As the 2 first Posts from Edinburgh were good, these two last to Berwick were bad: & after it beginning to alter, grew worse & worse.

What they have left of the old Fortifications deceiv'd us at our first coming toward Berwick; but we found new ones within. Have they 4? or 5? Batteries for cannon.—We mistook the Townhouse too for a church, from its cupola on top; but they allow of no steeple house in the Town. Tis a good handsome new building (date on it. 1754) We pass'd thorough the Town; & over a very large & strong (but not well built) bridge; (900 f. long, & with 16 arches;) to Mrs. Humphrys just on the English side, which they call Tweed-Mouth. The Tweed makes a good appearance there; with the sea just by, & points and jutting out wch at low water seen to the eye to meet. The Inn is much the best thereabouts; & is kept by 3 sisters; one a Widow, & 2 Maidens:[26] one of which wd not marry she said because she was afraid of agitations. I enquired for Mrs. Selwyn of her, (formerly Miss Compton;) she was but two mile off, with two of her daughters: she has 7 children in all; one of whom was Maid of Honour to the Princess of Wales, & is married to a Gentleman of 7th[d] a year. Miss Compton herself, she said, was reckon'd extremely pretty; & was married too for love by Mr. Selwyn. As soon as you rise upon the hill on this side of Tweed, we saw the Cheviot Hills, stretching along to the right. They are like a boundary between England & Scotland. On the left appeared the sea; & as we advanc'd twas just in the shape of an Amazon's shield. We then, at the 3rd m'stone began to see Holy-Island, & had several more distinct, views of it farther on. It has a town abt ye middle of it, & a Castle tow'd ye extremity on ye right: tis very evident still, that it was made an Island by the encroachment of the sea. Hitherto, & for a good way on, the country is bad, & but poorly cultivated; much like that before Berwick: perhaps, they are both still the worse for having been the Borders. This held for almost all the two first Posts; Belford & Alnwick: before the former of which, our axle tree had a good escape, tho I was forced to walk by the Gentleman's house with a serpentine avenue to it (& a Summerhouse wch we had mistook for a Light-house, on a neighbouring knole, that has a view of the sea.) Just before ye town, as in the latter, is Alnwick-Castle, wch my Ld. Northumberland is now repairing all over.[27] We saw but little of the sea after we had left Alnwick; (only one good piece, opposite to the Cock & Stars, alm. 6 mls on). Had a good view, as far more? into Castle Park (In this Post they rob slips, almost wherever they can, from the sides of the road, as they do on the other side of Durham; & sometimes so far, as not to leave any foot-path at all, on the side of ye faucet. What ill consequences may this have when the road becomes too close & too much shaded?) We had woods, on each hand of us as we came into Morpeth, & dells, (with woods, abt them) on each hand, going out.

The Town is well enough: (a long street, with two shorter at ye end.) a bridge, with pretty woods on each side (Sr Mathew Whites's) who has a good house near the road afterwards; & a plantation runs on each side of it; from 5th to 6th mile stones. The worse pieces of road we pass'd while fro Edinburgh to Durham was the dip at The Pees, & that vile descent in Newcastle. In these two last Posts ye country generally mended on us; & in ye latter part of the former, was the same sort of waving in ye ground that is the characteristic of the County of Durham.

NOTES

1. Farther in, is a higher (& finer) rock call'd Eagles-Cliff; which had the day been fine we might have gone to, (thorough the windings of the hills mentioned below) in a boat. There are a great many eagles about those Parks.

2. In this pass'd thro' a little piece of woods; (with dark passage, for a few paces,) Oaks like shrubs,—beech—poor alders etc.

3. Grass fields for mowing? or pasture?

4. In the dark opening in between the different mountains, on the right is ye Spa.

5. (The Skidaw?)—Toward the top, met with poor man carrying his sick boy (of 16) on his back and (2d) Glede, that cheated as for an Eagle.

6. Highland prisoner flung himself down the steep line that comes up to the road; & escapd both the breaking of his neck & the firing of ye 12 soldiers that had guarded him.

7. This almost always be cots, huts or caves, wch of them rise but little above the height or dignity of our hogs stys. The hills here look all barren & alpine. There is here & there an inter mixture of cultivation that about 4 and 5 miles from ye Crook, the plain grows wider & smoother; and the look of ye hills is softened.

8. This day the first flight of crows; & lost the music of birds, almost every where; (& indeed in a country so bare of trees, how cd. most of them build their houses?)

9. Saw clouds beneath the tops of hills every day, we travelled (& sometimes all day): fro Ullswater, quite to Edinburgh, partly on ye *Pentland*-Hills how high must that ground be, wch they call the Lowlands! Tis so often on hills, of a very moderate height from ye vale we pass; as these at ye Crook etc.? Query of the increase of height in a vale near Edinburgh, to one in Cheshire or the begin'g of Lancashire?

10. Mr. Fisher's House at a distance, with woods about it & rows of trees round the fields & on up to along the road-side. The woods look'd well; the single lines very ill (From these & many others I s'd imagine they shou'd always plant thick; in woods, groves, grovettes & clumps of various sizes: for you seldom see trees look thriftily there, unless they skreen one another.) Then a larger wood at a distance; beyond the (Pillar) Pidgeon house (Sr. James Clerk's): visible so long before to us:—And farther, a long wood of *lofty* trees; (unless they are the usual ones, growing up a bank)?

11. Beyond *Penicuik* Sr James Clerk's on ye right.

12. Moreton

13. Braid Hill

14. Craig House—Lockart's? (Mr Hamilton's Villa there.)

15. Part of Leith? the sea-port for Edinburgh. Why did not they extend ye Town to ye Seaside rather than build so high & pay so exces'ly for ground where they are?

16. This is ye middle point of a high Rocky Hill, that next to the City is call'd Salisbury Crag: & ye farthest has not any name—Sr Alexander Dick's seat is under ye middle one. Arthurs Seat (Formerly all cover'd with woody, Mrs. Balfour. Query of Maitland's History of Edinburgh; mentioned by ye same Folio—for any map of the town, or it is environs?)—The meadow & these parts all woods of oaks formerly; the whole town first built of wood & the wrights (or carpenters) liv'd there (Building & Firing, I suppose) had made the ground so bare of trees in so many other parts: wch pity, planting is not more in vogue among 'em!—They now give 3 prizes a year wch has had a great effect.

17. Caught, one after another, thro' the Port-holes in the Half-Moon; (that & the walk on parallel to the Town, like walking in a Picture-Gallery.)

18. Island (Inch-Keith) in ye middle (of a mile long, and 4 Gs. an Acres), between Keith & Kinghorn, the great Port for the Northern parts; and 4 mile from each. Kinghorn (in Fifeshire?)

19. The Mezzo Relievo of Antoninus & Faustina wt an Inscription (? Query in Maitland) agst a House to ye right in the High Street, before you come to the Netherbow?

20. Is for the schooling of 130 boys.

21. Mr. H. answers to my queries

22. but this query (Mr H. said) required more consideration, for a full answer.

23. Almost the double cube: 42 f. long 22 br. & 22 high.

24. 1st. Wood on a hill to ye right, that which the rebels came thorough before ye Battle of Preston-pans—dark field above 2 (& lower) wood, was Cromwell's Battle: of [blank] or Musselburgh.

25. (Ld Wintoun's seat & estate lay a good way farther on, below.)

26. How cheerful! after suffering so much for 14 yr. fr vapors & doctors.

27. G. Nicholson, (of the Swan, at Alnwick) the best postillion we had on ye road.

MICHEL BARIDON

History, Myth, and the English Garden

A study of historical myths in the English garden is an enterprise that stands in need of justification, for it may antagonize those for whom it is destined, the garden lovers themselves. Those who give a great deal of loving care to the tending of trees and flowers may object to the presence of historians in their favorite haunts. They may insist that a garden is meant to allow one to forget the battles of life, not to commemorate them, and they may add that the passing of time, as experienced in the quiet enjoyment of nature, has nothing to do with the linear time artificially conceived to record events. To abandon oneself to the cycles of the seasons, to follow the imperceptible operations of what Keats called "slow time" is to become part of the general movement of life; to resurrect dead societies is to withdraw from this movement in order to see things through the eye of memory.

And yet, the historian cannot help being fascinated by a fact that the garden lovers cannot deny: gardens are the most perishable of all art forms. Pictures are more fragile but they remain true to the intentions of those who painted them. Buildings and statues can be restored and made to look exactly like the models originally designed by architects and sculptors. But gardens change unceasingly. They change from morning to evening, becoming enchantingly mysterious at night; they change with the seasons and they change with the taste of the successive generations that tend them. "Slow time" proves indeed much more active and much more destructive than human time, and in the case of gardens both can often be seen to operate together.

If a personal anecdote may be allowed here, I shall try to show how my first visit to Stourhead started me on a train of thought from which the present paper originates. This was a memorable occasion as one may well imagine. I was in the company of the late Kenneth Woodbridge, as valiant a gardener and historian as one might

wish to be with on such a day. The whimsical gods who rule the English weather stood, at least for that morning, on our side. The full beauty of the garden suddenly revealed itself as we reached the top of the incline that gently slopes down to the Palladian bridge. The lake was before us, with the white Pantheon in the distance; the whole scene seemed as eternal as the English countryside and as immortal as the pagan gods on Mount Parnassus. Henry Hoare's rural paradise, with his dream of antiquity, had come down to us in its pristine state of perfection; it was indeed "a thing of beauty." Once the first moment of emotion was over, I turned to Kenneth and asked him whether the trees as we saw them produced the same effect as those originally planted. The answer was no, that the trees we saw looked darker, and this was due, he explained, to the Victorians' taste for romantic scenery.

This came as a kind of revelation. Gardens were not only responsive to "slow time" and to the revolutions of the seasons; they were also part of the historical pattern determined by social change. Once their designers had disappeared, they could be set to the taste of successive generations. They might even lose their original character in the process. But were not some gardens more susceptible to alterations than others? Versailles, for example, looked impervious to time, whereas The Leasowes seemed to make seasonal change and historical change part of the enjoyment of nature. Was it not intriguing to see André Le Nôtre's perfect geometry defy even the seasons while William Shenstone changed the itinerary of his visitors according to the moment when it was particularly suitable to see some trees or some plants? And did Shenstone not also take pride in the prospect of the small church of Saint Kenelm because it offered various historical associations? Was the French formal style time blind? If so, could the taste for ruins, so evident in the English garden, not be a reaction against the style that Versailles had imposed for such a long time? And how could this be explained? Since the English garden was indebted to Versailles and yet adverse to its taste for symmetry and regularity, there must be something deep in the intellectual life of the eighteenth century that explained why time, cosmic or historical, had suddenly become essential to the vision of nature presented by gardens.

It is the growing development of time awareness in the English garden that constitutes the subject of the present paper. Horace Walpole stands as a good example of this evolution. He admired Capability Brown as much as he disliked Le Nôtre, and when he justified his preference it was in *The History of the Modern Taste in Landscape Gardening*,[1] a book that proved the superiority of the "modern" style by putting all the others in historical perspective. The rise of the English garden runs parallel to that of historicism. It also runs parallel to the gothic revival, as the example of Horace Walpole proves. It is therefore no exaggeration to say that it was central to eighteenth-century aesthetics, and the best way to understand why this was so is to start from Le Nôtre. His influence was so often and so vigorously counteracted by English landscape designers that his style must have provided a good starting point for those who wanted to develop a new vision of nature.

If we transport ourselves to the French side of the Channel, we find that, when Le Nôtre died in 1700, the style of garden design for which his name stood was still universally admired. Vaux-le-Vicomte, Versailles, and Chantilly offered accomplished examples of a style to which all Europe was indebted. Indeed, so high was Le Nôtre's prestige that his *grande manière* influenced Charles Bridgeman and is clearly perceptible in the general layout of Stowe. It took a long time before it was definitely eclipsed by the creations of Shenstone, Capability Brown, William Mason, and Humphrey Repton. And yet, Le Nôtre was constantly under attack for political reasons. While Louis XIV was still alive, Stephen Switzer said that the French king turned Versailles into a splendid park "so that he might allure and dazzle the eyes of Europe and thereby carry on the scheme of universal monarchy."[2]

Joseph Addison equated regularity and symmetry with despotism. He painted Switzerland in *The Spectator* as a kind of dream world "inhabited by the Goddess of Liberty covered with a profusion of flowers, that, without being disposed into regular Borders and Parterres, grew promiscuously," and he described the Rhône as a river that "after having run to and fro in a wonderful variety of meanders" and:

after having made its progress through those free nations, stagnates in a huge lake at the leaving of them and no sooner enters into the regions of slavery, but runs through them with an incredible rapidity, and takes its shortest way to the sea.[3]

In the same way, Repton extolled the English constitution in which he found:

the happy medium betwixt the wildness of nature and the stiffness of art, in the same manner as the gothic constitution is the happy mixture between the liberty of the savages and the restraint of despotick government.[4]

There is no need to reproduce here all the attacks launched against the despotism of Louis XIV and against Versailles, which was presented as the very image of so rigid a tyranny that it constrained nature into a system in which "grove nods at grove and each alley has a brother."[5] Granted that this kind of argument was inspired by political propaganda, the real question that confronts us is not why the ideologues of the time simplified things so much, but rather why they found an echo in public opinion. If we try to answer this question we shall find that the attacks against regularity and symmetry invariably went hand in hand with the praise of the "mixed constitution" with which the Glorious Revolution had blessed England. And this entailed historical arguments of which Versailles had no need.

History is strangely absent from Versailles. In the very thorough study of the gardens that was made by Alfred Marie one finds that none of the statues was historical;[6] they were all mythological or emblematical. Not one single French king was there, apart from Louis himself; not one single French general, philosopher, or scientist. The marble effigies decorating the alleys were those of Hercules, Ceres, Apollo, Bacchus, and their consorts, the four elements, the four types of poetry, the animals of the creation, and the rivers of France, cast in bronze, the metal reputed to be eternal. Change and mutability had no place in a garden designed to celebrate the eternal character of the king's omnipotence. He wanted the creation of Versailles to strike all visitors, from the poorest of the Parisians, who were admitted once a week, to the proudest monarchs. He insisted on supervising everything

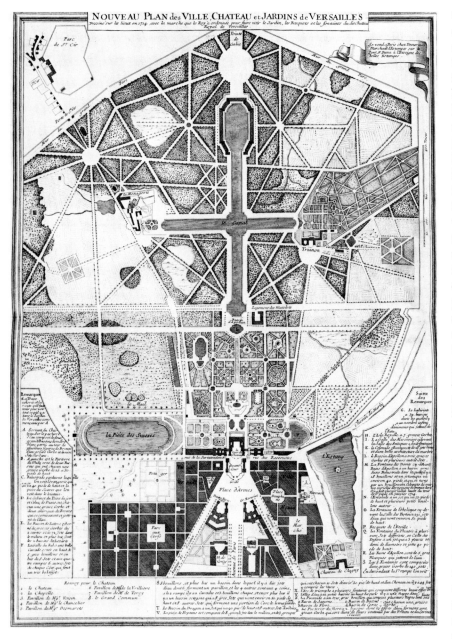

Fig. 1.
Plan of Versailles by Demortain,
1714 (Photograph: The Garden Library,
Dumbarton Oaks, Washington, D.C.)

to his dying day and he wrote the *Manière de montrer les jardins de Versailles* with his own hand, using Le Nôtre's *grande manière* to glorify his own political achievements.[7]

The king and his gardener shared the same ideal vision, a vision that curbed the energies of Nature to make her serve political ends. Eugène de Ganay tells us how Le Nôtre once proposed to his master to make the waters of the Loire valley flow into the *Pièce d'eau* at Versailles, thus trying to emulate the cutting of the canal that linked

the Atlantic to the Mediterranean.[8] This anecdote proves that in the eyes of both men Versailles was to serve as a microcosmic reproduction of the kingdom; it was meant to offer an image of ideal organization of space. France had been unified and civilized, it was implicitly alleged, by the will of the monarch, whose triumph was also the triumph of centralization (fig. 1). From this we may conclude that the English propagandists were right: Versailles was indeed an ideal image of absolutism. But what they did not say was that a large proportion of the middle class, at least among Catholics, had welcomed the changes brought about by the system. These changes leveled out provincial differences and reduced the importance of the nobility; they developed trade and industry by making communications easier; they purified the language from provincial accretions; they created an administration whose faultless mechanism enabled the *commis* and the *intendants* to implement the centralization from which so much was expected. One has only to read Voltaire's *Siècle de Louis XIV* to understand how the bourgeoisie appreciated the benefits of absolutism as long as it was not allowed to degenerate into ecclesiastical tyranny.

Versailles still bears the mark of this political vision, but it is surely an oversimplification to represent Le Nôtre as a mere illustrator of the king's political projects. His style was already formed when he arrived at Versailles, and the elements of his aesthetics had already reached a stage of complete coherence at Vaux-le-Vicomte, which was not designed for the king. The real task, then, is to analyze the ahistorical character of his style by tracing its relation to the scientific movement in which Descartes played an outstanding role. Descartes' influence was strongly established in France and it prolonged itself well into the eighteenth century.[9] Descartes, it will be remembered, had little use for history and he trusted what he called "the method of the geometricians." Nothing equaled in his eyes the perfection of a system logically worked out by this method. In the same way as he explained the life of a body by the well regulated flow of animal spirits, so in the second chapter of his *Discourse on Method* he accounted for the beauty of a town by the structural unity of a plan designed on flat ground by one single architect. According to him the preservation of old buildings inevitably resulted in irregularities that were a disgrace to the whole.[10] Whatever Etienne Lanson says,[11]

Fig. 2.
Versailles in winter, from Bernard Jeannel, *Le Notre,* Paris, 1985

this love of rational systems was central to the development of neo-classical aesthetics. Beauty, it was believed, could only be achieved by elaborating coherent principles that acted as so many constraints. A fine tragedy must conform to the three unities of time, place, and action. One might almost add the unity of references, since the ancients were supposed to provide the only models worthy of imitation. Even human nature was reduced to a system of passions whose expressions were studied by Charles Le Brun and turned into permanent images by Cesare Ripa and by antique statuary. Mount Olympus and the French court stood as two homological systems in which the passions of Man were displayed in their fullest perfection. Molière's *Amphytrion* caught this aspect of things by showing gods and the courtiers playing at hide and seek in the park; so did Watteau's *Fêtes galantes.*

All this resulted in unbounded admiration for the masterpieces of antiquity and almost equal confidence in the capacities of the age. In his *Mémoire de ce que le roi désire dans ses bâtiments de Versailles* Jean-Baptiste Colbert writes: "le roi se veut servir de tout ce qui est fait de neuf."[12] Old buildings had no interest for him; neither had the past history of the kingdom any interest for Racine, albeit he was historiographer to the king. Tacitus provided better subjects for tragedies than the antiquities of France. All this has to be kept in mind for a complete understanding of the French garden, because it shows how the method of the geometricians tallied with the proud creations of absolutism to give Nature the ideal form that the Sun King wished her to assume.

Versailles celebrates a great political creation that was to last forever because it was perfect and

because it rested on theological truths that had withstood the action of time. Once the truth of the Bible was acknowledged, the rights of absolute kings could not be disputed.[13] The aesthetics of the gardens was also expressive of the modernity of the times. The shape and the colors of evergreen trees hardly changed from one season to another (fig. 2). The impeccable geometry of the parterres, with their circles, their triangles, and their pyramids, was as eternal as mathematical equations. The symmetry of the whole allowed the eye to run from one side of the horizon to the other without finding any hiatus in the landscape, and the statues displayed the passions of Man under the immortal masks of the gods (fig. 3). The rational concatenation of forms gave a flawless unity to the whole. Seen from a terrace—and the king insisted that his visitors went from one level to another ("Il faut s'arrester sur le haut des degrez pour considérer la situation des parterres" says the *Manière de montrer les jardins de Versailles*")[14]—the whole extent of the gardens displayed an incomparable coher-

ence that identified itself with the eternal laws of the mechanistic world picture (fig. 4).

French absolutism was not as eternal as it wished itself to be, however, and once it had passed its zenith it came under the same attack as Stuart "tyranny" in England. This is not surprising, since there were many similarities between the systems of theological politics conceived by Jacques Bénigne Bossuet in France and Sir Robert Filmer in England. Those two systems justified absolutism by the fact that almost all men were born subjects while only a tiny minority were born kings because they descended from Adam in direct line. Such a conception of subordination did not suit the ambition of the nobles. A French aristocrat like Henri de Boulainvilliers was as violent as Lord Shaftesbury in his denunciation of what he called "the shameful system of the Lord Bishop of Meaux," and he advocated a recourse to history to prove the time-honored privileges to which the nobility was entitled. He

lamented the neglect in which the archives of the kingdom lay "under the vaults of the Sainte-Chapelle" and he called for the study of "such treasures." He added: "C'est ainsi que les Anglais justifient le droit de leur Parlement et la franchise de leurs personnes et de leur biens."[15]

In other words, the liberties of the kingdom lay buried in the archives because the king, ever since the establishment of a centralized monarchy, had gradually suppressed them by successive encroachments. The Duke of Saint Simon held similar views; he was a staunch defender of the privileges of the nobility and, quite naturally, he hated Versailles. He described it as a place that had neither air nor water and that was so little fitted to become a park that the king had had to

"tyrannize nature" in order to gain his own ends.[16]

The same arguments were used in England before and after the Glorious Revolution. But the revolution and the Civil War had made them even more central to political debates because they were used to justify, or to deny, the king's supremacy or the antiquity of Parliament. To take but one example: the political myth known as "the Norman yoke" presented English history as a long struggle to defend the liberties of the kingdom. Absolutism had first come to England with William the Conqueror; it had relented when the Magna Carta was conceded by John Lackland, and it had come into its own again with the accession of James I. Hence the

Fig. 4.
Chantilly, from Bernard Jeannel, *Le Notre*, Paris, 1985

historical battle fought in the 1680s between the king and his opponents. The names of Robert Brady, James Tyrrell, William Petyt, and Henry Neville are sufficient proof of the importance history came to assume in all the debates that concerned the future of the kingdom and the legitimacy of the king's power. Far from remaining confined to the field of antiquarian research, history had acquired a decisive role in England.

This role was fully confirmed when the Glorious Revolution limited the king's power. Since the political representation of the country was left unchanged, since power was essentially land based, the "great families who had supported the revolution"[17] became the great wielders of influence, and their role was expressly recognized by the invaluable mixed constitution of which the country was so proud. The House of Commons became the "peculiar club" of which Sir Lewis Namier speaks in the opening sentence of his *England in the Age of the American Revolution,* and the nobility could well appear as the bulwark of English liberty. It had stood for it heroically in the days of Lord William Russell and Algernon Sidney, and it could prove its case by history. In fact, history was more indispensible to the nobility than to any other participants in the debate on the nature of authority, for the king could make use of religion to establish his power, and the partisans of the "people" could lay the stress on the "natural rights of man" rather than on the argument from history. This, I believe, explains why Viscount Bolingbroke wrote *On the Study and Use of History,* and why Edmund Burke could say in his letter to Lord Richmond:

> You people of great families and hereditary trusts or fortunes, are not like such as I am who are . . . but annual plants. . . . You are the great oaks that shade a country and perpetuate your benefits from generation to generation.[18]

In the same letter he described the houses of the nobility as "the public repositories and offices of record of the constitution." If a text can show how the role played by the aristocracy had need of history to prove its validity, this is it. It has everything: the function of the country house in the immemorial past of the English countryside, the beauty of the park, and the constitutional right of the aristocracy to stand for the permanence of the country's liberties.

As was to be expected, the ruling circles lost no time in discovering the nature of their political role after the Glorious Revolution. The growing importance of Parliament, the prestige now attached to the function of the legislator, the possibility of turning castles and country houses into status symbols—all this made clubs such as the Kit-Cat intellectual centers of great importance for the connection between the world of active politics and the world of intellectual and artistic creation. It was at the Kit-Cat that John Vanbrugh met Lord Carlisle, and this encounter proved decisive because it brought into contact a leading politician (Carlisle had been First Lord of the Treasury twice and had been an efficient promoter of the Union with Scotland) and an enterprising architect who had been imprisoned by that bugbear of Whig England, Louis XIV. Vanbrugh was the ideal man to invent a suitable style for a great lord's castle. But who can give shape to an idea unless he resorts to myths? Vanbrugh resorted to myths with extraordinary success.

One has to be clear about the meaning one gives to the word *myth,* because it is essential to the relation of history to art criticism. To avoid endless theoretical discussions, a clear working definition can perhaps be borrowed from Henry Nash Smith's *Virgin Land: The American West as Symbol and Myth.* I shall use it as it stands, unwilling as I am to alter its brevity and its remarkable cogency: "A myth is an intellectual construction that fuses concept and emotion into an image."[19]

If a myth results from the coalescence of a concept, a feeling, and an image, we have all three in the first creations of Vanbrugh. The concept was that of freedom as guaranteed by the mixed constitution in which the aristocracy played such a great part; the feeling was one of pride and elation at the idea that England was now free from the tyranny of the Stuarts and that, having become a great nation in her own right, she might now challenge the power of France and conquer an empire which she would civilize by the power of commerce and by the wisdom of her laws. As to the images that sprung from the coalescence of the two, they were certainly not evocative of the regularity and the symmetry found in French neo-classicism. In the visual arts, as in anything else, one has one's positive values and one's negative values. The formality of the French style stood for the negative that had to be repulsed into nothingness by new positives. Of this Vanbrugh was acutely conscious; he was a prolific inventor of new images, and he tried to invent forms hitherto un-

Fig. 5.
Park wall at Castle Howard by
Vanbrugh, 1725, from Lawrence
Fleming and Alan Gore, *The English
Garden,* London, 1980

seen to concretize the new state of things. In a letter to Lord Manchester he discussed the plans of Kimbolton Castle in the following way:

As to the outside I thought twas absolutely best to give it something of the castle air. . . . I hope your Lordship won't be discouraged if any Italians you may shew it to find fault that it is not Roman. This will make a very Noble and masculine show.[20]

In other words, Vanbrugh intended to create forms expressive of the time-honored role of the aristocracy, and he wished to do so without resorting to foreign models. He quite naturally studied the examples of medieval architecture that he could find in the north of England and in Scotland, and he designed some interesting crenellated ramparts for the park at Castle Howard (fig. 5). He became interested in the remains of gothic castles just at the moment when William Stukeley was making similar discoveries in the English countryside. Feudal gothic was massive, warlike, irregular, and quite opposed in its style to the carefully designed finery of France and Italy. It had one even greater merit: it provided the imagination with visions of ages past; it established visual connections with the history of country houses and castles at the time when they stood for the liberties of the provinces against the encroachments of kingly power (fig. 6). Joshua Reynolds remarked in his *Discourses:*

Architecture certainly possesses many principles in common with Poetry and Painting. Among those which may be reckoned as the first, is, that of affecting the imagination by means of association of ideas. Thus, for instance, as we have naturally a veneration for antiquity, whatever building brings to our remembrance ancient customs and manners, such as the Castles of the Barons of ancient Chivalry, is sure to give this delight. Hence it is that towers and battlements are so often selected by the painter and the poet to make a part of the composition of their landscape; and it is from thence in a great degree that, in the buildings of Vanbrugh who was a great poet and an architect there is a greater display of imagination than we shall find perhaps in any other.[21]

Is it not interesting to find Reynolds putting his finger on what seems to have been the great originality of Vanbrugh, that is, the connection he established between feudal times, gothic architecture, and the landscape? For this is exactly what Vanbrugh did when he made Castle Howard "the top seat and garden of England" by capturing the poetic essence of the northern atmosphere of the place. Any visitor who enters the grounds of Castle Howard feels at once that Lord Carlisle's "place" is indeed a "flaunting symbol of territorial whiggery" (fig. 7), to quote Sir John Summerson's superb definition.[22] He cannot fail to realize at first glance that Lord Carlisle's family has indestructible links with the land over which it wields influence, because the

Fig. 6.
The Belvedize, Claremont
(The National Trust)

Fig. 7.
Grass walk to the Temple of the
Four Winds, Castle Howard, 1725,
from Lawrence Fleming and Alan
Gore, *The English Garden,* London,
1980

Fig. 8.
Woburn Farm   (The British Library)

Fig. 9.
The Exedra at Chiswick
House   (The National Trust)

Fig. 10.
Bristol High Cross and the Pantheon, Stourhead, from Miles Hatfield, *The English Landscape Garden,* Aylesbury, 1977

off by Trees and Flowers, that the soil was capable of receiving, a Man might make a pretty Landskip of his own Possessions.[23]

English garden designers thus turned to nature for guidance, but they did so because of the historical role played by the country house. "The wildness pleases," as Shaftesbury said,[24] but it pleased because it gave coherence to the relation of myth to form. The centralizing myths of the Sun King might well have given coherence and a sense of purpose to the perennial geometry of Versailles, but times had changed and history was now coming into its own in a way that reconciled past greatness with the hope of more greatness to come.

When we speak of past greatness we should not forget that the myth of English liberty conveyed a profusion of mental images. It could bring to mind battlements and crenellated walls reminiscent of the great barons; it could also project visions of temples and colonnades, because the mixed constitution so often referred to by the ideologues of Whig England was also said to be of Roman origin. We need only look at Chiswick or Stowe to realize that the antique balance so dear to James Harrington and to his eighteenth-century followers served as a reference that conferred much dignity on the hazardous warfare of English politics. After all, the mixed constitution, the palladium of English liberties, could be presented as a modern adaptation of the tripodic model of a lasting constitution as described by Polybius.[25] Monarchy, aristocracy, and democracy controlled one another and ruled together under the modern form of King, Lords, and Commons. The Grand Tour pilgrims came back with inspiring visions of greatness; they also came back with numerous statues that adorned their gardens—statues of Cicero and Caesar as well as statues of the gods, to say nothing of the obelisks, the pyramids, and the nymphs that decorated the bowers and the prospects of the Elysiums whose growing numbers changed the face of the countryside.[26] To Burlington, who put up a statue of Cicero at Chiswick (fig. 9), Robert Castell dedicated his *Villas of the Ancients,* and his book inspired many improvers with visions of Pliny's Tusculum.

The development and influence of the Roman myth has been so often described that the inspiring role it played in English politics need not be examined here. What is interesting about the Roman myth is that it acted in conjunction with the gothic myth (fig. 10), thus reinforcing the

house and the garden form a whole with the surrounding landscape. Vanbrugh put the historic house in its local context. He made it clear that the beauty of a park could no longer be the result of its adherence to ideal canons applied like an abstract formula. It had to create a link between an important political figure and the land he owned and over which he ruled (fig. 8). This point was clearly made by Addison (another eminent member of the Kit-Cat):

But why may not a whole Estate be thrown into a kind of Garden by frequent Plantations, that may turn as much to the Profit, as the Pleasure of the Owner? Fields of corn make a pleasant Prospect and if the Walks were a little taken care of that lie between them, if the natural embroidery of the Meadows were helpt and improved by some small Additions of Art, and the several Rows of Hedges set

historical stance that was fast developing among garden designers. Two quotations, both by Walpole, will prove this point. The first refers to Castle Howard:

Nobody had informed me that at one view I should see a palace, a town, a fortified city, temples on high places, woods worthy of being each a metropolis of the druids, the noblest lawns in the world fenced by half the horizon, and a mausoleum that would tempt one to be buried alive; in short, I have seen gigantic places before, but never a sublime one.[27]

The second refers to Rousham:

The whole is as elegant and antique as if the emperor Julian had selected the most pleasing solitude about Daphne to enjoy a philosophic retirement.[28]

These two quotations prove that Horace Walpole, who saw himself as the first historian of the English garden, yoked the two myths together. Antagonistic as they were—for there is a contradiction in praising both the emperors and the barbarians who ultimately triumphed over them—they promoted a new awareness of historical time as they effected deep transformations in the ideal vision of nature. A myth cannot contradict another myth, because it is only conceptual in part; but it can displace or obscure another myth if circumstances prove more favorable to its internal development. A typical instance of this kind will be found in the evolution of the gothic myth in eighteenth-century aesthetics.

The gothic myth was in fact twofold. It subdivided into Saxon and gothic proper, a discrimination not often clearly made in the eighteenth century. It was William Warburton who called attention to the confusion in one of his notes to Alexander Pope,[29] and he recommended that "Saxon" should be applied to what we now call romanesque, while "Gothic" would be given the sense that it now has. Be this as it may, "Saxon" and "Gothic" often went hand in hand when the limitation of the king's power was at stake. Jonathan Swift, at the same time as he applied the lessons of antiquity to the political situation in England, could declare that the British Parliament was a gothic institution;[30] Robert Molesworth said the same thing in his *Principles of a Real Whig,* whom he defined as "one who is exactly for keeping up to the strictness of the true old Gothick constitution;"[31] and Bolingbroke, who posed as the Cicero of the age, concurred in this general praise of the "gothick" constitution; he wrote in his *Remarks on the History of England:* "It must be a pleasure to reflect on that uniformity of spirit which created and has constantly preserved or retrieved, the original freedom of the British and Saxon constitutions."[32]

All eighteenth-century specialists know the importance King Alfred came to assume in the collective imagination of the time, particularly among those most opposed to any increase of the king's power. The Saxon myth represented Alfred as the king under whom the country had reached a state of almost perfect freedom; his political wisdom had preserved the original model of Saxon liberty in strict adherence to the principles of the *Witena Gemote* of the Germans, a mode of government described by Tacitus in a famous passage with which Whig propagandists were well acquainted; but it will also be remembered that the German model of Saxon liberty was described as a gathering that always took place in the woods.[33]

From this association with the forest, the Saxon myth derived connotations that proved important for the development of the English garden. For reasons already explained, the coalescence of concepts (the balance of monarchy, aristocracy, and democracy in the assemblies of the Germans) and of feelings (obvious enough in the text by Bolingbroke just quoted) generated images in which the forest appeared as the asylum of British liberty. Walter Scott and all the romantics made use of this relation of natural scenery to political myths, but long before them Montesquieu detected it with great subtlety. In the famous chapter of *L'Esprit des Lois* written in praise of the English constitution we find a somewhat cryptic comment: "Ce beau système a été trouvé dans les bois,"[34] and a footnote indicating "Tacitus, Germania cap. XI," is sufficient proof that Montesquieu was acquainted with a text that he must often have heard quoted when he was among his friends of the Bolingbroke-Pope-Kent-Warburton connection.

This brings us back to the garden. What could be more irregular and venerable, more evocative of the primitive Saxons, than the forest that had spread over the whole of British territory from time immemorial? The forest could well regenerate the ideal vision of nature because it had nothing regular or symmetrical about it. It had all that wildness could offer: the civilizing, regularizing hand of man could not be seen in it; it

was the abode of wildlife and it was, from the earliest events in British history, the sanctuary of the people's liberties. So that when Lord Cobham decided to build his Temple of Liberty at Stowe, he wished it to be in the gothic style, and he surrounded it with tall trees (fig. 11) to make the atmosphere around it reminiscent of a forest. By so doing not only did he confirm what Montesquieu had said about the origin of the Saxon model of government, but he also confirmed an observation made by the French traveler Pierre Grosley, according to whom, when the English designed a garden, they tried to imitate their native woods as closely as they could. "Les Anglais cherchent leurs modèles dans leurs forêts,"[35] he observed while on a visit to England.

This remark proves that he saw how references to the myth of Saxon liberty could be either expressive or emblematical. They could be emblematical when they took the form of a gothic temple, and they could be expressive when dark evergreen trees were planted around it. The categories used by Ronald Paulson in his classic study *Emblem and Expression* can plainly be seen to apply to the Temple of Liberty at Stowe.[36] The same could be said of Cirencester, with its ruinous gothic fabric (fig. 12), or of

Fig. 11.
Gothic temple at Stowe
(The National Trust)

Fig. 12.
Alfred's Hall at Cirencester Park
(The National Trust)

Vanbrugh's project to surround Woodstock manor with "a wild thicket."[37] The expressive character of woods, with their gloom and their evocation of Saxon times, proved perhaps one of the most fertile discoveries of English landscape designers. It certainly opened the way for the gothic revival, and its link with national history was evident, for Sir William Temple believed that "the Saxons had changed the face of the country."[38] Ever since the antiquarians had begun their tours and their enquiries into the antiquities of England, the idea that gothic architecture was related to the forest had been, so to speak, in the air. We find it in William Stukeley, who wrote as early as 1723:

The cloysters of this cathedral [Gloucester] are beautiful beyond anything I saw in the style of King's college Cambridge; nothing could ever have made me so much in love with Gothick architecture (as call'd) and I judg[sic] for a gallery, library and the like, 'tis the best manner of building, because the idea of it is taken from a walk of trees, whose branching heads are curiously imitated by the roof.[39]

The same idea was expressed twenty years later by Warburton who, being a friend of Montesquieu, Pope, and Bolingbroke had every reason to be conversant with the gothic myth of English liberty. It is interesting to quote him after Stukeley because his text, written as an annotation to Pope, shows how the merging of historical myths with natural scenery manifested itself in the perception of architectural styles:

When the Goths had conquered Spain . . . they struck out a new kind of architecture unknown to Greece and Rome; upon principles and ideas much nobler than what had given birth to classical magnificence. For this northern people having been accustomed, during the gloom of paganism to worship the deity in groves . . . when their new religion required edifices they ingeniously projected to make them resemble groves as nearly as the distance of architecture would admit . . . and with what skill and success they executed the project . . . appears from hence, that no attentive person ever viewed a regular avenue of well-grown trees, intermixing their branches overhead, but it presently put him in mind of the long vista through a Gothic cathedral.[40]

So, Lord Cobham was right: gothic architecture required the gloom of a forest to be seen in context; but the context reciprocated the relation, for it proved that the primeval forest of Great Britain still contained the unalterable germs of Saxon liberty and provided models for the national architecture of all northern countries. The hive of nations was also the cradle of political freedom. In Gibbon's phrase: "The most civilized nations of Europe issued from

the woods of Germany and, in the rude institutions of these barbarians we may still distinguish the original principles of our present laws and manners."[41]

But Gibbon is a case in point; willing as he was to supply historical references to the gothic myth, he would not trust himself with primitivism. He thought the barbarians were often idealized by "declaimers" who made dangerous use of Saxon references in order to attack not only absolutism but monarchy itself. He was right in a way, for the name of Alfred was often used by Thomas Jefferson, and Benjamin Franklin, with characteristic cunning, used the myth to serve his own political purposes when he declared roundly in the *Gentleman's Magazine* of October 1773 that: "Britain was formerly the America of the Germans."[42] Nothing could be more clear: if Britain was the America of the Germans, Liberty was undergoing a *translatio* which made it cross the Atlantic and stand by the side of the American "rebels." One may smile at Franklin's capitalizing on a myth by turning it against those by whom it was circulated, but one fact cannot be denied: the gothic myth was more popular among the friends of American liberty than among its foes; Gibbon had no eye for gothic architecture, and neither had Samuel Johnson, who never understood what the gothic revival, let alone landscape gardening, was all about. In the *Lives of the Poets* poor Shenstone was accused of giving too much time to "performances" that were "rather the sport than the business of human reason,"[43] yet Shenstone detected all the potentialities of the gothic myth with extraordinary perceptiveness. He liked what was wild and melancholy (fig. 13); he managed to offer, among his choice prospects, a view of the tower of the neighboring church of Saint Kenelm, whose Saxon name he loved because it was consonant with the native freedom of the country whose "hand attires the plain." He thought of a poem in praise of the history of gothic, Saxon, or even pre-Saxon times: "I long for some subject about the size of Philips's Cyder to settle heartily about it, something that I could enrich by episodes drawn from the English history: Stonehenge has some of the advantages I like but seems a dead lifeless title."[44]

Shenstone praised Sanderson Miller at Radway Grange for "turning every bank and hillock of his estate if not into classical at least into historical ground."[45] Hence his friendship with Mason, Walpole, and William Pitt, who also admired

Fig. 13.
Aquatint of *The Leasowes* by H. F. James and Stadler, c. 1880, from John Dixon Hunt and Peter Willis, eds., *The Genius of the Place,* London, 1975

Fig. 14.
Drawing of Wimpole Mock Castle by Sanderson Miller, 1749, from David Watkin, *The English Vision,* London, 1982

Sanderson Miller (fig. 14). The bringing together of such names enables us to see that the gothic myth of Saxon liberty had come to assume an ever-growing importance in the second half of the eighteenth century. It had its connections with the world of active politics. Mason and Walpole played with the idea of a republic, and there was a copy of Charles I's death warrant framed in the gothic library at Strawberry Hill. William Pitt was the "great commoner" and a staunch opponent to kingly power. At Radway Miller had a statue of Caractacus in a gothic niche, and he took his hero to be a striking illustration of the virtues of primitivism. William Beckford's great wealth enabled him to erect the megalomaniac gothic buildings of Fonthill Abbey, but did not prevent him from fraternizing with "the conquerors of the Bastille" in 1789. Mrs. Radcliffe, the gothic novelist, took care to discriminate between those who liked the

Fig. 15.
Alfred's Hall at Cirencester Park,
1763 (The National Trust)

English garden and those who did not. In the *Mysteries of Udolpho* she opposed Emily to the Marquise de Villeroy. The old lady admired the French formal garden and all the prejudices rejected by her young niece. There was no end to the progress of the gothic; after its humble beginnings in the garden, it had come to spread ruins everywhere (fig. 15) and to change the style of the house whose very bookshelves it was now invading.

The rise of the gothic myth was made inevitable by the political history of England. Once it was on the ascendant, its growing power over the collective imagination was governed by the events that marked the last decades of the eighteenth century. But a myth is an elusive creation of the mind; it is nobody's property, and the aristocrats who had circulated libertarian slogans to oust absolutism found themselves in the position of the sorcerer's apprentice when the gothic leaped the fence of their parks and was enlisted by the friends of the people. The takeover effected by Franklin was attempted by the partisans of parliamentary reform, men like Beckford, William Burgh, Horne Tooke, and Mason, or

like the members of the Lunar Society of Birmingham, who were readers of Rousseau. The paintings of Wright of Derby, himself a friend of the "Lunatics" of Birmingham, illustrate the new trends at work in the gothic imagination. His gloomy iron forges whose ruins are illuminated by fire, his moonlit scenes, and his strange night-pieces showing a monk discovering phosphorus (fig. 16) or a hermit piecing together the remains of a skeleton (fig. 17) all testify to the evolution that was leading England toward the times when the industrial revolution would make the Reform Bill inevitable.

As the example of Wright of Derby shows, the internal logic of political ideas is not enough to explain the spread of the gothic in the collective imagination of the time. Other factors have to be considered, such as the evolution of techniques, the development of productive forces, and the shaping of new mentalities by economic change. Essential to the general trend of innovations is the scientific movement. This study cannot be concluded without one last incursion into the world of science, for, in the same way as Cartesianism was at work in the systems of neoclassicism, empirical epistemology gave a struc-

Fig. 16.
The Alchemist by Joseph Wright of
Derby, 1771, oil on canvas
(Derby Art Gallery)

Ermenonville. These were the second generation of *philosophes—philosophes* of sentiment, not of reason. Their main interest was in natural history, biology, and botany, not in geometry; they took their inspiration from Locke and Newton by prospecting fields of research that Voltaire and Montesquieu had only begun to survey. The English garden was naturalized in France by those who proclaimed themselves men of sensibility.

The relation of sensibility to the scientific movement is demonstrated by the example of these French philosophers. It was evident to them that Locke's psychology was derived from Newtonian physics: the *Essay upon Human Understanding* states quite explicitly that sense impressions compose the basic material of mental life, and since sense impressions are produced by the impact of particles on sensory organs, they can only be explained by corpuscular physics. But corpuscular physics was the great innovation of empirical science; it was central to the discoveries of Robert Boyle, Thomas Sydenham, and Newton; it was one point, perhaps the most essential point, about which the Cartesians and the Newtonians were at variance. For Descartes space was a plenum, for Newton it was a void. Voltaire could say that he found it strange to see space full in Paris and empty in London, but his disciples saw nothing funny about that because they were consistent Newtonians who had need of corpuscular physics to develop their study of Lockean psychology.

Locke's connection with empirical science was established not only by Newtonian physics but also by his complete adherence to the methods of investigation of the Royal Society. In his introduction to the *Essay upon Human Understanding* he explained that his book had been conceived by "the historical plain method," that is to say, not by means of "systems" like the Cartesians, but by means of "histories" like the empiricists.[46] A history was a collection of observations made without any preconceived ideas, an enquiry into the "particulars" (the term was often used by Boyle) of a given set of phenomena. Particulars were essential to the true knowledge of things; a scientist proved his abilities not by composing systems, but by observing closely the processes by which change was taking place under his eyes. The Royal Society's *Philosophical Transactions* contain many such "histories," and the popularization of empirical methods of investigation could not fail to provoke changes in the mentalities of the age. Nature itself could not be

ture to the new vision of nature. This is, I believe, demonstrated by the success of the English garden in eighteenth-century France.

The leading intellectuals who favored the new type of landscape gardening—Rousseau, Diderot, Baron d'Holbach, Anne Robert Jacques Turgot—were all *anglomanes* of a new description: they preferred James Thomson to Pope, and Richardson to Fielding. The Marquis de Girardin, who gave shelter to Rousseau and took care of him to the very last, was an admirer of Shenstone, whose Leasowes he tried to imitate at

seen by the compilers of histories as it had been seen by the makers of systems.

If a garden stands for an ideal image of nature, it is quite understandable that the makers of systems should have wished to discover the garden from the vantage point of a terrace, or from a *haut,* as the Sun King put it. It was by an artifice of this kind that they were able to grasp the beauty and harmony of the landscape they had preconceived. Compilers of histories had no such ambition. They considered a garden as a place in which the particulars already in existence had to be considered. If a ruin stood somewhere, so much the better; if a river meandered its way through the grounds, it must not be forced into a geometrical basin. This tallied very well with the necessity, for political reasons, of merging a garden into the surrounding landscape. But what was true of space was also true of time.

Whereas a system must be seen as a whole, a history must be composed as one goes. To anyone visiting an English garden, the pleasure of discovering a prospect is offered from time to time. There is nothing systematic about it; the visitor is invited to take his pleasure in a perambulation that leads him from one surprise to another. It is only once he has gone over the grounds that he can compose, retrospectively, an image of the whole. The true amateur shuns what Pope called "the *a priori* road," the road of the Cartesians. The same desire to see things in chronological perspective led to the introduction of historicism in the creative imagination of the landscape gardeners. When Hoare erected Alfred's tower he knew he would make it stand on the very spot where the defender of English liberty had raised his standards against the Danes, because this was one of the particulars of Stourhead. By so doing he captured the original character of a landscape and opened the way for the free play of the association of ideas into which Locke's disciples were researching actively. Samuel Hoare carried things even further by his interest in the antiquities of Wiltshire. This was so original and so new a characteristic of the English garden that it was imitated by the French landscape designers of the late eighteenth century. Jean-Marie Morel, who did some work at Ermenonville and who was also active in Burgundy, encouraged the collection of local antiquities. This could be seen at Savigny-les-Beaune where, until very recently, Celtic remains stood in the garden. Morel did not see them as mere ornaments; he considered that they made the

country house true to its vocation, for not only did it occupy a central place in the culture of the whole neighborhood, but it contributed to a better historical knowledge of the region in which it stood. What was underground was also part of the particulars that interested the designers of English landscape gardens, for such particulars offered insights into the abysses whose subterranean waters and primeval fire were fit subjects for "philosophical melancholy." But those were meditations on cosmic time, and they would take us too far from historical myths, on which it is now time to conclude.

Fig. 17.
Hermit Studying Anatomy by Joseph Wright of Derby, c. 1771–1773, oil on canvas   (Derby Art Gallery)

A study of the transition from the French to the English garden shows that many causes were at work in so complex a phenomenon as the gradual change of the ideal vision of nature. Undoubtedly the prevalent taste for symmetry and regularity gave way to a disposition of plants, water, and relief that favored irregularity and variety. National character has not much to do with what B. Sprague Allen called "the tides of taste,"[47] for Englishmen designed regular gardens until the end of the seventeenth century and Frenchmen anglicized theirs for a few decades after that. The true causes of this evolution lie in the deep recesses of the creative imagination of some leading artists, whose vision was understood and circulated by a growing part of the public.

What makes the public receptive to innovation is the capacity of innovation to form an image of things to be by reshaping things that are. By this process of collective creation a certain conception of the modernity of the age emerges as an answer to the challenges of an ever-changing world picture. Nothing contributes more to the modification of the world picture than scientific discoveries and political ideas, because both compel men to adapt their mental apprehension of things to new objects. The political scene is never long at rest, and scientists do not long satisfy themselves with what their predecessors have found.

This is true of all epochs, but there are phases in human history when time undergoes considerable acceleration. Such was the case in England in the period from 1680 to 1715. The intense intellectual fermentation that preceded and immediately followed the Glorious Revolution (Newton's *Principia* were published in 1687, while Locke's *Essay concerning Human Understanding* and his *Two Treatises of Civil Government* appeared less than three years afterward) was accompanied by a reshuffling of the political structure of the country. The conditions were thus created for important changes in the collective imagination; even the ideal image of nature was modified, and gardens followed suit. New myths potentialized the need for change and they provided artists and designers with the material from which new forms were evolved. The English garden as it was shaped by innovators like Vanbrugh, Brown, Shenstone, and Mason offered endless creative virtualities; it provided the poets, the painters, and the architects with the possibilities they needed to make their creations explore and express what would now be called the modernity of the age. It is hoped that the present study has shed some light on the part played by the scientific movement and by political myths in the formation of a new ideal image of nature, an image that was essential to the aesthetics of sensibility.

NOTES

1. Horace Walpole, "The History of the Modern Taste in Gardening," in *Anecdotes of Painting in England* (London, 1826–1828).

2. Stephen Switzer, *Ichnographia rustica*, 3 vols. (London, 1742), 1:7.

3. Joseph Addison, *Spectator* 161 (April, 1710).

4. Humphry Repton, *An Enquiry into the Changes of Taste in Landscape Gardening* (London, 1806), 28.

5. Alexander Pope, "Epistle to Burlington," in *The Poems of Alexander Pope*, ed. John Butt (London, 1963), 592, line 117.

6. Alfred and Jeanne Marie, *Versailles au temps de Louis XIV*, 3 vols. (Paris, 1976), 3:348–355.

7. Simone Hoog, ed., *Louis XIV. Manière de montrer les jardins de Versailles* (Paris, 1982).

8. Eugène de Ganay, *André Le Nostre* (Paris, 1962), 48.

9. The enduring influence of Cartesianism in eighteenth-century France is analyzed in Aram Vartanian, *Diderot and Descartes* (Princeton, 1953).

10. The text in which Descartes praises regularity in the layout of cities is his *Discours de la Méthode*, trans. J. Veitch (London, 1953).

11. Etienne Lanson, *Etudes d'histoire littéraire* (Paris, 1929), 58.

12. Quoted by Alfred Marie, *Naissance de Versailles*, 2 vols. (Paris, 1968), 1:56.

13. Both Filmer and Bossuet justified the absolute rights of kings by their direct descent from Adam; both made use of the long genealogies found in Genesis. See Robert Filmer, *Patriarcha* (London, 1680); Jacques-Bénigne Bossuet, *Politique tirée des propres paroles de l'ecriture sainte* (Paris, 1709).

14. Hoog 1982, 19.

15. Quoted by Renée Simon, *Henry de Boulainviller* (Gap, 1940), 54.

16. Louis de Rouvroy, duc de Saint-Simon, *Mémoires*, ed. Yves Coirault, 8 vols. to date (Paris, 1983–), 4:1005.

17. According to Lord Chatham, George III thought that "the government cannot be carried out without the great families who have supported the Revolution government," quoted by R. W. Harris, *Political Ideas, 1760–1792* (London, 1963), 100.

18. Burke to Lord Richmond, 15 November 1772, *The Correspondence of Edmund Burke*, ed. T. W. Copeland et al., 10 vols. (London, 1960), 2:377.

19. Henry Nash Smith, *Virgin Land: The American West as Symbol and Myth* (Cambridge, Mass., 1950), v.

20. Quoted by Kerry Downes, *Vanbrugh* (London, 1977), 48.

21. Joshua Reynolds, *Discourses on Art*, ed. Robert R. Wark (New Haven and London, 1975), 241–242.

22. Sir John Summerson, "The Classical Country House in 18th Century England," *Royal Society of Arts Journal* 107.

23. Joseph Addison, *The Spectator*, ed. Donald F. Bond, 5 vols. (Oxford, 1965), 3:551–552.

24. Anthony Ashley Cooper, Earl of Shaftesbury, *Characteristics of Men, Manners, Opinions, Times, etc.*, ed. John M. Robertson, 2 vols. (London, 1900), 2:122. Christopher Thacker made use of this quotation as a title to his recent study of eighteenth-century primitivism.

25. Edward Spelman, *A Fragment out of the Sixth Book of Polybius* (London, 1743), preface. The text is in H. T. Dickinson, *Politics and Literature in 18th Century England* (London, 1974), 112.

26. For further discussion of the role of the Grand Tour in the decoration of English gardens, see John Dixon Hunt, "The British Garden and the Grand Tour," in this publication; idem, *Garden and Grove: The Italian Renaissance Garden in the English Imagination, 1600–1750* (Princeton, 1986).

27. Wilmarth Sheldon Lewis, ed., *The Yale Edition of Horace Walpole's Correspondence*, 48 vols. (New Haven, 1937–1983), 30:256–257.

28. Quoted by John Dixon Hunt and Peter Willis, eds., *The Genius of the Place* (London, 1975), 25.

29. Alexander Pope, *Works*, ed. William Warburton, 9 vols. (London, 1751), 1:29.

30. Swift wrote to Pope: "As to Parliament, I adore the wisdom of that Gothick institution," *The Correspondence of Jonathan Swift*, ed. H. Williams, 5 vols. (London, 1963–1965), 2:372.

31. Quoted by Dickinson 1974, 24.

32. Henry Saint-John, 1st Viscount Bolingbroke, *The Works of Lord Bolingbroke*, 4 vols. (London, 1844), 1:316.

33. Tacitus, *Germania*, trans. W. Peterson, Loeb Classical Library (Cambridge, Mass., 1914), 45:275, 279–283.

34. Montesquieu, *L'Esprit des Lois*, ed. Gonzague Truc, 2 vols. (Paris, 1956), 1:174.

35. Quoted by Eugène de Ganay, "Les jardins à l'Anglaise en France au XVIII° siècle" (Ph.D. diss., Musée des Arts Décoratifs, 1923), 55.

36. Ronald Paulson, *Emblem and Expression* (London, 1975).

37. Quoted by Hunt and Willis 1975, 120–121.

38. Sir William Temple, *Works*, 4 vols. (Edinburgh, 1814), 3:98.

39. William Stukeley, *Itinerarium Curiosum* (London, 1724), 64.

40. Pope 1751, 3:267–268.

41. Edward Gibbon, *The History of the Decline and Fall of the Roman Empire*, ed. J. B. Bury, 7 vols. (London, 1896–1900), 1:213.

42. See Albert Henry Smyth, *The Writings of Benjamin Franklin* (New York, 1905–1907), 6:127.

43. Samuel Johnson, *Lives of the English Poets*, ed. George Birkbeck Hill, 3 vols. (Oxford, 1905), 3:350–351.

44. William Shenstone, *Works*, 3 vols. (London, 1773), 3:63.

45. Shenstone 1773, 3:241.

46. John Locke, *Essay concerning Human Understanding* (London, 1694), 1.

47. B. Sprague Allen, *Tides in English Taste, 1619–1800* (Cambridge, Mass., 1937).

ALISTAIR M. DUCKWORTH

Gardens, Houses, and the Rhetoric of Description in the English Novel

*T*he immense trees which encircled Boot Magna Hall, shaded its drives and rides, and stood (tastefully disposed at the whim of some forgotten, provincial predecessor of Repton) singly and in groups about the park, had suffered, some from ivy, some from lightning, some from the various malignant disorders that vegetation is heir to, but all, principally, from old age. Some were supported with trusses and crutches of iron, some were filled with cement; some, even now, in June, could show only a handful of green leaves at their extremities. Sap ran thin and slow; a gusty night always brought down a litter of dead timber.

The lake was moved by strange tides. Sometimes . . . it sank to a single, opaque pool in a wilderness of mud and rushes; sometimes it rose and inundated five acres of pasture. There had once been an old man in one of the lodges who understood the workings of the water system; there were sluice-gates hidden among the reeds, and manholes, dotted about in places known only to him, furnished with taps and cocks; that man had been able to control an ornamental cascade and draw a lofty jet of water from the mouth of the dolphin on the south terrace. But he had been in his grave fifteen years and the secret had died with him.[1]

Evelyn Waugh's description of the landscape garden at Boot Magna Hall in his novel *Scoop* conceals beneath its satire a nostalgia for an aristocratic past that seemed, in 1938, irretrievably lost. The agricultural depression of the late nineteenth century, death duties (doubled or tripled in some instances by deaths in World War I), a dramatic decline in domestic and estate servants—these and other factors had led to the sale of millions of acres of land and to the demolition of hundreds of country houses.[2] Though the second National Trust Act had been passed in 1937, and the Georgian Group formed a year earlier, Waugh, naturally enough in the year be-

fore the Second World War, saw little hope for the resuscitation of the country house as an institution. Hence the condition of the park at Boot Magna Hall fully justifies Uncle Theodore's refrain: "Change and decay in all around I see."

The condition of Boot Magna Park reflects the condition of England in 1938, a country suffering from various malignant disorders and from old age, a country on crutches, its sap running thin and slow. Once, Waugh is suggesting, there had been those who understood the system, men who had the secret of control; but no more. Potentially, Waugh's description is adaptable to a liberal economic theory: the man furnished with taps and cocks so that he can regulate the water supply could be viewed as the Keynesian planner preventing a cycle of scarcity and overflow in the money supply; but Waugh's politics were far from Keynesian—or classical—liberalism. Though *Scoop* is less sentimental in its nostalgia than *Brideshead Revisited* (1945), it shares with the later novel a retrospective affection for an economic system controlled by an enlightened patriarchy. In the absence of such a system of order the modern world, represented by Lord Copper's journalism in *Scoop* or by the manners of Hooper and his kin in *Brideshead Revisited,* is fair game for Waugh's satire. Rather than accede in any degree to modern or progressive ideas, Waugh delights in the anarchism and amorality of characters like Mrs. Stitch and Basil Seal.

Waugh's dislike of modernity and progress appears in his criticism of architectural improvements of a Bauhaus or simply voguish sort. In *Decline and Fall* (1928), Margot Beste-Chetwynde modernizes an old country manor unchanged since "the reign of Bloody Mary." Desiring something "clean and square," she hires an architect after seeing a reproduction of his "re-

395

jected design for a chewing-gum factory . . . in a progressive Hungarian quarterly."[3] In *A Handful of Dust* (1934), Mrs. Beaver defaces Hetton, the ancestral home of Tony Last, by removing the fleur-de-lis mouldings from the morning room.[4] In *Brideshead Revisited* (1945), Celia Ryder converts an old tithe barn into a studio for Charles Ryder: oak boards now cover the earthen floor, a stone-mullioned bay window has been built in the north wall, and the great timbered roof stands out "stark, well lit, with clean white plaster between the beams."[5] Ryder regrets, however, that the old smell is lost.

Waugh's descriptions of gardens and houses are stylistically distinctive, but as a technique of social criticism and a way of expressing political allegiance, they are typical of fiction. Gardens and houses are the predicates of character and theme in English novels, and, as Roman Jakobson and Kenneth Burke have shown,[6] descriptive sequences allow novelists to deepen characterization and to communicate moral, social, and political ideas. Through the logic of the metonym, we may say, garden style is the man at Grandison Hall in Richardson's novel or at Pemberley in *Pride and Prejudice*. Through the same logic, the unimproved landscape of the moors in *Wuthering Heights* is at once an expression of Heathcliff's character and of his (and his author's) repudiation of the conventional culture represented by Edgar Linton at Thrushcross Grange.

The fictional role of the metonym is now generally understood; what is not so generally understood is the extent to which gardens and houses—and such alternative landscapes as moors and mountains, to which they may be opposed—play a variety of coded roles in the English novel. Considered as verbal structures, descriptions may be viewed as fragments from an anthology which, like the *topoi* Ernst Curtius discovered in medieval literature, migrate from work to work. In this perspective, novelists are not to be viewed as describing "real" houses or landscapes, nor, in their metonymic digressions, as constructing unique meanings; rather their descriptions exist and have meaning in relation to an intertextual field of available descriptive fragments that both constrain and enable fictional expression.[7] Existing as words or phrases, or inhering in longer sequences of prose, coded fragments allow novelists to achieve determinate effects. In Sir Walter Scott's fiction, for example, "docks and nettles" in a garden signify a condition of cultural neglect, while within a house "wainscot" signifies

a traditional society. Old brick walls and old trees are other backward-looking notations. In longer sequences an "irregular" house also carries conservative connotations (Appendix, 6). Scott's novels often provide a whole rhetoric of landscape, in which political positions are represented by scenic equivalents. In *Waverley* (1814), for example, "Jacobitism" finds its metonym in the bleak mountainous region of Fergus MacIvor's highland estate, while the prosperous Hanoverian establishment is signified by the "verdant, populous, and highly cultivated country" that arouses Waverley from his melancholy following the bloody execution of Fergus at Carlisle. That Waverley should ultimately prefer this English landscape to the "scenes of waste desolation, or of solitary and melancholy grandeur" he has experienced in Scotland is as much an indication of Scott's acceptance of the parliamentary union of 1707 as that Waverley should in the end marry Rose Bradwardine rather than Flora MacIvor.[8]

In this essay I shall follow the migrations of certain codes of representation from the time of Addison and Pope to that of Jane Austen and Scott, and then briefly indicate their persistence in later novels. I should first, however, pose some questions raised by the ideas of a "code of representation" or an "anthology of descriptive items." What do such ideas say to us regarding authorial originality? What are the political implications of an author's adoption of a particular code of representation? The rather too easy equation made above between Jacobitism and mountains suggests that novelists draw upon a kind of Flaubertian *Dictionary of Received Ideas,* and, if this is so, one would seem then to be required to conduct with regard to English fiction the sort of demystifying analysis Roland Barthes brings to the cultural codes used by Balzac in *Sarrasine.*[9] Barthes's criticism in *S/Z* is platonic in the sense that it distrusts the quality of the knowledge provided in "classic" novels, appraising such knowledge as vulgar *doxa* that formulaically repeats or recirculates ideas without being able to escape from ideological imprisonment. Is this the case when English novelists resort to descriptive cultural codes? In some instances the answer may be yes. In other instances, however—though we need not grant to fiction the capability of objective political analysis possessed by other forms of prose discourse—novelists may relate creatively to descriptive traditions. To rephrase T. S. Eliot, the most individual descriptions in an author's work may be those in which inherited codes of representation assert their immortality most vigorously.[10]

Invoking Eliot, moreover, we might conceive of a "mind of Europe," that changes but does not superannuate classic formulas of description. And indeed, as I shall note later, it is possible to discover in Jane Austen's prose descriptive sediments that date to the time of the Roman poets, or earlier. In what follows, however, I enter the intertextual field of fictional descriptions at the beginning of the eighteenth century, not because this is an absolute point of origin for the themes pursued, but because a number of significant events relevant to the rhetoric of fictional description occur at this time.

The early decades of the eighteenth century witnessed not only the emergence of the English novel and the English landscape garden, but also those sweeping changes in the English financial and political system, which, since the foundation of the Bank of England in 1694, had led to a series of confrontations between—in J. G. A. Pocock's terms—"virtue" and "commerce."[11] During this period a division appeared between those, like Addison and Defoe, who sought to give to merchants and men of business a civic role, and others, like Pope and Bolingbroke, who associated civic ideals with the possession of landed property and responded, therefore, to such innovations as the national debt, stockjobbing and moneyed corporations by viewing them as signs of modern corruption.

There is of course a danger—against which Pocock continually warns—of simplifying the politics of this period by presenting them as an opposition between squire and merchant, manor and market, polity and economy.[12] One needs to distinguish between financiers (the moneyed interest) and merchants, between speculators in public funds and dealers on the market; one needs also to be aware that not even the most extreme of court Whigs denied the importance of the land as a basis of civic personality, and that "commerce" as well as "virtue" could be defended on humanist grounds. The main threat to an ideology of real property was not trade but a system of public credit, and it was the latter that marked the shift from political to capitalist relations in the decades following the financial revolution of the 1690s.

Important as such caveats are, however, it is not always easy—nor was it easy for eighteenth-century writers—to separate "commerce" from "credit" and align it with "virtue"; it was even less easy to separate "credit" from "corruption." As Pocock observes:

Augustan political economics mark the moment when the trader—and, still more pressingly, the financier—was challenged to prove that he could display civic virtue in the sense that the landed man could. It was easy to visualize the latter, anxious only to improve his estate for inheritance, engaging in civic actions which related his private to the public good; much harder to ascribe this role to one constantly engaged in increasing his wealth by exchanging quantities of fictitious tokens.[13]

At such a moment, it seems fair to suppose, writers of a "Tory" or "country" persuasion might be led to collapse distinctions between merchant and rentier, market and stock market, in the interests of defending a traditional social order grounded in an ideology of real property. Basing their idea of a civic personality in a landed and precommercial past, such writers—Smollett and Goldsmith will provide later examples—might see history, directed by commerce, as departing from virtue, and respond with the call for a restoration of traditional values or perhaps, merely, with nostalgia.

At the same moment, other writers of a "Whig" sort might contest the "Tory" or "country" view in two ways; they might satirize a landed society unimproved by commerce (Macaulay seems to have accepted as true Addison's portrait of the boorish and otiose Foxhunter in *The Freeholder*); or they might rise to the challenge Pocock identifies of establishing the civic virtue of the trader and financier. In either case, they were as likely as their ideological opponents to conduct their arguments both discursively and—the possession and use of land being precisely in question—metonymically, that is, via descriptions of gardens, landscapes, and houses.

When, in 1712, Addison asked his celebrated question in *The Spectator*, No. 414—"Why may not a whole Estate be thrown into a kind of Garden by frequent Plantations, that may turn as much to the Profit, as the Pleasure of the Owner?"—he deliberately sounded a note different from that heard in seventeenth-century discussions of the garden, which turned rather on the idea of retirement, variously connected with the pursuit of spiritual or contemplative goals, or with Horatian or Epicurean notions of a country life divorced from the bustle of the city.[14] True, retirement is praised in *The Spectator*, No. 114, which also describes the old-fashioned garden of Sir Roger de Coverley; but that paper is by

Steele. Addison treats Sir Roger more critically. His Whig alternative to Sir Roger is Sir Andrew Freeport, the vigorous city merchant who, in *The Spectator*, No. 549, projects a very different kind of garden from Sir Roger's. Observing that the "greatest Part of [his] Estate has been hitherto of an unsteady and volatile Nature, either tost upon Seas or fluctuating in Funds," Sir Andrew is pleased that his fortune is now "fixt and settled in Substantial Acres and Tenements." He displays civic virtue in his plans to be a charitable landlord by building an Alms-house for a dozen "superannuated Husbandmen;" and he also intends to set his poor neighbors to work in his garden, fishponds, arable grounds, and pastures, so that they may earn "a comfortable Subsistence out of their own Industry." He writes to Mr. Spectator: "I have got a fine Spread of improveable Lands, and in my own Thoughts am already plowing up some of them, fencing others; planting Woods, and draining Marshes." Sir Andrew's projections resemble the practice of the wise and knowledgeable man in *The Spectator*, No. 94, who on looking back over an industrious life "beholds a beautiful and spacious Landskip divided into delightful Gardens, green Meadows, fruitful Fields, and can scarce cast his Eye on a single Spot of his Possessions, that is not covered with some beautiful Plant or Flower." By contrast, the man "grown old in Ignorance and Folly" is like "the Owner of a barren Country, that fills his Eye with the Prospect of naked Hills and Plains which produce nothing either profitable or ornamental."

Addison's writings on landscape are usually viewed as an important step in the development of an aesthetics of the beautiful and the sublime, but in passages like these Addison's appropriation of garden and field in support of an expansionist ideology favorable to commerce is more evident. Other writers also celebrate the Comforts of Industry and warn against the Miseries of Idleness.[15] The contrast between the two is central, for example, to Defoe's *Tour thro' the Whole Island of Great Britain* (1724-1726). Defoe's descriptions establish his citizens in rural settings, or so combine both natural and urban features as to deny divisions between land and trade. Thus (in a famous passage) the houses along the Thames are not only owned by gentlemen and businessmen alike, but "reflect beauty . . . and magnificence upon the whole country, and give a kind of a character to the island of Great Britain in general." And at Bushy Heath, where the prospect includes views of St. Albans and London, two foreign visitors express wonder that "England was not like other country's, but . . . was all a planted garden."[16] It is a short step from Defoe to James Thomson's *The Castle of Indolence* (1748), in which the Knight of Arts and Industry destroys the illusory land of the Wizard of Indolence, revealing it for what it is, a landscape of unproductive waste and bogs; on his retirement Thomson's Knight, like Sir Andrew Freeport, assumes "the amusing cares of rural industry," and under his direction, "Dark frowning heaths grow bright with Ceres' store;/And woods imbrown the steep, or wave along the shore."[17]

Is it possible—when one has been alerted by the arguments of E. P. Thompson and John Barrell[18]—to detect already in such descriptions the grounds for a conservative opposition to Whig expansionist methods? In book 3 of *Gulliver's Travels* (1726), Swift does seem to be satirically opposing the enthusiastic praise of prosperous landscapes and rural industry that Defoe provides in the *Tour*. On his way to Lord Munodi's house, Gulliver finds that, though there were "many busy Heads, Hands, and Faces . . . in . . . the Fields," he has never encountered "a Soil so unhappily cultivated, Houses so ill contrived and so ruinous, or a People whose Countenance and Habit expressed so much Misery and Want."[19] But while such perceived innovations as enclosures and habits of work discipline would later in the century be associated with modern agrarian methods and criticized from a moral position by those committed to traditional country customs and usages, such criticism does not seem to be prevalent in the 1720s and 1730s. Those who opposed Walpole comprised both Tories and country Whigs, and they were not opposed to an improved agriculture; John Trenchard was not alone, in *Cato's Letters* (1720-1724), in believing that "trade must be added to husbandry if the darker aspects of Gothic society [are] to be overcome."[20] Where agrarian improvement was concerned, conservative responses to Whig appropriations of garden and field were somewhat hampered.

Alexander Pope's position is of interest here. Pope was a Tory with Jacobite sympathies, and there was a gothic side to his thought that found expression in his love of "irregular" old houses like Sherborne and Stanton Harcourt (Appendix, 1, 2). He was a Tory, too, in his commitment to charity and benevolence, as exemplified in his portrait of the Man of Ross in the "Epistle III to Allen, Lord Bathurst" (1733). But there was also a Whiggish side to his thought.[21] Pope was a member of the Burlington circle that promoted the Palladian revival in architecture, and he was, like Addison, a significant influence on the development of the English garden by virtue of his practice at Twickenham, his advice at estates like Cirencester, Sherborne, and Prior Park, and his writings on the garden—especially his essay of 1713 in *The Guardian*,[22] which reinforced the growing dislike of topiary and Dutch formality, and his "Epistle IV to Richard Boyle, Earl of Burlington" (1731), which laid down criteria of hortulan taste for the rest of the century. The question arises whether his Tory ideals found—or could find—easy expression in the image of an "improved" garden or estate. Doubtless some of the estates of the Tory and Catholic noblemen he advised displayed his virtues of "use" and "sense," and could thus stand as moral examples against the putative inutility, extravagance, and folly of Whig estates like Houghton, Blenheim, and Chatsworth, which have been put forward as models for "Timon's villa" in the "Epistle to Burlington." Morris Brownell has even argued that Pope was responsible for transforming Ralph Allen at Prior Park from a Timon to a Man of Ross.[23] Yet, as Peter Martin has pointed out, the "Epistle to Burlington" is addressed to a Whig magnate, and in it Pope praises Stowe, the garden of another Whig lord (however "disaffected") as the model of "use" and "sense."[24] Moreover, in the concluding exhortation ("Bid Harbors open, public Ways extend"), Pope sounds an expansionist and imperial note that sits a little oddly with the Horatian role he played out on his five acres at Twickenham. Pope seems to have believed that benevolent paternalism might serve the cause of a "moral" economy both in particular estates at home and, on a much larger scale, in an expanding British empire. But the dialectic of retreat and expansion in his thought results in a rather puzzling political position.[25]

The literary consequences of Pope's writings on gardens are easier to locate. His political strategy was to align the aesthetic and the moral by apportioning taste and utility to the landed interest, and extravagance and vanity to the moneyed men. It succeeded brilliantly. In novel after novel in the eighteenth century Timon's villa is present either as a shadow warning to novelists not to convict their heroes of civic irresponsibility by leaving them open to charges of false taste, or in the negative form of a falsely improved estate, whose vitiated condition testifies to the corruption of a natural moral order by the forces of luxury and commerce.

Timon's villa is a shadow warning in Samuel Richardson's *The History of Sir Charles Grandison* of 1754. In his final volume Richardson provides us with a detailed presentation of Grandison Hall as a model of progressive farming and efficient but humane management. Sir Charles evidently inherits and puts into practice Sir Andrew Freeport's program of improvement. At the same time, however, Richardson, himself a citizen and man of commerce, obviously felt under some pressure to make his knight of arts and industry as impeccable in his aesthetic tastes as in his commercial undertakings. Thus his extensive landscaping is both tasteful and up-to-date, and might have been designed by Capability Brown, who had only recently set himself up in independent practice. Sir Charles has evidently consulted Pope's "genius of the place" and, unlike Sabinus' son in the "Epistle to Burlington," has been particularly careful not to cut down trees planted by his father.[26]

Timon's villa reappears as a negative example in the description of Baynard's estate in Smollett's *Humphry Clinker* of 1771. The estate is ruined after Baynard marries the daughter of a citizen whose ruling passion is vanity, and who has "no idea of a country life." Under Mrs. Baynard's direction the gardens have been so radically altered that Matthew Bramble does not recognize them when he visits. As Bramble writes to Dr. Lewis, Mrs. Baynard has:

pulled up the trees, and pulled down the walls of the garden, so as to let in the easterly wind, which Mr. Baynard's ancestors had been at great pains to exclude. To shew her taste in laying out ground, she seized into her own hand a farm of two hundred acres . . . which she parcelled out into walks and shrubberies, having a great bason in the middle, into which she poured a whole stream that turned two mills, and afforded the best trout in the country. The bottom of the bason, however, was so ill secured, that it would not hold the water, which . . . made a bog of the whole plantation.[27]

Like Bolingbroke and Pope, Smollett associated civic virtue with property-owning—and therefore independent—country gentlemen, and his novel allows for no rapprochement between a traditional and a commercial morality. While the luxurious Mrs. Baynard lives, the disorder and insubordination she has introduced into the estate will remain; only after her death will her "improvements" be reversed, the stream allowed to follow its natural course, the shrubbery extirpated, the pleasure grounds restored to cornfield and pasture, the garden walls rebuilt, and trees planted to cut off the east wind.[28]

The intensity of Smollett's animus against luxury gives some support to Pocock's suggestion that the emergence of a "bourgeois ideology" was hindered in England by a set of civic humanist values that were basically hostile to early modern capitalism.[29] If this is so, Smollett was not alone in using the garden as a vehicle of antibourgeois satire. In the second half of the eighteenth century—and with Capability Brown often cast in the role of butt or villain—landscape improvements are frequently the object of satire or criticism in essays, plays, poems, and novels.[30] In many instances accusations of false taste accompany attacks on city *arrivistes*. Francis Coventry, for example, writing in the periodical *The World* (No. 15) in 1753, asserts that, "in serious truth, the vast multitude of grotesque little villa's, which . . . swarm . . . on the banks of the Thames, are fatal proofs of the degeneracy of our national taste." Coventry goes on to tell the story of Squire Mushroom, once a city clerk, who buys an old mansion, improves it in execrable taste, and then shows his "genius . . . in the disposition of his gardens, which contain every thing"—including "a yellow serpentine river . . . near twenty yards in length"—"in less than two acres of ground." In Richard Graves' novel *Columella; or, the Distressed Anchoret* (1779), the absurdities of Squire Mushroom have become the ridiculous rural embellishments of another "cit," Mr. Nonsuch, who, in *one* acre of ground, has "contrived to introduce . . . a large shrubbery, a small serpentine river . . . a Chinese bridge . . . a Chinese pagod, a Gothic temple, a grotto, a root-house or hermitage, a Cynic tub or two."[31]

Graves' novel is better known for its satirical treatment of Shenstone's improvements at The Leasowes, and it also expresses a dislike of "eclectic" gardens, including Stowe; but there is a distinct difference in tone between the satire—often interspersed with appreciative comments—directed at Shenstone's garden and that directed at Mr. Nonsuch's. Another specimen of Graves' satire, clearly deriving from Coventry's essay in *The World,* suggests that Graves, like Coventry, was opposing the enthusiastic welcome that Defoe had accorded to citizens who retire to the country (Defoe's *Tour* was frequently updated and reprinted in the eighteenth century, by Samuel Richardson and others). Hortensius, one of the visitors to Columella's garden, objects to "this absurd passion for retirement" that makes "every little clerk in office [think he] must have his villa, and every tradesman his country house. A cheesemonger retires to his little pasteboard edifice on Turnham Green, and when smoking his pipe under his codling-hedge on his gravel walk made with coal-ashes, fancies himself a second Scipio or Cincinnatus."[32] Such fun at the expense of aspiring citizens could be extended indefinitely by references to descriptive passages in the plays of Garrick and the poems of Robert Lloyd, but the humor begins to pall when one sees it as serving a (no doubt unarticulated) program to discredit the efforts of writers like Addison, Defoe, and Richardson to promote through description the idea of commercial humanism.

The snobbery of Coventry, Graves, and other eighteenth-century writers who used taste in landscape as a shibboleth should doubtless be set against the sentiments of such writers as James Thomson—in *The Seasons* (1744)—or John Dyer—in *The Fleece* (1767)—who celebrated commerce, trade, and rural industry. Moreover, in the work of Adam Ferguson and other Scots theorists commerce was being identified as an inevitable and not necessarily pernicious stage in the course of history. Unlike Rousseau, the Scottish "speculative" historians believed that the opposition between a past civic virtue and a present commercial civilization could be managed.[33] Yet if we look at the episodic narratives of Henry Mackenzie, an Edinburgh lawyer and novelist who grew up in the midst of the Scottish school, we discover a repetition of the anticommercial prejudice already examined. Mackenzie's episodic stories in the two periodicals that he edited, *The Mirror* (1779–1780) and *The Lounger* (1785–1787), are the best of the eighteenth-century imitations of Addison and Steele, but they adopt a different posture toward social change. The characters of Mr. Umphraville and Colonel Caustic, like Sir Roger de Coverley, are open to gentle satire, but to be *laudator temporis acti* is to play a significantly more valued role in Mackenzie than in Addison. Nouveau riche families, on the other hand, like the Blubbers, who tell of their Highland tour in *The Mirror,*[34] or the Mushrooms, whose eldest son has returned a nabob from India in *The Lounger,*[35] are less sympathetically treated; there is no character in Mackenzie who resembles Sir Andrew Freeport. In a way increasingly typical of fiction, Mackenzie discovers traditional values in old-fashioned settings and suspect modern values among improved landscapes. Thus, the worthy Mr. Umphraville's house is gothic and his garden formal,[36] but the newly rich Lord Grubwell, "without the manners or the taste of a gentleman," has, to Colonel Caustic's disgust, improved his estate after the modern fashion, introducing a serpentine river and a Chinese bridge.[37]

Quite distinct from the satire of Coventry, Graves, and Mackenzie, but equally opposed to commerce, is the protest against the landscape garden that Oliver Goldsmith mounts in *The Deserted Village* (1770). Goldsmith's protest is accompanied by a mood of elegiac pessimism, and has sometimes been dismissed as sentimental self indulgence that is in any case false to history. Recent interpreters, however, have accepted the force of Goldsmith's claim that, in consequence of the extravagant and extensive landscape improvements of the "man of wealth and pride," "the country blooms—a garden and a grave."[38] Most contemporary reviewers tended to consider Goldsmith's political protest exaggerated; yet dozens of old villages were in fact removed to make way for Georgian pleasure grounds, and even if Goldsmith's charges of depopulation were excessive and his criticism of luxury contestable, he was both sincere and informed in his opposition to the effects of economic individualism in the country. In an essay of 1762 entitled "The Revolution of Low Life" he describes how one village had been forced to evacuate because "a Merchant of immense fortune in London, who had lately purchased the estate on which they lived, intended to lay the whole out in a seat of pleasure for himself."[39] In *The Traveller* (1764), too, he connects landscape gardening with depopulation, and in *The Vicar of Wakefield* (1766) he evokes a vision of a precapitalistic world as yet unaffected by enclosures, enforced habits of work discipline, and an improved agriculture.

No doubt there is more than a little mystification in Goldsmith's nostalgia, and, as a counter, one might recall that in the late eighteenth century landlords with an eye to improvement were transforming "a traditional and communal agriculture and a backward, truly reactionary peasantry, thereby promoting the forces of economic

individualism in the rural community."[40] Seen from this perspective, Goldsmith's social criticism is reactionary. On the other hand, Donald Davie has recently suggested that Goldsmith's *Traveller* may contain "the earliest and . . . most caustic indictment of the world of 'free enterprise,' unstructured and unrestricted competitiveness [and] the morality of the market."[41] For present purposes, it is of less consequence to decide how far Goldsmith's criticism is limited by its conservative cast than to observe how typical it was. We tend to think of this period as characterized in the matter of garden taste by Horace Walpole's *The History of the Modern Taste in Gardening* (1771–1780), which did more than any work to correlate the English garden with ideas of liberty and the Whig enlightenment. But against Walpole (and William Mason) may be set not only critics like Sir William Chambers and Richard Payne Knight, who for various reasons objected to the *style* of Capability Brown's landscapes, but also poets like William Cowper and John Langhorne, who joined Goldsmith in finding social and moral reasons for their disapproval of the modern garden.

At the beginning of the nineteenth century Wordsworth repeated Goldsmith's moral opposition to improvements in a long letter to Sir George Beaumont, who was then engaged in improving his estate at Coleorton. Basing his advice on the principle that the house should belong to the country, and not the country to the house (a reversal, in effect, of Addison's emphasis), Wordsworth argues that "it was a misconception of the meaning and principles of poets and painters which gave countenance to the modern system of gardening, which is now I hope on the decline." Referring to Brown's improvements of the 1760s at Alnwick, Wordsworth deprecates the attempt to "modernize" the ancient home of the Percys. The "man of wealth and influence" should "give countenance to improvements in agriculture" and "do his utmost to be surrounded with tenants living comfortably," but as to "that part of his estate devoted to park and pleasure ground let him keep himself as much out of sight as possible." And, in further echo of Goldsmith, Wordsworth asks: "What then shall we say of many great mansions with their unqualified expulsion of human creatures from their neighborhood, happy or not, houses of which what is fabled of the upas-tree is true, that they breathe out death and desolation. . . . I was glad to hear from Lady Beaumont that you did not think of removing your Village."[42]

Wordsworth's approval of agricultural improvements but disapproval of landscape improvements raises an obvious question. Did all the landlords who employed Capability Brown on their estates—at Alnwick, Althorp, Burghley, Chatsworth, Petworth, and scores of other places—breathe out death and desolation on the land? Obviously not. Brown was employed in 1762 at Holkham Hall, then an estate remarkable for its absence of trees, and it is Brown's planting, followed by Repton's improvements to the lake, that account for the park's "splendour and diversity."[43] Moreover, Holkham was the home of Thomas William Coke, otherwise known as "Coke of Norfolk," who achieved mythic status in the late eighteenth century as a Whig farmer whose agricultural improvements raised the value of his land tenfold in a generation (or so it was widely believed until recently).[44] At the same time he made the fortunes of his tenants who paid the high rents. Clearly, Addison's synthesis of pleasure and profit, of simultaneous improvement to garden and field, *was* achievable at a time when progressive and libertarian landlords were effecting agrarian changes central to the prosperity of the national economy.[45]

Wordsworth's moral criticism of landscape improvements, like that of Smollett, Goldsmith, and others, should not be dismissed, however, simply as reactionary Toryism. While it is true that, compared with the huge enterprise of agricultural reform, "landscape gardening was a minor department . . . of estate business,"[46] it was the department visible to novelists and poets— the space in which the widening gaps they perceived between, in Coleridge's terms, "cultivation" and "civilization" could be measured and criticized. Unlike the antibourgeois satirists, who used aesthetic discrimination in the protection of a hierarchical order, the moral critics of capitalism, finding its disruptive effects evident in the landscape, looked backward to an earlier organic society (or "moral" economy) for an ideal social model.

I would include Jane Austen among the moral critics of economic individualism. True, she existed in the midst of a capitalist money culture.[47] She observed the great good fortune of her brother Edward, who was adopted in his teens by a rich landowning kinsman and became, in consequence, the heir and eventual owner of a great estate at Godmersham in Kent and another more modest estate at Chawton in Hampshire. But she existed in a marginal relation to Edward Knight's prosperity, and her novels reveal a sense of traditional social values under threat from modern materialistic behavior. The values she admires and upholds are often expressed metonymically. Consider Delaford in *Sense and Sensibility* (1811), for example, which is to become the home on marriage of both Dashwood sisters. As Mrs. Jennings describes it:

Delaford is . . . a nice old fashioned place . . . quite shut in with great garden walls that are covered with the best fruit-trees in the country . . . there is a dove-cote, some delightful stewponds, and a very pretty canal; and every thing, in short, that one could wish for . . . it is close to the church. . . . A butcher hard by in the village, and the parsonage-house within a stone's throw. To my fancy, a thousand times prettier than Barton Park, where they are forced to send three miles for their meat.[48]

In 1811 Delaford is indeed old-fashioned. With its garden walls, dovecote, stewponds, canal, and its village still close to the house, Delaford has evidently escaped the improvements of Capability Brown and his imitators. Through Mrs. Jennings' description we recognize codes of value signifying organic growth and social community. One notation—the contrast between Delaford and the richer Barton Park—is as old as Martial's epigrams.[49]

Delaford resembles other old-fashioned estates in Jane Austen's novels, such as Sotherton Court and Thornton Lacey in *Mansfield Park* and Donwell Abbey in *Emma*, and while an old-fashioned condition is not invariably a virtue (Sotherton Court obviously needs "modern dress," if not of the kind Henry Crawford proposes), old-fashioned houses and gardens usually betoken value. By the same measure, extravagantly improved estates like John Dashwood's Norland Park in *Sense and Sensibility*, or General Tilney's Northanger Abbey, are presented negatively as the visible signs of social aggression and greed. Inheriting Norland Park, John Dashwood proceeds to enclose Norland common, engross a neighboring farm, and, to his sister Elinor's dismay, cut down the old walnut trees behind the house to make way for a greenhouse and flower garden for his wife. Abetted by his wife, John Dashwood is the most materialistic of Jane Austen's characters, and in associating him with improvements Jane Austen is criticizing members of the gentry who have forgotten their social obligations in the pursuit of profit and display. A similar criticism extends to General Tilney, whose house and grounds at Northanger Abbey are—to Catherine Morland's disappointment—the *dernier cri* in modern fashion. Perhaps a portrait of the inventor Count Rumford, and in other ways reminiscent of Pope's Timon, General Tilney is a modern, not a gothic tyrant.[50] Wrongly believing Catherine Morland to be an heiress of a great fortune, he displays to her his huge kitchen garden, countless hothouses and pinery as a mark of the magnificence she will acquire on marrying his son. But after he finds she is not an heiress after all, he dismisses her instantly from the Abbey.

Jane Austen was not, of course, an enemy of tasteful improvements either in her life or her fiction.[51] Among her heroes, Edward Ferrars, Henry Tilney, and Edmund Bertram are, or will be, improvers of their parsonages, and in *Pride and Prejudice,* Pemberley is a model of "modern," if understated taste. Elizabeth Bennet is delighted: "She had never seen a place for which nature had done more, or where natural beauty had been so little counteracted by an awkward taste."[52] Darcy, like Sir Charles Grandison, reveals his moral character in his aesthetic practice. Yet other value-laden places in Austen's novels are either inconspicuously improved or plain old-fashioned, and alongside the novelist's approval of Augustan taste there is a more romantic affection for places that have evolved gradually and harmoniously over the years without the help of the professional improver's hand.[53]

Mr. Knightley's Donwell Abbey, in *Emma,* is such a place. As his name implies, Knightley is committed to a traditional role, whose origin is feudal or chivalric. At the same time, he resembles Wordsworth's ideal landowner, who engages in agricultural improvements for the benefit of the community, but keeps himself out of park and pleasure ground. When Emma visits Donwell Abbey, she sees:

the respectable size and style of the building, its suitable, becoming, characteristic situation, low and sheltered—its ample gardens stretching down to meadows washed by a stream, of which the Abbey, with all the old neglect of prospect, had scarcely a sight—and its abundance of timber in rows and avenues, which neither fashion nor extravagance had rooted up.—The house was . . . rambling and irregular . . . and Emma felt an increasing respect for it, as the residence of a family of such true gentility, untainted in blood and understanding.[54]

What is remarkable about this famous description is that it comprises an anthology of codes of representation. Consider, for example, the abundance of timber and the low and sheltered situation. Trees, of course, had carried political meanings at least since the Restoration, when Royalist propagandists exaggerated their loss during the interregnum so as "to create an association between the wanton felling of trees and republican politics."[55] A low and sheltered situation is a later code, arising in reaction to the excesses of those eighteenth-century builders who sited houses on an eminence and then surrounded them with parks improved in the style of Capability Brown (whose "innovating hand," according to Richard Payne Knight, first "banish'd the thickets of high-bow'ring wood").[56] Of even more significance, however, is the code of the irregular house. From the time of Jonson's "To Penshurst" (1612), the irregular house—as opposed to the house "built to envious show"—has been a literary occasion for the transmission of conservative values. Migrating from text to text over the centuries, the code may be found in Pope (in his letter to Lady Mary Wortley Montagu describing Stanton Harcourt), in Defoe's *Tour* (where, as one might expect, it carries negative value), in Smollett, and above all in Scott, where Tully Veolan in *Waverley,* which "extend[s] its irregular yet venerable front along a terrace,"[57] is only one of a dozen irregular houses in his fiction (Appendix, 1, 3, 4, 6, 8).

According to Mavis Batey, "the Scots baronial mansion, in imitation of Tully Veolan . . . with its angle turrets, crow-stepped gables, and battlements, sprang up, seemingly overnight, in England and Ireland."[58] Abbotsford, too, the irregular house built from scratch for Scott by William Atkinson, was influential in reinforcing the literary and architectural associations now well established between old-fashioned houses and gardens and what Wordsworth, apostrophizing Lowther Castle, called "the strength of backward-looking thought."[59] After an admiring visit to Abbotsford, Washington Irving used it in *The Sketch Book* (1819–1820) as the model for Bracebridge Hall: "an irregular building," with gardens "laid out in the old formal manner of artificial flower-beds, clipped shrubberies, raised terraces, and heavy stone balustrades, ornamented with urns, a leaden statue or two, and a jet of water."[60]

Scott's role in the transmission of a conservative cultural outlook has been criticized at least since Mark Twain's *Life on the Mississippi* (1883). But in recent scholarship Scott has appeared less as a Burkean conservative than as a man educated by the Scottish philosophical historians, who theorized that society had moved through successive stages—from hunting to pasturage to agriculture to commerce—and could look, therefore, on the eighteenth-century shift from "land" to "credit" as diachronic and inevitable rather than as a sign of necessary decadence and corruption.[61] In this context it is possible to see Scott—far more than Mackenzie, the "Scottish Addison" to whom Scott inscribed *Waverley*—as a progressive thinker, who believed that the opposition between traditional ideals and a commercial civilization could be reconciled. Often, in fact, his novels reveal progressive intentions. When Jeanie Deans in *The Heart of Midlothian* (1818), for example, walks barefoot from Edinburgh to London to beg Queen Caroline for a reprieve of her sister Effie's death sentence, she passes through a landscape that unfolds historically as well as geographically. One of her stopping places is the clerical mansion at Willingham, and Willingham, with its old "irregular" house and its garden planted with "old oaks and elms," is a metonym for English heritage and tradition (Appendix, 6). But after meeting the Duke of Argyll in London, Jeanie is shown another landscape, that of the Thames near Richmond, and all the notations in this description—flocks of sheep, herds of cattle, rich pastures, prosperous villas—signify a Whig landscape of prosperity and compromise. (It is the Thames countryside as viewed by Defoe and Thomson, not Coventry.)[62] Moreover, from London Jeanie is transported by the charitable duke to the west of Scotland, where her father—old Davie Deans, the Covenanter—becomes head of an experimental farm. In historical fact the house of Argyll at this time (the fictional year is 1737) was a leader in landscape and agricultural improvements, and at Inveraray the duke had built a gothic castle, laid out parks and gardens, and built new towns, harbors, and canals. Scott's approval of his fictional duke's benevolent landlordism is not qualified by an awareness of the negative side of the historical duke's enterprise: at Inverary—as distinct from Holkham, later—stiff rents and competition for leases led to a high rate of insolvency among tenants.[63] The only dangers to Jeanie's happiness come from the highlands, which, as usual in Scott's novels, are the habitat of those who exist in, or have regressed to, a primitive historical stage of culture.

Other novels by Scott may be read as progressive also. In *Rob Roy* (1817), "virtue" and "commerce" vie for the hero's allegiance in the persons of Rob Roy, the Highland outlaw, and Bailie Jarvie, the canny Glasgow merchant and banker, who has plans for draining Loch Lomond so as to make available thousands of acres of arable land. In the end, however, Frank Osbaldistone opts for the commercial future rather than the adventurous past. The conclusion of the novel is reminiscent of Addison's irenic strategies. Frank, after his marriage to the Catholic Diana Vernon, transforms Osbaldistone Hall, the family estate, from an abode of drunken boors and foxhunters into a civilized house. In *The Abbot* (1820), Sir Halbert Glendinning deplores the barren hills of his native Scotland and holds up the industrious Dutch and Flemings, who have forsaken a life of arms for agriculture, as a model; and some indication of how progressive a notation this is may be gained if we recall that, for Goldsmith in *The Traveller*, the phlegmatic Dutch exemplified the corruption intrinsic to a commercial society.[64]

In other novels, however, Scott hardly welcomes commerce. In *The Pirate* (1821), for example, the agricultural improvements that Triptolemus Yellowley seeks to carry out on behalf of the Lord Chamberlain of the Orkney and Zetland islands are exposed by Scott, in a manner resembling that of Swift, as the visionary schemes of a crazy projector. With his plans for ploughing barren land and draining lochs, Yellowley sounds like the Defoe of the third volume of the *Tour*, who had his own schemes for improving primitive areas in Scotland. Part of Scott's intention, in keeping with "philosophical" history, was to conduct an exercise in comparative anthropology—Zetland is remote in space and, the period being the seventeenth century, time. Scott's sympathies nevertheless seem to be with Magnus Troil and the immemorial customs and rights he observes in his "irregular" mansion house at Jarlshof (Appendix, 8).

In the Scottish novels Scott seems genuinely to have sought for a political compromise that would grant civic consciousness to market man, but the utter failure of a novel like *The Bride of Lammermoor* to enact a dialectical resolution testifies to the difficulties he faced. At this time—the period of Peterloo—Scott's faith in progress was tested by the constitutional reforms proposed by the radical Whigs, and his view of what was permissible in the way of political improvement narrowed. Typically resorting to metonymic (and Burkean) techniques, he described the British constitution in a pamphlet as "an excellent old mansion, which had been founded in the feudal times, but by additions and alterations . . . had been adapted to modern ideas of convenience; so that, still retaining the exterior of a gothic castle, it was in the inside as warm and comfortable a habitation as you could desire." It is this fundamentally sound structure that the mob, inadequately controlled by Mr. Vitruvius Whigham (Henry Brougham?), wishes to demolish "with lifted levers, lighted torches, and every implement of destruction."[65]

A Burkean perspective on society, the constitution, and the law may also explain the criticisms Scott makes in the 1820s of the landscape garden. Culminating in 1828 in an essay on landscape gardening in the *Quarterly Review*,[66] his criticisms testify to the expertise he had acquired by virtue of his own improvements at Abbotsford, but also to his growing dissatisfaction with the commercial present, which had plunged him into bankruptcy late in 1825. Scott's animus against "the spade and mattock" school of gardening doubtless stems from his sense of its destructive relation to historical places. Thus, in his *Journal* he admires the trees on the *left* side of the river at Alnwick, "where they have been let alone by the capability villain,"[67] while in the introductory chapter to *Quentin Durward* he deplores the removal of terraces, sculptures, and parterres from before an old house, commenting that "fickleness of fashion has accomplished in England the total change which devastation and popular fury have produced in the French pleasure grounds."[68] In the *Quarterly Review* essay he accuses Horace Walpole of confounding the garden and the park, and defends the artificial garden near the house; and while he is no more willing than Pope or Addison to defend topiary, he argues that the gardens of London and Wise—where they still exist—should be preserved. He is critical of "capability-men" like James Robertson, "a pupil of Brown's," who, at Duddingstone, "twisted the brook into the links of a string of pork-sausages," and rejected the ruined Craigmillar Castle as a termination to a view, because—in the improver's words—"Craigmillar, seen over all the country, was a common prostitute." Scott also criticized Kent for his innovations, which inspired a disciple to

make Glamis "more parkish" by razing the exterior defences of the castle and bringing "his mean and paltry gravel-walk up to the very door."

Scott's novels of the 1820s for the most part take us to historical periods earlier than the eighteenth century, and they provide Scott with numerous opportunities for an affectionate reconstruction, through descriptions, of old houses and gardens. One may compare the cultural impact of these descriptions to the illustrations in Joseph Nash's *Mansions of England in the Olden Times* (1839–1849). The estate of the old royalist knight in *Woodstock* (1826) is, in fact, probably based on Compton Wynyates, as Henry James suggested in *English Hours* (1905).[69] To be sure, Scott remained a friend of progressive improvements under paternalistic direction, approving in his *Journal* of the changes in progress at Drumlanrig and Dalkeith and revealing his awareness of Coke's achievements at Holkham.[70] But Scott's view of the commercial present undoubtedly darkened after his bankruptcy, and it is of some importance in assessing his political legacy to fiction (and culture) to note his criticism of "the modern system of gardening" and his fondness for old mansions and formal gardens.

Following Jane Austen and Scott in the nineteenth century—and in some degree because of their example—many other novelists use old houses and gardens as metonyms of conservative values. Henry James loved actual "irregular" houses like Penshurst, Haddon Hall, and Wroxton Abbey, and described others in his fiction—like Gardencourt in *The Portrait of a Lady* (1881) and Medley Hall in *The Princess Casamassima* (1886)—that may be based on actual houses but probably owe more to the literary code under examination. In *English Hours,* particularly, James reinforced the association of the English landscape with traditionalist political beliefs. Of Warwickshire he wrote (in 1877):

One had no need of being told that this is a conservative county; the fact seemed written in the hedgerows and in the verdant acres behind them. . . . I had a feeling, as I went about, that I should find some very ancient and curious opinions still comfortably domiciled in the fine old houses whose clustered gables and chimneys appeared here and there, at a distance, above their ornamental woods.[71]

And in the same essay he provides one of the richest of the tributes to the romantic associations of the English country house in his description of Compton Wynyates. All the conservative codes are there—abundant trees, low situation, irregular architecture—yet so elaborated and filled with precisely observed details as to become James' own (Appendix, 10).

James' attitude to aristocratic rural life was not one of unambiguous veneration. He was aware of "the darker actualities of a hereditary and hierarchical order,"[72] as is most clear in *The Princess Casamassima* (1886), in which Hyacinth Robinson, child of the London slums, embraces violent anarchism as the answer to social injustice. But Hyacinth's revolutionary commitment is—not discredited—but immensely complicated by his experience, at Medley Hall, of an elegant world of heritage and culture, whose values, predictably, are expressed in and through descriptions of irregular architecture and old-fashioned gardens (Appendix, 11, 12).

As the sample descriptions in the Appendix may suggest, gardens and houses continue to serve in the English novel as transmitters, not primarily of progressive ideals—which was their role in Addison, Defoe, Richardson, and, arguably, Pope—but of cultural conservatism. They carry with them the freight of respect—often elegiac—for tradition, and of suspicion—sometimes satirical—of modernity. Of course there are significant exceptions; Chesney Wold in Dickens' *Bleak House* (1853) is hardly a metonym of an approved "moral economy." In conclusion, therefore, I wish to suggest briefly some of the ways in which descriptive traditions are opposed or qualified in the interests of political vision. Two of the novelists examined—Emily Brontë and D. H. Lawrence—are characterized by the intensity of their rejection of received culture; two others—George Eliot and William Morris—seek liberal or socialist reform in part via descriptions of houses and landscapes; and one—E. M. Forster—may unwittingly reveal the ways in which inherited structures hinder a commitment to progressive change.

In *Wuthering Heights* (1847), Emily Brontë totally repudiates connections between the *paysage riant* and an authentic society. The contrast between Heathcliff and Linton, Nelly Dean tells Lockwood, "resembled what you see in exchanging a bleak, hilly, coal country for a beautiful fertile valley."[73] This contrast is of less interest for being original than for the respective values Emily Brontë accords to the terms in question. When Defoe employs a similar contrast in his description of Chatsworth in the *Tour,* he shows a Whig preference for cultivated nature over waste hills and moorland. Arriving at Chatsworth, Defoe writes, the stranger from the north looks down in wonder "from a frightful heighth, and a comfortless, barren, and as he thought, endless moor, into the most delightful valley, with the most pleasant garden, and most beautiful palace in the world."[74] Catherine Earnshaw also exchanges the heights for a fertile valley when she marries Edgar Linton and becomes mistress of Thrushcross Grange; but she lives to regret her decision and dies having compromised her commitment to a reality transcending the shallow culture of Linton's society. Like other romantic writers, including her sister Charlotte, Emily Brontë repudiates conventional society by repudiating the garden, and seeks freedom on the heights and the moors.[75]

Yet the union Catherine and Heathcliff seek—unmediated by culture, education, or manners—is impossible, as Brontë recognizes, and, having assaulted culture, the novelist sought to reconstruct it on more authentic grounds in the relationship of the second Cathy with Hareton Earnshaw. Mistreated by Heathcliff, Hareton is described as "good things lost amid a wilderness of weeds," yet there is evidence of "a wealthy soil that might yield luxuriant crops"[76] Hareton's name, which is already a metonym, points the way. Unlike *Heathcliff,* which combines two extrasocial terms (heath and cliff), *Hareton* is a mixture of the wild (hare) and the social (ton or town).[77] Accordingly, he may be acculturated during the courtship with Cathy (he learns to read and be polite), just as the garden at Wuthering Heights, until now the home of wild currant and gooseberry bushes, may at the end of the novel be planted with stocks and wallflowers imported from Thrushcross Grange.

D. H. Lawrence's "apocalyptic" fiction is as far from suggesting a specific political program as Brontë's is. Yet when, in *Women in Love* (1921), Lawrence describes the rising smoke from the colliery that is visible across the garden and park from the old mansion at Shortlands, he describes a "prospect" far bleaker than Pope's, say, when Pope views the town of Sherborne from Sherborne Castle, or Emma's, when she views the Abbey Mill farm from the grounds of Donwell Abbey.[78] Of all English novelists, Lawrence is the most critical of the idea that benevolent paternalism can solve the problems caused by industrial capitalism; and for him there is no hope of a reconciliation between the garden and the colliery. The compromise between virtue and commerce variously proposed by Addison, Defoe, and Richardson—and represented by "prospects" combining rural and urban features—is unthinkable in the polluted countryside of the Midlands. In *Lady Chatterley's Lover* (1929) Lawrence seeks possibilities for cultural renewal in the "wood," a setting—and a meaning—quite separate from the garden of Wragby Hall or the colliery which is the basis of its riches.

Like Lawrence, on whom she was a significant influence, George Eliot was aware of the dangers posed to society by industrial technology; like him she held little brief for a system of benevolent paternalism. Her vision is in marked contrast to the neo-feudal vision of Disraeli and the Young Tories. Unlike Lawrence, however, she retained faith in society as an organic structure and sought to translate this faith into a political position. Though she believed in reform, she distrusted radical and Benthamite measures that endangered cultural continuity (in her distrust of radical reform she is kin to Wordsworth and Arnold). More important to her than the achievement of universal suffrage is the acquisition of knowledge and moral sensibility on the part of the electorate; these are the qualities that contribute to the maintenance of our "common estate," and, as Peter Coveney has well shown, these are the morally informed politics that the hero urges in *Felix Holt, the Radical* (1866) through speech and behavior.[79]

Felix Holt expresses Eliot's politics metonymically, especially in and through its descriptions of Transome Court, the magnificent house and estate rejected by the heroine, Esther, in favor of the life of social work and political dedication that she will experience as the wife of Felix Holt. With its ancient oaks and broad lawns, Transome Court seems to belong to the same descriptive paradigm as those great good places one encounters in the novels of Jane Austen and Henry James, and in the poems of Yeats; but Eliot invites such associations only to dispel them. The Tory Mrs. Transome, while waiting long years for her son's return, has "held every tree sacred on the demesne;"[80] Harold meanwhile has adopted radical politics and, on his return, plans to improve his inheritance by the felling of old and decayed trees. Harold has a touch of Jane Austen's Henry Crawford (that "capital improver") in his makeup; but neither preserver nor improver, trustee nor heir is admirable in *Felix Holt*. Even more significantly, trees, among the most positive of value signs in literature, take on unusual associations at Transome Court—associations with seclusion, imprisonment, and death.

At the climax of the novel, Esther, living at Transome Court, realizes that she is in "a silken bondage that arrest[s] all motive":

To be restless amidst ease, to be languid among all appliances for pleasure, was a possibility that seemed to haunt the rooms of this house, and wander with her under the oaks and elms of the park.[81]

But earlier the moral and political answer to such languor and despair had also been presented scenically in the description of a walk Esther takes with Felix:

They passed through a gate into a plantation where there was no large timber, but only thin-stemmed trees and underwood, so that the sunlight fell on the mossy spaces which lay open here and there.

"See how beautiful those stooping birch-stems are with the light on them!" said Felix. "Here is an old felled trunk they have not thought worth carrying away. Shall we sit down a little while?"[82]

Eliot's refusal of the usual association of old trees with values of heritage and organic growth is very effective; in this novel large old trees connote decay and corruption, and it is the thin-stemmed trees, the stooping birch stems, that signify growth and renewal. Yet one also notes that renewal and growth take place in the undergrowth near the old felled trunk, which has escaped, presumably, from Harold's sweeping measures of improvement; and the biological continuity of nature suggests a similar continuity in culture.

In *News from Nowhere* (1891), William Morris also disputes conservative and paternalist uses of landscape and houses. In the socialist future he imagines, all England has become "a garden, where nothing is wasted and nothing is spoilt, with the necessary dwellings, sheds, and workshops scattered up and down the country, all trim and neat and pretty."[83] Country houses have become collegial dwelling places, and their artificial shrubberies and rockeries are no longer to be seen; as for their landscaped parks: "why, the whole Thames-side is a park this time of the year; and for my part, I had rather lie under an elm-tree on the borders of a wheat-field . . . than in any park in England."[84]

Morris is not above antibourgeois commentary, similar to that conducted by Coventry and Graves in the eighteenth century. In the old days, we learn, the Thames had been defaced by "the hideous vulgarity of the cockney villas" of well-to-do stockbrokers.[85] Such commentary does not diminish the importance of Morris' influence on the idea and development of the garden city. But in seeking a model for his socialist future in the medieval world, Morris joined those critics who associated "improvements" with commerce and technology; and this may explain why, from Kelmscott Manor, too, the association of old houses and gardens with communal, precommercial values comes into modern culture. In the early twentieth century, traditional allegiance is expressed architecturally in the neo-vernacular houses of Blunden Shadbolt and Ernest Trobridge, who reused old tiles and timbers to give the instant effect of age and heritage,[86] and fictionally in the coded descriptions of houses to be found in the works of (among others) Vita Sackville-West, Ford Madox Ford, Joyce Cary, Evelyn Waugh, and Barbara Pym (Appendix, 13, 15).

No novel more clearly exhibits the force of inherited descriptive codes than E. M. Forster's *Howards End* (1910), a work avowedly seeking "connection" between such oppositions as past and present, Coleridge and Bentham, tradition and commerce. At Howards End the Wilcoxes are enthusiasts for sports and physical fitness; they play croquet on the lawn and—when not afflicted with hay fever—do calisthenic exercises on a machine they have attached to the greengage tree. They are keen motorists, belonging, in Forster's phrase, to a "civilization of luggage," and they have damaged the roots of the ancient wych-elm tree in building a garage. As prosperous businessmen committed to a laissez-faire economy, the plutocratic Wilcoxes are a modern version of those improvers who, with backgrounds in commerce and money, show disdain for heritage and community. Charles Wilcox bullies porters; his sister Evie (who has perhaps read Reginald Farrer's *My Rock Garden,* published in 1907, or E. Newell Arber's *Plant-Life in Alpine Switzerland,* of 1910) creates a rockery in the garden, which she fills with alpine plants. In a sense the reader is invited to recover; the faults of brother and sister are similar. Also reprehensible is the Wilcox action of filling in the gap in the hedge through which a path had once run from the lawn through the meadow to the farm.

At the end of the novel Howards End comes under new stewardship, that of the Schlegel sisters. The calisthenic machine has been removed from the garden, the wych-elm flourishes, only a few bumps in the grass recall the rockery, and the gap in the hedge is allowed to reappear. The last scene describes the cutting of the hay ("such a crop of hay as never"). Forster's conclusion is affirmative, but, despite the marriage of Henry Wilcox and Margaret Schlegel, no real connection has been made between business and culture, Bentham and Bloomsbury. The move has been backward from Great Britain to Little England—in Forster's terms, from the way of life of the "imperialist" to that of the "yeoman"; but the problems raised, including that of the emergence of the masses (symbolized by Leonard Bast) have been evaded rather than resolved, as Forster seems to concede at the end of the novel when he describes the "red rust" of London creeping toward his Hertfordshire idyll.

Forster's suspicion of improvements to house and garden accompanies his characterization of commerce as the enemy of tradition and virtue; but, as we have seen, he is not alone in making this equation. From Jane Austen he probably derives the motif of the house and garden endangered by the extravagant improvements of fashion-seeking owners; with Smollett and other novelists he shares the structure of the falsely improved garden returned to its simple and communal condition; like Scott, Trollope, and James, he describes an old house and garden to measure the limitations of utilitarian schemes or more radical measures (Appendix, 8, 9, 11, 12); and like Rousseau, he shows a xenophobic distrust of the importation of foreign plants into domestic soil.[87] Based on Forster's own childhood home, Rooksnest, Howards End is a characteristically modest metonymic ideal, hardly comparable to Pope's Sherborne Castle or Scott's Glamis, or even James' Compton Wynyates; but in seeing a house and garden as repositories of old values endangered by modern innovations, Forster is a very typical novelist.

NOTES

1. Evelyn Waugh, *Scoop* (Boston, 1977), 20–21.

2. Marcus Binney and Gervase Jackson-Stops, "The Last Hundred Years," in *The Treasure Houses of Britain,* ed. Gervase Jackson-Stops [exh. cat., National Gallery of Art] (Washington, 1985), 70–71.

3. Evelyn Waugh, *Decline and Fall* (Boston, 1949), 159.

4. Evelyn Waugh, *A Handful of Dust* (New York, 1945), 124.

5. Evelyn Waugh, *Brideshead Revisited* (Boston, 1973), 232.

6. Roman Jakobson, "Two Aspects of Language: Metaphor and Metonymy," in *European Theory and Practice,* ed. Vernon W. Gras (New York, 1973), 120–129; Kenneth Burke, "Container and Thing Contained," in *A Grammar of Motives and a Rhetoric of Motives* (Cleveland and New York, 1962), 3–20.

7. Roland Barthes, "L'Ancienne Rhétorique," *Communications* 16 (1970), 172–237.

8. Alistair M. Duckworth, "Scott's Fiction and the Migration of Settings," *Scottish Literary Journal* 7 (1980), 97–112.

9. Roland Barthes, *S/Z,* trans. Richard Miller (New York, 1974).

10. T. S. Eliot, "Tradition and the Individual Talent," *The Egoist* 6 (September/October, November/December 1919), 54–55, 72–73.

11. J. G. A. Pocock, *The Machiavellian Moment: Florentine Political Thought and the Atlantic Republican Tradition* (Princeton and London, 1975), 423–505.

12. The argument in this paragraph is indebted to J. G. A. Pocock, *Virtue, Commerce, and History* (Cambridge, 1985), as well as to Pocock 1975.

13. Pocock 1975, 445.

14. For detailed discussions of literary attitudes to seventeenth-century gardens, see Maren-Sofie Róstvig, *The Happy Man: Studies in the Metamorphoses of a Classical Ideal,* 2d ed., vol. 1 (Oslo, 1962); John Dixon Hunt, *The Figure in the Landscape* (Baltimore and London, 1976), chap. 1. Citations from *The Spectator* papers are taken from *The Spectator,* ed. Donald F. Bond, 5 vols. (Oxford, 1965).

15. Paintings by George Morland with this subject matter are at the National Gallery of Scotland, Edinburgh.

16. Daniel Defoe, *A Tour through the Whole Island of Great Britain,* ed. G. D. H. Cole and D. C. Browning, 2 vols. in 1 (London, 1974), 1:167, 2:8. For an argument that Defoe's landscape descriptions promote a Whig political program, see Alistair M. Duckworth, " 'Whig' Landscapes in Defoe's *Tour,*" *Philological Quarterly* 61 (1982), 453–465.

17. Canto 2, xxvii. J. Logie Robertson, ed., *The Complete Poetical Works of James Thomson* (London, 1963), 288.

18. E. P. Thompson, "Eighteenth-Century English Society: Class Struggle Without Class?" *Social History* 3 (1978), 133–165; John Barrell, *The Dark Side of the Landscape: The Rural Poor in English Painting, 1730–1840* (Cambridge, 1980).

19. Jonathan Swift, *Gulliver's Travels,* ed. Harold Williams (Oxford, 1941), 159.

20. Pocock 1975, 470.

21. Maynard Mack, *Alexander Pope: A Life* (New York and London, 1985), has noted Pope's Whig proclivities most recently; see his explication of "Lines written in Windsor Forest," 199–207.

22. *The Guardian,* No. 173, 29 September 1713, in *The Prose Works of Alexander Pope,* ed. Norman Ault (Oxford, 1936), 1:145–151.

23. Morris Brownell, *Alexander Pope and the Arts of Georgian England* (Oxford, 1978), 207–213.

24. Peter Martin, *Pursuing Innocent Pleasures: The Gardening World of Alexander Pope* (Hamden, Connecticut, 1984), 81–94, also suggests that Pope may have been uncomfortably aware of how close his friend Bathurst at Cirencester came to displaying the extravagances of Timon's villa. For a consideration of Pope in relation to the "greater house" and its "antitypes," see Brownell 1978, chaps. 8, 9.

25. Virginia Kenny, *The Country-House Ethos in English Literature: Themes of Personal Retreat and National Expansion* (New York, 1984), chaps. 2, 3. Pope's relation to paternalist values is also well treated in Howard Erskine-Hill, *The Social Milieu of Alexander Pope* (New Haven and London, 1975).

26. For a fuller discussion, see Alistair M. Duckworth, "Fiction and Some Uses of the Country-House Setting from Richardson to Scott," in *Landscapes in the Gardens and Literature of Eighteenth-Century England* (Los Angeles, 1981), 96–104.

27. Tobias Smollett, *The Expedition of Humphry Clinker,* ed. Lewis M. Knapp (London, 1966), 287, 292.

28. Smollett 1966, 343.

29. Pocock 1975, ix, 460–461; and (with important qualifications) Pocock 1985, 69–70. For Smollett's old-fashioned—in the 1770s—views on luxury, see John Sekora, *Luxury: The Concept in Western Thought, Eden to Smollett* (Baltimore and London, 1977).

30. Edward Malins, *English Landscaping and Literature: 1660–1840* (London, 1966), chap. 5; Elizabeth Wheeler Manwaring, *Italian Landscape in Eighteenth Century England* (1925; reprint ed., London, 1965), chap. 8.

31. Richard Graves, *Columella; or, the Distressed Anchoret,* 2 vols. (London, 1779), 2:65–66.

32. Graves 1779, 2:173.

33. Pocock 1975, 504.

34. *The Mirror,* No. 41, 15 July 1779, 161–164.

35. *The Lounger,* No. 17, 28 May 1785, 65–68.

36. *The Mirror,* No. 61, 7 December 1779, 241–244.

37. *The Lounger,* No. 31, 3 September 1785, 121–124.

38. Oliver Goldsmith, *The Deserted Village,* in Arthur Friedman, ed., *Collected Works of Oliver Goldsmith,* 5 vols. (Oxford, 1966), 4:298, lines 275, 302. In "The English Lord and the Happy Husbandmen," *Studies on Voltaire and the Eighteenth Century,* ed. Theodore Besterman, vol. 57 (1967), 1357–1375, esp. 1362, A. J. Sambrook claims that the English garden, though it was associated with English freedom and the revolt against the "tyranny" of formal gardens, "still devoured villages, and possibly devoured more than the formal garden had done"; see also Mavis Batey, "Oliver Goldsmith: An Indictment of Landscape Gardening," in *Furor Hortensis,* ed. Peter Willis (Edinburgh, 1974), 57–71.

39. Friedman 1966, 3:195–197.

40. David Spring, "Interpreters of Jane Austen's Social World: Literary Critics and Historians," in *Jane Austen: New Perspectives,* ed. Janet Todd (New York and London, 1983), 64.

41. Donald Davie, "Notes on Goldsmith's Politics," in *The Art of Oliver Goldsmith,* ed. Andrew Swarbrick (Totowa, New Jersey, 1984), 86.

42. Wordsworth to Sir George Beaumont, 17 October 1805, *The Letters of William and Dorothy Wordsworth: The Early Years*

1787–1805, ed. Ernest De Selincourt, 2d ed. (Oxford, 1967), 622–629.

43. Dorothy Stroud, *Capability Brown* (London, 1975), 112.

44. See R. A. C. Parker's *Coke of Norfolk: A Financial and Agricultural Study, 1707–1842* (Oxford, 1975) for a separation of the largely admirable fact from the myth, which Thomas Coke happily fostered.

45. Spring 1983, 64–65.

46. Spring 1983, 64.

47. Spring 1983, 65.

48. Jane Austen, *Sense and Sensibility,* ed. R. W. Chapman (Oxford and New York, 1982), 196–197.

49. Martial, Epigram 3:58: "Baiana nostri villa, Basse, Faustini." Like Bassus (and like Mrs. Baynard in *Humphry Clinker*), the Middletons of Barton Park have forsaken the ideal of "unbought provisions," the self-sufficient estate.

50. B. C. Southam, "*Sanditon:* The Seventh Novel," in *Jane Austen's Achievement,* ed. Juliet McMaster (London, 1976), 12–16.

51. John Dixon Hunt, "Sense and Sensibility in the Landscapes of Humphry Repton," *Studies in Burke and His Time* 19 (1978), 3–28; Alistair M. Duckworth, "Improvements," in *The Jane Austen Companion,* ed. A. Walton Litz et al. (New York, 1986), 223–227.

52. Jane Austen, *Pride and Prejudice,* ed. R. W. Chapman (Oxford and New York, 1982), 245.

53. Edmund Bertram distrusts the employment of a professional improver in *Mansfield Park,* and his distrust is shared by (among others) Alexander Pope (see Pope to the Earl of Strafford, 1725, in *The Correspondence of Alexander Pope,* ed. George Sherburn, 5 vols. [Oxford, 1956], 2:309), William Wordsworth (see Wordsworth to Sir George Beaumont in De Selincourt 1967, 622–629), and Sir Walter Scott, who, in a review-essay in the *Quarterly Review* 37 (1828), argues that landed proprietors should be their own improvers.

54. Jane Austen, *Emma,* ed. R. W. Chapman (Oxford and New York, 1982), 358.

55. Keith Thomas, *Man and the Natural World: A History of the Modern Sensibility* (New York, 1983), 209. Thomas' section on "Tree-planting," 198–211, is a mine of information. Defoe's attitude to trees in his *Tour*—in which he frequently advocates the felling of trees for profit and production—stands in marked contrast to the tree worship of Drayton, Evelyn, Pope, and many others.

56. Richard Payne Knight, *The Landscape: A Didactic Poem* (1794), 17. Even such an enthusiast for improvements as Horace Walpole could write to Montagu (15 June 1768): "How our ancestors would laugh at us, who knew there was no being comfortable, unless you had a high hill before your nose, and a thick warm wood at your back: Taste is too freezing a commodity for us, and depend upon it will go out of fashion again" (Wilmarth Sheldon Lewis and Ralph S. Brown, Jr., eds., *Horace Walpole's Correspondence with George Montagu* [New Haven, 1941], 2:262).

57. Sir Walter Scott, *Waverley* (London, 1912), 54.

58. Mavis Batey, "The High Phase of English Landscape Gardening," *Eighteenth-Century Life,* n.s. 2 (1983), 47.

59. Quoted in Mark Girouard, *The Return to Camelot: Chivalry and the English Gentleman* (New Haven and London, 1981), 49; chaps. 3 and 4 of this work are an excellent demonstration of Scott's role in establishing chivalric models for nineteenth-century behavior.

60. Washington Irving, *The Sketch Book* (New York, 1855), 252–253.

61. P. D. Garside, "Scott and the 'Philosophical' Historians," *Journal of the History of Ideas* 36 (1975), 497–512.

62. For a fuller discussion of Jeanie's journey through a variety of coded settings, see Duckworth 1980, 101–108.

63. Thomas Crawford, *Scott* (Edinburgh, 1982), 95–99; Eric Cregeen, "The Changing Role of the House of Argyll in the Scottish Highlands," in *Scotland in the Age of Improvement,* ed. N. Phillipson and R. Mitchison (Edinburgh, 1970), cited by Crawford.

64. Their much-loved wealth imparts
    Convenience, plenty, elegance, and arts;
    But view them closer, craft and fraud appear,
    Even liberty itself, is bartered here.
            (Oliver Goldsmith, *The Traveller,* lines 303–306)
    For a good reading of Scott's attempts to reconcile such oppositions as past and present, honor and credit, see Lawrence Poston III, "The Commercial Motif in the Waverley Novels," *English Literary History* 42 (1975), 63–84.

65. Sir Walter Scott, *The Visionary,* ed. Peter Garside (Cardiff, 1984), 20, 24. The ancient mansion is described in the first vision; in the second vision the consequences of the 10th Duke of Hamilton's misguided scheme to aid distressed weavers are described; employed to make alterations in the duke's park, the weavers "displayed the three-coloured flag . . . and declared their purpose was to divide the parks and grounds of the gentry into lots of ten acres to be appropriated to themselves" (32). Scott's image of the British constitution as an irregular house is picked up in the description of Abbotsford in John Buchan, *Sir Walter Scott* (New York, 1932), 148; see Appendix, 14.

66. Sir Walter Scott in *Quarterly Review* 37 (1828), 303–344. The essay comprises a large part of Scott's review of Sir Henry Stewart, *The Planter's Guide* (1828). Scott's reputation as an improver was high; on 13 December 1827 he mentions "a letter from Lockhart announcing that Murray of Albemarle Street would willingly give me my own terms for a volume on the subject of planting and Landscape gardening" (*The Journal of Sir Walter Scott,* ed. W. E. K. Anderson [Oxford, 1972], 395). For an informative treatment of Scott in relation to the history of the garden in Scotland, see A. A. Tait, *The Landscape Garden in Scotland, 1735–1835* (Edinburgh, 1980), 203–209, 239–240.

67. Anderson 1972, 362 (7 October 1827).

68. Sir Walter Scott, *Quentin Durward* (London, 1912), xxiv.

69. Henry James, *English Hours,* ed. Alma Louise Lowe (London, 1905), 139.

70. Anderson 1972, 188, 255, 480 (24 August 1826, 19 December 1826, 23 May 1828).

71. James 1905, 131.

72. Richard Gill, *Happy Rural Seat: The English Country House and the Literary Imagination* (New Haven and London, 1972), 4.

73. Emily Brontë, *Wuthering Heights,* ed. David Daiches (Baltimore, 1967), 110.

74. Cole and Browning 1974, 2:176.

75. Charlotte Brontë's (metonymic) rejection of *Pride and Prejudice* is well-known: "a carefully fenced, highly cultivated garden, with neat borders and delicate flowers; but no . . . open country, no fresh air, no blue hill, no bonny beck" (Brontë to G. H. Lewes, 12 January 1848, in B. C. Southam, ed., *Jane Austen: The Critical Heritage* [London, 1968], 126).

76. Brontë 1967, 231.

77. As noted by Susan Gubar and Sandra Gilbert, *The Madwoman in the Attic* (New Haven and London, 1979), 301.

78. For Pope's description of the prospect of Sherborne, see Pope to Martha Blount, 22 June 1724, Sherburn 1956, 2:37; for Emma's account of the Abbey Mill farm, see Austen 1982, 360; both are metonyms of a traditional paternalist social system and reinforce "English" values (for Jane Austen's description, which is not above some antibourgeois satire, see Appendix, 5).

79. George Eliot, *Felix Holt, the Radical,* ed. Peter Coveney (Harmondsworth, 1977).

80. Eliot 1977, 95.

81. Eliot 1977, 592.

82. Eliot 1977, 362.

83. William Morris, *News from Nowhere* (New York and London, 1903), 100.

84. Morris 1903, 194-195.

85. Morris 1903, 193.

86. Clive Aslett and Alan Powers, *The National Trust Book of the English House* (New York, 1985), 243-246. For an interesting discussion of how the traditional house persists as a code of appeal in modern advertisements, see Don E. Wayne, *Penshurst: The Semiotics of Place and the Poetics of History* (Madison, Wisconsin, 1984), appendix B.

87. Julie's "elysium" in Jean-Jacques Rousseau, *La Nouvelle Héloïse,* pt. 4, letter 10, contains plants "du pays" only.

APPENDIX

Migrations of a Code: The Irregular House

1. You must expect nothing regular in my description of a House that seems to be built before Rules were in fashion. The whole is so disjointed, & the parts so detachd from each other, and yet so joining again one can't tell how; that, in a poetical Fitt you'd imagine it had been a Village in Amphions time, where twenty Cottages had taken a dance together, were all Out, and stood still in amazement ever since.

Alexander Pope, Letter to Lady Mary Wortley Montagu describing Stanton Harcourt, 1718

2. I will conclude by saying of Shakespeare, that with all his faults, and with all the irregularity of his drama, one may look upon his works, in comparison to those that are more finished and regular, as upon an ancient majestic piece of Gothic architecture, compared with a neat modern building. The latter is more elegant and glaring, but the former is more strong and more solemn. It must be allowed that in one of these there are materials enough to make many of the other. It has much the greater variety, and much the nobler apartments; though we are often conducted to them by dark, odd, and uncouth passages.

Alexander Pope, Conclusion to *Preface to Shakespeare,* 1725

3. In this dull vale stands the antient, paternal estate and castle which gives name (and title too) to the great family of Douglass. The castle is very ill adapted to the glory of the family; but as it is the antient inheritance, the heads or chief of the name have always endeavour'd to keep up the old mansion, and have consequently, made frequent additions to the building, which have made it a wild, irregular mass.

Daniel Defoe, *Tour thro' the Whole Island of Great Britain,* 1724-1726

4. The house is old-fashioned and irregular, but lodgeable and commodious. To the south it has the river in front. . . .

Tobias Smollett, *Humphry Clinker,* 1771

5. She felt all the honest pride and complacency which her alliance with the present and future proprietor could fairly warrant, as she viewed the respectable size and style of the building, its suitable, becoming, characteristic situation, low and sheltered—its ample gardens stretching down to meadows washed by a stream, of which the Abbey, with all the old neglect of prospect, had scarcely a sight—and its abundance of timber in rows and avenues, which neither fashion nor extravagance had rooted up.—The house was larger than Hartfield, and totally unlike it, covering a good deal of

ground, rambling and irregular, with many comfortable and one or two handsome rooms. It was just what it ought to be, and it looked what it was—and Emma felt an increasing respect for it, as the residence of a family of such true gentility, untainted in blood and understanding. . . .—The whole party were assembled, excepting Frank Churchill . . . and Mrs. Elton, in all her apparatus of happiness, her large bonnet and her basket, was ready to lead the way in gathering, accepting, or talking—strawberries, and only strawberries, could now be thought or spoken of.

. . . .

and at the bottom of this bank, favourably placed and sheltered, rose the Abbey-Mill Farm, with meadows in front, and the river making a close and handsome curve around it.

It was a sweet view—sweet to the eye and the mind. English verdure, English culture, English comfort, seen under a sun bright, without being oppressive.

Jane Austen, *Emma,* 1816

6. The clerical mansion was large and commodious, for the living was an excellent one. . . .

It was situated about four hundred yards from the village, and on a rising ground which sloped gently upward, covered with small enclosures, or closes, laid out irregularly, so that the old oaks and elms, which were planted in hedge-rows, fell into perspective, and were blended together in beautiful irregularity. When they approached nearer to the house, a handsome gate-way admitted them into a lawn, of narrow dimensions, indeed, but which was interspersed with large sweet-chestnut trees and beeches, and kept in handsome order. The front of the house was irregular. Part of it seemed very old, and had, in fact, been the residence of the incumbent in Romish times. Successive occupants had made considerable additions and improvements, each in the taste of his own age, and without much regard to symmetry. But these incongruities of architecture were so graduated and happily mingled, that the eye, far from being displeased with the combinations of various styles, saw nothing but what was interesting in the varied and intricate pile which they exhibited. Fruit-trees displayed on the southern wall, outer staircases, various places of entrance, a combination of roofs and chimneys of different ages, united to render the front, not indeed beautiful or grand, but intricate, perplexed, or, to use Mr. Price's appropriate phrase, picturesque.

Sir Walter Scott, *The Heart of Midlothian,* 1818

7. It was an irregular building, of some magnitude, and seemed to be of the architecture of different periods. One wing was evidently very ancient, with heavy stone-shafted bow windows jutting out and overrun with ivy. . . . The rest of the house was in the French taste of Charles the Second's time, having been repaired and altered, as my friend told me, by one of his ancestors, who returned with that monarch at the Restoration.

Washington Irving, *The Sketch-Book,* 1819–1820

8. It was a rude building of roughstone . . . a large old-fashioned narrow house, with a very steep roof, covered with flags composed of a grey sandstone. . . . The windows were few, very small in size, and distributed up and down the building with utter contempt of regularity.

Sir Walter Scott, *The Pirate,* 1821

9. Ullathorne is a high building for a country house, for it possesses three stories; and in each story, the windows are of the same sort as that described, though varying in size, and varying also in their lines athwart the house. Those of the ground floor are all uniform in size and position. But those above are irregular both in size and place, and this irregularity gives a bizarre and not unpicturesque appearance to the building.

. . . .

There may be windows which give a better light than . . . these, and it may be, as my utilitarian friend observes, that the giving of light is the desired object of a window. I will not argue the point with him. Indeed I cannot. But I shall not the less die in the assured conviction that no sort of description of window is capable of imparting half so much happiness to mankind as that which had been adopted at Ullathorne Court.

Anthony Trollope, *Barchester Towers,* 1857

10. But of Compton Wyniates . . . I despair of giving any coherent or adequate account. . . . It sits on the grass at the bottom of a wooded hollow, and the glades of a superb old park go wandering upward away from it. . . . I said to myself that here surely we had arrived at the farthest limits of what ivy-smothered brick-work and weather-beaten gables, conscious old windows and clustered mossy roofs can accomplish for the eye. It is impossible to imagine a more finished picture. . . . The house is not large, as great houses go, and it sits . . . upon the grass, without even a flagging or a footpath to conduct you from the point where the avenue stops to the beautiful sculptured doorway which admits you into the small, quaint inner court. From this court you are at liberty to pass through the crookedest series of oaken halls and chambers, adorned with treasures of old wainscotting and elaborate doors and chimneypieces.

Henry James, "In Warwickshire," 1877

11. At one end of the garden was a parapet of mossy brick which looked down on the other side into a canal, a moat, a quaint old pond . . . and from the same standpoint showed a considerable

part of the main body of the house—Hyacinth's room belonging to a wing that commanded the extensive irregular back—which was richly grey wherever clear of the ivy and the other dense creepers, and everywhere infinitely a picture: with a high-piled ancient russet roof broken by huge chimneys and queer peep-holes and all manner of odd gables and windows on different lines.

Henry James, *The Princess Casamassima,* 1886

12. One of the gardens at Medley took the young man's heart beyond the others; it had high brick walls, on the sunny sides of which was a great training of apricots and plums, it had straight walks bordered with old-fashioned homely flowers and enclosing immense squares where other fruit-trees stood upright and mint and lavender floated in the air. In the southern quarter it overhung a small disused canal, and here a high embankment had been raised, which was also long and broad and covered with fine turf; so that the top of it, looking down at the canal, made a magnificent grassy terrace, than which on a summer's day there could be no more delightful place for strolling up and down with a companion—all the more that at either end was a curious pavilion, in the manner of a teahouse, which crowned the scene in an old-world sense and offered rest and privacy, a refuge from sun or shower.

Henry James, *The Princess Casamassima,* 1886

13. [The Pennistons' house] was nearer to the earth than most; it had, in fact, subsided right down into it, sinking from north to south with the settling of the clay, and the resultant appearance of established comfort was greater than I can describe to you. The irregularity of the building was the more apparent by reason of the oak beams, which should have been horizontal, but which actually sloped at a considerable angle. I found, after I had lived there no more than a couple of days, that one adopted this architectural irregularity into one's scheme of life.

Vita Sackville-West, *Heritage,* 1919

14. [Abbotsford] was growing piece-meal round the core of the old farm with the irregularity of the British Constitution.

John Buchan, *Sir Walter Scott,* 1932

15. More even than the work of the great architects, I loved buildings that grew silently with the centuries, catching and keeping the best of each generation, while time curbed the artist's pride and the Philistine's vulgarity, and repaired the clumsiness of the dull workman. In such buildings England abounded, and in the last decade of their grandeur, Englishmen seemed for the first time conscious of what before was taken for granted, and to salute their achievements at the moment of extinction. Hence, my prosperity, far beyond my merits.

Evelyn Waugh, *Brideshead Revisited,* 1945

Biographical Sketches

MICHEL BARIDON teaches English literature and cultural history at the University of Burgundy. He is the author of *Gibbon et le mythe de Rome: histoire et idéologie au siècle des lumières* (Paris, 1974) and his publications include articles on the Gothic revival, the theory of history in the eighteenth century, the genesis of the historical novel, and the relation of idea to form in the landscape garden. He is currently writing a book on eighteenth-century aesthetics.

Michel Baridon was awarded a fellowship at the Dumbarton Oaks Foundation in 1988. He has been a member of the Conseil National des Universités since 1980 and is currently General Secretary of the International Society for Eighteenth Century Studies.

JOHN CORNFORTH first wrote about country houses for *Country Life* in 1961. In the mid-1960s, as a member of the former Historic Buildings Committee of the National Trust, he became interested in the problems of country house interiors, their preservation, restoration, and display to visitors. This led to collaboration with John Fowler on *English Decoration in the 18th century* (London, 1974), *English Interiors 1790–1848, The Quest for Comfort* (London, 1978), and two considerations of twentieth-century attitudes and taste, *The Inspiration of the Past* (London, 1985), and *The Search for a Style* (London, 1988). He is a regular contributor to *Country Life,* and is at present expanding "A Georgian Patchwork" into a book.

ALISTAIR M. DUCKWORTH, professor of English at the University of Florida, Gainesville, is the author of *The Improvement of the Estate: A Study of Jane Austen's Novels* (1971) and of numerous essays on the English novel.

PIERRE DE LA RUFFINIÈRE DU PREY is professor in the department of art, Queen's University, Kingston, Ontario. His best-known writings in British architectural history concern Sir John Soane. He is currently engaged on two books, one about Nicholas Hawksmoor's churches and the other about the concept of the villa from Pliny to posterity.

SIR BRINSLEY FORD, C.B.E., F.S.A., was born in 1908 and educated at Eton and Trinity College, Oxford. He has been a member of Britain's National Art-Collections Fund for sixty-one years, twenty-eight of those as a member of the executive committee, from which he resigned in June 1988. He was for sixteen years secretary of the Society of Dilettanti, having been a member of the society for thirty-six years. From 1954 to 1961 he was a trustee of the National Gallery, London. Sir Brinsley is an Honorary Fellow of the Royal Academy, a trustee of the *Burlington Magazine,* president of the Walpole Society, and chairman of the National Trust's Foundation for Art. He has recently given to the Paul Mellon Center for Studies in British Art, London, the archive he has formed over thirty years on the English in Italy in the eighteenth century. From this archive he has published in the *Burlington Magazine* and in *Apollo* a number of articles on artists and patrons in Rome in the eighteenth century. He is also the author of *Drawings of Richard Wilson* (London, 1951), and edited "The Letters of Jonathan Skelton" for the Walpole Society (1960).

MARK GIROUARD was educated at Christ Church, Oxford, and the Courtauld Institute of Art. He was Slade Professor of Fine Art at the University of Oxford from 1975 to 1976, and has worked for *Country Life* and the *Architectural Review.* He is a member of the Victorian Society, the Royal Fine Art Commission, and the Commission for Historic Buildings and Monuments. Among his many works are *Robert Smythson and the Elizabethan Country House* (London, 1966; New Haven, 1983), *Sweetness and Light: The Queen Anne Movement 1860–1900* (London and New Haven, 1977), and *Life in the English Country House* (London and New Haven, 1978), for which he won the Duff Cooper Memorial Prize and the W. H. Smith Award.

ST. JOHN GORE, C.B.E., F.S.A., was advisor on pictures to the National Trust from 1956 to 1986, and historic buildings secretary of the National Trust from 1973 to 1981. He has served on the executive committee of the National Art-Collections Fund since 1964, and is a trustee of the Wallace Collection and the National Gallery, London. He is the author of various exhibition catalogues, including *English Taste in the Eighteenth Century* (London, 1955) and the "British School," in *European Paintings in the Collection of the Worcester Art Museum* (Worcester, Mass., 1974).

JOHN HARRIS was curator of the British Architectural Library's Drawings Collection and Heinz Gallery from 1960 to 1986, and was subsequently appointed consultant to the Canadian Centre for Architecture, Montreal, and chairman of Colnaghi's. His many publications include *Sir William Chambers, Knight of the Polar Star* (London and University Park, Pa., 1970) and *The Artist and the Country House* (London, 1979). He was Andrew Mellon Lecturer in Fine Arts at the National Gallery of Art, Washington, in 1981, and was awarded the O.B.E. in 1986.

JOHN DIXON HUNT is director of studies in landscape architecture at Dumbarton Oaks (Harvard University) in Washington, D.C. Previously he was professor of English literature at the universities of East Anglia, Leiden (in the Netherlands), and London. He is editor of both the *Journal of Garden History* and *Word & Image*. His main interests are the relationships between verbal and visual languages and the design history, meaning, and experience of gardens. He is currently working on studies of gardens in the city of Venice, an anthology of garden verse, and a general, theoretical book on garden art.

OLIVER IMPEY is senior assistant keeper in the department of eastern art at the Ashmolean Museum, Oxford, and a fellow of Green College. He is chairman of the International Committee for Museums of Applied Art of the International Council of Museums. He has written widely on various aspects of Japanese art, more especially on the export arts, and on the effect of oriental art upon European art. His publications include *Chinoiserie: The Impact of Oriental Styles on Western Art and Decoration* (Oxford and New York, 1977) and, most recently (with Arthur MacGregor), *The Origins of Museums: The Cabinet of Curiosities in Sixteenth and Seventeenth Century Europe* (Oxford, 1985). He is the editor (also with Arthur MacGregor) of the *Journal of the History of Collections*.

GERVASE JACKSON-STOPS was educated at Harrow and Christ Church, Oxford, and worked at the Victoria and Albert Museum before joining The National Trust as architectural advisor in 1972. He was curator of *The Treasure Houses of Britain* exhibition at the National Gallery of Art in Washington (1985–1986), and is the author of *The English Country House: A Grand Tour* (London and Boston, 1985) and *The Country House Garden: A Grand Tour* (London, 1987). He was awarded the O.B.E. in 1986.

ALASTAIR LAING has been advisor on paintings and sculpture to The National Trust since 1986. Prior to that he was one of the coorganizers and the chief author of the exhibition catalogue of *François Boucher* (New York-Detroit-Paris, 1986–1987). His publications include (with Anthony Blunt) *Baroque and Rococo* (London, 1978) and *The Arts and Living: Lighting* (London, 1982) for the Victoria and Albert Museum. He is currently preparing a gazetteer of all the paintings in the houses owned by The National Trust in England, Wales, and Northern Ireland, which, taken together, probably amount to the largest—but also the least known—collection in the British Isles.

BARBARA KIEFER LEWALSKI is Kenan Professor of History and Literature and of English Literature at Harvard University. Her many books and articles include: *Protestant Poetics and the Seventeenth-Century Religious Lyric* (Princeton, 1977), winner of the James Russell Lowell Prize of the Modern Language Association, and *Paradise Lost and the Rhetoric of Literary Form* (Princeton, 1985), winner of the James Holly Hanford Prize of the Milton Society of America. She is now at work on a book entitled, "Writing Women in Jacobean England: Social Roles and Literary Images."

WILLIAM MCCLUNG is professor of English at Mississippi State University and author of *The Country House in English Renaissance Poetry* (Berkeley, 1977) and *The Architecture of Paradise* (Berkeley, 1983). He holds a B.A. degree from Williams College and a Ph.D. from Harvard University. His recent work includes a catalogue essay on ephemeral architecture for the inaugural exhibition of the Canadian Centre for Architecture, Montreal (1989).

MICHAEL MENDLE is associate professor of history at the University of Alabama. His first book, *Dangerous Positions* (Alabama, 1985), explored the political implications of various formulations of the estates of the realm in sixteenth- and early seventeenth-century England. He is currently at work on a study of Henry Parker, the "Observator."

FRANCIS RUSSELL was educated at Westminster and Christ Church, Oxford, and has been a director of Christie's since 1978. He is a regular contributor to the *Burlington Magazine* and other publications, and is the author of *The Portraits of Sir Walter Scott* (London, 1987).

ANNA SOMERS COCKS is editor of *Apollo* magazine. She was for thirteen years an assistant keeper at the Victoria and Albert Museum, spending eleven of them in the metalwork department and the remainder in ceramics and glass. She has written numerous articles and organized various exhibitions, in particular, *Princely Magnificence: Court Jewels of the Renaissance* (1980). She is author of among other titles, *The Victoria & Albert Museum: The Making of the Collection* (London, 1980), and coauthor of *Renaissance Jewels, Gold Boxes and Objets de Vertu in the Thyssen Collection* (London, 1984).

DAMIE STILLMAN is professor of art history at the University of Delaware. A former president of the Society of Architectural Historians and winner of its Founder's Award, he is the author of the recent *English Neoclassical Architecture* (London, 1988), *The Decorative Work of Robert Adam* (London, 1966), *English Painting: The Great Masters, 1730–1860* (New York, 1966), and numerous articles and book reviews. He is currently at work on a study entitled "Neo-classicism in America: The Architecture of the Young Republic, 1785–1825."

A. A. TAIT is the Richmond Professor of the History of Art at the University of Glasgow. He works on eighteenth-century landscape and architecture, and his publications include *The Landscape Garden in Scotland* (Edinburgh, 1980; New York, 1989). He is a member of the National Trust for Scotland Garden Committee and of the Committee U.K. for the International Council on Monuments and Sites. He was a fellow of Dumbarton Oaks and a member of their advisory committee from 1978 to 1986.

RICHARD TUCK is a fellow of Jesus College, Cambridge and a university lecturer in history. He is the author of *Natural Rights Theories* (Cambridge, 1979), and *Hobbes* [Past Master Theories] (Oxford, 1989).

JOHN WILTON-ELY holds degrees from Jesus College, Cambridge and the Courtauld Institute, London. He taught at Nottingham University from 1963 until his appointment as chairman of the department of art history at Hull University in 1979. Since his retirement with an emeritus professorship in 1987, he has been director of Sotheby's Educational Studies in London. Professor Wilton-Ely helped arrange the exhibition *Age of Neo-Classicism* at the Royal Academy, London, in 1972, and organized and catalogued the *Piranesi Bicentenary Exhibition* at the Hayward Gallery, London, in 1978. Among his publications, *The Art and Mind of Piranesi* received the Banister Fletcher Prize in 1979. He has held visiting fellowships at the Institute for Advanced Study, Princeton, and at the Pierpont Morgan Library, New York, where he delivered the Franklin Jasper Walls lecture in 1980.